The
Plutonium Files

America's Secret Medical

Experiments in the Cold War

E I L E E N   W E L S O M E

THE DIAL PRESS

Published by
The Dial Press
Random House, Inc.
1540 Broadway
New York, New York 10036

Library of Congress Cataloging in Publication Data
Welsome, Eileen.
    The plutonium files: America's secret medical experiments in the cold
    war / by Eileen Welsome.
        p.   cm.
    Includes bibliographical references.
    ISBN 0-385-31402-7
    1. Radiation—Toxicology—Research—United States.   2. Human
experimentation in medicine—United States.   3. Radiation victims—
United States.   4. Informed consent (Medical law)—United States.
5. Radiation—Physiological effect—Research—Moral and ethical
aspects—United States.   I. Title.
    RA1231.R2W45   1999
    616.9'897'00973—dc21   99-10991
                                                CIP
Book design by Donna Sinisgalli

Manufactured in the United States of America
Published simultaneously in Canada

September 1999

10 9 8 7 6 5 4 3 2 1

BVG

To Jim, Joan,
and in memory
of Jane Margaret

CONTENTS

Prologue 1

PART FIVE: THE RECKONING

A long habit of not thinking
a thing wrong gives it a superficial
appearance of being right, and raises at
first a formidable outcry in
defense of custom.

Thomas Paine
Common Sense
1776

PROLOGUE

It came on suddenly, the desire to see Italy, Texas, again. The small town had grown indistinct in my memory, a place that had become more imagined than real as the months, then years, went by. I wanted to see the sagging storefronts on Italy's Main Street, feel the clap of air conditioning on my face as I stepped from the sun-blasted emptiness into the Uptown Café.

On a late summer afternoon in 1997, I went back to look around. As soon as I landed at Love Field in Dallas, I got in a taxi and headed south. Though five years had elapsed since my first visit, I knew Italy was close when I began seeing the rows of freshly plowed earth, the crows diving in and out of the spent cornfields. On the edge of town was the old sign that Fredna Allen had once pointed out. It was badly weathered and nearly invisible in the shimering heat, but there was still pride in its message: WELCOME TO ITALY. THE BIGGEST LITTLE TOWN IN TEXAS.

Then I was standing on Main Street. It was just as I remembered, especially the heat, which flattened and bent down everything before it. Drifting down through the thick air came the sound of a lawnmower, the metallic confusion of an engine that wouldn't start.

Film crews from all over the world had passed through Italy to interview Fredna, the widow of Elmer Allen, but the intense media exposure had left no outward mark, no trace of worldliness, on the small community. Italy looked punch-drunk and haggard beneath the ashy sky, too far gone for some Dallas investor to turn into a quaint version of what it was and always had been: a rural town tethered to the boom-and-bust cycles of cotton. Although there was nothing faintly Mediterranean about the place, many years ago someone from the post office in Washington,

D.C., had suggested the village change its name from Houston Creek to Italy.

Most of the stores were still vacant, the names of defunct businesses stenciled across the display windows. Out of a sense of respect, tact perhaps, sheets of brown paper were drawn down over many of the storefronts. Not all hope had been abandoned though. A new video store and a beauty salon had staked out space a few doors down from City Hall. And a block or two from the grim desolation of Main Street there were pockets of cool tranquility, neighborhoods with green lawns and white, two-story houses. With their awnings and screened-in porches, the homes had the stately air of Italy's more prosperous decades.

In this unlikely place, I had found the first solid evidence that would help me unravel a story that began at the dawn of the atomic age. Just four months before two bombs were dropped on Japan, the doctors of the U.S. Army's Manhattan Project, the top-secret wartime machine that built the first atomic bomb, embarked on a human experiment so closely guarded that many details remained classified for fifty years.

Beginning in April of 1945 and continuing through July of 1947, eighteen men, women, and even children, scattered in quiet hospital wards across the country, were injected with plutonium. Urine and stool specimens were collected in jars, packed into wooden crates, and shipped to the Manhattan Project's laboratory in Los Alamos for analysis. Some of the patients were close to death when they were injected; others, including some mistakenly believed to be mortally ill, would live for many years. Most went to their graves without knowing what had been done to them.

I came across the story in 1987, just a few months after I began working at the *Albuquerque Tribune,* a small afternoon newspaper in New Mexico. One late-spring morning, while thumbing through a dense report describing the Air Force's efforts to clean up its waste sites throughout the United States, I noticed that several dumps at Kirtland Air Force Base in Albuquerque were on the list. Buried in the dumps were radioactive animal carcasses. Although this didn't seem like much of a story, I have always loved animals and the disclosure caught my eye. What kind of animals were buried in those dumps, I wondered, and why were they radioactive?

I called around and eventually learned that the animals had been used in radiation experiments. Many of the technical papers written about the studies were stored at what was then called the Air Force Special Weapons Laboratory at Kirtland. When I made inquiries there, a spokesman for the weapons lab assembled a stack of these papers and told me I was welcome to come to the base and read them.

A couple of days later I drove over to Kirtland, showed my driver's license to the guards, and was waved on through. The official from the weapons lab escorted me to the basement, where I was told to take a seat at a long wooden conference table. On the table were the reports I had requested. Once the public information officer had departed, I looked around. Nearby was a walk-in vault where both classified and unclassified documents were stored. The heavy black door, which had a huge, 1950s-style tumbler lock, had been left ajar, and I could see hundreds of documents on the shelves. Although I didn't know it at the time, the base had been a major launching site for many Cold War missions.

The reports were stiff with age and smelled of dust. As I pried the pages apart, I felt certain they hadn't been read in many decades. I soon realized I wasn't going to find a story that afternoon, but, having requested all those papers, felt obliged to read on. I was about to pack it in when my eye fell on a footnote describing a human plutonium experiment. The information jolted me deeply. One minute I was reading about dogs that had been injected with large amounts of plutonium and had subsequently developed radiation sickness and tumors. Suddenly there was this reference to a *human* experiment. I wondered if the people had experienced the same agonizing deaths as the animals.

I jotted down the citation. The following day I began my research at the University of New Mexico library. Naively I thought I might be the first to "break" this forty-year-old story, but I soon discovered that *Science Trends,* a small publication in Washington, D.C., had gotten there first with an article in 1976. The injections had also been the centerpiece of a 1986 congressional report, which had attracted some press coverage.

In none of these places—*Science Trends,* the newspaper articles, or the congressional report—were the patients identified by name. They were known by code numbers only. I wondered who these people were; what happened to them after they left the hospital with the silvery, radioactive metal circulating in their veins—if they ever left at all, that is.

In the months and years that followed, I worked on the story in my spare time—tracking down technical reports, talking to scientists, and filing Freedom of Information Act requests with the Department of Energy, the modern-day successor to the Manhattan Project. The DOE sent me a few scraps of paper, on which anything that might have helped me to identify the patients seemed to have been deleted. Those scraps, they told me, were all the department possessed on the long-ago study. I knew from my reading that there was much more information available and that the DOE was not complying with either the spirit or the letter of the Freedom of Information Act. At Los Alamos, an official denied that such an experiment occurred—despite the fact that it had been described in the 1986 congressional report. The bureaucratic stone-walling was infuriating and only served to increase my determination to uncover the patients' identities.

I put the interview notes, the reports, the documents in a manila folder and filed it away. Every few months I'd pull out the folder, hoping to find something that had been overlooked. Using the skimpy data, I gradually developed profiles of the patients. I put the information on eighteen sheets of yellow, legal-pad paper—one for each patient. I knew their race and gender; their birth and, in some cases, their death dates; the hospitals where they were injected; and the diseases they suffered from. But I didn't know their names and, quite frankly, never thought I would.

In the fall of 1991, I went to Stanford University on a John S. Knight Fellowship and left my folder behind. It was a year in which we were encouraged to set aside the deadlines of daily journalism and explore the riches of the university. So I didn't work on the story at all that year. But my first week back on the job, in July of 1992, I pulled out the folder again. In an almost absentminded way, I shuffled through the papers. Suddenly, on the page in front of me, two words that the DOE had neglected to delete jumped out. These were the words that would finally unlock the story. There must have been something about seeing them afresh that jolted me into awareness. The document stated that one of the government scientists had written "to a physician in *Italy, Texas,* about contacting patient CAL-3. . . ."

I didn't know where Italy was, but I knew a lot about "CAL-3" from the crude profile I had developed. He was an African American who would be about eighty years old if he were still alive. Doctors plunged a hypodermic needle loaded with plutonium into CAL-3's left calf on July 18, 1947, in a San Francisco hospital. He was the last of the eighteen patients injected. Three days later the left leg was amputated at midthigh for what was thought to be a preexisting bone cancer.

I got out a map of Texas and began looking for Italy. It was a small dot nearly swamped by the snarl of interstate highways that spoked out from Dallas. I knew I could find CAL-3 in Italy even if it meant going door to door. But, as it turned out, locating him was not that difficult. I called Italy's City Hall and described the man I was looking for.

"You're looking for Elmer Allen," a woman on the other end told me, "but he died a year ago. Do you want his wife's number?"

Suddenly the windowless press room seemed to be swimming with light, but I think it was because I was holding my breath. The minute I got the number, I thanked the lady, hung up, and dialed Mrs. Allen. She answered on the first or second ring. Without going into a lot of detail, I described a little of what I knew about the experiment. Fredna Allen was very pleasant but didn't want to meet with me until she had discussed the matter with her daughter, Elmerine Allen Whitfield. When I asked Mrs. Allen if I could contact Elmerine directly, she readily agreed and gave me her number in Dallas.

Elmerine listened intently while I told her about the experiment and why I thought her father had been one of the patients. Finally, after what seemed like an eternity of silence, she said, "Okay. You can come on." She gave me instructions to her home and said that her mother would meet us there.

The following afternoon I arrived in Dallas and checked into a hotel near the airport. Since I wasn't scheduled to meet Fredna and Elmerine until the following morning, I decided to drive down to Italy. When I pulled into one of the parking spaces on Main Street, a glaze of heat and dust lay over everything. The town seemed completely deserted, as if everybody were off at a funeral. The storefronts looked like they had been punched from cardboard. Suddenly the possibility that Elmer Allen and CAL-3 were the same person seemed like a long shot. What could Italy, Texas, have to do with the Manhattan Project? But luck was with me that day.

When I stepped out of my car, I saw an African American man who could have been anywhere from sixty to eighty years old sitting on one of the benches. He had just slipped off his leather cowboy boots and was wriggling his feet in obvious relief. His name was Joe Speed. I asked him if he knew Elmer Allen. They had been good friends, he told me. We talked for a little while. Then I asked him if Elmer had ever said anything about how he lost his leg or the long-ago hospitalization in San Francisco.

Joe Speed's eyes swept the deserted street and then focused on a spot somewhere in front of his feet. Elmer, he began, had talked about the doctors who bustled in and out of his hospital room "practicing" to be doctors. "He told me they put a germ cancer in his leg. They guinea-pigged him. They didn't care about him getting well. He told me he would never get well." Joe Speed delivered this information swiftly, then looked at me sideways as if to say he didn't believe the story either. But his comments were a powerful confirmation that Elmer and CAL-3 were the same person.

The following morning I met with Fredna at Elmerine's house, a large, four-bedroom in the Oak Cliff section of Dallas. Before I arrived, Elmerine had gotten out a dictionary and looked up the word "plutonium" for her mother. As we sat at the kitchen table and talked, the awkwardness between us gradually evaporated. Fredna had taught school for thirty-five years and had a sweet, trusting disposition. Elmerine was a school teacher too, but she had come of age in the 1960s and had stood on picket lines in college. She was outspoken and had opinions on just about everything.

Fredna brought several documents to the interview, including an old blue mimeographed itinerary of a trip that she and Elmer had taken to a hospital in Rochester, New York, in 1973, some twenty-six years after the injection. I knew from my research that CAL-3 was one of the three survivors whom scientists had examined in Rochester as part of a follow-up study of the plutonium experiment. None of the doctors ever told Fredna that the real purpose of their study was to measure the plutonium circulating in her husband's body.

The dates on Fredna's records matched exactly the dates on my documents. Her recollections were also consistent with what I knew about CAL-3. By the time the interview was over, I was certain that I had finally found one of the patients. Fredna and Elmerine were also convinced. Although the knowledge of the experiment would cause her a lot of sadness in the years to come, Fredna was a deeply religious woman and her initial reaction was mild. "I'm not angry," she began carefully. "It just gives me a better view of how people will do you when they feel like you don't know better." But Elmerine's response was much harsher. In a curt voice that she undoubtedly used when she was trying to bring her eighth-grade class to order, she said, "I'm very upset, but being African American, I stay angry about a lot of things."

With the trip to Italy, Texas, the process of transforming the plutonium patients from numbers into human beings had begun. CAL-3 was not just a laboratory animal who provided scientists with a wealth of data about how plutonium was deposited in muscle and bone. He was husband to Fredna, father to Elmerine and her brother, William; a man who cleaned bricks, upholstered chairs, repaired shoes, and plowed the rich dark soil the farmers called black gumbo.

When I returned from Italy, I worked on the story full time for another two months. Then the political season was upon us and other assignments got in the way. But the story now had a momentum of its own. The newspaper's attorneys filed a new, meticulously worded Freedom of Information Act request with the Department of Energy. With near-daily prodding from attorney Loretta Garrison, the documents began trickling in. In the spring of 1993, I returned to the story full time; and, in the space of a few months, I had pieced together the identities of another four people who had been injected with plutonium. They too became real: Albert Stevens, an easygoing house painter; John Mousso, a mild-mannered handyman; Eda Schultz Charlton, a shy, nervous housewife; and Fred Sours, the much-beloved town supervisor of a suburb near Rochester. Although Sours died soon after the injection, the rest would live for decades, plagued by a myriad of physical ailments.

About sixteen months after that trip to Italy, the *Tribune* published the first of a three-day series on the experiment. When the first installment rolled off the press, I sat at my desk expectantly, waiting for calls from outraged readers. I didn't get one phone call from the public that day, but reporters from the hometowns where the five patients lived began calling to get more information, and a few reporters from Japan contacted me. Still, the story went largely unnoticed by the national media until Department of Energy Secretary Hazel O'Leary, who had been appointed less than a year earlier, officially condemned the experiment at a December 7, 1993, press conference, which she had called to announce the DOE's new policy of openness and candor. Speaking toward the end of the conference, O'Leary said what she had just learned of the experiment horrified her: "I was appalled and shocked. It gave me an ache in my gut and heart."

Soon after O'Leary's press conference, President Clinton directed the federal agencies to make public any records dealing with the human radiation experiments. He also appointed the Advisory Committee on Human Radiation Experiments to look into the controversy. As the documents on the plutonium experiment poured from the government warehouses and people used in other experiments came forward, it became apparent that the story was much bigger than anyone had imagined. It turned out that thousands of human radiation studies had been conducted during the Cold War. Almost without exception, the subjects were the poor, the powerless, and the sick—the very people who count most on the government to protect them, Clinton would later point out.

Many of the Manhattan Project doctors who took part in the plutonium injections showed up as advisors or participants in the postwar studies. Although they played a key role in the experiments, they had only supporting parts in the bomb project. They were on a first-name basis with such legendary figures as J. Robert Oppenheimer and Enrico Fermi, but they themselves have remained among history's obscure players. During the Manhattan Project, their job was to protect the health and safety of workers at a time when little was known about the effects of radiation on healthy people. Fearing a cancer epidemic among the project's employees, they embarked upon a crash course to learn everything they could about the effects of radiation delivered externally or internally through the ingestion or inhalation of radioactive materials. The bombings of Hiroshima and Nagasaki only intensified the urgency of their research. What did radiation do to human genes, reproductive organs, and fetuses?

With the building of the atomic bomb, an industry equivalent in size to General Motors had been born in the United States. After the war, the lavishly expensive atmospheric testing of atomic bombs began at the Pacific Proving Ground, and the Nevada Test Site. Responding to these developments, medical researchers found ever-new areas of inquiry to pursue. In closed-door meetings in Los Alamos and Washington, D.C., they and other scientists investigated such issues as how much radioactive strontium America's children were collecting in their bones from fallout and how many more bombs could be exploded before the radioactivity would exceed a level that the doctors had deemed safe.

In addition to studies focused specifically on issues relating to the bomb and its fallout products, many other experiments used supposedly harmless amounts of radioactive materials, so-called tracer doses, to investigate questions relating to human metabolism. Officials of the early Atomic Energy Commission, the civilian department that succeeded the Manhattan Project in 1947, promoted radioisotopes with a missionarylike zeal. Doctors and scientists desperately hoped the splitting of the atom would produce something good for humankind, possibly even a cure for cancer. Radioisotopes produced in the Manhattan Project's nuclear reactor in Oak Ridge, Tennessee, were shipped to qualified scientists throughout the world. Over the years the "radioisotope distribution program," which began partially as a public relations ploy to show that the bomb builders were willing to share information with civilian outsiders, grew by leaps and bounds.

Some radioisotope research conducted by civilian scientists contributed to a better understanding of how the human body works and to the development of new diagnostic tools to detect cancer and other diseases. But many studies were repetitive, poorly conceived, and frequently the subjects did not know what they were being given. Like the plutonium experiment, which was flawed in design and led to some erroneous conclusions, they were not just immoral science, they were bad science.

The Army, Navy, and Air Force also funded numerous experiments designed to help them learn more about how to fight effectively on the nuclear battlefield. What were the effects of shock, blast, and radiation on ships, planes, tanks, and, most critically, men? Were there efficient ways to decontaminate men and machinery? As the narrator of one recently declassified film about the testing program explained in 1952, "We're trying every angle and every gadget we can to find out what really happens when an atomic bomb kicks out fiercely at the world around it."

Radiation experiments on soldiers began in 1951, the year atomic bomb tests began in Nevada. They continued until 1962, when aboveground tests were halted. Military troops were used in psychological tests, decontamination experiments, flashblindness studies, research involving flights through radioactive clouds, and studies aimed at measuring radioisotopes in their body fluids.

Many of the military experiments also were repetitive and poorly planned. Thomas Shipman, the Los Alamos scientist who guided the lab's health division through much of the Cold War, complained in 1952 that some of the armed forces' studies appeared to be the "same old chestnuts being pulled out of the fire again and again." Five years later Shipman was still complaining about the military's haphazard involvement. "From past experience we know all too well that everybody wants to get into the act. And all too frequently we find within [the] military establishment anxious souls who have had no opportunity to familiarize themselves with what has already been done."

The researchers were a curious blend of spook, scientist, and soldier. Many were physicians who swore by the Hippocratic Oath, yet were willing to administer to their unwitting patients everything from radioactive arsenic to radioactive zinc. Those who were motivated by patriotism, especially scientists who had seen the ravages of two world wars, firmly believed the development and testing of nuclear weapons was essential to maintaining the security of the United States. Shrewd and sophisticated, they were preoccupied with public relations and obsessed with the fear that someone would file a lawsuit against the Manhattan Project or its successors for some imagined illness arising from radiation exposure. Negative publicity and lawsuits, they worried, would jeopardize the nuclear weapons program.

They downplayed the amount of radioactive pollution emanating from the bomb factories and the health risks of fallout, reasoning that a few extra leukemias, bone cancers, or genetic mutations were an unfortunate but unavoidable side effect in the struggle against communism. "People have got to learn to live with the facts of life, and part of the facts of life are fallout," said Willard Libby, a chemist who was awarded the Nobel Prize for developing the radiocarbon dating technique.

When I returned to Italy, Texas, in August of 1997, ten years had elapsed since I found the footnote describing the plutonium injections. Thanks in large part to the massive releases of material that began in 1994, my thin manila envelope had grown to eight filing cabinets. As I sat on Main Street, listening to the late-afternoon, end-of-summer sounds and the deep silence of the country, I wondered what the people of Italy thought of Elmer's story.

Though it was not yet six o'clock, nearly every store on Main Street was closed. City Hall was locked tight. So was the Uptown Café. But several women were talking quietly in the Magic Mirror Beauty Salon, one of the new businesses that had come to town. When I asked them if they had ever heard of Elmer Allen, they all began talking at one. *"I read something about that in the* Fort Worth Star-Telegram.*" "Didn't they test something on him when he was in the Army?" "His widow still lives here, I think." "Isn't she rich on account of that?"*

Fredna did still live in Italy and had received a substantial settlement from the government. But she had not moved out of the small house that she shared with Elmer for so many decades. She had aged rapidly and had begun using a walker to get around. While she was still gracious, a guardedness had crept in and she no longer gave interviews. But Elmerine, who as a child had been sent out to Italy's fields with her brother to pick cotton, had become more outspoken than ever. She often said she couldn't imagine going through life without knowing what had happened to her father. Although theirs had been a complicated and combative relationship, the knowledge had helped her better understand him.

On my way out of town, I swung by the cemetery. Sitting astride a lawnmower, a man in a broad-brimmed hat was working his way around the headstones. Down a hill behind this beautifully manicured swath of green is another collection of graves where Italy's African Americans are buried. Elmer Allen is there. On my first trip to Italy, Elmer had been dead only a year and the grass had not yet grown back over the chalky soil where he was buried. Now the grass lay thick and undisturbed. At the head of his grave was a beautifully carved tombstone that wasn't there during my first visit. Next to the Allen family name, the inscription read:

ELMER

JAN. 26, 1911

JULY 18, 1947

"CAL-3"

JULY 18, 1947

JUNE 30, 1991

ONE OF AMERICA'S

HUMAN NUCLEAR "GUINEA PIGS"

The inscription was his family's shorthand way of telling visitors how Elmer had been transformed by the U.S. government from a man into a number after he had been injected with plutonium. This was the story of injustice that Fredna, Elmerine, and I had pieced together at the kitchen table. Strangers, though, might have a hard time deciphering the tombstone's meaning. Even in Italy, the story was already fading from memory.

Would any of what we had learned from the thousands of documents made public over the last several years be remembered? I don't know the answer. The granite, at least, will last.

Eileen Welsome
Albuquerque, N.M.
March 1999

PART ONE

The

"Product"

1

THE ACID TASTE OF PLUTONIUM

The accident occurred on August 1, 1944, a morning like any other in Los Alamos: hot, dry, the sky an indigo bowl over the sprawl of wooden buildings and barbed-wire fences that constituted the core of the Manhattan Project. At seven thousand feet, the New Mexico air smelled of sun, pines, a trace of frost. Occasionally the scent of dust spiraled up from the desert, where temperatures hovered around 100 degrees.

In twelve months, two atomic bombs would be dropped on Japan, and the secret work being carried out in the wooden buildings would be revealed to the world. On the morning of the accident, the atomic bomb had progressed far beyond mathematical theories but was still an unproven weapon. Plutonium, a silvery metal discovered about four years earlier, was one of the key elements that would transform the theories into a fireball.

In Room D-119, a cheerful young chemist named Don Mastick was standing over a sink chatting with his laboratory partner, Arthur Wahl, a chemist not much older than himself and one of the four scientists from the University of California at Berkeley who had discovered plutonium. Mastick was just twenty-three years old, a "bushy-tailed kid," as he would later describe himself, with short blond hair and an alert, friendly face. He had been one of Berkeley's most promising chemistry graduates and was just about to enlist in the Navy when J. Robert Oppenheimer approached him and asked if he would like to join the scientific team being assembled in Los Alamos, the most secret site in the vast network of laboratories and factories established to build the bomb.

Oppenheimer, a brilliant theoretical physicist, was already a legend on the Berkeley campus, and Mastick was thrilled at the idea of working with him. When he arrived in Los Alamos in the spring of 1943, Oppenheimer had designated him the lab's ultra microchemist. Working with amounts of plutonium that were too small to be seen with the naked eye, he studied the chemical reactions of the new material under a microscope. His glass test tubes were no bigger than sewing needles and his measuring instruments looked like a child's toys. Even his laboratory was small: a claustrophobic box at the end of a hallway, ten feet wide and twelve feet long.

In Mastick's hand that day was a small vial containing ten milligrams of plutonium—an amount so small it would have fit on the head of a pin. But it was far more plutonium than Los Alamos had had to work with only a year before. In fact, the radioactive material was still so scarce that a special crew had been assembled whose only job was to recover the material from accidents and completed experiments and then repurify it through chemical processes so it could be used again. The crew developed a flow chart to help separate plutonium from every other element in the Periodic Table. "They were prepared to tear up the floor and extract the plutonium, if necessary. They would even dissolve a bicycle. I mean, plutonium [was] so valuable that they went to great extremes to recover everything," physician Louis Hempelmann recalled decades later.

Inevitably some of the radioactive molecules seeped out into the laboratory, spread by a starched sleeve, the scuff of boots, even the dust that blew in from the desert. Nervous and preoccupied with their efforts to construct a workable bomb, Oppenheimer and his colleagues viewed the spreading contamination with consternation. Their concerns were twofold: They didn't want to lose any material, and they were just beginning to understand its potential hazards. Joseph Kennedy, another member of the Berkeley team who had discovered plutonium, acknowledged that it was "not pleasant" to think that unaccounted-for plutonium was floating around the lab. On the day of this particular accident—which would be the most serious of any thus far—it was not the lost plutonium that would be the problem. It was the plutonium in Mastick's vial.

A purplish-color liquid that gave off an eerie, animallike warmth when concentrated in larger amounts, the plutonium in the vial had undergone an unanticipated transformation overnight. Some of the liquid had been converted into gas and was pushing against the walls of the bottle. Other molecules were tunneling into the sides of the glass itself.

Unaware of the small bomb he was holding, Mastick snapped the slender neck of the vial. It made a small, popping sound in the quiet laboratory. Instantly the material spewed out of the bottle and onto the wall in front of him. Some of the solution ricocheted back into his mouth, flooding his lips and tongue with a metallic taste.

Not overly alarmed, Mastick replaced the vial in its wooden container. Then he trotted across the hard-packed ground of the technical area to knock on the door of Dr. Hempelmann's first-aid station. He had just swallowed a significant amount of the world's supply of plutonium. "I could taste the acid so I knew perfectly well I had a little bit of plutonium in my mouth," he said in an interview in 1995.

Louis Hempelmann's office was just a few minutes' walk from D Building, where Mastick worked. With its "deluge shower baths" and clothes-changing rooms, D Building was one of the most elaborately ventilated and costly structures at Los Alamos. Except for the forest of metal pipes protruding from the roof, it looked no different from the other green clapboard structures in the technical area.

Hempelmann was the medical doctor in charge of protecting technical personnel on the bomb project from "unusual hazards," and he reported directly to J. Robert Oppenheimer. With his long, narrow face and wide jaw, Hempelmann wasn't handsome, but there was something refined and pleasing about his appearance. He was the son and grandson of doctors and a fine physician in his own right, although he was known to grow queasy at the sight of blood. ("Louie did his first sternal puncture on me and he almost fainted. He's one of those doctors that can't stand the sight of blood—he should have been a psychologist or something," said Harold Agnew, one in a line of laboratory directors who succeeded Oppenheimer.)

Taking great pains to keep his long face expressionless, Hempelmann listened to Mastick's account of what had happened and then left the room for a moment in order to make a frantic phone call to Colonel Stafford Warren, the affable medical director of the Manhattan Project. Hempelmann often turned to Warren, who was nearly two decades older, for advice and reassurance. In his late forties when he was commissioned as an Army colonel, Warren was a big man, well over six feet tall, who exuded a breezy confidence. Unlike many of the scientists on the bomb project, who refused to join the armed forces and chafed under military control, Warren loved being in the Army. He liked the rough feel of his starched uniform, the silver eagles on his collar, the .45 revolver tucked in a holster on his belt.

Speaking on a secure telephone line from his office at the Manhattan Project's headquarters in Oak Ridge, Tennessee, Warren tried to calm Hempelmann down. He thought about the accident for a moment and then suggested that the young doctor try using a mouthwash and expectorant to remove the plutonium from the chemist's mouth. Hempelmann hung up and hurried back to the examining room where he prepared two mixtures. The first was a sodium citrate solution that would chemically combine with the plutonium in Mastick's mouth to form a soluble liquid; the second was a bicarbonate rinse that would render the material insoluble again.

Mastick swished the solutions around in his mouth and then spit them into a beaker. The first mouthful contained almost one-half microgram of plutonium. A microgram of plutonium, which is a millionth of a gram, was considered in 1945 to be the maximum amount of plutonium that could be retained in the human body without causing harm. Eleven more times at fifteen-minute intervals Mastick swished the two solutions around in his mouth and then spit them into the beaker.

After the accident, Mastick's breath was so hot that he could stand six feet away and blow the needles on the radiation monitors off scale. His urine contained detectable plutonium for many years. In one of several interviews Mastick said that he was undoubtedly still excreting "a few atoms" of plutonium but had suffered no ill effects.

When the mouth washings finally were finished, Hempelmann ordered the young man to lie down on a cot. Then he pumped out his stomach several times. Carefully he transferred the stomach liquids into a tall beaker. The plutonium would have to be chemically separated from the organic matter in Mastick's stomach and mouth so it could be reused in future experiments. No scientist at the lab had ever undertaken such a task.

Hempelmann gave the young chemist a couple of breakfast waffles for his empty stomach and some Sippy alkaline powders to be taken during the day. Then he turned and handed him the four-liter beaker of murky liquid.

Go, he said, retrieve the plutonium.

Mastick returned to his lab with the beaker and opened his textbooks. It took a "little rapid-fire research," as he put it, to figure out how to separate the plutonium from the organic matter. But he didn't flinch from the task, despite the ordeal he had just been through. "Since I was the plutonium chemist at that point, I was the logical choice to recover it." From Mastick's perspective, the mood in which all these events took place was calm, deliberate, and "almost humorous." But other people did not feel nearly so relaxed about what had occurred.

The day after the accident, Hempelmann sat down and wrote Stafford Warren a thank-you note. "I was sorry to bother you but was anxious to have your help and moral support. In retrospect, I think that the chances of the fellow's having swallowed a dangerous amount of material are slight." Hempelmann told Warren that he believed about ten micrograms of plutonium had entered Mastick's mouth. The mouth washings had removed all but one microgram, an infinitesimal but nevertheless hazardous amount. More important, Hempelmann thought the chemist had not inhaled any plutonium. At that time scientists knew that plutonium was extremely hazardous if it was breathed in and deposited in lung tissue. But they also were discovering that the radioactive material was not readily absorbed through the gastrointestinal tract and that it could not penetrate beyond the outer layer of human skin. Thus, most of the microgram of plutonium in Mastick's mouth undoubtedly would have passed through his digestive system and out of his body without being absorbed.

A catastrophe had been avoided, but the accident was a vivid reminder of the invisible dangers that scientists and workers were confronted with at "Site Y," the code name for Los Alamos. The responsibilities seemed overwhelming to Hempelmann, who was only twenty-nine years old and a neophyte when it came to understanding radiation. He had been working with radioactive materials for three years. As for plutonium, he had only about six months of hands-on experience. "There were all sorts of problems," he admitted years later, "which I just couldn't handle because of limited experience."

2

THE RAD LAB

Research into the atomic bomb had begun in piecemeal fashion at various U.S. college campuses in 1939 when news reached America that two chemists in Nazi Germany had split the uranium atom. But an all-out effort to build the bomb did not really get under way until the U.S. Army Corps of Engineers was brought in and a newly promoted brigadier general named Leslie Groves took charge in September of 1942. With Groves at the helm, the Manhattan Project, or Manhattan Engineer District, as it was more formally known, began the frenetic race to build an atomic bomb.

By then Nazi Germany controlled much of Europe. Many of the scientists working on the bomb project were European refugees who believed Adolf Hitler's scientists were working on a similar bomb. With such a weapon, they feared it would only be a matter of time before Hitler controlled the world.

J. Robert Oppenheimer, who had been selected by General Groves to head the Los Alamos laboratory, had crisscrossed the country in early 1943 trying to lure the nation's most eminent scientists to the remote outpost. His charisma was so great that his opponents claimed he had the uncanny ability to turn bright men, even geniuses, into slavish followers. But, in fact, he had to use all of his persuasiveness to get experienced chemists, physicists, engineers, metallurgists, and explosives experts to go to the remote laboratory.

Many were already engaged in important war work. Others thought the project was preposterous and wanted no part of it. But younger, less established men such as Don Mastick leapt at the chance to do something exciting that would also contribute to the war effort. Mastick was one of the many scientists recruited for the atomic bomb project who had been educated or worked at the premier center for nuclear physics in the United States: the Radiation Laboratory at the University of California at Berkeley.

In the early 1930s, when the "Rad Lab" was just beginning to make a name for itself in the European-dominated world of physics, the young, idealistic scientists working in its sunny classrooms and laboratories dreamed not of weapons of mass destruction but of unlocking the secrets of the universe. From the atom, they sought to learn more about the enormous energy that binds protons and neutrons together, hoping that energy could somehow be used to benefit humankind and perhaps even cure cancer. Dressed in the uniform of their generation—unpressed suits, ties, and clean white shirts—they labored from dawn until dusk, sustained only by an encouraging word from one of their revered leaders, Ernest Lawrence or J. Robert Oppenheimer.

Lawrence, an experimental physicist who was only twenty-seven years old when he first arrived in Berkeley, and Oppenheimer, a theoretical physicist three years younger, were transforming what had been a second-rate school into one of the most renowned institutions in the world for nuclear physics. Both scientists were tall, blue-eyed, ambitious, and inspired a cultlike following among their students. Beneath the surface, though, were distinct differences in their personalities that would emerge over time.

Lawrence was vigorous looking, with his blond hair swept back from his forehead and his face tanned and regular as the Great Plains upon which he was raised. Save for the wire-rimmed glasses, which gave him an intellectual appearance, he could easily have been mistaken for a businessman or football coach. His father was the president of a small teachers' college in Springfield, South Dakota; his mother, a practical matron who taught him to save water and not to swear. He worked his way through the University of South Dakota selling kitchenware from farm to farm. He continued his studies at the University of Minnesota, the University of Chicago, and finally, Yale, where he was offered an assistant professorship. Dissatisfied with the complacency of the students and the snail's pace of his career, Lawrence packed up a bright red coupe in 1928 and headed West. He picked up his mother and father in South Dakota, stashed his younger brother, John, in the rumble seat, and drove on to Berkeley.

Lawrence had an infectious enthusiasm and the quirky, imaginative mind of an inventor. He was convinced from work being done in England that the next great frontier was the atomic nucleus, a dense speck of matter composed of protons and neutrons surrounded by a protective cloud of negatively charged electrons. The atomic nucleus, Lawrence observed in one lecture, was like a "fly inside a cathedral." The only hope of entering the hallowed ground was to pierce the barrier with a particle moving at an enormous speed. In 1929, while he was flipping through foreign publications at the library, Lawrence hit upon the idea of the cyclotron, a contraption that would use a magnetic field to accelerate particles in a circular pattern. With each loop, an electric field would give the particles another push, making them go even faster. When the particles were going fast enough, they would be directed off the circular field and hurled onto targets, which could then become radioactive and eject other particles. With the help of a graduate student named M. Stanley Livingston, Lawrence had his cyclotron, or "atom smasher" as it was called in the popular press, up and running two years later. By the early 1930s, Lawrence had become one of America's best-known physicists. Eventually he was awarded the Nobel Prize for his invention.

Driving a gray battleship of a car, Julius Robert Oppenheimer, known as "Oppie" or "Opje" to friends, arrived in Berkeley the year after Lawrence. He was slender, almost emaciated looking from a long string of illnesses, which included appendicitis, dysentery, and colitis. He had a dreamy, choirboy face and a cloud of black hair when he was young. As he matured, the years wore the softness away and he came to resemble a gaunt medieval scholar.

Oppenheimer was a chain-smoker, his teeth and fingers stained with nicotine. He liked hot, spicy food and ice-cold martinis, and refused to teach a class before 11:00 A.M. The nights, he said, were for thinking and physics. On campus, he wore a gray suit and round-toed black shoes, at home a blue work shirt and faded blue jeans. He was the son of a wealthy New York merchant, but his voice had a strange, slightly foreign accent.

Absorbed in his science and free from financial worries, Oppenheimer was initially so detached from world affairs that he didn't learn of the 1929 stock market crash until after the event. Through a girlfriend, he became sensitized to the plight of the masses and began contributing funds to Loyalists in the Spanish Civil War and migrant workers in California. His ex-girlfriend, his future wife, and even his brother, Frank, became members of the Communist party. Oppenheimer's political activities, which were common among liberal intellectuals of that time, would come to be viewed with deep suspicion by the Manhattan Project's intelligence agents years later.

Oppenheimer was a brilliant though erratic student. After he graduated from Harvard, he went to the Cavendish Laboratory in Cambridge, England, where he floundered badly when he tried his hand at experimental work. Eventually he found his calling in quantum mechanics, a branch of physics dealing with the interaction of radiation and matter, the structure of the atom, the motion of atomic particles, and related phenomena. By the time he reached Berkeley, he had developed a solid international reputation as a theoretical physicist. He predicted the existence of black holes and neutron stars long before astronomers had the instruments to confirm their existence.

In 1935 John Lawrence, the kid brother Ernest had stashed in his rumble seat, went to Berkeley for a visit. Having acquired a medical degree from Harvard, he was a little startled to discover that the men working around the cyclotron appeared to have no inkling of the dangers of radiation—or of the potential medical benefits from the radioisotopes produced on the cyclotron. With the enthusiastic support of his famous brother, John Lawrence and a small group of medical doctors began exploring whether neutrons and radioisotopes could be used to treat cancer patients. (Scientists at that time used the word "radioisotope" to refer to any radioactive element. But technically speaking, a "radioisotope" refers to the radioactive isotopes of one specific element. A "radionuclide" refers to any kind of radioactive isotope and is the term used by contemporary scientists.)

In the cyclotron, radioisotopes were created by bombarding ordinary elements such as iron, phosphorous, and iodine with fast-moving particles. When the speeding particles crashed into a nonradioactive element, the element absorbed the moving particle, lost one of its own subatomic particles, or broke into pieces, thus becoming radioactive. The radioactive version of the element, known as a radioisotope, would "decay," or return to a stable condition after it had rid itself of the energy it had absorbed from the collision, in a process that would take place over minutes, days, or even years. The energy was released in the form of X rays, gamma rays, alpha particles, and beta particles.

Radioisotopes are chemically identical to their stable counterparts. In other words, radioactive iron, phosphorous, carbon, and sodium are metabolized in the human body in exactly the same way as their nonradioactive counterparts. Since radioisotopes emit energy when they decay, they can be easily followed, or "traced," through the body with a Geiger counter.

Many doctors at the time compared radioisotopes to microscopes, hoping they could be used to unlock the hidden, biochemical processes of the human body. By administering a tracer dose of radioactive sodium to a patient, for example, a doctor could follow the path of sodium with a Geiger counter and uncover blockages in the circulatory system. The same principle could be applied to animals, plants, or even industrial processes.

The diagnostic potential of radioisotopes had long been recognized. But Ernest and John Lawrence, as well as other scientists throughout the world, also hoped that radioisotopes might have an even more important function: They dreamed that one of the new radioisotopes might become a "magic bullet" that would find its way to malignant cells and destroy them.

A couple of years after Ernest Lawrence had his first cyclotron operating, he decided that it was time to build a bigger machine that could accelerate particles at an even faster rate. But to build a new cyclotron, he needed money. And what better way to get money than to tout the medical applications of materials made by the cyclotron? Waldo Cohn, a graduate student in Berkeley at the time, remembered dryly, "Lawrence, with his cyclotron, was very anxious to get money to support not only the building of the cyclotron and its maintenance, but also to continue the running of the laboratory. Any possible use of radioactive materials, [any] practical use, he [would] use as a gimmick to convince donors to contribute money to his project."

A masterly salesman, Lawrence began holding a series of public lectures in Berkeley on the medical benefits of the cyclotron-produced materials. As Nuell Pharr Davis, one of the more colorful chroniclers of the Lawrence-Oppenheimer years tells it, Lawrence was up on stage one afternoon with a bottle of liquid containing sodium-24 and a Geiger counter. With a flourish, Lawrence put the counter next to the bottle. Then came an embarrassing moment of silence. One of his assistants had apparently made the solution so radioactive that it swamped the counter's detection abilities. Without losing a beat, Lawrence scanned the audience and saw his tall, blue-eyed friend, J. Robert Oppenheimer, slumped in one of the chairs. "He got me on the platform and used me as a guinea pig," Oppenheimer recalled. "He had me put my hand around a Geiger counter and gave me a glass of water in which part of the salt had radioactive sodium in it. For the first half minute all was quiet, but about fifty seconds after I drank, there was a great chattering of the Geiger counter. This was supposed to show that in at least one complex physiochemical system, the salt had diffused from my mouth through my bloodstream to the tip of my fingers and that the time scale for this was fifty seconds."

Despite an occasional glitch, Lawrence's showmanship paid off handsomely, and the money started flowing in from foundations and wealthy patrons. One of his earliest supporters was Lewis Strauss, a New York businessman who would go on to become a close friend of Lawrence's and an important figure in the Atomic Energy Commission. "We thought or hoped there might be a specific isotope for every part of the body," Strauss said. "I suppose I had the medieval notion of the fencing thrust, or of a magic bullet that would strike straight at the disease."

John Lawrence injected his first leukemia patient with radiophosphorous on Christmas Eve of 1937. Kenneth Scott, a pudgy, young scientist who worked in the laboratory at the time and whose recollections of many of the key personnel and events of the Rad Lab are tinged with bitterness, described the Christmas Eve treatment as a "big grandstand act" designed to attract money and fame for the Lawrence brothers. But Scott's views were not shared by everyone. According to records and interviews with a number of doctors who were practicing medicine at the time, radiophosphorous was genuinely thought to have some therapeutic value for the treatment of certain kinds of leukemia and blood disorders.

Indeed, Ernest and John Lawrence believed enough in the curative power of the neutrons produced by the cyclotron to use it to treat their mother, Gunda. The sixty-five-year-old woman was put on a train for California as soon as the doctor informed her she had cancer of the pelvis. After first undergoing X-ray therapy at the University of California Hospital in San Francisco, located across the bay, she was transported to the Rad Lab, where her sons arranged for a neutron beam from the cyclotron to be turned upon her. Gradually her health improved and she lived for another eighteen years. "She was the very first to be given neutron treatment. It was kept completely confidential," an unidentified physicist told author Davis.

Notwithstanding the apparently successful treatment of Gunda Lawrence, many medical doctors at the University of California Hospital in

San Francisco viewed the use of radioisotopes and neutrons by the Berkeley experimenters with skepticism. A few UCSF doctors, however, became intrigued by the research going on at the Berkeley Rad Lab. UCSF physicians Robert Stone and Joseph Hamilton were among those who would find the Lawrences' work inspiring. In fact, even before John Lawrence had performed his much-ballyhooed phosphorous experiment, Stone and Hamilton had quietly injected two leukemia patients with radioactive sodium. According to a scientific paper written by the two men, the radioactive material did not seem to alter the course of the patients' disease, but neither did it cause any severe side effects. There is no indication whether the patients knew what was being administered or gave their permission.

The sodium experiment, performed in 1936, would mark the beginning of a long relationship between the two men. Stone was nearly a decade older than Hamilton, but he said in a tape-recorded memoir that it was Hamilton who "stimulated me into working with him on radioisotopes." Stone was a small, benign-looking radiologist who wore glasses and had a thick head of gray hair. Although he had a gentlemanly demeanor and was well liked by his colleagues, he grew extremely angry when anyone challenged his medical judgment.

Born in Canada in 1895, Stone went to Europe with the Canadian Expeditionary Forces during World War I, was wounded, and returned to Canada, where he resumed his education. By 1924 he had a bachelor's degree, a master's degree, and a medical degree from the University of Toronto. He joined the faculty at the University of California at San Francisco in 1928, becoming the hospital's first full-time radiologist. Almost immediately, he was drawn into the research across the bay at the Rad Lab. "Ernest Lawrence was a great stimulus to our department from the very beginning," Stone recalled in his tape-recorded memoir.

Like the Lawrence brothers, Stone believed that neutrons had great potential for deep-seated cancers. More biologically effective than X rays by a factor of ten or more, neutrons interact readily with human tissue, causing a series of physical and chemical changes in the body.

With the help of a young scientist named Paul Aebersold, Stone began using the neutron beam from the Rad Lab's cyclotron for his human experiments. Between December of 1939 and September of 1941, he bombarded some 128 patients with neutrons. They were irradiated in a small lead-lined chamber adjacent to the cyclotron. Some of the patients came from the UCSF's outpatient clinic and were in good or fair condition. Others came from the "Visible Tumor Clinic" and were deemed to be suffering from cancers that could not by cured by normal surgical or X-ray treatment. Still others were apparently well-to-do individuals who had been referred to Stone by other doctors.

At first, everything seemed to go well. As Kenneth Scott recalled of that period, "Dr. Stone's wealthy patients used to roll up with chauffeurs and their iced champagne. In the laboratory they had a big field day that afternoon; we all got smacked on champagne and I thought it was wonderful."

As the experiment progressed, however, it became clear that Stone had underestimated the biological effects of neutrons. Although they are effective at killing cancer cells, they are difficult to control and can cause a lot of collateral damage to healthy cells as well. Nearly half of the patients died within six months of the treatment period. Many of the subjects suffered horribly from the side effects. Some developed gruesome skin damage that one radiobiologist likened to armor plates. Others eventually died of malnutrition rather than their underlying disease because they had such painful ulcers in their mouths they couldn't eat. Although Stone acknowledged the statistics were discouraging, he nevertheless recommended that neutron therapy be continued because the neutrons did shrink tumors and, in some cases, caused them to disappear altogether.

While Robert Stone was discovering the good and bad effects of neutrons, his young sidekick, Joseph Hamilton, continued to explore the medical possibilities of radioisotopes. According to Scott, Hamilton had become interested in radioisotopes almost by accident. Scott was analyzing mouse tissue at his laboratory bench one day when Hamilton, dark-haired and smooth-looking, slipped onto the stool behind him and asked him what he was doing. "He was just a young resident in neurology interested in doing something interesting," Scott remembered. Scott later worked for Hamilton but the two men never became close friends: "He was the kind of guy who gets his zipper stuck in the men's room, he won't let anybody help him. I caught him in the men's room one day and he couldn't get his zipper up, and he wouldn't let me help him with it. So I got him a pair of scissors. I guess he cut himself out of there one way or another."

To the casual observer, Hamilton seemed like any other affluent, urbane doctor; he enjoyed fine wine, drove a convertible, played poker. But documents written by Hamilton himself as well as recollections of his colleagues reveal a suspicious and brooding side to his personality. As his hairline receded and pouches formed beneath his eyes, he developed a scowling and remote appearance that seemed a more accurate reflection of the inner man.

Hamilton was trained as a medical doctor to heal the sick, yet he recoiled from human touch. He was taught to respect the sanctity of human life, yet he plotted ways to poison the food and water supply of enemies with radioactive materials. Anne de Gruchy Low-Beer, a contemporary and wife of one of his colleagues, said, "He didn't have any warm friendships. He was not the kind of person to make them." Patricia Durbin, a Berkeley scientist who as an undergraduate washed glassware in Hamilton's lab and is to this day one of his most devoted fans, saw the same qualities but in a more positive light. Hamilton, she said, "would have been very much at home in mid-Victorian Sweden, hard bound, bound by rules of conduct, narrow, not to show in public that you had either emotions or affection."

Hamilton's guarded nature may have been a defense mechanism developed in response to the probing eyes of his father, Gilbert Van Tassel Hamilton, an author, scientist, and avid experimenter. A contemporary of Sigmund Freud, the elder Hamilton was a "psychopathologist" who specialized in the study of human sexuality. Hamilton Sr. moved to southern California sometime before 1914 and began treating many well-known personalities, including playwright Eugene O'Neill. In a live-oak woods in Santa Barbara, the elder Hamilton also maintained a spacious laboratory where he did observational experiments on monkeys and baboons. He would place various combinations of animals—even different species—in cages together and then record their behavior and sexual couplings in steamy, overwrought language. Joseph Hamilton was an only child and undoubtedly served as an experimental subject for his father— at least on an observational level. In a discussion about the suckling behavior of animals, the elder Hamilton once wrote that his son had sucked both his thumb and his Teddy bear until early adolescence.

Hamilton attended schools in Santa Barbara and then enrolled in the University of California at Berkeley. He graduated with a bachelor's degree in chemistry and then crossed the bay, where he obtained his medical degree from the University of California at San Francisco in 1936. During medical school, he married painter Leah Rinne, who had had rheumatic fever as a teenager and suffered from ill health for much of her life. The couple owned a log cabin in the Sierra Nevada where Hamilton liked to pan for gold.

Although Hamilton's colleagues thought he was a bright and imaginative scientist, he didn't have the patience for painstaking research nor did he possess the originality that produces great scientific discoveries. "We considered him a kind of explorer," Stafford Warren remembered years later. "He didn't want to do any of these long-term, big-scaled things. He was not that kind of an operator. He had a mind that was very quick and very imaginative." Toward the end of his life, he told Patricia Durbin on several occasions, "what he liked to do was get in there early and skim off the cream and go on to something else."

Like Ernest Lawrence, Hamilton often gave public talks about the benefits of radioisotopes. Instead of sodium, he used radioactive iodine, which has a longer half-life and concentrates in the thyroid gland. As for the guinea pig, Hamilton used himself. He would pour the radioactive iodine into a water glass and then hold a Geiger counter up to the glass so the audience could hear the clicks. "Then he would walk across the room and put it up to himself and there were no clicks," recalled Patricia Durbin. "He would drink the water, and in order to demonstrate how valuable this tool was with respect to the thyroid metabolism, at the end of his lecture he would put the Geiger counter up to his neck—lots of clicks."

Hamilton was cold, sober, serious-minded. Yet, at the edges of his life, there was a giddy recklessness. He immersed himself in radiation, gulping down "radioactive cocktails" and flying through radioactive clouds in the postwar years. But where he really pushed his luck was around the cyclotron. He raced into the bombardment area to grab samples while the room was still radioactive and slouched against the hot, ticking parts of the machine with a nonchalance that radiologist Earl Miller still found staggering decades later. "I tried to talk to him about the danger," Miller told interviewers from the Department of Energy in 1994. "This was massive doses of radiation that he exposed himself to."

Perhaps as he watched the delicate starlike shapes from plutonium emerge on film, or when he looked up from a microscope late at night in the stillness of the laboratory, the knowledge suddenly came to Hamilton that he was carrying the irradiated cells of his own death within him or, as colleague Kenneth Scott bluntly put it, that he "had already had it."

Hamilton was one of the many Manhattan Project veterans who often boasted after the war about how safe the nuclear weapons industry was, but he was to become one of its first casualties. Sometime in the 1950s, he grew pale and wan, plagued by infections, bleeding gums, and bruises. He had contracted a fatal form of leukemia, a disease that can be induced by exposure to radiation. His sister-in-law, Christine Alan, said Hamilton diagnosed the illness himself. John Gofman, a Berkeley scientist who has written extensively on the effects of small doses of radiation, said Hamilton "looked like a ghost" after he became ill. Patricia Durbin added, "I would be willing to bet that his [radiation exposure] would have been if not the highest, among the highest ever recorded in Berkeley."

Through the 1930s and into the early 1940s, the Rad Lab continued to attract eager new students interested in working with one of the great masters, Ernest Lawrence or J. Robert Oppenheimer, or with the lesser-known physicians who were using the side products of the cyclotron to forge a new discipline that came to be known as nuclear medicine. The students came not only from California but from other parts of the United States and even Europe.

One of the pilgrims was Hymer Friedell, an extremely bright and talented young doctor with a medical degree and a doctorate in radiology from the University of Minnesota. Friedell began hearing about Berkeley while he was working in New York at Memorial Hospital (today known as the Memorial Sloan Kettering Cancer Research Institute) and thought he had better get himself to California. "I wrote to Dr. Stone and asked him if he would accept me. And he did. So I came and became a member of the staff."

Friedell helped Stone with his neutron experiment and treated a few of his patients. With John Lawrence and other doctors, he also administered radioactive phosphorous and radioactive strontium to cancer patients. The radiophosphorous seemed especially effective in the treatment of breast cancer, Friedell recalled. But the radiostrontium, which behaves like calcium in the body, was a failure. Joseph Hamilton, in a letter written years later, said one of Friedell's patients had almost died from too much radiation after he gave her a small amount of radioactive strontium. When Friedell was asked about Hamilton's remarks, he said Hamilton was confused and must have been talking about radioactive phosphorous. But in an interview with fellow scientist J. Newell Stannard more than a decade earlier, Friedell said, "I was assigned a project very early working on radiostrontium. In fact I did some terrible things in my day. I took radiostrontium, and I was going to cure some tumors because it was going into bone, bone tumors. I got some into the bone (tumors), but I also got a hell of a lot into normal bone, too."

While Hymer Friedell was doing his apprenticeship, Louis Hempelmann was finishing his residency in Boston, Massachusetts. One day he got an inquiry from a medical colleague back home in St. Louis. Washington University was building its own cyclotron; would Hempelmann be interested in treating cancer patients with the radioactive materials created by the machine?

Hempelmann was intrigued by the offer. Washington University was his alma mater and St. Louis was his hometown. He had received his undergraduate degree in 1934 and his medical degree in 1938 from the university. He also had many friends and well-established acquaintances in St. Louis. His wife, Elinor Wickham Pulitzer, was the daughter of Joseph Pulitzer, publisher of the *St. Louis Post-Dispatch,* for whom the Pulitzer Prizes are named.

The idea of returning to St. Louis was attractive, but Hempelmann had absolutely no experience with cyclotrons or radiation therapy. So he decided to get a fellowship and find out more. He spent three months working in St. Louis and then struck out for the Rad Lab where all the breakthroughs were being reported and little, if anything, was being said of the failures.

Like Hymer Friedell, Hempelmann worked with Robert Stone and John Lawrence. Hempelmann was modest and unassuming and probably said little as he made the medical rounds in San Francisco or crossed the bay to Berkeley where the patients were being bombarded with neutrons. The neutron exposures left deep marks, like an iron that had burned through a sheet, on the patients' skin. Hempelmann had a first-rate mind and would soon see for himself how hazardous radioactive materials could be if they were not carefully administered. Nevertheless, he viewed the Berkeley research as the wave of the future.

After four months in Berkeley, Hempelmann went to Memorial Hospital in New York (where Hymer Friedell had just been) and spent another month studying radiation physics. Then he returned home to St. Louis. Before the year was out, on Sunday, December 7, 1941, the Japanese attacked Pearl Harbor. Nearly twenty ships and 292 aircraft were destroyed, and 2,403 Americans killed and 1,178 wounded. The following day the United States declared war on Japan, Germany, and Italy. Hempelmann, like millions of other young men, would soon be drawn into the war.

3

1942: THE MET LAB

Arthur Holly Compton, a handsome man who was just entering his fiftieth year, sat up as straight as he could in his sickbed as the group of scientists climbed the stairs to the third floor of his Chicago town house for the meeting he had called. With the visitors came a blast of wintry air and the sense of urgency that had seemed to grip the entire country since President Roosevelt's declaration of war six weeks earlier. Ernest Lawrence, his handsome face reddened by cold and excitement, sat down on the bed opposite Compton. Luis Alvarez, one of Lawrence's protégés, sat down next to his mentor. Standing close enough to participate in the discussion but far enough away to reduce the risk of catching cold was Leo Szilard, a brilliant Hungarian physicist known to his friends as "Leo the Lizard." Two other scientists also had squeezed into the room.

The date was January 24, 1942. The scientists had met at Arthur Compton's home to decide where a central laboratory should be located for further investigations into the chain reaction. Compton was the head of a National Academy of Sciences committee that had just finished a study concluding that an atomic bomb could be built. It was the most positive and concrete report written to date, providing estimates of the time it would take to build such a weapon, the amount of fissionable material needed, and what it would cost. Although the United States was now officially at war and President Roosevelt recognized that raw materials and manpower would soon be in short supply, he nevertheless was so impressed by Compton's report that he had given his approval for the project to proceed to the construction phase on January 19, just five days before the meeting in Compton's sickroom.

Many scientific advances had been made since December 1938 when radiochemists Otto Hahn and Fritz Strassman split the uranium nucleus in their Berlin laboratory. The German scientists could hardly believe what had happened. They checked and rechecked their findings, and then Hahn contacted a trusted colleague, Lise Meitner, a superb physicist who had been forced to flee Nazi Germany and was living in Sweden. Meitner thought deeply, conducted numerous calculations, and talked the matter over with a nephew, Otto Frisch, also a physicist. She suspected the uranium atom, when it captured the neutron, had become unstable and divided into two parts. Using Albert Einstein's theory of mass and energy, she calculated the energy released from one atom was equal to 200 million electron volts. Meitner was convinced that Hahn and Strassman had indeed split the uranium atom and wrote them a letter of congratulations. Then her nephew set out for Copenhagen to tell Niels Bohr, the great Danish physicist, of the discovery.

Bohr, who was about to board a boat for America, struck his forehead in sudden understanding when he heard the news. As his ship lurched across the Atlantic, Bohr pondered the scientific implications of the discovery. When he reached the United States, Bohr inadvertently leaked news of the Hahn-Strassman experiment and the Meitner-Frisch interpretation to fellow scientists. The information spread like wildfire. The profound ramifications of the discovery were immediately understood by scientists in the United States as well as those working in England, France, Germany, Russia, and Japan.

The physicists suspected that when a uranium atom splits, it might eject two or three more neutrons. Those neutrons could smash into other atoms and break them up. Soon a chain reaction would be ignited in which geometrically increasing amounts of energy would be released. A controlled reaction could be used to generate heat and power. An uncontrolled reaction could lead to an explosion of unimaginable proportions.

Leo Szilard, a balding, portly scientist, had prophesied such a chain reaction even before the German chemists had split the uranium nucleus. When he heard the results of the Hahn-Strassman experiment, his mind leapt ahead to Hitler, whose September 1939 invasion of Poland was still some months away. The Nazi leader would be unstoppable with an atomic weapon in his arsenal.

Szilard, who had an imaginative, restless mind and an uncanny ability to see into the future, was deeply worried by the news. After discussing the matter with fellow Hungarian scientists Eugene Wigner and Edward Teller, he asked Albert Einstein, then working at Princeton University, if he would use his enormous scientific prestige to help him get a letter of warning to President Roosevelt. Einstein, who had known Szilard for many years, agreed. In a letter dated August 2, 1939 and delivered several months later through an intermediary, Einstein warned Roosevelt that "extremely powerful bombs of a new type" could be constructed. The Germans, he added, were already investigating the chain reaction phenomenon.

Responding cautiously at first to Einstein's appeal, Roosevelt authorized a group of civilian and military representatives to look into the potential military applications of nuclear fission. Scientists working in laboratories at Columbia, Princeton, and Berkeley soon realized that while a bomb was theoretically possible, constructing such a weapon was fraught with enormous technical difficulties. Chief among them was finding a way to enrich uranium to the point it could be used in a fission bomb.

While work progressed on this difficult task, a young chemist in Berkeley named Glenn Seaborg continued the promising research which had been started by his colleague, Edwin McMillan. As soon as news of the German breakthrough reached Berkeley, McMillan had begun bombarding uranium with neutrons produced by the cyclotron. During the process, McMillan and fellow scientist Philip Abelson discovered a new element that lay beyond uranium, then the heaviest known element in the Periodic Table. McMillan called the ninety-third element neptunium, after the planet Neptune. McMillan suspected there was another, even heavier element beyond neptunium, but before he could confirm his hunch, he agreed to go to MIT's newly established radar laboratory to help with defense work.

After McMillan moved east, Seaborg wrote to him and asked for permission to continue his research. McMillan said he would be "pleased" to have Seaborg's help. Seaborg enlisted the aid of Arthur Wahl, then a graduate student, and Joseph Kennedy, an instructor in UC-Berkeley's chemistry department, and the assault on the new element began.

Seaborg, a tall scientist with blond hair and hazel eyes who had received his Ph.D. in chemistry at the age of twenty-five from University of California at Berkeley, had been chagrined when he learned that the

Germans were the first to report splitting the uranium atom. But he soon suspected that there was still-uncharted country beyond uranium where new elements were waiting to be identified. Seaborg, who would go on to identify many of those elements, recalled years later, "The new land had not really been discovered."

Seaborg's team began their backbreaking attack on the ninety-fourth element in the fall of 1940. First the uranium had to be bombarded in the cyclotron, where some of it would be transmuted to plutonium. Then the plutonium would have to be isolated through a series of tedious chemical processes. By Tuesday, February 25, 1941, the team had solid evidence that they had isolated the ninety-fourth element. It was later confirmed to be plutonium-238, a very radioactive isotope of plutonium with a half-life of about eighty-six years.

But Seaborg was not yet through with his labors. With the help of Emilio Segré, one of Enrico Fermi's colleagues, he continued to bombard uranium samples in the cyclotron in order to isolate a second isotope, plutonium-239. As the radioactivity increased, the men donned goggles and lead gloves and worked behind lead shields. They placed the radio-active mixture in a centrifuge tube, which was inserted into a lead beaker. Then they carried the lead beaker from room to room in a wooden box with long poles, which served as handles. Seaborg and his colleagues finally isolated a minuscule speck of plutonium-239 on March 6. About two weeks later, they completed tests showing that plutonium-239, with a half-life of about 24,000 years, would fission violently.

Although it would be nearly a year before the new substance got its formal name, Seaborg's team followed McMillan's lead and called the ninety-fourth element plutonium, after the small planet Pluto that orbits the sun at the outer edges of the solar system. "It really should have been called 'plutium,'" Seaborg said, "but we liked how plutonium rolled off the tongue." Pluto was also the name of the Greek god of the under-world. Deaf to prayers and unmoved by sacrifices, Pluto was the most hated and feared of all the gods. He owned a helmet that rendered him invisible.

Plutonium, also feared and invisible when it was first discovered, offered scientists a second and perhaps more plausible way to build a bomb. Ernest Lawrence immediately recognized its potential. Pluto-nium-239, he told government officials, could be used to create a "super bomb." But how would plutonium be produced? Assuming a cyclotron could make a milligram a month, it would take about 500,000 years to scrape together enough plutonium for a bomb. But some other apparatus that could be used to produce plutonium—a nuclear reactor, for example—might do the trick.

At Columbia University, Enrico Fermi was already hard at work on the problem. Fermi, who was awarded the Nobel Prize in 1938 for the discovery of new radioactive substances and his work with slow neutrons, had actually been the first to split the atom in 1934 but didn't recognize it as such. He was an undisputed genius, a small, wiry man who had learned English from reading Jack London stories. In a drafty laboratory, Fermi and his assistants were engaged in the grimy job of trying to build a crude nuclear reactor by layering chunks of uranium and graphite on top of each other. Fermi called his towering creations "piles" because that's exactly what they looked like. Fissioning uranium would produce the neutrons; graphite would act as a moderator and slow the neutrons down. Fermi believed the "pile" would be able to sustain a controlled chain reaction once the technicalities were worked out. And then they would have the plutonium they needed to build the bomb.

On the day the scientists crowded into Arthur Compton's sickroom (actually the bedroom of one of his children), all of these facts were known. With Compton listening, each of the men began pitching his respective university as the best place to build the chain-reacting pile and perform the chemical research on plutonium. Szilard, who was working at Columbia with Fermi, argued that the project should remain in New York. To disassemble the experimental piles, pack up the scientists' families, and move halfway across the country would mean a loss of valuable time.

But Ernest Lawrence countered that the project should be established in Berkeley. After all, it was Glenn Seaborg, one of Lawrence's young colleagues, who had isolated plutonium (and would marry Lawrence's secretary in a few short months). Besides, there was something undeniably magical about Berkeley. The classrooms and laboratories were filled with Nobel laureates and future Nobel laureates, and scientific discoveries seemed to occur as effortlessly as the ripe apricots that dropped from trees in nearby orchards.

Compton, himself a Nobel Prize winner, already had his mind made up. He insisted that the project should be housed at the University of Chicago for a number of reasons: The school's administrators had promised full cooperation; housing was adequate; more scientists were available in the Midwest than on the eastern or western seaboards; and the city was not as vulnerable to military attack as the coastal cities.

Lawrence objected. "You'll never get the chain reaction going here. The whole tempo of the University of Chicago is too slow," he told Compton.

"We'll have the chain reaction going here by the end of the year," Compton retorted.

"I'll bet you a thousand dollars you won't," responded Lawrence.

When Compton accepted the bet, Lawrence dropped the stakes to a five-cent cigar. As soon as the scientists left, Compton climbed out of bed and called Enrico Fermi—the man upon whose shoulders the success of the whole plutonium project rested. Everything would flow from his chain-reacting pile, if only he would agree to move from New York. Fermi was a congenial man and eager to do his part. Reluctantly he agreed to make the move.

"The project for producing plutonium, as yet unseen even under a microscope, using a nuclear reactor that was still imaginary, and of fashioning this plutonium into bombs whose explosiveness had never been tested, was now ready to go," Compton wrote in his memoirs. The coordinated effort was given the code name of the "Metallurgical Project." Eventually the research would be spread out among some seventy groups located throughout the country, but the most critical work would be done at the University of Chicago, in a group of buildings that came to be known simply as the Met Lab.

Within a matter of weeks, the scientists began arriving. Compton's wife, Betty, found rooms in a friend's home for Enrico and Laura Fermi and their two children. Fermi's two assistants shared a room in Compton's house. On a racket court under the West Stands of Stagg Field, Fermi's men began building a series of piles that were far below the size needed for a chain reaction but would help them better understand the behavior of neutrons.

Compton also persuaded Glenn Seaborg to move his research from Berkeley to the Met Lab. Seaborg and a colleague, Isadore Perlman, arrived in Chicago on April 19, 1942—Seaborg's thirtieth birthday—following a two-day train trip aboard the *City of San Francisco*. As the two scientists left the station, they scanned the Chicago newspapers: Tokyo was being bombed by Allied troops and the flimsy Japanese homes were going up in flames.

In a few short months an extraordinary collection of scientists was working at the Met Lab. They would be eclipsed in brilliance only by those eventually assembled at Los Alamos. They included Eugene Wigner, a future Nobelist known for his almost painful politeness; James Franck, a highly respected German physicist and a 1925 Nobel Prize winner; and, of course, Leo Szilard, who roamed from lab to lab, offering advice and opinions to anyone who would listen. One scientist, distracted by Szilard's talk, suggested putting him in a state of suspended animation and then reviving him for two minutes each year. "He could give us enough ideas to keep us busy for the rest of the year. For two minutes he'd be fantastic, but how marvelous life in the lab would be for the rest of the year."

Compton also asked J. Robert Oppenheimer to take over the theoretical studies necessary to construct the actual bomb. He had quizzed Oppenheimer about his Communist connections, but the scientist assured him those days were over. "I'm cutting off all my Communist connections," Compton quoted him as saying. Oppenheimer assembled a group of scientists in Berkeley whom he called "the luminaries" to help him with his theoretical work. Among them were Edward Teller, Hans Bethe, Robert Serber, and John Manley.

Before Glenn Seaborg's chemists began their laboratory experiments, they spent two days with the project's top leaders discussing how to go about studying plutonium. Met Lab officials decided that plutonium research was to have a "special category of secrecy," Seaborg wrote in his journal, and information about it would be strictly limited to a small circle of people within the lab itself. To further ensure its secrecy, the leaders decided a new terminology was needed. He wrote:

> At Berkeley, we have been using the code names "silver" for neptunium (element 93) and "copper" for plutonium (element 94), but this is often confusing and we have been forced to resort to such expressions as "honest-to-God" silver and "honest-to-God" copper when referring to these elements themselves. It was agreed that the names "neptunium" and "plutonium" should not be used as code words for elements 93 and 94 because they might be revealing if overheard.

The group came up with new code words for those elements derived from the last digit in the atomic number and the last digit in the atomic weight for each isotope. Thus plutonium-239, with an atomic number of 94 and an atomic weight of 239, became known for the duration of the bomb project as 49. Soon another code name for plutonium emerged: the product.

The Chicago chemists worked with amounts of plutonium even smaller than those available to the Los Alamos chemists a year and a half later. Since the machine shops were already swamped with requests from the physicists, Seaborg's men fashioned their own tiny instruments. They made balances from quartz fibers to weigh their precious millionths of a gram. Miniature pans were created from very thin platinum foil cut and shaped under the microscope. To protect the delicate instruments from air currents, they surrounded them with small cases constructed from wood and glass.

While the chemists were making their instruments, five kilograms, or about eleven pounds, of uranyl nitrate hexahydrate was being bombarded with neutrons in Berkeley. From those eleven pounds, the Berkeley group extracted one microgram of plutonium, or one-millionth of a gram. The precious microgram was forwarded to Chicago. Since the sample was too small to be seen with the naked eye, radiation counters were used to determine its presence. The Met Lab then turned to Washington University in St. Louis for additional help. The St. Louis cyclotron had a more powerful beam than the one at the Rad Lab, and by early August it had produced 50 micrograms of plutonium, a collective amount that was about one-tenth the size of a grain of salt.

To make the micrograms of plutonium, the St. Louis cyclotron crew worked around the clock. It was hot, dirty work, and it gave Louis Hempelmann, one of the crew members, a lifelong appreciation for imponderably small amounts of plutonium. Hempelmann had begun helping out on the cyclotron soon after returning to St. Louis. He also had established a clinic where cancer patients were treated with radiophosphorous made in the cyclotron. Hempelmann injected the radioactive material into the veins of patients two to three times a week. He soon grew uneasy when some of the patients developed dangerously low blood counts and even hemorrhages. While he was convinced that radiophosphorous was still a valuable tool, he nevertheless warned doctors in a scientific paper to monitor blood counts carefully so that treatment could be halted before "irreversible toxic effects on the bone marrow are produced."

By August 20, 1942, Seaborg's microchemists had isolated their first visible speck of plutonium. It was pink in color. Wrote Seaborg, "It is the first time that element 94 (or any synthetic element, for that matter) has been beheld by the eye of man. I'm sure my feelings were akin to those of a new father who has been engrossed in the development of his offspring since conception." A holiday spirit soon enveloped the Met Lab. One of the team brought in flood lamps and photographed every-thing in sight.

The chemists' elation turned to wrenching disappointment five days later when Isadore Perlman went to his lab one morning to work with his microscopic allotment of plutonium and found the contents spilled on a Sunday edition of the *Chicago Tribune*. Someone who was concerned about radiation apparently had surrounded the beaker with lead bricks, one of which had fallen over and smashed the glass. Perlman placed the newspaper into a large dish and poured nitric acid over it. Once the Sunday paper had been dissolved, he could retrieve the plutonium through a chemical process.

The chemists soon discovered that plutonium was an "absolutely crazy" metal. Small amounts undergo spontaneous combustion in air; therefore, it must be handled in an atmosphere devoid of oxygen. De-pending on its chemical compound, it can be blue, green, purple, yellow-brown, red, or pink. "Plutonium is so unusual as to approach the unbelievable," Seaborg once observed:

> Under some conditions, plutonium can be nearly as hard and brittle as glass; under others, as soft and plastic as lead. It will burn and crumble quickly to powder when heated in air, or slowly disintegrate when kept at room temperature. It undergoes no less than five phase transitions between room temperature and its melting point. Strangely enough, in two of its phases, plutonium actually contracts as it is being heated. It also has not less than four oxidation states. It is unique of all the chemical elements. And it is fiendishly toxic, even in small amounts.

No one who held plutonium ever forgot its seductive warmth. Leona Marshall Libby, one of the few female scientists at the Met Lab, said it felt like a "live rabbit." But Arthur Compton thought it was much hotter. "I held in my hand a heavy lump of plutonium, gold-plated to protect me from the alpha particles. Its temperature was so high from its own radio-activity that it almost burned my fingers."

Through the summer and fall of 1942, while Seaborg's team contin-ued their plutonium research, Fermi's group continued its work on the chain reaction under the West Stands of Stagg Field. A towering pile of graphite blocks embedded with uranium was erected. Flat on top and bulging at the sides, the edifice resembled a huge crushed bowling ball. On December 2 Fermi was ready to conduct his first test to see if the pile would actually sustain a chain reaction. It was cold in Chicago that day, about ten degrees above zero. Gas rationing had begun the day before, and the streetcars and elevated trains were jammed.

Threaded down through the pile were cadmium rods that absorbed neutrons and would be used to control the reaction. As Fermi ordered one rod after another removed, the clickety-clack of the neutron counter soon became a roar. When the pile had achieved a sustained reaction for a few minutes, Fermi ordered the control rods reinserted. As the counters subsided, the Met Lab scientists stood around in dazed silence. A bottle of Chianti in a brown paper bag was presented to Fermi. One of the greatest barriers to building a successful bomb had just been hurdled. The unflappable Fermi later said operating a pile was as easy as driving a car.

With the successful operation of Fermi's pile, the stage was set to build a pilot plant where grams of plutonium could be produced. Less than three months later, construction began on a graphite reactor, code-named the X-10 plant, at the Clinton Engineer Works in Oak Ridge, Tennessee. The Clinton Engineer Works, which subsequently became the official headquarters of the Manhattan Project, was a 56,000-acre tract of land located in the foothills of the Smoky Mountains, ancient hills covered with forests and teeming with deer. Several vast factories where uranium-235 would be produced also were located in the rolling hills and valleys. The bomb builders, still unsure whether enough uranium or plutonium could be produced to make a weapon, were hedging their bets and pursuing several ways to produce enriched uranium, as well as plutonium.

The construction on the Tennessee reactor was still in its initial stages when a decision was made to build a full-scale plutonium facility in an even more isolated region. A huge windswept chunk of land in eastern Washington state near the small town of Hanford was selected. This site became known as the Hanford Engineer Works. There the chemical separation methods that Seaborg's team developed in Chicago would be scaled up a billionfold.

4

A TOLERABLE DOSE

In the summer of 1942, when it looked as if Enrico Fermi's pile would actually work, the physicists began to worry about their own safety. The scientists realized that the crude nuclear reactor would be a source of copious amounts of radiation. Fermi's pile would not only create the highly desirable plutonium, it would also create many different radioactive fission products from the middle of the Periodic Table. Extracting plutonium from this radioactive stew would be an extremely hazardous undertaking.

The physicists, Arthur Compton wrote in his memoirs, "knew what had happened to the early experimenters with radioactive materials. Not many of them had lived very long. They were themselves to work with materials millions of times more active than those of these earlier experimenters. What was their own life expectancy?" Compton decided there was only one thing to do: "We must bring to Chicago the most competent men we could find in the field of the physiological effects of ionizing radiations."

Compton put out feelers to various scientists and medical doctors. Several advised him that Robert Stone was the man for the job. As a member of the National Cancer Advisory Council, Compton knew of Stone's experimental use of neutrons for cancer treatment. Although the neutron experiment could hardly be considered a success, Compton nevertheless was impressed by Stone's work at the Rad Lab and invited him to come to Chicago and take over the Met Lab's new Health Division, which would be on an equal footing with the physics, chemistry, and engineering divisions. Stone would have a seat at the table with Compton, Fermi, Seaborg, and the other members of the innermost sanctum. "Stone's exceptional qualification for this work on which the very lives of our workers depended was evident," Compton wrote.

Robert Stone accepted Compton's offer but was slow to immerse himself in the bomb project. Initially he divided his time between Chicago and San Francisco, spending three weeks at the medical school and only one week at the Met Lab. As the pace at the Met Lab increased, Stone reversed his schedule, spending three weeks in Chicago and one week in San Francisco. Eventually he joined the Manhattan Project full time for the duration of the war.

Soon after Stone arrived in Chicago, he realized that a scientist of extraordinary skill would be needed to investigate the new fission products that Fermi's pile would produce. Stone knew of no scientist better qualified for the job than his old partner, Joseph Hamilton. Two months after Stone was hired, Hamilton was put under contract by the Met Lab to do the biological studies on the fission products.

Unlike Robert Stone, Hamilton did not move to Chicago. Instead he remained in Berkeley, where he did his research and then forwarded his reports to Stone. Using the cyclotron, Hamilton produced micrograms of the same radioactive isotopes that would be cooked up in Fermi's pile. Then he exposed rats to the isotopes, killed them, and studied how the radioactive materials were distributed in their bodies. A year or so into this assignment, Hamilton and Stone were among the scientists tapped by the bomb builders to investigate the possibilities of using the fission products as a weapon against the enemy. This investigation was known as radiological warfare, or RW. Hamilton advised Robert Stone in a May 26, 1943, report that radioactive isotopes sprayed from aircraft "offer the possibility of infecting to dangerous levels, large areas such as cities." He added, "The poisoning of water supplies such as reservoirs, wells, etc., and food must be kept in mind."

Radiological warfare was seriously considered by other Manhattan Project scientists and military officials early in the bomb-building effort, when there were still real doubts about whether a workable weapon could be made. J. Robert Oppenheimer and Enrico Fermi once debated whether to use radioactive strontium to poison food supplies. "I think that we should not attempt a plan unless we can poison food sufficient to kill a half a million men, since there is no doubt that the actual number affected will, because of non-uniform distribution, be much smaller than this," Oppenheimer wrote in a May 25, 1943, letter to Fermi. Rad warfare was put on a back burner as the construction of the atomic bomb progressed, but Hamilton continued to nurse the idea for years.

While Joseph Hamilton conducted his rat experiments in Berkeley, Robert Stone was busy organizing the Met Lab's Health Division. There were three major sections: the medical section, responsible for the health of the workers; the health physics section, which monitored the labs and developed new radiation measuring instruments; and the biological research section, which undertook a massive program to better understand the effects of external and internal radiation from materials inhaled or ingested. Each of these sections was working in uncharted territory and making decisions with potentially profound implications for the health of those they were charged with protecting.

The doctors working in the medical section performed routine pre-employment exams and regularly collected blood samples from employees. Generally speaking, low white-cell counts suggested that a worker had been overexposed to radiation, but Stone and his medical team soon suspected blood counts were not a reliable indicator because they varied so widely. He nevertheless ordered the Met Lab doctors to continue collecting blood samples because there was no other way to detect a possible overexposure. At the same time, he directed his staff to start looking for other biochemical changes in the blood, urine, or liver that might be indicators. This inquiry, begun legitimately enough, was the start of a long and ultimately fruitless search for a so-called biological dosimeter. The effort would cost millions of dollars and occupy scores of civilian and military researchers for the next thirty years.

The health physics section had the job not only of monitoring the labs for radiation but also translating what those results meant to exposed workers. This was not an easy task, given the fact that little or nothing was known about some of the different kinds of radiation they would encounter. To further complicate matters, the various forms of radiation differ greatly in the damage they can cause in human tissue.

As radioactive materials decay, energy is liberated in the form of X rays, gamma rays, alpha particles, or beta particles. When these rays and particles strike human cells, a tremendous transfer of energy occurs. The incoming energy can disrupt the delicate latticework of chemical bonds that hold atoms and molecules together and start a chain of events with several possible and quite distinct outcomes: a harmless dead cell, an impaired cell, or an altered cell that triggers the runaway growth known as cancer.

Alpha particles are ejected from radium, plutonium, uranium, and many fission products as they decay into another form. One milligram of plutonium, which was a tenth of the amount in Don Mastick's vial, emits 140 million alpha particles per minute. Each alpha particle consists of two protons with two positive charges and two neutrons with two neutral charges. Although an alpha particle can travel only about three or four cell lengths, or about half the width of a strand of human hair, because of its large mass and charge, it can create extensive damage in a very small amount of human tissue through a process called ionization.

Beta particles are high-speed electrons that are 7,000 times smaller than alpha particles. They can penetrate human skin and cause burns, which are called beta burns, or cause damage within the body if they are inhaled or ingested.

Although their origins differ, X rays and gamma rays are essentially identical forms of energy. They are photons, or bundles of energy, moving at the speed of light. Traveling great distances, they can cause damage when they strike the body from the outside or from the inside, when radioactive materials are inhaled or ingested.

When Robert Stone's team began their research at the Met Lab in the late summer of 1942, the basic unit of radiation was known as the roentgen. Named after Wilhelm Roentgen, the discover of X rays, the roentgen measures the ability of X rays to ionize air. Eventually the roentgen was supplanted by the "rem," a term coined by Herbert Parker, one of Stone's employees. The rem takes into account not only the amount of radiation but also its biological impact. (The roentgen, the rem, and the rad, another unit, were considered roughly identical and the terms were used interchangeably through the 1940s, 1950s, and even into the 1960s.)

For Stone and his team, the most challenging part of the job was the biological research into the hazards of radiation. While some knowledge had been gleaned from Berkeley's medical experiments, Stone knew there was still little knowledge about the so-called tolerance dose for neutrons, alpha particles, and beta particles. "It must be remembered," he wrote in a 1943 formerly secret report, "that the whole clinical study of the personnel is one vast experiment. Never before has so large a collection of individuals been exposed to so much irradiation."

That serious hazards existed had long been known. Soon after Wilhelm Roentgen discovered X rays in 1895, the workers who handled the equipment began to exhibit injuries. The operators began noticing peculiar skin conditions, soreness around the eyes, strange muscle spasms, and loss of hair. Within a few years, there were reports of anemia, tumors, and even several deaths. One of the most dramatic examples was the case of H. D. Hawks, an 1896 graduate of Columbia University. Mr. Hawks had been giving public demonstrations of his X-ray apparatus in the New York area until forced to stop work because of the physical effects of the X rays:

> The hair at the temples has entirely disappeared, owing to the fact of Mr. Hawks having placed his head in close proximity to the tube to enable spectators to see the bones of the jaw. The eyes were quite bloodshot and the vision was considerably impaired. The eyelashes began to fall out and the lids to swell. The chest was also burned through the clothing, the burn resembling sunburn. Mr. Hawk's disabilities were such that he was compelled to suspend work for two weeks. He consulted physicians, who treated the case as one of parboiling.

Within a year of Roentgen's discovery, nearly every city in the United States had an X-ray center. The use of X rays increased dramatically in World War I. While the new equipment helped physicians locate bullets and bone fractures, the casualties were mounting among the men who operated the machines. By 1922 one researcher estimated that no less than a hundred radiation pioneers had succumbed to cancer caused by their occupation.

In the mid-1920s, German physicist Arthur M. Mutscheller found injuries from X rays so appalling that he decided it was time to create scientifically valid protection standards. Mutscheller, like many scientists both before and after him, scoffed at the idea of absolute safety. Rather, the idea was to strike a balance between the amount of shielding needed to protect workers and a "tolerance dose" that, while not zero, would not harm X-ray operators.

Mutscheller then surveyed a few facilities and a couple of operators who seemed healthy. From this cursory examination, he concluded that workers could receive with impunity a dose that was translated by other scientists to be roughly the equivalent of six roentgens a month or 0.2 roentgens daily.

In 1934 the United States Advisory Committee on X-Ray and Radium Protection recommended the daily tolerance dose be limited to 0.1 roentgen. Physicist Gioacchino Failla defined a tolerance dose as "that dose of radiation which experience has shown to produce no permanent physiological changes in the average individual."

Stone and others used the concept of "tolerance dose" during the Manhattan Project. The concept evolved into what was called the "maximum permissible exposure" for external radiation or the "maximum permissible body burden" for internally absorbed materials. These concepts imply that there is some safe level of radiation, and they have since been discarded. Most scientists today generally agree that any amount of radiation, no matter how small, has the potential of causing harm.

Robert Stone knew the standard for external radiation was based upon "very sketchy" scientific data. In the 1943 report, he wrote, "It is our hope that the tolerance dose based on very scanty previous knowledge will be found correct—when we have the actual dose carefully followed by the physicists and the clinical conditions followed by the physicians." Knowing that the standard for external radiation was built on such a shaky foundation must only have increased Stone's worries. Added to this burden was the other half of the horrifying equation: The protection standards for radioactive materials absorbed internally were built on equally skimpy scientific data.

Much of what was known about internal exposure was based on the strange case of the radium dial painters. At about the same time the public began learning that X-ray workers were succumbing to fatal anemias and leukemias, reports began surfacing in New Jersey about young, seemingly healthy women who were dying from a strange affliction that first manifested itself with unhealed infections in the mouth. A New York oral surgeon named Theodore Blum was the first to recognize that something was amiss. In 1924 a young woman who painted luminous figures on watch dials had come to him because her jaw had failed to heal following some dental work. Blum took one look at her mouth and realized he was seeing something he had never seen before. "Clinically, I couldn't diagnose a thing, but she told me where she worked, and I surmised that her jaw had been invaded—yes, and pervaded—by radioactivity."

Blum wrote up his findings in a medical journal, ascribing the young woman's afflictions to "radium jaw." His report caught the attention of Harrison Martland, a scrappy medical examiner in Orange, New Jersey, whose suspicions had been aroused by the unexplained deaths of several young women living in the area. Family doctors had attributed the deaths to syphilis, Vincent's angina, anemia, and other diseases. But Martland wasn't satisfied with those explanations and began examining stricken dial painters himself.

The nation's largest dial-painting company, the United States Radium Corporation, was located in Orange, New Jersey, where Martland worked. Other dial-painting companies were in Connecticut, Illinois, and New York City. The dial-painting industry began around 1915 and probably employed some 4,000 women, 800 of whom worked at the Orange plant.

The dial painters applied a luminous paint mixture containing a phopshorescent zinc sulfide and minute amounts of radium to watch dials, buttons, military instruments, even religious artifacts. When the alpha particles emitted by the radium struck the zinc sulfide mixture, they caused tiny scintillations, or flashes. When there were large enough numbers of the flashes, the eye would see them as a uniform illumination.

The dial painters at the Orange plant, almost all of whom were working-class women, worked in a large, airy room on the second floor of the factory called the "Studio." Wearing shirtwaists and skirts, they sat at heavy wooden benches, dipping their camel's-hair brushes into pots of yellowish paint. Since they were paid piecemeal, they worked very rapidly, sometimes painting as many as 250 to 300 watch dials a day.

The women often licked their paintbrushes into a point many times during the course of a work shift. This procedure, which was called tipping, allowed them to better follow the shaded script numbers on a finely made watch. Over the weeks and months, they would swallow many micrograms of radioactive material.

"Depending on their skill, the workers tipped the brush from 1 to 15 times per dial, and painted 250 to 300 dials per day. A worker who licked one milligram of paint from her brush 4 times per dial, 300 dials per day, 5 days per week, would therefore ingest about 4,000 micrograms of radium in 6 months," a young scientist named Robley Evans would later calculate in a paper published in 1933.

Their dresses spattered with the radium paint, the young women would go home and amuse their families by showing them how they glowed in the dark. A few applied the paint to their lips, eyelids, and teeth when they went out on dates.

One of the first dial painters examined by Martland was a thirty-five-year-old woman who was suffering from rapidly progressing anemia. She had worked as a dial painter for six years and was in good health until June of 1925, when bruises began appearing on her body. Soon her gums began to bleed and the tissue on the roof of her mouth and throat began to slough off. Knowing that she had been exposed to radium, Martland performed some tests on her before she died. When a radioactive counter was placed near her body, the instrument began clicking. Although she was exhausted and near death, the woman was asked to blow into a rubber tube that fed into a large glass container. Her captured breath contained significant amounts of radiation in the form of radon gas.

When Martland conducted the autopsy, he found hemorrhages on the woman's abdomen and legs and on her internal organs. Her bones were so radioactive that when he wrapped a bone sliver in a piece of dental film, the material fogged the film. Martland was convinced that the woman's death had been caused by radium and mesothorium, a shorter-lived and hotter isotope of radium also used in the luminous paint mixture.

Radium, which had been discovered in 1898 by Pierre and Marie Curie, behaves like calcium in the body. While most of it is excreted rapidly, some is absorbed in the bloodstream and deposited mainly on the skeleton. As radium decays, it produces radon, an alpha-emitting gas that diffuses through the bloodstream, enters the lungs, and is expelled. Radium also emits gamma rays, which can be detected outside the body.

When Martland examined other young dial painters, he found their bodies and breath were also highly radioactive. The physical effects of the high doses were devastating: Although many of the women were not yet thirty years old, they were so crippled from bone fractures they couldn't stand without the aid of canes. Their bone marrow, the life-giving factory that produces the red and white blood cells and platelets, failed. Their jaws were so damaged from the constant bombardment of the alpha particles that the bones were in danger of snapping when the women yawned or rolled over in their sleep.

Soon after the first grisly deaths were reported, several families filed lawsuits. The cases were widely publicized and the dial painters deluged with nostrums promising a cure. In France, Madame Curie advised the girls to eat raw calf's liver to counteract the anemia. "I would be only too happy to give any aid that I could," she said. Eventually the lawsuits were settled out of court, but the paint companies refused to accept legal responsibility.

Even though Harrison Martland had issued a stern warning about the dangers of radium, the radioactive material continued to be mixed into vaginal jellies, face creams, elixirs, and candy sold throughout the United States. Doctors prescribed radium for every imaginable ailment ranging from arthritis and gout to "debutante fatigue." In 1932, the horrifying death of Eben Byers, a Pittsburgh millionaire, finally brought the dangers of radium to the attention of the American people.

A bon vivant and ladies' man, Byers began consuming a tonic called Radithor for an old football injury. Each bottle contained a microcurie of radium and a microcurie of mesothorium. The radiation initially irritated Byers's blood-forming organs, producing a temporary increase in red and white blood cell production and a momentary sense of well-being. The concoction made Byers feel so good that between 1927 and 1931 he consumed perhaps 1,000 to 1,500 bottles of Radithor and began giving it away to his girlfriends.

Soon the devastation set in. Byers's athletic frame withered to ninety pounds and he turned a ghastly shade of yellow as his bone marrow and kidneys failed. His jaw and part of his skull were surgically removed in an effort to stop the advancing disease, but the operations were useless, and he died.

Officials at the Los Angeles County Health Department, fearing they might soon be swamped with similar cases, sought help from Robert Millikan, a famous Nobel scientist from Cal Tech. Millikan referred the officials to one of his promising graduate students, Robley Evans, who had developed some of the most sensitive radiation detection equipment in the world. As a result, Evans developed a lifelong interest in the dial painters and became one of the world's experts in radiation biology.

After completing his Ph.D. under Millikan at Cal Tech in 1932, Evans moved to Berkeley, where he spent the next two years doing postgraduate work. Ernest Lawrence and J. Robert Oppenheimer were just beginning their remarkable careers, but Evans did not succumb to the charms of either man. He was hard-headed, cold to the point of rudeness, but not without a sly sense of humor. In 1934 Evans, his wife, and two young children piled into his four-cylinder Plymouth and drove east to MIT, where he became a professor of physics and founded the Radioactivity Center. There Evans continued his research on the radium poisoning victims. In his 1933 paper on the dial painters, he reported that as little as two micrograms of radium in the body, or two millionths of a gram, had proved "fatal" in some women.

By the spring of 1941, with the armed forces preparing for a war that had not yet been officially declared, Evans's work on radiation was deemed so important that a Navy medical officer approached him and threatened to draft him if he didn't provide the Navy with maximum permissible levels for radium and radon. The Navy was interested because it used many kinds of luminous instruments on its ships. Evans rapidly assembled a committee, which included Harrison Martland as well as representatives of the radium industry. By then Evans had data on twenty-seven dial painters who had radium burdens in their body. Seven had less than 0.5 microcuries; the other twenty had amounts greater than 1.2 microcuries. (A microcurie is a millionth of a curie. Named after Madame Curie, the curie measures the activity, or rate of decay, of a radioisotope. By contrast, a microgram measures the actual weight.) Evans reviewed the data on the dial painters and then turned to the committee and said:

> Well, my feeling would be that we should set a number which if it was the amount of radium in the body of our wife or daughter, we would feel perfectly comfortable about it. And for me, this is a tenth of a microcurie. "What about you, [Harrison] Martland?" He thought for a moment and said, "Okay." And I said, "What about you [Gioacchino] Failla?" He said, "Okay." We went around the table one at a time like this, and they all agreed one hundred percent. So the secretary of the committee wrote down on that line 0.1 microcurie. So . . . that's how it was done.

Although twenty-seven cases were certainly too small a sample upon which any scientific conclusions could be drawn, over the next four decades Evans and his colleagues examined some 2,000 people with radium in their bodies. He reported in 1981 that he had never seen any symptoms in people with less than 0.1 microcuries in their bodies. Therefore, he concluded, the standard was still good.

But Robert Stone, the worried leader of the Met Lab's Health Division, did not have the benefit of four decades' worth of information. All he knew was that the so-called tolerance dose for radium had been based on only twenty-seven cases. And that was the only data the Met Lab had upon which to base its own protection standards for a wide range of internally absorbed radioisotopes—including plutonium.

Given the scanty data, Robert Stone turned to human experimentation to get the information he needed. His first experiments were aimed at better understanding the effects of small doses of external radiation on humans. By 1943, a year after he took over the Met Lab, he was supervising three experiments at hospitals in San Francisco, New York City, and Chicago. Most subjects used in these experiments were cancer patients who were undergoing radiation treatment for their diseases but had relatively normal blood counts. Stone explained the problem this way in the introduction to the California study:

> The Health Division of the Metallurgical Project was faced with the problem of what changes would occur in individuals exposed to more than the tolerance dose of 0.1 roentgen on one or more days. It was thought that the blood picture of such individuals would show a rapid and radical change. The literature, however, contained very little information on the effect of X-ray exposure on persons with relatively normal hematological pictures, and such investigations as were reported were rather confusing because of the objectives of the studies. Hence it was considered necessary to study the effects of total-body irradiation with X-rays of varying energy on hematologically normal individuals.

In each of the three Met Lab–sponsored experiments, the patients were subjected to radiation administered over their entire bodies in a procedure called total body irradiation, or TBI. Stone maintained that total body irradiation was a bona fide procedure aimed at benefiting the patients. The Manhattan Project, he asserted, was merely taking advantage of the treatments to do blood studies. But statements made by researchers at the time suggest exactly the reverse was true: The blood studies seemed to be the primary focus of the exposures and little, if any, benefit accrued to the patients.

Not surprisingly, the first experiment was conducted at the University of California Hospital in San Francisco. The study began in October of 1942, shortly after Stone joined the Met Lab, and continued through June of 1946. Bertram Vojtech Adelbert Low-Beer, a mild-looking scientist with a round face and a dark fringe of neatly trimmed hair, ran the experiment while Stone was in Chicago.

Low-Beer had fled Czechoslovakia in 1939. At the urging of Mark Oliphant, an Australian physicist who had strongly encouraged the Americans to pursue the atomic bomb, Low-Beer had joined the University of Birmingham. He had just begun his radioisotope research when war broke out in England. John Lawrence invited him to the Rad Lab in

Berkeley in 1941, and with a recommendation from Robert Stone, he was appointed to the medical faculty at UCSF two years later. He was a pleasant man, even jovial at times, but was known to get "extremely worked up" over sloppy or careless work, according to Stone. Like Robert Stone and Joseph Hamilton, Low-Beer had close ties to both the San Francisco hospital and the Rad Lab. He was an expert in the physics, chemistry, and biology of how radioactive substances behaved in human tissue.

Over the four-year period, twenty-nine patients, ranging in age from twenty to seventy-five, were irradiated at UCSF. The exposures per sitting varied from 5 to 20 roentgens and the total dosages ranged from 27 to 394 roentgens. (To put this in perspective, scientists believe 350 roentgens, delivered at one time and without counteractive measures, such as antibiotics, fluids, and bone marrow transplants, will kill 50 percent of those exposed.)

The physical effects of the irradiation on the patients are unknown because the scientific paper written by Stone and Low-Beer addresses only the blood changes. Many blood samples were drawn before the radiation was administered, during the treatment itself, and for a number of weeks afterward. The two experimenters found that radiation exposure did reduce the number of blood cells, particularly white cells, circulating in the body.

A second TBI experiment was conducted from December of 1942 until August of 1944 at Memorial Hospital in New York—the hospital where Hymer Friedell and Louis Hempelmann had worked before the war. The lead experimenter was Lloyd F. Craver, a doctor who had just co-authored a paper stating that TBI was a "discouraging" treatment for patients suffering from generalized cancer. Despite his negative results, Craver conducted an experiment in which eight patients were to be irradiated with a total of 300 roentgens. The planned doses ranged from 10 to 15 roentgens per sitting. The selection of patients was the "most difficult part of the project," Craver wrote, because the subjects had to be in good enough condition to survive "the combined effects of their disease and the irradiation for at least six months in order that some conclusions might be drawn as to later effects of the irradiation."

The experiment didn't work out the way Craver had hoped. Three patients died within two months of the treatment. The others continued to live for a while but did poorly. Craver blamed the deaths and deterioration to the patients' diseases and not the radiation, concluding that "such doses of radiation should be well tolerated by healthy persons."

A third TBI experiment was conducted at the Chicago Tumor Clinic beginning in March of 1943 and continuing through November of 1944. The lead investigator was J. J. Nickson, a young doctor who was only three years out of medical school. The fourteen subjects used in the experiment were divided into three groups. The first consisted of eight cancer patients who had "neoplasms that could not be cured but still were not extensive enough to influence general health." The second group consisted of three patients who had illnesses that were "generalized and chronic" (one of the three was a twenty-five-year-old woman who had a history of "pain and stiffness of the joints"). The third group was composed of three healthy young white men who volunteered to be irradiated with seven roentgens a day over a three-day period. That group was of "particular interest," Nickson wrote, because the men most closely resembled the Met Lab workers themselves. Nickson found no changes in the blood counts of the three men.

Except for these three men, the TBI experiments involved sick people. Although they provided the Met Lab doctors with needed information, many questions about radiation remained:

> What are the first changes produced by exposures just above the tolerance level? Is the peripheral blood picture as reliable an indicator of over-exposure as radiologists have considered it to be? Are there any other changes produced that can be detected by known or newly developed clinical tests? Can a person ever recover completely and entirely from any dose of radiation big enough to produce detectable effects? Are there any methods of treatment that will aid in recovery? How much radiation is necessary to kill a man?

That was Stone, writing in 1947, when answers to those questions were still not known.

5

THE MANHATTAN PROJECT IS LAUNCHED

At about the same time that the Met Lab's Health Division was formed, government officials and scientists involved in the bomb-building effort decided it was time to bring in someone aggressive to oversee the entire project. The Army's Corps of Engineers had been chosen to build the production facilities. But Colonel James C. Marshall, who was supervising the bomb project, was inclined to move cautiously. With the growing wartime demand for recruits and raw materials, the whole effort was in danger of foundering.

On September 17, 1942, Leslie Groves, a tall, pear-shape Army general who had overseen the construction of the new Pentagon building in Washington, was appointed to head the project. Groves, a West Point graduate, had been desperately hoping for an overseas assignment and was bitterly disappointed by the appointment. But the general, like Arthur Compton, was a minister's son who had been schooled in the importance of duty. He swallowed his disappointment and got to work the next day.

Groves was a brilliant administrator who was accustomed to working long hours and handling huge budgets. He had the ability to quickly grasp situations and was willing to make decisions based on incomplete information. Unfortunately, he also had an enormous ego, an abrasive and tactless personality, and a predilection for humiliating people. Although he developed a fairly good working relationship with the company engineers and scientists who were brought into the project from Du Pont, Union Carbide, and Eastman Kodak, his relationship with the Met Lab scientists deteriorated quickly. He considered them "prima donnas" and "crackpots." To Groves, Leo Szilard—a man who wouldn't flush his own toilet because he considered it maid's work—was one of the worst offenders.

Groves often used one of his aides, Colonel Kenneth Nichols, as a go-between with Arthur Compton and the Chicago scientists. He told an interviewer in 1967, "I suspected that Compton liked Colonel Nichols more than he did me. Primarily because Colonel Nichols had a Ph.D. and looked very scholarly and still does, everything done with Compton was generally done through Colonel Nichols; that is, anything that was difficult. That didn't mean that I didn't see a lot of Compton. But if there was anything that was particularly touchy, I always had Nichols do it."

Groves said in his memoirs that soon after he was assigned to the project he realized that he would need a scientist to coordinate the actual design, construction, and testing of the weapon. Because the other scientists who might be suitable candidates for the job were already engaged in other facets of the bomb project, he selected J. Robert Oppenheimer. "It must have been a bitter blow to Compton to have his project pulled away from him, especially after the major success of the chain reaction at Chicago," Leona Marshall Libby, the young scientist at the Met Lab, speculated. "One should remember, in dealing with the Department of Defense, that they are trained to be killers. Especially in wartime, it is almost their duty to leave a trail of bodies behind. In a sense, Compton was a body along Groves' trail."

Groves also decided to establish a new laboratory to design and construct the bomb in New Mexico. An isolated state, it was nevertheless accessible by train, plane, and automobile. The choice could not have pleased Oppenheimer more. He had spent summers as a youth in the Sangre de Cristos, one of the southernmost ranges of the Rocky Mountains, and had grown to love the blues and grays of the desert. Although the two labs would physically look very different, their functions were actually quite similar: The Met Lab's job was to achieve a controlled chain reaction; Los Alamos's mission would be to produce an uncontrolled chain reaction.

In November of 1942, General Groves, Major John Dudley, a Manhattan District officer, Oppenheimer, and Edwin McMillan, who was helping to organize the new lab, arrived in Albuquerque and began driving in a northwesterly direction toward Jemez Springs, one of the proposed sites. Although Jemez Springs was lovely and had plenty of water, it was hemmed in by tall canyon walls. Oppenheimer felt it might have a "depressing effect" on laboratory workers; Groves gave it a thumbs-down because there was no room to expand. Oppenheimer then suggested that they drive over the mountains and take a look at the Los Alamos Ranch School, a private school for boys. When they arrived, it was snowing lightly and the surrounding mountains were vague as clouds. The general immediately endorsed the site for numerous reasons, including its remoteness. "The geographically enforced isolation of the people working there lessened the ever-present danger of their inadvertently diffusing secret information among social or professional friends outside." Oppenheimer was also satisfied. "My two great loves are physics and desert country," he once confided to a friend.

As soon as the owners agreed to sell the boys' school, the Manhattan Project began making plans for the new lab. It would be located on a high plateau near the lip of the Jemez caldera, a huge, collapsed volcano. To the west were the Jemez Mountains; to the east, the blue, slumping line of the Sangre de Cristos; below, the muddy curl of the Rio Grande. Dominating everything was a 360-degree sky and the desert light, harsh as a camera flash at noontime, luminous in the gathering dusk.

Oppenheimer quickly began assembling his team. As in Chicago, the physicists and chemists were recruited first. Then came the medical doctors. Oppenheimer wanted John Lawrence, Ernest Lawrence's brother, to oversee the health and safety aspects of Los Alamos, but Lawrence was already working on high-altitude studies for the Air Force. He suggested that Oppy look up Louis Hempelmann in St. Louis. Oppenheimer went to St. Louis and talked with Hempelmann. Impressed by the young physician's quiet intelligence, he offered him a job.

Ever the pragmatist, Hempelmann decided to do some sleuthing around before he committed himself. He went to Chicago and talked to Robert Stone and his colleagues. They assured Hempelmann his duties would be rather simple; his main task would probably consist of taking blood counts from fifty to sixty people who might be at risk.

Hempelmann then took a westbound train to New Mexico to have a closer look. Oppenheimer, who had arrived in Los Alamos with a few staff members on March 15, 1943, picked Hempelmann up in Santa Fe. Up the canyon they went, following a primitive road that the Corps of Engineers was trying to make passable for the heavy trucks that would soon be arriving with cyclotrons, accelerators, tons of steel, and miles of piping. Until enough housing could be built, the scientists lived at nearby ranches and dined on box lunches brought in from Santa Fe. Often they were forced to go hungry because the automobiles carrying the food broke down or had flats on the rough roads.

The lab was little more than a military post. The crude living conditions and barbed-wire fences may have given Hempelmann some pause, but he nevertheless agreed to take the job. He returned to St. Louis and packed up his belongings. He and his wife, Elinor, arrived in Los Alamos in April of 1943.

While Hempelmann was setting up his small office, Allied forces were winning key victories in the Pacific and in Eastern Europe. During the first week of April, more than one hundred bombers had swarmed over an outlying area of Paris, France, raining destruction on a Nazi-controlled Renault factory. General Douglas MacArthur reported another devastating assault on the Japanese fleet near New Guinea. And a furious air battle had raged in Tunisia between Nazi dive-bombers and American Spitfires as General George Patton's troops hurried toward a rendezvous with the British Army.

Louis Hempelmann's first year at Los Alamos was uneventful and unhurried. He split the work with another doctor named James Nolan, a gynecologist who was an old friend and classmate. Nolan oversaw the small post hospital. Hempelmann was in charge of protecting the workers from the radiation hazards. As in Chicago, that meant establishing "safe tolerance levels" for exposure to radiation, monitoring workers, and carrying out blood tests.

Hempelmann had a small staff—himself, four to five blood technicians, and a part-time secretary. One of his employees was Laura Fermi, the beautiful wife of Enrico Fermi. The Fermis, like other scientists, moved to Los Alamos as work at the Met Lab slowed down and the pace in New Mexico increased. Laura Fermi was struck by Hempelmann's shyness. In a memoir, she remembered, "He was my first paying boss . . . and we both acted shy. His embarrassment showed in his easy blushing, which made him look little older than a schoolboy."

Behind Hempelmann's boyish demeanor, however, was the mind of a shrewd administrator who quickly recognized that radioactive contamination drifting off site might provoke possible lawsuits and create public relations problems down the road for Los Alamos. He fumed when his advice wasn't taken and chafed under the yoke of the plodding bureaucracy.

That first year was so leisurely that Hempelmann undoubtedly had time to explore the remote country that lay outside the laboratory's fences. Many of the Manhattan Project scientists, particularly those raised and educated in Europe, were stunned when they got off the train at the little station near Santa Fe, New Mexico. The intoxicating light, the buoyant air, and the high elevation combined to produce a momentary vertigo. The vast distances glittered like the bottom of an ancient sea and blue mountains floated on the edges of the horizon. Here the skin of the world felt so thin it seemed that a bigger reality was about to break through. As they looked out upon the vastness, the thoughtful among them no doubt contemplated their own mortality and the fearsome weapon they had come to build.

In the winter the scientists and their wives organized ski trips across snow so light and powdery it seemed artificial. During those cold winter months, when the earth lay barren and the planet was tilted farthest from the sun, the New Mexico skies grew soft, filled with feathery clouds the color of mangos and tangerines. As the sun dipped below the horizon, the mountains east of the lab turned a luminous rose color. It was that extraordinary color which had prompted the Spanish settlers to name them the Sangre de Cristos, or blood of Christ.

In the summer the scientists hiked into the mountains or picked their way on horseback through forests and canyons filled with fantastic stone shapes. This was wild country, intimidating and lonely, country one had to acquire a taste for. "Nobody could think straight in a place like that," the urbane Leo Szilard predicted. "Everybody who goes there will go crazy." But once the brilliant landscape had permanently imprinted itself on their minds, some scientists yearned ever after to stand on ground that seemed to offer a vision of the four corners of the earth. Many never left. Others, such as Louis Hempelmann, bought second homes in New Mexico.

Hymer Friedell, a reserve officer for several years, was still working for Robert Stone in California when Pearl Harbor was bombed. Day after day he waited to be called up for active duty, but the orders never materialized. Friedell soon learned he had been put on an "essential list" by the dean of the medical school. Just thirty-one and feeling obligated to enlist in the military, Friedell told UCSF officials he must be removed from the list or he would resign. Sometime in the late summer of 1942, he got what he later described as "rather odd orders." He was inducted into the Army at the Presideo in San Francisco and then instructed to don civilian clothes and report to a Captain Craftan at 5125 University Avenue in Chicago. The address was the Met Lab, where his boss, Robert Stone, had begun to visit periodically. Friedell was immediately told to continue on to the Manhattan Engineer District offices in New York

City. When he arrived, he learned that the Army had plans to create its own medical program.

Friedell was the first Army doctor assigned to the Manhattan Project. After his trip to New York, he returned to the Met Lab, where he served as a liaison between the Army and the laboratory and helped out with medical tasks. One of his patients was Edward Teller. "He thinks I'm the world's greatest doctor—because I can recognize a hernia the size of my fist," he once said.

Friedell was eventually transferred to Oak Ridge, which in mid-1943 became the new headquarters of the Manhattan Engineer District, or MED, as it was often referred to in documents. Soon after that, Colonel Nichols named him the executive officer of the Manhattan Project's newly established Medical Section. General Groves liked Friedell but felt he was too inexperienced to head the section. "You're too young for this racket," Friedell quoted the general as saying.

Groves had first wanted Robert Stone for the job. During a train trip to Chicago in early 1943, the general spent several hours trying to convince Stone to enlist in the Army so that he could supervise all of the Manhattan Project's medical programs. But Stone wasn't interested. In a letter to Arthur Compton, he explained, "General Groves was not entirely satisfied but agreed with me that he would not push the Army appointment, especially since this would mean a very great financial sacrifice on my part with no greater ability to serve the country."

General Groves's next choice to head up the Medical Section was Stafford Warren, who was then a professor of radiology at the University of Rochester medical school. Warren was a man's man, garrulous and full of bravado, just the kind of doctor Groves was looking for. He had a handsome, square face that was just beginning to loosen, a small brushy mustache, and a large, well-shaped nose. He was an extraordinary blend of contradictions: flamboyant and cautious, amiable and shrewd, a storyteller who kept secrets.

After some negotiation, Warren agreed to serve as a consultant to the project, but said he would not join officially unless he was given the rank of colonel. With Hymer Friedell as his guide, over the spring and summer of 1943 he gradually learned more about the bomb-building effort. At that time, Los Alamos still resembled a crude military encampment; Oak Ridge was little more than a muddy construction site filled with lumber and bulldozers; and Hanford, struggling with labor shortages and sandstorms, had yet to drive a stake for its first nuclear reactor.

On November 3, 1943, Warren received his commission as a colonel in the Army, at which time he moved his family to Oak Ridge and became a full-time member of the project. According to one written account, he showed up for work on his first day wearing combat boots and a .45 revolver strapped to his waist. Like the crackpots and prima donnas at Los Alamos, Warren was also a scientist, but he clearly saw himself as a military officer whose loyalty belonged to General Groves.

Although Stafford Warren was living in Rochester when Groves recruited him, he was actually another member of the ever-increasing tribe of Berkeley-trained scientists working on the bomb project. His California roots were deep, dating back to his adventurous grandfather, for whom he was named, who had lit out with his brother from Wellsville, New York, to join the California gold rush. The two brothers made about sixty-five dollars panning for gold before they turned their attention to more practical ways to earn a living: burning charcoal and tanning hides. Eventually they purchased a small ranch in Hayward, a little town near Oakland, California, and planted cherry, apricot, and pear trees. Warren grew up on that ranch, digging stumps, milking the family cow, and listening to his grandfather's stories—tall and uncomplicated tales of the frontier. Later he breezed through the University of California at Berkeley and just as effortlessly sailed through four years of medical school at the University of California at San Francisco. After obtaining his medical degree in 1922, he spent three years doing postgraduate work at Johns Hopkins and Harvard. Then he was offered an assistant professorship in radiology at the new medical school being built at the University of Rochester. Before settling into Rochester, where he remained from 1925 to 1943, he toured the famous radiation laboratories in Europe with his wife, Viola.

In Paris, he met Madame Marie Curie, the recipient of two Nobel Prizes. The first, awarded in 1903, was a joint prize given to Curie, her husband, Pierre, and Henri Becquerel, for the discovery of radioactivity. The second, awarded in 1911, was for the isolation of pure radium. Marie Curie died of radiation-induced leukemia in 1934. By the time Warren met her, "She was very anemic and yellowish looking," he recalled. "She had some burns on her hands and her skin was very rough." The memory of her appearance would haunt him during his Manhattan Project days.

At the Rochester medical school, Stafford Warren had pursued several lines of experimentation, including "fever therapy" to treat gonorrhea. In a 1937 paper, he reported that fever therapy had shown some promise but warned that it should be undertaken only in a hospital setting and under close medical supervision. When the gonorrhea sufferers checked into the hospital for treatment, they were given lots of water, salt, and a sedative. Then they were taken to a "radiant energy cabinet," where they were put into restraints and a thermometer was inserted in their rectums. The subjects were periodically examined by nurses and given additional water and salt when it was needed. When the sedatives wore off, they were given whiskey.

By increasing the patients' body heat, the doctors hoped they could kill the infection. But some patients died first. Warren reported that a twenty-two-year-old boxer ("normal except for the presence on the right temple of an unhealed wound produced by a blow received during a recent boxing match") was comatose after spending twenty-four hours in the radiant heat closet. Twenty-two hours later he died.

When the Army surgeon general learned that Warren was to be in charge of the MED's health and safety programs, he asked Colonel Nichols, "Why do you want that clap doctor?" Nichols, unwilling to explain why they wanted a radiologist, responded stiffly that they had chosen Warren "for good and sufficient reasons."

Stafford Warren and Hymer Friedell were in charge of all matters relating to health and safety for the Manhattan Project. In Oak Ridge itself, a town of some 70,000 people that sprang up overnight, that meant overseeing everything from fly control to toxicology studies. Warren was particularly dismayed by the diet of the "colored people" who worked in Oak Ridge. Many drank Coca-Cola and ate potato chips and chocolate bars for breakfast, a menu so intolerable to Warren that he sent some of his men out to lecture on the advantages of drinking milk. On the subject of their diet, he recalled:

> Of course, the colored people wanted chitlins. It took us about a month to figure out what "chitlins" were. Finally the cafeteria manager ordered a barrel of entrails of chicken from the Chicago chicken cleaning place. It just stunk like the devil when it was opened; but by this time they had a colored person there, too, to supervise it. This was just deep-fried. The stench going downwind was fantastic, but they thought it was wonderful. And after that we had peace.

General Groves enforced a policy of strict compartmentalization in order to protect the secrecy of the project: "My rule was simple and not capable of misinterpretation—each man should know everything he needed to know to do his job and nothing else. Adherence to this rule not only provided an adequate measure of security, but it greatly improved overall efficiency by making our people stick to their knitting."

But Warren and Friedell were not required to adhere as rigidly to their "knitting" and actually knew more of what was going on than many senior scientists. Recalled Friedell, "When the general decided that the Army would keep its finger on everything, we really didn't have operational authority, but we had, if you will, informational authority. That is, we found out everything that was going on, and we became aware of it, and every once in a while he would ask us what was going on." Groves seemed to have a soft spot for the doctors, Friedell added. "He thought we had some special secret, the laying on of hands or whatever."

But the doctors often fell to squabbling among themselves. Louis Hempelmann didn't get along with Joseph Hamilton. And Stafford Warren and Hymer Friedell were forced to handle Robert Stone with kid gloves. Aware of Stone's prickly and stubborn nature, they attempted to guide his research program by gentle suggestions rather than outright orders. "We wouldn't go and say, 'Hey, don't do work on these rats—do this.' We wouldn't do it that way. We would really have to go and say, 'We think there is more need to do this, or our basic problems are as follows . . .'" Friedell once told a colleague.

Stafford Warren and Hymer Friedell traveled freely to the Met Lab, to Berkeley, and to Hanford. But they had to get permission to go to Los Alamos. "The rest of the places really were at our discretion," Friedell recalled, "but if you wanted to go to Los Alamos that was not easily done."

In Los Alamos, Stafford Warren occasionally stopped in to say hello or drink a cup of coffee with Oppenheimer. But most of the time he simply checked in with Oppenheimer's secretary and then went off with Louis Hempelmann or James Nolan. Oppenheimer, who could be as cruel and condescending as General Groves, didn't share the general's soft spot for doctors; in fact, he didn't like having a hospital on the laboratory grounds and didn't even like to acknowledge that disease existed. His distrust extended to the most basic medical precautions. Oppenheimer refused to have his dog vaccinated for rabies, even though it was official policy and all the other dogs had been inoculated. Recalled Warren: "We didn't know what to do; so finally I made a special trip out there. Oppie told Hempelmann he just wouldn't do it. He didn't believe in it. He didn't want to risk his dog, and it wasn't necessary. So we decided the best thing to do under the circumstances was to ignore this one dog. We didn't want to have Oppie upset by this emotional hassle, since it was only this one dog. . . ."

Stafford Warren and Hymer Friedell also went frequently to Rochester, New York, to confer with scientists at a top-secret biomedical research facility called the "Manhattan Department" or "Manhattan Annex." Located at the University of Rochester medical school and formally established in April of 1943 by the Manhattan Project, this laboratory had a large experimental animal colony. Many of the scientists who worked there were Warren's former students or colleagues. Scientists at the Manhattan Annex in Rochester focused some of their first experiments on the toxicological effects of uranium. This effort was no doubt spurred by the vast uranium plants in Oak Ridge that were about to begin operating. Other radioactive isotopes, including plutonium, were also investigated. Unlike the other sites, the Rochester facility was not involved in the design or production of the bomb. Its concerns were strictly health-related.

6

PLUTONIUM RISING

All the medical doctors knew that plutonium would be extremely hazard-ous, but it really didn't pose much of a problem throughout most of 1943 because there was so little of it. In the beginning, most of the cyclotron-produced material was going to Chicago. Los Alamos scientists were forced to use "stand-in" isotopes, such as uranium, for their chemical studies while they waited for the graphite reactor in Oak Ridge to come on line.

Tired of waiting, Oppenheimer finally took a trip to Berkeley in the fall of 1943 and demanded that the chemists make him half a milligram of plutonium on the cyclotron. John Gofman, then a young Berkeley scientist, asked Oppenheimer why he needed it. "You're going to have grams of it in a half-year to a year from Oak Ridge," he argued. "Yes, I know," he quoted Oppenheimer as saying. "But right now we need half a milligram and there's only a twentieth of a milligram in existence."

During September and October of 1943, scientists at Berkeley bom-barded a ton of a uranium compound in the cyclotron. When they were finished, they had produced about 1.2 milligrams of plutonium—little more than one-tenth of the amount Don Mastick had in his vial a year later. Remembered Gofman, "After about three weeks of around-the-clock work, we had it down to about a quarter of a teaspoon of liquid." Oppenheimer took one milligram back to Los Alamos and left the Berke-ley group with the remaining two-tenths to use in their chemistry experi-ments.

At about the same time the Berkeley group was bombarding the uranium compound, Robley Evans published a follow-up study on the radium dial painters in the September 1943 issue of the *Journal of Industrial Hygiene and Toxicology*. The paper sent a ripple of fear through the bomb complex. Evans had included in his article a horrifying photograph of a female radium dial painter who had developed a grapefruit-size tumor in her chin from only 1.5 micrograms and died soon thereafter. He compared the alpha particles emitted by radium to the "first bullet of a repeating gun," warning that so-called bullets could strike the human body not only through ingestion but also through inhalation.

Evans assured his readers that not all radium dial painters were condemned to such a fate. With proper precautions, such as spotlessly clean rooms and elaborate ventilation systems, radium could be handled safely. The Manhattan Project doctors, who had yet to conduct their first animal experiment with plutonium, knew from its chemical makeup that it might pose the same dangers as radium. Like radium, plutonium was a heavy metal with a long half-life and was expected to deposit in human bone. Most important, it emitted alpha particles—the same kind of atomic bullets that radium emitted. Once an alpha emitter such as plutonium lodges in human tissue or bone, three or four cells in the immediate area get an enormous blast of energy for a very long time. Whether an alpha particle produces cancer is a chance event. It may be the first or the millionth particle that produces the crucial mutation that leads to cancer; or such a mutation may never occur.

Glenn Seaborg became aware of Robley Evans's paper soon after it was published. He said it was "quite likely" that Joseph Hamilton brought it to his attention. "I'm pretty sure that even without that article I would have realized the danger of working with alpha particles of plutonium. I had been working with radioactivity ever since 1934 and wasn't a neophyte."

There were probably no more than two milligrams of plutonium in existence by the end of 1943. But Seaborg knew that that situation was about to change. As he looked around the Chicago laboratory, he recognized the grave hazards his discovery would soon pose to workers. "It was only when the plutonium appeared, and I could see it, or see solutions, you know, where people are stirring the solution and beginning to work with it, that it shook me like a thunderclap," Seaborg recalled many years later.

As 1943 gave way to 1944, a year that would lay the groundwork for the final Allied victories in Europe and in the Pacific, Glenn Seaborg wrote a brief note to Robert Stone. "It has occurred to me," he began in the January 5, 1944, memo:

that the physiological hazards of working with plutonium and its compounds may be very great. Due to its alpha radiation and long life it may be that the permanent location in the body of even very small amounts, say one milligram or less, may be very harmful. The ingestion of such extraordinary small amounts as some few tens of micrograms might be unpleasant, if it locates itself in a permanent position. In the handling of the relatively large amounts soon to begin here and at Site Y, there are many conceivable methods by which amounts of this order might be taken in unless the greatest care is exercised. In addition to helping to set up safety measures in handling so as to prevent the occurrence of such accidents, I would like to suggest that a program to trace the course of plutonium in the body be initiated as soon as possible. In my opinion, such a program should have the very highest priority.

When Seaborg was asked decades later whether he had meant human experiments, he exclaimed, "Oh, God, no." The memo, he said, referred to experiments with animals. Seaborg added in a subsequent interview that he knew nothing about the human experiments. "We were working in a compartmentalized atmosphere. We weren't told anything other than those things that related directly to what we were doing."

Robert Stone, by then known by his Manhattan Project moniker of Dr. Rock, responded to Seaborg's memo a few days later, saying that the Health Division had been planning to do experiments with plutonium. "The question of tracer studies to find its distribution in the body have long been planned as part of Dr. Hamilton's program, although it has never been mentioned in official descriptions of the program." Hamilton, he added, didn't see any point in doing tracer studies until several milligrams of plutonium could be made available to him.

As Seaborg and Stone were exchanging memos, the first milligram amounts of plutonium were being produced in the X-10 reactor in Oak Ridge. At a high-level meeting in Oak Ridge on January 19, Robert Stone emphasized the "poisonous nature of product." He noted that one to two micrograms of radium had proved fatal in the dial painters. Fortunately, Stone believed, plutonium was less hazardous by a factor of fifty. On the negative side, he pointed out, radium could be measured through the breath or with Geiger counters placed outside the body. But plutonium, which did not decay to radon or emit gamma rays, would be difficult to detect.

Arthur Compton advised during that same meeting that the project leaders should consider plutonium "potentially extremely poisonous." Using Stone's rough estimate as a guideline, they then established the so-called tolerance dose for plutonium at five micrograms—an amount that was exactly fifty times *higher* than the tolerance dose for radium established by Robley Evans's committee three years earlier.

On February 10 Joseph Hamilton received eleven milligrams of plutonium for animal experiments from the Manhattan Engineer District. The allocation, approved by J. Robert Oppenheimer and Arthur Compton, represented a significant portion of the plutonium in existence at the time and reflected not only the bomb makers' concern about plutonium's toxicity but Hamilton's high ranking within the inner circle. He was the first scientist to receive plutonium for studies unrelated to the actual task of constructing the bomb.

Over the next few weeks, Hamilton and his colleagues in Berkeley diluted the plutonium, divided it into batches, and used it in dozens of animal experiments. The material was injected into the jugular veins, tails, and hind legs of rats. Fine aerosols containing plutonium were concocted, and the animals were forced to breathe in the deadly mist. The rodents were killed at intervals and their organs analyzed to find out where the plutonium went. Most of the injected material gravitated to the skeleton. The plutonium from the aerosols settled in the alveoli, the tiny blood-rich sacs in the lungs, where oxygen and carbon dioxide are exchanged.

The same month Hamilton received his first allocation of plutonium, Hempelmann and several scientists from the Met Lab and Oak Ridge visited the Luminous Paint Company in Boston. Their escort was none other than Robley Evans. Evans had a good hunch why the Manhattan Project officials were there, but the word "plutonium" was never mentioned. "We were always very careful in talking with each other," Evans once told an interviewer. "We gave the other fellow enough information so that intelligent responses could be given, and that was it. Really, the less we knew the better."

Evans no doubt pointed out the Luminous Paint Company's fastidious housekeeping procedures. The floors and walls of the plant were scrubbed regularly; the young women wore kerchiefs and caps to keep their hair from touching the paint; eating and smoking in the work area was forbidden; and special ventilation hoods were installed above each desk to suck out dust particles and gases.

Although Evans understood the hazards of radium better than any other scientist in the world, he nevertheless sent a proposal later that year to Joseph Howland, a young Manhattan Project physician who worked with Stafford Warren and Hymer Friedell in Oak Ridge. Evans wanted to administer one microgram of radium to "conscientious objectors or other volunteer human subjects" in order to better understand the effects of a small dose. The amount would be perfectly harmless, he wrote in a letter declassified in 1994, "because we can be absolutely sure that the subject will excrete more than 90 percent of this material, and will be left with a perfectly harmless amount of radium in his system." There is no evidence that the Manhattan Project took Evans up on his offer. But Evans was an ardent believer in the poet Alexander Pope's maxim that the "proper study of mankind is man," and he would have ample opportunity to gratify his penchant for human experiments in the postwar years.

The month after Hempelmann and his colleagues returned from Boston, the first whole gram of plutonium, a small ampoule of green-colored liquid, arrived at Los Alamos from Oak Ridge. Before the vial was shipped, Arthur Compton, General Groves, Colonel Nichols, and a few others went down to the plant to have a look at it. Compton removed the vial from under its ventilation hood and placed it in the colonel's hands. Then, wrote Colonel Nichols, Martin Whitaker, one of the project leaders, "hurriedly picked up a stainless steel pan and held it under my hand, saying, 'For God's sake, don't drop it on the floor.' As Groves reached for it [the vial], Whitaker grabbed it and replaced it safely under the hood."

Although the other Manhattan Project sites would also be confronted with plutonium contamination, the problem would prove particularly serious in Los Alamos, which was responsible not only for designing and putting the bomb together but for the final purification and shaping of plutonium metal. Acutely aware of the tragedy that befell the radium dial painters, Louis Hempelmann and his Los Alamos colleagues did what they could to prepare for the plutonium. They held lectures and passed out safety pamphlets, instructed employees to don coveralls, booties, and surgical caps, ordered plate-glass covers for the desks of people working with plutonium, installed swinging doors to eliminate contamination from "hot" doorknobs, and imported monitoring devices, air dust samplers, and respirators from other sites. Although these and other safety regulations were put into place, they were hard to enforce—especially among the scientists. Hempelmann said years later that many of the scientists were "individualists" who didn't like to follow rules. "Unfortunately, the more scholarly and inquisitive the person, the greater the tendency to ignore the recommended procedures. The janitors, I am sure, always did what we told them to do."

Sometimes the plutonium that spilled onto floors was so hard to retrieve that maintenance crews simply enameled over the contaminated area. Some of the material was carried offsite by employees who were leaving the tech area with "very high counts on their street clothing." (A "count" reflects the detection of an energy particle or a photon emitted from an unstable radioactive atom.)

Spotty and crude though it was, oiled paper, in the form of swipes, was one of the only ways to detect the presence of plutonium. The paper was swept over contaminated surfaces and placed under counters for measurements. Similarly, the nostrils of employees were swabbed twice a day with paper glued around the ends of sticks. The paper was then spread out and placed under detection devices. Decades later Thomas Shipman, the head of Los Alamos's health division, could still recall in vivid detail the woman who performed the nose swipes: "She was well endowed with the more important female sex characteristics and she saw to it that they were properly exhibited. When she would appear in a laboratory and shout out 'Nose Swipes,' strong men could be trampled in the rush."

The counts registered on the paper were sometimes shockingly high: 1,578 in a worker's nose, 1,000 on a laboratory floor; 40,000 on a desk; "infinite" in some rooms. Evidence of contamination was even found inside workers' respirators. The readings taken from the nose weren't considered significant, Hempelmann said, unless they were more than fifty counts per minute.

The monitoring, decontamination, and record keeping were not just humanitarian measures implemented to protect the workers. Hempelmann and his colleagues also wanted to protect themselves and the Manhattan Project from possible lawsuits. In a seventeen-page account of the history of the Los Alamos health group from March 1943 to November 1945, Hempelmann observed three times that inaccurate, incomplete records could entangle the lab in lawsuits. "The lack of records of non-exposure of persons not working with radiation or radioactive materials means that we do not have important legal evidence in case of future claims against this project," he wrote.

Stafford Warren also worried about lawsuits, as did J. Robert Oppenheimer. The lab director kept a tight rein on information that might reveal health problems or suggest that Los Alamos was contaminating his beloved desert. After Oppenheimer left Los Alamos, employee J. F. Mullaney asked Norris Bradbury, Oppenheimer's successor, for guidance on the handling of health reports. "Mr. Oppenheimer, I believe, directed that all reports on health problems be separately classified and issued only at his request. I do not know the reason for this special treatment, but I believe it is to give added security protection to safeguard the project against people claiming to have been damaged."

The Manhattan Project officials had reason to worry. The results of Joseph Hamilton's initial rat studies contained some disconcerting news. As the medical doctors expected, plutonium, like radium, did lodge in the skeleton. But it was excreted much more slowly, which meant that plutonium would stay in the body longer and cause more radiation damage. Hamilton advised in May of 1944 that wounds contaminated with plutonium be treated like snake bites. "I realize that analogies are frequently dangerous for the purposes of comparison, but the superficial similarities of the parenteral introduction of product [a code word for plutonium] into the body to snake bite come to mind."

By the end of August 1944, the month that Don Mastick's accident occurred, Los Alamos had received fifty-one grams of plutonium from the Oak Ridge reactor. In metal form, that amount would not have filled a spoon, but it had been divided up and used in 2,500 separate experiments.

Mastick's accident was the most alarming the medical personnel at Los Alamos had faced, but there had been other terrifying moments. One of the first occurred on May 26, 1944, when a metallurgist and his technician began trying to reduce a plutonium solution into metal. The experiment succeeded but the metallurgist was exposed to large amounts of plutonium dust. Two other minor accidents occurred the same month as the Mastick explosion. On the afternoon of August 19, a small amount of plutonium in powder form spilled on the floor of Room D-101. An open beaker containing ten milligrams of plutonium cracked the night of August 28 in Room D-117, just two doors down from Mastick's laboratory.

In a monthly health report for August, Hempelmann noted the rising levels of contamination in D and H buildings. D Building was the elaborately ventilated plant where Mastick worked. It had five miles of piping and a complex ventilation system designed to remove dust particles from the air. Despite the efforts to maintain a clean environment, the building grew hopelessly contaminated and had to be torn down after the war. H building contained other laboratories and offices. "As has been anticipated the amount of contamination throughout both of these buildings is much greater now that larger amounts of material are being used," Hempelmann wrote.

After Mastick's accident, Louis Hempelmann had a near mutiny on his hands. In an August 16, 1944, memo, he advised Oppenheimer that Mastick's colleagues were deeply alarmed:

> A great deal of concern has been expressed during the past two weeks by members of the Chemistry Division about the inability of the Medical Group to detect dangerous amounts of plutonium in the body. This concern was occasioned by the accidental explosion of 10 milligrams of plutonium in Don Mastick's face with the subsequent ingestion of an unknown amount of this material. The questions which have been raised by the chemists are: 1) how much plutonium was absorbed by the gastro-intestinal tract in this case, 2) what fraction of a serious dose does the absorbed plutonium represent and 3) is it safe for Mastick to go back to work in Building D at his old job?

Hempelmann had several discussions with Mastick and other chemists, including Joseph Kennedy and Arthur Wahl. Then he recommended to Oppenheimer that the biological research program be expanded. The program initially called for more animal experiments and the development of a chemical method to detect plutonium in urine, stools, and lungs. "It would not seem out of place to raise this question now as accidents similar to [Mastick's] are bound to happen again despite the most elaborate precautions."

Oppenheimer, who had little use for medical doctors, immediately agreed. He made it clear, though, that he didn't want the work done at Los Alamos. "As for the biological sides of the work, which may involve animal or even human experimentation, I feel that it is desirable if these can in any way be handled elsewhere not to undertake them here," he wrote Hempelmann.

Practical considerations, rather than moral or ethical questions, undoubtedly dictated Oppenheimer's decision. In a telegram written several months earlier to the Met Lab's Arthur Compton, Oppenheimer noted that the Los Alamos lab was "not equipped for biological experiments." With its clutter of houses, barracks, trailers, and huts, Los Alamos was bursting at the seams. In January 1943 the population was 1,500. By the end of 1944 it had nearly quadrupled to 5,675. (By 1945 it would be 8,200.)

Louis Hempelmann, Stafford Warren, Joseph Kennedy, and J. Robert Oppenheimer met on August 25, 1944, to further discuss the medical research program on plutonium. At Warren's suggestion, Hempelmann summarized the program in an August 29 memo to Oppenheimer. The project was to have three parts: the development of chemical methods to determine the amount of plutonium in urine, feces, tissues, and lungs; animal experiments to cross-check the chemical methods; and "tracer experiments on humans to determine the percentage of plutonium excreted daily." After Los Alamos had developed "satisfactory analytical methods," Hempelmann added, further metabolic studies would be turned over to another medical group, presumably the Manhattan Annex at Rochester.

Los Alamos scientists plunged into the project and, by January of 1945, had completed the first step—the development of a chemical process that could detect one ten-thousandth of a microgram of plutonium in urine and stool samples. The detection method was a long, tedious process that involved drying the sample and converting it to ash before dissolving it in acid. Although several people were involved in the effort, Wright Langham, a young chemist from Oklahoma, received the credit for developing the process. Scientists in Chicago and Berkeley also developed their own detection methods.

The Los Alamos group could not try out their approach until a contamination-free laboratory was ready in February. The test was first used on Los Alamos employees in March of 1945, and the initial results shocked Hempelmann. "They were just frightfully high. My God, we were just terrified because they suggested—I mean, if they were true—if that much plutonium was being excreted, the workers would have God knows how much plutonium. . . ."

The lab began sending employees home for two days. Then the workers reported back to the hospital, where they showered and washed their hair, changed into hospital garments, and provided urine specimens for the next twenty-four hours. With those procedures in place, the plutonium detected in the urine dropped dramatically, suggesting the contamination was coming from the workers' hands and clothes.

Still, the Langham test was inconclusive. With the process, the Manhattan Project doctors could measure the level of plutonium in urine or stools. But what fraction of the total body burden did the excreted amount represent? To answer that question, they needed a human being in whom they could inject a known amount of plutonium and measure the rate at which the material was excreted. If scientists knew the excretion rate, they would then be able to extrapolate from urine and stool samples how much plutonium remained in the body of a worker who had suffered an accidental exposure.

The time had come to take the inevitable next step—a step that would cast its shadow over the Manhattan District and its successor agencies for the next five decades. Only a human experiment would confirm the usefulness of Langham's test. "It was not until the first human tracer experiment had been performed in April 1945 (with the help of the medical section of the Manhattan District) that the above tests could be evaluated with any degree of certainty," Hempelmann later wrote.

7

PLANNING THE EXPERIMENT

In late March of 1945, Louis Hempelmann checked out a sedan from the motor pool and drove down to Santa Fe to pick up Hymer Friedell. The trip down the canyon was harrowing even for those scientists who didn't have Hempelmann's delicate constitution: thirty-five miles of dust and curves and one swooping bridge, ten feet wide and two hundred fifty feet long, to cross.

Friedell, clad in a brown Army uniform, had come from Oak Ridge, Tennessee. Warren had come to rely heavily on Friedell: "I used him for my 'crying wall,' you might say," Warren remembered years later. "I tried my ideas out on him and if he thought they were good, fine; if he didn't then I'd look for the problem."

Hempelmann and Friedell rumbled past the Indians hawking their wares on the Santa Fe Plaza and then headed in a northwesterly direction back toward Los Alamos. Despite the Corps of Engineers' efforts to smooth the road, it was so narrow and bumpy from rainstorms and heavy traffic that the sedans often had to be sent to the motor pool for repairs following the punishing trips. The two doctors stopped once to fix a flat tire somewhere between the bosque, the lush cottonwood forest that outlines the Rio Grande, and the bone-colored cliffs that mark the last dusty miles into Los Alamos. Above them, hawks rode the spring thermals, their eyes probing the powdery red vistas for prey. The air was dry enough to cause nosebleeds.

As the dark sedan inched up the switchbacks, climbing higher and higher into the sky, now a vast blue, the two doctors may have talked of the upcoming meeting. Or they may have judged the matter too sensitive and stuck to chitchat about the war. The nation's attention had been riveted on Iwo Jima, a small island in the Pacific, where one of the bloodiest battles of the war was winding down. The Fourth and Fifth Marine divisions had gone from hole to hole and from cave to cave trying to wrest the small island from the Japanese. They had succeeded, but at a heavy price: 5,885 Marines had been killed and 17,272 wounded. Using Iwo Jima as a forward air base, Major General Curtis LeMay's B-29s began their devastating, nightly firebomb raids on Tokyo and other major Japanese cities. Although Japan soon realized it was doomed to be defeated militarily, its troops fought on ferociously, determined to take as many Americans to the grave with them as they could.

In Europe, the war was drawing to a close. The Allies were massing at the Rhine River, Germany's traditional western frontier. Staring defeat in the face, Hitler vowed to continue the war and ordered that anything which might be of use to the enemies of Germany be destroyed. Fortunately, Albert Speer, his minister of armaments and war, and a handful of Army officers were able to convince industrialists and politicians to ignore Hitler's scorched-earth instructions.

In Los Alamos, the atomic bomb project was moving forward at a relentless pace. Beginning on February 2, 1945, the first kilogram amounts of plutonium had begun arriving from Hanford. The bomb material, which was in the form of a thick, jellylike mixture, was placed into shielded, wooden boxes and transported by Army ambulances. Ambulances were chosen because they were seen all over the country and raised no suspicions. As an added precaution, the drivers, who did not know what they were transporting, were instructed to take different routes and avoid stopping at the same places to eat. Occasionally Colonel Franklin Matthias, the military officer in charge of Hanford, would have counterintelligence officers tail the ambulances to make sure the drivers weren't developing habits that might endanger their precious cargoes. At Fort Douglas, Utah, the ambulance drivers would deposit their boxes with a military officer and drive back to Hanford. Los Alamos drivers then would pick up the boxes and take them on to the lab. There were usually two trips per week.

The deliveries, Hempelmann admitted in a sworn deposition taken in 1979 on behalf of a former worker who was suing the lab, were about ten times what the laboratory could handle safely. The contamination grew so severe, he added, that "if it had not been that we had to get the bomb made as soon as possible, all work would have stopped."

The plutonium quickly spread beyond the confines of the technical area. The wind, always an unpredictable companion in the desert, undoubtedly picked up a few stray atoms and scattered them beyond the fences. But most of the plutonium that slipped beyond the site came from the lab's waste water, which initially was dumped into the streams and canyons that angled down from the mesa. Los Alamos and Pueblo creeks were crackling with radioactivity. It was highest where the water from the contaminated laundry drained into Los Alamos Creek. Along the laundry ditch, plutonium measured 144,000 disintegrations per minute per liter, about 325 times the allowable amount of plutonium that can be released into sewers today. Hempelmann warned that the contaminated canyons, while not a health hazard, presented the lab with serious legal problems:

> It's quite possible that future illnesses or diseases contracted by a person who has blundered into a contaminated area may be connected by this person with his contact with radioactive materials. Unless we can state categorically that all contaminated areas have been completely enclosed by child-proof and dog-proof fences, it will be extremely difficult to convince a jury that the project was not at fault. The cost of good fencing, although considerable, would undoubtedly be less than that of one or two successful lawsuits against the project. In addition to the monetary aspects of such court proceedings, the bad public relations which would result would cause the project inestimable harm.

At a laboratory meeting more than two decades later, Thomas Shipman said, "Everybody had his own contaminated dump. Today we think we know where all of these were, but I wouldn't want to guarantee it." The contamination drifted down the canyons, swept along in the raging waters that materialized suddenly when storms lashed the mesa. Scientists detected plutonium in the Rio Grande, one of the great rivers of the West, only four years after the material had been discovered by Glenn Seaborg and his colleagues in Berkeley.

Friedell had made the long, arduous trip to Los Alamos to discuss the human plutonium experiment the laboratory had been moving toward even before the vial had exploded in Don Mastick's face. Friedell, like the Los Alamos scientists, knew that human guinea pigs would be needed to learn more about how plutonium was metabolized and excreted in the body. In a memorandum written two months before the meeting, which was not declassified until 1994, Friedell stated: "In conjunction with the experiments conducted on animals, it is expected that on selected human subjects tracer studies with product [plutonium] would be made."

On Friday, March 23, 1945, Friedell sat down with Louis Hempelmann and other Los Alamos doctors and scientists to hash out details of the proposed experiment. Oppenheimer, who had grown so anxious over the bomb project that he sometimes was forced to take sleeping pills, "occasionally" dropped in, recalled Friedell, who was one of the only people still alive in the 1990s who attended the meeting and had firsthand knowledge of the experiment. The animosity between Los Alamos and Manhattan Project headquarters in Oak Ridge had been increasing steadily, and the meeting undoubtedly was tense. Both Hempelmann and Oppenheimer felt the Manhattan Project had not come through with the help they had been promised. Originally Los Alamos had planned to leave the biological studies to other sites, but the lab was not getting the answers it needed quickly enough and had begun its own research program.

Friedell told DOE interviewers in 1995 that he wasn't "terribly enthusiastic" about the experiment but felt it needed to be done. "Now my own recollection is that Dr. Hempelmann was in favor of the program, but he wasn't wildly enthusiastic. I would say that the one that was more enthusiastic, was pushing this more, was Wright Langham."

Until the war intervened, Langham's future had looked like an unbroken stream of quiet days on the plains, studying the swirling patterns of sun-parched soil and conferring with ranchers on improving the yield of their cattle herds. Born in Winsburro, Texas, in 1911, Langham graduated in 1934 from Oklahoma Panhandle A&M College in Goodwell and received a master's in chemistry from Oklahoma A&M College in Stillwater a year later. His "ingenious studies of patterns of soil drifting in the dust bowl," wrote Louis Hempelmann, so impressed the head of the University of Colorado's biochemistry department that Langham was invited to enroll as a Ph.D. candidate. After obtaining his doctoral degree in organic chemistry, Langham worked for a year as a research chemist at the Met Lab in Chicago and then transferred to Los Alamos in March of 1944 where he helped to develop the detection technique for plutonium. Over the next decades, he became one of the world's leading experts in the toxicology of plutonium, earning him the nickname Mr. Plutonium from his colleagues.

Langham was extremely bright but unsuited for the delicate tasks of the laboratory. His hands trembled so much that once he accidentally pricked himself with a needle filled with plutonium while trying to inject a rat, Louis Hempelmann recalled. "He came over to see me, and he was the most embarrassed person I think I have seen in my life." Langham was hard driving, immensely ambitious, and often impatient. But beneath the exterior, Hempelmann observed, was an "underlying gentleness and good will." By the time Langham reached Los Alamos, the Oklahoma Panhandle, with its stench of feed lots and sound of bawling cattle, was a distant memory. Langham was a pipe-smoking scientist, all tweeds and bowties, with a thin mustache stenciled across his upper lip.

Now here he was taking part in a discussion about a human experiment. In the preceding months, at laboratories in Rochester, Chicago, Berkeley, and Los Alamos, dogs, rats, mice, and even rabbits had been injected with plutonium or forced to breathe in large amounts of plutonium-contaminated air. Then their bodies or organs were reduced to ashes in ovens and dissolved in acid, and the plutonium was extracted and measured. As expected, the animals who received the largest amounts suffered severe damage and death. Hemorrhages appeared on internal organs. Spleens, thymus glands, and adrenals shrunk dramatically. Livers turned yellow and necrotic. Lymphomas and bone sarcomas were induced. Precancerous conditions appeared at injection sites, and rats that breathed in the vapors developed acute pneumonia.

Although the scientists initially believed that plutonium was fifty times less hazardous than radium, by the spring of 1945 they had begun to realize that plutonium in larger amounts could actually be thirty times *more* hazardous than radium. From their animal studies, they had discovered that plutonium gravitated to more vulnerable parts of the body than radium. Radium deposited itself in mineralized bone, which is generally considered resistant to radiation. But plutonium in a soluble chemical form settled in the liver and the parts of bone associated with the production of blood cells. That phenomenon was particularly serious, Joseph Hamilton later wrote, because it meant that the alpha particles would be bombarding the "radio-sensitive bone marrow."

The Los Alamos scientists asked Friedell to take back a request to Manhattan Project headquarters. They wanted help in arranging an experiment: "It is suggested that a hospital patient at either Rochester or Chicago be chosen for injection of from one to ten micrograms of material and that the excreta be sent to this laboratory for analysis." Oppen-

heimer gave his approval to the human experiment in a memo forwarded
to Stafford Warren:

> I should like to add my personal indorsement [sic] to the re-
> quests outlined in the accompanying memorandum. We all have
> the feeling that at the present time the hazards of workers at Site
> Y [the code name for Los Alamos] are probably very much more
> serious than those at any other branch of the Project, and that it
> would be appropriate that the medical program of the Manhat-
> tan District consider some of our problems rather more inten-
> sively than they have in the past. I think that you yourself know
> the reason for some of these hazards, and we tried to give Colo-
> nel Friedell [sic] a picture of them. . . . Although we would
> have some ideas of how to pursue all of the topics mentioned,
> we have, as you know, neither the personnel nor the facilities
> which would be involved in this. It was our impression that if
> other workers on the medical program were better informed
> about what was important from our point of view they would
> probably be glad to help us out. Certainly we will appreciate any
> help that you can give us.

Usually Stafford Warren was the medical officer who made the jar-
ring trip up the canyon to Los Alamos. But according to Hymer Friedell,
Warren was having prostate surgery on the day the scientists decided to
go ahead with the plutonium injection experiment. His role in the decision is hard to pin down. In a 1950 Los Alamos report, Warren is
credited as the official who was "primarily responsible" for the initiation
of the program. Yet few records have surfaced that were written by Warren, or to him, about the experiment. One document that has been found
is a December 2, 1944, memo to his files entitled "Medical Experimental
Program on Radium and Product." Writing about five months after the
Mastick accident, Warren summarized efforts by scientists in Rochester,
Chicago, Los Alamos, and Berkeley to obtain data that would clarify the
relative toxicity of radium and plutonium and help establish "tolerance"
standards for workers. Task "a" involved using intravenous injections to
determine the lethal dose for radium and "product" in rats. Task "b" was
to establish the ratios of blood level to urine and fecal excretion following
injections of radium and "product" into rats. And the final task was
"Tracer experiments on humans like b. above so that the comparison
(factor) can be made between the rat data and human data."

The role of Warren's boss, General Leslie Groves, is even more obscure. Groves kept tabs on all aspects of the atomic bomb project and probably knew about the experiment being planned. But so far his name has not surfaced on any documents related to the injections. John Lansdale, a lawyer who had been in charge of Groves's intelligence operations and once interrogated Oppenheimer about his Communist connections, said in 1995 that the experiment was "not the kind of thing that should have been initiated without the approval of Gen. Groves, yet I find it hard to believe he did—moreover it is the kind of thing he would have discussed with me but I knew nothing of it."

Hymer Friedell told DOE interviewers that he believed Groves was aware of the plan. "I think he was. I think he would be. But I don't know [it] from the record. If I recall correctly, I never communicated with him. But Stafford Warren almost certainly did."

8

Ebb Cade

In Oak Ridge, Tennessee, the day after the Los Alamos meeting, Ebb Cade and his two brothers got ready for work. It was a Saturday and they were tired and stiff from a long week of hard labor. But soon the three men slipped out of the house and piled into a car driven by Jesse Smith, a friend who lived and worked with the Cade brothers.

Ebb was a soft-spoken man with powerful shoulders and callused hands who worked as a cement mixer for the J. A. Jones Construction Co., a contractor based in Charlotte, North Carolina, which had built the Oak Ridge Gaseous Diffusion Plant, a gigantic U-shape building where uranium was enriched. Ebb was only fifty-five, but his left eye was completely blind, a daub of cloudy blue. A cataract was starting to creep over the right eye too.

On the way to the job site, they picked up another man and woman. About 6:30 A.M. they pulled up to the guard shack leading to the classified project. The occupants showed their badges to the guard and were waved on through. At 6:40 A.M., one to two miles from the plant, Smith spotted a stalled government truck blocking his lane. One of its rear wheels was jacked up, and Smith started to edge around the vehicle. That's when he saw the dump truck barreling straight toward him. It was too late to turn, too late to brake.

Ebb may have been napping in the backseat, squeezed between the warm bodies of his two brothers, dreaming of Sunday, when the head-on accident occurred. The injuries suggested it was a violent collision, full of the shriek of brakes and squealing metal. Then a shuddering stillness filled the blue Tennessee dawn.

Everyone in Ebb Cade's vehicle was taken to the Oak Ridge Army Hospital, a bustling facility built two years earlier and staffed with 20 civilian dentists, 141 nurses, 54 nurses' attendants, 8 dietitians, and 41 medical officers. Ebb's nose and lip were cut. His right kneecap, forearm, and his left femur, the long, heavy bone that extends from the hip to knee, were fractured. The injuries suffered by the other occupants are unknown. But one record indicates the driver, Jesse Smith, was hospitalized for nine months.

Ebb was coherent enough to give the doctors some of his family history. He told them he had always been in good health except for a chronic urethral discharge. Upon examination, physicians noted that the lens of his left eye had been "completely obliterated" by a cataract. He had marked tooth decay, gum disease, and a touch of arthritis in his left knee. Ebb said he didn't have any problems with his kidneys or liver, but a urine test indicated that he had a "somewhat diminished" kidney function. A doctor wrote: "He was a well developed, well nourished colored male."

A couple of days after the accident, Los Alamos chemist Wright Langham sent Hymer Friedell a detailed set of instructions on the "49" [plutonium] experiment. On April 6, twelve days after the sit-down meeting in Los Alamos, he sent a second set of instructions, according to a memo declassified in 1994. Langham was particularly concerned that the plutonium injected into the human subject be accurately measured. The syringe containing the plutonium, he advised Hymer Friedell, should be allowed to sit for five to ten minutes so that the plutonium would saturate its inner walls. "My experience has been that a syringe always delivers 5–10% less than indicated by the graduations," he wrote. "There is also the problem of 49 [plutonium] absorption by ground glass surfaces."

The subject's urine and stool samples should be bottled separately for the first thirty-six hours after injection. Mason fruit jars would make good containers, but "you may have a better idea on this," Langham wrote. "The samples should be packed about twice as securely as normally necessary because the packages coming into this place are hardly recognizable after the truckers get through with them."

Four days later, on April 10, a small amount of plutonium was removed from an ampoule that Langham had sent to Oak Ridge and mixed into a solution containing distilled water. Approximately 0.25 cc of the plutonium mixture was drawn up into a syringe, then the solution was injected into Ebb's left arm. During the injection, a document later noted, "care was taken to avoid leakage."

Denser than lead and with a 24,000-year half-life, the plutonium immediately began circulating through Ebb's bloodstream. Eventually the radioactive molecules would settle in his liver and bones. Ebb Cade, later assigned the code name HP-12, had been injected with 4.7 micrograms of plutonium—nearly five times the amount scientists at the time felt could be retained without harm in the human body and a dose equal to eighty times what the average person receives in a year from natural and man-made radiation sources.

The day after Ebb's injection, Hymer Friedell sent Louis Hempelmann a copy of the protocol and a brief note: "Everything went smoothly, and I think that we will have some very valuable information for you," he wrote. "I think that we will have access to considerable clinical material here, and we hope to do a number of subjects."

No one is sure now who actually administered the injection. Joseph Howland, the young doctor who was in charge of the Manhattan Project's "special problems," told AEC officials many years later that he did it under protest, and only after he received written orders from Hymer Friedell. No consent was obtained from Cade, Howland said.

Friedell has denied Howland's allegation for more than two decades. He contends a physician named Dwight Clark from the University of Chicago performed the injection. In August of 1994 Friedell was asked again about the injection by staffers from President Clinton's Advisory Committee on Human Radiation Experiments:

Interviewer: Were you there at Oak Ridge at the time of that injection?

Dr. Friedell: I was there.

Interviewer: Did you actually witness it?

Dr. Friedell: No, no. For some reason I didn't know about it until afterwards.

Interviewer: One of the other stories was that you actually were the one to give that [plutonium injection].

Dr. Friedell: Never did.

Interviewer: Okay.

Dr. Friedell: The one who actually gave it was Dwight Clark.

Interviewer: Dwight Clark gave an injection under . . . ?

Dr. Friedell: He gave the injection simply under the . . . on the direction of [Stafford] Warren.

After the war, Howland returned to the University of Rochester where he had worked before and took over the medical division of Rochester's Atomic Energy Project. Some years later he suffered a nervous breakdown. He eventually returned to the laboratory, but on the advice of his physician did not resume his practice.

In an undated autobiographical sketch, Howland described the injection of Ebb Cade as "a command performance": "I injected a five-microcurie dose of plutonium into a human and studied his clinical experience. (I objected, but in the Army, an order is an order.)"

Howland also stated that Dwight Clark carried out parallel experiments on animals at the University of Chicago. Both Howland and Clark are dead now, but a declassified transcript of a telephone conversation appears to support Howland's version of the injection.

Three years after Ebb Cade's injection, Albert Holland, a medical doctor in Oak Ridge, contacted Joseph Howland at the University of Rochester and asked him about the case. Although the conversation appears casual, the telephone call was transcribed and may have been part of a surreptitious investigation into the experiment by Shields Warren, the Harvard pathologist who assumed control of the Atomic Energy Commission's biological and medical programs after the war. (Shields Warren was not related to Stafford Warren.) The following is an excerpt of the January 9, 1948, telephone call:

> Holland: One other thing which comes up. What do you know about this Cabe [sic] case? Wasn't that one of the cases that . . .
>
> Howland: That was one of the cases that Friedell had me put "49" [plutonium] in. What are they doing about it?
>
> Holland: Nothing. I think it is about time we dig it up. I was talking with Dwight Clark when I was up in Chicago and he said the last he heard this boy [Ebb Cade] was practically completely blind.
>
> Howland: I hadn't heard anything. The last I saw Dwight was when we were discharged from the Army and he hadn't heard anything from Cabe.
>
> Holland: I saw Dwight on Dec. 22 when I was up in Chicago; and we were just casually chatting and he wanted to know what was new on him. I thought when I heard that of course that it was something I would look up.

Howland: I think the fellow had senile cataract in both eyes, as I
    remember.
Holland: I don't know; we are in the process of getting the file
    out now and I just wondered if you had any additional back-
    ground information.
Howland: All I know is how much he got.
Holland: What was that—90?
Howland: He got 4.7 [micrograms] once a day, which was 49
    [plutonium] . . .
Holland: Well, we will get it out and find out where he is and
    what he is doing and I'll let you know.
Howland: Louie Hempelmann . . . has medical results on him.
    They've got the most complete work-up results, because
    they did all the chemical analysis out there. . . . Dwight
    should have the rest of the information.
Holland: The fellow's name was what?
Howland: Eb [sic] Cade.

A month after Cade's injection, Langham gave a classified talk in
Chicago to other Manhattan Project doctors about the experiment: "The
subject was an elderly male whose age and general health was such that
there is little or no possibility that the injection can have any effect on
the normal course of his life," he began. Langham said the plutonium
solution that he prepared was designed to produce the "maximum deposition" in human bone. "This presumably would produce an excretion
rate comparable to that of a worker having absorbed the material at a
slow rate thereby depositing a maximum amount in the bone where it is
probably the most damaging." In charts accompanying the talk, Langham
noted that 332 counts per minute were detected in Ebb's urine in the
first twenty-four-hour period after injection, declining to 119 counts
three months later. By contrast, exposed laboratory workers—individuals
with nose counts in excess of 50 counts per minute—showed only an
average of 2.2 counts per minute in their urine samples. The excretion
rate of human beings was surprisingly low, Langham said, and the level-
ing off was much slower "than with rats."

Despite the elaborate planning, the experiment was flawed. Samples
of Ebb's urine from before and after the injection were accidentally
pooled together, providing no control sample. Scientists also worried that
Ebb's kidney damage could have affected the excretion rate.

Five days after the injection—and nearly three weeks after the accident—Ebb's bones were set. The timing of the surgery enabled the scientists to complete one critical component of the experiment: obtain bone samples from Ebb after the plutonium had circulated in his body. The samples showed the plutonium had indeed gone to the bone. In one fragment, scientists detected 82 counts per minute. Fifteen of Ebb's teeth also were pulled, purportedly because Ebb was suffering from gum inflammation and tooth decay. The teeth, as well as portions of his gum tissue and jawbone, were analyzed for plutonium content. Plutonium also goes to the jawbone where the teeth are embedded.

Lawrence Suchow, a young enlisted man, spent about a week in June emptying Ebb's bedpan. He had been cautioned to be very careful taking the urine away and never saw any family members or doctors stopping in to see Ebb. Two months or so had elapsed since the accident and Ebb still appeared to be in great pain. "He was just moaning," Suchow remembered. "He seemed in terrible shape. He looked to me like he was not going to make it for a few days."

One of the still-unexplained aspects of the case is what happened to Jesse Smith, the driver. He was hospitalized for approximately nine months with a fractured hip. In a letter written two years after the accident, a Major William Clarkson in Oak Ridge asked Hymer Friedell about Smith's case. X rays taken in January 1946 and March 1947 showed that Smith's bones still had failed to heal. And a colleague, he added, "is at a loss to explain the failure of the bone to unite and because of the large amount of laboratory work done while he was hospitalized, was wondering if, perhaps he had received 'some stuff' given by a member of this office." In a response to Clarkson written three days later, Friedell said he couldn't remember the man's name who had received the material and suggested that Clarkson contact Joe Howland or Wright Langham. "Joe Howland actually gave the material and he might remember the man's name," Friedell added. "As I remember it, the individual who received the material was an older Negro and had multiple fractures."

Although Clarkson had asked for information on Jesse Smith, the driver, Friedell's response seems to refer to Ebb Cade. Friedell does not mention the patient's name or the word "plutonium," so it is not absolutely certain to which of the men he was referring. No written evidence whatsoever has been found suggesting that Smith received plutonium. And if Friedell was referring to Cade, it would be further confirmation of Howland's version of the story.

9

NEXT IN LINE: ARTHUR AND ALBERT

It's not clear why the Manhattan Project doctors abandoned their plan to use a hospital patient in Rochester or Chicago and chose Ebb Cade instead. But sixteen days after Cade was injected, Arthur Hubbard, a bespectacled and distinguished-looking white businessman from Austin, Texas, was injected with plutonium in Chicago by Robert Stone's group.

As a young man, Arthur had been recruited to play baseball for St. Edward's University, a small college in Austin. During one game, he glanced up and saw a determined-looking girl named Selma watching him from the stands. The couple fell in love and got married. Eventually they had seven children, one of whom died as a toddler after eating mistletoe at Christmas.

When Arthur's baseball days were over, he purchased land in the hill country outside Austin where he cut down cedar trees, split them into posts, and sold them for fences and firewood. When gas heaters replaced woodstoves, he moved to town and opened Hubbard's Baseball Inn, which sold beer and barbecue sandwiches and became a watering hole for the police chief and the county commissioners.

Arthur had enjoyed excellent health until the latter part of June 1944, when he noticed a swelling under the front part of his chin. The swelling increased to the size of a "hen's egg" and was excised four months later. Doctors diagnosed Arthur with squamous cell carcinoma and subsequently exposed the affected area to two thousand roentgens of localized radiation. Within two weeks the cancer was back, and Arthur underwent another surgical procedure and another round of radiation.

A friend who was a surgeon urged Arthur to get treatment at University of Chicago's Billings Hospital. The hospital was just a few minutes' walk from the Met Lab, and many of the doctors who worked at the lab also had privileges at the hospital. "We knew they were experimenting with some new treatment," Arthur's daughter, Ripple Guess, said. But neither Ripple nor any of Arthur's other children suspected the so-called treatment consisted of an injection of top-secret material that would be used in a weapon soon to be dropped on Japan.

In his late sixties when he contracted cancer, Arthur underwent "seven different plastic operative procedures," including the removal of his lower jaw. Eventually he was fed by tube because his throat and mouth had become so painful that he could no longer swallow. At 9:17 A.M. on April 26, 1945, several weeks after he entered the hospital, he was injected with 6.5 micrograms of plutonium in a citrate solution, a dose equal to 120 times the radiation an average person receives in a year. Afterward, his urine was collected in gallon bottles filled with hydrochloric acid and samples of his stool were placed in "seal-fast" cardboard containers. He was assigned the code name CHI-1, a number that signified that he was the first Chicago patient injected with plutonium. A year later Met Lab scientists explained the logic behind the injection in a secret report:

> Since people were of necessity exposed to some degree to plutonium and since plutonium is known to be very radiotoxic it was obviously desirable to have some method of determining whether or not a given person had any plutonium in him. It was equally desirable to be able to estimate as accurately as possible how much was deposited in any person. Animal experiments were used to procure as much data as possible. Some human studies were needed to see how to apply the animal data to the human problems.

Soon after Arthur Hubbard was injected, Joseph Hamilton and his colleagues in Berkeley began scouting the corridors of the University of California Hospital in San Francisco for a suitable human candidate for their own plutonium experiment. For more than a year, Hamilton and his associates had been injecting plutonium into rats. Now Hamilton, a compulsive and impatient experimenter, was eager to ratchet the studies up to the next level. In January of 1945, the very month that Los Alamos's Wright Langham perfected the chemical technique for detecting plutonium in human urine and feces, Hamilton notified the Met Lab's Arthur

Compton that he was ready "to undertake, on a limited scale, a series of metabolic studies with product [plutonium] using human subjects." Although Compton was a religious man, his moral scruples apparently were overridden by his fear of plutonium and his conviction that the human experiments were necessary.

Joseph Hamilton held dual academic appointments: He was a professor of medical physics at UC-Berkeley and a professor of experimental medicine and radiology at UCSF. This arrangement, he said, allowed him access to "clinical material." The "clinical material" that caught his eye in May of 1945 was house painter Albert Stevens, a shrunken, pale man on Ward B of the University of California Hospital in San Francisco.

Albert had long been a familiar figure in the small town of Healdsburg, California, his bladelike body rattling up and down ladders with cans of paint or slouching in a block of shade with an unfiltered cigarette between his fingers. In the 1920s Albert had set off for California in a skinny-wheeled Model T with a bird's nest of furniture piled on top after a doctor told him his asthmatic wife would not survive another year in Ohio. The West was still an uncharted wilderness then, and the rutted roads often bloomed into lakes or vanished in the prairie grasses. The journey took a year and it was one of the happiest times of his life. In the old photographs, he is tall and slim and always grinning.

The years had taken their toll on Albert, and by the spring of 1945 he bore little resemblance to the smiling young man in the photographs. For several months he had been experiencing extremely sharp pains in his stomach. The pain was so fierce, so consuming, it was as if the finches and canaries he kept were free and he, Albert Stevens, were in the cage. He talked to the birds often, coaxing them to sing for his young grandson. Now the musical notes spilled over his shoulders, sweet and clear. But Albert was listening to the drab complaint within him. The pain weakened him, draining the color from his face and hair, until finally he was a prematurely old man.

One doctor said he had lost fifteen pounds; another put it at forty. A local physician suspected Albert had a malignant ulcer that had spread to the liver and advised him to consult specialists at the University of California Hospital. Albert reluctantly agreed. It meant he would miss part of the spring. In his backyard, lumps of hard fruit hung from the orange tree and in the tangled blackberry bushes along the wall. The seventy-five-mile trip south to San Francisco was beautiful. The hills were still a vivid green, and splotches of yellow mustard spilled across the slopes.

Albert arrived at the hospital in San Francisco the first week of May 1945, the week Germany announced its surrender. Just three weeks earlier, President Franklin D. Roosevelt, who had guided the nation during the war and had approved the atomic bomb project, died. President Harry Truman was briefed on the new weapon on April 25 by Secretary of War Henry Stimson and Army General Leslie Groves.

Albert was slated to undergo a battery of tests in the hospital. The cost was $5.25 a day plus a $30 deposit. The medical expenses were reasonable, but Albert was unemployed and it was a lot of money to scrape together. The hospital also insisted that Albert's family replace any blood used for transfusions, so his son and daughter-in-law flew down from Michigan to donate. Afterward they paced the corridors and waited for the results of the diagnostic tests.

In the first few days of his hospital stay, Albert underwent a routine workup. A urinalysis and chest X ray were normal. His abdomen was concave and tender to the touch. Small curds of milk and coffee grounds were found in his stomach. He was placed on a standard hospital diet and after a few days felt "substantially improved." An upper gastrointestinal series was conducted. Both a radiologist and a surgical consultant concluded that Albert probably had cancer but suggested a gastroscopy be done to confirm the diagnosis. For some reason, however, the procedure, which involves inserting a scope through the mouth to visually inspect the stomach, was not done. When the other diagnostic tests were completed, the doctors relayed the bad news to the family: Albert had stomach cancer and would probably not live more than another six months. He was fifty-eight years old.

Through some invisible network, perhaps nothing more than a hallway conversation, scientists working on top-secret research for the Manhattan Project learned of Albert. While doctors in San Francisco were doing their diagnostic tests, Joseph Hamilton's group in Berkeley began preparations for their first human plutonium experiment. Hamilton's team prepared a solution that consisted of mostly plutonium-238 and a small amount of plutonium-239. Plutonium-238 is 276 times more radioactive than plutonium-239 and therefore has the potential to cause much more biological damage. Plutonium-238 probably was used because it was easier to measure with the crude instruments of the time.

Kenneth Scott, the chubby scientist who had been working at the Rad Lab since John Lawrence had injected his first human patient with radiophosphorous, transported the plutonium from Berkeley to the hospital. The son of an aspiring beautician and a locomotive engineer, Scott had worked his way through high school and the University of California at Berkeley and later claimed to have successfully cured animal tumors with LSD. Like Hamilton, Scott's interest in radioisotopes was accidental, having begun after he went to a "beer party with a bunch of physicists."

On May 14 the mixture that Scott had brought to the hospital was injected into one of Albert's veins. Patricia Durbin, the scientist who as an undergraduate worked in Hamilton's lab, said years later the injection was the equivalent of a "carcinogenic dose." Albert was designated CAL-1, the first California patient injected with plutonium.

On the day Albert was injected, five rats were injected with the same solution. Two of the rats were killed a day later and the plutonium in their lungs, liver, kidney, and skeleton was measured. The other three rats were allowed to live for the remainder of the experiment.

In an interview several decades later, Kenneth Scott said that UCSF radiologist Earl Miller injected the plutonium into Albert's body. Miller had been hired at the University of California at San Francisco in 1940 by Robert Stone and was acting chief of the radiology department while Stone was at the Met Lab. For decades Miller denied that he had any involvement in the experiment. "I never, never, never injected any radioactive material into anybody," he said in May 1995, about two months before his death. "These people," Miller told other interviewers, "the people that were chosen usually in these studies, they were doomed. They were ready to die."

Four days after the injection, with the plutonium coursing through his bloodstream and already settling in his bones, Albert was wheeled into surgery. He was lain on his right side and a pillow placed under his chest. Then a long incision paralleling the ninth rib was made. Surgeons found a "huge, ulcerating, carcinomatous mass" that had grown into his spleen and liver.

Initially the doctors were planning to remove his entire stomach, but halfway through the operation, they decided against it. Half of the left lobe of the liver, the entire spleen, most of the ninth rib, lymph nodes, part of the pancreas, and a portion of the omentum—an apron of fat covering the internal organs—were taken out.

According to a note written by the surgeon, the specimens were handed to Earl Miller as they were removed from Albert's unconscious body. Miller was to take a portion of each specimen and then send the remainder to the hospital pathology department, where the cancer diagnosis was to be confirmed. The surgeon apparently agreed to the division because he erroneously thought that Albert had been given radioactive phosphorous by the X-ray department for "special studies."

The operation was expertly done. The incision along the ninth rib was sutured with fine cotton thread and a small catheter was inserted in an opening so that penicillin could be administered for the next forty-eight hours. "The patient withstood the procedure exceedingly well. He was returned to the ward in good condition," the surgeon wrote.

On May 19, the day after the operation, there is a verbal order from Miller in Albert's medical records instructing that urine and stool samples are to be "saved for Mr. Scott who will collect them each day." On May 21 there is another notation in Albert's medical records that states: "All specimens going to Dr. Miller."

The hospital pathologist, James F. Rinehart, found evidence of a huge, cheeselike ulcer in Albert's stomach. But after carefully examining the specimens under a microscope, he came to a startling conclusion: Albert didn't have cancer. He had a "benign gastric ulcer with chronic inflammation." The mass removed by surgeons was apparently part of the ulcer.

Disbelief rippled through the medical staff. The surgeon noted that the operation was a "radical procedure to do for a benign process." Earl Miller became extremely upset by the findings and spent days looking at Albert's slides, thinking there was a mistake. But "he just didn't have it," Scott recalled of the cancer diagnosis.

Scott, too, seems to have been troubled by what happened to Albert Stevens. After he retired, he was interviewed for an oral history by Berkeley medical historian Sally Hughes. The interview was conducted in December 1979 at Scott's bedside in Novato, California. Scott, who was then about seventy years old, was diabetic, disabled by a stroke, embittered—and drunk. Lying in a hospital bed with his wife hovering nearby, Scott told Hughes that he left the Crocker lab in part because Hamilton wanted to do some "incautious experiments":

Scott: I thought they were morally wrong.
Hughes: Are you talking now about the human experiments?
Scott: Yes.
Hughes: And he went ahead and did those?
Scott: Yes, he did, and he did the first one with my help.
Hughes: That was the plutonium?
Scott: Plutonium-248 [sic], which we gave to this nice man who
    was scheduled for stomach surgery. They were sure—Earl

Miller, for example, was sure—that he had cancer of the stomach and his probable survival wasn't very great. He was fifty-five, maybe, when I first found him. We injected him with plutonium-238, and the story of it is that he didn't have a cancer that anyone could demonstrate. Earl Miller got very upset with that and looked for days at slides of this man's post-op remains, and he just didn't have it. I got very interested in him as a person, and I contracted through the laboratory to buy all of his urine and feces, for which he would get a monthly check. We would go up once a week and pick it up in acid carbolase in various bottles we left up there with him.

Hughes: Did he know what was going on?

Scott: Never told him.

Hughes: What was the outcome?

Scott: Finally the laboratory wouldn't pay for his feces any more. He was in excellent health. His sister was a nurse and she was very suspicious of me. But to my knowledge he never found out, and he slipped through our fingers at the age of eighty-eight. He died of something.

Hughes: Nothing to do with the plutonium?

Scott: He got many times the so-called lethal textbook dose of plutonium. Patricia Durbin knows more about that. She's kept up with his data.

Hughes: In those days it was possible to do experiments on human beings with such ease?

Scott: Yes, yes.

Hughes: What did it involve?

Scott: It involved getting a needy patient who had a known disease, or thought it was known. He came out of the clinic for us at UC. I took the plutonium over there and gave it to Earl Miller, who injected it into this guy.

Albert's medical records show that he signed consent forms for both the anesthesia and surgery. But there is no mention of informed consent for any injection of radioactive material. A document declassified in 1994 also strongly suggests that neither Albert nor the second California patient injected with plutonium were told of the injections.

Albert was discharged from the hospital a month after his admittance. Hamilton soon grew worried that he might leave the Bay area, and on July 7, 1945, wrote a letter to Robert Stone asking whether it would be possible to pay him fifty dollars a month to make sure he stayed in the Berkeley area:

> Kenneth [Scott] and I are very much afraid that the man may sell his house and go to live at some distant point which would, of course, put an end to our most interesting series of experiments. This proposal may be totally irregular and out of keeping with Army policy, but since we have, to date, maintained daily collections of all excretions, it would seem most unfortunate not to have the assurance of his continued presence within a reasonable distance from Berkeley.

A couple of days later, Hamilton also wrote to Joseph Howland at Oak Ridge about the problem. Howland responded with a memo suggesting some possible ways to solve Albert's "financial embarrassment":

> 3a. Pay for his care in a hospital or nursing home as a service.
>   b. Place this individual on Dr. Hamilton's payroll in some minor capacity without release of any classified information.
> 4. It is not recommended that he be paid as an experimental subject only.

If Scott's memory is accurate, the solution they apparently arrived at was to pay Albert for his urine and stool samples. Albert's son, Thomas, said he remembered that his father kept the samples in a shed behind the house. His father believed the collections were part of his follow-up care. "They sent an intern and a nurse down once a week from the hospital. He was led to believe it was all done because of the operation he had. They kept saying he was doing very well, that it was an unusual operation."

Thomas and his sister, Evelyn, who were both in their thirties at the time of the experiment, said their father seemed completely unaware that he was part of a medical experiment. All that they knew for sure was that their father's medical care was free. "My mother and I figured they were using him for a guinea pig," Evelyn said. "We knew they were using things they weren't sure of. But he was dying, and we were praying that something would help. And it did help." So they believed, because Albert's children were never told that their father did not have cancer. For decades, Thomas said he checked "yes" on every medical form asking if there was a history of cancer in the family.

In 1946, almost a year after Albert's injection, the Berkeley group published a classified report titled "A Comparison of the Metabolism of Plutonium in Man and the Rat." The abstract begins: "The fate of plutonium injected intravenously into a human subject and into rats was followed in parallel studies."

A description of the body parts removed from Albert on the operating table—the specimens that were not delivered to the pathology department—appears in the report. "Four days after the plutonium had been administered, specimens of rib, blood, spleen, tumor, omentum, and subcutaneous tissue were obtained from the patient."

Albert's rib was scraped with a sharp instrument, split longitudinally, and the marrow removed. The different parts of the bone were ashed and analyzed for plutonium. Most of the material had gravitated to the marrow and trabecular bone, the lacy spongelike bone threaded with marrow. The experiment showed that rats excreted plutonium more quickly than human beings, the report noted, thus making "the problem of chronic plutonium poisoning a matter of serious concern for those who come in contact with this material."

The authors of the "Man and Rat" paper included Josephine Crowley, H. Lanz, Kenneth Scott, and Joseph Hamilton. In 1947 C. L. Marshall, an AEC deputy declassification officer in Oak Ridge, Tennessee, refused to declassify the report: "It contains material, which in the opinion of the management of the United States Atomic Energy Commission, might adversely affect the national interest," he wrote. The refusal is one of the only documents made public so far in which national security is cited as a reason for not declassifying information related to a human experiment.

10

TRINITY SITE

While Ebb Cade, Arthur Hubbard, and Albert Stevens struggled to regain their health, the Manhattan Project's medical doctors turned their attention to the desolate area in southern New Mexico where the world's first atomic bomb would be tested. The war in Europe was over, but the beaches on the small island of Okinawa, the stepping-stone to the Japanese mainland, were red with blood. The casualties were horrendous on both sides. While Marines went from cave to cave with flame-throwers and grenades, suicidal kamikaze pilots were inflicting heavy casualties and unspeakable terror on American ships.

At the Met Lab, scientists had grown divided over whether the atomic bomb should be used against Japan. A subcommittee headed by Nobel laureate James Franck was formed to examine the social and political implications of the revolutionary new weapon. Its members included Glenn Seaborg, James J. Nickson, the young medical doctor involved in the TBI experiment at the Chicago Tumor Clinic, and, of course, Leo Szilard. After much debate, the group concluded the bomb should not be used against Japan for two reasons: First, such a powerful weapon would necessarily involve the killing of thousands of people and engender an attitude of fear, suspicion, and hate toward the United States. Second, the United States might wish to outlaw the use of atomic weapons by international agreement after the war, but its position would be weakened if the bomb had already been used. The Franck committee urged that the United States demonstrate the power of the new weapon before the eyes of the world on a barren island.

No one lobbied harder for this position than Leo Szilard, the Met

Lab's enfant terrible and the scientist who had done so much to get the entire bomb project going. Arthur Compton, who was trying to hold his tumultuous staff together, disagreed with Szilard but presented his views fairly in his postwar memoirs:

> There were few who sensed as clearly as did Szilard the shock that would be felt throughout the world if the atomic bomb destroyed large numbers of Japanese lives. This he thought of as an international crime and believed that many in all parts of the world would share this view. He had been willing to approve and even to urge the use of the bomb against the Germans, for in this case it would be an evil less than that of the human destruction he felt sure would result if the Nazis should gain the victory. He could not persuade himself that the case was the same with regard to the Japanese.

The Met Lab's debate was mirrored at the national level by members of the innocuously named Interim Committee. The all-civilian group, which was headed by Secretary of War Henry Stimson, had been created to consider issues relating to the use of the new weapon. Ernest Lawrence, Enrico Fermi, J. Robert Oppenheimer, and Arthur Compton acted as scientific advisors. The committee bandied about the idea of demonstrating the weapon's power on a uninhabited island but rejected it for several reasons: First, even if the initial atomic bomb test was successful, there was no guarantee the second bomb wouldn't be a dud. Second, the Japanese might attempt to interfere with the delivery of the weapon or put American prisoners of war at the detonation site. Third, the panel thought it was doubtful that Japan's fanatic military leaders would be inclined to surrender after witnessing a bloodless demonstration. And finally, the group believed such a test would eliminate the important element of surprise. Although Ernest Lawrence would become a powerful advocate of bigger nuclear weapons after the war, his hard-line nature had not yet emerged and he was the last of the scientific advisors to give up on the idea of a peaceful demonstration.

In Los Alamos, the debate over using the bomb was muted, in part a testament to the charismatic leadership of J. Robert Oppenheimer as well as the crushing workload. Los Alamites were working twelve hours a day, seven days a week. The momentum of the technology itself was driving the project forward, and many scientists were intensely curious to see if the "gadget" would work.

Stafford Warren knew the detonation of an atomic bomb could release radioactivity equivalent to a ton of radium, or a million grams, into the atmosphere. "Now before the war, hospitals and doctors treating cancer thought they were in marvelous shape if they had a quarter of a gram or maybe a few milligram needles . . . and when you thought of a ton and a million grams, my God!"

Trinity site, the place where the first atomic test would be conducted, was about 230 miles south of Los Alamos in the Jornada del Muerto (Journey of Death) valley. The Jornada was a treacherous shortcut on the Camino Real, the King's Highway that linked old Mexico to Santa Fe, the capital of New Mexico.

By early May, the engineers were constructing the tower from which the weapon would be dropped. Oppenheimer established a new organization within the lab called Project TR to oversee test preparations. The laboratory's official history indicates that Project TR did not include a medical group until a month later, a small oversight that again demonstrates the second-class status of the medical doctors. They were the last hired, the last to be brought into planning on critical projects. Although the physicians grew accustomed to their lowly status, a tinge of bitterness often crept into their voices when they discussed their roles with historians after the war. "Everybody was too busy with getting the bomb fabricated to worry about what happened afterwards. In fact, we'd get brushed off," Stafford Warren recalled years later. Hymer Friedell, his sidekick, described the men assigned to oversee health and safety operations as "hangers on."

High-level officials at Los Alamos did not give serious attention to fallout hazards until a few months before the detonation, when two of their physicists, Joseph O. Hirschfelder and John Magee, did a wide-ranging study and concluded that radioactive debris might pose a more severe hazard than anyone had predicted. "In spite of all this work," Hirschfelder remembered, "very few people believed us when we predicted radiation fallout from the atom bomb. On the other hand, they did not dare ignore this possibility."

Leslie Groves assigned Stafford Warren the task of making sure none of the test participants or nearby residents was injured by the radioactive fallout. Hirschfelder said that he and Magee were Stafford Warren's "chief helpers," but their mission had such low priority that they had to borrow an automobile from a friend to get to Trinity. Warren also received help from Louis Hempelmann and members of his health group, who included James Nolan, Wright Langham, and Paul Aebersold, the

Berkeley scientist who had lent Robert Stone a hand in his prewar neutron experiment and had recently transferred to Los Alamos.

In the weeks leading up to the test, the men toured the blast area, studied topographical maps, consulted with meteorologists, and read everything they could about the 1883 eruption of the volcano Krakatoa, the largest explosion ever recorded. Although they were both deathly afraid of flying, Warren and Hempelmann flew over the Trinity site. From their light aircraft, the doctors could see that there were "a lot of people" living in the vicinity of the test area. "We suddenly discovered Indian reservations there with lots of people. And then there were dude ranches that somebody hadn't thought to mention," Warren remembered.

After Warren developed a reasonably good idea of what the fallout pattern would be, he spent twenty-four hours drafting an evacuation plan for Leslie Groves.

> I asked for a couple of hundred troops, jeeps, and trucks, because General Groves had told me that he would have the power of marshal law—he had talked with the governor—and that I would operate under that at that time. So I said to myself that if I needed to evacuate people, I would have to have armed troops to go in and take them out. Suppose grandma was cooking dinner and she says, "The heck with you boys." These were independent people and had been living that way. They frequently had a rifle behind the door and wouldn't take any nonsense.

General Groves initially scoffed at Warren's safety plan, but eventually he ordered a couple of military trucks and more than 150 troops to stand by in case the surrounding towns needed to be evacuated. Leaving nothing to chance, Warren also directed that two planes remain on standby in Oak Ridge in order to ferry four psychiatrists to New Mexico in the event the bomb failed and the scientists had nervous breakdowns. "One of the big problems that kept nagging my group," he explained, "was the fact that if the first bomb test was a fizzle we would have a tremendous trauma and a psychological disintegration, really, of a great many of the scientists who had been working so hard on this bomb."

By early July, word had come down that the bomb was to be detonated on July 16, 1945, providing weather conditions were permissible. On that date, President Truman would be in Potsdam, Germany, meeting with British Prime Minister Winston Churchill and the Soviet Union's Joseph Stalin. On the negotiating table were postwar concerns in

Europe, surrender terms for the Japanese, and Russia's planned entry into the Pacific campaign. If the Trinity test was successful, Truman would have more bargaining power and less reason to bring the Soviets into the war with Japan.

But mid-July also happened to be one of the worst times in New Mexico to test such a weapon because of the frequent summer thunderstorms. True to predictions, a fierce thunderstorm blew in from the Gulf of Mexico in the early morning hours of July 16, bringing lightning, high winds, and several inches of rain. Oppenheimer was beside himself with worry. Groves was furious. And many scientists advocated canceling the test. When Jack Hubbard, a meteorologist, finally advised Groves that the storm front would pass and that the weather would be acceptable at dawn, the general snarled that Hubbard had better be right "or I will hang you."

Fortunately, Hubbard's prediction was correct. The skies cleared and the stars came out. The atomic bomb test was back on schedule.

At 5:15 A.M., Warren placed a call to Hymer Friedell, who was standing by at a hotel in Albuquerque. Friedell had been stationed there in case the bomb destroyed the southern half of the state and incinerated all the scientists. "Let's synchronize watches," Warren suggested. "It's five-fifteen here, fifteen minutes to zero." Warren told Friedell that field monitors were in position for the blast and everything was going according to schedule. "Keep this line open, no matter what," he added, reminding Friedell before he hung up that he would be in charge if Warren was killed in the blast.

Fifteen minutes later Warren lay in a ditch filled with hay and leaves nine miles from Ground Zero. His feet were toward the blast area; his eyes were protected by dark welder's glasses. As the seconds ticked away, many of the other scientists sheepishly crept down in the ditch as well. "They were embarrassed, you know, to lie down; so I lay down, myself, so there would be no question, then Dr. Hempelmann and Nolan. Then it went off. And, at first, of course, there was a feeling of great heat as if you had just opened a big furnace door, and then it was shut. There was a funny squeezing sensation to the ears, in the mastoids, that I have noticed several times since and never was able to identify as anything real. Then the fireball developed."

The scientists watched the awesome cloud as it rose into the sky and then turned to each other. Knowing their words would be recorded for posterity, some had thought in advance about what they were going to say and their language is filled with self-consciousness. Oppenheimer remembered a line from the *Bhagavad-Gita:* "Now I am become Death, the destroyer of worlds." While the scientists stood about congratulating each other, Leslie Groves bustled off to see how Stafford Warren and his monitors were doing. Warren, it seemed, was the one who might soon be in need of a psychiatrist. Remembered Groves:

> When I went to Warren's headquarters in the base camp soon after the explosion, I was not pleased to discover that he had been so busy getting ready that he had gone without sleep for almost forty-eight hours. Although his decisions were sound and his instructions were clear, I was sure from listening to them as he talked over the telephone, that—quite understandably—his mind was not working so quickly as it normally did, by any means. Fortunately, we had at Alamogordo a Navy doctor who was familiar with our activities—Captain George Lyons, and I suggested that he spell Warren for a few hours to give him some rest. I was displeased, too, with myself, because I felt that I had fallen down in not making certain that Warren would be in first-class physical shape to handle the situation.

While Warren napped, his monitors spread out across the countryside. Hirschfelder and Magee, driving the borrowed sedan, stopped at the Bingham store, which was located about fifteen miles north of Ground Zero. An old man came out and looked at their white coveralls curiously. Then he broke out laughing and said, "You boys must have been up to something this morning. The sun came up in the west and went on down again."

The monitors also stopped at William Wrye's ranch, which is about nine miles north of the Bingham store. Wrye and his wife had been on a trip and had just gotten home several hours earlier. When Wrye saw the monitors waving their bulky counters over his property later that morning, he went out and asked them what they were doing. "They told me they were checking for radioactivity. I told him that we didn't have the radio on," Wrye remembered in an interview in 1998. In a rocky gorge that was subsequently dubbed Hot Canyon, the monitors came across fallout readings of fifteen to twenty roentgens per hour. Since maps indicated the area was uninhabited, they turned around and left quickly.

In a few hours, the cloud had disappeared from sight. Feeling elated and yet strangely empty, many of the scientists piled into cars and headed back to Los Alamos. Wright Langham spotted a sedan with a flat tire on the side of the road just south of Albuquerque. It was Enrico Fermi's car. Using methane gas from one of his radiation counters, Langham inflated the tire and Fermi, who had been christened the "Italian Navigator" after the Chicago pile went critical, was on his way. The automobile that Hirschfelder and Magee had borrowed was so hot from fallout that it read four roentgens per hour in the driver's seat. Back in Los Alamos four days later, the car was still hot enough to throw sensitive Geiger counters in nearby laboratories off the scale.

Troubled by the high readings in Hot Canyon, Louis Hempelmann decided to spend the night at the Trinity base camp and do some further investigation. The following morning he met Hymer Friedell, and the two men drove into the rock-strewn gorge. To their dismay, they discovered a two-room adobe house, which the Army had somehow overlooked and omitted from the monitors' maps. An elderly couple named the Raitliffs and their grandson lived there. The grandson had left for the Bingham store on horseback on the morning of the explosion, Hempelmann wrote:

> By being at Bingham during the day and indoors at night, he missed most of the heaviest exposure of the first day in "hot canyon." During this day, Mr. Raitliff had spent most of the day outdoors but Mrs. Raitliff was indoors a large portion of the time. During the following two weeks there was no change in their usual habits of going indoors about 7:00–8:00 o'clock to dinner, retiring after hearing the evening news broadcast and arising at about 6:00 AM.

During the next six months, Hempelmann and his fellow Manhattan Project doctors were to make several visits to the Raitliffs' ranch. Mr. Raitliff told Hempelmann that the ground and fence posts had the appearance of "being covered with light snow, or of being 'frosted' for several days after the shot," particularly at sunrise and sunset. Although the family seemed healthy, Mr. Raitliff complained of "nervousness, tightness in the chest and poor teeth." Hempelmann did not think Mr. Raitliff's symptoms were related to his radiation exposure since the symptoms had been present before the detonation. But in a later memo, Hempelmann was less certain. The color of Mr. Raitliff's hands and lips, he wrote, indicated he might be "slightly anemic."

Hempelmann also examined the family's animals and realized that they had been injured by radioactive debris from the cloud. The paws of two black house dogs were raw and bleeding from beta burns. "One of the dogs was so badly affected that she was unable to walk except with extreme difficulty." A milk cow and heifer and one of the dogs also had white hair on their back or patchy areas where the radioactive particles had sifted through their coats and irradiated their skin. Hempelmann estimated that the members of the Raitliff family each received about forty-seven roentgens, or nearly fifty rem, of whole-body radiation in the first two weeks after the Trinity test. It's not known whether the family was ever informed of the exposure or urged to take precautions, although fifty rem can cause nausea in some people and increase the risk of contracting cancer.

William Wrye, who still lives on his ranch, said in 1998 his beard fell out three months after the Trinity explosion. "I was slick-faced except for the corner of my chin. When my beard grew back it came in gray, and a couple of months later, it came back black again." Wrye told newspaper reporters the same thing in 1945, but the Manhattan Project doctors dismissed his statement as tomfoolery. Wrote Louis Hempelmann in a December 1, 1945, memo to the files:

> According to neighbors, this man, Bill Wrye, is a relatively young man who is turning gray prematurely. When teased about "getting old," early in the spring of 1945, he attributed the change in color of his beard to the fact that he had accidentally rubbed "dehorning paste" on his face. When the cattle began to show the effects of beta radiation, he changed his story and attributed the color change to the atomic bomb. According to the neighbors, Mr. Wrye is having fun at the expense of the newspapers. Since the radiation levels in the region of the Wrye Ranch are quite low, it has been decided not to investigate the story further.

The fallout from the Trinity test spread much farther than even an alarmist like Warren had dared to imagine. Some was discovered 1,100 miles away in the Wabash River in Vincennes, Indiana. When infuriated Eastman Kodak officials reported that radioactive particles from the river water had been absorbed into paper used in packaging and made tiny black spots on film, atomic scientists got their first hard data about how far fallout could travel.

11

A "SMALL PIECE OF THE SUN"

Following the Trinity explosion, the action shifted to Tinian in the Mariana Islands, some 1,300 miles southeast of Tokyo. Tinian, along with Guam and Saipan, had been captured in August of 1944 from the Japanese, and the three were being used as air bases for America's newest long-range bomber, the B-29 Superfortress. Six runways, each two miles long and as wide as a ten-lane highway, had been constructed. Next to the runways were rows of glittering silver planes. For an hour and a half each evening at roughly fifteen-second intervals, the bombers would roll down the runway and lift off for Japan with bellies full of incendiary bombs.

Leslie Groves had sent a thirty-seven-member team of civilians and military officials to Tinian to help assemble and load the atomic bombs onto specially modified B-29s. One of the people at Tinian was Don Mastick, who had been assigned the job of analyzing urine samples after his accident. The task was so revolting that one day he stormed into J. Robert Oppenheimer's office and said, "I can't stand what I'm doing. It stinks." Oppenheimer was sympathetic; it seems the smell of the boiling urine was going up Mastick's ventilating hood and then blowing back down into Oppenheimer's office. He agreed to transfer Mastick to the crew in charge of dropping the bombs. Another Manhattan Project scientist at Tinian was Philip Morrison, one of Oppenheimer's former students. In the evenings, Morrison would sit on a coral ridge overlooking Tinian and watch the planes take off. Every so often he would see one of the bombers go careening into the sea or onto the beach where it burned like a torch. The implications of such a disaster happening to an airplane loaded with atomic bombs were almost too horrible to contemplate.

The components for two types of atomic weapons, a uranium and a plutonium bomb, were being shipped to Tinian at about the same time the Potsdam Declaration was issued. That document called upon Japan to surrender unconditionally or face "prompt and utter destruction." When the Japanese vowed to continue fighting, the United States moved ahead with preparations to drop the two bombs.

On the morning of August 6, the *Enola Gay*, one of the specially modified B-29s, lumbered down the runway with its payload. At 8:15, it dropped the payload—a uranium bomb—on Hiroshima. The city was immediately engulfed in roiling clouds of smoke and flames. "The mushroom itself was a spectacular sight, a bubbling mass of purple-gray smoke and you could see it had a red core in it and everything was burning inside," recalled Robert Caron, a tail gunner on the *Enola Gay*.

Below the veil of clouds and smoke was an inferno of unimaginable proportions. At the hypocenter, the place on the ground directly below where the bomb was detonated, thousands of Japanese citizens were instantly incinerated. Those who were not killed on the spot suffered grotesque injuries. Their skin, burned by the flash and torn loose by the blast, hung like rags from their bodies. In an effort to ease the agony of burned flesh touching burned flesh, they walked through the city like sleepwalkers with their arms and hands held out in front of them, their skin hanging from their fingertips and chins. Many were killed by material from collapsing buildings or were impaled by flying debris. Injured residents who were pinned beneath roofs and walls were soon burned alive by firestorms that engulfed the city.

P. Siemes, a German Jesuit priest who lived in a novitiate about a mile from Hiroshima, later organized a nightmarish trip into the city to rescue two injured priests. When the sun came up the morning after the bombing, he saw a wasteland of ashes and rubble that extended as far as the eye could see: "The banks of the river are covered with dead and wounded, and the rising waters have here and there covered some of the corpses. On the broad street in the Hakushima' district, naked burned cadavers are particularly numerous. Among them are the wounded who still live. A few have crawled under the burnt-out autos and trains. Frightfully injured forms beckon to us and then collapse."

Although the Japanese did not yet know what kind of a weapon had caused such destruction, Manhattan Project scientists had a pretty good idea of what they had unleashed. It was as if "a small piece of the sun" had descended upon the city, Philip Morrison told members of the Special Senate Committee on Atomic Energy, which began meeting in the fall of 1945:

> There is formed what we have called the ball of fire, which is a hot, glowing mass something about one-third of a mile across, with a temperature of about a hundred million degrees Fahrenheit in the center of it. The effects from this small sun are as you would expect. In the first place, there is a sudden creation and expansion which pushes away with terrible violence the air that once occupied this region. This air, shocked into motion, as we say, moves just like a blast wave from a great explosion of TNT. . . . This pushing air creates enormous pressure, even a great distance away. Behind the wave of pressure, which travels rapidly through the air, there comes great winds, 500 to 1,000 miles per hour, winds which damage and destroy all structures. . . . If you are near the sun, you must expect to get burned. . . . There are two more effects. At the instant of the explosion there is emitted from this small sun not only the great push through the air, the violent blast, which is the violent explosion—there is not only the concentrated heat which you would expect from being close to the sun, there is also a great amount of radiation, like the radiation used by doctors, like the X-ray radiation used for the treatment of cancer. This radiation is very penetrating. There is no protection behind a foot of concrete, for example.

Although communication with Hiroshima was severed and it would take the Japanese government several days to figure out what had happened, the U.S. military decided that a "one-two" punch was the only way to defeat Japan. On August 9, three days later, another B-29 named *Bock's Car* rolled down the runway at Tinian carrying a plutonium implosion bomb. It exploded over Nagasaki at 11:02 A.M.

Once again the roiling clouds quickly obliterated a city. The destruction was so unbelievable that the bombing victims could find no words to describe it. Many compared the devastation to the agonies of hell depicted in Buddhist paintings. The survivors made their way to air raid shelters where in the stifling gloom amid the groans and screams, they died. Thousands of others plunged into rivers. "A human dam! A human dam!" survivor Chie Setoguchi remembers thinking when she saw thousands of corpses bobbing in a river. "Who masterminded the atrocity of blocking a river with the corpses of human beings?"

A sixteen-year-old postal worker named Sumiteru Taniguchi was blown off his bicycle and knocked unconscious. When he came to, he realized the skin from his shoulder to his fingertips had been peeled off and was hanging down "like a tattered old rag." He managed to survive the first chaotic days and eventually was taken to a hospital, where he spent the next twenty-one months lying facedown on his stomach. He developed bedsores that penetrated to his bones and was in and out of the hospital for decades with mysterious skin lesions that would not heal.

Hisae Aoki, just eighteen years old, was pinned beneath the rubble of her house. As she felt the heat of the approaching fires, she struggled frantically to free herself. When her hair began burning, she managed to wrench herself free and ran from the house. She had been spared, only to watch as one after another of her family members died from radiation overexposure.

Within hours of the bombings of the two cities, surviving relatives began streaming back into the burning rubble looking for the remains of their loved ones. Japan is a predominantly Buddhist country, and dead family members are usually cremated and their ashes interred in a family grave. In the ensuing years the survivors offer prayers for the repose of their souls. One of the most anguishing experience for relatives of the bombing victims was the inability to find the remains of their loved ones. If a person's body is not found, the relatives feel the deceased person's soul can never rest peacefully in the world of the dead.

On August 15—August 14 in the United States—the Japanese people heard the voice of Emperor Hirohito, the venerated symbol of supreme authority in Japan, broadcast over the radio. He told them that the country had surrendered. The enemy, he said, had begun to "employ a new and most cruel bomb, the power of which to do damage is indeed incalculable, taking the toll of many innocent lives. . . ."

Even before the people of Japan heard the lugubrious voice of their emperor, the United Press was reporting that Japan was preparing to surrender. On August 12 Stafford Warren and Louis Hempelmann were about to embark upon another round of interviews with ranchers near the Trinity site when Warren received an emergency call from Leslie Groves. The general wanted Warren to go to Japan after the surrender to survey the radioactivity and damage from the weapons. Warren left

Hempelmann at Trinity and hurried back to Los Alamos. Eventually a team of about forty Manhattan Project officials, including Hymer Friedell and Joseph Howland, was assembled. They stripped nearly all the Manhattan Project sites of detection equipment and then boarded a plane in San Francisco for Tinian. Once on the island, the doctors joined up with the Manhattan Project scientists who had helped prepare the bombs for delivery. Then they split into two parties. Hymer Friedell was with one group; Stafford Warren with another. From Tinian, both teams went to Hiroshima, and then Warren's group continued to Nagasaki.

Meanwhile, back at home, Louis Hempelmann, ever the diligent doctor, proceeded to interview the Raitliff family and then returned to Los Alamos to write up his findings. No doubt he felt disgruntled about being left behind, but soon he would have an opportunity to see at home the same dreadful stages of radiation sickness that Warren and Friedell were about to encounter on a grand scale in Japan.

At about 9:00 P.M. on August 21, a young Los Alamos physicist named Harry K. Daghlian left the regular Tuesday evening colloquium and returned to the "49 Room" at Omega site, a building in a remote canyon where experiments with the cores of atomic bombs were conducted. At one end of the twenty-five-foot by twenty-five-foot room was the critical assembly where Daghlian worked. At the other was a guard, Robert Hemmerly, sitting at a desk with his back turned to the apparatus.

Daghlian began to lower a brick onto the assembly with his left hand when his instruments began chattering. The clicking sound told him a chain reaction was about to begin, and he started to withdraw his hand. Suddenly the brick slipped from his grasp and fell into the center of the assembly. Daghlian brushed the brick off with his right hand, but it was too late. A brief chain reaction was ignited, bathing the assembly in an unearthly blue glow.

It was the second time the blue glow had been seen at Omega site. On June 4, eight people were exposed to neutrons and gamma rays during an experiment to measure the critical mass of enriched uranium. Although the doses were large, especially to the two experimenters standing closest to the assembly, they were much smaller than what Daghlian received.

After brushing the brick away, the young scientist felt a deep "tingling sensation" in his right hand but no immediate pain. He was taken to the hospital by a companion, where he was examined by Louis Hempelmann and Paul Aebersold. Robert Stone is named as an "assistant" in one report, indicating that he may have flown in to Los Alamos to help.

There wasn't much the doctors could do to counteract the radiation damage, and Daghlian's condition deteriorated quickly. Ice pads and "grease gauze dressings" were applied to his hands, but they didn't stop his arms from swelling to painful proportions. His hair fell out, he suffered intense abdominal pains, and eventually he slipped into a coma.

Even as Harry Daghlian's physical condition was deteriorating, General Groves began receiving disquieting news reports based on broadcasts by Radio Tokyo: Mysterious "rays" were coming from the rubble; residents uninjured by the bomb were suddenly collapsing and dying; rescue workers were developing dangerously low blood counts. Fearful he would be yanked before Congress to explain why he had used such an inhumane weapon, Groves placed two phone calls on August 25 to Army Major Charles Rea, a surgeon in charge of the Oak Ridge hospital. He read line by line from one of the articles, trying to get the physician to explain to him the strange medical symptoms being reported by Radio Tokyo. The following is an excerpt from one of those phone calls:

G: [Reading from article] "The death toll at Hiroshima and at Nagasaki, the other Japanese city blasted atomically, is still rising, the broadcast said. Radio Tokyo described Hiroshima as a city of death. 90% of its houses, in which 250,000 had lived, were instantly crushed." I don't understand the 250,000 because it had a much bigger population a number of years ago before the war started, and it was a military city. "Now it is peopled by ghost parade, the living doomed to die of radioactivity burns."

R: Let me interrupt you here a minute. I would say this: I think it's good propaganda. The thing is these people got good and burned—good thermal burns.

G: That's the feeling I have. Let me go on and give you the rest of the picture. "So painful are these injuries that sufferers plead: 'Please kill me,' the broadcast said. No one can ever completely recover."

R: This has been in our paper, too, last night.

G: Then it goes on: "Radioactivity caused by the fission of the uranium used in atomic bombs is taking a toll of mounting deaths and causing reconstruction workers in Hiroshima to suffer various sicknesses and ill health."

R: I would say this: You yourself, as far as radioactivity is concerned, it isn't anything immediate, it's a prolonged thing. I
think what these people have, they just got a good thermal
burn, that's what it is. A lot of these people, first of all, they
don't notice it much. You may get burned and you may have
a little redness, but in a couple of days you may have a big
blister or a sloughing of the skin, and I think that is what
these people have had.

G: You see what we are faced with. Matthias [the young engineer in charge of the Hanford Engineer Works] is having
trouble holding his people out there.

R: Do you want me to get you some real straight dope on this,
just how it affects them, and call you back in just a bit?

G: That's true—that's what I want. . . . Then they talk about
the burned portions of the bodies are infected from the inside.

R: Well, of course, any burn is potentially an infected wound.
We treat any burn as an infected wound. I think you had
better get the anti-propagandists out.

G: This is the kind of thing that hurts us—"The Japanese, who
were reported today by Tokyo radio, to have died mysteri-
ously a few days after the atomic bomb blast, probably were
the victims of a phenomenon which is well known in the
great radiation laboratories of America." That, of course, is
what does us the damage.

R: I would say this: You will have to get some big-wig to put a
counter-statement in the paper.

Groves planned to do just that, but first he needed more reliable
information on what was happening in Japan. On September 2 two Japanese representatives signed surrender documents on the deck of the USS
Missouri in Tokyo Bay. Six days later, on September 8, Stafford Warren's
team landed in Hiroshima. Always eager to please his volatile boss, Warren cabled Washington on September 10 and reported: "Number dead or
injured by radiation unknown, but preliminary survey indicates that there
are only a small percent of injured survivors."

On the same day the cable arrived, Groves led a caravan of thirty-
seven reporters and photographers to the Trinity site. Accompanying him
were J. Robert Oppenheimer, Louis Hempelmann, and many other scientists and military officers. The scientists and newsmen donned white

booties and shuffled "like kittens with paper shoes tied to their feet" across the fused green sand of the Trinity crater. The green glass, which covered an area eight hundred yards in diameter, was strewn with globs of glazed soil. For three weeks the area had reeked of the stench of death from the small desert animals killed in the blast. The site was still so radioactive, an Associated Press science writer reported, that it made "spending a day and night right in the crater a possibly risky business." The writer continued:

> The tour's purpose was dual. One, to tell the almost incredible story. Two, to show first hand that the facts do not bear out the Japanese propaganda that apparently tried to lay the foundation for claims that Americans won the war by unfair means. This New Mexico bomb was big, its effects comparable to those bombs dropped on Japan. What happened here was studied purposely to avoid the chances the actual bombings would inflict bizarre and non-military suffering.

His brown Army uniform rumpled and stained with sweat, Groves allowed the photographers to take a few pictures of the crater, warning them to be quick or their film would fog. He explained that the lingering radioactivity at Trinity was due to the fact the bomb was detonated from a tower at a much lower height than the two bombs dropped on Hiroshima and Nagasaki. The Japanese bombs were exploded high above the two cities, he said, thus allowing the heat of the blast to carry the radioactive debris upward and away. "There were evidences of some Japanese deaths due to radioactive rays, but the information now available indicates that this number was relatively small," he told the newsmen.

Wearing his famous pork-pie hat to ward off the sun, Oppenheimer added that the heights of the Japanese detonations were selected specifically to ensure "there would be no indirect chemical warfare due to poisoning the earth with radioactive elements and no horrors other than the familiar ones due to any great explosion." Oppenheimer said that one hour after the blast it was probably safe for rescue workers to enter the area. Satisfied with the pronouncements by the two prominent leaders, *Life* magazine opined: "It seemed certain that the Japanese in Hiroshima and Nagasaki had died within the grotesque legality of wartime killing."

In reality, Oppenheimer and Groves were engaged in a wholesale distortion of the facts. While it is true that air bursts, such as the Hiroshima and Nagasaki explosions, produce less residual radiation than weapons detonated from towers, some radioactivity nevertheless occurs when neutrons are captured by atoms in the air and soil. Radioactive fallout from the two bombs also delivered significant doses of radiation to Japanese who lived downwind of the two cities. Furthermore, Groves told members of the Special Senate Committee on Atomic Energy that the weapons were detonated above the Japanese cities not to protect the inhabitants from radiation effects but to "give us the maximum possible explosive force." And finally, Groves's statement that only a few Japanese were dying of radiation injuries was patently untrue. Even as Groves and Oppenheimer were walking like kittens across the green sand, a second wave of bombing victims was dying from internal complications caused by severe radiation damage. But it would be years, even decades, before the rest of the world learned the full extent of the injuries because on September 19, General MacArthur prohibited any further press reports on the bombings.

On September 15, shortly after the publicity show staged by Groves and Oppenheimer, Harry Daghlian died. When General Groves learned of his death, he instructed Los Alamos officials to cut a $10,000 check for Daghlian's mother and sister and to prepare a legal document that family members were to sign releasing the University of California, the War Department, and the federal government from liability. The transaction was completed on the same day as Daghlian's death.

Notwithstanding the optimistic cable he had sent General Groves on September 10, Stafford Warren had found thousands of Japanese dying from radiation exposure when his team arrived in Hiroshima. Many had already been cremated. Thousands more were lying on mats, anywhere there was a roof over their heads. Those who could eat and drink were given rice and tea. The floors of the first-aid stations were slick with vomit and bloody diarrhea. Outside the relief stations were piles of wooden sandals from cremated patients. "When we got there it stunk terribly, and there were flies everywhere," Warren remembered. "The flies were so bad that we had to close up the windows of the car to keep them out. You would see a man or a woman with what looked like a polka-dot shirt on, but when you got up close, there was just a mass of flies crawling over a formerly white shirt."

The Japanese who were close to the hypocenter and received the largest doses of radiation often began vomiting within half an hour of the bombing. They suffered from severe and bloody diarrhea and intense thirst. The downward spiral closely paralleled the symptoms suffered by Harry Daghlian: coma, delirium, and death.

By the time of Stafford Warren's arrival, the second wave of death had begun taking its toll, due to the lethal effects of the radiation on victims' bone marrow and gastrointestinal (GI) tract. The bone marrow is the blood-making factory where new cells, called stem cells, are produced. These cells mature and differentiate, becoming red cells, white cells, and platelets. When the whole body is irradiated, the number of cells in the bone marrow drops immediately, sometimes disappearing altogether. The bone marrow can regenerate itself if the damage is not too great. But if the exposure is large and nothing is done to counteract the damage, eventually fewer cells will be circulating in the bloodstream. The loss of red cells will cause anemia and fatigue; the reduction in white cells will reduce the body's ability to fight infection; and the lack of platelets can lead to hemorrhages. The effects of radiation on the bone marrow are most noticeable between twenty and sixty days after exposure.

The GI tract, which contains many cells being created and undergoing cell division, also can suffer dramatic damage if the radiation dose is high enough. After 100 rem have been delivered, changes can be seen in the cells lining the mucosa of the small intestine, but the production of new cells will compensate for any cells that are killed or damaged. At doses ranging from 500 to 1,000 rem—the radiation exposures received by many Japanese near the hypocenter—the cells that make up the epithelial layer of the small and large intestine are killed or unable to replenish themselves fast enough. Diarrhea and dehydration begin. Bacteria from the intestine can flood into the bloodstream, greatly increasing the risk of infection, called bacteremia, or toxic shock syndrome. With the depletion of white cells, the body is even less able to fend off the infection.

Some of the effects of the bombing would not become visible for weeks, months, years, or even decades. Unlike the bone marrow and GI tract, many organs and tissues are composed of mature cells which are relatively resistant to radiation. These organ systems may not show damage until they require new cells, at which time the stem cells of these organs may be unable to divide. Then the organ may not have all the cells it needs to function efficiently, and its overall performance will be diminished. The result: a shortened life—one of the major biological consequences of radiation.

The Japanese doctors who were treating the injured with penicillin and transfusions did not yet understand the mysterious sickness that the survivors were suffering from. To their dismay, they discovered that treatment seemed only to increase the suffering. Needle punctures caused "oozing that continued to death," Warren observed. "Even pricks to obtain blood for blood counts caused oozing that could not be checked."

Warren's job was not to minister to the sick but to find out whether the two bombs had left any residual radiation, and if so, whether the radiation was causing deaths. Donald Collins, a member of the survey team, said many years later that the group had been instructed by General Thomas F. Farrell, one of Groves's top aides, that their mission was to "prove there was no radioactivity from the bomb." Apparently they didn't even have to go to the bombing sites to offer that proof because while the team was still waiting to enter Japan, Collins said, "we read in the Stars and Stripes the results of our findings."

Stafford Warren told members of the Special Senate Committee on Atomic Energy that it was impossible to develop meaningful statistics on the death rate because all the records and all the record-keeping organizations had been destroyed. What made the mortality survey even more difficult, he said, were the unreliable memories of the Japanese. "It often took an hour of careful questioning of a patient, even an intelligent one, like a doctor or a nurse, to find out precisely what happened on that day. . . . Our conclusion was that we could trust very little of the factual information that came to us through interpreters, from these Japanese, these patients." He estimated that only 5 to 7 percent of the fatalities were caused by radiation. "I think the radiation has been exaggerated," he testified. (The number of people killed in Hiroshima and Nagasaki is still a matter of dispute; the U.S. Strategic Bombing Survey, which had assessed the damage of the air attacks on Germany and was ordered by President Truman to survey the destruction in Japan, estimated that 140,000 to 160,000 people in Hiroshima were killed or injured and 70,000 killed or injured in Nagasaki.)

Two weeks after the Manhattan Project doctors began combing the bombed-out cities, a contingent of Navy officers and scientists arrived in Japan to do their own independent survey. That group, which included Shields Warren, the Harvard doctor who would take over the AEC's new Division of Biology and Medicine after the war, reached a quite different conclusion: Most of the deaths in Japan were caused by radiation.

Shields Warren was deeply shaken when he saw Nagasaki. To reach the ruined city, his team first drove through miles of terraced hillsides and farming country. Then they passed through a tunnel that had been converted to a war workshop. "When we came out the other side of the tunnel we shifted from a view of a peaceful countryside to utter devastation," he recalled. "It was almost like stepping from the eighteenth century say, into the twentieth century—the countryside on the one side, and on the other, modern power."

Shields Warren moved from hospital to hospital, examining survivors and studying slides and autopsy notes made by Japanese doctors. As he toured the devastated city, he recorded his impressions in a small diary. At the front of the diary are Japanese words that he apparently learned while waiting off the coast of Japan for armistice to be declared: *ketsueki,* blood; *fushosha,* wounded person; *babsudan,* bomb; *ikutsu,* how many. Warren sent transmittal letters and specimens from the bombing victims to the Naval Medical Research Institute in Bethesda, Maryland. According to Warren's diary, copies of the letters were also sent to the director of naval intelligence.

Radiating outward for two miles from the hypocenter was a scene of total destruction, he wrote. "Rats, flies, mosquitoes killed. No larvae on bodies." "Weeds + a little grass starting back." "Horses & dogs died just like people, only protected ones lived. Even moles etc. were supposed to have died." "No crawling bugs. No vermin."

With scant medical supplies and no knowledge of the illness, little could be done for the victims. "Few transfusions given, no plasma. Used saline freely and injectable vitamin ABC," Warren wrote. "Skin ripped off & viscera out from blast effect." "Most had amnesia 1–2 days." "Blast broke tympanun." "Hemorrhages came back." "Much GI irritation." "Some complained of heat—enough to ignite clothes, others felt only mild warmth." "Brightest light they had ever seen." "Some ocular hemorrhages, 3 blind, others see dimly at about one meter." He also jotted down the conflicting death tolls that were being reported at the time: "175,000 killed at Nagasaki." "40,000 killed instantly." "Estimates dead at 30,000 +."

Sometimes huge, mottled patches of purple appeared on the bombing victims' skin. Observers reported that blood often poured from nasal passages, eardrums, uteruses, and urethra. Ulcers soon developed in gums, throats, and tonsils. Before some patients died, their tonsils and tissues in the throat area became gangrenous. Those who survived the critical period often succumbed to pneumonia or some other infection, which their weakened immune system could not fight off.

Warren saw the same astounding damage on the internal organs removed during autopsies: lungs filled with fluid; kidneys, liver, and hearts covered with bright red hemorrhages; depleted bone marrow; congestion in the brains; bizarre-looking cells and massive nuclei spawned by the huge radiation doses. The injuries were "diverse and confusing," he recalled in an article published in September 1946:

> A greater number of injuries was probably caused by ionizing radiation-blast effects, gamma rays, and neutrons than by any other type of injury resulting from the explosion of the bombs. However, since the effects of this ionizing radiation take hours, days, or even weeks to appear, their importance was largely masked by the great numbers killed by flash burn, fire or wreckage of buildings well before the time that symptoms due to irradiation could develop.

Soon after the Manhattan Project team and the Navy group completed their preliminary surveys, the War Department dispatched 195,000 soldiers to Japan to aid in the demilitarization effort and help supervise the cleanup. The first troops arrived in Hiroshima about sixty days after the bomb had been dropped. GIs landed in Nagasaki forty-five days after that city had been bombed.

Bill Griffin, a Marine who survived the fierce fighting on Iwo Jima, arrived in Nagasaki on November 1, 1945. Occasionally he was ordered to patrol the bombed-out area. "I don't know what the purpose of it was. There were no people. All the people had perished," he said. "There were no birds, no wildlife, no crickets, no nothing. It's hard to explain what complete silence is like. You have to experience it." Griffin said he saw civilians wearing white coveralls and divers' helmets ("They were all covered up") taking radiation measurements of soil and water. Japanese who came down from the mountains often wore menstrual pads over their faces to avoid breathing the dust. He said the bombing victims, particularly those who were horribly disfigured by thermal burns, had been whisked out of sight so the American soldiers could not tell people back home what they had seen.

As Bill Griffin and other American GIs patrolled the desolate streets of Nagasaki and Hiroshima, top officials of the Manhattan Project went to Capitol Hill to testify before the Special Senate Committee on Atomic Energy that was investigating the problems related to the development and control of the atomic bomb. Brien McMahon, a freshman Democrat from Connecticut, chaired the hearing. General Groves took a seat at the witness table in Room 312 of the Senate Office Building at 10:00 A.M. on November 28, 1945.

By then Groves knew a great deal more about the effects of radiation on the human body than he did when he placed the two panicked phone calls to Oak Ridge the preceding August. He knew, for example, the details of Harry Daghlian's death. He knew fallout from the Trinity bomb had injured livestock and exposed families such as the Raitliffs to a significant amount of radiation. And he was also aware that thousands of Japanese were dying from medical complications caused by radiation from the bomb. Intent upon calming the public's fears and keeping the Manhattan Project's laboratories and factories open, however, Groves chose to downplay the dangers from radiation.

"The radioactive casualty can be of several classes," Groves testified. "He can have enough so that he will be killed instantly. He can have a smaller amount which will cause him to die rather soon, and as I understand it from the doctors, without undue suffering. In fact they say it is a very pleasant way to die. Then we get down below that to the man who is injured slightly, and he may take some time to be healed, but he can be healed."

"Does that come about through treatment or through time?" Eugene D. Millikin, a conservative Republican senator from Colorado, asked.

"Through time," responded Groves. "Anyone who is working with such materials, who accidentally becomes overexposed, just takes a vacation away from the material and in due course of time he is perfectly all right again."

Later in the hearing, when Senator Harry F. Byrd, a Virginia Democrat, asked the general if there had been any "operating accidents" during the Manhattan Project, Groves gave a response that was a study in obfuscation: "We had no operating accidents throughout this project that were directly attributable to the unusual nature of the material that was a fatal accident. We had one after the bomb was exploded. We then had one we should not have had; there was no reason for having it. It was like all accidents, industrial or home accidents."

The committee was especially interested in the question of whether the two bombs had left any residual radiation in Japan. In fact, a transcript of the hearing shows that was the first question Groves was asked when he took a seat at the witness table. The general stuck to the line that he and Oppenheimer fed to reporters during the Trinity tour. "There is none. That is a very positive 'none,' " he snapped.

When Richard Russell, a Democratic senator from Georgia, pressed Groves about the injuries, he responded, "There was no radioactivity damage done to any human being excepting at the time that the bomb actually went off, and that is an instantaneous damage."

"Let me ask you," said Senator Millikin, "would the effect be different had the bomb exploded in the ground?"

Groves replied, "If the bomb had exploded on or near the ground, that is, within a hundred feet or so, the effect would have been the same as at New Mexico, I believe; there you would have had lasting effects for a considerable period of months. You would have had a considerable number of radioactive casualties, and I think that you would have had an area which should have been banned from traffic. The first mission given to our organization that went over there was to determine that the cities of Hiroshima and Nagasaki were 100 per cent safe for American troops, and to know absolutely that that was a fact so that the men themselves would know everything was all right."

But many of the men who were sent to Hiroshima and Nagasaki do not believe that "everything was all right." Not long after Bill Griffin was discharged, his skin flaked off and his hair and teeth fell out. One of his grandsons was born with a club foot; another appears to have an impaired immune system. Griffin is certain that he received a significant dose of radiation while in Nagasaki and that the exposure damaged his reproductive cells. "We were the first issue of guinea pigs."

Other soldiers stationed in the bombed-out cities said they developed rare cancers and blood disorders, or suffered from premature heart attacks, chronic fatigue, lung diseases, and inexplicable skin afflictions. Many believe their diseases and illnesses are due to the radiation they received in Japan. For decades the Defense Department has vigorously denied that occupation troops were exposed to dangerous levels of radiation, maintaining the doses ranged from a "few tens of millirem" to a "worst case" dose of up to one rem. The Pentagon's desire to prove the two Japanese bombs left no residual radiation became one of the prime motivating factors in the atomic maneuvers that began at the Nevada Test Site in 1951. Thousands of troops were marched through the swirling radioactive dust at Ground Zero over a decade or so. Instead of quelling fears, however, the military's strategic plan backfired and thousands of soldiers came to believe that they, too, had been used as unwitting guinea pigs by their government.

12

THE QUEST CONTINUES

When the news of the Hiroshima bombing reached Los Alamos, the scientists rejoiced. Some raced to the telephone and booked tables at La Fonda Hotel in Santa Fe. Others stayed at Los Alamos and celebrated. They substituted dynamite for fireworks and snaked through the streets banging garbage-can lids. "Everybody had parties, we all ran around. I sat on the end of a jeep and beat drums and so on," recalled Richard Feynman, a math wizard and future Nobel laureate.

As the devastation from the bombings became better understood, some of the scientists' elation began turning to guilt about the past and fear about the future. No one better demonstrated these conflicting emotions than J. Robert Oppenheimer. Deeply fatigued and more emaciated than ever, he departed Los Alamos in mid-October of 1945. In a ceremony before he left, he warned his colleagues: "If atomic bombs are to be added as new weapons to the arsenals of a warring world, or to the arsenals of nations preparing for war, then the time will come when mankind will curse the names of Los Alamos and Hiroshima."

General Groves selected Norris Bradbury, a Berkeley-trained physicist who had worked on the explosives aspects of the plutonium bomb, as the interim laboratory director. Bradbury agreed to take the job for six months, but those six months eventually turned into twenty-five years. While politicians, military leaders, and even the scientists themselves debated the future of the atomic bomb at public forums and congressional hearings that would continue for the next year, the physicists, chemists, metallurgists, and explosives experts who had built the bombs drifted from day to day, uncertain of their future.

But the project's second string of scientists—the medical researchers who had been shunted to the sidelines while the great bomb-building drama unfolded—seemed moved to redouble their efforts at this stage. If anything, the Trinity fallout, the deaths in Japan, the demise of Harry Daghlian, had made it even more imperative to obtain accurate information on the effects of radiation. In addition, nose counts and urine counts taken from Los Alamos workers that summer had shown that some employees had been seriously overexposed to plutonium. Were those workers going to come down with the same grisly cancers the radium dial painters had developed? The thought terrified Louis Hempelmann. The contamination was so severe, he warned Joseph Kennedy, "that the situation seems to be getting completely out of hand."

Ebb Cade, Arthur Hubbard, and Albert Stevens were more or less on their own as the cataclysmic events of the summer of 1945 unfolded. Toward the end of his hospital stay, Ebb Cade developed infectious jaundice. But by the time he was discharged, "the patient was ambulatory and in good condition," an Oak Ridge physician observed. Ebb moved back to Greensboro, North Carolina, with his wife after he was released from the hospital. On Sundays, he brought sacks of oranges to his nieces and nephews. He encouraged them to stay in school and warned them to be careful when they got behind the wheel of a car. "We just loved to talk to him," recalled his niece, Mary Frances Cade Derr. "He would throw his head back and laugh with us."

On April 13, 1953, almost exactly eight years to the day of the injection, Ebb Cade died of heart failure. He was sixty-three years old. His brothers and sisters outlived him by decades. One sister, Nanreen Cade Walton, lived to be more than one hundred years old and went to Washington in 1979 to speak with the House Select Committee on Aging. On the eve of her 107th birthday, she told a reporter, "I believe the old days was pretty hard but these days are more wicked."

Arthur Hubbard remained in fair condition until August of 1945, when he began complaining of chest pains. Despite the radical surgical procedures he had undergone, the cancer continued to spread rapidly. Confused and in considerable pain, he died on October 3, five months after the injection. Twelve hours after he died, his body was autopsied and his organs harvested and examined for plutonium deposition. The hottest parts were his bone marrow and liver, but scientists were convinced the injection had not affected the disease or hastened his death.

They did note that the plutonium did not seem to concentrate in the tumor area, an observation that seemed to rule out the possibility that the radioactive substance could be used for therapeutic purposes.

Albert Stevens began painting houses again but was soon forced to give it up. "It got to the point where he wasn't strong enough anymore," his daughter said. Periodically he returned to UCSF for follow-up visits. Robert Stone ordered that a GI series be done without charge whenever Albert returned to the clinic. He had no specific complaints except for his inability to gain weight. Ten years after he was injected, a radiologist noted "rather marked" degeneration in the lumbar region of his spine and several degenerating discs.

Albert was to live nearly twenty-one years after he was diagnosed as terminal and injected with a so-called lethal dose of plutonium. His long survival rate is astonishing considering the amount of radiation he received. In 1995 two Los Alamos scientists calculated that Albert received a dose equal to 6,400 rem during his lifetime. That translates to 309 rem per year, or 858 times what the average person receives during the same period.

Just how the plutonium affected Albert's day-to-day health is unknown. The radiation probably caused his bones to thin and become brittle. But it was his heart that gave out first. On January 9, 1966, he died of cardiorespiratory failure in Santa Rosa, California, twelve miles from the town of Healdsburg where he had brought his ailing wife and children so many decades before. He was seventy-nine years old. His body was cremated, and his ashes were placed in a bronze urn and stored in a niche in Santa Rosa's Chapel of the Chimes.

The Manhattan Project medical doctors were not satisfied with the data they had acquired from the three injections. Ebb Cade's impaired kidney function may have skewed his excretion results, and for some unknown reason, Albert Stevens was excreting plutonium much more slowly than the other two patients. The physicians and scientists soon developed a list of things they needed to find out: What was the minimum amount of plutonium necessary to produce damage in the body? How could it be quantified and detected in wounds or lungs? Did diet affect plutonium's distribution? How was the liver damaged after intravenous injection? Did existing kidney damage diminish the elimination rate? And as a corollary, should people with kidney damage be excluded from working with plutonium?

The human experiments and ongoing animal studies had only confirmed fears that plutonium was indeed more carcinogenic than radium. On May 21, 1945, less than two weeks after Albert had been injected, Wright Langham wrote a letter to Hymer Friedell recommending that the so-called tolerance dose for plutonium be lowered to one microgram. Although Langham agreed with Friedell that the limit was probably much too conservative, he nevertheless supported it because "the medico-legal aspect will have been taken care of, and of still greater importance, we will have taken a relatively small chance of poisoning someone in case the material proves to be more toxic than one would normally expect."

Toward the end of June 1945, after the Manhattan Project's Medical Section had received data on Albert, it officially lowered the tolerance dose to one microgram. (In 1949 a group of researchers recommended that the tolerance dose be lowered again, to one-tenth that amount, or 0.1 microgram, after former Met Lab scientist Austin Brues presented results of a rat study suggesting plutonium was fifteen times more damaging than radium. Wright Langham and other scientists vigorously opposed the adoption of such a conservative standard, arguing, among other things, that it would produce "serious delays" in the lab's plutonium operations. The AEC's Shields Warren struck a compromise and lowered the maximum permissible dose to 0.5 micrograms.)

Sometime in the summer of 1945, the Manhattan Project Medical Section decided to inject more humans with plutonium. In making the decision, the doctors probably were thinking about overexposures that had already occurred as well as exposures that might occur in the future. Stafford Warren knew as early as April of 1945, even before the successful detonation of the Trinity bomb, that the Manhattan District would continue in some shape or form. "It has been indicated by properly qualified individuals that the operations of the Manhattan Engineer District should and will continue on for peacetime purposes," he wrote in a letter declassified in 1995. In short, plutonium and its hazards were not going to go away.

Over the next two years, an additional fifteen patients would be injected with plutonium: two in Chicago by Robert Stone's group; another two in San Francisco by Joseph Hamilton's group; and eleven patients in Rochester. Before the program ended in the summer of 1947, a total of eighteen people would be injected with plutonium without their informed consent.

13

THE ROCHESTER PRODUCTION LINE

On September 5, 1945, just three days after Japan formally surrendered, Los Alamos chemist Wright Langham sat down with scientists working at the Manhattan Annex, the secret research facility at the University of Rochester to plan the most comprehensive set of plutonium injections yet undertaken. This new round of injections would be a collaborative effort. Langham would supply the plutonium; the Rochester doctors, the patients. According to documents made public in 1994–1995, the Rochester segment of the plutonium experiment was part of a larger, planned study in which fifty patients were to be injected with radioisotopes of plutonium, polonium, uranium, lead, and radium.

Rochester's Manhattan Annex was originally located across the street from the medical school and connected by a tunnel. There, as at all Manhattan Project sites, secrecy was closely guarded. Constructed in five months, the Annex employed 350 people by the end of the war. Its activities were shielded from intruders by Army guards, and the occupants' backgrounds were thoroughly investigated to make sure "they were loyal American citizens, that they were discreet, and that they could be depended upon to keep secret work which contributed toward the development and production of the atomic [bomb]."

Rochester was far from the noisy industrial plants and hectic laboratories of the Manhattan Project. Oddly enough, though, the cold, industrial city had numerous links to the bomb project. Rochester was the home of George Eastman, the founder of Eastman Kodak Co. A subsidiary of his company, the Tennessee Eastman Corp., was the first operating contractor of the gigantic Y-12 plant in Oak Ridge where enriched uranium was produced.

Stafford Warren, who had gotten to know Eastman when he was in Rochester, said Eastman had been a man so painstakingly meticulous he painted the shapes of tools on the walls of his workshop so he could tell immediately whether things were in their proper position. At home, diagrams of cutlery were outlined on the kitchen walls. In his hunting lodge, the shadows of his guns were painted behind the gun rack. On March 14, 1932, Eastman asked his personal physician to draw the image of his own heart on his skin. Then, at the age of seventy-eight, according to Warren, he shot himself in the middle of that drawing. "He, of course, was very meticulous about his own hygiene and was always dressed very nicely and properly, shaved and barbered, and so on," recalled Warren. "But then he began to get feeble and developed some incontinence and had to hire a nurse to take care of him. After a while, he began to wear the equivalent of diapers so that he wouldn't have a mess on his hands. He decided he wasn't going to tolerate this." William McCann, the physician who drew the heart on Eastman's chest, was one of the men present at the September 5 planning meeting.

At the time of the meeting, less than six months had elapsed since Wright Langham had sent that first ampoule of plutonium to Oak Ridge to be injected into Ebb Cade. But the world had changed radically in those months, and Langham, the young chemist who once seemed destined for a mundane career on the Oklahoma Panhandle, now found himself in the vanguard of that change. He had bucked across the desert at the Trinity site in an Army jeep, bulky radiation detector in hand, as the purples and golds of the first atomic bomb ascended into the New Mexico sky. He had worked alongside the scientists responsible for Little Boy, the bomb dropped on Hiroshima, and Fat Man, the bomb that exploded three days later over Nagasaki.

The meeting that Langham attended in Rochester had been ordered by Stafford Warren (who was to land in Hiroshima in three days). Most of the men present were Warren's colleagues or students from his prewar days. Among them were Robert Fink, William Bale, Andrew Dowdy, and Harold Hodge. At the request of the Manhattan Engineer District, Bale had "activated" a metabolic ward at Rochester's Strong Memorial Hospital to carry out "certain tracer studies" with long-lived radioisotopes. The ward, at least in the early years, appears to have been used exclusively for the radioisotope studies.

The protocol for the plutonium injections, which was written by Wright Langham and not made public until 1995, disclosed that the experiment was a result of the Rochester meeting as well as "numerous conversations with Col. Warren, Col. Friedell, and Dr. L.H. Hempelmann." According to that protocol, only two subjects were to be admitted to the metabolic ward during the first six weeks of the program. Once the technicalities were worked out, however, scientists hoped to handle four patients simultaneously.

The patients were generally transferred to the ward from other parts of the hospital. The small ward where the injections were administered and the excretion samples collected was supervised by Samuel Bassett, a pleasant-looking doctor educated at Cornell University who had also attended the September 5 planning meeting.

Each patient was assigned the initials "HP" followed by a number. According to one document, the "HP" stood for "human product." The doctors were on the lookout for patients who had relatively normal metabolisms. Langham wrote:

> At the meeting it seemed to be more or less agreed that the subjects might be chronic arthritics or carcinoma patients without primary involvement of bone, liver, blood or kidneys. It is of primary importance that the subjects have relatively normal kidney and liver function, as it is desirable to obtain a metabolic picture comparable to that of an active worker. Undoubtedly the selection of subjects will be greatly influenced by what is available.

Under the tentative plan, the group decided that each patient was to be injected with an average of five micrograms, or five millionths of a gram of plutonium. That was *five* times the amount of plutonium the Manhattan Project scientists had just declared could be retained without harm in the human body and was also more than what Wright Langham and other scientists were willing to risk putting into their own bodies. "We considered doing such experiments at one time," Langham wrote in 1952, "but plutonium is considered to be sufficiently potentially dangerous to discourage our doing absorption experiments on ourselves."

Though five micrograms was the planned dosage, the actual amount of plutonium injected into the patients varied from 4.6 to 6.5 micrograms. The cumulative radiation dose received by each patient was dependent on two factors: the amount of radioactive material injected into the body and how long the subjects lived. The longer the patients lived, the larger their cumulative dose.

Six weeks following the Rochester meeting, the program became operational when the first patient was injected with plutonium. In all, eleven patients would be injected there between October 16, 1945, and July 16, 1946. But before that first injection could take place, many housekeeping details had to be worked out.

The patients' initial two weeks on the metabolic ward were slated as a control period in which they were to be trained to collect their own urine and stool specimens. "The period of indoctrination," Bassett later wrote, "usually required about ten days." After collection, the urine samples were heated in a steam bath for two hours and then cooled. An adhesive mortar was then placed around the top of the jars so that "any leakage which might have occurred would be revealed to the person receiving the urine for analysis." A preservative was added to the stool samples, and the mixture was boiled for ten minutes before it was transferred to half-gallon fruit jars. The excretion samples, as well as periodic blood samples, were to be collected on a strict schedule and shipped in wooden crates to Los Alamos.

According to the protocol prepared by Langham, Stafford Warren had suggested a Lieutenant Valentine perform the injections. But Hannah Silberstein, a woman who apparently worked on the metabolic ward, wrote that Bassett made the first injection. It's not clear from the documents, however, whether Bassett injected all the patients. When Louis Hempelmann was asked about the experiment by AEC investigators in 1974, he said Bassett prepared the syringes and handed them to a physician who injected the patients. Hempelmann said he was "quite positive" that the physician making the injections did not know the contents of the syringe.

There is no evidence that any of the Rochester patients gave their consent for the experiment or knew what was being injected into them. In fact, Hempelmann told investigators that a "deliberate decision was made not to inform the patient of the nature of the product that was injected."

Amedio Lovecchio, a sixty-seven-year-old Sicilian immigrant whom Bassett described as "well preserved for his years," became the first of the Rochester plutonium injectees. A proud-looking patriarch, Lovecchio had two fig trees in his backyard. Each fall he bent the trees to the ground and buried them deep in the soil to protect them from the harsh winter. Each spring he gave the first fig to a pregnant daughter-in-law. Lovecchio was admitted to the hospital after an ulcer hemorrhaged so severely that he required a transfusion. Code-named HP-1, Lovecchio was injected at 3:30 P.M. October 16 by Dr. Bassett "with no ill effects," Hannah Silberstein reported. Lovecchio lived for another fourteen years after the plutonium was administered. He was working as a maintenance man when he contracted pneumonia and died on January 12, 1960.

William Purcell, a forty-eight-year-old hemophiliac who was assigned the number HP-2, was injected five days after Lovecchio. Purcell was a cheerful, red-haired Irishman who had been admitted to the hospital thirty-eight times. He was well known and well liked by the staff and was listed as the proprietor of a cigar store on his death certificate. Bassett confessed in a letter to Wright Langham and Louis Hempelmann that he had been unable to get the three control samples of blood from Purcell prior to the injection. "The reason being that he is a hemophiliac who has been in the hospital for studies of blood clotting. This had led to a thrombosis of one of his veins which we felt should be given time to heal, and hence, we kept our venous punctures down to a minimum. I will be able to furnish the requisite number of post injection blood [samples]." Purcell's condition eventually improved, and he was injected with plutonium on October 23. He died on August 4, 1948, two and a half years later, from what doctors described as "brain disease."

Eda Schultz Charlton, HP-3, and Jean Daigneault, HP-4, were both injected on November 27. Charlton, a housewife, was to live for another four decades. Daigneault, who was only eighteen years old, died on April 19, 1947, a year and a half after the plutonium was administered. Daigneault suffered from Cushing's syndrome, a metabolic disorder characterized by a moon-shaped face and excessive weight in the trunk. She was studied intensively by doctors interested in that disease. On one occasion, when she was put on a rice and raisin diet, she told her sister that she craved a hot dog. As a teenager, she had won the western New York women's breast stroke swimming championship.

Paul Galinger, HP-5, a tall, thin man with trembling hands and slow speech, was fifth in line. He was a machine shop foreman whose handicapped son had died the previous year. Doctors diagnosed Galinger, then fifty-six, as suffering from depression and an incurable nerve disorder now called Lou Gehrig's disease. "So far he has cooperated quite well but has a difficult personality," Bassett confided to Langham. "The prognosis is poor and fatal termination can be expected within a year." Galinger was injected on November 30, 1945, and died on April 29, 1946. Even before he was dead, Bassett had begun making plans to retrieve his organs. "This may be counting our chickens before they are hatched but I thought it might be well to settle on some of these details before we are confronted with the necessity of obtaining specimens. I presume you would like a sample of blood from the heart or lungs?" Bassett inquired in a letter to Langham.

His carefully laid plans notwithstanding, Bassett learned only by chance that the much-anticipated autopsy was under way, and he had to rush to the hospital to lay claim to the specimens he wanted from Galinger's body. "We arrived after all the dissection had been completed and only had about thirty minutes in which to get the material together," he told Langham. In another letter he added, "The specimens from both the large and small bowel so nearly filled the jars that there was an insufficient space for the alcohol and hence a good deal of decomposition has occurred. This probably holds true for the liver samples also. I have added a little formalin to each of the intestinal samples to try to reduce formation of gas."

By the end of 1945, five of the eleven injections had been completed and the Rochester program was beginning to have the efficient feel of an assembly line. But there were still a lot of messy details to work out, even acts of God to cope with. As the holiday season approached, Bassett worried the experiment would grind to a halt. "It begins to look now as if we might be without patients at Christmas. No one seems to want to be in the hospital on that particular day. I will do what I can, however, to keep the production line going."

Bassett's efforts were unsuccessful and there were no new injections in Rochester during the month of December and January. They resumed February 1, 1946, with John Mousso, HP-6, a gentle-tempered handyman from East Rochester, a village seven miles east of the city. Mousso, forty-four at the time, was admitted to the hospital for multiple infections on his eyelids and toes, but the underlying illness that plagued him was Addison's disease, an adrenal gland disorder that made him nauseated, lethargic, and achy. Mousso was a familiar figure in East Rochester: sweeping out the fire hall, shoveling snow from the church steps, emptying the penny meters along leafy streets named Elm, Oak, and Hickory. Bassett described Mousso as a "well developed, but thin male with deeply pigmented skin." Supported by his deep love for his wife, Rose, Mousso was to live for many decades after the injection was administered. But he returned to the hospital often, and on several occasions, doctors surreptitiously gathered excretion samples from him.

Edna Bartholf, HP-7, was injected February 8. Edna was fifty-nine years old and suffered from rheumatic heart disease. Except for the "marked" swelling that extended from her hips to her feet, she looked healthy. But when Bassett placed his stethoscope to her chest, he heard the irregular heartbeat. Bartholf had spent her life in Morganville, a tiny hamlet near Rochester that today has a population of 150. She was active in the Congregational Christian Church, the Women's Christian Temperance Union, the Ladies' Aid Society, and other groups. "Her church was the thing she was most interested in," her niece, Winifred Thater, recalled. Bartholf lived another nine months after the plutonium was administered, dying on October 27, 1946, of pulmonary failure.

Next was Harry Slack, a sixty-nine-year-old janitor at a local YWCA and an alcoholic suffering from malnutrition and cirrhosis of the liver. Little is known about Slack's life. He enlisted in the Army at the age of twenty-one to fight in the Spanish-American War, but his company made it only as far as Virginia. Slack had been admitted to the hospital on December 12, 1945, because he had been having trouble breathing and his abdomen was enlarged. Bassett described him as a "poorly nourished, weak, thin male who is slightly confused."

Slack's health continued to decline while he was in the hospital, and he was "moribund" when the plutonium injection was administered on February 20, 1946. Six days later he died of pneumonia. Apparently surprised by Slack's sudden death, Bassett dashed off a letter to Wright Langham: "I hope this next part of the letter will not prove too much of a shock to you since we have run through an acute experiment. No collections of urine or feces were made in this instance."

The experiment hadn't been a total loss, however. An autopsy had been performed less than six hours after Slack's death, and researchers would have his organs to analyze. "We were somewhat pressed for time and perhaps did not obtain as much in the way of bone samples as we might have," Bassett added. He was certain, though, that the plutonium had mixed sufficiently in Slack's body and would be detectable in the harvested organs.

Langham *was* a little startled by the news. But he in turn had something even more startling to suggest, which apparently was inspired by rumors he had heard about the experiments taking place in Chicago: Inject the next terminal patient with fifty micrograms of plutonium, he instructed. Such a dose would be equal to fifty times the amount that several researchers, including Langham himself, had estimated could be tolerated without harm in the human body: "This would permit the analysis of much smaller samples and would make my work considerably easier. I have just received word that Chicago is performing two terminal experiments using 95 micrograms each. I feel reasonably certain there would be no harm in using larger amounts of material if you are sure the case is a terminal one."

Bassett, in a reply dated March 27, appeared to have been troubled by the idea that the plutonium may have hastened Slack's death but nevertheless agreed to try to implement Langham's plan:

> This case did turn out to be terminal, but at the time I started the experimental period, there was sufficient uncertainty regarding the outcome to make me feel that the dose should be within the range of tolerance. . . . The larger doses that you mention, particularly 50 micrograms, might be given if a suitable opportunity occurred and if you are very anxious that I should carry it through, I will see what can be done.

Slack was actually the eighth person injected but was given the code number HP-11. The reason for the inconsistency is unknown. Perhaps the experimenters originally planned not to include Slack in their study because of the failure to obtain any urine or stool samples but then changed their minds as they were compiling their data for their final report.

About two weeks after Slack's demise, Janet Stadt, HP-8, a forty-one-year-old woman suffering from scleroderma, a chronic skin disease that hardens and fixes the skin to underlying tissues and eventually disrupts the functioning of the internal organs, was injected. Bassett described Janet Stadt as a "thin and pale female" and carefully chronicled the symptoms of her disease: Her eyelids were tight and the skin was drawn around her mouth. The flesh on her hands was so thick and taut her fingers could not uncurl completely.

Stadt's son, Milton, said at a public hearing in 1995 that his mother's disease was so painful that she eventually became addicted to painkillers. "I had to get up in the middle of the night, sterilize needles, fill them with Demerol, and she would inject herself with Demerol for the pain," he said. To add to her misery, Janet Stadt received 1,000 rem of radiation during her lifetime, the highest dose of any of the Rochester patients, according to calculations performed in 1995 by the Los Alamos scientists. She died on November 22, 1975, nearly three decades after the injection was administered. Her death certificate states that the cause of death was malnutrition caused by cancer of the larynx.

Milton Stadt did not learn that his mother had been injected with plutonium until he received a call from Energy Secretary Hazel O'Leary in 1994. "My mother," he said, "went in for scleroderma, which is a skin disorder, and a duodenal ulcer, and somehow she got pushed over into this lab where these monsters were."

Fred Sours, HP-9, was injected April 3. In the town of Gates, a suburb of Rochester, Sours held the position of supervisor, a job roughly equivalent to mayor. He was sixty-four years old and suffering from dermatomyositis, a rare disorder in which the skin becomes inflamed and the muscles grow weak. His face was red; his eyelids and ears also were red and swollen. "Man appears chronically ill, skin is dry and loose," wrote Bassett. Sours died on July 2, 1947, of pneumonia, a year and three months after the injection. When the townspeople of Gates heard the news, they lowered the town flag to half mast for four days and the town board issued a proclamation stating: "His honesty was known to all, and the well-being and interests of the town, of which he was the chief executive officer, were his early aim during his official life." While the people of Gates were mourning Sours's demise, Manhattan Project doctors were harvesting his organs. The plutonium was everywhere—in his liver, spleen, kidneys, and bones—everywhere except for his heart.

Bassett received a steady stream of polite but critical letters from Langham while the injections were under way. The Mason jars containing the urine and stool samples often arrived at the New Mexico laboratory broken or leaking. The samples were sometimes mislabeled, and in some cases, the labels were missing altogether. Too much human material had been stuffed into some of the containers and not enough preservative had been poured into others. Only a month after the injections started, Langham found himself overwhelmed by the volume of urine and stool samples. "I would like to suggest," he said in a letter to Bassett, "that the next patients selected be individuals whose conditions will not require high fluid intake and extremely high diet levels of mineral or nitrogen."

On another occasion, Langham complained that the iron content in the patients' diets was interfering with the radiochemical analyses. Bassett then began sending Langham an inventory of the patients' diets. Among other things, Jean Daigneault was getting pineapple juice, potatoes, squash, ground round steak, and macaroni. William Purcell, the hemophiliac, was getting lots of vegetables, a slice or two of American cheese, and an occasional cup of coffee. Amedio Lovecchio, the Sicilian immigrant who suffered from a bleeding ulcer, *was* on a "very peculiar" diet prior to the injection, Bassett conceded. "We took him on short notice with the understanding that we would carry out the medical treatment as already planned."

Before the human injections began, three rats were injected in their tail veins with the same plutonium solution that Langham and Bassett planned to administer to the patients. Only a small percentage of the plutonium went to the rodents' livers, which made the two scientists more confident that the plutonium injected into the human subjects "would not be taken up in high concentration by a single organ such as the livers," Bassett wrote. Belatedly, after ten of the eleven injections had been completed, Langham recognized that they had been overly confident. Dangerous amounts of plutonium were, in fact, accumulating in the patients' livers: "The amazing feature regarding the tissues [of Paul Galinger] was that 48 percent of the material was found in the liver. This result is extremely alarming to me. Results obtained at Chicago more or less confirm the finding. The results indicate that complexing the Plutonium with citrate does not prevent the deposition in the human liver as it does in the case of the rat."

Wright Langham and Samuel Bassett kept their fears about possible liver damage and other long-term consequences to themselves, and eventually the patients were discharged from the hospital without ever having been told what had been done to them. For the rest of their lives, the injectees carried within their bodies the plutonium they had received on Samuel Bassett's metabolic ward. "With regard to ultimate effects [of plutonium], it is too early to predict what may occur," Bassett wrote in a secret, unpublished report.

For the five decades that followed, it was widely assumed, and reported in the scientific literature, that the patients were very ill and not expected to live much longer. Incredibly, documents released in 1994 and 1995 reveal that that false impression was perpetuated largely by a 1950 Los Alamos report written by Wright Langham, Samuel Bassett, and two other scientists. The Los Alamos report, entitled "Distribution and Excretion of Plutonium Administered Intravenously To Man," was classified secret and not declassified until 1971.

Three of the eleven Rochester patients did die within one year; but three others lived for thirty years or more. After the experiment was completed, Bassett wrote up a rough draft of what had taken place. In that draft, he noted that the patients selected for injection were "a miscellaneous group of male and female hospital patients for the most part with well established diagnoses":

Preference was given to those who might reasonably gain from continued residence in the hospital for a month or more. Special treatments and other therapy thought to be of benefit to the patients were carried out in the normal manner. The necessity of studying urinary and fecal rates of excretion of Pu [plutonium] automatically excluded cases of advanced renal disease or disturbance in the function of the gastrointestinal tract. Patients with malignant diseases were also omitted from the group on the grounds that their metabolism might be affected in an unknown manner.

Bassett also confessed in his draft report that one of the patients had been misdiagnosed. But his draft was never published. Thus the only published account was the one that came out of Los Alamos under the names of Langham and Bassett and the two other scientists. It omitted Bassett's description of the patient selection process and his mention of the misdiagnosis. The Los Alamos version, considered for decades the authoritative source on the experiment, states that the patients were "suffering from chronic disorders such that survival for ten years was highly improbable." Other statements later made by Langham himself furthered the impression that the patients' conditions were terminal. At a chemical conference in 1956, Langham described the patients as "hopelessly sick." And in a 1962 paper, he described them as "terminal."

The plutonium experiment was temporarily interrupted in the early summer of 1946 when Langham and Bassett were pressed into service by Stafford Warren for Operation Crossroads, a joint military exercise in which the first two atomic bombs of the peacetime era were detonated on an remote atoll in the Pacific Ocean. Warren had found it so difficult to recruit radiation monitors that he had been reduced to asking anyone who could read or write to join the operation. Langham was hopeful that he and Bassett might be able to talk with Warren about the experiment. It's likely the three men did spend a little time together, although there are no documents describing such a meeting.

In their absence, a Rochester physician named Helen E. Van Alstine continued to look for "suitable" subjects. In a July 10 letter to Wright Langham, she said, "We were finally successful and had admitted to the special metabolic division on July 8th, a 52-year-old negro male with a diagnosis of severe heart disease. . . ."

The subject was Daniel Nelson, who was recuperating from a heart attack when he was shipped to the metabolic ward for "special studies." The transfer to that ward was the last of a string of misfortunes suffered by Nelson. A cook for most of his life, he had lost all his money in the

stock market shortly before the heart attack. He was injected with plutonium on July 16 and given the number HP-10. When he was discharged
from the hospital, he had no place to convalesce and finally sought help
from a now-defunct rest home for veterans in Mount McGregor, New
York. Nelson lived for ten years and eleven months after he was injected,
dying of heart disease on June 2, 1957.

Bassett returned to the United States soon after the first atomic bomb
was detonated during Operation Crossroads, and was in Rochester by
the time Nelson was injected. But Langham remained to see the second
shot, an underwater explosion that pushed a dome of radioactive water
high into the sky. "The second test at Bikini was really a great show. I am
sorry that you did not stay to see it," Langham told Bassett when he
returned to Los Alamos. Reinvigorated by their Pacific adventure, the
two men were ready to increase the dosage level.

"Shall we try for a terminal case or two?" Bassett queried.

"I think we should get some terminal cases if possible," Langham
responded.

But for unknown reasons, Nelson turned out to be the last patient
injected with plutonium. The following month Bassett began an experiment in which enriched isotopes of uranium were injected into six people with good kidney function. The uranium injections were apparently
part of the larger study that had been planned by the Manhattan Project
after the war and their function was to find the minimum dose that
would produce detectable kidney damage. Thousands of people were
working with uranium in Oak Ridge, and the bomb doctors were eager to
find out more about both its radioactive and chemical toxicity.

While the uranium injections were under way, Langham kept nagging Samuel Bassett to collect more urine and stool samples from pluto-
nium-injected patients whenever they were readmitted to the hospital.
Additional samples were obtained from hemophiliac William Purcell
when he returned to the hospital in early January of 1946 for bleeding of
the intestinal tract. Samples were also collected from John Mousso, the
East Rochester resident, whenever he was readmitted. Eda Schultz
Charlton, a lonely, depressed widow, turned out to be one of their most
fruitful subjects.

14

A MISDIAGNOSED HOUSEWIFE

Eda Schultz Charlton sat on a high stool all day, legs tucked beneath her, inspecting camera shutters at the Kodak plant. As she hurried home at night, she may have sensed the winter gathering over the black waters of Lake Ontario. She was a middle-age woman, slightly overweight and filled with vague fears about the future. The war was finally over and the whole country was celebrating, but it was an unhappy time for Eda. Her husband had died of a heart attack a year earlier and her son had not yet been discharged from the Navy. Sometimes she sat up alone in her living room eating handfuls of peanuts and candy. Other nights she just crawled into bed early.

Eda had a touch of hypochondria and a tendency to go on food binges. The hypochondria, almost indiscernible at the time, would flower into a painful obsession during the last two decades of her life. No diagnostic test, no doctor's words, could staunch the fear of cancer that eventually grew weedy and strong in her mind. Eda camouflaged her insecurities with clothes. She wore beautifully tailored suits, stylish felt hats, and carried small pocketbooks with gold latches. Her permanents were always fresh and her nails well-buffed ovals. Even when she was in her eighties, she continued to wear a tortuous corset of lace and elastic that left deep red marks on her body. The youngest of four sisters, Eda had serious dark eyes and wavy brown hair. She was twenty-three years old when women won the right to vote, and she dutifully walked the narrow path laid out for women of her generation. Except for the brief stint at the Kodak plant, she was a housewife for most of her life.

As the autumn turned into the winter of 1945, Eda had developed numerous minor physical complaints and went to doctor after doctor. One physician had given her a thyroid medication that apparently increased her nervousness. Another had given her three or four injections of B vitamins for back pain. She had gained ten pounds from the peanuts and candy.

Not long after the vitamin injections, she broke out in a rash. Small pimples spread from her hairline, down the back of her neck and shoulders, and over her abdomen. Then her legs swelled abruptly. The swelling suggested something serious might be wrong, and she was admitted to the University of Rochester's Strong Memorial Hospital on November 2 for diagnostic tests. The doctors were puzzled by her symptoms but suspected her diet was the culprit. "Her nutrition has been poor because she eats alone, lives alone, has little interest in food, poor appetite, has subsisted largely on sandwiches and coffee and an occasional glass of milk—poor protein, poor vitamins," states the first of many hospital admission notes.

Her eyes were clear, her lungs and heart normal. With just two days of bed rest and the hospital's high-protein, low-salt diet, the rash and swelling in Eda's ankles subsided. The doctors thought the swelling was caused by hypoproteinemia, a condition in which abnormally small amounts of protein are found in the circulating blood plasma. That condition, in turn, could have been caused by her poor diet. She might also have been suffering from a mild case of hepatitis.

On the eleventh day of her hospital stay, she was transferred to E-3—Dr. Samuel Bassett's metabolic ward—for "protein studies." Bassett, in a classified letter written to Wright Langham a day later, confided, "We have also taken in another patient, Eda Schultz, #239876, and expect to begin collection within a few days if she proves to be sufficiently cooperative."

At home, Eda was rigid and controlling, setting aside a day for laundry and a day for ironing. She was upset when she found dust under her bed or saw dandelions on the front lawn. She was so formal that even in the presence of family and friends, she referred to her first husband as "Mr. Schultz" and her second as "Mr. Charlton." But in the hushed hospital wards or doctors' waiting rooms, she acquiesced to the most intimate probing of her body. "I think she had an inferiority complex," Helen Schultz, her daughter-in-law, speculated. "She was kind of shy and timid around people. She might have done what they told her to do."

Samuel Bassett was juggling several patients when Eda arrived on E-3. The plutonium-laced urine and stool samples from Amedio Lovecchio and William Purcell were being packed and sent to Los Alamos. Control samples were being gathered from Jean Daigneault and Paul Galinger.

Bassett instructed that Eda be placed on the "house diet" until further notice. An ice bag, codeine, and aspirin were ordered for a pain in her left shoulder. Two days later Bassett told the nurses to begin the collection of urine and stool samples. "Cover with acid at the end of 24 hr period. Have pt. void directly into collection jar." Twice she went on shopping excursions. "She feels that her ankles have not been as swollen recently in spite of increased activity including two shopping trips," wrote Helen Van Alstine, the doctor who selected Daniel Nelson for injection.

Eda celebrated Thanksgiving on Bassett's ward. She may have exchanged a few words with Jean Daigneault or Paul Galinger. On November 27, five days after Thanksgiving, a needle filled with sterile saline was slipped into one of her veins. The saline was injected slowly to ensure smooth entry into the vein. Then the syringe was detached and another containing plutonium was substituted. "The plutonium solution was injected rapidly, after which the syringe was rinsed once by drawing it full of the patient's blood and discharging the blood back into the vein," the Los Alamos report written by Wright Langham and Samuel Bassett stated. "For obvious reasons," Langham had pointed out before the experiment even began, "extreme care should be taken to make sure the vein has been entered before the material is discharged." The syringe injected into Eda contained 4.9 micrograms of plutonium, an amount that delivered a total lifetime dose of 880 rem. The radiation exposure that she received each year from the plutonium was equal to sixty-six times what the average person receives annually.

Eda's medical records contain no information about the injection. In fact, nothing in the 314 pages of medical records maintained by Strong Memorial Hospital from 1945 to 1979 reveals she was in the plutonium experiment. Only a slight change in the urine collection schedule suggests that anything unusual was afoot on the day of the injection. "Collect urine Spec. in 2–12 hr periods today. Collect the second 12 hr Spec @ 8:00 PM. tonight. Tomorrow resume the 24 hr collection," Bassett wrote.

The decision to keep references to the experiment out of the patients' medical files was apparently made by the Manhattan Project doctors before the experiment began. In an October 25, 1946, letter to Samuel Bassett, Wright Langham wrote:

> I talked to Colonel Warren on the phone yesterday and he recommended that I send copies of all my data to Dr. Dowdy where it would be available to you and Dr. Fink to observe. He thought it best that I not send it to you because he wanted it to remain in Manhattan Project files, instead of taking a chance on it finding its way into the hospital records. I think this is probably a sensible suggestion.

Life on the ward resumed its humdrum pace following Eda's injection. Seconal was authorized for her if she requested it, as was a water enema, if necessary. On December 11 a young doctor named Christine Waterhouse performed a routine kidney test. A couple of days later Bassett said Eda could start using salt on her food again. With the plutonium circulating in her body, Eda was discharged on December 20, 1945, five days before Christmas.

Several years later, when Bassett wrote up his version of the experiment, the misdiagnosis that he mentioned was a reference to Eda. "A woman aged 49 years may have a greater life expectancy than originally anticipated due to an error in the provisional diagnosis," he wrote. But it is not clear what Bassett meant by the "provisional diagnosis." Although the doctors were uncertain about what was wrong with Eda, nowhere in her medical records is there a suggestion that she was terminally ill. Both Langham and Bassett knew Eda was not terminally ill at the time they were writing the Los Alamos report, but they omitted the fact from their published paper. The misinformation was hidden from Eda's family, the scientific community, and the public until 1995.

Eda was not terminally ill, she was not chronically ill, and she may not even have been seriously ill. The shopping excursions certainly seem to suggest that her health was not badly impaired. Her daughter-in-law, Helen, never recalls Eda having hepatitis. And her son, Fred, said his mother seemed fine when he finally arrived home from the war. "I don't remember her being sick at all after my father died. I lived with her for two years when I got home from the Navy," he recalled.

The error proved to be a stroke of good fortune for the Manhattan Project doctors, however. Since Eda's metabolism was normal, scientists would be able to get a more accurate picture of how a healthy worker metabolized and excreted plutonium. She was to become one of the most intensely studied of the injectees. From 1945 until she died in a nursing home in 1983, she was tracked by doctors and scientists working for the Manhattan Project or its successor agencies. She was not told about the plutonium injection for nearly thirty years.

On July 25, 1946, eight months after she had been injected with plutonium, Eda fell down her basement stairs. She told doctors she didn't recall striking her head or losing consciousness, but afterward she became dizzy and vomited. Blood trickled from her right ear and her spinal fluid was bloody. X rays revealed no evidence of an old or new fracture.

Eda was hospitalized for two weeks and complained frequently of a severe headache and upset stomach. Doctors settled on a diagnosis of cerebral concussion. The physical effects apparently caused by the injury plagued her the rest of her life. She suffered from severe attacks of vertigo, nausea, blurred vision, and unsteady gait. Eventually she learned to control the vertigo by first raising her head from the pillow in the morning before turning it from side to side. Dr. John Cobb, a medical doctor and radiation expert who reviewed Eda's medical files, said it was unlikely that the plutonium contributed to the fall or the nausea and vertigo.

Bassett's name does not show up in Eda's chart during the July 1946 hospital visit because he was at Crossroads. But he was clearly behind her third admittance in October 1946 for "liver function" studies. "I am still hammering away at the Hp patients and now have Hp3 in again for about a week," Bassett confided to Langham. "You should soon receive some urine specimens and I hope at least one four-day collection of feces."

Eda's red blood cells appeared to be within normal limits, but years later, another test would indicate the cells were of "very rare" shapes and sizes. The red blood cell changes—which can be indicators of numerous diseases, including anemia—could have been caused by the radiation from the plutonium.

In the spring of 1950, a few months before Bassett and Langham completed their work on the Los Alamos report, Langham asked the Rochester doctors to secure several additional urine samples from Eda and John Mousso. "Even one sample from one or two of these individuals after this late date," Langham wrote, "will be extremely valuable data to have. It will afford a basis of checking mathematical expressions that we have derived and will give us some confidence in our extrapolations."

Bassett, who by then had left Rochester and had gone to work in a Veteran's Hospital in Los Angeles at Stafford Warren's urging, enlisted the aid of Christine Waterhouse. A 1938 graduate of Mount Holyoke College, Waterhouse had earned her medical degree from Columbia University's College of Physicians and Surgeons in 1942. She joined the staff of the University of Rochester School of Medicine and Dentistry in 1943 and remained in Rochester for the rest of her professional career.

Waterhouse was the young doctor who did the routine kidney test on Eda when she was hospitalized during the injection period. Her name also appears on the cover of the Los Alamos report as one of the fifteen doctors or scientists who did work related to the study. But Waterhouse has stated emphatically that she had nothing to do with the original injections. "I never knew the top people in this affair," she said during one of several interviews. "This was already a done thing. The people making the decisions, I didn't have much to do with. I was told to take care of the patients."

Waterhouse examined Eda for the first time in 1950 at about the time the excretion samples were shipped to Los Alamos. It was the beginning of a patient-doctor relationship that continued until 1979. Waterhouse saw Eda sometimes as often as twice a month in the later years, listening to her heart, her lungs, the steady stream of her complaints. Yet, over the course of three decades and throughout the 300-plus pages of Eda's medical records, Waterhouse never mentions the word "plutonium."

Waterhouse said she did not refer to plutonium because the experiment was "classified information" until 1972. After that, she said she still didn't mention it because she didn't think any of Eda's medical problems were related to the injection. "It wouldn't have occurred to me to put it in the chart unless I thought it was related to the symptoms," she said.

Waterhouse said she took a practical view toward the experiment after the injections had been completed. "My feeling was once the initial act was done, then it was my job to get all the information I could get. In other words, there was no way anybody was going to take the plutonium back. As long as it's there, you might as well, I felt, get the maximum amount of information that I could to try to help in the future."

In October 1950 Langham asked former Manhattan Project doctor Joseph Howland, who by this time had rejoined the University of Rochester medical school, to help him obtain X rays of Eda and John Mousso. The "most likely symptoms" resulting from the injections, he said, would be changes in the bones—a generalized inflammation, thinning in the bones of the feet, the jaw, and the heads of the long bones, and a coarsening of the trabeculae. "The X rays seem to be the all important thing, but please get them in a completely routine manner. Do not make the examination look unusual in any way."

In April 1953 X rays again were taken of Eda's elbows, hands, both feet, and ankles. "There are some interesting changes in the chest," a radiologist noted. A "distinctly abnormal" mass, he added, had been detected on the left side of her rib cage. The radiologist's findings were delivered to Waterhouse and to Louis Hempelmann, who had left Los Alamos in October of 1948 to become a professor of experimental radiology at the University of Rochester's medical school. Hempelmann, in turn, relayed the information to Charles Dunham, a top AEC official in Washington, D.C.: "The patient in question was brought in for a skeletal survey, and turned out to have a 'coin-like' lesion inside the chest wall. . . . It is undoubtedly an incidental finding, but she must be explored by the chest surgeon here at Strong. In the course of the operation, he will remove a rib which we can analyze. Her films show the same type of minimal indefinite change in the bone the others have had."

Eda was admitted to the hospital in June of 1953 for surgery. She was anesthetized and a four-inch incision made along her left side. A "soft, rubbery mass" on the third rib was removed as well as two inches of the rib itself. The mass turned out to be benign. Her medical records don't indicate what became of the rib.

At about the time of the operation, Eda moved forty miles away to Canandaigua, a bucolic town on the shores of Canandaigua Lake, the "gem" of New York's Finger Lakes. Settled soon after the end of the Revolutionary War, Canandaigua has a history long enough to give an antique patina to the entire town. Just blocks from the town center, sweeping lawns are anchored by carriage barns that once sheltered horses from snow. But the stately homes, the fresh wind blowing in off the lake, and the town's lovely shoreline did little to improve her health. "I'm sick to my stomach all the time," Eda complained when she was admitted to Strong Memorial Hospital in August 1962. It was her fourth admittance since the 1945 plutonium injection.

Her second husband, Howard, had died three months earlier and Eda was acutely depressed. She had lost ten pounds and was experiencing early-morning awakenings and feelings of despair. "Patient is a thin, anxious appearing female who looks somewhat younger than her stated age of 65," one doctor observed.

Month after month she complained of morning nausea, dizziness, tension, and anxiety. She had many other odd symptoms as well. She frequently complained of a burning sensation on her lips and the tip of her tongue. She had spasms in her throat, severe pain on the side or top of her head, and a prickly sensation in her face. She went to countless dentists with complaints, but the doctors could find nothing wrong. It's not clear whether the plutonium, which can be deposited around the tooth sockets and bone surfaces of the mouth, was causing her discomfort. But dogs injected with large amounts of the material have experienced loosening of the teeth and other dental problems.

In Canandaigua, Eda also began seeing Dr. Joseph Guattery, an internist who once taught at the University of Rochester medical school. Now retired, Guattery said that Christine Waterhouse referred Eda to him. "Because Mrs. Charlton lived in Canandaigua, it was much easier for somebody to give her regular daily care and whatnot here, so she referred her to me."

Helen Schultz, Eda's daughter-in-law, said Eda told her that she first learned that she had been injected with plutonium from Guattery. Helen said she couldn't remember the year her mother-in-law first mentioned it. "She said to me one day, 'What is plutonium?' and I told her. Then I said, 'Where did you hear that?' and she said, 'Dr. Guattery said that's what they gave me at Strong.'"

But Guattery said he didn't inform Eda of the plutonium injection. Rather, Eda told him and then "Dr. Waterhouse gave me a little information," Guattery said. "I can see her very plainly as you're talking to me. She was a moderately stout woman, though not very fat. She was well-built, soft-spoken. She had dark skin, dark hair, wore glasses and didn't always seem to have very much energy."

Eda's son and daughter-in-law also continued to take her to Rochester for her checkups at Dr. Waterhouse's office. In the early years, Eda usually visited Waterhouse once a year. But as she grew older and sicker, the frequency of the visits increased. Waterhouse chronicled her complaints and ordered numerous tests—X rays, blood tests, barium enemas, liver and brain scans.

In early January 1967, after Eda's weight had ballooned to 144 pounds, she confided to Waterhouse that she was afraid she had cancer. ". . . she feels that this weight increase is all localized in the abdominal area, in other words, she wonders if she has a tumor growing in her abdomen," Waterhouse wrote.

Dr. John Cobb said Eda's fear of cancer could have been something that she picked up unconsciously from Waterhouse. "The doctor was being very careful and not leaving any stone unturned. The patient could have been worried about cancer because her doctor was worried about cancer."

But Waterhouse said she requested a lot of tests because Eda had so many symptoms. "Patients of this character who tend to have a lot of symptoms, you work them up and you don't find anything to cause their symptoms and you tell them. They come back three months later with a different set of symptoms."

According to Dr. Waterhouse's notes, Eda mentioned "experimentation" to her during an October 18, 1975, office visit. This is the sole written proof that Eda had some idea she had been involved in an experiment. "Mrs. Charlton says she feels terribly from the mental point of view, that she is forgetting things and is confused much of the time. She again mentions the problem of experimentation but does not push this at the present," Waterhouse wrote.

Eda's physical and emotional problems seemed to accelerate in the 1970s. She felt plain terrible. She was chronically depressed and suffered from fatigue and shortness of breath. The morning nausea continued along with the discomfort in her bowels.

Her diet worsened. She lived on milk, crackers, and bread and subsequently developed anemia. "She fails to cook vegetables because it's too much trouble and the same goes for meat," Waterhouse jotted down after one visit.

Eda also began taking up to eight aspirin a day for the ever-increasing pain from her arthritis. New X rays showed bony outgrowths on each hip and other degenerative changes. The plutonium had delivered twice the amount of radiation to her bone cavities theoretically needed to induce a tumor. Roland Finston, a retired Stanford University health physicist, said it was quite possible her bones could well have developed a "moth-eaten" appearance from the radiation. But the arthritis didn't worry Eda as much as cancer. Despite the negative tests, Dr. Waterhouse's notes show that Eda continued to worry about a possible malignancy:

• 1976 [Day illegible]: "The patient continues to be obsessed with the idea that she has received [illegible] much radiation and that she has a cancer in her neck." (The reference to "radiation" is ambiguous; Eda may have been talking about the experiment or the exposure she had received from the many diagnostic tests.)

• June 28, 1976: "Mrs. Charlton complains of excessive fatigue today. She feels worse than she has ever at any time in the past. She states that she is fairly convinced from Dr. Guattery and myself that she does not have a cancer, but on the other hand, she has never felt worse in her life."

• November 21, 1978: ". . . she has had symptoms of a 'creepy crawly' feeling up the side of her face, tremendous anxiety probably associated with these symptoms. When asked point blank if she were afraid she had cancer, she denied this but repeatedly brings up the possibility of cancer."

Tormented and obsessed, Eda was to live another four years. She developed serious physical problems that were compounded by the life-long depression. She was moved to a health-related facility at a local hospital after she underwent surgery for a bowel obstruction. A second surgery followed. Then she had a heart attack, fractured her hip, and finally suffered a stroke. At 7:30 P.M. on January 24, 1983, just two months shy of her eighty-sixth birthday, Eda Charlton died of "acute cardiac arrest," her death certificate states.

After her death, Guattery sent a clinical summary of Eda's final years to scientists at Argonne National Laboratory in Chicago. "At no time during the years that I was Mrs. [name deleted] physician did I see any evidence of carcinoma," he wrote. "This was specifically looked for, especially with her background history."

Eda's funeral was small and poorly attended. Other than Fred and Helen and their immediate family, only one other nephew was present. The business with plutonium, the name of the radioactive material that Nobel laureate Glenn Seaborg said rolled off the tongue better than "plutium," had vexed her until the very end. Sometime before she died, she asked her son, "Do you suppose that stuff they gave me did anything to me?"

15

CHICAGO: UPPING THE DOSE

Less than a week after Eda Schultz Charlton was injected with plutonium, Una Macke, a frightened and desperately ill woman, pushed
through the doors of Chicago's Billings Hospital. She was hoping to find
a doctor who would help her. Instead she unwittingly delivered herself
into the hands of Manhattan Project scientists who were on the lookout
for "moribund" patients. A petite, thoughtful-looking woman, Una had
traveled to Chicago from Ohio several months earlier to consult a hematologist after experiencing pain around her ribs, sternum, and the small
of her back. The hematologist diagnosed her as having infectious mono-
nucleosis, but the diagnosis didn't fit her symptoms. She began experiencing fevers at night, a raging thirst, and a loss of appetite.

On December 3, 1945, she was admitted to Billings Hospital for
diagnostic tests. Beneath the hospital gown, her body was shockingly
frail. There was a faint bluish tint around her lips and nose and her face
was deeply lined, making her look a full decade older than her fifty-six
years. Una had no husband, no children. Her father, John H. Macke,
was a manager of the John Shillito Company, a department store in
Cincinnati, Ohio, and author of a book on how to measure and cut
carpets.

The antiseptic smells and the polished corridors of the hospital
might have seemed familiar to Una. When she was young, she had been
extremely ill with tuberculosis of the spine and lungs. She had licked the
disease and, with the exception of occasional sinus problems, had enjoyed good health since.

Soon after she was settled on the ward, doctors performed a biopsy, removing tissue from her head and left armpit. The results were ominous: Una had widespread cancer, which had probably originated in the left breast. As she tossed in her hospital bed, soaking her gown with perspiration, a solution called "U" medication was prepared by scientists at the Met Lab, a ten-minute walk from the hospital.

Christmas came and went. The scant records don't indicate whether she had any visitors. Two days later, on December 27, the "U" medication was started. Almost immediately Una began to vomit. She was unable to eat, unable to drink, unable to hold anything down in her stomach. Seventeen days later, on January 13, 1946, she died.

Two hours after her death, her body was whisked to an autopsy room. On the slab, she was hardly bigger than a child: five feet one inch tall and eighty-five pounds. "On the head," wrote a pathologist, "is a large quantity of graying red hair."

Her mouth and teeth were in good repair, the tongue covered by a dark brown coating. In her right armpit and groin, several walnut-size nodes were palpable to the touch. "The muscles are thin, somewhat pale and poorly developed." "The emptied heart weighs 250 gms."

The cancer had spread to her liver, small intestine, spinal column, and pelvis. The bone marrow had been almost completely replaced by tumor. The pathologist examining the tissues also made a surprising but not unheard of finding: Una was suffering from a second cancer called lymphoblastoma. The pathologist compared postmortem tissues taken from Una with biopsy material removed before the "U" medication had been administered. He found lymphoblastoma in the biopsy tissue, a finding that ruled out the possibility that the second cancer "was induced by the medication."

Una's organs were scooped from her body and placed into containers filled with a 95 percent alcohol solution. Alcohol was used because the Rochester studies had revealed that formalin tended to leach plutonium out of the specimens. The body parts later were dried, ashed, and converted into an acid solution. Then they were measured for radioactivity. The bone marrow was the hottest, emitting 1,399 counts per gram of tissue.

The "U" medication administered to Una was not a medication at all; it appears to have been a code word for plutonium. A health physicist who reviewed Una's medical records concluded the dose could have delivered enough radiation to Una's liver to cause nausea. The nausea and the inability to eat may, in turn, have hastened her death.

The same day Una was injected, a young man suffering from Hodgkin's disease was also injected with plutonium. The man, who died about 170 days after the injection, is the only one of the eighteen plutonium patients whose identity remains unknown. Una was assigned the code number CHI-2 and the Hodgkin's patient, CHI-3. They were the last two people injected with plutonium in Chicago.

What distinguishes the injections of Una and CHI-3 from those that occurred at other Manhattan Project sites was the size of the doses— 94.91 micrograms of plutonium. That was nearly one hundred times what scientists in 1945 believed that a healthy worker's body could tolerate without harm and equal to more than 1,700 times the radiation that the average person receives in a year from natural and man-made sources. It was out of envy of the superior data he thought such doses might yield that Wright Langham had written to Samuel Bassett asking him to be on the lookout for terminal patients whom they could inject with larger doses.

The records that have been made public so far do not reveal who authorized the doses. The lines of authority between the Met Lab's Health Division and the Manhattan Project were fuzzy, and it could have been either Robert Stone or Stafford Warren who gave the go-ahead. As for the doctor who actually performed the injections, the scientists gave conflicting statements to AEC investigators many years later when they were asked about them. Scientists Edwin Russell and J. J. Nickson are listed as authors of a 1946 scientific report describing the injections and postmortem analyses of Arthur Hubbard and Una Macke. Leon Jacobson, R. Lesko, and W. Monroe are listed as assistants.

Edwin Russell told AEC investigators that he prepared the plutonium solutions and that Leon Jacobson injected the material into the patients. But Jacobson, who went on to become chairman of the Department of Medicine at the University of Chicago's Pritzker School of Medicine, denied any involvement in the experiment. He said he "knew very little about it, next to nothing."

In 1946 six Met Lab employees drank a plutonium solution concocted by Edwin Russell. The study was probably done so scientists could confirm that plutonium was not readily absorbed by the GI tract. One of the volunteers was Robert Carr Milham, of Augusta, Georgia. Now in his seventies and in good health, Milham said in 1995 he was clearly informed about the nature of the experiment. The drink tasted like "lemonade," he added. "Some people who were near terminal death, I believe, preceded us."

16

POSTWAR BERKELEY:
THE FINAL INJECTIONS

Joseph Hamilton was in the Sierra Nevada panning for gold with his wife and sister-in-law when a neighbor came running up and breathlessly informed them that some kind of fantastic weapon had just been dropped on Japan. Hamilton knew perfectly well what kind of weapon his neighbor was talking about, but like virtually every other scientist on the Manhattan Project, he been so indoctrinated in the ways of secrecy that he had not told anyone about the bomb, including his wife, Leah. At last, the secret was out. He turned to his wife and sister-in-law and said, "That's been my work." The women began talking excitedly, but Hamilton soon returned his attention to the trout-filled creek and the glittering pan of rocks in his hand.

As he breathed in the brisk mountain air, Hamilton's mind no doubt raced ahead to the postwar period. Although he knew there would be changes, Hamilton acted as if the war was not over when he returned home to Berkeley. In the days and weeks to come, he continued to run the Crocker lab, the heavily guarded facility that he oversaw, with his usual secrecy, locking his papers each evening in a heavy office safe. Like clockwork, he filed his dry, technical reports with the Manhattan Engineer District, updating project leaders on ongoing experiments and informing them of the additional studies he was planning. In September of 1945, the month that Wright Langham went to Rochester and Stafford Warren and Hymer Friedell were in Japan, he sent the Manhattan Project the following memo on his next study:

The next human subject that is available is to be given, along with plutonium 238, small quantities of radio-yttrium, radiostrontium and radio-cerium. This procedure has in mind two purposes. First, the opportunity will be presented to compare in man the behavior of these three representative long-lived Fission products with their metabolic properties in the rat, and second, a comparison can be made of the differences in their behavior from that of plutonium.

Hamilton hoped to perform his next injection within two months, but for unknown reasons, the experiment was not carried out until April of the following year. The patient targeted to receive the multiple injections was Simeon Shaw, a four-year-old boy who arrived in the United States on April 16, 1946, on a U.S. Army Transport Command plane from Sydney, Australia.

Simeon, or "Simmy" as he was called, was the youngest of three children, a lively little boy with sparkling eyes and dark hair. He was from Dubbo, Australia, a small farming community in western New South Wales, 260 miles northwest of Sydney. Around January 6 of that year, Simmy's six-year-old sister, Helene, was rocking him in a hammock on their front porch when he tumbled out and onto the ground. Simmy began to cry loudly, alarming his father, who came out to the porch and scolded Helene severely for her carelessness. The commotion so frightened Joshua, the oldest child, that he ran into the garden and stood in front of a green chili bush. Then he plucked off a chili and ate it. "There is a whole blank from there," Joshua recalled.

Simmy complained of pain in the right leg, but in a few days he was careening around the farm again with his usual, wild happiness. A week or so later his mother, Freda, noticed a tender, swelling mass on the inside of the boy's knee. She took him to a local doctor who diagnosed the injury as a fractured femur. Simmy's leg was placed in a cast and the X rays forwarded to a radiologist in Sydney.

After carefully studying the film, the radiologist came up with a shocking finding. Simmy appeared to have an osteogenic sarcoma, a form of bone cancer, and probably would not live for more than nine months. Desperate and disbelieving, the Shaws sought other medical opinions. Eventually they decided to take the child to the University of California Hospital in San Francisco for treatment.

How the family learned of UCSF or who in Australia referred them remains a mystery. An Australian doctor, whose name has been deleted from medical records released by the Department of Energy, had consulted his counterparts in the United States. Perhaps contact was made through this conversation. A note in Simmy's medical records states that the child was referred from Australia by a "Major Davis through the Red Cross."

Once the decision was made to go to the United States, events moved at lightning speed. Freda applied for a nonimmigrant visa, and within a matter of hours, the two were boarding the U.S. Army plane in Sydney. So grave was the plight of the small boy that American troops headed home from the Pacific campaign had been off-loaded to make room for them. Once they were in the air and the roar of the engines had lulled Simmy to sleep, Freda, a young woman with long dark hair, may have begun playing and replaying in her mind the blurred events of the last four months, searching for an explanation for the unthinkable prognosis her son had just been handed.

Freda's husband, Samuel, was a wool buyer from Gorki, Russia, who had immigrated to Australia years earlier. Freda, who was fifteen years younger than her husband and a British citizen by birth, was a gifted musician. She had a lovely singing voice and played the piano, cello, and violin. Although she was only thirty-two years old, the extra flesh she carried around her shoulders and hips had dragged her into an early middle age.

The large plane flew east for eight thousand miles across the blue wrinkled expanse of the Pacific Ocean, stopping for fuel in Brisbane, New Caledonia, and Fiji. When they reached Honolulu, Red Cross officials took mother and son sightseeing and then prepared a fresh bed for the child's last lap to San Francisco. The ragged brown edge of a new continent appeared in their plane window just four days after Freda had applied for the visa.

The transport plane touched down at a small airfield north of San Francisco. A Red Cross ambulance was pulled up nearby and a knot of reporters and photographers were milling about. Freda tottered down the ramp with her child. She was wearing an old-fashioned hat, a print dress, and a dark coat. Draped around her shoulders was a slender braid of mink.

Simmy looked like a character out of a Charles Dickens novel, skin and eyes glittering with fever, his right leg swaddled in a cast. The photographers moved in with their boxy cameras. The boy giggled, reaching for the spent bulbs. Someone gathered up a whole bag of bulbs and shoved them into his hand. Freda, exhausted and disoriented, was brimming with gratitude. She thanked the Army and the Red Cross for helping to arrange the flight. The doctors in Australia, she said, had told her it was urgent to get to UCSF within a week. "Inside of one hour, American Army officers and Red Cross workers had arranged priorities for us as paying passengers," she said. "I want everybody to know how kind they have been." Freda refused even to acknowledge the possibility that UCSF would not be able to help her son. "I'm hopeful," she said, "because I have to be."

The next day the story of the arrival of mother and son was carried in newspapers around the United States: "Mercy Flight Brings Aussie Boy Here"; "Sydney Boy Admitted to U.S. Hospital After Flight"; "Specialists Hope to Cure Boy, 4." Then the reporters moved on to the next assignment. For Freda and Simmy, though, the story was just beginning.

Once he was in the hospital, the experiment on Simmy had to proceed quickly. Ships and men were already massing in the Pacific Ocean for Operation Crossroads. Many of Hamilton's assistants would be going. Even Hamilton himself, on one occasion toting a bottle of bourbon for the sweaty troops, would be flying back and forth.

Still carrying the bag of spent flashbulbs, Simmy was placed in a wheelchair and rolled to his hospital bed. The admittance office waived a lot of the paperwork. "Their traveling expenses, previous specialists, etc. have been tremendous," one official hurriedly noted. Freda gave the physicians the X rays and medical reports she had carried with her from Australia. Curiously, there was no letter of referral or summary of Simmy's illness.

The child was given a detailed physical examination. Codeine and aspirin were prescribed for his pain and an elixir of phenobarbital was ordered to help him sleep. Freda stayed at the Parnassus Guest House across the street from the hospital. Her joy at arriving in the United States evaporated quickly when doctors allowed her to see Simmy only three times a week. "They say if I go more often they will not be able to do anything," Freda told her husband in a telephone conversation. Simmy was also distraught by the separation. "He wants to see his mother continually," an entry on his medical chart states.

Simmy began to grow more feverish a few days after he was admitted. Additional aspirin was ordered. Ice packs were placed on his forehead. Alcohol rubs were administered. A severe infection materialized in his middle ear, and ten days after his arrival, his left eardrum was punctured so pus could drain out.

Incredibly, on April 26, the same day his ear was punctured and his temperature was hovering at 104 degrees, Simmy was injected with three radioisotopes: plutonium-239, cerium, and a third isotope believed to be yttrium. He was the youngest of the eighteen plutonium patients and the only foreign citizen. CAL-2 was his code name.

The radioisotopes injected into Simmy were slightly different from the ones Hamilton outlined in his memo. Instead of plutonium-238, plutonium-239 was injected. Radioactive strontium was eliminated, and one of the scientists involved in the experiment suggested the yttrium injected into Simmy may actually have been rubidium.

Simmy's fever continued to seesaw after the injections. It dropped to normal a day later, and then rose again to 104 degrees. The infection spread to the right ear, which was also drained. Although his temperature kept fluctuating, surgeons decided to go ahead and do a bone biopsy. Australian doctors had specifically recommended against a biopsy, but the reason for their objection is not clear. After Freda signed a consent form for the anesthesia, the child was wheeled into surgery and a rubber tourniquet was wrapped around his upper leg. Surgeons removed an "oblong section" of bone. "Then with curved gouges more material was removed from the center of the tumor for radioactive studies as well as biopsy." Small bits of muscle and tissue were also taken out for study. Finally the incision was closed and the child was returned to the ward.

A note in Simmy's medical records states that some of the specimens were sent to Earl Miller. Another document states that the data on the uptake of the radioactive materials could be obtained from Miller by "responsible individuals." But Miller said in an interview shortly before his death that he was not involved in Simmy's case. "If I had any contact with this kid it might have been through reading his films."

Freda placed two calls to Australia, the first on April 25 and the second on May 9. Samuel's secretary listened to the conversations and transcribed them. Simmy's brother, Joshua, said this was probably done because his Russian-born father didn't speak English well and the phone connections were terrible. Some of the transcripts contain blank spaces, which Joshua said probably represented words the secretary couldn't understand. The transcripts are filled with a poignant sense of confusion and urgency. They were kept by Simmy's father for decades and were handed down to his surviving children after he died.

The day after the radionuclides were injected, Freda placed the first call to her husband. "They have given him an injection and will be giving him another one on Saturday," she reported. There is no further information about what Freda was told about the injections; nor has any evidence made public so far indicated that Freda was informed about the plutonium.

Simmy's diagnosis, unlike Albert Steven's and Eda Schultz Charlton's, was accurate. X rays showed the child had two additional lesions— one in the upper thigh and one in his left arm. The disease probably had nothing to do with the fall from the hammock.

Freda's agitation, meanwhile, continued to mount. In the second conversation with her husband, she said, "This afternoon they said they have not any hope at all. The resident specialist has told me there is no hope."

Simmy's fever continued to fluctuate during the rest of his hospital stay. He was given large doses of penicillin and more aspirin for the pain in his leg. There was a debate about whether to administer "deep X-ray therapy" or to amputate the leg. Both options were discarded because it was felt that the cancer was too far advanced. Freda was advised, however, that if Simmy's tumor became excessively large or ulcerated through the skin, amputation might be necessary.

A fresh plaster cast was placed over Simmy's leg and he was discharged on May 25. The child seemed improved and was trying to put weight on the injured leg. Ominously, though, an X ray done four days after the discharge suggested the tumor actually was increasing in size. Six weeks had elapsed since Freda's joyous, hopeful arrival in the United States. "Sailing June 14th Need Money Cable Immediately Love," she wrote in a telegram to her family.

Simmy and Freda took a slow boat back to Australia. The journey took a month, and the two may have passed some of the Navy vessels transporting scientists and sailors to Operation Crossroads. Somewhere in the middle of the Pacific Ocean, Simmy celebrated his fifth birthday. When they reached Australia, Simmy and his mother took up residence in the Riverview Hotel on the outskirts of Sydney. Simmy's father joined them there. The eight-room hotel, which is still standing, was owned by Samuel's sister. Joshua, the eldest son, said the family probably stayed in Sydney because they were strapped for cash.

Through the summer, fall, and winter, Freda, Simmy, and Samuel were together, sharing a large room in the front of the hotel. There were cooking facilities, perhaps a hot plate in the room. Simmy slept in the only bed.

Freda, who had had her fill of doctors and mercy flights, used homeopathic remedies in a desperate attempt to ease the child's pain. Mrs.

O. S. Adams, a Californian who may have befriended Freda while she was in the United States, sent her a packet of clover bloom. "At last I have the clover bloom for your little boy," she wrote. "Cover with water, boil two or three minutes strain and serve when cool enough." The letter and the envelope, with its six cents' worth of stamps, were also kept by Simmy's father.

The clover bloom was fragrant and full of hope, but no match for the bone cancer. The disease did its work, brutally and efficiently. Finally there was nothing left to do but hold Simmy. "The last time I went into his room, Simmy was screaming with pain. I couldn't stand it," said Joshua. "The next thing we were driving back to Dubbo. I was sitting in the backseat and I asked my mother where Simmy was. She said he was staying in Sydney for a while. I could see she was very upset."

Simmy died on January 6, 1947, a year after the fall from the hammock. His death deeply affected the Shaw family. Samuel never mentioned Simmy's name again and shut himself off from his two other children. If Joshua or Helene touched him, he went to the sink and washed his hands. "From Simeon's death onward, there was a void. I can't remember one happy moment," Joshua said.

A couple of years later, a secretary for Bertram V. A. Low-Beer, the UCSF radiologist who conducted the TBI experiment for the Met Lab, wrote to Freda. Low-Beer was interested in how Simmy was feeling. "We realize you may have been busy and overlooked the letter, but we are very interested in knowing how your son, [name deleted], is feeling at the present time." Low-Beer's secretary told Freda she was welcome to use the bottom of her letter for her reply. A stamped, self-addressed envelope was enclosed. "Hoping to hear from you soon," she added. Freda never responded.

Soon after the experiment on Simmy was completed, Joseph Hamilton and his colleagues headed to the beautiful lagoon in the Pacific Ocean where the world's first peacetime atomic bombs were detonated during Operation Crossroads. But his human experiments were not over yet. In November of 1946, some five months later, he was again pleading with the Manhattan Engineer District for small amounts of plutonium-238 so he could continue his studies. The next human guinea pig in Berkeley was injected not with plutonium, but americium, a radioactive element discovered by Glenn Seaborg in 1944, which is created by bombarding plutonium-239 with neutrons. The subject was Hanford Jang, a sixteen-year-old boy from Canton, China, who spoke no English. Often referred to as CAL-A, Jang was suffering from the same disease as Simmy: an osteogenic sarcoma. The cancer was located in his left femur and had spread to other parts of his body.

According to the scant records on the case, Jang was injected with americium on June 10, 1947, at the Chinese Hospital in San Francisco's Chinatown. On the day of the procedure, a note in his medical records states: "An injection has been given this patient at 10:30 a.m. today, henceforth all urine and feces shall be collected separately daily in individual containers provided to be collected daily at 9:00 a.m. by messenger from the radiation laboratories of the University of California at Berkeley. Please date all bottles." Another note in his records states: "Keep clear of urine. Keep cool. Keep in container and in bucket of ice."

Scientist Kenneth Scott instructed researcher Josephine Crowley to "make arrangements for daily car trips to S.F. for excreta for first two weeks." He continued, "We will use the same procedure as with Mr. S. See JGH for particulars." "Mr. S." was probably a reference to Albert Stevens. "JGH" was Joseph Hamilton.

Although doctors had decided not to amputate Simmy's leg because the cancer was too widespread, they went ahead and amputated Hanford Jang's leg despite the fact that his cancer, too, had metastasized. The amputation was performed two days after the injection. The limb was then sent to Berkeley, where it was dissected and the americium measured in the bone, tumor, connective tissue, and muscle. The teenager died eleven months later, on June 15, 1948, and was buried in the Six Companies Cemetery, a Chinese cemetery in San Francisco. The Department of Energy admitted years later there was "no evidence of disclosure" about the experiment in Jang's medical records.

Although Hamilton certainly supervised the human experiments, it's not clear whether he actually injected the patients. "I don't think Dr. Hamilton, himself personally, ever injected anybody with anything. I don't think he ever wanted to practice medicine after he finished his internship," Patricia Durbin speculated in an interview with government officials in 1994. "He basically turned [away from] medical practice and became a laboratory bench scientist. He was terrified of patients. He was terrified of people." Hamilton was so afraid of human touch, Durbin added, that he once wanted to fire one of his pregnant secretaries because he was worried he would have to deliver the baby himself.

Within weeks of the Hanford Jang injection, Joseph Hamilton and his associates began looking around for another human subject. They eventually set their sights on Elmer Allen, an African American railroad porter originally from Texas whose life had been turned upside down by an accident. Code-named CAL-3, Elmer was the third and last patient injected by the Berkeley group and the final subject used in the entire experiment. Elmer outlived the other seventeen patients and the doctors who injected him, succumbing to pneumonia in 1991. But his was one of the most tragic stories of all.

As the fog streamed in over the hills of San Francisco, blanketing the city in a cloud of swirling whiteness, Elmer Allen hobbled from doctor to doctor, hoping to find somebody who could help him get back on his feet again. He and his young wife, Fredna, had moved to Richmond, California, in the East Bay area after World War II. The color of their skin didn't seem to matter as much in California as it did back home in Texas, where segregation was still rigidly in place. They had met in a bustling train station in El Paso. Fredna had missed her connection and was crying when Elmer, his eyes serious and thoughtful beneath the porter's cap, appeared at her side. "I can get you on the next train," he said. He followed Fredna back to her hometown of Italy, Texas, where they were married.

Everything went well those first two years in California. Elmer was working as a railroad porter for the Pullman Company and Fredna as an aide in a health clinic. They had two children, a four-month-old son and a daughter who was not yet two. "We were optimistic about the future," Fredna recalled. But then an accident occurred on September 3, 1946, a minor accident really, which would set in motion a chain of events that would forever alter their lives. Elmer was trying to get off a train in Chicago when the train jolted suddenly and threw him to the side, injuring his left knee.

He went to the company doctor in Chicago and saw another when he returned to Oakland. The Oakland doctor diagnosed the injury as a fracture and advised Elmer to wrap his knee in an Ace bandage and apply heat. But the pain and swelling didn't go away. Finally Elmer was referred to a private physician named Lloyd Fisher. Puzzled by the knee's inability to heal, Fisher removed some fluid and sent it off to a pathologist for a second opinion. The consulting pathologist diagnosed the wound as a bone cyst and found no evidence of cancer. "The principal picture is that of newly forming bone, organizing hemorrhage, and chronic inflammation." Fisher then referred Elmer in June of 1947 to

UCSF's outpatient clinic. "Of great teaching value," one clinician later penned on Elmer's medical records.

The injury had put a terrible strain on Elmer and his young family. The Pullman Co. had discontinued his checks and stopped paying his doctor's bills. Rent was $35 a month; insurance, $4.20; and his union dues, $3. His net assets consisted of $25 in cash. He was $60 in debt, most of which represented doctors' bills.

One of the first things that the UCSF doctors did was take another set of X rays. By that time, Elmer was taking painkillers and his knee had swollen to three or four times its original size. The radiologist concluded the changes could have been due to infection superimposed by a surgical defect, "but the probability of a bone sarcoma must be seriously considered." The same radiologist reversed his opinion a few days later when he did a second set of X rays: "This is probably an osteogenic sarcoma . . . however, the possibility of a chronic infections process superimposed on a surgical defect must be seriously considered." A biopsy was performed July 14 to settle the question. Following a microscopic examination of the cellular material, a pathologist concluded that Elmer did indeed have bone cancer. Doctors told Elmer that his left leg would have to be amputated in order to halt the spread of the disease, a procedure that is still considered an acceptable treatment for patients suffering from cancer of the long bones. Although the disease usually is fatal by the time it is diagnosed, X rays showed that Elmer's cancer had not metastasized.

It's not clear how Joseph Hamilton and his associates learned of Elmer Allen. Probably someone in UCSF's radiology department became aware of his case because of the numerous X-ray studies. Several Manhattan Project veterans were working in the radiology department at that time, including Robert Stone, Earl Miller, and Bertram Low-Beer.

The doctors did not immediately schedule Elmer for surgery after the definitive cancer diagnosis was made. Ray Mullen, one of Elmer's primary physicians, wrote in his medical chart that the amputation would be "postponed until Monday in order to have radioactive tracer substances prepared (plutonium) and standardized. Pt. will have tumor uptake studies done." This is the only time in which plutonium is specifically mentioned in Elmer's medical records.

At 3:30 P.M. on Monday, July 18, 1947, Bertram Low-Beer and several other doctors gathered around Elmer's hospital bed. According to a lengthy note that appears to have been written by Low-Beer, Elmer was told the following: "The experimental nature of the intramuscular injection of the radioactive tracer sample was explained to the patient, who agreed on the procedure. The pat. was in fully oriented and in sane mind."

The so-called consent form does not state what the radioactive material was, and relatives said it was unlikely that Elmer, who had a limited education, would have understood what the doctors were talking about anyway. "If they told my father that he was injected with plutonium, that would be like telling him he was injected with ice cream," said his daughter, Elmerine.

The plaster cast on Elmer's left leg was split down the side and removed. After flecks of plaster were sponged away, a bull's-eye was drawn in the middle of his calf. Then a syringe loaded with plutonium was plunged into the center of the circle. The needle sunk down two centimeters, or eight-tenths of an inch, depositing the plutonium deep into the calf. When the needle was withdrawn, a physician wrote, "No blood appeared on aspiration and no bleeding after removal of needle."

Elmer was observed carefully for three days following the injection. On the first evening Dr. Mullen noted that Elmer was experiencing "no pain or discomfort whatsoever." The next day Mullen scribbled: "A good day with only slight throbbing pain in region of knee." On the third day Elmer was taken to surgery.

A tourniquet was wrapped around the upper thigh, then the skin and underlying muscles were peeled back and severed. The nerves and arteries were isolated and snipped off. Finally, a saw was used to cut through the thigh bone. Following the amputation, Elmer was wheeled out of the operating room in "good condition" and given morphine, codeine, and aspirin to relieve the pain. The severed limb was sent "to pathology and radiological study."

Elmer was a model patient. Mullen, who witnessed the plutonium injection, was delighted with his speedy recovery. On July 28 he scrawled: "Feeling much better. Anxious to get up on crutches." Two days later he wrote: "Has been up in wheel chair with great joy. Wound dressed and appears to be healing well [without] any infection . . . a fine patient." On August 1, Elmer was "in wheel chair most of day. No pain from stump. Penicillin [discontinued]. Afebrile. Eager to find work after convalescence—not depressed."

Elmer's leg was taken to Berkeley, where the plutonium at the injection site was carefully measured. When Patricia Durbin was asked how the Berkeley scientists managed that, she responded, "It just takes big beakers, that's all."

Elmer was the only patient injected in a muscle rather than a vein.

The reason is not clear, but Manhattan Project doctors had been concerned about plutonium-contaminated wounds and punctures ever since the spring of 1944, when Joseph Hamilton had advised they should be treated like snake bites. The Met Lab's J. J. Nickson had warned his colleagues the following year: "For large, grossly contaminated wounds on the hand, the satisfaction of the dictates of this method of treatment might well necessitate the amputation of the hand." In Los Alamos, Louis Hempelmann had begun excising wounds that were only potentially contaminated. Between 1944 and 1945, seventy-eight wounds were excised, but only three contained significant amounts of plutonium and the practice was discontinued because it discouraged employees from reporting minor injuries.

On August 7, Elmer was discharged from the hospital. Soon the flush of exuberance faded and the impact of the amputation began to sink in. For Elmer, an African American trying to fish up a livelihood in a segregated country, the railroad job had been a godsend. Now there would be no more graceful leaps onto moving trains, no evening strolls through the sleeping cars. He haunted the wharves in San Francisco, where he bought and sold fish. But that didn't bring in enough money to support his family. A couple of years later Elmer and his wife bundled up their two children and went home to Italy, Texas. "He wanted to make a good living for his family," Fredna said. "After he lost his leg, he just gave up all hope."

Wearing a new prosthesis from California's vocational rehabilitation department, Elmer tried to readjust to life in Italy. The intense humidity, which made the summer heat feel more like gravity than air, was particularly hard on the young couple. They had grown used to California's blue skies and tangy breezes. Then there was Italy's rampant segregation. The little town had two mayors and two city councils in the 1950s—one for whites and one for African Americans. "He was disgusted. He never wanted to come back here. He had so many hopes and dreams for his family," Fredna recalled. For his children, those dreams would come true. His son, William, and his granddaughter, April, became engineers. His daughter, Elmerine, became a school teacher. But for Elmer himself life would hold little promise.

"He could do anything," recalled his friend Joe Speed. "But there was nothing for him to do." One job after another fell through. Elmer began having epileptic seizures and could no longer commute to Dallas, where work was more plentiful. When the seizures occurred, Fredna would put a spoon in his mouth. "He would chew the spoon to pieces—his tongue, too," Elmerine remembered. Elmer made toys for schoolchildren, kites from brown paper bags, lampshades from Popsicle sticks, and flower baskets from egg cartons.

Soon Elmer began drinking heavily. Eventually he became one of Italy's town characters, slumping on a bench on Main Street, telling outlandish stories about the amputation and the doctors who flew in and out of his room "practicing" to be doctors. He told his friend, Joe Speed, that he had been used as a guinea pig. But no one, not even his family doctor, believed him.

David Williams, a doctor in Waxahachie, Texas, who treated Elmer for the last twenty years of his life, said Elmer informed him during one of their first visits about the plutonium injection. The physician said he put the information "in the back of my bonnet" and watched him for indications of the long-ago exposure. Williams didn't know whether to believe Elmer or not. "I wondered. I also wondered if it was a portion of his paranoia and whether or not it was a crutch for him to not function as he should have functioned. His conscience needed a salve to where it was O.K. for his wife to be teaching and so forth."

Williams also didn't encourage Elmer to talk about the experiment. "I didn't think there was a lot of gain there. Do you follow? In other words, I didn't turn him off, I'd listen, but I felt like he had other more ongoing problems that were more pressing and that we needed to deal with day-to-day rather than going back to that." Williams eventually wound up diagnosing Elmer as a paranoid schizophrenic. "What I saw was a fellow who had a loss of limb and became an emotional cripple because of it. He took to the bottle and then got off that. He probably had paranoid schizophrenia all of his life. As far as doing things, I thought he was using this possible exposure as a crutch, a reason, rather than doing as well as I would have liked to have seen him do."

Medical authorities in California attempted to keep in touch with Elmer but eventually communication ceased—possibly due to the fact that the physicians overseeing his case died. Dr. Bertram Low-Beer, who was at Elmer's bedside on the day of his injection and wrote the consent form that was placed in his medical file, died of leukemia in 1955. The disease, which is believed to have been caused by an accidental overexposure to radiation in Czechoslovakia, was discovered during a routine blood test and came as a terrible shock to the scientist and his wife. Low-Beer was "passionately dedicated" to the idea of safety, his widow said. "It's extremely ironic that he should have been a victim."

Joseph Hamilton was diagnosed with leukemia the year that Low-

Beer died. After years of watching Hamilton play Russian roulette with radioactive materials, none of his colleagues was surprised by his illness. Hamilton was melancholy, though. "He became sad when he was dying," Earl Miller said.

Hamilton continued to work up until a month before his death. His secretary, Grace Walpole, carried his papers back and forth to the hospital. "He was very sad. But he just sort of went along as though nothing was wrong. And, of course, he seemed to work a little more frantically." Hamilton died February 18, 1957, at the age of forty-nine. The University of California listed his death as an "industrial accident," but no one could explain the accident or when it happened. "You know," he told Patricia Durbin in a conversation before he died, "the sad part is that all the easy experiments have been done."

With the injection of Elmer Allen, the first phase of the plutonium experiment was completed. In 1967, exactly twenty years later, a second phase would begin when Patricia Durbin, who had washed dishes in Joseph Hamilton's lab and went on to coauthor twenty papers with him before he died, began looking into the whereabouts of the patients. To her amazement, she would discover that Elmer Allen, Eda Schultz Charlton, John Mousso, and Janet Stadt were still alive.

PART TWO

Atomic
Utopia

17

AT A CROSSROADS

Within days of the bombings of Hiroshima and Nagasaki, politicians, military leaders, scientists, and newspaper editors across the United States began the acrimonious debate over the future of the atomic bomb. Out of the year-long discussion would emerge the Atomic Energy Commission, a powerful new department that one congressional witness proclaimed to be possibly "the most important federal bureau in the history of the republic." The Atomic Energy Commission would indeed have godlike powers, controlling virtually every aspect of the nuclear weapons program for the next three decades.

Although few in Congress understood the excruciating deaths caused by radiation or the bomb's long-lived and dangerous by-products, many developed a quasi-religious view toward the new weapon. "God Almighty in His infinite wisdom [has] dropped the atomic bomb in our lap," Senator Edwin Johnson of Colorado enthused. "It's our opportunity right now to compel mankind to adopt the policy of lasting peace . . . or be burned to a crisp."

Nearly everyone recognized that the atomic bomb was a revolutionary weapon that would change the nature of war and the United States' relationship to other nations. Perhaps no country better understood this than the Soviet Union. Although the United States did not yet realize it, its former wartime ally had already obtained many of the bomb's secrets from Manhattan Project scientist Klaus Fuchs and other atomic spies.

The issues immediately after the war revolved around the following questions: Should the bomb be placed under military or civilian control? Should the United States relinquish the bomb and its secrets to an international commission in an effort to prevent an all-out arms race? Just how would the new weapon change the nature of war?

The Navy was the first branch of the military to recognize that it might be rendered obsolete by the bomb. Two days after Japan announced that it would surrender, Lewis Strauss, the astute businessman who had supported Ernest Lawrence's prewar cancer research, urged Navy Secretary James Forrestal to conduct atomic tests on surplus ships. "If such a test is not made," cautioned Strauss, who served as a rear admiral during the war, "there will be loose talk to the effect that the fleet is obsolete in the face of this new weapon and this will militate against appropriations to preserve a postwar Navy of the size now planned."

Eager not to be left behind or see its own budget cut, the Army Air Forces pounced on Strauss's idea and proposed that two atomic bombs be used to sink captured Japanese vessels. Eventually a compromise was worked out between the two fierce rivals: a joint Army-Navy test involving two, possibly three, atomic bombs would be conducted and supervised by the Joint Chiefs of Staff. The test series was dubbed "Operation Crossroads," a name that accurately described the confusing period immediately after the war.

While the military branches began planning for Operation Crossroads, several bills were introduced in Congress that would establish and define the parameters of the Atomic Energy Commission. The first major piece of legislation, the May-Johnson bill, was introduced in October of 1945 by Democrats Andrew J. May of Kentucky and Colorado's Edwin Johnson. Using a corporate model, the bill called for a general manager with sweeping powers who was not subject to removal by the president, and nine full-time commissioners who could be either civilians or retired or active military officers.

The May-Johnson bill alarmed many atomic scientists. They were disturbed by the severe restrictions imposed on the dissemination of information and the heavy penalties for inadvertently disclosing atomic secrets. Above all else, they believed the legislation was nothing more than a power grab by Leslie Groves, who would eventually succeed in installing himself as the general manager.

Still smarting from Groves's wartime policies of secrecy and compartmentalization, the atomic scientists began traveling to Washington to lobby against the bill. Although Groves repeatedly denied that he was trying to set himself up as the atomic energy czar, many of the Manhattan Project veterans didn't believe him. Silenced for too long, the atomic scientists were an exceptionally eloquent and effective lobbying group that became known as the "reluctant lobby."

On November 1, 1945, they established the Federation of Atomic Scientists in a warren of poorly heated offices in downtown Washington. When they began attracting support from scientists in other disciplines, they changed their name to the Federation of American Scientists, an organization that still exists today and continues to closely monitor nuclear issues. William Higinbotham, the federation's executive secretary, said in an interview in 1946 that the scientists' lobby had no interest in politics: "The question is: Are you pro- or anti-suicide?"

The earnest young men soon became the toast of Washington's social scene. David Lang, who was covering atomic issues for the *New Yorker* magazine at the time, wrote, "The scientists quickly discovered, to their embarrassment, that 'atom' was a magic word in Washington and that they, the only ones who fully understood its meaning, were looked upon as glamour boys." But the scientists' curmudgeonly boss, Leslie Groves, did not fare as well. Anti-Groves sentiment began to spread through Washington, and many a social gathering ended with an obligatory excoriation of the general. Wrote one scientist after a typical outing, "His nibs (G.G.) took quite a beating."

As opposition mounted to the May-Johnson bill, Senator Brien McMahon, the ambitious Democrat from Connecticut, proposed the creation of the Special Senate Committee on Atomic Energy. McMahon, who had introduced the first piece of atomic legislation, also had quasi-religious sentiments about the bomb and often told his fellow senators that the bombing of Hiroshima was the greatest event in world history since the birth of Jesus Christ.

The Senate soon approved McMahon's idea and made him the chairman of the committee he had suggested. When it became clear that the May-Johnson bill would not pass, the action shifted to McMahon's committee, where a new atomic energy bill would be hashed out over the next few months. The Special Senate Committee on Atomic Energy began its work in November of 1945 by first trying to educate itself about the Manhattan District. It took trips to the bomb project's production sites and invited a remarkable number of the project's stars and supporting cast to Washington to testify. From Philip Morrison, for example, the committee learned the new weapon resembled a "small piece of the sun." From Leslie Groves, it heard that radiation was a "pleasant way to die."

The McMahon committee, composed of mostly conservative senators, supported a strong military involvement in the new Atomic Energy

Commission. But committee staffers, as well as McMahon himself, wanted an all-civilian commission that would have absolutely no military representation. The atomic scientists threw their support behind the McMahon bill. "They felt that an army, being an agency for waging war, would naturally and properly concentrate on the improvement of atomic weapons," wrote David Lang.

While the members of the McMahon committee were thrashing out details of the new legislation, other officials in Washington were engaged in the equally demanding task of trying to formulate a policy on international control of the atomic bomb. As early as 1944, scientists such as Albert Einstein and Niels Bohr recognized that an arms race was inevitable unless some kind of agreement could be reached among all the nations of the world. Such a pact would require that all countries renounce the bomb, open their borders to inspections, and be willing to accept heavy penalties for violations—including an atomic attack if necessary.

President Truman had expressed his support for putting the bomb under international control. As a result, Undersecretary of State Dean Acheson had appointed a committee of consultants to develop a workable plan. Among the consultants were J. Robert Oppenheimer and David E. Lilienthal, who would eventually be appointed the first chairman of the new Atomic Energy Commission.

Working eighteen hours a day for nearly two months in early 1946, the group had developed a detailed plan that became known as the Acheson-Lilienthal Report. "The study was a peculiar one," wrote Lang, because the consultants, working in almost complete secrecy, were trying to come up with "a way for the nations of the world to get along together without the dread of being blown up at any moment."

The plan the consultants came up with called for the creation of an international commission that would control the world's supply of uranium sources, aggressively support the peaceful uses of atomic energy, and conduct inspections to make sure rogue nations weren't surreptitiously trying to build a bomb. Bernard Baruch, a seventy-five-year-old Wall Street businessman, was appointed by President Truman to present the plan to the newly formed United Nations Atomic Energy Commission. Both Oppenheimer and Lilienthal were appalled by the choice; they had wanted someone younger and more dynamic to lead the U.S. negotiations. The elder statesman supported the Acheson-Lilienthal plan, but he wanted to make sure violators would face swift and certain punishment. Over time, the Acheson-Lilienthal proposal became known as the Baruch plan.

Under the terms of the plan, the United States would stop making nuclear weapons, destroy its existing weapons, and transfer its nuclear materials to an international authority *after* the Soviet Union had agreed to an in-depth inspection and verification program. But the Soviets, who were secretly engaged in their own bomb-building effort, didn't like the idea of U.S. inspectors snooping around. Andrei Gromyko, the young Soviet negotiator, offered a substitute that turned the U.S. proposal on its head and effectively challenged whether the United States was sincere about handing the bomb over to an internationally respected authority. The Soviet Union, Gromyko said, would be willing to subject itself to an intrusive system of inspections and controls provided the United States first agreed to halt its bomb production program and destroy all of its existing weapons. In other words, the United States wanted controls first, then disarmament; the Soviets wanted it the other way around.

The Baruch plan and legislation that would provide the blueprint for the domestic Atomic Energy Commission were both in their most delicate stages of negotiation when Operation Crossroads began. Unlike the Trinity test, which was conducted in complete secrecy, Crossroads was to be a highly publicized event. Scores of journalists, foreign observers, and congressmen were invited to witness the two detonations. Many people in other countries viewed the upcoming event with a mixture of horror and confusion. On the one hand, the United States was claiming that it was willing to destroy its atomic arsenal once proper controls were put into place. On the other, it was preparing to host a military extravaganza unlike any the world had ever seen.

Through the spring and early summer months of 1946, ships loaded with men and supplies sailed from California toward Bikini Atoll, a tropical paradise in the middle of the Pacific Ocean some 2,500 miles southwest of Hawaii. On May 29, the USS *Haven,* a ship that had been converted into a floating laboratory, departed from San Francisco, her hold filled with medical supplies, Geiger counters, and test tubes. On board were Stafford Warren and several hundred other men who would serve as radiation monitors. Warren may have had a little more swagger in his step as he ambled over the ship's wooden decks. He had been a member of the supporting cast only during the Manhattan Project, but would have a starring role during the joint Army-Navy exercise. Warren was the chief radiation safety officer for Crossroads and had orders from President Truman himself to make sure that no one was harmed by the "special attributes of the atom bomb." Considerably older than the rest of the passengers, Warren celebrated his fiftieth birthday aboard the *Haven* and was given a "Mark III" lead jockstrap.

Warren had begun recruiting radiation monitors for Crossroads soon after he returned from Japan. But with the rapid downsizing of the armed forces and the desire on the part of many civilian scientists to return to academia, he had run into problems. Warm bodies were so hard to come by that he had pressed his own son into service: "I had to practically browbeat Dean to do it," he told a historian. Warren also had to do some fancy talking to get his Manhattan Project colleagues to sign on. Louis Hempelmann reluctantly put aside some pressing problems he was working on to help out. Wright Langham shelved his chemical analyses of the Rochester patients. Samuel Bassett left his assistants in charge of the metabolic ward. And Joseph Hamilton and Kenneth Scott temporarily halted their analyses of the data gathered from Simeon Shaw. In return, Warren tried to spare his medical colleagues from the rigors of daily work. "I felt they might be kind of soft, physically, and that it might be kind of hazardous, so I didn't want them to get hurt."

As the floating laboratory plowed west across the glassy blue ocean, lectures were held on the balmy navigation deck. The first talk, on security, so intimidated many of the men that they threw their scientific notebooks and cameras overboard. The slow somnolent days were filled with lessons on nuclear physics, radioactivity, and the intricacies of the detection instruments. The evenings were filled with murder mystery films, poker games, and coffee drinking.

On June 12 the bored and restless passengers on the *Haven* spotted the gray silhouettes of ships and the low line of Bikini Atoll. "A little eggshell of coral, like hundreds of others out here; hitherto unknown, unremembered for glamour or sorrow, it now suddenly becomes a pinpoint in the sea of human affairs, truly a crossroads," wrote David Bradley, one of the radiation monitors.

One of the twenty-nine atolls and five islands in the Marshall Islands, Bikini Atoll consists of a circular chain of small, low-lying islets surrounding a gorgeous blue lagoon. The atoll began forming hundreds of thousands of years ago when a coral shelf began growing on top of a submerged volcano. The coral eventually protruded beyond the sea and attracted vegetation. Approximately 160 people lived on Bikini when the

Americans arrived. In short order they were moved off, the palm trees bulldozed, and the low-lying islets scraped smooth as a "porcelain table top in a physics laboratory." Tall metal towers were erected where the palm trees once swayed, and cameras and radiation detection equipment were mounted atop the towers.

But it was the sepulchral collection of ships anchored in the middle of the lagoon that was the real focus of this vast exercise. This was the ghost fleet, ninety-five doomed vessels that were soon to experience the fury of two atomic bombs equal in size to the weapon dropped on Nagasaki. Bobbing on the gentle currents were American aircraft carriers, Japanese battleships, and a German cruiser. On the decks of the ships were cages containing goats, sheep, pigs, and rats.

Despite the manpower shortages, the mighty armada that was eventually assembled at Bikini consisted of 42,000 men, 156 airplanes, and 242 ships. Crossroads was so extravagant that it seemed like a once-in-a-lifetime event, but actually it turned out to be the first of a series of lavishly expensive bomb tests that would continue for more than fifteen years at both the Pacific Proving Ground and at a second proving ground in the United States, which came to be known as the Nevada Test Site.

In the days leading up to the first atomic detonation, the men checked their equipment, attended briefings, and undertook dress rehearsals. In their off hours, they hunted for shells, went snorkeling, and swam in the warm lagoon. They ate steak three times a day, washing it down with a foul-tasting coffee called "scald." To clean their clothes, they simply hung them out in the frequent rain squalls.

Shot Able, the first atomic test, was detonated on July 1. Dropped from an airplane, the bomb missed its target by a half mile and sank only a few ships. The general response among the observers was one of disappointment. But those who stuck around for the second detonation saw an unforgettable sight, a foaming, white mushroom cloud that would forever be seared in the public's mind as *the* archetype of an atomic bomb explosion.

On July 25, a little more than three weeks later, Shot Baker was detonated ninety feet below the water. On the deck of the *Haven*, the Manhattan Project doctors watched in awe as a mighty geyser of water burst from the sea. When the white plume was a mile high, it suddenly collapsed and dropped a million tons of radioactive seawater onto the fleet of target ships anchored in the middle of the lagoon. Instantly a cloud of radioactive steam and spray surged out from the base of the explosion and enveloped the vessels. When the roar of the bomb had subsided, the doctors heard the faint cries of the animals that had been sheared of their coats and placed on the decks of the doomed vessels. The animals were alive, but not for long.

Through his binoculars, Stafford Warren watched a launch carrying Louis Hempelmann and Rear Admiral T. A. Solberg speed toward the *Saratoga,* a venerable Navy carrier anchored only 350 yards from where the bomb had been detonated. The ship was listing badly and the admiral, who was in charge of salvage operations, wanted to cut the anchor and save her. Remembered Warren:

> Through the glasses you could see this tug going like mad with a big bow wave toward the *[Saratoga],* and all of a sudden it looked as if it put its heels in the water, slowed down, stopped, and then backed up furiously. Dr. Hempelmann had been standing on the bow with a Geiger counter and had suddenly run into this contaminated water which was quite high in radioactivity. We got out without any trouble, but this was the way the rest of it went. You couldn't get near these ships.

Shot Baker turned the beautiful and pristine Bikini lagoon into a radioactive stew. The bomb destroyed nine ships outright, and the highly radioactive water that crashed back down into the decks essentially put the remaining vessels out of commission. Neutrons from the detonation converted the saltwater in the lagoon into radioactive sodium and radioactive chlorine. Algae, small marine animals that lived on the coral reef, and larger fish soon became radioactive. Neutrons from the blast even made the soap on the ships radioactive. Alpha and beta particle contamination stuck to ropes and rusty metal and became embedded in the wooden decks. Despite these hazards, the first patrol boats were recovering instruments forty-one minutes after the blast, and salvage groups were working in the area two hours later. Forty-nine ships carrying 15,000 men had returned to the lagoon by the end of the first day.

The Navy tried to decontaminate the target ships by blasting them with seawater, coffee, rice, cornstarch, lye, boiler compound, diesel fuel, ground corncobs, coconut shells, barley, soap, sulfuric acid, flour, and charcoal. Oftentimes wearing little more than shorts and sailor caps, thousands of young enlisted men boarded the ships with mops and soap and water to scrub the decks. They also scraped radioactive paint from the hulls, radioactive rust from the propellers, and recovered underwater monitoring equipment and gauges.

The Navy's cleanup efforts were no match for the tasteless, odorless, and invisible contamination that engulfed the target vessels. Soon the contamination spread to support ships where the sailors, scientists, officers, and journalists slept and ate. It got so bad that Stafford Warren began confiscating shirts and shoes. "They might have passed under a bit of superstructure and have water drip down their backs or something; so their clothes were all contaminated and so was the skin of their back. They would not wear gloves, so they would get the palms of their hands contaminated." The radioactive mist and water seeped into ships' ventilating systems and into boilers that converted the seawater to drinking water. Soon even the scientists on the *Haven* were finding minute doses of radiation in their food. "Our cook had never been off the ship; but, apparently, somebody had contaminated the handrails of the ladders and other places in such a way that he and his helpers had gotten their hands contaminated so that when they peeled the potatoes, it got into the mashed potatoes," Warren remembered.

The Geiger counters did not work well in the tropical humidity. What's more, the counting instruments had trouble detecting alpha and beta particles. Only 15 percent of the task force, or about 6,000 people, were given film badges—and these also failed to register alpha and beta particles. The target vessels, with their uneven surfaces, gave off wildly fluctuating exposure rates. To make matters worse, many Navy officers were uncooperative and began ignoring the monitors' advice about how long cleanup crews could remain on the contaminated ships. "Since they couldn't taste, feel, see etc. anything, the officers then began to take advantage of their numbers and my green men," Warren confided in an August 11, 1946, letter to his wife, Viola. The relationship between the monitors and the Navy men grew so strained that one day Warren was called before 1,400 officers and petty officers. He told an interviewer later, "You could just feel a kind of wall of hate when I walked in; the tension was terrific . . . I was just a dirty stinker, you know."

The Navy brass were finally convinced Warren's concerns were real when they saw some of the radioautographs he made from the fish. The fish were sliced longitudinally down the middle, dried in a warm blast of air, and then placed facedown on a piece of film. Several hours later their gills, coiled intestines, liver, and gonads could be clearly seen on the film.

Ever conscious of litigation, Warren created a "Medico-Legal Board" for advice. Its members included Louis Hempelmann, James Nolan, and Joseph Hamilton. According to documents, the board's function was to "reassure Col. Warren that the safety measures adopted by RadSafe were such as to attract no justifiable criticism and to give what assurance was possible that no successful suits could be brought on account of the radiological hazards of Operations Crossroads."

Warren also prepared a paper trail of classified memos that would exonerate him from any future blame. He described the radiological hazards in detail and advised the task force leaders to halt the operation. In one memo he wrote that many of the men had exceeded the 0.1 roentgen per day "tolerance limit." Alpha particles were "insidiously toxic in very minute quantities," he cautioned in a later memo. Speaking of a "lethal dose" as an amount that could be deadly if inhaled or ingested by one person, Warren wrote:

> Where only one or two lethal doses are spread over a whole ship the problem is small and of no consequence. However some of the most important ships have had many lethal doses deposited on them and retained in crevices and other places involved in the final clean up stages where scraping and other dry methods of removal will be used. Here the inhalation hazard will be extensive and unpredictable.

He also pointed out to Navy officials that as little as 0.5 roentgens per day for three months or less could result in defective children in successive generations. "The majority of personnel exposed at Bikini are young, and their heredity is of prime importance to them and their families."

Dale Beaman, just seventeen at the time, would later wish that such information had been conveyed to him before he swabbed the decks of the *Saratoga*. "We worked there all day and took our lunch. When we got back to the *Fulton*, they checked us with a Geiger counter and they said we were too hot and they told us to go below and take a shower." Beaman subsequently developed colon cancer, and his three children have experienced serious health problems. Charles McKay, a young Navy diver, made fifteen or twenty descents into the middle of the lagoon to measure the radiation on the sunken ships. A dosimeter was fastened to the back of his diving suit, and he was instructed to press his back against the sides of the vessels so the instrument could pick up the radiation. "Mac, that's hot. Get the heck away from there," he once heard someone say through his headset. McKay also developed colon cancer and believes the disease was caused by the exposure he received on the underwater expeditions. Boley Caldwell III, one of Crossroads' 386 radiation safety monitors, told a reporter, "It was often a matter of just several minutes before you got above a tenth of a roentgen." Harvey Glenn, a young sailor who for two weeks had scraped paint from the USS *Carteret,* said a Geiger counter measured their exposure after they were abruptly ordered off the vessel. "They checked our clothing, and that thing was going mad," he recalled. "Then we stuck our bare hands underneath and it did go crazy." Glenn knew something was wrong when his tonsils began "rotting" in 1964. Three years later he was diagnosed with cancer.

Operation Crossroads was terminated in August 1946. A third test, Shot Charlie, was canceled in large part due to Warren's constant haranguing. Exhausted and relieved, he slept for almost the entire journey home. Despite memos to the contrary, a decade later Warren denied that any of the Crossroads participants received more than 0.1 roentgen per day.

As far as the Manhattan Project was concerned, the Crossroads tests signaled an end to its exclusive monopoly of the bomb. For the Navy, the tests confirmed that a strategically placed nuclear weapon could indeed kill every sailor on board and coat its great ships with a potentially lethal layer of contamination. As for the Soviets, they were convinced the tests were nothing more than a dress rehearsal for the nuclear battlefield. Andrei Gromyko rejected the Baruch Plan on July 25, the same day the white geyser produced by Shot Baker burst from the sea. Thus began the arms race between the superpowers and decades of disarmament talks.

Shots Able and Baker made Bikini so radioactive that residents were not allowed to return to their paradise home. The atoll was used for subsequent nuclear tests and became too contaminated for anyone to live there safely. Except for a brief period in the 1960s and early 1970s, the Bikinians never did go home again.

Radiation from the underwater blast killed large sections of the exquisite coral reef and made all the fish for miles around radioactive. David Bradley, who wrote a controversial book about Operation Crossroads called *No Place to Hide* when he returned home, stumbled across another type of desecration. On the lagoon side of a beautiful little island called Cherry, which was less than a half-mile wide and covered with a glade of pine trees, he found an urban dump:

Boxes, mattresses, life belts, tires, boots, bottles, broken-up landing craft, rusting machinery and oil drums, all the crud and corruption of civilization spread out on the sands, and smeared over with inches of tar and oil . . . In the lavish expense account for Operation Crossroads, the spoilage of these jeweled islets will not even be mentioned, but no one who visited them could ever forget it.

While the Pacific tests were under way, politicians in Washington worked out the final details of the McMahon bill, which would define and establish the scope of the new Atomic Energy Commission. Ultimately the AEC wound up having a general manager and five commissioners. The commissioners were appointed by the president, approved by the Senate, and served staggered five-year terms. The general manager was chosen by the commissioners themselves and served at their pleasure. The new legislation also created three permanent committees: a General Advisory Committee, composed of civilian experts who would advise the AEC on scientific and technical matters; a Military Liaison Committee, consisting of officers chosen by the secretaries of the military branches who would advise the AEC on the military applications of atomic energy; and the Joint Committee on Atomic Energy, a permanent standing committee in Congress. A fourth committee, the Advisory Committee for Biology and Medicine, which provided advice on health and safety matters, would be added in late 1947.

Although the atomic scientists and many other lay groups favored keeping the military out of the AEC altogether, the compromise legislation provided for ample input from the armed forces. First, there was the Military Liaison Committee, which was to become an extremely powerful force in the late 1940s and early 1950s. Second, there was the Military Applications Division, one of the AEC's major headquarter divisions, which would be headed by a military flag officer and coordinate military planning with the AEC's production programs.

On August 1, with members of the Special Senate Committee on Atomic Energy looking on, President Truman signed the Atomic Energy Act of 1946. With the president's signature, the AEC was officially born. But the factories and laboratories and equipment belonging to the Manhattan Project would not be transferred into civilian hands until January of 1947. During those five months, there would be more political battles over appointments to the new commission and last-minute arguments with Leslie Groves.

Although he had been much maligned by the scientists, Groves had acted quickly in the transition period after the war to prevent scientists and doctors from leaving the Manhattan Project by offering them new equipment and an opportunity to spend part of their time on fundamental research. "That is part, as far as I am concerned, of their salary," he told the Special Senate Committee on Atomic Energy. "These men have very active minds, they border on the genius type and unless we do that, we just cannot keep these men." Groves warned that it would be "national suicide" to close the bomb factories. Los Alamos, Oak Ridge, and Hanford were not rifles that could be cleaned, put away, and then reassembled some day, he pointed out. "We cannot shut down the Los Alamos laboratory and ever assemble a laboratory like it again, except in time of war."

During the limbo period of 1945 and 1946, Groves had continued to run the Manhattan Project with his usual efficiency, shutting down some facilities in Oak Ridge and shoring up others in Los Alamos. With the signing of the Atomic Energy Act, however, it was clear that there would be no place in the civilian-run organization for the so-called "Atom General." Consequently Groves found the waning months of 1946 among the most difficult of his career. "For I was no longer simply a caretaker awaiting a final decision—I was a caretaker who could make no major decisions during a period when decisions were vital."

Groves managed to stay involved with the nuclear weapons program for another year or so as the first director of a new interservice agency called the Armed Forces Special Weapons Project. Created from the military remnants of the Manhattan Project, AFSWP (pronounced af-swop) was in charge of all the Defense Department's nuclear programs. With its field offices at Sandia Base in Albuquerque, New Mexico, AFSWP was within driving distance of Los Alamos and flying distance of the Nevada Test Site. "The whole purpose of the operation," recalled General Groves, "was to make absolutely certain that in case of war, or even the threat of war, the Defense Department would have at its instant disposal teams ready and trained to assemble atomic weapons."

AFSWP, which was staffed by officers and enlisted men from the Army, Navy, and Air Force, did much more than that. The agency coordinated the Pentagon's nuclear weapons research, conducted troop maneuvers at the Nevada Test Site, and churned out reams of propaganda. AFSWP was one of the most secretive and powerful entities to emerge in the developing Cold War and most of its records are still classified.

18

COMINGS AND GOINGS

Stafford Warren had stuck by Leslie Groves through 1945 and most of 1946. But by then the novelty of being in the Army had worn off, and he longed to return to civilian life. After he had recovered from Operation Crossroads, he hit the lecture circuit and began warning select audiences about the dangers of the atomic bomb. Having witnessed Trinity, the devastation in Japan, and the massive contamination from the Pacific tests, Warren seemed to have developed—at least temporarily—a dread of nuclear weapons. Some of his more candid speeches were reserved for scientists and military personnel with security clearances. But other talks were given to carefully selected groups of nonmilitary people: medical students at Massachusetts General Hospital—"no reporters"; the Rochester Medical Society—"students and MDs—no reporters"; the Chatterbox Club—"Women's Semi-professional Club—no reporters."

Warren asked General Groves for permission to tell some of the lay groups about the hazards of plutonium, noting that when the medical research was declassified it would show that plutonium "is probably the most toxic metal known, and that extremely small amounts deposited in the marrow will eventually cause progressive anemia and death years later." He continued, "I believe a frank statement of this sort should be made now to professional and intelligent lay groups as part of the general discussion on the effect of the bomb as a whole. Sooner or later one of your favorite columnists will focus attention on product [plutonium] alone and the effect on public relations will be difficult to combat. Merged with the rest, it does not appear so startling."

During a classified speech given in "Building X" on a Sunday afternoon in October 1946, Warren sketched the apocalypse he feared would come. "Soon the number of bombs which will have been let off will have made available so much radioactivity that it will seriously damage our food supplies and make serious changes in our world economy. This is not a figment of the imagination at all." To the security-cleared audience, he added the following warning:

> You need only to absorb a few micrograms of plutonium and other long-life fission materials, and then know that you are going to develop a progressive anemia or a tumor in from 5 to 15 years. This is an insidious hazard and an insidious lethal effect hard to guard against. It has a tremendous morale-destroying effect. Would you want to live in an area which was contaminated with something that was all around you which you couldn't eliminate and which would get on your clothes, in your house, in the water, in the milk, and all the food?

Warren's dire pronouncements upset many scientists at the time and have continued to rankle researchers down to the present day who feel the hazards of plutonium have been exaggerated. One person who was particularly upset when the remarks were first made was Los Alamos chemist Don Mastick. In a letter to Louis Hempelmann, Mastick wrote:

> It has recently come to my attention that Dr. Stafford Warren has made a very serious and deeply implicated statement; namely, that the long lived component of the atomic bomb (Pu, 24,000 year) is of such a nature, physiologically speaking, that all life on this planet, as we know it, would probably be extinguished by the detonation of 1,000 (one thousand) Nagasaki type atomic bombs. Thus, we have only 995 bombs to go by this reasoning . . . Due to the hidden implications in such a statement, I would like some information on this matter, purely for personal consumption.

Hempelmann dismissed Warren's comments, saying that he was surprised that Mastick gave any serious consideration to what the colonel said. "You know Staff better than that. I think that the plutonium from the thousand bombs scattered universally over the earth would do us all good (stimulates the spermatocytes—not for publication)," he wrote.

"Plutonium, next to alcohol is probably one of the better things in life. We are using it for toothpowder out here."

After getting permission from General Groves, Stafford Warren mustered out of uniform on November 3, 1946. He had spent three years and two days in the Army. Homesick for his native state of California, Warren accepted a job as the first dean of the still-to-be-built medical school at the University of California at Los Angeles.

At UCLA, Warren maintained close ties to the Atomic Energy Commission, using his wartime connections to bring lucrative AEC contracts and researchers to the university. In fact, Warren disclosed in his oral history, all of the start-up medical school faculty that he hired were funded by the AEC. He also established a classified Atomic Energy Project at UCLA modeled after Rochester's Manhattan Annex. One of the first tasks undertaken by the UCLA group was an investigation of how the radioactive fission products at Trinity were moving into the food chain, a study that AEC attorneys were initially reluctant to fund. Recalled Warren, "They were afraid we might find something. And I said, 'Well, you've got to look, because if there is something, you'd better find it and prevent further things, or pay off, and face it before there is some scandal.'"

UCLA scientists also did yearly fallout studies at the Nevada Test Site and examined people who claimed to have been injured by the radioactive debris. How committed Warren was to the Atomic Energy Project is unclear. Years later one AEC official doing a field review noted bitterly the project's *"extremely* low morale." Warren, he was told, had used the Atomic Energy Project as a place to employ his staff until the medical center was built. "Those that are left are the unwanted leftovers."

Hymer Friedell, Warren's second in command, also returned to academic life in 1946. He, too, maintained close ties with both civilian and military officials involved in atomic energy issues. He participated in some of the secret debates that occurred in the late 1940s over whether healthy prisoners should be used in total-body irradiation experiments and served on a joint military-civilian panel that oversaw biomedical research at the bomb tests. In Cleveland, at what is today known as Case Western Reserve University, Friedell established another large program called the Atomic Energy Medical Research Project. Under an AEC contract, he brought together a team of researchers to study the toxic effects of internally deposited radioisotopes and their possible applications in medicine. Every once in a while he would get a letter or a phone call from someone interested in Ebb Cade, the Oak Ridge patient injected with plutonium.

With both Stafford Warren and Hymer Friedell gone, General Groves was forced to appoint an interim director of the Manhattan Project's Medical Section for the few remaining months of its existence. He chose James Cooney, a career Army officer and radiologist who had been assigned to his staff in February of 1946. Cooney's first experience with the atomic bomb had occurred at Crossroads, where he served as one of Stafford Warren's assistants. Warren told an interviewer years later that Cooney would take off about 4:00 P.M. every afternoon for the beach club. "He wasn't about to stay up all night to see if anything was going to happen." Ironically enough, James Cooney, a stout, middle-aged man from Iowa, would go on to become one of the most powerful military leaders in the Cold War testing program.

In the ensuing years, Cooney blamed Stafford Warren for much of the public hysteria about nuclear weapons. He believed Warren "was so conservative he was a disaster," recalled Herbert Scoville, an employee in the Armed Forces Special Weapons Project and later the Central Intelligence Agency. Cooney's son, James P. Cooney Jr., said his father believed one of the biggest fear mongerers was David Bradley, the physician who wrote the 1948 book about Operations Crossroads. "He was tremendously upset about the misinformation," the son recalled.

Robert Stone returned to San Francisco, where he conducted additional human experiments with both radioisotopes and X rays. As irascible as ever, Stone locked horns with Shields Warren, the new director of the AEC's Division of Biology and Medicine, over an experiment in which Stone was administering dangerously large amounts of radiophosphorous to arthritis patients. Stone would also become a leading advocate of a controversial proposal put forth by a civilian-military group to perform total-body irradiation experiments on healthy prisoners. Lined up behind him would be many of his old allies from the Manhattan Project and the admirals and generals of the Army, Navy, and Air Force who were preparing to wage the next war on a nuclear battlefield.

The nuclear battlefield, an unthinkable Armageddon that Albert Einstein predicted would return civilization to the Stone Age, was uppermost on the minds of civilian and military war planners after Japan surrendered. How would the armed forces wage such a war? How could they defend against it? One of the scientists they turned to for advice was Joseph Hamilton, who had acquired an encyclopedic knowledge of how radioactive materials unleashed in bombs behaved in the human body. Hamilton maintained close links with the AEC and the military, frequently flying back and forth to meetings in Washington, D.C. He had become, according to his protégé, Patricia Durbin, a "walker in the corridors of power."

Hamilton's old dream, radioactive warfare, had been revitalized by Shot Baker, the spectacular underwater atomic bomb detonated at Operation Crossroads. On New Year's Eve of 1946, the day before the Manhattan Project's sprawling factories and laboratories were transferred to the AEC, Hamilton wrote a long memo to Colonel Kenneth Nichols, who directed the daily operations of the Manhattan Engineer District, describing how radioactive materials could be used to destroy cities, poison food supplies, and render uninhabitable thousands of square miles. Trivial amounts of fission products absorbed in the body could irradiate the bone marrow and produce "lethal effects," he wrote. Aerosols of radioactive materials mixed with smokes could be fatal when breathed into the lungs. "One of the principal strategic uses of fission products will probably be against the civilian population of large cities," he continued. "It can be well imagined the degree of consternation, as well as fear and apprehension, that such an agent would produce upon a large urban population after its initial use."

In his New Year's Eve memo, Hamilton advised that a full-scale investigation of rad warfare (RW) be launched by the armed services in an isolated region. His suggestion was taken seriously and implemented by the U.S. Army Chemical Corps at the Dugway Proving Ground in Utah. As an added bonus, Hamilton himself was made chairman of a panel charged with overseeing the safety for the RW experiments. On at least one occasion he flew in a plane tracking the radioactive cloud. According to the Clinton Advisory Committee, sixty-five tests were conducted at Dugway between 1949 and 1952 and more than 13,000 curies of radioactive tantalum were released into the atmosphere. The program was kept secret out of fear that the rad warfare program might cause "public anxiety," "undue public apprehension," and even "public hysteria," the committee reported. The program remained under wraps until 1974 and was largely unknown by the public until 1993. Funding for the RW program was cut in 1953, just as the Chemical Corps was proposing a huge expansion in its testing program. Its demise was probably due to budget cuts as well as practical questions about its military effectiveness, the presidential panel speculated.

Wright Langham was to make Los Alamos his base of operations for the rest of his life, becoming a familiar figure at the scene of some of the world's most hair-raising nuclear accidents. In 1966 he flew to Europe when four thermonuclear weapons were dropped near Palomares, Spain, during a midair refueling collision over the Mediterranean Sea. Two of the weapons were found intact. The other two underwent nonnuclear explosions, which resulted in the release of some fissionable fuel and some burning. Langham was also sent to Greenland in 1968 when a B-52 bomber from the U.S. Strategic Air Command that was carrying four unarmed nuclear weapons crashed seven miles west of Thule Air Force Base. The explosives in the unarmed weapons detonated, and considerable plutonium spewed over the ice.

Louis Hempelmann left Los Alamos briefly in 1946 to return to Washington University in St. Louis, but was persuaded by lab director Norris Bradbury to come back for a couple more years. With few paved streets, no sidewalks, and only a limited number of telephones, living conditions were still primitive on the mesa. Residents shopped at the post exchange and purchased other items through the mail. A series of calamities, including a water shortage, had driven all but the heartiest out of town. Robert Bacher, the unflappable scientist whom Oppenheimer confided in during the dark and uncertain days of the bomb project, later told Congress, "The technical developments during 1946 had slowed not to a stop but were so slow the motion was hard to detect."

Hempelmann and fellow physician James Nolan were almost overwhelmed by the paperwork and physical exams associated with processing civilian and military personnel who were leaving the site. Although they weren't always successful, the doctors tried to obtain blood and urine samples from departing workers to protect the project from possible lawsuits. Nolan wrote:

> With the lifting of security and the lack of pressure afforded by the war, employees at this laboratory now have many qualms about special hazards. It has been necessary for the protection of the contractor and for the morale of the worker to do things which are not absolutely necessary for the protection of workers' health. This office has attempted to make more of a "show." Nurses have been employed in the first aid rooms of outlying sites rather than G.I. first aid men.

The Los Alamos doctors also established a "milk route" to obtain urine specimens from the homes of recalcitrant employees who worked with polonium, a highly radioactive material, and consciously attempted to make safety procedures part of everyday life.

Just when the two physicians thought they were bringing the "chaos" under control, another devastating criticality accident occurred on May 21, 1946. Because the accident occurred on the eve of Operation Crossroads and at a time when sensitive negotiations were occurring over the domestic and international control of the bomb, many details of the incident remained unknown to the general public for decades.

Louis Slotin, a young Canadian-born scientist and a close friend of Harry Daghlian, had his passport ready and his bags packed for Crossroads when he decided to show his colleagues how to perform an experiment know ominously among physicists as "tickling the dragon's tail." On that fateful day in May, Slotin and a number of other scientists gathered around a table at a remote laboratory in Pajarito Canyon. One of the men standing nearest to Slotin was Alvin Graves, a member of the so-called Chicago suicide squad who had stood on a platform above Fermi's pile, ready to halt the chain reaction with neutron-absorbing cadmium.

Slotin was an intense-looking young man who had the reputation of being a daredevil. He had served in the Spanish Civil War as an antiaircraft gunner and had joined the Royal Air Force when World War II broke out. When authorities discovered he was nearsighted, he was forced to resign. On his way home to Winnipeg, Canada, he visited with a colleague in Chicago who encouraged him to join the Met Lab. Eventually Slotin transferred to Los Alamos, where he became the resident expert at the "tickling the dragon's tail" test, which was done to determine the exact amount of fissionable material needed to ignite a chain reaction. Enrico Fermi believed the test was so dangerous that he had warned Slotin, "Keep doing that experiment that way and you'll be dead within a year." Slotin shrugged off Fermi's words of caution; he had already performed the test successfully some forty times before.

Wearing a loose, open shirt and his trousers tucked into cowboy boots, Slotin stood in the middle of a large, sun-filled room and slowly lowered the upper half of a hollow beryllium hemisphere around a mass of fissionable material that was resting in a similar lower hemisphere. He held the upper sphere in his left hand with his thumb and fingers inserted in the plug hole at the top. In the other hand he held a screwdriver, which he used to keep the two shells apart. Suddenly the screwdriver slipped and the telltale blue halo appeared. "You can guess the rest," Norris Bradbury confided to several colleagues two days later. "The hemisphere fell, there was the familiar blue glow and feeling of heat in his hands."

Slotin knocked the two spheres apart and then made for the exit. Four other scientists, a technician, an engineer, and one guard who also were in the room raced out the door. Ten minutes later Slotin gathered the group around him and drew a sketch of where everyone was standing in order to help estimate how much radiation each had received.

Los Alamos scientists believed Slotin received a dose of about 800 roentgens, more than twice the lethal dose. Alvin Graves received an estimated 100 roentgens; junior scientist Allan Kline, 60 roentgens; Dwight Young, a technician, 50 roentgens; Patrick Cleary, a security guard, 30 roentgens; junior scientist Marion Cieslicki, 12 roentgens; scientist Raemer Schreiber, 8 roentgens; and Theodore Perlman, an engineer, 6 roentgens.

Alvin Graves was standing about a foot behind Slotin and was shielded from some of the radiation by Slotin's body. After Harry Daghlian was killed, Slotin and other scientists had kicked around the question of whether it was better to run away or knock apart the assembly once a chain reaction had begun. They concluded it was better to stop the reaction. "This is not because there was any possibility of an explosion," Graves once explained. "It is because one cannot run fast enough to decrease the radiation exposure as much as it would increase from the reaction itself. It is very much to his [Slotin's] credit that he had the presence of mind to remember this conclusion at such a moment. It is unquestionably true that I and perhaps others of those present owe our lives to his action."

Louis Hempelmann was in charge of the stricken scientists when they arrived at the hospital. For the third time, the doctors would have a chance to observe what would happen to a healthy person exposed to radiation from an atomic weapon without the confounding effects of blast or burn.

Slotin knew he was dying but maintained a cheerful demeanor even as his blood counts dropped, his body began to swell with fluid, and giant blisters appeared on his hands. "When we were alone together in a hospital room," Graves wrote, "he said, 'Al, I am sorry I got you into this. I am afraid I have less than a fifty-fifty chance of living. I hope you have better than that."

Slotin's decline mimicked the course followed by the Hiroshima and Nagasaki victims. A tube placed in his throat soon became painfully irritating because of the ulcers that developed on his tongue and the back of his mouth. He developed uncontrollable diarrhea, and his hands became gangrenous after the swelling had shut off the blood supply. Morphine was his only relief. "Nothing could be done to stop the steady progress of total disintegration of body functions," J. Garrot Allen, one of the treating physicians, later wrote.

On May 30, nine days after the accident, Slotin died. Philip Morrison, the scientist who had testified so eloquently on Capitol Hill about the "penetrating" effects of radiation, helped pack up Slotin's belongings and return them to his parents. Among his possessions were a pair of opera glasses and three mounted glass containers filled with Trinity sand.

Several of the other scientists who had been in the room also grew sick. Alvin Graves suffered from nausea and intermittent vomiting while he was hospitalized. He developed a fever on the fifth day, a rash on the ninth. He was discharged two weeks later but was so weak that he had to remain in bed for sixteen hours a day. Eventually the hair on his head and his beard began to fall out and his sperm disappeared altogether. Eventually he regained his strength, returned to work, and fathered healthy children.

Louis Hempelmann warned Graves to avoid further exposure in the years that followed, but Graves ignored his advice and waded more deeply into the world of atomic weapons. In 1948 he was named the leader of the Los Alamos weapons testing division and was the man considered by many to be the most influential scientist in the atmospheric testing program. Having survived his own exposure, Graves came to believe fallout worries were "concocted in the minds of weak malingerers" and recommended that radiation exposures be compared to on-the-job accidents. A dose of fifteen roentgens, for example, could be the equivalent of a "cut finger not requiring stitches," he suggested. "Such a guide would not only be useful for operational decisions but would be extremely useful for public relations purposes." But the radiation damage Graves received was not a figment of his imagination; he died about twelve years after the accident at the age of fifty-four from medical complications caused by the exposure.

Allan Kline, who was standing about four feet from the assembly, was also nauseous when he was admitted to the hospital. Like Alvin Graves, he, too, experienced a marked weakness when he was sent home. The hair on his head and eyebrows fell out, his eyes watered continually, and he complained of an inability to concentrate for more than a few moments at a time.

Kline's life took a radically different turn from Graves's. He left Los Alamos soon after the accident and returned to Chicago. According to a *New York Times* article, Kline entered Billings Hospital in December of 1946 for a battery of tests. Convinced he was being used as a guinea pig, though, he stormed out of the hospital and soon became embroiled in a dispute with Los Alamos over compensation and access to his medical records. Documents obtained from Los Alamos under the California Public Records Act show that his physician was J. J. Nickson, one of the doctors involved in the Met Lab's TBI experiments and the Chicago plutonium injections.

An attorney representing Kline charged in a 1949 letter to Brien McMahon, who by then was chairman of the new Joint Committee on Atomic Energy, that Kline had received "unusually shabby treatment" from the Manhattan Project, the AEC, and the University of California, which manages Los Alamos. "Mr. Kline was refused medical care and information at a time when he was dangerously ill from radiation and was emitting enough radiation from his body to cause a Geiger counter to react with some force," the lawyer wrote. "This refusal of treatment, dropping him from the payroll with little reserve funds about 2,000 miles from his home, in an extremely weakened radioactive and dangerous condition, and the subsequent indifference to his existence and well being constitute a very tarnished chapter in the history of the development of the atom."

In an attachment, Allan Kline described in detail the physical ailments he had suffered. The neutrons had made many molecules in his body radioactive; his teeth were so hot that a metal shield had to be placed over them to protect delicate mouth tissues; his skin became so sensitive to the sun's ultraviolet rays that it swelled perceptively; he was completely sterile; he required frequent naps or sleep totaling up to twelve to fifteen hours a day; and he was unable to walk up a short flight of stairs without becoming completely exhausted. Worst of all, Kline was not even allowed to see his own medical reports. As a consequence, he began seeing private physicians. Ironically, those doctors were not informed of the origins of Kline's physical complaints because of secrecy rules. He wrote:

> I was actually used as a guinea pig during this whole period as no medication or treatment was given me for my recovery, nor was any advised. All any of the physicians did was to check my physical condition and subject me to very long, uncomfortable tests

and the results of these tests then became the property of the U.S. Government, and I was not given access to them. This condition still exists. This amounted to a denial of medical care.

Records that were not declassified until the mid-1990s show that Kline was being used as a guinea pig in other ways. Louis Hempelmann carefully collected the data from Kline's exposure and the other healthy men injured in the criticality accidents and used it in later years when military and civilian officials in Washington were trying to predict what would happen to soldiers on an atomic battlefield.

Kline, who is still alive and living in California, spoke in general terms about the accident, but did not answer specific questions about his health or legal issues related to his case. He is a classic example of what President Clinton's Advisory Committee came to refer to as an "experiment of opportunity." That is, he was not the subject of an experiment per se, but his exposure provided scientists with a unique opportunity to collect data.

Louis Hempelmann remained at Los Alamos until 1948, when he joined the University of Rochester medical school, where he was to remain for the rest of his career. Like the other Manhattan Project doctors, Hempelmann maintained his close ties with the AEC. He was always one of the first experts called upon whenever someone was injured by radiation.

19

THE AEC AND
THE POLITICS OF SECRECY

At the stroke of midnight on January 1, 1947, the wartime empire belonging to the Army's Manhattan Engineer District was officially transferred to the new, civilian-run Atomic Energy Commission, which was headquartered in Washington, D.C. The complex was scattered over thirteen states and included more than 2,000 military personnel, 4,000 government employees, and 38,000 employees of contractors. On December 24, six days before the transfer, U.S. Army Col. Kenneth Nichols, who directed the daily operations of the Manhattan Project from a rambling administration building in Oak Ridge known as the castle, sent the following memo to the Manhattan District's representative in Berkeley:

> The first paragraph of this report indicates that certain radioactive substances are being prepared for intravenous administration to human subjects as part of the work of the contract. . . . It is felt that such work does not come under the scope of the Manhattan District Program and should not be made a part of its research plan. It is therefore deemed advisable by this office not only to recommend against work on human subjects but also to deny authority for such work under the terms of the Manhattan contract. You will take immediate action to stop this work under this contract, and report to this office upon compliance.

The stop-order apparently was triggered by a progress report written by Joseph Hamilton and sent to Oak Ridge a month earlier. In his usual dry language, Hamilton had advised his superiors that "suitable solutions" of uranium, americium, and plutonium were being prepared for "intravenous administration to human subjects." He had sent many similar reports to the Manhattan Project, and there was nothing remarkable about his statements. But suddenly, the bomb builders found that the research was unacceptable. The abrupt policy change is one of the most inexplicable events surrounding the plutonium injections. Were Colonel Nichols and General Groves, who were about to lose control of their empire, trying to clean up the paper trail so it would appear as if they hadn't known about or supported the human experiments? Was Nichols objecting to the ethical implications? Did he feel that the injections did not fall within the wartime contract between the Rad Lab and the Manhattan District? Or could there have been other reasons for the stop order?

Records that have surfaced so far don't fully explain what was going on, but at least one document suggests that Nichols, who had been appointed by Groves to serve as a liaison to the AEC, may have felt that the decision to continue such studies should be made by the Manhattan Project's civilian successor. In fact, a memo sent to Berkeley on January 8, 1947, indicates that AEC officials did want to review the human studies: "Until the Atomic Energy Commission is able to consider sponsoring this type of experimentation, authorization cannot be given for the use of radioactive materials in human subjects under this contract."

Other events going on in the world might have been making General Groves and Colonel Nichols jittery. Throughout the summer and fall of 1946, American prosecutors were preparing for a historic trial in Nuremberg, Germany. In December of that year, twenty-three medical doctors, including Hitler's personal physician, went on trial for assorted crimes involving murder and torture performed in the name of medical science. Even before the trial began, the American Medical Association (AMA) went on record with guidelines for ethical human experiments. The three rules published by the AMA required the voluntary and understanding consent of the subject, prior animal experimentation, and appropriate medical supervision.

An editorial writer for the *Journal of the American Medical Association* pointed out that the guiding principle behind ethical human experiments was the voluntary consent of the subject. "In the American army," he wrote, "the tradition is well established that human beings, even under military conditions, are not ordered to submit to procedures that violate the sanctity of their own persons." Alluding to the medical experiments conducted in Nazi Germany's concentration camps, the editorial writer pointed out that the medical profession in the United States would rally behind any enlisted officer who refused to conduct an unethical human experiment, even if ordered to do so by the "highest political leaders."

It's likely that some Manhattan Project officials saw the editorial. One AEC official, writing years later, noted that as early as 1946, "doubts were expressed concerning the ethics of the [plutonium] study. At one time, consideration was given to referring the matter to the A.M.A. ethics committee but this was not done."

But Stafford Warren, who was just getting settled in at his new job at UCLA, had no ethical qualms, at least initially, about the radioisotope injections and wanted to continue them. Warren chaired an interim committee that provided advice to the AEC on the future course of its research. Not surprisingly, much of the proposed research was slated for the doctors who had done the wartime work, including Stafford Warren himself. "It is the opinion of this Committee," Warren wrote on January 30, 1947, "that in the further study of health hazards and of the utilization of fissionable and radioactive, and other materials, final investigations by clinical testing of these materials will be necessary under the proper and usual safeguards."

Always conscious of litigation, Warren suggested that the AEC's legal department determine what the commission's "financial and legal" obligations were when "clinical testing" was done. Warren didn't explain what he meant by "clinical testing," but presumably he was referring to the kind of studies being done by Joseph Hamilton, Robert Stone, and scientists at Rochester's Manhattan Annex.

Warren's request landed on the desk of Carrol Wilson, the AEC's boyish-looking general manager. An engineer and an MIT graduate, Wilson had been appointed by President Truman just days before the transfer occurred. His uncle, Frank J. Wilson, one of the AEC's security consultants, had headed up the income tax investigation of Al Capone and also was responsible for the recording of the serial numbers of the bills that led to the capture of the Lindbergh baby kidnapper.

Under Carroll Wilson's direction, the AEC developed new rules for human experiments, which were summarized in a letter sent to Stafford Warren at UCLA on April 30, 1947. The commission would allow human experiments with radioactive materials to continue provided several conditions were met. First, no experiment could be undertaken unless the procedure was expected to benefit the patient. Second, the medical file should contain documentation showing the patient understood the procedure and agreed to it. The experiment, Wilson cautioned:

> should be susceptible of proof from official records that, prior to treatment, each individual patient, being in an understanding state of mind, was clearly informed of the nature of the treatment and its possible effects, and expressed his willingness to receive the treatment. In view of your recommendation, the Commission does not request that written releases be obtained in such cases, but it does request that in every case at least two doctors should certify in writing (made part of an official record) to the patient's understanding state of mind, to the explanation furnished him, and to his willingness to accept the treatment.

Wilson's guidelines were strong and unambiguous, but when Joseph Hamilton and his Berkeley colleagues injected Hanford Jang and Elmer Allen a few months later, they flatly ignored this first rule. Wilson had made it clear that radiation experiments could proceed only if the patients might benefit. Neither the americium nor the plutonium was expected to benefit the two California patients.

The Berkeley experimenters could not plead ignorance, because Wilson had ordered the letter outlining the new guidelines to be circulated to all of the AEC's area managers. And it is obvious that the letter had been disseminated to the Berkeley scientists because the so-called consent form in Elmer Allen's file repeats almost verbatim parts of Wilson's directive. The records made public so far do not explain why the Berkeley group ignored AEC policies. But it was not the first time, nor would it be the last time, such a violation occurred.

About the time that Hanford Jang and Elmer Allen were injected, a new blue-ribbon panel of experts was brought together to help the AEC further define its research goals. This panel, called the Medical Board of Review, urged that even more restrictive guidelines governing human radiation experiments be implemented. The review board recommended that doctors obtain not only the patient's informed consent in writing but also the written informed consent of the most responsible nearest of kin. It is not known if the review board recommended the tighter restrictions in response to Hamilton's continuing experiments, or if the board even knew about those studies. But it is clear that this recommendation became part of the official AEC policy. In a November 5, 1947, letter to Robert Stone, who was also at Berkeley, Carroll Wilson summarized the review board's guidelines and explained why and under what conditions it was allowing human radiation experiments to proceed:

> The atmosphere of secrecy and suppression makes one aspect of the medical work of the Commission especially vulnerable to criticism. We therefore wish to record our approval of the position taken by the medical staff of the AEC in point of their studies of the substances dangerous to human life. We believe that no substances known to be, or suspected of being, poisonous or harmful should be given to human beings unless all of the following conditions are fully met: (a) that a reasonable hope exists that the administration of such a substance will improve the condition of the patient, (b) that the patient give his complete and informed consent in writing, and (c) that the responsible nearest of kin give in writing a similarly complete and informed consent, revocable at any time during the course of such treatment. Were it not for the extreme value and pressure for securing reliable information on the limits of human tolerance of radioactive substances there would be no need for explicit reference to this subject. We wish to see immediate and steady increase in this gravely important subject of human tolerance to radioactivity, but we believe that since secrecy must of necessity mark much of the medical research supported by the federally-sponsored AEC, particular care must be taken in all matters that under other circumstances would be open to investigation and publicity.

Thousands of human radiation experiments, many of them unethical and without therapeutic benefit, were funded by the AEC over the next three decades of the Cold War. But Wilson's two letters show unequivocally that within the first year of its creation, the commission had clear, strongly worded rules governing such experiments. Although President Clinton's Advisory Committee on Human Radiation Experiments pointed out that Wilson's second letter contained the earliest known use of the term "informed consent," the historic significance in this document seems to have been lost on them. They mentioned the letter then all but dismissed it, saying the standards it enunciated may not have received wide circulation. "Maybe it means Wilson was just a good writer," speculated Ruth Faden, who chaired the panel. But Joseph Volpe, who worked as an attorney at AEC headquarters at that time and knew Carroll Wilson personally, said that it was "inconceivable that [Wilson] didn't see that this policy reached everyone in the organization."

At the same time Carroll Wilson and his lawyers were drawing up new rules for ethical human experiments in the future, the commission began to cover up any evidence of the plutonium injections from the past. The cover-up is well documented in memos, many of which remained classified for fifty years. What's not clear is who specifically decided that the experiments should be kept secret and who ordered the cover-up.

The Atomic Energy Commission had squeaked into existence following a year of congressional battles and behind-the-scenes struggles. Not surprisingly, the general manager and the appointed commissioners were eager to prevent news of a possible scandal from reaching a public already apprehensive about atomic bombs. The AEC was intent upon making atomic energy as unthreatening as electricity; public disclosure of the injections would have damaged the commission's bomb-building program and its efforts to build a civilian nuclear power industry.

With the ruthlessness of a political ward boss, the AEC suppressed all evidence of the plutonium injections and other human experiments and embarked on a deliberate campaign to squelch information that could tarnish its prestige, promote lawsuits, or cause embarrassment. Scientific reports were regularly scrutinized by the commission's classification officials as well as by employees who worked in its medical and insurance departments. Wrote the medical advisor in Oak Ridge:

> There are a large number of papers which do not violate security, but do cause considerable concern to the Atomic Energy Commission Insurance Branch and may well compromise the public prestige and best interests of the Commission. Papers referring to levels of soil and water contamination surrounding Atomic Energy Commission installations, idle speculation on the future genetic effects of radiation and papers dealing with potential process hazards to employees are definitely prejudicial to the best interests of the government. Every such release is reflected in an increase in insurance claims, increased difficulty in labor relations and adverse public sentiment. Following consultation with the Atomic Energy Commission Insurance Branch, the following declassification criteria appears desirable. If specific locations or activities of the Atomic Energy Commission and/or its contractors are closely associated with statements and informa-

tion which would invite or tend to encourage claims against the Atomic Energy Commission or its contractors, such portions of articles to be published should be reworded or deleted.

Three scientific papers on the plutonium injections had been completed at the time of the advisor's warnings: The Chicago scientists had written a 1946 report describing the injections and postmortem analyses of injectees Arthur Hubbard and Una Macke. The Berkeley group had written the 1946 "Man and Rat" paper describing the injection of house painter Albert Stevens. And Samuel Bassett and Wright Langham were putting together the collaborative report on the Los Alamos–Rochester injection program, which would be published in 1950. The paper describing the plutonium injections of Macke and Hubbard, which had been declassified and then reclassified "restricted," was one of the first articles to set off the AEC alarm bells. An AEC declassification official, C. L. Marshall, warned that the distribution of the report could have dire consequences for the fledgling commission. (Marshall is the same official who blocked the release of Hamilton's "Man and Rat" paper on grounds that it might adversely affect the national interest.) Marshall's memo proves conclusively that AEC officials covered up the experiment because of fear of lawsuits and adverse publicity:

> This document appears to be the most dangerous since it describes experiments performed on human subjects, including the actual injection of the metal, plutonium, into the body. The locations of these experiments are given and the results, even to the autopsy findings in two cases. It is unlikely that these tests were made without the consent of the subjects, but no statement is made to that effect and the coldly scientific manner in which the results are tabulated and discussed would have a very poor effect on the general public. Unless, of course, the legal aspects were covered by the necessary documents, the experimenters and the employing agencies, including the U.S., have been laid open to a devastating lawsuit which would, through its attendant publicity, have far reaching results.

The declassification officer's opinion was seconded by Birchard Brundage, an Army major in Oak Ridge who went on to work with Stafford Warren at UCLA. "It would be unwise to release the paper," he agreed, "primarily because of medical legal aspects in the use of plutonium in human beings." Brundage added that Warren felt that since plutonium was not available for offsite work, it was not "essential" to distribute the paper. Norris Bradbury, Oppenheimer's successor, had doubts about the wisdom of completing the Los Alamos report on the injections because of the "attitude taken by the AEC in regard to this type of research." And Andrew Dowdy, the supervisor of the University of Rochester's Manhattan Annex, requested on February 18, 1947, that the report not be declassified for general distribution outside the AEC without Rochester's foreknowledge. "I make this suggestion because of possible unfavorable public relations and in an attempt to protect Dr. Bassett from any possible legal entanglements," he stated.

But some of the experimenters were eager to have their work published, and a dispute, only vaguely discernible from the exchange of memos, arose between the bureaucrats and the scientists. The AEC on April 17 then issued a blanket order:

> It is desired that no document be released which refers to experiments with humans and might have adverse effect on public opinion or result in legal suits. Documents covering such work field should be classified "secret." Further work in this field in the future has been prohibited by the General Manager. It is understood that three documents in this field have been submitted for declassification and are now classified "restricted." It is desired that these documents be reclassified "secret" and that a check be made to insure that no distribution has inadvertently been made to the Department of Commerce, or other off-Project personnel or agencies.

It's not clear what three documents the AEC memo was referring to, but undoubtedly one was the Arthur Hubbard–Una Macke paper written by the Chicago group, and a second may have dealt with the uranium injections administered at Rochester. An additional item in the memo further confirms that the AEC knew the plutonium experiment was of no medical benefit and clearly distinguishes between such experiments and studies that might help patients: "These instructions," the memo added, "do not pertain to documents regarding clinical or therapeutic uses of radioisotopes and similar materials beneficial to human disorders and diseases."

20

SHIELDS WARREN:
"PATRIOTIC ENOUGH TO LIE"

While bureaucrats within the Atomic Energy Commission were putting together new rules for future human experiments and trying to bury the evidence of old ones, Shields Warren, who had been part of the first Navy inspection team to go to Japan shortly after the bombings, returned to that country for another look. His mission this time was to help set up a study of the surviving bombing victims and their descendants. Japan was rebuilding itself when Warren arrived in the spring of 1947. Freshly cut lumber was being brought into the cities. New buildings were going up, their sides covered with corrugated iron or flattened tin cans. The roads had been greatly improved. "People more alert, many smiling, look fat and well-fed. Striking change," he wrote.

Warren worked with a "compulsive zeal," a colleague recalled, snacking on "cranberries in any form and crackers." He visited hospitals and doctors in Nagasaki and Hiroshima, occasionally examining patients who were still suffering from injuries received during the bombings. Many still had low blood counts and keloids, ugly overgrowths of scar tissue that occurred following thermal burns. Warren examined fifty-seven people. Some underwent sternal bone marrow biopsies, a procedure in which a small core of marrow is removed from the thin bone of the breast. During one biopsy, a needle broke and had to be extracted with pliers. When the patient shunned a second biopsy, Warren noted in his diary, "Stoicism of the Japanese not too marked."

Soon after he returned to the United States, Albert Baird Hastings and Alan Gregg, both members of the AEC's Medical Board of Review, the panel that had been convened briefly in 1947 to help the commission chart its new research program, approached Warren with a job offer. Was he interested in becoming the interim director of the AEC's Division of Biology and Medicine? This was not the first time Warren had been approached to do work for America's nuclear establishment. When the United States entered World War II, Shields Warren was a reserve officer in the Navy. In early 1943 Stafford Warren paid him a visit. He "told me that I had exactly the skills that he needed for a project that he was involved with but couldn't tell me anything about it and would I leave the Navy and take this on? Well, I told him that I thought I was being useful where I was and didn't feel that while the war was on I could move around like a free agent and so I did not come into early contact with the Manhattan Project." In 1947, however, the time was right. "There were so many opportunities and such fine people to work with in this new Atomic Energy set-up that it was one of those challenging things I couldn't pass up," he said in an interview which was filmed in 1974 and later converted to videotape.

Warren was a pathologist at that time with the New England Deaconess Hospital in Boston, a position he maintained on a part-time basis during his AEC years. He commuted from Boston to Washington, D.C., lugging back and forth a fat briefcase filled with documents. At the age of forty-nine, the expressive face of his youth had been winnowed down by the years: the full lips thinned and pressed against words that sometimes came haltingly, the eyes inscrutable behind spectacles, and lines of fatigue coursing down his cheeks. He could function efficiently on five hours of sleep but confessed that as he grew older, he had been forced to lengthen his usual rest to six or six and one-half hours a night. He worked six days a week, as he would continue to do until his seventies, and spoke in a slow deliberate voice in order to camouflage what one colleague described as a "gentle stammer."

Warren was the ideal man to head up the AEC's biomedical programs. He was a highly regarded scientist who had already made several important discoveries related to cancer. Early in his career, he had discovered that cancerous cells might be transported through the body by the lymphatic system, a finding that led to the practice of removing lymph nodes near cancerous tissue. He was also an expert on the effects of radiation on the human body. But even more important, he had the sophistication to navigate Washington's political waters.

Warren was probably the most influential biomedical scientist in AEC history and one of the enigmas of the Cold War. From 1947 to 1952 he helped the commission cobble together a vast network of national laboratories, universities, and hospitals that would investigate every imaginable effect of radiation over the next three decades. The research was part of the AEC's dual mandate under the 1946 Atomic Energy Act to both promote atomic energy and protect the public from its harmful effects. Through grants, fellowships, contracts, construction projects, and the funding of huge machines, the AEC created a new industry and became one of the largest sponsors of scientific research in the United States.

Warren arrived at the AEC when the nuclear weapons program was in its infancy. Only five atomic bombs had been exploded—one at Trinity, two in Japan, and two at Crossroads. By the time he left in June of 1952, the arms race with the Soviet Union was well under way and the atmospheric testing program had become part of American life. Policy decisions Warren and other postwar researchers made during those years have affected the health of generations of Americans. For the atomic veterans and residents who lived downwind of the test site and the weapons plants, those decisions would have tragic consequences and spawn a bitter debate that continues to this day.

After overcoming his initial doubts, Warren supported the first atomic bomb test in Nevada, in 1951, during which dangerous amounts of fallout were released and people living downwind were put at risk. The "ominous" implications of inhaling alpha particles from fallout, which had been brought to Warren's attention by Joseph Hamilton in 1949, were glossed over and the food chain dangers ignored. Warren also participated in the debates over the placement of troops in Nevada. He repeatedly protested the reckless, short-sighted plans of the armed forces, only to capitulate or be overruled by his superiors. In time, volunteer soldiers would find themselves crouching in trenches one mile from Ground Zero, and specially trained pilots would be directed to fly straight into the hot, gaseous heart of thermonuclear clouds.

During the highly emotional fallout controversy that began in the mid-1950s, Warren aligned himself with such passionate advocates of the testing program as Edward Teller and Nobel laureate Willard Libby. He agreed with the no-danger chorus of scientists who claimed that the biological risks from fission products were negligible. He also took the position, which has since been largely rejected by the scientific community, that there exists a threshold dose of radiation below which no damage will occur.

Records show that Warren routinely suppressed information that might provoke lawsuits or harm the AEC's public image, and dealt brutally with outsiders. Yet documents declassified in 1994 and 1995 also reveal a courageous scientist who spoke out in secret meetings against proposed human radiation experiments. One of his most heroic battles centered around the ill-fated plan supported by Robert Stone and others to expose prisoners serving life sentences to total-body irradiation, a process that undoubtedly would have led to the shortening of the subjects' lives and the possible development of cancer. Warren's admirers viewed him with a deferential awe; his enemies saw an opportunist who shifted with the political wind. "He was a god to me," recalled fellow pathologist Clarence Lushbaugh, who worked at both Los Alamos and Oak Ridge. "I considered him a saint," said retired Air Force Colonel John Pickering.

"I was never quite sure what he was up to," remembered physicist Howard Andrews. "I shouldn't say that, but I never really quite trusted this man. I worked with him, and we wrote a couple of papers together having to do with frogs and oysters and things of that sort. But as far as things that went on in some fields, I thought he was a little slippery."

San Antonio physician Herman Wigodsky said he didn't think Warren "was too swift." And retired physiologist Nello Pace said Warren was "kind of a turkey, full of himself—not like Stafford. Stafford was just wonderful. But Shields was very old-fashioned in his attitude that some M.D.s have: 'Only M.D.s and God can touch people.'"

Even in 1950, when Joseph McCarthy was making charges in the Senate about the Communist leanings of AEC scientists, documents show Warren was fearless in the closed-door showdowns with admirals and generals. But he was at heart a practical man, flinty and cold as the New England soil his forefathers settled on in the 1600s and fully capable of playing the villain. "You must realize," fellow scientist Merril Eisenbud once said of Warren, "some people are patriotic enough to lie."

Shields Warren was born in 1898, just two years after Stafford Warren, into an old New England family of Methodist ministers, educators, and farmers. His baby name was "Shewannie." One of his grandfathers was the first president of Boston University; the other was a friend of Theodore Roosevelt and the "unwilling lawyer" for Mark Twain. His father was a philosophy professor at Boston University and dean of the school of liberal arts.

His earliest memories were of Cape Cod: the smell of salt marshes and tide pools and the choppy north Atlantic, somnolent and calm under a June sky. Using a cloud as a light source, the young Warren focused the lens of his first mail-order microscope on the organisms in the tide pool.

Their translucent, geometrical shapes burst into view and he was hooked. Between Greek and Latin classes at a public school in Brookline, Massachusetts, he crammed in science courses, preparing himself for a career in zoology.

Like his father and grandfather, Warren also attended Boston University. He graduated in 1918 with a bachelor's degree and immediately enrolled in the Army. He came down with the flu in artillery training camp, and while he was recovering, Armistice was declared. "The mortality was terribly heavy," he remembered in a 1972 oral history interview. "This convinced me that there ought to be a better way of doing medicine than this, and while I was convalescing I made up my mind that medicine was what I wanted to do."

Warren decided to enroll in medical school at Harvard. In the meantime, he had a small "grubstake" from the Army and nearly a year off, so he decided to see America—by rail. "I decided the best way of doing this would be to hobo." Warren worked his way across America, experiencing a slice of life that young, well-bred men such as himself rarely saw. He stoked a freight train through the Rockies, worked in the shipyards in Portland, flipped pancakes in a lumberjack camp in the Pacific Northwest, picked fruit in California, and cut wheat in Oklahoma. The hobo life left him with a sense of self-sufficiency and the feeling that he could meet any challenge.

Warren graduated from medical school in 1923. Following another trip, this time to Europe, he joined the faculty of Harvard Medical School and continued to teach there until he retired. When he was a young resident, he autopsied several patients with Hodgkin's disease and learned to his amazement that they had died not from the disease, but from the radiation treatment they'd been given. "Apparently nobody knew what happened when anybody had been irradiated," he recalled. At the time of his AEC appointment, he was the author of "The Effects of Radiation on Normal Tissues," a compilation of scientific papers, which the AEC considered the definitive work of the time regarding the effects of radiation on the human body.

Warren maintained a punishing schedule during his first few years on the job, making regular loops to the Manhattan Project's laboratories at Los Alamos, Chicago, and Berkeley and its monolithic uranium and plutonium-producing factories in Oak Ridge, Tennessee, and eastern Washington state. During the trips, he tried to assess the health risks to workers and pollution problems. One of the first things he wanted to make sure of, he told AEC officials years later, was that there were no "epidemics" brewing at the former Manhattan Project sites.

By 1947 the AEC was acutely aware that radioactive waste was going to be a huge problem. Government officials debated whether to dump the material in the oceans, store it in vaults until radioactive decay had progressed sufficiently, collect it in garbage cans and bury it on federal property, or shoot it into space by "interplanetary rockets." At Hanford a biologist had discovered that radioactivity levels in fish in the nearby Columbia River were on an average 100,000 times greater than the radioactivity in the water itself. But Hanford officials were determined to keep the information from becoming public: "It is recommended that all river contamination studies indicating the extent to which aquatic life in rivers concentrate and hold radioactivity should be classified 'Secret,' " an official wrote in 1948. "It is further suggested that all problems related to radioactive contamination of our rivers be tightly held until reasonable solutions to these problems are available."

Warren spent the first few months on the job trying to get a handle on what was going on. "When I took over at AEC, we had to pick up threads at each installation, and find out from the people there what had been going on, what the local practices were," he said. "There were zero records that I received when I came to AEC and [I] had to depend primarily on word of mouth and the medical regulations and what medical history I could get from contractor personnel of the various installations."

Around Christmas of 1947, Shields Warren met with Joseph Hamilton. The two doctors, both lean, well-dressed men, were reminiscing about the early days of radioisotopes when suddenly the conversation veered into dangerous territory. Warren told AEC investigators, who interviewed him in 1974 about the plutonium injections, that he and Hamilton had been discussing "isotopic injection" when Hamilton made an oblique reference to the "utilization of plutonium." Hamilton began the conversation by saying that Warren must have a "shrewd suspicion" about the radioisotope research the Berkeley group had done during the war. Warren replied that he was aware of the work from Hamilton's published reports. "Yes, but there are some unpublished things that you probably haven't heard of," Warren remembered Hamilton saying.

Then Hamilton plunged into the details of the three plutonium injection cases in California. At the time of Hamilton's disclosure, Albert Stevens was trying to restart his house painting business, Simmy Shaw was dead, and Elmer Allen had just been seen in UCSF's outpatient clinic several weeks earlier. (". . . feels fine, has gained weight, has good stump," a doctor noted in his medical chart.)

"I had not known of any work in humans in plutonium up to that time. So I talked with him a little bit about it, and we did not get any facts, figures or numbers," Warren told AEC investigators. The two men did discuss whether the California patients gave consent for the injections because doctors at the time were "reasonably sensitive" about that issue. "You know," he quoted Hamilton as saying, "we have had something of a problem in this because there were very rigid restrictions on the use of the word 'plutonium' and the handling of the material and letting anyone know that there was any such stuff." Warren continued:

> Dr. Hamilton told me that he had explained to the patients that they would receive—now I've got to put my thoughts in order in this—that they would receive an injection of a new substance that was too new to say what it might do but that it had some properties like those of other substances that had been used to help growth processes in patients, or something of that general sort. You could not call it informed consent because they (the patients) did not know what it was, but they knew that it was a new, and to them, unknown substance.

Warren said he became concerned when he heard about the injections. "All I knew about plutonium—there was practically nothing written down that was available—was that it was very nasty stuff." Following the meeting, Warren talked the matter over with his trusted colleague, Alan Gregg. "We've got a sticky problem here," Warren quoted Gregg as saying.

Warren said he eventually learned by "osmosis" that additional patients had been injected with plutonium in Rochester, Chicago, and Oak Ridge. "One might say I would pick up a stray bit of information one place or another." He said he assumed records on the experiment existed, but he did not see them. "And when I inquired of Bob Stone, he said he thought it depended primarily on people's memories."

Warren and Gregg ordered new rules drawn up by the radioisotope distribution committee, a panel that approved the use of radioisotopes in human research. Then the two men let the matter drop. "We saw no point in bringing this up after the fact as long as we were sure that nothing of this sort could happen in the future. This is because we assumed that those patients were all dead at that time."

Warren said he did not know of the "continuing contact" some of the scientists had with the plutonium patients during his tenure. "To the best of my knowledge, from the time that I took over, there were not any injections made. And I would have insisted that they not be made if this had been brought up to me at that time."

Documents and excerpts from Warren's own diaries reveal that events surrounding Joseph Hamilton's disclosure were not quite the way Warren described them. Nor was his role quite so innocent. These records suggest that Warren learned the full extent of the plutonium experiment almost immediately, not years later as he implied in his interview with AEC investigators. Recently released documents also show that Warren's employees at AEC headquarters in 1950 authorized additional metabolic studies on Eda Schultz Charlton and John Mousso, two of the Rochester plutonium patients. The documentation makes it highly unlikely that Warren himself was not aware of the "continuing contact" with those patients or that he did not know that some subjects were still alive. Some newly declassified records also suggest that Warren may have even directed trusted colleagues to make low-key inquiries. One such document is the 1948 transcript of the telephone conversation with Rochester physician Joseph Howland in which he is asked about Ebb Cade.

Autocratic by nature, quiet and self-contained, not prone to emotional outbursts or idle chatter, Shields Warren quickly adapted to the AEC's culture of secrecy, maintaining the classification policies that had begun to be formulated in early 1947, before he arrived. Biological, medical, and environmental reports that might promote lawsuits or have an adverse affect on public relations were routinely classified and locked away from public view. Shields Warren was just as determined as AEC general manager Carroll Wilson to keep the plutonium experiment concealed. In 1948, for example, he refused to declassify two reports dealing with the injections and agreed to the publication of the 1950 Los Alamos report coauthored by Wright Langham and Samuel Bassett provided the document be given a "confidential" classification and that its circulation be limited.

A wealth of records released in the mid-1990s show unequivocally that the AEC covered up the plutonium experiment in part because of embarrassment. But Warren denied in the AEC interview that embarrassment was a factor: "I don't think we thought of it from that angle carefully at that time. We regarded it [the experiment] as an accomplished fact that we would not ourselves do."

Warren was also hesitant about letting Robert Stone publish a paper on one of the wartime TBI experiments because he feared the report would bring adverse publicity or lawsuits. Stone was infuriated by Warren's hesitation and dashed off a heated letter: "With regard to the first statement concerning adverse publicity, I thought this item was taken care of when we stated in the paper that the patients were incurable by any known means of therapy," he said. "With regard to the lawsuit part of the program, I think that this could be taken care of readily by the elimination of the initials of the patients. I must confess that the inclusion of the initials of the patients slipped past my editorial eye or they would have been taken out. With the initials removed, there will be no means by which the patients can ever connect themselves up with the report."

Shields Warren was also worried about releasing a report by Los Alamos scientist Norman Knowlton that described the blood changes in a group of chemists exposed to an average of 0.2 roentgens of gamma rays per week in Bayo Canyon. Located three miles east of Los Alamos, Bayo Canyon is the site where the implosion studies for the atomic bomb were done. Knowlton had found "highly significant decreases" in the blood counts of ten scientists who worked there between December 1946 and June 1948 in comparison to a control group of twenty-four individuals who received no exposure. An AEC insurance official cautioned against the release of Knowlton's report:

> The results of the studies indicate that the tolerance levels for chronic exposure to gamma radiation which have been accepted both within the A.E.C. and elsewhere may be too high. We can see the possibility of a shattering effect on the morale of the employees if they become aware that there was substantial reason to question the standards of safety under which they are working. In the hands of labor unions the results of this study would add substance to demands for extra-hazardous pay. We can also see the definite possibility that general knowledge of the results of this study might increase the number of claims of occupational injury due to radiation and place a powerful weapon in the hands of a plaintiff's attorney.

(Knowlton's report eventually was published, and none of the terrifying scenarios predicted by the AEC declassification officer materialized. Knowlton, who now lives in St. Louis, Missouri, said that he still has "no idea" what caused the blood changes. He said he subsequently obtained "piles of blood counts" from exposed and nonexposed workers and took them to a statistician in New York to analyze, but they could find no correlation between exposures and blood changes.)

Warren used friendly persuasion to get what he wanted and raw power when necessary. He maintained cordial relationships with many Manhattan Project scientists, including doctors like Robert Stone with whom he had strong professional disagreements. But in early 1952 Warren allegedly attempted to ruin the career of one scientist outside the inner circle who raised serious questions about radiation hazards in the uranium mines.

Wilhelm Hueper, an outspoken scientist at the National Cancer Institute, had been invited by the Colorado State Medical Society to present a paper at its annual meeting in Denver on the cancer hazards that workers in the unventilated mines on the Colorado Plateau faced. Drawing on a seventy-five-year history of lung cancer incidents among miners at Schneeberg, Germany, and at Joachimsthal, Czechoslovakia, Hueper described the similar hazards that U.S. miners, many of whom were Native Americans, were exposed to from the radioactive gas and dust. In his unpublished autobiography, Hueper said that the director of the AEC's Division of Biology and Medicine then ordered him to eliminate all references to hazards in the mines, and subsequently suggested that he be dismissed for using bad judgment. Shocked, Hueper told his supervisor at the National Cancer Institute that he had not joined the organization "to be made into a scientific liar."

Hueper did not lose his job, and went on to warn against other radioactive materials that were potentially hazardous. One was nasopharyngeal irradiation, a practice in which radium applicators were inserted in the nostrils. Thousands of Navy submariners and Army Air Force pilots underwent the procedure in order to alleviate obstructions of the eustachian tube; and hundreds of thousands of children with chronic colds and sore throats or inflammatory changes in the tonsils and adenoids were also subjected to the procedure.

The treatment of the uranium miners remains one of the scandals of the Cold War. Hundreds of miners have died, and many are still dying, from lung cancer caused by radioactive dust and gases trapped in the unventilated mines. Stewart Udall, a former Interior Secretary who waged a decade-long battle to obtain compensation for the miners, questioned Shields Warren about Hueper's allegations a year before Warren died. Warren did not dispute the accuracy of Hueper's story, Udall later wrote.

21

"WRAPPED IN THE FLAG"

Under Shields Warren's steady hand, a vast new empire devoted to radiation research sprang up in the United States. The research, Warren informed Congress, was necessary not only for the advancement of science but to ensure "our very survival." With the terrible visions of Hiroshima and Nagasaki still fresh in their memories, the Manhattan Project doctors and scientists already had staked out their own large piece of the action in this burgeoning new world. But the money was flowing freely and there was plenty of room for newcomers. In fact, the AEC actively encouraged them. Recruitment and training of young scientists was one of the five major components of the commission's biomedical program. The others were: continuation and expansion of wartime research into the effects of ionizing radiation; follow-up studies of the Japanese bombing victims; the development of a nationwide cancer research program; and the distribution and sale of radioisotopes for medical and industrial research. (Plutonium and uranium, which could be used in weapons, were not for sale.)

In mid-1946, the Manhattan Project began aggressively hawking radioisotopes produced in its Oak Ridge reactor to qualified researchers. These isotopes, which included such materials as radioactive iron, iodine, phosphorous, calcium, and sodium, were used as diagnostic tools to help locate a malignancy or malfunctioning organ and, in basic research, aimed at better understanding the body's metabolic processes. By tagging red blood cells with radioactive iron, for instance, researchers could learn more about how long those blood cells lived. Or, since radioactive iodine has an affinity for the thyroid gland—a small butterfly-shaped gland at the base of the throat—by measuring the rate at which the iodine was absorbed they can learn a lot about how well the thyroid was operating. As MIT scientist Robley Evans explained in a 1946 *Atlantic Monthly* article, "The radioactive isotopes are actually spies which go around unrecognized in the company of normal atoms of the same chemical type and at a later time reveal in detail the movements of the normal atoms which they accompany." When scientists first began investigating the medical uses of radioisotopes in the 1930s, they hoped they might find the proverbial magic bullet that would destroy cancer cells, but by the end of the 1940s they realized that most isotopes would function primarily as diagnostic tools.

Researchers throughout the United States used the radioisotopes in thousands of human experiments. As these experiments involved minute amounts of radioactive materials, they are often called "tracer studies." A few of the radioisotope experiments did involve large amounts of radioactive materials, which caused severe injury and death.

The Manhattan Project's first shipment of radioisotopes went to the Barnard Free Skin & Cancer Hospital in St. Louis, Missouri. Within twelve months, 1,092 shipments of more than "100 varieties" of radioisotopes had been sent from Oak Ridge to research facilities around the country. The radioisotope distribution program was one of the commission's most widely touted success stories. Radioisotopes were seen as an antidote—an inoculation of sorts—against the public's fear and apprehension of the atomic bomb. Recalled Oak Ridge scientist Marshall Brucer: "The liberal establishment was in the depths of shame for having ended the war by killing people. Radioisotopes didn't kill people; they cured cancer." The AEC's Medical Board of Review said the program "would aid in showing the scientific world that the Atomic Energy Commission is effectively contributing to the advancement of knowledge despite the impression often left by security regulations."

Congress allocated $175 million to the AEC in 1947, with up to $5 million to be reserved for cancer research that did not duplicate the work of other public or private agencies. At that time the $5 million was a huge sum, and more money than some AEC officials believed could be spent on legitimate projects. Under Shields Warren's direction, three AEC cancer hospitals were eventually set up: the Argonne Cancer Research Hospital, a fifty-eight-bed facility located in an AEC-owned building in Chicago next to Billings Hospital; a thirty-bed hospital at the Oak Ridge Institute of Nuclear Studies in Tennessee; and a forty-bed facility at Brookhaven National Laboratory near Upton, New York. During the next three to four decades, scores of human experiments using radioisotopes and external radioactive sources were conducted at these facilities.

Armed with $1.1 million annually in AEC fellowship funds, Warren and his colleagues sought to encourage young science and medical students to pursue a career in some aspect of radiation research. From the moment of its inception, the AEC had recognized the obstacles to recruitment of scientists. "The emphasis on the responsibilities of the Atomic Energy Commission for atomic warfare and the consequent fear and distaste which is engendered in the public mind brings added difficulties to the work of the Commission," intoned the Medical Board of Review, the blue-ribbon panel. Rochester's Andrew Dowdy believed scientists weren't interested in radiation research because there was "no romance" to it. He said: "There are no Nobel prizes. There are no great discoveries to be made. Few people want to take that sort of thing. . . . You merely sit for months without seeing anything happening. You have nothing to report. You go to meetings and everybody else has something to report, and you just sit there. It takes you months or years to accumulate information."

Stafford Warren, Shields Warren's predecessor, knew long-term experiments were needed to properly assess the dangers of low-level radiation but warned in an April 1, 1947, speech at Yale University that such studies were going to be "time-consuming and rather unspectacular." Returning again to one of his favorite subjects, Warren said the research had to be done in order to protect the government from lawsuits by scam artists and freeloaders: "Particularly if we have a depression, we will have a lot of people who will want to coast along on the government charities, and who will come up with the story that they worked for the Manhattan District somewhere, or they passed down the street to windward of the plant, and therefore they deserve compensation. It is going to be a very serious problem."

Unbelievably, the AEC in early 1948 found itself in the position of having too much money. What is even more unbelievable is that it considered returning some of the cash to the federal treasury. "Several members [of the Advisory Committee for Biology and Medicine] told me that the cancer money might prove to be very embarrassing to AEC since there is already more money for cancer research than there are original and legitimate research projects upon which to spend it," AEC official Bob Tumbleson wrote. "In fact [A. Baird] Hastings went so far as to suggest that it might be well if the Commission would refuse to accept cancer money for the coming year."

Soon enough, scientists hungry for grant money and job advancement managed to overcome their distaste for atomic warfare and the tedium associated with radiation research. Proposals poured into the AEC and the money flowed out. "One had the feeling that almost anything could get supported if it had any smattering of sense behind it," recalled William Bale, the Manhattan Project scientist who opened the metabolic unit at Strong Memorial Hospital. Stanton Cohn, another Manhattan Project veteran, said, "It was fantastic—we could buy any piece of machinery or equipment, and you never had to justify it." A deliriously happy Los Alamos scientist returning from Washington after the launching of Sputnik once remarked, "I am black and blue from being pelted with money." By the 1950s the commission's budget for biomedical research was around $25 million per year. About 37 percent of that went to studies of radiation effects; 34 percent to studies of the benefits of radiation; 21 percent to research related to industrial health and safety; and 8 percent to studies aimed at combating radiation's harms.

The Atomic Energy Commission wasn't the only federal agency with deep pockets. The Army, Navy, and Air Force established their own research laboratories and entered into generous contracts with universities following the war. With preparations for the atomic battlefield in full swing, a lot of the money went to the development of nuclear weapons and radiation research. "Never before in history have the interests of the weaponeers and those who practice the healing arts been so closely related," crowed a medical doctor in the 1949 volume *Atomic Medicine*. The symbiotic arrangement was fraught with danger, however. What was good for the armed forces wasn't necessarily good for the patient, and vice versa. Some experiments went on too long. Others wouldn't have been done at all without military or AEC funding. The melding of medical know-how and military dollars produced "dual-purpose" experiments—studies with both a medical and a military component. Many of the Manhattan Project's human experiments had dual purposes, as did other experiments conducted in the postwar years.

Much of the atomic research was initially classified, creating cliques on college campuses of people who spoke mostly to each other. Sometimes even college presidents didn't know what kind of research their professors were doing. Secrecy prevented adequate oversight and enabled sloppy, incompetent, or unethical experiments to go unquestioned or to be swept under the rug. Oak Ridge scientist Karl Morgan, often called the father of health physics, said in an interview many years ago that weapons scientists worked in a closed society where the same ideas were passed from researcher to researcher. "Pretty soon it makes the circle, and you're literally talking to yourself." In addition, he said: "I realize now that we were rather conceited as a group. We grew up during the war years and in an environment which only we were interested in or knew anything about these problems, problems of nuclear energy. The outside world, at least during the early security days even in physics departments, they hardly knew what was going on in this field."

After the war the physicists needed big machines like cyclotrons and accelerators to do their work and were growing ever more dependent on military largesse. Philip Morrison was one of the first Manhattan Project physicists to warn of the dangers of military-supported science. At a forum on public affairs sponsored by the New York *Herald Tribune* in October 1946, he said, "The backers—Army and Navy—will go along for a while. Results, in the shape of new and fearful weapons, will not justify the expenses and their own funds will begin to dwindle. The now amicable contracts will tighten up and the fine print will start to contain talk about results and specific weapon problems. And science itself will have been bought by war on the installment plan."

The infusion of money, combined with the advances in medicine and science during World War II, spawned an orgy of human experimentation in almost every medical field in the postwar years. "This was, to borrow a phrase from American political history, the Gilded Age of research, the triumph of laissez-faire in the laboratory," writes Columbia University's David Rothman.

The vastness of the human experimentation became clear only in 1994, when the General Accounting Office reported that hundreds of thousands of Americans were used in military-related experiments involving radiation, blister and nerve agents, biological agents, and LSD between 1940 and 1974. "In some cases, basic safeguards to protect people were either not in place or not followed. For example, some tests and experiments were conducted in secret; others involved the use of people without their knowledge or consent or their full knowledge of the risks involved."

With the expansion in medical research came a new breed of physicians who were interested not in treating patients but in finding cures that would benefit mankind. Original research and frequent publication put physicians and scientists on the fast track to academic advancement.

"Some of my peers were quite immoral or perhaps amoral. I realize many would do anything for academic advancement," recalled William Silverman, a retired physician who did pediatric research at Columbia University in the 1940s, 1950s, and 1960s.

Silverman was one of the nearly two dozen prominent researchers who was interviewed by the Clinton Advisory Committee on Human Radiation Experiments about the ethos of human experimentation during that era. The physicians, all considered leaders in their field, were drawn from a variety of disciplines, including radiology, infectious diseases, pharmacology, and hematology. Like William Silverman, many of the researchers spoke with a startling frankness about past practices. Leonard Sagan, a doctor who worked for the AEC and the Atomic Bomb Casualty Commission, or the ABCC, the organization set up to monitor the Japanese bombing victims, told committee staffers that getting informed consent often conflicted with a researcher's professional goals:

> Doctors who were doing research wanted to be professors, and in order to be a professor, you have to have lots of publications, so your highest priority is to conduct research and publish it. You're the doctor. Here's a patient that you want to experiment on. . . . Is it going to contribute to your research if you inform that patient? What can happen is the patient says, "No, I don't want to do that." That's not in your interest. Your interest is to have that patient participate, so do you tell him or her? No. Does anybody care? No. So you don't tell them. So that's why they [ethical rules] were ignored, because there's a conflict between informed consent and the ability to conduct research and the physician is interested not in the patient's welfare, he's interested in his or her welfare. So he doesn't inform him.

Although times were heady and money was plentiful, doctors should have been reminded of their obligations to their patients by medical codes dating back to antiquity, and familiar to them since their days in medical school. Hippocrates, a physician who lived in ancient Greece and is often called the Father of Medicine, is credited with articulating the core principles regarding a doctor's relationship to patients. The Hippocratic Oath states, "I will follow that system of regimen which, according to my ability and judgment, I consider for the benefit of my patients, and abstain from whatever is deleterious and mischievous. I will give no deadly medicine to any one if asked nor suggest any such counsel. . . ."

Los Alamos chemist Don Mastick inadvertently swallowed a significant proportion of the world's existing supply of plutonium when a vial he was holding exploded on August 1, 1944. (LOS ALAMOS NATIONAL LABORATORY)

J. Robert Oppenheimer and Louis Hempelmann examine a Geiger counter during a trip to the Trinity site on September 10, 1945. (AP/WIDE WORLD PHOTOS)

Albert Stevens, "CAL-1," stops to enjoy the scenery en route to his new life in California in the 1920s. On May 14, 1945, when he was fifty-eight, Stevens, who had been mistakenly diagnosed with terminal cancer, became the first of three people injected with plutonium at the University of California Hospital in San Francisco. He lived for almost twenty-one years. (COURTESY OF EMMA STEVENS)

Simeon Shaw, "CAL-2," an Australian boy suffering from an osteogenic sarcoma, arrives in San Francisco with his mother, Freda. He was injected with plutonium and two other radioisotopes on April 26, 1946, when he was two months shy of his fifth birthday. He died eight months later. (COURTESY OF JOSHUA SHAW)

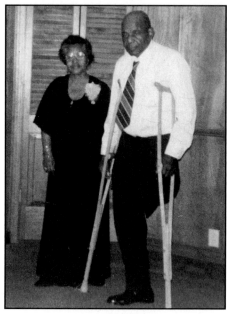

Elmer Allen, "CAL-3," and his wife, Fredna, whose dreams of a better life on a Pullman's salary were cut short when Elmer's leg was amputated because of an osteogenic sarcoma. Elmer was injected with plutonium on July 18, 1947, and lived another forty-four years. (COURTESY OF ELMERINE ALLEN WHITFIELD BELL)

Arthur Hubbard, "CHI-1," was a sixty-eight-year-old businessman whose love of baseball dated from the years he played on his college team. He was injected on April 26, 1945, at Billings Hospital in Chicago, where he had gone for treatment for mouth cancer. He died five months later. (COURTESY OF RITA DELMAR)

Una Macke, "CHI-2," was injected on December 27, 1945, when she was fifty-six and suffering from two kinds of cancer. The dose she received was equivalent to nearly one hundred times what scientists then believed could be tolerated without harm. She died seventeen days later. (COURTESY OF MARCIA SULLIVAN)

Amedio Lovecchio, "HP-1," a sixty-seven-year-old Sicilian immigrant with a bleeding ulcer, was injected with plutonium on October 16, 1945, becoming the first of eleven patients injected at Rochester's Strong Memorial Hospital. He lived another fourteen years. (COURTESY OF CARMELLA M. HEHIR)

William Purcell, "HP-2," a forty-eight-year-old hemophiliac who owned a cigar store, was injected on October 23, 1945, during his thirty-eighth trip to the hospital. He died two and a half years later. (REPRINTED WITH PERMISSION OF THE *DEMOCRAT AND CHRONICLE*, ROCHESTER, NY)

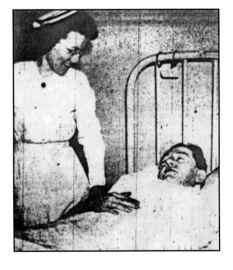

Housewife Eda Schultz Charlton, "HP-3," was injected on November 27, 1945, when she was forty-eight. Described in an unpublished report written several years later as "having a life expectancy [greater] than originally anticipated," Eda lived thirty-seven years after her injection. Toward the end she became obsessed with "that stuff they gave me" and what it might have done to her. (COURTESY OF DAVID SCHULTZ)

Eighteen-year-old Jean Daigneault, "HP-4," was suffering from Cushing's syndrome, a metabolic disorder, when she was injected November 27, 1945. She died a year and a half later. Scientists found plutonium in her hair when her body was exhumed many years later. (COURTESY OF RUTH DAIGNEAULT BROWN)

Paul Galinger, "HP-5," was a machine-shop foreman still grieving over the death of his son when he was injected on November 30, 1945, at the age of fifty-six. He had what is now known as Lou Gehrig's disease and died five months later. (COURTESY OF KENNETH A. PULLMAN)

John Mousso, "HP-6," was injected on February 1, 1946. The forty-four-year-old handyman survived another thirty-eight years. (COURTESY OF ROBERT MOUSSO)

Edna Bartholf, "HP-7," was injected on February 8, 1946. Diagnosed with rheumatic heart disease, she was fifty-nine years old. She died nine months later. (COURTESY OF DOUGLAS O. THATER)

Janet Stadt, "HP-8," was suffering from scleroderma, a painful skin disease, when she was injected on March 9, 1946, at the age of forty-one. She died of cancer of the larynx some thirty years later. (COURTESY OF MILTON STADT)

Fred Sours, "HP-9," town supervisor of a Rochester suburb, was injected on April 3, 1946. He was sixty-four, suffering from dermatomyositis, and died a year and three months later. (REPRINTED WITH PERMISSION OF THE *DEMOCRAT AND CHRONICLE*, ROCHESTER, NY)

Daniel Nelson, "HP-10," a fifty-two-year-old cook, was transferred to Samuel Bassett's metabolic ward after suffering a heart attack. He was injected on July 16, 1946, and survived nearly eleven years. (COURTESY OF BENJAMIN QUAMINA)

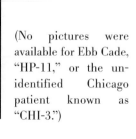

Mary Jeanne Connell was twenty-four years old and in good health except for being underweight, when she was injected with a large dose of enriched uranium on October 1, 1946. Still living, she is the only known survivor of those experiments. (COURTESY OF MARY JEANNE CONNELL)

(No pictures were available for Ebb Cade, "HP-11," or the un-identified Chicago patient known as "CHI-3.")

Col. Stafford Warren (right), the director of the Manhattan Project's Medical Section, boards the USS *Haven*, a ship bound for Operation Crossroads. (UCLA/SPECIAL COLLECTIONS)

Robert Stone (far right) looks on as General Groves pins the Medal of Merit on Enrico Fermi. The others who received the medal are (from left to right) Harold Urey, Samuel Allison, Cyril Smith, and Stone himself. (UNIVERSITY OF CHICAGO/SPECIAL COLLECTIONS)

Kenneth Scott transported the plutonium used in the human experiments at the University of California Hospital in San Francisco. (BANCROFT LIBRARY, UC-BERKELEY)

Samuel Bassett was the doctor who oversaw the plutonium and uranium injections at Rochester's Strong Memorial Hospital. (UNIVERSITY OF ROCHESTER)

Inveterate experimenter Joseph Hamilton used both rats and human beings for his studies of radiation exposure. (LAWRENCE BERKELEY LABORATORY)

Wright Langham, a Los Alamos chemist obsessed with finding a test to measure plutonium levels in the human body, examines a "plastic man" used in radiation exposure simulations. (LOS ALAMOS NATIONAL LABORATORY)

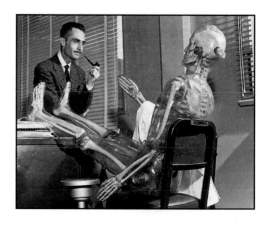

As clear as it is, the Hippocratic oath pertained only to patients and not experimental subjects, bioethicist Michael Grodin writes, and it wasn't until 1803 that an English physician named Thomas Percival developed a code specifically directed at experiments in which the subject might not benefit. In 1833 William Beaumont, an American physician, developed a more elaborate code of ethics that had as one of its requirements the "voluntary consent" of the subject, Grodin points out. By the turn of the century, doctors recognized that the consent of the subject was needed before an experiment could be conducted. The *Journal of the American Medical Association* in 1890 cautioned that even consent "will not protect the physician in performing bizarre operations, or reckless experimentation."

In 1908 a woman named Mary E. Schloendorff sued the Society of New York Hospital, claiming that she had not given her consent for an operation in which a fibroid tumor was removed from her stomach. Following the procedure, she developed gangrene in her left arm and several fingers were amputated. Upon appeal, Benjamin Cardoza, who later went on to become a Supreme Court judge, issued his now-famous ruling: "In the case at hand, the wrong complained of is not merely negligence. It is trespass. Every human being of adult years and sound mind has a right to determine what shall be done with his own body; and a surgeon who performs an operation without his patient's consent commits an assault for which he is liable in damages."

Under general manager Carroll Wilson, the AEC had developed strong guidelines for human experiments. The military branches also had rudimentary principles. The Clinton Advisory Committee located documents showing that by the 1920s the Army had developed guidelines for the use of "volunteers" in medical research. The Navy had rules by 1932. The Committee on Medical Research, which funded studies related to the war effort, warned in 1942 that only fully informed volunteers should be used in human experiments.

If these precedents seemed remote in time, the doctors could look to the Nuremberg Code, ten eloquent principles handed down in 1947 at the conclusion of the Nazi doctors' trial. In his closing argument, James McHaney, the chief prosecutor at Nuremberg, said, "It is the most fundamental tenet of medical ethics and human decency that the subjects volunteer for the experiment after being informed of its nature and hazards. This is the clear dividing line between the criminal and what may be non-criminal. If the experimental subjects cannot be said to have volunteered, then the inquiry need proceed no further."

But many American doctors believed the Nuremberg Code was written for barbarians, not for them. Columbia University's William Silverman recalled, "The connection between those horrendous acts and our every day investigation was not made for reasons of self interest, to be perfectly frank. As I see it now, I'm saddened that we didn't see the connection, but that's what was done. We wrapped ourselves in the flag. . . ."

The 1940s, 1950s, and 1960s were decades when doctors were treated like gods and patients like children. Adults suffering from fatal diseases often were not told they were dying; children were never told. With few drugs available, doctors consciously tried to increase a patient's confidence in their medical skills to help bring about a cure. "The model was in religion," remembered Silverman, "that is, faith in the priest who will speak to God and get the answer. We were encouraged to behave like priests. We never told patients everything. On the contrary, we told them as little as possible. Just enough so they would get the general drift of what we were doing. This was conscious. It was a conscious effort to make patients feel they were in the presence of healers."

Physicians performed experiments on healthy people and sick patients without informing them of what was going on or getting their consent. Sick patients were preyed on most frequently. They were convenient, plentiful, and vulnerable, since nontherapeutic procedures could be administered easily under the guise of medical treatment. A fuzzy line existed between bona fide treatment and full-blown experimentation, and researchers often slipped over the line, rationalizing that the experiment was harmless, the procedure was no more harmful than some other accepted medical treatment, or the knowledge gained from the experiment would benefit mankind.

Terminally ill patients were perhaps the most vulnerable group of all. Stuart Finch, a physician who specialized in research related to iron metabolism, leukemia, immunology, and radiation effects, told the Clinton Committee, "It's very easy when you have a dying patient to say, 'Look, you're going to die. Why don't you let me try this substance on you?' I don't think if they have informed consent or not it makes much difference at that point."

Women, children, unborn fetuses, minorities, the mentally retarded, schizophrenics, prisoners, alcoholics, and poor people of all ages and ethnic groups were targeted. Several doctors told the Advisory Committee that poor patients often were selected because they were easily intimidated, didn't ask questions, and belonged to a different social class.

Acknowledged Silverman, "I must also tell you that I am ashamed about the fact that those on the lowest rungs of the social ladder had their rights trampled on much more than those who were on high rungs."

"In what way?" asked committee staffer Gail Javitt.

"When doctors' children or young children of important persons were enrolled in studies, the parents were informed."

"Because you couldn't get away with it?"

"Exactly," he responded. "Most of these clinical experiments were carried out in children whose parents didn't know what questions to ask."

"Patients on charity wards?"

"Charity wards, the so-called ward patients."

Paul Beeson, a renowned physician who specialized in infectious diseases and immunology, said that attitude also prevailed among his colleagues. At Emory University's Grady Hospital, where Beeson worked from 1942 until 1952, researchers flocked to the emergency room on hot summer nights to study the effects of shock in stabbing and gunshot victims. They biopsied syphilis patients not to cure them but to study the disease, and inserted catheters and needles into organs to study blood flow or the circulation of bacteria. "We were taking care of them and we felt that we had a right to get some return from them, since it wouldn't be in professional fees and since our taxes were paying their hospital bills," Beeson told Susan Lederer, a historian and member of the Advisory Committee.

Sometimes accidents occurred. Beeson told Lederer about an investigator who was studying the effects of potassium, which can stop the heart from beating and is used today to kill prisoners sentenced to die by lethal injection. "One of the fellows in the cardiac section was following the effect of intravenous drip of potassium on the electrocardiogram and the patient died," Beeson disclosed. The admission appeared to startle Lederer, who interviewed Beeson in November of 1994 at the Seattle airport: "I may be phrasing this crudely but I'm struggling to get this right. Is it your sense that clinical investigators felt they could do anything they wanted to these patients?" "Pretty much, yes," responded Beeson, continuing:

> It brings up the sociological aspects of it. This was before Medicare, Medicaid, and academics and medical students did their work with patients in charity hospitals. I feel that I am right in saying that we medical students and our teachers looked upon ourselves as belonging to another social class from the patients

we were taking care of. That they were lucky to be getting care of the best doctors in the community. . . . But without ever saying it, still it was felt that we didn't belong to the same class. . . . I really felt that had a little to do with the fact that we felt we were free to test these people and carry out studies on them.

The total-body irradiation experiments, such as the wartime studies sponsored by the Met Lab at hospitals in New York, Chicago, and San Francisco, also caused suffering and premature deaths. As for the radio-isotope experiments—the so-called tracer studies—many contemporary scientists contend the doses were too small to have caused harm.

But some of the tracer studies delivered whopping doses of radiation to the patients. In Memphis, Tennessee, for example, researchers gave two young African American mothers 100 microcuries of iodine-131 as part of their "routine medical follow-up." Both mothers had four-month-old infants whom they were breast-feeding. The younger mother received another 100 microcuries two months later. A dose of 100 hundred microcuries would have delivered approximately 200 rads to the adult thyroid, or twenty times the amount that the Agency for Toxic Sub-stances in 1997 said could cause thyroid nodules. The two infants would have been subjected to even larger doses because their thyroids were so much smaller.

The Advisory Committee compiled a data base of some 4,000 radia-tion experiments, including both the radioisotope and TBI studies con-ducted during the Cold War. But this list does not represent all the studies that were done. The Department of Health and Human Services, for instance, was unable to determine how many experiments the depart-ment or its predecessors had sponsored because much of the information was on paper and would have required tens of thousands of hours to retrieve.

To make matters more complicated, various federal agencies used different criteria in compiling their lists of radiation experiments. Some agencies included experiments in which radioisotopes or external radia-tion were administered for bona fide medical purposes, even though these studies were not what the Advisory Committee was looking at.

Only fragmentary records exist on the thousands of experiments per-formed after World War II. But in cases where documents have been retrieved, the evidence indicates overwhelmingly that the radioactive ma-terials were administered without the subjects' informed consent. The experiments violated the consent rules promulgated by the AEC's Carroll

Wilson and the blue-ribbon Medical Board of Review. Furthermore, an extraordinary memo that was made public only recently shows that AEC officials were aware of the contradiction. The 1947 memo, which appears to have been written by Albert Holland, the medical director at Oak Ridge and an ally of Shields Warren, laid out the pros and cons of tracer research, "some of which," he admitted, "is of no immediate therapeutic value to the patient." The pros and cons included:

Pro
1. Tracer research is fundamental to toxicity studies.
2. The adequacy of the health protection which we afford our present employees may in a large measure depend upon information obtained using tracer techniques.
3. New and improved medical applications can only be developed through careful experimentation and clinical trial.
4. Tracer techniques are inherent in the radioisotope distribution program.

Con
1. Moral, ethical, and medico-legal objections to the administration of radioactive materials without the patient's knowledge or consent.
2. There is perhaps a greater responsibility if a federal agency condones human guinea pig experimentation.
3. Publication of such researches [sic] in some instances will compromise the best interests of the Atomic Energy Commission.
4. Publication of experiments done by Atomic Energy Commission contractors' personnel may frequently be the source of litigation and be prejudicial to the proper functioning of the Atomic Energy Commission Insurance Branch.

How could the AEC, on one hand, have established new rules to prevent experiments like the plutonium injections from reoccurring while simultaneously promoting a program that would encourage thousands of similar experiments? No documents have surfaced to adequately explain the contradiction. Some records suggest that AEC researchers didn't really consider the tracer studies as bona fide experiments because they believed the doses were harmless. But if the experiments were harmless, researchers should have had no qualms about informing patients or using themselves as the test subjects.

When the Manhattan Project began distributing its radioisotopes in 1946, scientists who wanted to use the materials in humans had to submit a request to what became known as the Subcommittee on Human Applications. At one time or another, committee members included Hymer Friedell, Andrew Dowdy, Joseph Hamilton, and Paul Aebersold, the scientist who had assisted Robert Stone on his prewar neutron experiment and was assigned to help Stafford Warren at Trinity. Dubbed "Mr. Isotope," Aebersold was almost fanatical in his support of the program. Scientist Merril Eisenbud, one of the AEC's fallout experts, many years later described Aebersold as a "nut." Eisenbud added, "He committed suicide, which is probably the extreme of his nuttiness. But he was very fanatic about the importance of radioisotopes and what it was going to do for you."

Scant records of the subcommittee exist. But documents that have been found show that the subcommittee developed its own rules governing tracer research. Larger doses of radionuclides could be used on terminally ill patients and on "mentally deficient" subjects, the panel decreed. But by 1949 researchers were discouraged from using radioactive materials in normal children and pregnant women. For more than 800 women in Nashville, Tennessee, who were given radioactive iron "cocktails" to drink at a clinic where they went for prenatal checkups, this advice came several years too late.

22

THE VANDERBILT WOMEN

The waiting room at the Vanderbilt University Hospital Prenatal Clinic was always crowded in the jubilant years after the war, row after row of young women dressed in their Sunday best sitting in straight-back wooden chairs waiting for their doctors. There were no magazines to read or music to listen to, but soon the room filled up with girlish chatter as the young women turned to each other and began talking in soft, southern accents about their husbands, the new homes they were hoping to buy, the children they would soon give birth to. Segregation was strictly enforced, and the clinic treated white women only. But these were not women from Nashville's well-to-do neighborhoods. Many were poor and their fees were based on what they could pay. Shy and eager to please, they felt lucky to have Vanderbilt doctors taking care of them and followed their orders without question.

In late July of 1946, Helen Hutchison signed in at the reception desk and took a seat in the waiting room. A ceiling fan spun lazily overhead but did little to relieve the muggy Nashville heat. Helen's husband had landed in Europe on D-Day and had helped liberate two concentration camps, including Buchenwald. Although they weren't exactly poor, money was tight. Helen plucked at her damp clothes and fanned her face. Just twenty years old, she was a willowy woman with long curly hair who talked in a slow, unhurried voice. She had experienced so much nausea and vomiting during her pregnancy that she actually had lost fifteen pounds. The doctors prescribed liver shots, vitamins, thyroid medication, and plenty of bed rest, but the nausea continued unabated. When Helen's name was called, she followed the nurse down the hallway to an examining room. Soon a doctor came in, mixed something into a cup, and handed it to her to drink.

As Helen sat on the examining table holding the cup in her hand, she looked out the window at Gartland Avenue. Parked at the curb were De Sotos, Packards, and Studebakers. Beyond were the lovely brick homes and deep green lawns of Nashville. At the corner of Gartland Avenue and 21st Street was a pie wagon, a street car that had been converted to a soda fountain. After her checkup at the clinic, Helen sometimes slipped onto one of the stools and ordered a Coke, hoping the carbonated sweetness would staunch the nausea welling up inside her. It was such a beautiful day, she thought, as the physician urged her to swallow the drink.

"What is it?" she asked.

"It's a little cocktail. It'll make you feel better," she recalled the doctor saying.

"Well, I don't know if I ought to be drinking a cocktail," she responded, her voice light and bantering.

"Drink it all," he told her. "Drink it on down." The concoction was fizzy and sweet, like a cherry Coke. It wasn't bad tasting.

Three months later Helen was rolled into the delivery room. The nausea had not let up during her pregnancy. She had gained only six pounds and never even had to wear maternity clothes. Six hours after her labor began, a "lusty cry" announced the entrance of her daughter, Barbara, into the world. The infant's skin was so smooth and white she looked like a porcelain doll. The mother and her newborn were discharged five days later. Both seemed healthy.

The bizarre health problems that were to plague mother and daughter began several months later. Helen's face swelled up and water blisters appeared on the right side. "You could draw a line right down through the middle of my face," she remembered. Then her hair fell out and she began to tire easily. In the ensuing years she had two miscarriages. The internal hemorrhaging was so severe during the second one that she had to have sixteen blood transfusions. She now suffers from pernicious anemia and is extremely sensitive to sunlight.

Barbara also felt exhausted through most of her childhood and now suffers from an immune system disorder and skin cancer. When she was about eleven, the lymph nodes under her arms swelled inexplicably. "She was always really sleepy," Helen remembered. "She'd come in from school in the afternoons and have to lay down and take a nap. The other kids would say, 'Why don't you come out and play?' and she'd say, 'I will, after I take my nap.'"

As it turns out, Helen was one of 829 women who passed through the prenatal clinic between roughly September 1945 and May of 1947 and were given the strange-tasting cocktails to drink. Like Helen, many of the women were led to believe that the drinks contained something nutritious that would benefit them and their babies. But nothing could have been farther from the truth. The drinks actually contained varying amounts of radioactive iron. Within an hour the material crossed the placenta and began circulating in the blood of their unborn infants.

Paul Hahn, an enthusiastic researcher in his thirties, may have looked down the hall and seen the rows of young female patients as he dashed back and forth between the clinic and his laboratory. He had arrived at Vanderbilt University in 1943 with a stack of published reports and five years' experience using radioisotopes. He was five feet eleven inches tall, weighed 185 pounds, and was described by a colleague as "an energetic and competent investigator equipped with imagination and ingenuity and fired by an insatiable curiosity."

Hahn had been a protégé of Stafford Warren's at the University of Rochester, where he obtained his Ph.D. in biochemistry in 1936. There, he had collaborated on several experiments with William Bale, the dour-looking scientist who oversaw Strong Memorial Hospital's metabolic ward, and Joseph Howland, the young Manhattan Project doctor who later said he injected Ebb Cade with plutonium. Hahn had also studied under Robley Evans at MIT. During the war he frequently attended Manhattan Project meetings in Oak Ridge, and after it ended he was recruited for Operation Crossroads. One of the first scientists to take advantage of the Atomic Energy Commission's radioisotope distribution program, Hahn had received the largest number of radioisotope shipments in the country in 1947.

The radioactive iron experiment Hahn was doing at Vanderbilt was a subset of a large nutrition study. Partially funded by the Rockefeller Foundation, the study focused on how a woman's diet and nutrition would affect her pregnancy and delivery, and the condition of her infant. William Darby, a young nutritionist, was in charge of the overall study. Many decades later he said that one reason he undertook the study was because the poor living conditions, eating habits, and water supplies of people living in the South at that time were equivalent to those found in underdeveloped countries. "There were signs on the roadside showing which towns had healthy water."

The radioactive iron experiment was simple and straightforward. During the first visit to the clinic, a baseline blood sample was drawn and physical exam conducted by William Darby or one of his colleagues. The radioactive iron was administered during the second visit, and on the third visit, blood samples were drawn from the women to measure how much iron had been absorbed. Hahn wrote in a scientific paper published several years later that anywhere from 200,000 to 1,000,000 "countable counts" per minute were administered.

Darby stated in a sworn deposition taken in 1994 that the radioactive mixture was prepared in Hahn's office and brought to the clinic. He said researchers referred to the drinks as "cocktails" because that was the commonly used term. "We just used it. I mean, this is like—would you like to have a sweet?"

Darby told reporters that he was "certain" that the women were told the cocktails contained radioactive iron. But in his deposition taken several months later during a class-action lawsuit, he said, "We did not decide that we would not inform [the women]. We simply felt it was— felt it was unnecessary. . . ."

"Is it your testimony, sir, that you and the planning committee didn't decide to tell the women about the radioactive iron nor did you decide not to tell them?" Don Arbitblit, an attorney representing the women in the class-action lawsuit, asked.

"That's right. Neither," Darby responded.

Under questioning, Darby also stated that the radioactive iron had no therapeutic purpose and that he didn't know much about radiobiology. "In fact, it was not my field," he admitted.

In the early stages of the experiment, Hahn conferred with Stafford Warren, who was still medical director of the Manhattan Project. It's not known whether the two men specifically discussed the Vanderbilt experiment, but according to an entry in one of Warren's notebooks, they discussed "isotopes."

Vanderbilt University was proud of the radioiron study and on December 13, 1946 issued a press release describing the experiment. Most of the radioactive iron came from the cyclotron at the Massachusetts Institute of Technology, the press release noted, "while a recent supply has been received at Vanderbilt from the Oak Ridge chain reacting uranium pile."

Officials in Oak Ridge had become increasingly concerned about the radioactive iron manufactured in their reactor. In mid-1947 they discovered the iron-59 being distributed for medical purposes contained more iron-55 than had been expected. Iron-55 was thought to be too hazardous to be administered to humans because it had a half-life of five years. That meant that it would take five years for half of the iron-55 molecules in any given amount to decay to a nonradioactive compound, five more years for half of the remaining iron-55 to decay, and so on. By contrast, iron-59 was believed to have a half-life of forty-seven days, which meant that it would return to a stable form more quickly and subject the body to less radiation.

Oak Ridge officials were aware that any iron-59 contaminated with the longer-lived isotope was dangerous because it subjected the body to "considerable radiation." And Paul Hahn, even while the Vanderbilt experiment was ongoing, was advising a Florida doctor in 1947 not to treat his patients with radioactive iron. "Radioactive iron regardless of the amount of activity contained is, to my knowledge, of no value whatsoever in therapy," he wrote. Hahn believed that the half-lives of both iron-55 and iron-59 were "far too long." Iron-55 was believed at that time to have a half-life of about five years and iron-59 a half-life of forty-seven days. An isotope's half-life, wrote Hahn:

> must not be too long. Neither should there be an associated component of long half-life or a long-lived contaminant whose separation is difficult or impossible to effect. Such long-lived materials prevent good control of the supplied radiation and also might prove ultimately to be carcinogenic in themselves. We have arbitrarily set about 10 days as the upper limit of half-life which is desirable from this point of view.

If Hahn had any similar concerns about the radioactive iron administered to the pregnant women, no correspondence has yet been made public describing those concerns. He transferred to Nashville's Meharry Medical College in 1948, about a year after the Vanderbilt study ended, and the women were largely forgotten. Many of the mothers and children exposed to the radioiron developed strange afflictions that were similar to those described by Helen Hutchison and her daughter. They lost their teeth and their hair. They developed bizarre rashes, bruises, strange blood disorders, anemia—and cancer.

Around Christmas of 1955, a young Nashville child named Carolyn

Bucy developed a lump about the size of an orange on her upper thigh. Her mother, Emma Craft, a pretty woman with small, delicate features, had gone to the Vanderbilt prenatal clinic in early March of 1946 to find out if she was pregnant. Vanderbilt doctors had delivered her other three daughters, and she thought Vanderbilt was the best hospital in the world. At that time, she was married to Floyd Bucy, a carpenter and musician who made five dollars on Saturday nights playing at the Grand Ole Opry.

After examining her, the doctors at the prenatal clinic told her she was indeed pregnant with her fourth child and instructed her to return seven days later. On her second visit, she testified in a videotaped deposition taken in 1994, doctors gave her the cocktail to drink. Her daughter, Carolyn, was then a thirteen-week-old fetus.

"What is it that you were told about the drink?" asked attorney Don Arbitblit.

"It was vitamins," responded Emma.

"Were you told anything else about the drink?"

"No."

"Did they say anything about whether the drink was good for you or not?"

"Yes. They said it was good for me."

Later in the deposition, she was asked, "Before March of 1946, had you ever heard of radiation?"

"When they dropped the bomb was the first I knew anything about radiation."

"What was it that you knew about radiation?"

"Well, if you can drop something like that and kill people, well you know you don't want to take it."

Carolyn was born September 15, 1946, three weeks premature. Emma breast-fed the infant and she began to put on weight quickly. Both mother and daughter were healthy when they were discharged from the hospital eight or nine days later, but Emma's eyes soon turned swollen and black. "They had to carry me back to the hospital. My eyes looked like somebody had beat me. They were so swollen and black. I thought, 'Lord, I'm going blind.'" Eventually the swelling subsided and Emma's life returned to normal. A year after Carolyn was born, she began working in a box factory so she could better provide for her children.

Blessed with a loving disposition and her father's musical ear, Carolyn quickly became the center of the family's attention. "She liked doing for people," Emma recalled. She was about nine years old when her older sisters discovered the lump on her right thigh. The child begged her sisters not to say anything about it until after the holidays. When Emma was finally shown the growth, she was deeply frightened and took her daughter to Vanderbilt Hospital the following day. The mass would have to be removed, the doctors told her. Emma got a second opinion from another physician, named Elkin Rippy. He also felt the lump should be removed and agreed to do the surgery.

During the operation, Rippy discovered Carolyn had cancer. Emma, who was in the waiting room, fainted when he told her what he had found. "When I came to, he told me, he said, Emma, 'I got it all.' " But the cancer eventually came back. The disease spread into the child's spine, then moved up through her lungs, heart, throat, and finally, into her mouth. Emma prayed constantly and her husband went on a forty-day fast, drinking only fruit juice and water. Emma believed, "If God can make us, then God can heal us."

Carolyn underwent radiation therapy and four more surgeries. Eventually she became paralyzed from the waist down and was forced to use a wheelchair. A catheter was connected to her bladder and she was fed intravenously. The doctors cut the cancer out of her mouth several times. "It was black. Black cancer inside of her mouth just growing," Emma recalled in her deposition. As the child's body withered, her face grew swollen and misshapen from the disease. She was fed intravenously, but sometimes Emma would spoon a little malt water into her mouth. Carolyn finally went into a coma and died on August 28, 1958, about two and one-half years after the cancer was discovered. She was eleven years old.

Emma slipped into a deep depression after her daughter's death. Her foreman at the box factory often told her to go for a ride when the grief threatened to overwhelm her. She would drive for hours wondering why God allowed her daughter to die such a horrible death. She often thought about killing herself by running her car into a brick wall or tree. But the knowledge that she had other daughters at home who needed her kept her from such an unthinkable act. Eventually she came to accept the loss of her daughter as God's will and went on with her life.

In 1964, six years after Emma's daughter died, a new group of researchers at Vanderbilt University decided to do a follow-up study of the women who had been given the radioactive iron cocktails. The study began at a critical juncture in the history of the nuclear weapons program: Atmospheric testing had ended in 1963, but scientists were just beginning to make the connections between fallout and excess cancers in exposed populations.

The research community was also in an uproar over the controversial findings first reported in 1956 by Alice Stewart, a British researcher and physician. Stewart and her colleagues had conducted a vast survey of all children in England and Wales who died of leukemia or cancer between 1953 and 1955 before their tenth birthday. They discovered that one to two rads of radiation delivered to the fetus in utero caused a 50 percent increase in childhood cancer and leukemia.

The findings had enormous ramifications. Scientists had long known that the fetus, with its rapidly dividing cells, was extremely sensitive to radiation. But many physicians were incredulous that such small doses could have such dire consequences. Some raised questions about how Stewart collected the data, arguing that the women who got X rays were a "medically selected group," or women who had an underlying constitution or disease that predisposed their children to cancer. An independent study by Brian MacMahon of the Department of Epidemiology at the Harvard School of Public Health confirmed Stewart's findings. But studies of two other groups of "medically selected" women whose babies had been exposed in utero showed no significant relationship between cancer mortality and exposure.

Vanderbilt researchers thought the radioiron study might shed light on the controversy. The women who passed through the clinic and were given the radioactive iron cocktails were also a "medically unselected" group of patients. That is, the radioactive material was administered randomly to any pregnant woman who passed through the clinic doors regardless of her health or nutritional status.

Ruth Hagstrom, a medical doctor in her early thirties, pulled together the old records and set about collecting the epidemiological data. A scientist named A. Bertrand Brill, who had joined Vanderbilt in 1964 following a seven-year stint at the Public Health Service and had done research on the Japanese bombing victims, attempted to ascertain the doses given the mothers and fetuses. "Ruth Hagstrom did all the sleuthing," he said. "My involvement was in the dosimetry part of it."

The follow-up study was supported by the AEC and the Public Health Service where, as it happened, Paul Hahn had taken a job after leaving Nashville's Meharry Medical College in 1960. At the time the Vanderbilt follow-up study began, he was chief of the research grants staff of the Public Health Service's Division of Radiological Health. His division actually funded the follow-up study and Hahn also helped the Vanderbilt researchers to decipher the old data. "He helped to find the records and interpret what his notations meant and things like that," Brill said.

The data collection began in 1964 and took three years to complete. First the researchers had to dig out the records of the pregnant women given the radioactive iron. They found records on 751 mothers. Next they gathered records on a "control" group of pregnant women of roughly the same age who were seen at the prenatal clinic at about the same time who did not receive the radioactive iron. Records on another 771 mothers were obtained.

Both groups of mothers were then sent detailed questionnaires. If the women did not respond, the researchers attempted to contact them and obtain the information through interviews. According to a journalist who questioned them in 1994, both Ruth Hagstrom and officials from Vanderbilt claimed the mothers were informed of their earlier exposure to radioactive iron when the follow-up study was done. But Helen Hutchison and Emma Craft said they were never told the true purpose of the follow-up study. "This lady called and told me she was doing a paper on the children that were born at Vanderbilt after the war," remembered Helen. "She called and said, 'I'm researching the baby boomers.'" Emma Craft said the questionnaire she received dealt mostly with cancer and did not mention anything about radioactivity or the radioactive iron. "I filled it out to the best of my ability and sent it back."

A January 29, 1965, form letter from Hagstrom to the mothers who received the radioiron begins: "You may remember taking part in a study of diet and eating habits while attending Vanderbilt Obstetric Clinic in the years between 1945 to 1949." The letter goes on to say that the university is doing a follow-up project and is interested in finding out more about the health of the mothers and children. The mothers are asked to fill out an enclosed survey and are told the information will be kept confidential. But nowhere in the letter is there any mention of radioactive iron cocktails given decades earlier or that the true purpose of the follow-up is to find out what harmful effects, if any, were caused by ingestion of the radioactive material.

When the vast amount of data was analyzed, the scientists discovered four fatal malignancies among children who had been exposed to prenatal radiation and no cancers in the nonexposed group. Childhood cancer is extremely rare, and in a 1969 paper published in the *American Journal of Epidemiology*, Hagstrom and her coauthors concluded that the results "suggests a cause and effect relationship." The findings, they continued, represent a "small, but statistically significant increase . . . and is consistent with previous radiobiologic experience." The deceased children included:

• An 11-year-old boy who contracted liver cancer. The Vanderbilt scientists said the tumor was probably unrelated to the radiation because two of his older brothers also died of liver cancer. However, attorneys representing the mothers noted the other two brothers died at ages twenty-two and twenty-six, suggesting the radioactive iron may have brought on the cancer prematurely.

• A girl, five years and eleven months old, who died of acute lymphatic leukemia. Her mother received the radioactive iron in the twenty-third week of gestation.

• A boy, age eleven, who died from lymphosarcoma. His mother received the radioactive iron in the twentieth week of pregnancy.

• A girl, age eleven, who died of synovial sarcoma of the right thigh that spread to the lungs. Her mother received the radioactive iron when she was thirteen weeks' pregnant.

The fourth child fit the description of Emma Craft's daughter. Carolyn had the same kind of cancer. It started in the same place and in the same leg. She was the same fetal age when the radioiron was administered and the same age when she died. Emma Craft would have immediately spotted the similarities between the child described in the report and her own daughter—but she would not see the journal article for nearly twenty-five years.

23

THE FERNALD BOYS

Kneeling on the bare mattress springs, holding his young body in a prayerful stillness so that it wouldn't sway, wouldn't sink deeper into the coils, Gordon Shattuck dreamed of flight; the adrenaline-filled plunge down the hill behind the boy's dormitory, through the hole he had dug beneath the barbed-wire fence, across the fields, and onto the railroad tracks that led away from the red-brick institution. The dream, if he concentrated hard enough and long enough, blotted out the throbbing pain in his knees. All of the Fernald boys, many of them grandfathers now, remember the mattress springs; their squeaky unsteadiness as they clambered on top of coils looking for a solid purchase. The punishment was meted out for the slightest infraction, a smart-alecky remark, a disrespectful shrug. If their bodies swayed—and it was hard for them not to—the attendants would slap the soles of the boys' bare feet with switches. A week or so often passed before the crescent-shaped bruises faded from their knees.

Gordon came from an unstable home. His father was an alcoholic and sometimes abusive. His mother, Henrietta, had had her first child at the age of fifteen. By the time she was thirty-six, she had given birth to twenty-one children. Gordon was transferred from foster home to foster home. He kept running away and finally wound up at the Walter E. Fernald State School in Waltham, Massachusetts. The barred windows and gloomy buildings touched off an explosion of emotions within him.

Part English, part Irish, and part Native American, Gordon became one of the ringleaders at Fernald. He was small and wiry with black hair and hazel eyes. The institution was tolerable if the boys obeyed the rules and did what they were told. But for youths like Gordon, life was hard and filled with punishing abuse that left deep grooves of rage in his mind. Especially vivid is the evening an attendant locked him in the men's room, threw open the windows to the subfreezing temperatures, and poured bucket after bucket of cold water on him until he submitted to the man's sexual demands. "He molested me, I don't know how many times," he said.

Able-bodied youngsters who were not mentally retarded and had been stashed in Fernald by poverty-stricken families, or the courts, helped run the school. They worked on the farm, picking the corn, tomatoes, turnips, and peas that were canned and fed to residents the following winter. They toiled in the kitchen, repaired the buildings, mowed the grass, and delivered the mail. One boy even reportedly worked in the morgue, slicing human brains into paper-thin sections that were pressed between glass slides. It wasn't the physical hardship so much as the lugubrious tedium that got to them; like the 1950s sitcoms blaring from black-and-white TVs, the steamed food, the long afternoons in the workshop making wallets, brooms, and mattresses.

Often Gordon was ordered to polish the floors with a heavy block of carpeted wood that hung from a rope harness around his neck. "Rope rubbing," as the boys called it, was both a punishment and a chore. Back and forth across the wooden floors of the dormitories and hallways Gordon lugged the covered wood. Rope rubbing the floors of the upstairs rooms, Gordon could look down into an exercise yard and see the less fortunate inmates of the institution that staff members once divided into "idiots" (intelligence quotient less than 20), "imbeciles" (IQs of less than 50), and "morons" (IQs over 50). They moaned to themselves and chugged in endless circles, their hands on the shoulders of the person in front of them.

Seven times Gordon had wriggled under the barbed-wire fence and run toward home, a place that in his child's mind still represented warmth and security despite its total chaos. His escapes usually lasted until dark. He was afraid of the dark, and when night came on, he turned himself in to the local police. A state car was dispatched from Fernald to bring him back to the institution. "You're a state boy, Gordon," Malcolm J. Farrell, the school superintendent and physician, would tell him. "Nobody wants you. You're gonna die here." Still haunted by the murky dark rooms, the smells, the human suffering he witnessed, Gordon began to believe it. "It was like a Hitler camp, I tell you," he said.

Into this dreary march of days came the Science Club. The name alone conveyed the kind of belonging unwanted boys such as Gordon yearned for. The brainchild of scientists from the Massachusetts Institute of Technology, the Science Club offered Gordon and his young friends a legal way to escape from the hated institution for a few hours. The youngsters were taken to the beach, to ball games at Fenway Park and Christmas parties at the MIT faculty club. They got Mickey Mouse watches and armbands that showed they were wanted. But these weren't the kind of boys who got something for nothing. In return for the trips and the trinkets, the boys had to eat the specially prepared oatmeal scooped into their bowls each morning. They also had to submit to X rays and blood tests and collect their urine and stool samples in special containers for the scientists. The Science Club, they would learn many years later, was never designed to assuage their loneliness. It was part of a scheme concocted by MIT scientists to get the boys to participate in their radiation experiments.

Like Paul Hahn and his colleagues in Tennessee, researchers in Massachusetts had readily embraced the use of radioisotopes. Robley Evans, the founder of MIT's Radioactivity Center, and one of the world's experts on radium poisoning, was closely involved in overseeing the preparations for experiments at the school.

Between 1946 and 1953, seventy-four Fernald boys were used in experiments in which trace amounts of radioactive iron or calcium were mixed into their oatmeal. The function of the initial experiments was to find out whether phytates—chemicals found in cereals that can combine with iron and calcium to form insoluble compounds—were robbing the children of important minerals. The oatmeal was scooped out of square metal pans into the boys' bowls. Then the milk, foamy and cold, was poured over the cereal. Sometimes the radioactive isotopes were mixed into the cereal and sometimes they were mixed into the milk. The scientists had impressed upon the attendants how important it was that the boys clean their bowls. "You had to drink the milk. That was the thing," Gordon remembered. There was nothing unique about the MIT study at Fernald. Indeed, the school had been a veritable laboratory for medical researchers from nearby Boston for many years.

Founded in 1848 by Samuel Gridley Howe, Fernald was the first permanent school for the "feeble-minded" in North America. Howe was a social reformer who named one of his children after his good friend Florence Nightingale, and was guided through the prisons and institutions of England by none other than Charles Dickens. His wife was Julia Gridley Howe, a famous suffragette and outspoken opponent of slavery. Edward W. Emerson, the physician son of Ralph Waldo Emerson, at one time was a member of the school's board of trustees.

Howe believed that retarded children could be rehabilitated through education, fresh air, and work. But as the decades passed and the political climate changed, the institution evolved into a very different kind of school from the gentle learning environment Howe had envisioned. Civil servants replaced the high-minded reformers. The long periods of prayer and classroom lessons shrank to a few desultory hours per day. The goal was no longer to help the mentally retarded but to protect society from them. Walter E. Fernald, a respected figure in psychiatry and superintendent for whom the school eventually was renamed, illustrated the harsh sentiments of the era in a speech:

> The social and economic burdens of uncomplicated feeble-mindedness are only too well known. The feeble-minded are a parasitic, predatory class, never capable of self-support or of managing their own affairs. The great majority ultimately become public charges in some form. They cause unutterable sorrow at home and are a menace and danger to the community. Feeble-minded women are almost invariably immoral and if at large usually become carriers of venereal disease or give birth to children who are as defective as themselves. . . . Every feeble-minded person, especially the high-grade imbecile, is a potential criminal, needing only the proper environment and opportunity for the development and expression of his criminal tendencies. . . .

In addition to the mentally handicapped, Fernald also became a dumping ground for troublesome children and adults deemed unacceptable by society or the Massachusetts courts. Prostitutes and alcoholics, "deviants and defects," children from large immigrant families, and even youngsters found by the judiciary to be too stubborn were shipped to Fernald.

In the early twentieth century, as scientific research into the causes and treatment of "mental diseases" began to expand, doctors and scientists from the ivy-covered schools in Boston began to take an interest in the disabled residents living in the institution twenty to twenty-five miles away. Here was an ideal population—a captive population—that could be studied in detail. Here were humans suffering from such rare physical deformities and diseases that they were regularly paraded before photographers who snapped their pictures for medical textbooks. The diversity and range of ailments was so great that researchers began referring to the brick institution as the "zoo."

A laboratory was set up in one of the buildings. Downstairs was the morgue where autopsies were performed and human organs stored in jars of formaldehyde. Two air-conditioning repairmen inadvertently discovered several "artifacts" from that era on a summer day in June 1986 in a storage room at what is now called the Eunice Kennedy Shriver Center on the grounds of the Fernald campus. In the unused storage room, the repairmen found two enamel cooking pots eleven inches wide and nine inches high. On the lid of one of the crocks, which was caked with dust and "old brown spatters," the word "Pedro" was written in orange grease paint. Inside was a decapitated human head in formalin solution. The head was covered with gray and brown scalp hair about one inch long. All the upper teeth were missing and a stubbly beard covered the face. The other crock, labeled "Sexto," also contained a human head.

According to documents and news reports, the heads were from prisoners decapitated by General Francisco Franco in Spain and had been brought into the United States in the 1950s by Harvard neurosurgeon Hannibal Hamlin, who was researching a new treatment for Parkinson's disease. Hamlin subsequently turned the heads over to Paul Yakovlev, one of Fernald's former researchers. Yakovlev had acquired a collection of 1,000 brains, which eventually was given to the Armed Forces Institute of Pathology. He and his successors had tried on numerous occasions to give the heads away to a medical institution but were unsuccessful. Eventually the heads were put in storage and forgotten.

Many human experiments were conducted at Fernald, including lobotomies and vaccine studies for diphtheria, whooping cough, and measles. New drugs were used in nasal discharge studies on children with Down syndrome. Prepubescent girls and boys were subjected to hormone studies and biopsies. Scientists also used the institutionalized population for a "synthetic food" study.

The radioactive iron used in the initial cereal studies was produced by MIT's cyclotron, but scientists had to go through the AEC's radioisotope distribution program in Oak Ridge to obtain the radioactive calcium. While the AEC Subcomittee on Human Applications discouraged the use of radioactive material in normal children, it allowed larger doses to be used on patients institutionalized for "mental inadequacy" and on "moribund" patients.

At Fernald, for example, the AEC subcommittee not only approved the use of trace amounts of radioactive calcium for the boys in the Science Club, but also gave MIT scientists the go-ahead to administer a vastly larger amount of radioactive calcium to a young boy described as a "moribund gargoyle patient." Gargoylism is an archaic term used at that time to describe patients suffering from Hurler-Hunter syndrome, a metabolic disorder that causes severe skeletal abnormalities, dwarfism, and mental retardation. The child was two months shy of his tenth birthday and weighed thirty-three pounds. He was completely unaware of his surroundings and could communicate only with a "birdlike whine." Clemens Benda, Fernald's medical director and an instructor at Harvard Medical School, asked the AEC subcommittee for permission to inject the child with 50 microcuries of radioactive calcium, but a published scientific paper later stated the child was actually injected with 80 microcuries. Urine, stool, and blood samples were obtained from the boy at set intervals. Cerebrospinal fluid also was collected periodically through spinal punctures. The boy died sixteen days following the injection, apparently from his disease. Bone samples, teeth, and other body parts were removed during an autopsy and studied for calcium deposition.

At Robley Evans's insistence, researchers had spent a year conducting radioactive calcium studies on rats, guinea pigs, and dogs before the tracer doses were administered to the Fernald youths. While doing the animal experiments, the MIT group discovered that radioactive calcium concentrated in certain parts of the skeleton, creating "hot spots" that were six to ten times higher than surrounding bone.

Nevertheless, Evans believed the calcium doses targeted for the boys would cause no damage. Each youth was to be given the equivalent of one-hundredth of a microcurie of radium. Since "deleterious effects" from radium did not appear until one microcurie was retained in the body, the proposed radioactive calcium doses were "perfectly safe," he assured the AEC's Paul Abersold. (During a classified meeting on fallout years later, Evans reported that boys at the Fernald school had been used in the radioactive calcium studies and noted that "additional studies might be possible there.")

The Fernald boys were thrilled to have been among those selected to eat the specially prepared breakfasts. Gordon Shattuck believed the studies were for the 4-H club. Others thought they were participating in a vitamin study. Although they didn't like the X rays, the blood tests, or the collection of their urine and stool specimens, they endured the inconveniences because the payoff was admittance to the Science Club. The scientists viewed the Science Club as an innocent way to repay the boys for the minor inconveniences suffered during the experiments. But the outings and gifts were not available to other children confined to the institution and were viewed as a "potentially coercive factor" by a Massachusetts task force that investigated the experiments in 1994.

The task force also uncovered documents showing that the school provided misleading information to the parents about the experiment. In one 1953 letter, radioactivity is not mentioned and the researcher implied the studies would benefit the boys. "Dear Parent," the letter begins:

> In previous years we have done examinations in connection with the nutritional department of the Massachusetts Institute of Technology, with the purpose of helping to improve the nutrition of our children and to help them in general [function] more efficiently than before. For the checking up of the children, we occasionally need to take some blood samples, which are then analyzed. The blood samples are taken after one test meal which consists of a special breakfast containing a certain amount of calcium. We have asked for volunteers to give a sample of blood once a month for three months, and your son has agreed to volunteer because the boys who belong to this Science Club have many additional privileges. They get a quart of milk daily during that time, and are taken to a baseball game, to the beach and to some outside dinners and they enjoy it greatly. . . .

With the possible exception of the experiment on the "moribund" patient, most contemporary scientists maintain the radioactive iron and radioactive calcium used in the experiments delivered extremely small doses of radiation to the youths. When considered against the grim backdrop of the school itself and the other more invasive studies, the radiation experiments seemed almost harmless. Still, there was something opportunistic about scientists from a prestigious university using institutionalized boys into whose lives so much misfortune had fallen.

For Gordon and the other boys who participated in the experiments, the years passed slowly. They worked in the buildings, labored on the farm, and occasionally scraped together enough players for a baseball game. The thin, frightened children became young men. Sometimes the parents came and took their sons and daughters back home. More often the youths were "paroled" into the community at the age of eighteen, nineteen, or twenty. They had learned how to reweave chairs, cut meat, make key chains, wallets, brooms, coat hangers, and mattresses. But the institution had not taught them to read or write, a deficiency that practically guaranteed a lifetime of low-paying jobs. Some former residents "rehabilitated" themselves by attending night school after they were discharged. Eventually the memories of Fernald faded or were deliberately banished as the boys married and started families. Many never spoke of their boyhood at Fernald because of the stigma of mental retardation that it carried. None of them ever gave a second thought to the special breakfasts they had consumed so long ago.

PART THREE

The

Proving

Ground

24

STALIN'S LABOR DAY SURPRISE

On the afternoon of September 3, 1949, Washington, D.C., resembled the sleepy southern town it once had been. It was a Saturday, and nearly everyone had left for the Labor Day weekend. In the hot stillness, a teletype machine began clattering in a nearly deserted Air Force building. A weather reconnaissance plane on patrol from Japan to Alaska had picked up some unexplained radioactivity. One filter paper read 85 counts per minute; another showed 153 counts per minute. Over the next couple of days, the Air Force dispatched as many planes as it could in the direction of the Soviet Union to gather samples. Then they were analyzed in utmost secrecy by numerous experts. Eleven days later, on September 14, the experts had completed their analysis. The radioactivity could mean only one thing: The Soviets had detonated their first atomic bomb. The news spread quickly among those with top security clearances. In a panic, Edward Teller called Robert Oppenheimer. Talking in his thick Hungarian accent, he asked Oppenheimer what he should do. "Keep your shirt on," Oppenheimer counseled.

The detonation of "Joe I," named after Soviet leader Joseph Stalin, spelled the end to America's brief monopoly of atomic weapons. The Soviet bomb did not surprise many Manhattan Project veterans, but caught several military men by surprise, including Leslie Groves, who had predicted it would take the Soviets twenty years to build an atomic bomb. Soon after the detonation was announced to the American people, a profound debate began in military and scientific circles over whether the United States should move ahead with the development of the hydrogen bomb, or "Super," as it was then called.

Edward Teller, who had been toying with the idea of the hydrogen bomb since the earliest days of the bomb-building project, believed an all-out effort was essential. But Oppenheimer and other scientific members of the AEC's prestigious General Advisory Committee were morally opposed to building such an immensely destructive weapon. Oppenheimer considered the hydrogen bomb a "weapon of genocide." Enrico Fermi and Isidor Rabi, also members of the committee, declared it "necessarily an evil thing considered in any light."

Echoing the doomed aspirations of the Baruch plan, the General Advisory Committee held out the hope that perhaps the United States might be able to work out an agreement with the Soviet Union so that both countries would forego the building of the H-bomb. But that hope faded quickly in Washington's anti-Communist atmosphere. Ernest Lawrence lined up behind Edward Teller. So did Lewis Strauss, who had been appointed by President Truman to the first AEC Commission. The State Department, the Joint Chiefs of Staff, Brien McMahon, and the Joint Committee on Atomic Energy also felt that the United States had no choice but to build the weapon. (McMahon, who had aspired to the presidency, said on his deathbed in 1952 that if he were president, he would direct the AEC to produce "hydrogen bombs by the thousands.") On January 31, 1950, President Truman reluctantly gave the new weapon the green light. The president believed the United States should never use thermonuclear bombs but felt it was in the nation's best interests to have them in its atomic arsenal.

Just days after President Truman made his decision, the United States learned that physicist Klaus Fuchs, a quiet bachelor who baby-sat children at Los Alamos, had been spying for the Soviet Union. Fuchs was a German-born scientist who had fled to England in the 1930s and eventually became part of the British bomb-building effort. He was a member of the British team sent to Los Alamos during the war and consequently knew nearly everything there was to know about the atomic bomb. He had even participated in high-level discussions at Los Alamos in 1946 about the H-bomb. His treason, many scientists and politicians believed, made it all the more imperative that the United States move as quickly as possible to develop the hydrogen bomb. Reflecting on the controversy years later, Teller said that three men had helped to overrule the opinion of Robert Oppenheimer and the General Advisory Committee: Lewis Strauss, Brien McMahon, and Klaus Fuchs.

The creation of a successful thermonuclear weapon required prodigious mathematical calculations. Since the computer age had not yet arrived, initially this meant slide rules and long, tedious hours of work. As the early months of 1950 wore on, it appeared as if the technical hurdles were too great to be overcome. Edward Teller blamed the stalled effort on the lack of theoreticians and dearth of imagination among his peers. But the bomb-building effort was soon to be intensified.

While Teller and his colleagues continued their work, North Korean Communist forces, equipped with Soviet-made weapons, invaded South Korea on June 25, 1950. President Truman immediately ordered U.S. troops into Korea and thus began a bloody war in a distant country, a war few Americans wanted. Truce negotiations began a year later, on July 10, 1951, and would continue for two more years amid charges and counter-charges of inhumane practices. In all, the brief conflict claimed the lives of a total of 2 million men.

The Korean War gave an even greater sense of urgency to the bomb-building program and ultimately led to a huge buildup in weapons and a vastly expanded budget. Truman vowed that the United States would go to any lengths to resist the Chinese Communists, who had intervened when the United States and U.N. forces crossed the 38th parallel, the demarcation line between North and South Korea. "Will that include the atomic bomb?" asked one reporter. "That includes every weapon we have," the president responded.

Since the 1946 Crossroads extravaganza, only one additional nuclear test series had been conducted. In the spring of 1948, another huge armada of men, ships, and airplanes converged on Enewetak Atoll, a small ring of islands about 200 miles from the still-contaminated Bikini Atoll. There three atomic bombs with yields of 37, 49, and 18 kilotons were detonated from April 15 to May 15, 1948, in a test series called Operation Sandstone. This time the responsibilities for radiological safety fell to Colonel James Cooney, the career Army officer who had assisted Stafford Warren at Crossroads and served as Warren's replacement in the Manhattan Project's Medical Section before the project was dissolved.

A lover of epic poetry and sad Irish ballads, Cooney was born in Parnell, Iowa, on St. Patrick's Day in 1903. He attended public schools in Iowa, received a bachelor's degree from the University of Iowa in 1925 and his medical degree in 1927. That same year he joined the Army Medical Corps and was commissioned as a first lieutenant twelve months later. Cooney missed out on combat during World War II but leapfrogged through the ranks after the war was over.

After Crossroads, Cooney was sent on a special mission to Japan to study the survivors of Hiroshima and Nagasaki. Years later he said one reason the bombs did so much damage was because the Japanese were not prepared, a ludicrous statement given the fact the United States had deliberately chosen not to warn the Japanese. Following his stint with the Manhattan Project, Cooney returned to the Army Office of the Surgeon General, where he became chief of Special Projects Division in 1947 and also served as chief of the medical section of the Armed Forces Special Weapons Project. In 1948 he served briefly as chief of the radiological branch of the AEC's Division of Military Applications.

With the thunderous crack of each atomic detonation, Cooney's military career advanced. His personnel file grew thick with commendations from President Truman, James Forrestal, Leslie Groves, Kenneth Nichols, and other top military officers. Even J. Edgar Hoover dropped him a note, thanking him for permission to reprint Cooney's article on the psychological factors in atomic warfare in the FBI's monthly bulletin. By 1955 he had been promoted to major general and was deputy surgeon general of the Army.

"He was a wonderful doctor, a great radiologist," recalled retired Army Major General Charles Gingles. "I called him every St. Patrick's Day to wish him happy birthday." Cooney kept his pockets filled with change, which he doled out liberally to small children, and often showed up at parties with a puppet. "Friends remember him for singing those wonderful songs and having the jumping jack [puppet] on his knee. He could manipulate it and make it tap dance," Gingles recalled. "He always brought it to every party. And he had it colored, you see. A black man."

During Operation Sandstone, fallout was heavy, but the tests were completed safely due largely to good luck and good weather. The most serious accident involved four men who suffered severe beta burns to their hands while trying to remove filter paper from the unmanned drone planes that had flown through the mushroom clouds. Huge blisters appeared and over the next decade several of the men had to undergo skin grafts and plastic surgery.

Like Stafford Warren, James Cooney also went on the lecture circuit when he returned home from the Pacific. Instead of warning of the dangers of radiation, Cooney took the opposite position, arguing that there was no reason for the public to be so afraid of atomic bombs. He also began calling for psychological training for the troops in future atomic tests. The idea had come to him during Crossroads when he spotted two soldiers with rosary beads around their necks. "An Irishman is no good when you frighten him to that extent," he said several years later. Before a Boston audience, Cooney noted:

> I have observed the reactions of the military, who were not acquainted with the technical details, on two missions, Bikini and [Eniwetak], and the fear reaction of the uninitiated is appalling. The fear reaction of the uninitiated civilian is ever evident. It is of such magnitude that it could well interfere with an important military mission in time of war. . . . If we are to live with this piece of ordnance and ever have to use it again in the defense of our way of living, we must acquire a practical attitude, not only toward its efficiency or limitations as a bomb, but also toward the possible effects and limitations of this "mysterious" radiation.

Following the 1948 Sandstone tests, military and civilian officials began looking for a place closer to home where they could explode nuclear weapons. The cost of mounting the huge operations at the Pacific Proving Ground was prohibitive, and weapons scientists wanted to speed up the development of the hydrogen bomb. Concerned that the Korean War might interfere with testing, the Pentagon was also worried that the Soviets might try to kidnap U.S. nuclear scientists or sabotage the tests in the Pacific.

The Armed Forces Special Weapons Project, in a 1948 top-secret study called "Nutmeg," narrowed the possible continental test sites to five locations: the White Sands Guided Missile Range in Alamagordo, New Mexico, which included the Trinity site; Dugway Proving Ground at the Wendover Bombing Range in Utah; the Tonopah Bombing and Gunnery Range near Las Vegas, Nevada; another area in Nevada extending from Fallon to Eureka; and the Pamlico Sound–Camp Lejeune area in North Carolina.

Although the Nutmeg study did not specifically recommend any one site, a portion of the Las Vegas gunnery range came closest to fulfilling the criteria set out by the weaponeers. The land was already controlled by the government and would not require any tedious acquisition process; the site had a relatively low population density and favorable weather conditions; and most important, it was reasonably close to Los Alamos.

The future continental test site lay in a transitional zone between the Mojave and the Great Basin deserts and had been written off by many officials as useless real estate. "A good place to throw used razor blades,"

Gordon Dean, chairman of the Atomic Energy Commission from 1950 to 1953, once observed. In truth, the region was a thriving ecosystem that was home to many species of mammals, reptiles, birds, and water-fowl. Gray-headed juncos, buffleheads, and great yellowlegs swooped through the blue vastness. Tortoises, lizards, and snakes made their homes in the shade of sagebrush and four-winged saltbush. Mule deer, coyotes, bobcat, wild horses, mountain lions, and bighorn sheep roamed the higher elevations.

The plans for a continental test site were put on a back burner after the Nutmeg study was completed. Sumner Pike, one of the AEC com-missioners, remarked in 1949 that atomic tests could be justified on the North American continent only in the event of a national emergency. The Korean War provided just such an emergency.

On August 1, 1950, some five weeks after the outbreak of hostilities in Korea, some of the elder statesmen of the Manhattan Project and the boosters of the burgeoning nuclear weapons program gathered in Los Alamos to discuss the "radiological hazards" associated with such a test site. Among those present were Edward Teller, Enrico Fermi, Joseph Kennedy, and Wright Langham.

Shields Warren did not attend the meeting, nor did any of his repre-sentatives from AEC headquarters. Warren's absence was conspicuous given the enormity of the pending event and the fact that the AEC's Division of Biology and Medicine was charged with overseeing the health and safety of the nuclear weapons program. Warren's exclusion probably was deliberate; he had not yet come around to the idea that atomic bombs could be detonated with impunity within the continental United States and may have argued against such a program. But shortly before his death, in an interview with Stewart Udall, who was representing people who lived downwind of the test site in a class-action lawsuit, Warren refused to concede that his absence was a "serious oversight" by those who convened the meeting.

Chairing the meeting was Alvin Graves, the scientist who was peer-ing over the shoulder of daredevil physicist Louis Slotin when the screw-driver slipped. Graves, who combed his longish, unkempt hair over a bald spot caused by the radiation exposure, instructed the participants to restrict their comments to the radiological hazards "omitting insofar as possible the psychological and political implications." Then he turned the meeting over to the Army officer who had found his identity in the postwar confusion of the Manhattan Project and whose career had flowered in the deepening Cold War: General James Cooney.

Breezy and confident as ever, Cooney assured the group that atomic bombs could be safely detonated in Nevada, pointing out that the medical profession "generally accepted" the position that an individual, no matter what his or her physical condition, would suffer no harm if exposed to twenty-five roentgens. Cooney said he felt certain Warren and others in the radiobiology field would accept this figure, but years later Warren said the general was "quite wrong" in his opinion. Nevertheless, records show that Cooney's twenty-five roentgen figure was adopted by Los Alamos and the AEC as the upper-level dose that civilians could receive in an emergency.

Cooney was also confident the tests would not result in any serious internal contamination. "One would have to ingest a kilogram of the material immediately under the shot tower in order to ingest enough plutonium to cause physical damage," he is quoted as saying in notes taken at the meeting.

To buttress his argument, after the meeting Cooney asked University of Rochester professor William Bale to prepare a memorandum on the radiation dose a person in the path of fallout might theoretically receive. Bale, an old-timer from the University of Rochester, had obtained one of the first biophysics degrees in the country under Stafford Warren's tutelage and had supervised the metabolic ward where Samuel Bassett had conducted the Rochester plutonium injections. When he later worked as an AEC consultant in the early 1950s, Bale discovered radon levels in a mine in Marysvale, Utah, that were more than 4,000 times greater than the exposure allowed for radium dial painters. But he applauded Public Health Service officials for not "unduly alarming miners as to hidden hazards that may exist, or in any way impeding mining operations."

In the memo he prepared for Cooney, Bale inexplicably limited his discussion of radioactive dangers to beta particles, even though he and the other scientists knew that atomic bomb detonations also released gamma rays and alpha particles. At Rochester's Manhattan Annex, Bale's colleagues had investigated the potential biological damage caused by both alpha and beta particles. Mild exposure to beta particles can cause erythema, a reddening of the skin that resembles sunburn. Severe or prolonged exposure can cause dryness of the skin, wartlike growths, chronic ulcerations, and skin cancer. "It should be emphasized," wrote Simeon Cantril, one of the Manhattan Project scientists, "that beta particles of the average energy associated with the long-lived fission products will penetrate well below the skin, and hence there is real potentiality for injury if due caution is not exercised to avoid overexposure."

Bale further limited his discussion by confining it to only three possible scenarios: He analyzed the potential exposures people living downwind from an explosion might receive from beta particles if the fallout was uniform, if the fallout was uneven, or if residents were in their homes when the radioactive cloud passed overhead. (For some reason he had concluded that most human exposures in contaminated areas would occur when the residents were inside their homes or when the fallout was uniformly distributed. Curiously, he did not explain why he believed the fallout would be uniform. Scientists knew dating back to the Trinity test that fallout did not come down uniformly and that areas of intense radioactivity, called hot spots, could develop.) "Even the lightest type of house construction gives close to perfect protection from beta rays," Bale wrote optimistically. "The soles of shoes are thick enough that substantial to complete protection to beta rays is given the bottoms of the feet when walking on contaminated ground."

The scientists attending the August conference concluded that a twenty-five-kiloton bomb dropped from a tower would expose residents in a hundred-mile radius to no more than six to twelve roentgens. They did concede, however, that some "people will receive perhaps a little more radiation than medical authorities say is absolutely safe."

Enrico Fermi wanted the report to stress the "extreme uncertainty" upon which the conclusions were based. Apologizing for bringing up "psychological implications," Fermi added that "his impression was that if conditions are such that 10 r will be received, people should be warned to stay indoors, take showers, etc." His suggestions were not followed.

With little fanfare and no input from the public, the Nevada site was approved for bomb tests by President Truman in December of 1950. Before the first weapons were detonated in January of 1951, the Atomic Energy Commission embarked upon a highly sophisticated public relations campaign—approved by the National Security Council—to gain public acceptance for the tests. The whole thrust of the PR program, according to one memo, was "to make the atom routine in the continental United States and make the public feel at home with atomic blasts and radiation hazards. . . . It appeared that the idea of making the public feel at home with neutrons trotting around is the most important angle to get across."

The weaponeers originally envisioned the Nevada Test Site, as it later became known, as a place where they could conduct quick experiments with relatively small atomic bombs. The information obtained from the Nevada tests would then be applied to the development of bigger atomic bombs and thermonuclear weapons that would be exploded in the Pacific. But the atmospheric tests and the corresponding military maneuvers became routine events and continued for more than a decade. What's more, a number of the bombs exploded in Nevada were significantly larger than what the Graves Committee had anticipated.

Two series of atmospheric tests were conducted in Nevada in 1951. Subsequently, one atmospheric test series per year was conducted in Nevada in 1952, 1953, 1955, 1957, 1958, and 1962. Atmospheric tests were conducted in the Pacific in 1946, 1948, 1951, 1952, 1954, 1956, 1958, and 1962. In addition, a thirty-kiloton bomb was exploded underwater off the coast of San Diego, California, in 1955 during Operation Wigwam, and three bombs, ranging from one to two kilotons, were detonated on rockets hundreds of miles above the South Atlantic Ocean in 1958 during Operation Argus. Some 35 other nuclear devices were detonated at and near the test site, as well as in Alaska, Colorado, New Mexico, and Mississippi as part of the Plowshare Program, a project aimed at investigating the peaceful uses of nuclear explosives.

It turned out that William Bale was wrong even in the very limited risk analysis he provided. Hundreds of downwind residents suffered from both external and internal beta burns caused by fallout during the testing period. AEC investigators later attributed the complaints to "sunburns," "gastro-intestinal disturbance," "hysteria," and "hypothyroidism."

For Shields Warren and his biomedical colleagues at AEC headquarters, the continental testing program posed a whole new set of problems. Although Warren argued strenuously against some of the military maneuvers, particularly the plan to put troops closer to Ground Zero, he ultimately could shrug those off as the Pentagon's responsibility. Fallout was another matter. Eventually the radioactive debris circled the globe, creating an international furor by the mid-1950s. Incapable of engaging in an honest debate and unwilling to level with the American public, the AEC retreated behind its walls of secrecy, sowing a legacy of distrust that still exists toward its modern day successor, the Department of Energy. Many residents who lived downwind of the bomb tests contend they were used as laboratory animals by their government. Likewise, thousands of atomic veterans allege they were used as unwitting guinea pigs by the military.

Documents that were not declassified until the mid-1990s reveal that in 1951, the year the bombs began raining down on Nevada, Shields Warren had grave concerns about the health risks from fallout. But by the time the fallout controversy was in full bloom, he had become firmly committed to the idea that whatever the risks, the tests were necessary to keep the United States safe from the Soviet Union and a world dominated by communism.

25

THE FIRST GI GUINEA PIGS

Huddled in the cold night air, with galaxies of stars wheeling above them, Jerry Schultz and his two friends listened for the sound of approaching aircraft. The three enlisted men had left their wooden shack and taken refuge in a small hollow in the desert when the man on the red phone told him the aircraft would be arriving at 0547. The red phone was a direct link to the Atomic Energy Commission offices in Las Vegas. The AEC official had warned Schultz that the atomic bomb the aircraft was lugging toward them would be the biggest ever dropped from a plane. Be sure to protect yourselves, he had warned. "How do we do that?" Schultz asked. There was a long pause and then the voice said, "Frankly, we don't know."

Jerry Schultz, Jack Richards, and Lewis Woods had been assigned to gather weather data during Operation Ranger, the first atomic bomb tests ever held in Nevada. They were just kids, between nineteen and twenty-one years old, who had been handpicked by their commanding officer at Edwards Air Force Base and told to pack their bags for a top-secret assignment. The next day a plane picked them up and brought them to Indian Springs Air Force Base in Nevada. They worked in a wooden building about six and one-half miles from Ground Zero.

In the last days of January and the first days of February of 1951, the three young men witnessed the fiery glory of Ranger's first four detonations. With yields ranging from one to eight kilotons, the bombs were firecrackers compared to the weapon an aircraft was hauling toward them at that very moment. This fifth and final bomb, code-named Shot Fox, would have a yield of twenty-two kilotons, one kiloton bigger than the bomb that devastated Nagasaki. Although Schultz's recollection differs in some details from the official account of the shot, the following is what he remembers:

At 0540 the three men spotted a blinking light coming in from the east. All commercial airliners within a hundred-mile radius had been banned from the air space. They were certain this was their bomber. Schultz harbored the irrational hope that the aircraft was making a dry run, but the sudden high-pitched whine of the engines and the plane's bank to the right told him the bomber had dropped its payload. The men had no radiation badges, no Geiger counters. Schultz made a quick act of contrition and then looked at the fading stars, the burst of gold along the eastern horizon, and the scared eyes of his two young companions. It was February 6, 1951.

The bomb split open the soft cantaloupe of darkness with a searing light and an unearthly roar that was capable of rupturing human eardrums within six-tenths of a mile of Ground Zero. "The entire landscape around us was lit up in an eerie unrealistic light from horizon to horizon as far as the eye could see. The light was so intense that THERE WERE NO SHADOWS," Schultz later wrote.

He dropped to one knee. As he did so, the first shock wave struck him. It felt like a hundred-pound bag of sand hitting him in the chest. He staggered backward and his fur cap was blown from his head. His buddy, Jack Richards, began running back toward the wooden shack. The shock wave from the blast slammed Richards into the door, shoving his hand through one of the windows.

The black floor of the desert pitched and rolled. Two lightning bolts appeared in the rising mushroom cloud. The wintry air, sharp as cut glass only seconds earlier, grew thick with dust. As the cloud rose into the sky, its billowy mushroom shape turned the color of lava and then faded to a muddy brown.

When they regained their senses, the three young men returned to their duties. They bandaged Richards's hand. They filled out reports. And they began picking up the debris. The doors and windows and the wall of the shack facing the blast had been blown out. Schultz later estimated that if the pilot had missed his target by a tenth of a degree, the bomb could have landed on them—or near enough to kill them. "When I close my eyes, I can still see it," he said of the atomic explosion. "I will never forget it."

Operation Ranger lasted just thirteen days and involved less than 400 Department of Defense personnel. The test series was predominantly a Los Alamos–run show, designed to help weapons scientists work out some of the technical bugs for the larger atomic tests planned at the Pacific Proving Ground later that spring. Those Pacific tests, in turn, would yield critical information needed for the construction of the hydrogen bomb.

The armed forces had little involvement in Operation Ranger, a fact that several military leaders found unacceptable. Determined never to let such an opportunity slip by again, the Pentagon began mapping out plans for its first large-scale atomic exercise with troops. The first maneuvers would be held in the fall of 1951 during Operation Buster-Jangle, the second test series ever held at Nevada Test Site, and would continue for another eleven years. During that period thousands of soldiers would be shipped to Nevada to participate in atomic maneuvers that were often as haphazard and ill-conceived as the bomb drop Jerry Schultz and his two friends had witnessed. With temperatures sometimes exceeding 100 degrees, the soldiers marched across saltbush and sage toward imaginary invaders waiting for them near Ground Zero. Sometimes they were lost in the dust and wind, driven off course, only to find themselves dangerously close to the scorched center of the blast.

Because the exercises often took place in areas where previous nuclear detonations had occurred or fallout activity remained, the potential exposures of the soldiers increased with each test series. Blast waves from the detonations dispersed into the air one to two inches of earth containing plutonium, uranium, and long-lived fission products from earlier explosions. Some of the troops were loaded into trucks and transported to display areas where they witnessed the bizarre and uneven destruction left by the blasts. They saw trucks, Jeeps, even planes overturned with headlights melting and leather seats burning. They smelled the singed wool of sheep placed in cages close to Ground Zero. One of the eeriest spectacles was "Doom Town," a make-believe suburb filled with tract homes, school buses, and J.C. Penney's mannequins substituting for Mom, Dad, and the kids.

In all, approximately 205,000 enlisted men participated in the atmospheric testing program in Nevada or the Pacific Proving Ground. The Advisory Committee on Human Radiation Experiments estimated 2,000 to 3,000 troops were used in actual human experiments. But many participants allege the entire testing program was one vast experiment.

Public relations, the issue that so consumed the Manhattan Project, was one of the driving forces behind the atomic maneuvers. The military hoped the bomb tests would be an emotional vaccination of sorts. Richard Meiling, chairman of the Armed Forces Medical Policy Council, a powerful group located within the Office of the Secretary of Defense, summarized the problem in a June 27, 1951, memo: "Fear of radiation is almost universal among the uninitiated and unless it is overcome in the military forces it could present a most serious problem if atomic weapons are used for tactical or strategic purposes."

The military was also eager to prove to the world that atomic bombs left no residual radiation on the ground beneath the point of detonation. Ever since the bombings of Hiroshima and Nagasaki, the armed forces had asserted that Ground Zero could be occupied soon after the blast. Meiling urged that the soldiers be marched in the vicinity of Ground Zero to prove this point:

> A tactical exercise of this nature would clearly demonstrate that persistent ionizing radiation following an air burst atomic explosion presents no hazards to personnel and equipment and would effectively dispel a fear that is dangerous and demoralizing but entirely groundless. The necessity of destroying this fear is considered to be of great importance and should be accorded the highest priority possible."

Such thinking could not have been more in line with General Cooney's. In July of 1951, just months before the large-scale maneuvers began, Cooney went to Fort Monroe, Virginia, the headquarters of the Army's training command, to sketch out goals for the upcoming exercises. Finally, the nation's troops and "Mr. and Mrs. America" would see that their foreboding about nuclear weapons was nonsense. The time had come, Cooney told his fellow officers, to replace the "negative, defensive attitude" toward the bomb with a "positive offensive type of thinking." The way to accomplish the change, he said, was by:

(1) Re-emphasizing the extreme unlikelihood of radiation injury from lingering radiation even from bursts close to the ground.

(2) Familiarization of as many troops as possible with the weapon by active participation in future tests (for example, tactical exercises in burst area immediately following the explosion).

(3) The orientation of radiologic defense thinking away from the infinitesimal "tolerance" doses used in industrial and labora-

tory practice and towards vastly larger military acceptable doses. (Later discussion urged acceptance of 100 roentgens for a single exposure and 25 roentgens weekly for eight weeks for repeated exposures.) [Parenthesis found in memo].

Cooney's proposed doses were huge, and there is no written evidence that any troops in Nevada were ever exposed to the amounts he suggested. At the time the AEC would not allow its employees to receive more than 3.9 roentgens for any thirteen-week period. And today's nuclear worker is not allowed to receive more than five rem in a year.

As for inhalation hazards, the Army Chemical Corps had been pressuring the Army's Surgeon General for "more realistic tolerance levels" for airborne radioactive materials. The Surgeon General's office acquiesced—completely capitulated might be a better term—to their demands, stating that hazards from ingested or inhaled radioactive material could be "completely discounted" and the hazard of lingering radiation was "insignificant." General Cooney and the other military men at Fort Monroe also decided it was time to jettison some of the safety precautions used at earlier tests:

> It was generally agreed that radiologic protection measures (the use of sensitive detection devices, gas masks, disposable clothing) commonly used at prior tests did more to frighten the participants than to reassure them. The question of beta radiation detecting instruments was raised. General Cooney considers that gamma detectors of *low sensitivity* (and very few of them) are the only worthwhile instruments for field use.

Thus the comments made at Fort Monroe show that even before the first large-scale troop maneuvers were held, the armed forces planned to ignore inhalation hazards and considered collecting the data with instruments that would result in lower reported exposures for troops. These remarks, when combined with the cavalier attitude exhibited by Cooney and other high-ranking officers toward radiation hazards, strongly suggest that some troops received greater doses than what has officially been reported.

Before the maneuvers began, the Pentagon's Joint Panel on the Medical Aspects of Atomic Warfare met to thrash out a shopping list of questions that needed to be answered at the upcoming bomb tests. "It is, of course, obvious," the panel acknowledged, "that a test of a new and untried atomic bomb is not a place to have an unlimited number of people milling about." The top-secret panel was formed in 1949, the year the Soviets exploded their first bomb, but it's not clear when it was dissolved. Little was known about the Joint Panel until 1994, when a stack of its records was obtained by the Clinton Committee. Those records show that James Cooney, Louis Hempelmann, Robley Evans, and Hymer Friedell served as members or consultants.

Among other things, the "shopping list" prepared by the Joint Panel called for an investigation into the psychological effects of nuclear explosions on troops, research into the efficiency of protective clothing and devices, the measurement of radioisotopes in the body fluids of weapons test personnel, orientation flights in the vicinity of nuclear explosions, and studies on the effects of the atomic flash on the human eye. It so happened that the psychological tests, the orientation flights, and the flashblindness studies would all begin in the fall of 1951 and continue for the next decade.

26

"HOT PARTICLES"

In late May of 1951, when the dust from Operation Ranger had settled, Shields Warren went to Los Alamos, New Mexico, to discuss the fallout hazards from several underground detonations planned for that fall. A lifelong New Englander, he must have marveled at the raw ugliness of a western spring: the stinging wind, the leafless willows and cottonwoods, a gauzy brown veil draped over the Sangre de Cristos. In Albuquerque, local officials were trying to tell residents what to do if an atomic bomb were dropped on the state. "A person in the vicinity of an A-bomb can protect himself by turning and falling away from the explosion," the *Albuquerque Journal* quoted a local official as saying on May 23, "thus cutting down on the danger from flying debris, burns and radiation."

Like so many before him, Warren followed the switchbacks that led up from the Rio Grande Valley to the tangled jumble of buildings on top of the mesa. In the arroyos that gouged their way down to the river, wild asters and prairie zinnias clung to the chalky soil. As Warren looked across the arid expanse toward the blue granite mountains, he may well have pondered the memo he had written three months earlier in which he had warned that the desert was no place to explode an underground atomic bomb.

At the time of the Los Alamos meeting, the outcome of the Korean War was still uncertain. General Douglas MacArthur had just been re-called after threatening Communist China with a naval and air attack. Many people, including Warren, believed another war was imminent. Los Alamos had once again become a beehive of activity. Dejected and uncertain about its future in the years following World War II (some even talked of making the lab a monument or museum), the lab staff had been bucked up by the atomic blasts in Nevada and at the Pacific Proving Ground. "In Los Alamos, a sort of status symbol evolved from the Pacific tests," the Los Alamos Historical Society wrote. "If you had a giant clam in use as a bird bath or garden ornament, you were a bona fide Bikini veteran." With the continental test site in its backyard, the laboratory's future was secure at last.

Many of the security precautions enacted during the war were still in place when Warren arrived. The entire community of Los Alamos was off limits to outsiders. Miles of fences, set in concrete and topped by barbed wire, enclosed both the town and the laboratory. The main gate to Los Alamos, with its four lanes, resembled a turnpike toll barrier. Residents and visitors, both coming and going, were required to show their passes to guards. The town itself would not be declared an open city until February 18, 1957. Accustomed to their isolation by then, Los Alamos residents were chagrined at the prospect of unannounced visits from "meddlers, peddlers, [and] mothers-in-law."

The five atomic bombs that had been exploded in Nevada in January and February of 1951 had all been dropped from airplanes. The so-called air drops did not create the immense amount of contaminated dust that underground explosions were expected to generate. The planned underground explosions were the brainchild of the Armed Forces Special Weapons Project. Ever since Crossroads, military planners had wondered if a bomb buried deep within the earth would create the same spectacular contamination as Shot Baker. In November of 1950, a month before the Nevada Test Site was officially approved, AFSWP had received authorization from President Truman to conduct two twenty-kiloton detonations on the island of Amchitka in the Aleutian Islands. One bomb would be detonated on the surface and the other buried dozens of feet underground.

But once the Nevada site opened, AFSWP officials decided they wanted to conduct the tests there. It was a much more convenient location, but even more important, it would allow AFSWP to develop a comprehensive map of fallout, something that couldn't be done properly on an island.

But Shields Warren objected to the underground test precisely because of the fallout hazards. "It is not possible for us to disregard a potential long-term inhalation hazard," he told General James McCormack, director of the AEC's Division of Military Application. "There would be a continually recurring problem of dust contaminated with material of long half-life being blown around by the winds. The arid character of the region increases this hazard."

The dispute was one of the first of many arguments between civilian and military planners at the Nevada Test Site. Since both had legitimate interests in the nuclear weapons program, they generally came up with compromises or tried to carve out mutually exclusive areas of responsibility. In this case, the two sides reached a compromise: The two twenty-kiloton tests were canceled; instead, three bombs with yields of approximately one kiloton each were to be detonated. The first bomb, at the insistence of the AEC, was to be buried deep underground and would be used to assess the radiological hazards of the subsequent tests. The second bomb was to be exploded at the surface and the third a few feet below the ground. Although they were small, all three bombs were expected to generate significant fallout because of the tons of dirt that would be sucked up into the fireballs. The radioactive dirt, being heavier than usual fallout dust sucked up in the fireball, was expected to fall to earth more rapidly instead of being carried up and away with the wind, thus posing more danger to area residents.

The meeting was so important that many of the lab's top officials were there. They included Norris Bradbury, the Navy officer who succeeded J. Robert Oppenheimer as director of Los Alamos, and Thomas Shipman, the physician who had taken over the lab's health division. Louis Hempelmann, who by then had gone to the University of Rochester, returned for the discussion. Even more impressive was the presence of Gioacchino Failla, a scientist who helped set the United States' first radiation standards. Edward Teller, who was hard at work on the hydrogen bomb, made a cameo appearance on the second day.

Fifty-five pages of notes taken at the May 21–22 meeting were declassified (with deletions) by Los Alamos in 1995 and show how shockingly little scientists really knew about fallout at the dawn of the atmospheric testing program. They also reveal that even though scientists were aware that fallout from the tests could pose serious hazards to nearby communities, they chose not to evacuate residents because they apparently feared such a move would harm public relations and jeopardize the test site.

Despite his initial reservations, Warren appeared to be solidly behind the shots by the time he arrived in Los Alamos. As chairman, he was tactful and accommodating, artfully nudging the group toward the conclusion the detonations could be carried out without "undue hazard." But a transcript of the discussion shows that several scientists, including

Louis Hempelmann, had grave concerns about the "hot particles" the bomb would throw into the atmosphere.

Scientists at the time were most concerned about particles measuring about one to two microns in diameter. A micron is a millionth of a meter. Radioactive particles of one to two microns can lodge in the alveoli, the tiny air sacs in the lungs where the blood receives fresh oxygen and eliminates carbon dioxide. Once lodged in the air sacs, the particles can continue to irradiate the lung for a long time or they can gravitate to the lymph nodes on either side of the sternum. There the particles can irradiate the white blood cells that pass through the nodes and the red blood cells in the bone marrow of the sternum. Larger particles will not enter the body; smaller ones will be brought up by the mucus system of the airways coughed out. Some of the smaller particles are swallowed and eliminated through the digestive system. The digestive system, in turn, is exposed to some radiation as the particles pass through the GI tract.

Joseph Hamilton, in a secret report delivered to Shields Warren on October 4, 1949, had warned that radioactive particles in the one-micron range "would appear most ominous particularly with respect to the possibility of carcinogenesis." Hamilton had glossed over the dangers, though, by suggesting that it would take many hot particles in the lung to start a cancer. Warren and other scientists subscribed to the same theory.

Throughout the testing program, scientists focused on the external exposures to radiation and not on internal exposures from radioactive particles inhaled or absorbed through open wounds. The prevailing philosophy was that if the external dose was within a "permissible" range, the internal dose would be negligible. But the notes of the May 21–22 meeting suggest that even during the early period of the testing program, scientists knew internal doses posed a serious hazard.

"The particle size problem is a great worry, primarily because we don't know much about the effect of small hot particles in the lungs," began Walter Claus, one of Warren's chief aides from AEC headquarters. "However, one can always say that there have been so many of these particles spread about the country (from past tests), that so many people have already breathed pretty hot particles (why be concerned with it now). [The parentheses in this quote and others cited below are in the transcript of the notes taken at the meeting and apparently represent the completion of a thought or statement.]

From his examinations of the Raitliff family, Louis Hempelmann knew fallout was unpredictable and was disturbed by the fact that the group had no hard data on which to base its recommendations. "One point makes me unhappy," he said. "All the discussion of particle size indicated that we had absolutely no idea whether breathing these things in was serious or not. I think we should at least have some philosophy or basis for saying that we think people twenty miles downwind would be safe."

Hempelmann would not let the issue go. When the debate resumed the following morning, he again brought up the fact the committee had no hard data upon which to base its recommendations: "Our safe region is based upon how many particles this committee is willing to let another person breathe."

Shields Warren, apparently fed up with Hempelmann's hand-wringing, retorted, "Let persons breathe one particle, because chances of that happening anywhere in the northern hemisphere is a good possibility."

Warren's group considered evacuating residents within a forty-four-mile radius from Ground Zero, but Thomas Shipman advised against any postshot evacuation, because it would cause "bad public relations" and might expose the residents to even greater amounts of fallout. He said, "From our experience with the fallout after the first shot on Enewetak, we found most of the people had fallout in their hair. I think we could gain more by urging the people to take baths. (Again, bad public relations)."

Along the same lines, another participant suggested that gas masks be issued if the fallout risks were high, but Warren immediately quashed the idea. "I don't think so—it is psychologically bad and also almost impossible to enforce." Although Warren acknowledged the "possibility of external beta burns is quite real," he nevertheless argued that the underground shot should proceed because scientists needed the data to prepare for nuclear war.

He added, "We are faced with a war in which atomic weapons will undoubtedly be used, and we have to have some information about these things. With a lot of monitoring, the end instrumentation will give us the information we want; if we look for perfect safety, we will never make these tests."

In the end, the participants agreed and decided to move ahead with the tests. But after Warren returned to Washington, several scientists at Los Alamos performed some additional calculations and concluded that the deep underground test—the initial shot that was supposed to be used to assess radiological dangers—might prove to be the most hazardous of all. Subsequently that shot was scrapped, but preparations for the surface test and the shallow underground test continued.

One of the participants, identified as L. Thompson, wanted to insert a disclaimer in the final report stating that the committee's conclusions were "based on conjecture and incomplete data." But Warren felt such a disclaimer might be misunderstood. "One thing I'm afraid of is that in stating our scientific caution here, we overdo it from the standpoint of lay and political feeling. Although in our final wording we have to give due regard to our gaps in knowledge, we must not make these overly prominent so as to mislead those who are not used to scientific caution." The final report was amazingly blunt nevertheless:

> The hazard in the lung is that of carcinogenesis. It was pointed out that isolated particles retained in the lung would probably not be carcinogenic, owing to the small number of cells affected by each, even though an effective total dose of radiation might be provided in the immediate vicinity of a given particle. It was further pointed out that there already exists an opportunity for appreciable portions of the population of the Northern Hemisphere to inhale and retain particles as a result of previous tests, but the significance of this event and its statistical probability are so slight as to render the actual hazard negligible. The actual risk involved is currently under study.

In the ensuing years, as he had already begun to do in this meeting, Shields Warren took the side of the scientists and politicians who contended that fallout was a small price to pay to keep America safe. In 1956, on the eve of a presidential election in which fallout was one of the most hotly debated issues, Warren said that if the atmospheric tests were to continue for another thirty years, the genetic dose to the human race would still be insignificant. "Distant or worldwide radioactive fallout is not a controlling factor in bomb testing," he said in a telegram to Lewis Strauss. "To permit us to fall behind Russians is disastrous; to wait for them to catch up to us is stupid."

27

SCORCHED EARTH MANEUVERS

While Shields Warren and scientists at Los Alamos were discussing fall-out hazards, General James Cooney and other military leaders were mapping out their strategy for the first large-scale maneuvers that would be held at the Nevada Test Site. Unlike Operation Ranger, which involved only a few hundred men, the military exercises that began in the fall of 1951 would involve thousands of troops and specific activities designed to acclimate soldiers—both psychologically and physically—to atomic weapons.

During September and October of that year, thousands of troops from military installations throughout the country were trucked to the test site. Among them were cooks, mechanics, radar operators, machinists, and paratroopers. The operation was so secret that most of the soldiers barely had time to pack a duffel bag. Few knew where they were headed or why. Most were too young to care.

The GIs lived in a hastily erected camp dubbed Camp Desert Rock, which was located some thirty miles from where the atomic bombs were detonated. The soldiers slept in rows of tents that had been staked out in the middle of the desert. With dirt floors and one pot-belly stove for heat, the tents were freezing in winter. In an effort to keep warm, GIs lined their cots with newspapers and wrapped bath towels around their necks. In the days leading up to the shot, they dug foxholes and beautified the campsite with cactus transplanted from the surrounding desert.

Fresh fish and jumbo shrimp were flown in for the military brass and dignitaries. The troops had 16-mm movies and trucks to ferry them into Las Vegas during the waiting period. For many, the visions that greeted them in the casinos were as dazzling as the dawn explosions. The GIs got free drinks, free admittance to the shows, but no free betting, recalled Venlo Wolfsohn, then a public information officer for the 11th Airborne Division from Fort Campbell, Kentucky.

The first military exercise began on November 1, 1951. In the frigid, predawn hours, some 3,000 troops were ordered out of their bunks and trucked to Frenchman Flat. As they sat on the cold desert floor, a man on a P.A. system began talking about the atomic explosion they would soon witness: Shot Dog, the fourth bomb detonated during Operation Buster-Jangle. The briefing officer emphasized the safety of their position. Within ninety seconds of the blast, any danger from the radiation would be over, he said. With simple protective clothing, they could have been positioned much closer to Ground Zero. Most important, they were told the detonation would not make them sterile. Ribbing each other good-naturedly and passing binoculars back and forth, the helmeted GIs had no reason to doubt their officers. As the soldiers jostled each other impatiently, the darkness receded, revealing the contours of a wide valley enclosed by ragged mountains. Five minutes before detonation, the men were ordered to turn away from Ground Zero. Some had film badges and goggles; most did not. Seven miles from where the men knelt in the sand, the twenty-one-kiloton bomb exploded 1,417 feet in the air.

Even with their backs to the explosion, their eyes shut and arms flung over their faces, they could feel the presence of the white light obliterating the long shadows of the morning sun. From the direction of the rising cloud of dust came a tremendous blast of heat. Thirty seconds later the first shock wave rolled over the troops. Some of the men were knocked over like bowling pins. "The ground was running at you like a roller coaster," recalled William Brecount, an equipment operator from Washington state. Robert Saunders, a Marine, said it felt like an oven door suddenly had opened behind him. Ubaldo Arizmendi, a small plane mechanic from California, remembers rocks falling on him.

A few moments later, the soldiers were instructed to turn around and look at the fireball. It was beautiful and terrifying, capped by a thin layer of ice. High winds sliced off the mushroom cap and carried it "dangerously close" to a mountain range on which reporters stood. "Though they drove frantically away, the newsmen were slightly contaminated," *Life* magazine reported. A young corporal later told *Life* he was surprised troops could enter the blast area so soon after detonation—unwittingly lending support to the no-residual-radiation argument put forth by the generals.

A short while after the detonation, some 2,796 men who had

watched the explosion were transported to Ground Zero, where they were instructed to walk through a display area where make-believe fortifications and equipment had been subjected to the blast. Meanwhile, a combat battalion composed of nearly 900 troops who had also observed the test then "attacked" in the direction of Ground Zero where imaginary enemy soldiers were waiting.

Afterward, the troops went to a decontamination station where they were swept off with brooms and monitored for radiation. "If the radiation intensity could not be lowered to 0.01 r/hr the individual was to shower and change his clothing, and vehicles were to be washed," an official summary of the test noted. Some of the soldiers underwent psychological testing to determine the effectiveness of indoctrination programs. Researchers from HumRRO, the Human Resources Research Organization, an Army contractor based at George Washington University, found the troops' confidence in the use of atomic weapons had "increased materially." But psychologists from the John Hopkins University Operations Research Office, known as ORO, claimed their studies showed deep worry and anxiety among the troops despite the indoctrination lectures.

Many of the troops returned to their home bases following Shot Dog. But several hundred remained behind to observe the last two explosions of the Buster-Jangle series—the small surface detonation and the shallow underground detonation that Shields Warren had gone to Los Alamos to discuss the previous spring. As expected, both of these shots produced huge amounts of radioactivity. One hour after firing, the lips of the two craters measured 7,500 roentgens per hour. The troops waited until the radioactivity had decayed, but as a precautionary measure, they toured Ground Zero by bus instead of on foot. That arrangement, wrote DOE historian Barton Hacker, prevented the soldiers from getting much exposure, but he acknowledged, "The absence of film badges for most of these troops . . . leaves much uncertainty."

The armed forces, not satisfied that the atomic maneuvers were realistic enough, pressured the AEC at the conclusion of each test series for permission to move the troops closer to Ground Zero. During the 1951 Operation Buster-Jangle, the soldiers were seven miles from the blast. The following spring, during the 1952 test series, they were four miles. They were moved up to two miles from Ground Zero during the 1953 series. And for a select group of "officer volunteers," eventually the gap was narrowed to one mile or less.

Military leaders also chafed under the dose limits that had been set by Shields Warren, arguing that soldiers should be allowed to receive higher doses than AEC employees because they would be receiving only "infrequent" exposures. With the Cold War in full swing and the three branches of the military jockeying for their share of the atomic arsenal, Warren and the other members of the AEC were no match for the pressure. In the end, they gave the generals what they wanted, then they washed their hands of the problem.

The push to put the soldiers 7,000 yards, the equivalent of about four miles from Ground Zero, started almost immediately at the conclusion of Buster-Jangle. "So strong is the feeling about the importance of being at a tactically realistic distance from Ground Zero that the Marines have stated they would not participate if the seven mile limitation fixed during Desert Rock were again imposed," said Brigadier General Kenneth Fields, the AEC's director of Military Application.

Shields Warren would not relent on the distance. He was worried not so much about fallout hazards as the potentially harmful effects of the blast on the troops—not to mention the potentially negative publicity attendant on any such disaster. "Accidents occurring at the time and place of an atomic explosion are magnified by the press out of all proportion to their importance, and any injury or death during the operation might well have serious adverse effects," he wrote. "The explosion is experimental in type and its yield cannot be predicted with accuracy."

But the military representatives were adamant, and after a lengthy debate, AEC commissioners overruled Warren. AEC Chairman Gordon Dean, in a letter to Brigadier General Herbert B. Loper, chief of the Armed Forces Special Weapons Project, formally approved the 7,000-yard stipulation as well as the military's request to maneuver on foot in the vicinity of Ground Zero as soon as practical after detonation. He cautioned, though, that the 7,000-yard line meant the soldiers would be "from two and one-half to three miles to a bomb run."

The following year nearly 11,000 Defense Department personnel participated in Operation Tumbler-Snapper, the 1952 test series in Nevada governed by the four-mile limit. Afterward the military decided that four miles was still too far from Ground Zero for soldiers to get a realistic sense of the nuclear battlefield. "Here again," explained Lieutenant General L. L. Lemnitzer in a letter to U.S. Representative Carl Durham, "we found that we had not yet reached the point where the atomic explosion itself had any significant effect, psychological or otherwise, on the ability of the troops to maneuver after the explosion."

The military began lobbying to put soldiers even closer to Ground Zero for Operation Upshot-Knothole, the 1953 test series. In conjunction with this plan, they also launched a campaign to force the AEC to waive its 3.9 roentgens limit.

The Department of Defense felt the AEC was "not realistic" in setting exposure limits. The AEC had authorized up to 20 roentgens of exposure for crews of sampling aircraft, but ground crews had been limited to 3.9 roentgens. The AEC eventually capitulated to the military's demand, provided the armed forces issue a public statement announcing that it had assumed responsibility for troop safety. "Our position," said one AEC official, "is that we probably cannot dictate exposure limits to the military, but we do have the responsibility of informing them of the hazards in order that they may be fully aware of the responsibility which they assume."

Before the 1953 Upshot-Knothole series began, the Pentagon conducted a study to determine the "minimum distance" from Ground Zero that troops could be placed. The armed forces knew how soldiers would respond if a nuclear weapon were detonated miles away, but what about soldiers who were called upon to provide *"close atomic weapon support"* mused Colonel John Oakes, secretary of the Army General Staff. "Under conditions of a tower explosion, such as currently being conducted in the Nevada tests, it may be possible to place troops in deep foxholes as close as 800 yards from Ground Zero without these troops suffering serious injury."

General Kenneth Nichols, the officer who had run the Manhattan Project's daily operations, recommended that selected soldiers—who subsequently became known as "officer volunteers"—be allowed to receive up to ten roentgens per test and no more than twenty-five roentgens for the entire series while maneuvering within 1,500 yards of Ground Zero. "The Surgeon General has agreed that it is highly improbable that such exposure will result in any injury to these selected individuals," he wrote.

The officer-volunteer experiments, which began during Upshot-Knothole, were carried out in a democratic fashion: The volunteers themselves calculated the distance from Ground Zero from which they felt it would be safe to watch the detonations. The proposed distances then were approved by their commanding officers. The officer-volunteers, a memo later stated, "must have sufficient indoctrination in weapons effects to be fully aware of all the risks involved in exposure of this nature including possible latent effects, and must volunteer for such duty."

In 1955 Army Major R. C. Morris suggested that humans be used to validate tests conducted on dummies and animals at Ground Zero: "Volunteers in foxholes and prone on the surface of the ground can be exposed to low levels of blast and thermal effects until thresholds of intolerability are ascertained." The Armed Forces Special Weapons Project was vehemently opposed to the idea. "It is evident that the injury threshold cannot be determined without eventually exceeding it," an official succinctly observed.

Although atomic maneuvers would continue for another seven years, the Armed Forces Special Weapons Project felt by 1955 that no more "useful data" could be obtained at the Nevada site, according to a memo declassified in 1995. Like the scientists in the Atomic Energy Commission, AFSWP was also obsessed with the possibility of future lawsuits, that memo reveals:

> In particular it is significant that the long range effect on the human system of sub-lethal doses of nuclear radiation is an unknown field. Exposure of volunteers to doses higher than those now thought safe may not produce immediate deleterious effects; but may result in numerous complaints from relatives, claims against the government, and unfavorable public opinion, in the event that deaths and incapacitations occur with the passage of time.

The statement was a harbinger of events to come. Following their tours of duty in Nevada or at the Pacific Proving Ground, the military participants returned home with mysterious rashes, blisters, and allergies that still plague them today. Some have said in sworn testimony that their hair and teeth fell out and they suffered from nausea and vomiting. Many believe they carried away damaged cells that over the decades have developed into cancer and other diseases. These veterans also believe that the radiation they were exposed to at the bomb tests resulted in genetic mutations that have caused a vast assortment of diseases among their children and grandchildren.

Ubaldo Arizmendi, the airplane mechanic who witnessed the detonation of Shot Dog, said his face turned bright red and he came down with an extremely high fever twenty-four hours later. He was sent to the camp hospital, where he said he saw other men with similar symptoms. He has had skin and joint problems ever since. William Brecount, the young equipment operator, developed blisters on his feet. Forty-five years later the blisters still plague him, and sometimes his feet burn so much at night he can't keep a blanket over them. He said, "At that age, I didn't think there was anything big enough to whip me." Robert Saunders, the Marine who said it felt as if an oven door had opened behind him, had a melanoma on his back removed seventeen years ago and now has skin cancer.

The Defense Nuclear Agency, a successor to the Armed Forces Special Weapons Project, contends that only 1,200 of the approximately 205,000 military personnel who participated in at least one test in Nevada or in the Pacific got more than five rem of radiation. Based on that data, President Clinton's Advisory Committee calculated that only a handful of excess cancer deaths would have been caused by doses received during the troop exercises.

But the veterans claim the data are inaccurate. Documents show unequivocally that many veterans were not issued film badges, and the records for some film badges are missing altogether. Los Alamos scientist Harry Jordan in 1981 said one person in a platoon or company was often given a badge, and that dose was assumed to be the same for all other members of the group. "There were also innumerable instances," he recalled in an interview, "in which arbitrarily the executive decision was made—that those people had no exposures—and therefore they weren't given film badges." Newly declassified records, such as memos describing General Cooney's comments at the Fort Monroe conference in which he recommended using "gamma detectors of *low sensitivity* (and very few of them)" show that some exposures were surely underestimated. Film badges in general could not measure the radiation from the alpha particles, beta particles, and neutrons. What's more, many reports, including the military's own official accounts, show that unexpected fallout blew over the trenches or was found in the areas where the troops maneuvered. Despite the shifting winds, unpredictable fallout, hot spots, inaccurate recording instruments, and insensitive or missing film badges, the official doses assigned to the soldiers were always and invariably low.

Even more unconscionable, internal doses received by military participants as they marched toward Ground Zero on maneuvers or through equipment display areas have been ignored. This practice continues today even though the government knows participants were not wearing respirators and that extremely high blast winds blew radioactive material from past tests into the soldiers' faces. William Jay Brady, a scientist at the test site for many years, said internal doses would be much higher than external doses but appear to have been ignored to prevent paying the veteran or his survivors the benefits mandated by Congress. Brady began working at the Nevada Test Site in 1952 and actually observed many of the military exercises. During his nearly forty-year career, he served as a radiation monitor, a security officer, an expert witness, and a health physicist. When he retired from the nuclear weapons program in 1991, he began helping atomic veterans and their widows with their claims. With his scientific background and firsthand knowledge of what went on, he has proved to be a powerful ally for the veterans. When asked why he switched sides, Brady responded, "I thought it was time to even the score."

No comprehensive epidemiological study has ever been done of the atomic veterans. The National Academy of Sciences in 1985 concluded a mortality study of 46,186 veterans who participated in five test series— Operations Upshot-Knothole, Plumbbob, Greenhouse, Castle, and Red-wing—but the study had serious flaws. It erroneously included 4,500 veterans who had never participated in an atomic test and excluded 15,000 individuals who participated in one or more of the test series. Another serious flaw was using the general public as the control cohort. Soldiers are healthier than civilians and generally have less cancer. Even so, excess leukemia cases were detected in the 1957 Plumbbob series.

In 1996, the federal government released the results of a mortality study of Crossroads participants, which produced equally confusing results. The study concluded that Crossroads veterans had a higher death rate but lower cancer rate than nonexposed veterans. Although the authors were unable to fully explain the higher mortality rate, they said the findings do *not* support the notion that radiation exposure caused the increased deaths among Crossroads participants.

Congress has passed several major laws aimed at compensating veterans suffering from cancer possibly related to the radiation exposure they received while participating in the atmospheric testing program or the American occupation of Hiroshima and Nagasaki. The Veterans Dioxin and Radiation Exposure Compensation Standards Act of 1984 requires that veterans prove that they received at least five rem of radiation exposure, an expensive and all-but-impossible task for vets. The Radiation-Exposed Veterans Compensation Act of 1988 provides compensation if a veteran can show that he or she participated in the occupation or testing program and suffers from certain specified cancers. Although the 1988 law does not require a dose reconstruction, many atomic veterans feel the list of cancers is too restrictive.

According to Pat Broudy, the widow of an atomic soldier and long-time lobbyist for the veterans, fewer than 500 of the 450,000 military personnel who participated in the occupation of Japan or the atmospheric testing program are receiving awards under the two laws established by Congress. Hundreds of thousands of veterans who helped clean up the Marshall Islands following various detonations or were involved in other nuclear weapons activities are not even covered by these laws, she added.

The Department of Defense has opposed compensation for atomic veterans for many years. In 1981 William Taft IV, general counsel for the Defense Department, warned that proposed legislation to compensate the veterans would have a disastrous and far-flung effect on military and civilian programs. The proposed legislation, he wrote:

> creates the unmistakable impression that exposure to low-level ionizing radiation is a significant health hazard when scientific and medical evidence simply does not support that contention. This mistaken impression has the potential to be seriously damaging to every aspect of the Department of Defense's nuclear weapons and nuclear propulsion programs. The legislation could adversely affect our relations with our European allies, impact upon the civilian nuclear power industry, and raise questions regarding the use of radioactive substances in medical diagnosis and treatment.

According to documents obtained by Pat Broudy, the Defense Nuclear Agency paid $13.6 million between 1978 and 1994 to a contractor called Science Applications International Corporation to "reconstruct" the doses needed by veterans to qualify for compensation under the 1984 law. To arrive at the doses, a whirl of data about the atomic explosion and the soldier's whereabouts are fed into a computer. The results have been overwhelmingly in favor of the government; fewer than fifty veterans or their widows have qualified for awards under the 1984 law.

Scientist William Jay Brady said the internal dose estimates developed by Science Applications are based on incorrect assumptions. The contractor used the amount of radiation delivered to the bone to decide whether an internal dose reconstruction was necessary, but most veterans who participated in the Nevada tests received the largest doses of radiation to their lungs and lymph nodes from inhaling the so-called hot particles that Shields Warren and others were so worried about. In testimony submitted to Congress in 1996, Brady said that many of the internal organ doses "were in the hundreds or thousands of rads, certainly high enough to cause concern regarding incidence of radiogenic as well as nonradiogenic disease."

28

CITIZEN VOLUNTEERS

The military maneuvers at the Nevada Test Site captured the nation's imagination. Letters poured into Washington, D.C., from citizens throughout the United States who wanted to witness the fury of an atomic bomb. The commission had a stock response for the letter writers: "The Atomic Energy Commission does not deliberately expose any human being to nuclear radiation for research purposes unless there is a reasonable chance that the person will be benefited by such exposure. Needless to say, we are interested in exploring all possible means of evaluating the biomedical effects of atomic blasts, but we have restricted such experimentation to laboratory animals." The following are excerpts from some of those letters:

> *Dear Sirs: Please inform me how to apply for a job in the experimental department (guinea pig). Yours truly, Walter, East Liverpool, Ohio, April 6, 1953.*

> *War Dept., Army, Pentagon Building: If you would like a guinea pig for the next A explosion—I'm your boy. Jacob, Washington, D.C., no date.*

> *Dear President Eisenhower: I hope you don't think I'm crazy. But I am offering myself to be used as a "guinea pig" to an atomic bomb blast. . . . P.S. My age is 13. Gary, Carlsbad, N.M., June 8, 1953.*

Dear Sir: . . . With all of these tests that are being made with the atomic bomb would you have any need for a live human to be placed in the target area where you make the tests? If you do, I would like to be that person. Clarence, Minneapolis, Minn., July 20, 1953.

Dear AEC chairman: Was greatly disappointed that you did not acknowledge my letter dated March 25th in which I volunteered to expose myself in the next atom blast. I am as anxious as the government to learn the biomedical effects from an atomic blast. Robert, Beloit, Wis., April 6, 1953.

Sirs: You are experimenting these days with human beings near atom bomb blasts. Will you let me be one of your human guinea pigs? . . . I will not be "at home" to newspapermen or anyone wanting to play up my volunteering to be a human guinea pig. . . . I will also volunteer to be a passenger on a rocket being sent into the stratosphere, or for any other dangerous mission anywhere on earth. Lloyd, Indianapolis, Ind., March 26, 1953.

Gentlemen: . . . I have been wondering exactly how close a human being can be to an exploding atomic bomb, absorb its effects (radiation) vibrations, etc. and still live. I suppose you might have wondered, too! . . . I also suppose it would benefit mankind a great deal to know how much the human being can take and what can be done for him (if anything) after its effects. That, to me, sounds like a real experiment you, too, may like to find out. If you are further interested, I may be your "guinea pig." Ernest, no address, Aug. 8, 1953.

29

THE CLOUD SAMPLERS

Sandwiched between the soft blues of sky and ocean, four fighter pilots cruised toward a tower of mud and water directly in front of them. The column was twenty miles wide and 45,000 feet high. As they drew closer to the unearthly shape, the jets looked no bigger than flies. In groups of two, they pierced the curtain of dirty clouds and entered the dull red glow of the world's first thermonuclear detonation.

It was the morning of November 1, 1952, in the Pacific Proving Ground, October 31 in the United States—and three days away from a presidential election. Atop the muddy column of water floated a diaphanous cloud that eventually flattened out to more than 150 miles in diameter. The apparition, shockingly incongruous in the middle of the tropical mildness, was "Mike," the first shot in Operation Ivy and the most powerful explosion ever experienced on Earth. The blast incinerated the island of what was then called Elugelab and left a huge crater on the ocean floor. Its yield was estimated at 10.4 megatons, or five hundred times the size of a Nagasaki-type bomb. A "monster," declared an Air Force historian a decade later.

The four pilots were members of the "Red Team," the first wave of samplers who were scheduled to penetrate Mike and gather radioactive debris and gases for scientists back in the United States. A "White" and "Blue" team were also slated to enter Mike later that morning. The leader of the Red Team was Virgil Meroney, code-named Red One. His fellow pilots included a Captain Brenner, Red Two; Captain Robert Hagan, Red Three; and Captain Jimmy P. Robinson, Red Four.

Jimmy P. Robinson was a newcomer to the Pacific Proving Ground where the wind and rain were often fickle companions. Just twenty-eight years old, Robinson had a little over six hundred hours of flying time. At Bergstrom Air Force Base in Austin, Texas, his home base, he had completed a course in water survival. After attending a weeklong ground school for Radiological Indoctrination at Kirtland Air Force Base in Albuquerque, New Mexico, he had flown to Nevada where he participated in one sampling mission during the 1952 tests. Nearly six feet tall and 170 pounds, Robinson thought he was ready for the nuclear tests. But the Pacific blasts were bigger and more dangerous than those held in Nevada. And Mike was the biggest explosion yet.

The day before the shot, the four men had been briefed on what to expect by Dr. Harold Plank, a Los Alamos scientist who was in charge of the scientific aspects of the sampling operations. ("A dingaling but a brillant one," retired cloud sampler William Wright described him.) As the men listened intently, Plank reviewed the shot with them, but no one—not even Plank—knew how big Mike would be or whether it would actually work. Be sure to keep your canopies closed until the aircraft have come to a complete stop, he cautioned the men. The planes were extremely radioactive following the sorties, and potentially harmful amounts of alpha and beta particles could be blown back into their faces.

The sampler pilots were buckled into their cockpits. Then ground crews draped lead-filled gowns over their shoulders and placed lead-lined helmets on their heads. The gowns weighed fifty-five pounds each and the helmets six pounds, a combined weight that was equal to nearly a third of what some of the pilots weighed. Although the gear provided the participants with some degree of protection and psychological comfort, the scientists at Los Alamos undoubtedly knew the lead would not fully protect the pilots from the penetrating radiation in the heart of a thermonuclear cloud.

When the Red team arrived in the sampling area "one hour after 'H' hour," they split into pairs. Virgil Meroney and Captain Brenner were the first to fly into Mike's stem. Filled with many tons of water, debris, and the coral remains of Elugelab, the stem was highly radioactive and extremely turbulent due to the convective forces set up by the temperature changes. When the head of the cloud moved off, a 1963 declassified Air Force history of the cloud sampling program states, the stem remained in the upright position, pouring down into the ocean the radioactive water and muddy debris for one to two hours.

It took Meroney and his teammate about fifteen minutes to make contact with the roiling column of mud and water. "When he reached the cloud, Colonel Meroney was in for a busy time," the Air Force history reported. The two men put their planes on automatic pilot while they hastily gathered information. There were three radiation instruments to monitor, data to be recorded on a report sheet, and numbers to be radioed back to Harold Plank, who hovered in the nearby scientific control aircraft. The pilots also carried a stopwatch to time their stay in "radiation over one roentgen in intensity." Wrote the Air Force history:

> Inside the cloud Colonel Meroney was impressed with the color. It cast a dull red glow over the cockpit. His radiation instruments all "hit the peg." The hand on the integron, which showed the rate at which radioactivity was being accumulated ". . . went around like the sweep second hand on a watch . . . and I had thought it would barely move!" the colonel reported. With "everything on the peg" and the red glow like the inside of a red hot furnace, Colonel Meroney made a 90-degree turn and left the cloud. He had spent about five minutes in radiation over one roentgen intensity.

The "radiation over one-roentgen intensity" could refer to anything from 1 to 1,000 rads, and the history does not disclose how much radiation Colonel Meroney was subjected to during his five-minute sortie. When Meroney cleared the cloud, he turned his jet around to watch Robert S. Hagan and Jimmy P. Robinson make their runs. Meroney cautioned them not to go too far. Soon he heard Hagan, the Red Three pilot, tell a controller that he was changing direction, indicating that he, too, had run into a pocket of intense radiation. Next he heard heavy breathing over the radio, as if someone were holding his mike down. Jimmy Robinson also apparently had run into a hot spot while gathering scientific data. When he made a tight turn to escape, he somehow overtaxed the abilities of the plane's autopilot. The aircraft stalled and went into a spin.

It was a nightmare come true. The jet tumbled down 20,000 feet through the radioactive steam, mud, and coral smithereens of Elugelab. Finally it leveled out.

Meroney radioed Robinson and asked him if he was okay. The pilot responded, "I am O.K. and the aircraft is O.K. except it flies as if my flaps are dragging." Meroney then instructed Robinson and Hagan to get together, return to the control aircraft, and then head for the tanker plane for refueling. Both pilots acknowledged the instructions and switched to a different station. It was the last time Meroney heard Robinson's voice. The young pilot was to become a footnote in history, a tragedy quickly forgotten on the day when the fusion that burns deep within stars was first harnessed on earth.

When Red Three and Red Four exited the thermonuclear stem, the skies were filled with rain clouds. Neither could visually see the control aircraft or the refueling tankers. According to a 1952 accident report that was declassified in 1998, the electromagnetic interference from Mike had disrupted the electronic equipment on their jets and also had caused the radar equipment on the nearby control aircraft to malfunction. The two pilots could not pick up the electronic signals that would tell them where the refueling aircraft was or the emergency landing strip at Enewetak. Nor could the military controllers, who suddenly found their radar inoperative, give the pilots accurate directions.

The two men circled in the "soup" for nearly an hour. As they circled aimlessly, their jets, which burned 1,200 pounds of fuel per hour, grew dangerously low on fuel. Suddenly Red Three picked up a signal for Enewetak. With only 600 pounds of fuel in his tanks, he made a beeline for the emergency landing strip. Then Jimmy Robinson's aircraft picked up the beacon. The spinout in the cloud and the climb back up to altitude has cost him more fuel; he had perhaps 400 to 500 pounds of fuel left. He, too, raced toward Enewetak.

The island was covered in rain squalls. With his fuel tanks on empty, Captain Hagan landed on the runway. The touchdown was so rough that his right main tire blew out. Then it was Robinson's turn. He radioed the tower at 19,000 feet and told them his fuel gauge was on empty. At 13,000 feet he reported that his engine had just "flamed out." At 10,000 feet he was given steering instructions to the runway. At 3,000 feet Robinson radioed the tower and said that he couldn't make it. At 2,000 feet he said he could see a helicopter pilot who had been dispatched to look for him. Then, a second later he screamed, "I'm bailing out."

Donald Foss, the helicopter pilot, spotted Jimmy Robinson's plane just north of the atoll. The jet was in a level glide at 150 knots. Foss jumped in behind the aircraft and followed it. He assumed Robinson was attempting a water landing and thought he saw the wing tanks and canopy being released. Other observers later told accident investigators they saw what looked like a seat being ejected from the aircraft. If Robinson were in that seat, he would have been weighed down by an extra 61 pounds of lead.

The jet landed with a "great deal of force" on the water, Foss told authorities, skipping like a stone for another 100 to 300 yards. Then the belly of the plane slammed onto the sea again. The nose plowed into the water, flipping the aircraft on its back. Rapidly it began to sink. The helicopter pilot kept circling the plane, calling for aid. He watched helplessly as Robinson's plane disappeared into the lagoon three and one-half miles from the runway.

In the rain, the rescue teams kept looking for Robinson. Other units arrived to help. One aircraft, in an effort to reach the search area as fast as possible, knowingly took the shortest route: through a fallout zone. The seven-member crew received exposures ranging from 10 to 17.8 roentgens. Long after the muddy stem of Mike had collapsed back into the sea and the four winds had shredded the diaphanous mushroom cap, the rescue crews kept searching for the downed pilot. They found an oil slick, a couple of maps, and one glove. The small coral island of Elugelab and Jimmy P. Robinson were gone.

For Edward Teller, the successful detonation of Mike was the culmination of a lifetime and a deeply satisfying victory over naysayers like J. Robert Oppenheimer, who had once called the H-bomb a "miserable thing" that could be gotten to battle only by "ox cart." Although Mike was a bona fide thermonuclear detonation, it still could not be gotten to the battlefield: It weighed sixty-five tons and occupied an entire building on the soon-to-be vaporized island of Elugelab.

Teller, like Oppenheimer, was a brilliant physicist, but he had none of the former Los Alamos leader's charisma. With his volatile temper and huge ego, Teller had grown so estranged from his Los Alamos colleagues that he had not flown out to the Pacific to watch the detonation. Instead he sat in a darkened basement in Berkeley, his eyes trained on a seismograph in front of him that would tell him whether the thermonuclear device had worked. As Teller watched the small point of light on the seismograph, he felt as if he was aboard a "gently and irregularly moving vessel." Suddenly the light began to move erratically, recording the shock waves from Mike as they struck the California coastline. For many minutes Teller watched the dancing point of light. When the light finally grew still, the film was taken away and developed. In an article for *Science* magazine, Teller later wrote that he was unsure if what he had seen "was the motion of my own hand rather than the signal from the first hydrogen bomb. . . ."

Back in the United States that evening, there were phone calls, telegrams, whispers of congratulations following Mike's successful detonation. Officials in the State Department, Pentagon, and White House immediately began discussing "how to take psychological advantage of this tremendous stride in weapons development," wrote Kenneth Nichols, the Army officer who directed the Manhattan Project's daily operations and went on to become the Pentagon's atomic czar. The test was not announced to the public because of fears that it might influence the presidential election. Truman, who had been shown a model of Mike at the White House five months earlier, was delighted when he heard the news. He wrote in his memoirs: "It was an awesome demonstration of the new power, and I felt that it was important that the newly elected President should be fully informed about it. And on the day after the election I requested the Atomic Energy Commission to arrange to brief President-elect Eisenhower on the results of the test as well as on our entire nuclear program."

Of the thousands of enlisted personnel who participated in America's atmospheric testing program, perhaps no humans got closer to the exploding heart of a nuclear weapon than the sampler pilots. Straight into the heaving, turbulent clouds they flew. Built into the wings of their aircraft were special tanks equipped with filter paper attached to meshed screens. As the aircraft passed through a radioactive cloud, the pilot opened the valves to the tanks, allowing the debris to accumulate on the filter paper. Radioactive gases were collected by long, hollow probes located in the nose section of the aircraft. When the planes returned from the sampling missions, ground crews removed the bottles and filter paper and sent them back to weapons scientists in the United States for analysis. As Robinson's flight showed, the sampling missions were dangerous and unpredictable, and the pilots received some of the largest doses of anyone in the nuclear testing program. The cloud samplers were used in several actual experiments, but it goes without saying that the entire program was highly experimental. The General Accounting Office estimated that some 4,000 people were involved in units responsible for manning or decontaminating aircraft.

Although Robinson was relatively inexperienced, many of the sampler pilots were combat-hardened veterans who had dodged aircraft fire over the skies of Korea, Germany, and Italy. A sortie through a nuclear cloud, a flight that one scientist said would give the air crews a radiation dose equal to a couple of chest X rays, was supposed to be a breeze. But on their maiden voyages, many of the pilots were "simply overwhelmed—so badly that they could not function satisfactorily—by the awesomeness of the cloud interior," recalled Los Alamos scientist Paul Guthals. One officer, he remembered:

> volunteered to get an early sample (H + 45 minutes). It was his first sampling mission. As he entered the cloud, he, in a normal voice, reported an "R" reading of 30. In rapid succession his "R" reading reports came over the radio—each report higher in radiation intensity and each report in a voice of higher pitch. As his instruments passed 100 roentgens per hour readings, his voice was pitched so high that it didn't seem possible that a man was transmitting.

Enrico Fermi, the brilliant Italian physicist, might be said to be the first sampler of the nuclear age. J. Robert Oppenheimer had warned before the Trinity explosion that airplanes "must maintain a minimum distance from the detonation in order to avoid radiation." So Fermi rumbled to Ground Zero in a lead-lined Sherman tank. A mechanical arm operating from inside the tank scooped up samples of sand from the desert floor. The radioactive debris was then taken back to Los Alamos, where it was analyzed in order to help its creators determine what happened in the first milliseconds of the bomb's birth. Louis Hempelmann had talked "very seriously" with Fermi about the potential exposure, Stafford Warren remembered. "As I recall, he would not wear a film badge; but he took along a meter and in he went . . . he came back later with the statement that he'd gotten a little bit but not very much. He never said how much or how long he was in there." Fermi developed stomach cancer that is believed to have been caused by his many years of exposure to radioactive materials. He died in 1954 at the age of fifty-three.

During Operation Crossroads, drone aircraft operated by remote control were used to analyze the radioactive fission products from shots Able and Baker. The material was captured by filter paper placed within boxlike holders attached to the top and bottom of the aircraft fuselages. Radioactive gases were collected by large rubber bags capable of gulping ninety cubic feet of air during a pass through an atomic cloud. Manned flights began in 1948 during Operation Sandstone when a young lieutenant colonel named Paul Fackler accidentally flew through a cloud and suffered no "ill effects." Just to be on the safe side, though, Fackler flew his aircraft through several rain squalls before landing.

Organized sampling missions began in 1951 and continued at both the Pacific Proving Ground and at the Nevada Test Site for more than a decade. Weapons scientists came to depend on the fission products and radioactive gases that the pilots brought back from their sorties. Occasionally the sampler pilots scooped up radioactive debris on overseas missions in order to obtain scientific intelligence on the atomic bombs and hydrogen bombs being detonated by the Soviet Union and China.

The program was still in its rudimentary stages when Jimmy P. Robinson made his fatal flight. Often the procedures and equipment were modified following each test series. The year after his flight, for example, a lead-glass vest covering the sides and front of the men replaced the shroud, and the cockpits were lined with thin sheets of lead. Film badges were placed on the pilots and scattered throughout the cockpit. The aircraft also were equipped with several other devices that measured radiation. The pilots kept a close watch on an instrument called an "integron," which measured the cumulative amount of radiation they were absorbing.

The samplers donned rose-colored glasses to help them hunt down the shapes of mushroom clouds. Eventually the glasses were replaced with face shields embedded with gold dust. Langdon Harrison, a retired sampler pilot, said the gold face shields enabled the samplers to better see the reddish hues that distinguish an atomic cloud from a regular cloud. The dirty colors signified the presence of nitrogen dioxide, oxides from iron, and the condensed oxides from the casings of the nuclear devices and other equipment.

The pilots also got spotting help from the scientific control aircraft that usually hovered anywhere from ten to fifty nautical miles from the cloud. A military director and a scientific director normally rode in the aircraft. Harold Plank, who helped develop many of the innovations used in the sampling program, was Los Alamos's scientific director from about 1950 to 1957. Paul Guthals succeeded Plank in 1957 and continued until the program was terminated. In an Air Force newsletter, Plank praised the squadron that performed the cloud sampling. "Its members during test operations have an urgent and important mission, which is to pursue and penetrate the bomb cloud as a target. This mission has inherent elements of risks and of personal devotion to duty which are not normally required during peacetime."

The sampling program was fraught with tension caused by conflicting goals. The weapons scientists were interested in obtaining radioactive debris and gases emitted in the first seconds of a detonation. However, this was also the time in which the radiation levels in the clouds were so high that pilots could be killed or seriously injured. As the Air Force history explained: "Needed for planning purposes was an 'optimum time' at which an acceptable radiation exposure would not necessarily or accidentally be exceeded but at which it would always be possible to collect the required sample." One Los Alamos official said the preplanning was so well done that the pilots' doses were known before the mission started. "The same for ground personnel and natives was not always true, although no serious and long-lasting illnesses have resulted from unplanned fallout or routine contamination."

Other documents, however, indicate that, in the early days of the testing program, the estimations for expected yields from atomic or hydrogen bombs could be off by as much as 50 percent, or so approximate as to be almost useless. Mike's designers, for example, estimated the thermonuclear device would have a yield of between four and ten megatons. Such uncertainty made dose predictions mere guessing games, a fact that was acknowledged in the Air Force history: "A scarcity of information on the dimensions of, and radiation intensity in clouds, from megaton devices at operational altitudes for times up to one hour after detonation made 'the prediction of air crew radiation doses in transit through such clouds questionable.' "

During most of the atmospheric testing period, the AEC limited the "permissible doses" test personnel received to no more than 3.9 roentgens during a thirteen-week period. But the dose limits were waived for air crews. The Air Force Surgeon General permitted up to 50 roentgens for air crews during the 1956 Redwing test series, but no participant received that high a dose.

The actual exposures the pilots received are a matter of controversy. The Defense Nuclear Agency, a successor to the Armed Forces Special Weapons Project, could not provide an average dose received by the samplers but said the largest dose any one pilot got was 42.5 roentgens. Several retired sampler pilots believe their exposures were much higher than that. And the General Accounting Office uncovered evidence in the mid-1980s that bolstered the claims that exposures were underestimated.

When the pilots completed their flights, they continued to be irradiated on the way home from the debris that collected in the engines and on the external surfaces of the planes. "As a result a radiation flux or 'cockpit' radiation background existed within the interior of a sampling aircraft after its departure from the cloud," the Air Force history stated.

"While returning to base the pilot received additional radiation exposure."

When the planes landed, special forklifts were rolled up so that the pilots could step from their cockpits onto the platform and be rolled away without touching the sides of the planes. Air Force officials, embarrassed when visitors saw the pilots being wheeled away on platforms, eventually tried to do away with the forklifts. "Those aircraft never calmed down completely for 10 or 20 years," pilot William Wright remembered.

If time permitted, the aircraft usually were towed to an isolated area and the radioactive debris allowed to decay overnight. Then the planes were scrubbed down by ground crews. One pilot said Duz, a common laundry detergent, was used on the exteriors of the planes and ground walnuts shoveled into the engines. But the Air Force history said a special compound called "Gunk" was applied. Proper cleansing was important, the Air Force noted, because "grease spots collected more than one hundred times as much contamination in passage through a radioactive cloud as a clean surface of equal area." The soapy water, contaminated with radioactive debris, was often allowed to run into the desert sand.

The Air Force sought to eliminate the decontamination procedures in 1957 to save money and time. "Our experience in nuclear tests in developing knowledge of the psychological effects of radiation on humans, indicates that aircraft decontamination is not required for reasons of personnel safety except in unusual circumstances," wrote Air Force Colonel William B. Kieffer. ". . . We believe it is imperative that we take the lead in establishing a reasonable attitude toward decontamination requirements. . . . Furthermore, substantial economics may result from a reduction in aircraft decontamination efforts."

The Air Force proposal provoked a heated argument with Los Alamos scientists, among them Harold Plank, Alvin Graves, and Thomas Shipman. Shipman, a patrician-looking scientist with a biting wit, intensely resented the military's involvement in the weapons testing program. "We have always gone on the theory that the only good exposure is zero," he began.

If this means that the Air Force is trying to indoctrinate its personnel with the belief that moderate exposures may be received with impugnity [sic], I could not disagree more violently. Perhaps this means that the Air Force is so superior that exposure which might hurt other people do not damage them and that rules necessary for other people do not apply to Air Force Personnel.

The ground crews who removed the filter papers with tongs and rolled them into lead "pigs" were also in danger of being overexposed. The filter papers were extremely radioactive. At a distance of one foot, some of the filter paper emitted a gamma radiation intensity of 100 roentgens per hour. At twenty-five feet, the background intensity from the paper was approximately 0.5 roentgens per hour. Even the lead pigs did not completely shield all the radiation. During the flights back to the States, the samples were marked so that "neither crew or passengers would get close enough to the pigs to receive more than one week's tolerance dose during the flights." The samples were flown straight back to Los Alamos or Lawrence Livermore, another weapons lab established in California in the early 1950s. The samples were removed immediately from the pigs, placed in acid solutions, and dissolved.

Following the flights, the air crews went to a decontamination area where they stripped down and showered. "After we went through the showers, we were washed down and they checked us through the dosimeter on the Geiger Counter. Then we'd go through the showers again until finally it got down to what they considered an acceptable rate. Still we were emitting radiation even when it was an acceptable rate," Langdon Harrison recalled at a 1985 Veterans Administration hearing.

Harrison's recollections are partially confirmed in the Defense Nuclear Agency's official reports. For example, air crews during the 1951 Operation Ranger were emitting an average of 0.2 to 0.3 roentgens per hour following their sampling missions. Without scrubbing, the men could have exceeded today's 5-rem-per-year limit in about twenty-four hours.

Like the Army generals who kept nudging the troops closer to Ground Zero, the Air Force brass had a burning desire to find out what happened to a pilot who flew through an atomic cloud minutes after detonation. "Since there is a lack of knowledge concerning the homogeneity of the radioactivity in early thermonuclear clouds, there is a further requirement that at least part of the cloud penetrations should be straight through on a horizontal flight path at altitudes of interest to SAC [Strategic Air Command]," Air Force Brigadier General W. M. Canterbury stated in a letter to the Air Force Surgeon General.

Air crews eventually flew through atomic and thermonuclear clouds as early as seventeen minutes after detonation in an experimental project called the Early Cloud Penetration Program. Before the human studies began, mice and monkeys were flown through the nuclear clouds in remote-controlled aircraft. The animals then were killed and examined for internal contamination. Scientists concluded the internal hazard was negligible, although on what basis they came to that conclusion is difficult to say, since it would have taken years for cancers to have developed.

The first early penetration experiments with humans were conducted during Operation Teapot, a 1955 test series in Nevada. Among other things, scientists wanted to find out if the internal doses air crews received on a pass through an atomic cloud were equal to external doses measured on film badges. Before penetrating the cloud, pilots and technical observers swallowed a film packet consisting of nine small disks of film enclosed in a watertight capsule attached to a string. A similar capsule was attached to the outside of the flight suits. Seven penetrations were made from seventeen to forty-one minutes after detonation. Dose rates in the mushroom cloud were recorded as high as 1,800 rad per hour. Afterward, the two packets of film were analyzed. Scientists concluded that the external film badges accurately reflected the internal radiation doses the crews were receiving. Crews also rubbed their bare hands on the radioactive surfaces of the returning planes as part of an experiment to evaluate the radiation meters and "define exactly" what dangers existed for men working around contaminated aircraft.

Los Alamos scientist Wright Langham was brought in for a second group of experiments during Operation Redwing, a series of atomic and hydrogen bomb tests conducted in 1956 at the Pacific Proving Ground. During those experiments, scientists sought to measure the hazard from inhaling or ingesting radioactive particles on a sortie through a thermonuclear cloud. Before departing for the Pacific, the pilots and observers were sent to Los Alamos, where twenty-four-hour urine samples were collected and each participant's internal radioactivity measured in the lab's whole-body counter, a device that can measure the radiation of an entire body. The air crews then made twenty-seven penetrations of thermonuclear clouds from twenty to seventy-eight minutes after detonation. Radiation dose rates as high as 800 rads per minute were measured. Urine samples were collected from each subject immediately after the cloud penetrations and shipped back to Los Alamos for analysis.

Upon their return to the States, the radioactivity in the participants' bodies was measured again by the whole-body counter at Los Alamos. The pilots had absorbed a "wholly insignificant" amount of internal material from the flights, the scientists concluded. The exposures were so negligible, in fact, that Langham and his colleagues recommended that "no action" be taken to develop filters for aircraft pressurization systems nor "to develop devices to protect flight crews from the inhalation of fission products."

The cloud samplers continued to swoop in and out of the mushroom clouds until 1962. Like the ground troops, many of the pilots developed cancer or other diseases that they feel were caused by their radiation exposure. Langdon Harrison, who contracted prostate and bladder cancer, believes wholeheartedly that he received more than the 8.5 roentgens listed on his official reports. He said often he was ordered to circle in the dirty-looking clouds for up to fifteen minutes while trying to fill his tanks with radioactive gases. All the while he watched as the numbers on his radiation monitors climbed.

Harrison said he would never have volunteered for the sampling missions if he had been informed of the risks. "The whole thing was fraught with peril and danger and they knew it was, and this I resent quite readily," he told one interviewer. "There isn't anybody in the United States who isn't a downwinder, either. When we followed the clouds, we went all over the United States from east to west and covering a broad spectrum of Mexico and Canada. Where are you going to draw the line? Everyone is a downwinder. It circles the earth, round and round, what comes around goes around."

DISPATCH FROM GROUND ZERO

The sampler pilots returned to Nevada in the spring of 1953 along with thousands of ground troops for one of the longest and dirtiest test series yet. Eleven atomic bombs were detonated during Operation Upshot-Knothole. Seven were dropped from towers, three from airplanes, and one was fired from a cannon. With so many detonations, the military leaders had ample opportunity to try out the new "officer volunteer" program, a project in which officers witnessed the blasts at close range. It's not known how many officer volunteers participated or whether they suffered any long-term effects. President Clinton's Advisory Committee estimated that fewer than 100 people were involved. One of the participants was Robert Hinners, a young Navy captain, who hunkered down with seven other officer volunteers in a trench 2,000 yards, or a little over a mile, from Ground Zero when Shot Simon was exploded on April 25, 1953. Simon had an "official yield" of forty-three kilotons, but Hinners estimated the yield to be fifty to fifty-five kilotons. Other records support his numbers.

The military allowed the eight officer volunteers to observe the explosion 2,000 yards *closer* to Ground Zero than the Army had concluded was a safe distance for bombs in the thirty-five- to forty-kiloton range. Hinners estimated that he and his fellow officers received 13.6 roentgens of radiation, but a memo declassified in 1995 stated the officers probably received "24 rem initial gamma plus neutron radiation." (Neutrons are at least ten times more effective at causing biological damage than gamma radiation.)

Hinners prepared a report on his experience for the Armed Forces

Special Weapons Project, which provides an extraordinary firsthand account of the light, the radiation, and the dust from an atomic detonation witnessed at close range. The following are some excerpts from his account:

> 3. *Prior to final acceptance as a member of the group, each officer was required to personally and individually compute the effects to be expected in an open trench on the basis of the expected yield of 35 to 40 KT, and to recommend a distance for positioning the group which would not exceed the effects criteria which had been established for this exercise. Each officer also was required to execute a certificate confirming his volunteer status. . . . In submitting my own forms, I recommended a distance of 2,000 yards.*
>
> 4. *General Bullock reviewed the computations at a briefing conference held in his office on the day before the shot. Since there was substantial agreement between all of the officers of the group as to the 2,000 yard distance, this distance was approved by the General. . . . Trenches previously had been prepared at 500-yard intervals, so that the final decision could be made with some flexibility on the basis of the weather conditions and any other last-minute considerations having any bearing on the predicted effects. At the final briefing, General Bullock also informed us that although there had been a rather complete press release on the volunteer program following the first Desert Rock V exercise, more recent security restrictions precluded public release of the exact distance at which we would be positioned relative to Ground Zero or of any of the other details of our position and observations. . . .*
>
> 8. *On the morning of the shot, we rode to the forward area on one of the buses of the regular troop observer convoy. The Army psychologists accompanied us as far as the main troop positions at the 4,000-yard point. Our group continued on alone by truck to the general vicinity of the 2,000-yard position, arriving there about one hour before shot time. . . . We remained above ground until about 15 minutes before shot time, at which time we entered our trenches. There were two trenches in line, each about 20 feet long, 3 feet wide and 6 feet deep, with their adjacent ends separated by about five yards of unexcavated earth. One was reinforced with a solid wood lining on the front and rear faces and cross-braced with wood timbers at about 4-foot intervals. The other one was unrevvetted. Each trench had a row of sandbags placed flat on the ground*

around its top perimeter, and had a loose fill sloped to about a 45 degree angle at each end to facilitate climbing in and out. We were permitted to choose our respective positions. I chose the unrevvetted trench, along with two other officers of the group. Both trenches were bare of any equipment except for several shovels. . . .

10. The following is a summary of the various effects as we observed them at 2,000 yards from Ground Zero, in the positions described:

a. Light—The intense white light was the first manifestation of the explosion, and seemed to persist for at least six seconds, as it continued well beyond the time of arrival of the shock wave. I was wearing Navy safety goggles with clear glass lenses, as I was carrying a high-range experimental type of radiation survey meter and had hoped to get an early reading of the prompt nuclear radiation by opening my eyes very slightly. This proved to be impossible; I not only could not see the meter scale or pointer, but could not even see the profile of the instrument, the bottom of the trench, nor any other surrounding objects. There was nothing but white light on all sides. However, I had no sensation that it was hurting my eyes; it merely blanked out all vision for the duration of the fireball. When the fireball finally cooled off and the light gradually diminished, I had no sensation of any momentary flash-blindness; so far as I could tell, my eyes adapted to the rather dim early morning light (which was further reduced by the heavy dust cloud) as fast as the fireball disappeared.

b. Earth shock—This was the second manifestation of the explosion to be felt at our position, and in our case never exceeded a rather slight trembling motion. I was squatting on the balls of my feet with one shoulder braced lightly against the forward wall of the trench. In spite of this rather unstable position, at no time did I lose my balance due to ground motion, nor did I feel any appreciable ground shock against my shoulder. . . .

c. Heat—There was no sensation of heat in the trench; not even on my face, which was entirely exposed except for the small area covered by the frames of my safety goggles. . . .

d. Nuclear radiation—The first reading which I was able to obtain on my survey meter was exactly 100 r/hr. I estimate this to have been at about 8 seconds after the detonation, as soon as the light had diminshed enough for me to regain my sight. At this time, the pointer on the instrument was moving smoothly downward. The decrease in the reading was fairly rapid at first—down to 50 r/hr. during the next 10 seconds or so—but the rate of decrease then gradually slowed down so that it required about one additional minute for it to drop down to a reading of between 20 and 25 r/hr. I was calling the readings over to the group leader in the other trench and at this point he directed us to leave the trenches. I watched the meter as I climbed out, and it moved up to 40 r/hr. as I left the trench for the open ground. We stopped briefly to examine some sheep which had been tethered in a dugout, in shallow trenches, and in the open in the vicinity. As we did so, I noticed that the meter reading was gradually increasing, so that it was again up to about 50 r/hr. by the time we started walking down the road away from Ground Zero. It was then about four or five minutes after the burst. During all this time, particles of sand or other debris were continually raining down on our helmets; the sound resembled light sleeting.

11. As we walked away from Ground Zero, the survey meter reading steadily decreased, but whenever we stopped to look at something, it would gradually increase again which indicated that a substantial amount of fallout was still being deposited at those distances (between 2,000 and 2,500 yards from Ground Zero). After we had walked for about a quarter of a mile, we were met by our two evacuation trucks; by this time the instrument reading was down to about 10 r/hr. The reading continued to decrease rapidly as we moved away from Ground Zero by truck, and was down to less than 1 r/hr. by the time we reached the main body of troops at the 4,000-yard position. . . .

14. The principal effects visually observed above-ground after we had emerged from the trench were:

a. Sheep—Those in the vicinity were singed to a dark brown color on those portions of their bodies which had been exposed to line-of-sight thermal radiation, but they were all on their feet and showed no other evidences of physical injury.

b. Trees—A large Joshua tree just outside our trench was partly broken off and on fire. . . . Other Joshua trees were burning on all sides of our position.

c. Dust—The dust was sufficient to make the visibility very poor beyond a hundred yards or so in any direction, but was not heavy enough to be suffocating. I did not feel the need of putting on my gas mask, and did not use it.

15. *A stop was made for a monitoring check at the Desert Rock station across from the control point on our way back to camp. It was found that sweeping off our clothing and shoes with a broom was sufficient to bring the reading down to an acceptable level.*

16. *Following our return to camp, we were given an "exit interview" by the Army psychologists, and filled out questionnaires, Tab [illegible]. With respect to the question concerning the ability of the troops to carry on immediately after emerging from trenches under these conditions, it was the consensus of opinion that there should have been no difficulty except a reduction in efficiency for about the first five minutes due to the heavy dust cloud and resultant poor visibility. . . .*

31

THE INVERTED MUSHROOM

A young Army lieutenant shepherded his platoon into a trench 1,700 yards behind the officer volunteers on the morning that Shot Simon was being readied for detonation. The desert was blanketed in darkness. Two miles away, a small light glowed at the base of the 300-foot tower cradling the bomb. Normally the weapons were exploded about thirty minutes before sunrise. That way the flash from the bomb would trip the photoelectric cells that started the recording equipment and give the sampler pilots enough daylight to see the mushroom cloud.

The lieutenant, identified only as S.H., was the last man to march down the ramp into the five-foot-deep trench. He had been warned by his commanding officer not to look at the blast. Just twenty-two years old and two months out of officers' training school, the lieutenant found the temptation irresistible. As the loudspeaker counted down the last seconds, S.H. turned and glanced over his left shoulder. At that very moment, Simon was exploded in a fury of light and sound.

Before the young officer had time to blink, the light flooded into his eyes. His pupils, which were dilated for night vision, instantly absorbed more than fifty times the energy they would have during daylight. The flash bleached his retinas, turning the world white. Momentarily blind, S.H. staggered down into the trench to join his platoon. When his sight began to return, his men resembled white shadows. His vision remained blurred for the rest of the day, and his left eye began to swell. That evening when he tried to read, the print appeared distorted and a spot on the page seemed to move with his eyes. When he reported the problem to the camp medical officer the following day, he was whisked to a hospital in Fort Hood, Texas, immediately.

At the military hospital, he was placed on a salt-free diet and administered cortisone and atropine. The swelling in his left eye decreased markedly. But radiating tension lines soon appeared around the burn, suggesting that he might suffer a retinal detachment in the future. The lieutenant was released from the hospital about four weeks after the accident. Soon after his hospital discharge, he was separated from the service. Branded forever onto his left retina was a small blind spot. When an eye doctor from Brooklyn, New York, examined the young man's eyes two years later, he discovered something astonishing: The blind spot resembled an "inverted mushroom."

Long before the inverted mushroom appeared on the young lieutenant's eye, scientists had been concerned about the flash from the atomic bomb. At Trinity, observers had been cautioned to wait a few seconds before looking at the fireball through pieces of dark welder's glass. Everyone heeded the instructions except Richard P. Feynman, the future Nobel laureate. Feynman climbed into a truck, reasoning that the windshield would protect his eyes from the harmful rays. "I'm probably the only guy who saw it with the human eye," he later wrote. One historian said Feynman was temporarily blinded, but Feynman doesn't mention such a problem in his autobiography.

Radiation emitted by the cyclotron and other sources were also extremely damaging to the eye. Early in his tenure at the AEC's Division of Biology and Medicine, Shield Warren was confronted with the unsettling news that cyclotron workers were developing cataracts at an alarming rate. "Calls about cyclotron eyes," he jotted in his diary December 19, 1948. The eyes of eleven scientists were examined. Three had very severe cataracts, four had mild ones, and four had none. The findings prompted the AEC to begin a preliminary investigation of 1,000 people in Hiroshima who were believed to have been within 3,000 feet of the hypocenter. Forty "certain" cases of radiation cataracts and an additional forty "suspected" cases were found.

Military leaders had grave concerns about the effects of the atomic flash on soldiers and airmen. How could soldiers fight wars if the enemy's A-bombs blinded them? How could pilots fly? "Should the central vision of a soldier or airman be temporarily disabled and the visual acuity reduced below 20/400, he becomes useless as a fighting man and easy prey to the enemy and potentially a danger to his own forces," a document declassified by Los Alamos in 1995 states.

Like all light, the energy from an atomic flash passes through the lens of the eye, where it is projected in an upside-down image on the retina, a layer of tissue at the back of the eyeball. The retina, which acts much like a piece of film, contains the rods and cones that turn light into an electrical impulse that is then carried to the brain by the optic nerve. Because of the focusing ability of the eye, retinal burns occurred at far greater distances from Ground Zero than skin burns. William Jay Brady, the scientist who worked at the Nevada Test Site for many years, said he was injured twice by the flash from atom bombs. His eyes felt like they had sand in them for the first two weeks or so. Then "floaters" or black spots, appeared in his vision, which remain to this day.

The "flashblindness" experiments began almost simultaneously with the first atomic maneuvers in the fall of 1951 and were conducted through at least 1962. They continued even after the military officers and their scientific colleagues knew with certainty that the flash from the atomic bomb could cause permanent eye damage and even blindness.

The Air Force School of Aviation Medicine in San Antonio, Texas, today known as the School of Aerospace Medicine, was the lead investigator in the early experiments. Scientists at the school were particularly interested in the effects of flashblindness because one of its most renowned scientists, Hubertus "Strugi" Strughold, had suffered a retinal burn during an eclipse. "That's the thing that gave us curiosity," recalled retired Air Force Colonel John Pickering, who joined the school in the 1940s and subsequently became director of medical research.

As it happens, Strughold was a German scientist who had directed the Third Reich's Aeromedical Research Institute in Berlin during World War II. He was brought to the School of Aviation Medicine in 1947 under the auspices of a controversial project that became known as Operation Paperclip. Hundreds of German scientists were imported into the United States, courtesy of Operation Paperclip and its related programs, to work on scientific and industrial projects. Many of the foreign scientists, including Strughold, were alleged to have had connections with the Nazi Party. Some were accused of participating in the human experiments conducted in the concentration camps. Strughold, who died in 1986 in San Antonio, repeatedly denied that he had any connection to the Nazi Party or the concentration camp experiments. But a 1947 intelligence assessment report on Strughold observed, "His successful career under Hitler would seem to indicate that he must be in full accord with Nazism." Scientific reports and personnel records on file at the National Archives show that at least three Paperclip scientists—Heinrich Rose,

Paul A. Cibis, and Konrad Buettner—were involved in flashblindness research at the School of Aviation Medicine.

Heinrich Rose, a diminutive scientist with blond hair and blue eyes, worked for Strughold when he was in the Luftwaffe from 1939 to 1945. He was an expert in visual acuity, night vision, and depth perception, all problems of vital concern to the U.S. Air Force. According to intelligence reports, Rose was a member of the Nazi Storm Troopers from 1933 to 1935 and achieved the rank of *Sanitatsoberscharfuhrer,* or "sanitary red cross corporal." A denazification court in Heidelberg, Germany, classified him as a "follower" after the war and fined him 500 Reichmarks.

But in an affidavit for an immigrant visa, Rose stated that he had been urged to join the Storm Troopers by the local party leader in Berlin who was also his supervisor at the hospital where he was doing an internship. "While a member of the SA [Storm Troopers], I did not participate in any other activities than in those of a medical nature," he wrote. According to a security report prepared by U.S. Office of the Military Government, Rose was a member of the Nazi Party from 1937 to 1945. But Rose said in an affidavit he was not a party member, and no records were found indicating party membership. The Air Force awarded Rose the Exceptional Service Award, its highest civilian honor, ten years after his arrival in the United States for his studies on visual aids in aircraft landings, depth perception, night-vision training for pilots, and flashblindness arising from atomic bomb explosions.

Paul Cibis, whose last name also appears as "Zibis" on some military records, was brought to the United States some time after 1949. Cibis was "especially qualified in the field of time relationships and vision," wrote Walter Agee, a brigadier general working in the Air Force's Directorate of Intelligence. "His services are also desired in connection with studies in relation to the recognition and identification of aircraft flying at supersonic speeds. Dr. Zibis is further qualified in studies on the adaptation to darkness and has recently published a paper of fundamental importance in this field."

Konrad Buettner, a slender, serious-looking scientist with a ruddy complexion and brown hair, arrived in the United States in June 1947. His records state that he was a member of the Nazi Storm Troopers from 1934 to 1938, the Nazi Party from 1933 to 1939, and a major in the Luftwaffe from 1939 to 1945. At the height of the war, he was involved in experiments studying the pressure changes on pilots pulling in and out of dives and the "climatization" of airplane cabins and cockpits.

Buettner, who eventually moved on to the University of Washington in Seattle, said he joined the Storm Troopers and the Nazi Party "under pressure" from party organizations. He said he was expelled from the Storm Troopers and resigned from the Nazi Party. "When invited to re-enter the party during the war, I declined," he stated in an affidavit for an immigrant visa.

One of Buettner's colleagues described him as a dedicated scientist who cared little for "material advantages." But another remembered his "very elegant dwelling" and how he "paid all the expenses for social festivities among his circle of friends." A security report states that Buettner was not in "sympathy with Nazism but of necessity maintained a discreet silence."

From 1931 to 1947 Buettner, a meteorologist, conducted experiments at the University of Kiel on the effects of heat, cold, and moisture on human beings. According to Buettner's personnel records, his research included "Experiments with human beings in Arctic (Norway), subtropic (Sahara), and tropic (Bel. Congo), climate, climatic chambers and in aircraft. Erythema and solar-ultraviolet aerosol and static electricity (dust, fog, and salt crystals.)"

Buettner was assigned to two projects when he arrived at the School of Aviation Medicine. One involved the development of clothing and goggles to protect against intense heat. The second was the "correlation of skin temperature with pain threshold of skin." Part of the second project involved determining how "White and Colored Human Skin" would react to the atomic flash. For his experimental subjects, he used pigs because their skin behaves like human skin.

Focusing an intense beam of light on the black skin of young anesthetized pigs, Buettner observed that "blisters began to rise after 2.2 seconds, and they exploded with a light popping noise after 4 seconds." When the beam of light was aimed at the white skin on the same pig, Buettner found no signs of blistering even after ten seconds. "Its significance in civil defense," he said of the finding, "is obvious when one considers the close microscopic similarity of black pig and heavily pigmented human skin."

The first flashblindness experiment took place during the 1951 Buster-Jangle series. Approximately twenty-five volunteers watched the blast from a C-54 aircraft nine miles from Ground Zero. Some subjects wore goggles; others were given no eye protection. The initial study concluded that air crews who witnessed atomic detonations during daylight did not suffer any "serious visual handicap."

During the 1952 Tumbler-Snapper test series, the armed forces wanted to conduct flashblindness experiments at night in order to "determine accurately what temporary or permanent effect the flash of an atomic explosion has on the human eye." The AEC, which had demanded a written release from the military during the first experiment, had reservations about the second but eventually agreed to the military's demands.

A light-tight trailer was constructed and hauled to a location ten miles from Ground Zero. With twelve portholes punched into one side, the trailer bore a crazy resemblance to an oceangoing vessel that somehow had washed up on the Nevada desert. Inside the trailer, twelve stools on runners were positioned in front of the portholes. Directly behind the stools were visual charts, aircraft instruments, and other devices designed to measure the visual acuity of the test subjects after they witnessed the flash.

The portholes were fitted with shutters that exposed the left eye of each subject to the detonation. Half the subjects wore protective goggles while the other half did not. "The shutters remained open 2 seconds which allowed maximum bleaching of the retina and then the shutters closed." The experimental subjects then turned on their stools and attempted to operate the aircraft instruments.

The experiment was aborted after two shots when two men developed retinal burns. Air Force Colonel Victor Byrnes stated in a formerly classified report that both men had "completely recovered." But a scientific paper published three years later suggests that wasn't the case. That article disclosed that five of six people who suffered eye injuries from watching atomic blasts had developed a permanent blind spot or scar tissue. "Consequently, we assume that in these areas visual function is permanently destroyed," the authors wrote.

The injuries should have discouraged further experimentation, but the School of Aviation Medicine forged ahead with even more elaborate preparations for the 1953 Upshot-Knothole tests, the series during which S.H.'s eye was imprinted with the upside-down mushroom. Before the test series began, Heinrich Rose and Konrad Buettner calculated that at night the flash from a twenty-kiloton bomb could produce retinal burns forty miles away. "Due to the concentration of the energy in the image formed on the retina, skin burns and retinal burns follow different laws," they wrote.

The light-tight trailer was again used for the experiments. But instead of remaining stationary, it was moved from distances ranging from seven to fourteen miles from Ground Zero. Once again the shutters opened briefly to expose the subjects' left eyes. But this time the participants viewed the detonations through a double filter that reduced the light transmitted to the retina by 75 percent. Only one person, an officer with darkly pigmented eyes and the initials C.B., sustained a "slight retinal" burn. The injury occurred during "Climax," the largest shot in the Upshot-Knothole series and the largest nuclear weapon detonated in Nevada up to that date. The trailer was seven miles from Ground Zero at the time of the May 31 explosion—the shortest of the distances at which the trailer was deployed.

The School of Aviation Medicine's John Pickering said he volunteered for one of the experiments and signed a consent form before the study began. "When the time came for ophthalmologists to describe what they thought could or could not happen, and we were asked to sign a consent form, just as you do now in the hospital for surgery, I signed one. I'm damned sure everybody in that trailer signed one."

At the same time the human experiments were being conducted in the trailer, the School of Aviation Medicine was also coordinating a massive flashblindness experiment with rabbits. About 700 rabbits were trucked to the test site and placed in boxes at two, three, five, eight, ten, eighteen, twenty-seven, and forty-two miles from Ground Zero. The rabbits' heads were fixed through openings in the boxes so that they could not look away from the fireball. Moments before the bomb was detonated, alarm clocks woke the animals from their slumber. With their long ears twitching lazily, the rabbits were gazing toward Ground Zero when the searing white light flooded into their eyes.

When scientists decapitated the rabbits and removed the eyes, they made some shocking discoveries: The light was delivered so rapidly that tiny explosions occurred on the surface of the animals' retinas. The fluids in the eyes of the animals closest to Ground Zero began boiling and turned to steam. The flash had burned deep holes into the eyes of the animals stationed at eight miles or closer to Ground Zero, and retinal burns resembling a "yellowish white plaque" appeared at greater distances. In all, more than 75 percent of the rabbits sustained retinal burns, with some burns detected in animals as far as forty-two miles from the blast. Heinrich Rose, Paul Cibis, and two military officers cautioned, "One must consider the possibility of an atomic flash burn occurring directly on the optic nerve head. This would, if of sufficient size, result in complete blindness of the affected eye."

The flash from the hydrogen bomb was even more dangerous. Following Shot Bravo, which was detonated in 1954 at the Pacific Proving Ground, the deputy commandant of the School of Aviation Medicine sent an urgent message to the Atomic Energy Commission. "It can be assumed that all persons who viewed the actual fireball without eye protection have received permanent chorio-retinal damage," wrote Colonel John McGraw.

McGraw also disclosed that air crews flying at high altitudes within 1,000 miles of the detonation could have received retinal burns and urged that people who were within 100 miles of Ground Zero be examined by competent eye doctors. "It must be emphasized," he concluded, "that an immediate examination is of utmost importance. Such early data would greatly add to our present knowledge of this economically important eye injury in the human."

The injuries from the flashblindness experiments caught the attention in 1954 of Colonel Irving Branch, an official at the Armed Forces Special Weapons Project headquarters in Washington, D.C. In a letter to the assistant Secretary of Defense, Branch noted that in two instances volunteers were injured. "Because of the implications involved due to these injuries, it is felt that a definite need exists for guidance in the use of human volunteers as experimental subjects," he wrote. Attached to Branch's memorandum was an unsigned note that began:

> In Nov. 53, it was learned that there existed a T/S [top secret] document signed by the Secretary of Defense which listed various requirements and criteria which had to be met by individuals contemplating the use of human volunteers in Bio-medical or other types of experimentation. Since this information was of particular importance to this office in classifying and/or releasing information on the Flash Blindness programs at weapons tests, attempts were made to learn the nature of these requirements. . . . It was learned that although this document details very definite and specific steps which must be taken before volunteers may be used in experimentation, no serious attempt has been made to disseminate the information to those experiment-

ers who had a definite need-to-know. The lowest level at which
it had been circulated was that of the three Secretaries of the
Services. . . .

Incredibly, the document that was being so closely guarded was a
version of the Nuremberg Code, the principles guiding ethical human
experimentation that had been handed down by the U.S. judges presiding over the trial of the Nazi doctors. Defense Secretary Charles Wilson
had signed a memorandum embracing the principles on February 26,
1953. The provisions contained in the Wilson memorandum were circulated in unclassified Army documents beginning in 1954, but the Wilson
memorandum itself was not declassified until 1975.

Although records are sketchy, the flashblindness experiments apparently stopped for four years and then were resumed by other military
groups during Operation Plumbbob, a 1957 test series conducted in
Nevada, and Dominic I, a test series conducted in 1962 in the Pacific. At
least sixteen human subjects appeared to have been used in the Plumbbob experiment and three in the Dominic study. Official reports do not
say whether any injuries occurred. Rabbit experiments also continued
during the high-altitude nuclear shots detonated in the Pacific Ocean.
John Pickering said that rabbits on barges 325 miles from Ground Zero
got retinal burns from the flash.

32

BODY-SNATCHING PATRIOTS

The fallout from the bomb tests drifted down over the Earth. The radioactive debris found its way into starfish, shellfish, and seaweed. It covered alfalfa fields in upstate New York, wheat fields in North Dakota, corn in Iowa. It seeped into the bodies of honeybees and birds, human fetuses and growing children. The atom had split the world into "preatomic" and "postatomic" species.

At Los Alamos, Oak Ridge, Hanford, and AEC headquarters in Washington, scientists were growing uneasy. Could the fallout from the bombs already detonated be creating a health hazard? If not, how many more bombs could be detonated before the human race would be put at risk? In the summer of 1953, as the radioactive debris from the Upshot-Knothole tests gusted across the continent, a group of military and civilian scientists convened at the RAND Corporation headquarters in Santa Monica, California. Willard Libby, a brash scientist who passionately supported the testing program and would be awarded the Nobel Prize seven years later for the radioactive carbon dating technique, chaired the meeting. The group decided the only way they could properly ascertain worldwide hazards from fallout was by collecting and analyzing plants, animals, and human tissue from the four corners of Earth. Thus was born Operation Sunshine, one of the most bizarre and ghoulish projects of the Cold War. The source of its name is a matter of debate, but some say it was derived from the fact that fallout, like sunshine, covered the globe.

According to a 1995 General Accounting Office study, Operation Sunshine was the largest of fifty-nine "tissue analysis studies" conducted by atomic scientists during the Cold War. Collectively, the body parts of more than 15,000 humans were used in those studies. In countless instances, scientists took the corpses and organs of deceased people without getting permission from the next of kin.

For Operation Sunshine alone, approximately 9,000 samples of human bones, entire skeletons, and nearly 600 human fetuses were collected from around the world. Since the project was initially classified secret, researchers concocted "cover stories" that they used in order to acquire human samples from abroad. The military later began its own top-secret collection program of human urine, animal milk, and tissue samples under the guise of a "nutritional" study.

Willard Libby believed that "next to weapons," Sunshine was the AEC's most important mission. "This statement is made in all seriousness," he once told fellow Sunshiners, "because if the problems surrounding fallout are not properly understood and properly presented to the world, weapons testing may be forced to stop—a circumstance which could well be disastrous to the free world."

Raised on a ranch in northern California, Libby entered the University of California at Berkeley on the advice of his father, a successful farmer with only a third-grade education. One of his teachers while he was an undergraduate was J. Robert Oppenheimer. Although he enjoyed Oppenheimer's lectures, Libby still thought of Oppenheimer as "an active Communist" when he was interviewed for an oral history project in 1978.

After receiving his bachelor's degree in 1931 and his Ph.D. in 1933, Libby remained at Berkeley and taught classes. In 1940, he joined a team of Manhattan Project researchers at Columbia University who were trying to develop a method to separate uranium isotopes. He went on to serve as a member of the AEC's General Advisory Committee and as an AEC commissioner. The commission appointment came about because of his support of the H-bomb, he said. "For some reason, Oppenheimer had decided against the hydrogen bomb, and I fought him, tooth and nail. And I won. That's why I was appointed to the AEC."

Following the 1952 Mike detonation, it took weaponeers nearly two years to develop a slimmed-down hydrogen bomb that could be delivered by airplane. The perfected weapon, code-named Bravo, was detonated on March 1, 1954, at the Pacific Proving Ground. With a yield of fifteen megatons, Bravo was the largest bomb ever detonated by the United States. Not only did it endanger the eyesight of observers within 1,000 miles of Ground Zero, but it also dumped large amounts of fallout on several inhabited atolls and on a Japanese fishing vessel. A number of American soldiers and scientists were exposed as well.

Two days after the shot was fired, 236 Marshall Island residents were finally rescued. A number of them were found to be suffering from severe radiation sickness. The crew of the *Fukuryu Maru No. 5* (Fortunate Dragon), a Japanese fishing boat that was only eighty miles from Ground Zero at the time of the detonation, also suffered from acute radiation sickness. The fallout from Bravo covered the trawler's decks with a deep white powder that was so thick that the men left footprints when they walked on it. The fishermen pulled in their nets and headed for home. But before they did, they rinsed down the decks, a precautionary measure that probably saved the lives of many of them. According to Japanese scientists, the crew members received anywhere from 200 to 500 roentgens. Aikichi Kuboyama, one of the crew members, died seven months later.

The Bravo shot and five subsequent hydrogen bomb blasts in the Castle series had a combined yield of forty-eight megatons and distributed fallout over the globe. The fallout triggered an international furor that was to increase in intensity in the ensuing years and eventually culminated in an end to above-ground testing. Prime Minister Nehru of India, Albert Schweitzer, Albert Einstein, and Pope Pius XII were among those who called for an end to nuclear tests. As recently as 1994, the Bravo shot and what the AEC knew about an unexpected wind shift prior to the blast were the subject of a hearing before the House Natural Resources investigations subcommittee.

Ten months after the Bravo fallout disaster, Libby and his fellow scientists met in Washington, D.C., for a classified conference to discuss the latest Sunshine findings. By that time researchers had analyzed some fifty-five stillborn babies from Chicago, one from Utah, three from India, and three adult human legs from Massachusetts. According to a transcript of the conference, which was declassified in 1995, Libby told the group that they needed to procure more human samples, particularly from children. Although he didn't explain why, Libby said the "supply" of stillborn infants had been cut off and "shows no signs . . . of being rejuvenated." He added, "If anybody knows how to do a good job of body snatching, they will really be serving their country." Libby then turned his attention to the radioactive strontium accumulating in the oceans. Atomic scientists had believed the sea was an "infinite sink" but were discovering that wasn't true. Soluble fission products from the bombs probably would remain in the top 100 meters of sea water "essentially indefinitely," Libby said. Then he returned to the question of procuring human bodies:

> I don't know how to snatch bodies. In the original study on the Sunshine at Rand [Corporation] in the summer of 1953 we hired an expensive law firm to look up the law of body snatching. This compendium is available to you. It is not very encouraging. It shows you how very difficult it is going to be to do it legally. We may be able to help—I speak now of the Commission—in that we hope to downgrade the Sunshine classification. At least the existence of the project I hope we will get away with revealing. Whether this is going to help in the body snatching problem, I don't know. I think it will. It is a delicate problem in public relations, obviously.

J. Laurence Kulp, a scientist at Columbia University's Lamont Observatory, reassured Libby that researchers could obtain bone and tissue samples from humans of all ages in Houston and other cities. "Down in Houston they don't have all these rules," he said. "They intend to get virtually every death in the age range we are interested in that occurs in the city of Houston. They have a lot of poverty cases and so on." (Kulp told a reporter in 1995 that the term "body snatching" was "meant to be a joke.")

With a casualness most people reserve for the weather, the Sunshiners often talked about the number of bombs that could be detonated before mankind would be wiped out. One scientist had calculated that 100,000 weapons the size of the bomb dropped on Nagasaki could be detonated before the "doomsday" level was reached. But AEC scientist Forest Western told fellow Sunshiners he didn't believe fallout would kill everyone:

> I think you will find a few Eskimos or a few Patagonians or a few people in some isolated part of the earth who will keep the race going. They might not populate the earth with just the descendants we would like to see. They might not be highly civilized like we are. They might not know anything about atomic warfare, for example. But I think the concept of wiping the race out with nuclear weapons is a little bit far-fetched.

The Sunshiners focused on strontium-90, one of the hundreds of fission products released during an atomic detonation. Strontium-90 was considered a "bad actor" because it is deposited in human bone and has a half-life of twenty-eight years. In other words, half of the radioactive strontium released during the 1954 tests would have decayed by 1982; half the remaining radioactive strontium would decay by 2010; and so on.

Strontium-90 is chemically similar to calcium and is readily assimilated in the bones of growing children who drink contaminated milk. For that reason, the Sunshiners were particularly interested in procuring the body parts of young children. Eventually they learned that children on average had three to four times more strontium-90 in their bones than adults.

Scientists soon realized that other fission products could cause biological damage. One was radioactive iodine. The British were the first to detect radioiodine in the urine of children. Then it was discovered in animals near the Nevada Test Site. The military found radioiodine in their personnel in Hawaii and Washington. And finally Lester Van Middlesworth, a former student of Joseph Hamilton's, detected it in cattle thyroids.

Van Middlesworth, an enterprising scientist, was working in his laboratory in Memphis, Tennessee, in the spring of 1954 when a Geiger counter began ticking frantically. The device had picked up radioactivity from the thyroid gland still in the head of a slaughtered steer that had been grazing on Tennessee grass. Van Middlesworth suspected immediately that the radioactivity in the steer's thyroid came from the fallout from the 1954 Pacific tests. Hundreds, then thousands of thyroid glands begged from packing plants confirmed his hypothesis. "We knew in one week the entire country was contaminated," Van Middlesworth said. "Nobody believed you could contaminate the world from one spot. It was like Columbus when no one believed the world was round."

Van Middlesworth informed his mentor, Joseph Hamilton, of his suspicions. Instead of sharing Van Middlesworth's alarm, the older man attempted to throw his former student off the track. "Dr. Van Middlesworth is a very energetic and enterprising young man with a penchant for rather abruptly making decisions," Hamilton told an AEC official in a June 18, 1954, letter. "I saw the possible implications of what he brought to my attention and attempted to subdue his marked degree of enthusiasm by suggesting the traces of radioiodine in the Memphis area might have arisen from airborne contamination from the Oak Ridge National Laboratories."

Hamilton thought he had successfully diverted Van Middlesworth's attention but later learned his former student had obtained some thyroid glands from the Armour Packing Co. in San Francisco. "Again I indicated a lack of interest in the topic feeling that this was probably the best way such matters should be handled," Hamilton wrote.

An AEC official thanked Hamilton for "playing down" the matter with Van Middlesworth. But the AEC eventually embraced Van Middlesworth's findings and began sending him thyroid glands from throughout the world. From those thyroids, Van Middlesworth could not only detect above-ground atomic blasts set off anywhere in the world but could also estimate the size of the explosions. "It was not as helpful as high-altitude airplanes, but it was a biological indication of what was going on," Van Middlesworth said.

Although the weapons scientists admitted the atomic tests carried some health risks, they invariably underestimated the danger. Los Alamos chemist Wright Langham, in a paper apparently written sometime after the 1956 presidential elections, calculated that fallout might produce an additional thirty cases of leukemia and ten cases of bone cancer per year. "There is no doubt but that the world population is receiving a small exposure to radioactive materials originating from nuclear weapons testing. Fission products from bomb detonations have and are depositing over the surface of the earth. . . . these effects may result in an increase in genetic mutations, shortening of life expectancy and increased incidence of leukemia and bone sarcoma," he wrote. The paper said nothing about the hundreds of other radioisotopes released by the bomb, including radioiodine.

As the fallout controversy raged, the scientists continued to collect their human samples, often covertly. Some 1,165 human thyroid glands were collected during autopsies around the world and sent to the Oak Ridge Institute for Nuclear Studies for analysis. A human finger, which had been amputated after being pierced with plutonium metal, also was sent to Oak Ridge. With the help of a cooperative local pathologist, scientists at the Hanford Reservation analyzed the plutonium in the tissues and organs of nearly 350 people who lived near Hanford or worked at the nuclear facility. University of Utah researchers examined the tissues of some 75 residents to determine radioactivity from the weapons tests. At a uranium processing plant in Cincinnati, Ohio, the kidneys, livers, and spleens of workers were taken during autopsy and analyzed for uranium deposition. But one of the most extensive and long-lived body parts collection programs of the Cold War began at Los Alamos in 1959 after a plutonium worker named Cecil Kelley was fatally injured in a criticality accident.

Cecil was on his way to a New Year's Eve party on December 30, 1958, when someone called and asked him to fill in at the DP West Site, a facility where plutonium was chemically separated and recovered from waste products. Reluctantly he agreed. Snowy footprints crisscrossed the technical area and the Sangre de Cristos were beginning to take on their luminous, other-worldly color. From somewhere came the spicy scent of burning piñon wood. The building where Cecil worked resembled a huge boiler room. Large steel tanks containing varying amounts of plutonium in solution stood about the room and hundreds of pipes crossed the ceiling.

Just ten minutes earlier there had been about a half-dozen maintenance workers in Room 218, but they had left when their 4:30 P.M. shift ended. Cecil pulled on a pair of shapeless coveralls. He was thirty-eight years old, an ex-paratrooper and infantryman who had worked as a ski guide and instructor in Sun Valley, Idaho, before joining the Army in 1940. Afterward he had worked as a plutonium processing operator from 1946 to 1949, and again from 1955 through 1958.

Cecil mounted a small stepladder and looked down through a viewing window into one of the tanks. Normally the tank contained only a small amount of plutonium, but for some reason approximately seven and one-half pounds of plutonium had been washed into the vessel. The plutonium was sitting in a layer of organic solvents at the top of the tank.

Still looking through the viewing window, Cecil reached out and flicked a switch on the side of the tank that rotated a paddle inside the vessel. It was a simple, mechanical movement, which he had performed at least seventy-five times before. As the stirrer began turning, the liquids on the bottom were pushed outward and up the walls of the tank. A bowllike depression formed in the middle of the tank and the plutonium solvent rushed into the bowl. With a lot more plutonium molecules jostling each other, the solvent suddenly went critical. A chain reaction had begun.

A blue halo—the same blue halo that had anointed the brows of Harry Daghlian and Louis Slotin when they were fatally injured—filled the room. A muffled *thump* was heard as the 225-gallon tank jumped about three-eighths of an inch. Cecil either fell or was knocked to the floor. He got up, turned the stirrer motor off, then turned it on again. A rumbling noise came from the tank and he ran outside into the snow screaming, "I'm burning up. I'm burning up."

Scientists later calculated that between 10,000 and 12,000 rad struck Cecil's head and chest area. The neutrons and gamma rays ripped through his body, turning the sodium in his blood, the phosphorous in his hair, the calcium in his bones, and the silver-mercury fillings in his mouth radioactive. Two men working nearby took Cecil to a shower, passing by the tank where the chain reaction had occurred. One of them turned off the stirrer. By then Cecil could no longer stand. The workers laid him on the floor while they waited for an ambulance. A lab nurse observed he was in shock and unconscious but "with a nice pink skin."

Cecil was almost dead when he arrived at Los Alamos Medical Center a few minutes later. His eyes were so red they looked as if they had been damaged by a welder's arc. His lips were dusky blue. "The skin of the chest and abdomen was reddened as though it had been exposed to sunlight and received a first degree burn," his medical records state. The strange sunburn also covered his back.

The hospital doctors and nurses tried to make Cecil as comfortable as they could. "I was on call at the time. I had never seen anything like it before," said John S. Benson, a physician who still lives in Los Alamos. "He was miserable and scared. We were unhappy that he was in such a sad state. We were trying to make him comfortable."

The emergency room nurses were initially unable to check Cecil's blood pressure because he was so restless and agitated. Dr. Benson later wrote in his admission note, "When seen in the E.R. physical examination was impossible due to the fact that the pt. retched violently every few moments and was hyperventilating to the extreme, was quite restless and very agitated. His lungs were clear but pulse and blood pressure were not obtained. He was pale, moist, although he had taken a cold shower prior to being brought over."

As Cecil thrashed wildly in the emergency room, a contingent of Los Alamos scientists arrived at the hospital and hurriedly began gathering the "data." Using a tongue depressor, chemist Don Petersen, a friend of Wright Langham's, scraped Cecil's vomit from the floor and his explosive diarrhea from the walls. "We weren't going to lose anything but the groans," Petersen recalled in a deposition taken in 1997 by an attorney representing Cecil's family in a lawsuit. Numerous blood samples were taken and all of his urine was saved, including three ccs squeezed from his bladder after death. A portable Geiger counter placed next to him showed that he was emitting some 15 millirad per hour.

The massive irradiation of Cecil Kelley provided Los Alamos scientists with their third "experiment of opportunity." Once again they could chronicle what happens to the human body when a bomb was exploded without the confounding effects of burn and blast. But there was an even more intriguing experiment they could pursue once Cecil was dead. They planned to harvest his organs to find out whether the plutonium he had accumulated in his body matched the predictions derived from exposure records and Wright Langham's mathematical equations extrapolated from the plutonium injectees.

Langham, who had risen from his lowly Manhattan Project status to become one of the movers and shakers in Operation Sunshine and the world's authority on plutonium, coordinated the collection and analysis of data. When Cecil's wife, Doris, got to the hospital, Langham met her at the doors to the emergency room.

Do you know anything about this? he asked her.

Yes, she knew a lot, she responded.

Then you know he's not going to live, she recalled Langham telling her.

"I knew from the very beginning that he wasn't going to live," Doris said in an interview in 1994. "He was retching in the hospital emergency room. They wouldn't let me in. I was right outside the door. I don't know what they gave him. Morphine, I suppose. They settled him down and took him upstairs."

Cecil was taken to a private room where he was laid in a bed supported by "shock blocks" and enclosed in an oxygen tent. A saline solution dripped into his veins. Thorazine was administered to curb the nausea. Hot water bottles were placed on his swelling arms. Still, the pain and restlessness continued. At 6:30 P.M. Dr. Benson noted that Cecil was suffering from "severe chills—still retching, shocky, restless, moaning."

Gradually the vomiting and nausea subsided. Cecil began taking small sips of water but could not urinate and complained of severe pain in his right upper abdomen. A nurse wrote, "He described it as a hard knot in his lowest rib which wouldn't relax." By midnight Cecil was coherent enough to give his group leader a description of what had happened. He described the heavenly blue glow that had filled the room and the rumbling sound he heard from the tank. Sometime after the interview, he vomited on the floor. The floor was measured for radioactivity. Wrote Benson, "Vomitus area monitored and is 'O.K.' "

Don Petersen, who retired from the laboratory in 1990 but still serves as an advisor to the Army's chemical and biological warfare programs, said in his deposition that doctors were having trouble stabilizing Cecil's blood pressure. The only way they could keep the blood pressure up was to administer fluids. But as Cecil's body began to shut down and his kidneys failed, the infusion of liquids began creating other problems.

Doris, who was allowed into Cecil's room after he had been stabilized, remained at his bedside through most of the ordeal. She said her husband knew he was dying. He told her to take good care of their two children, a seven-year-old daughter and a boy about eighteen months old. His brother from Indiana arrived about 3:00 A.M. and they talked quietly for an hour or so.

Cecil occasionally napped or dozed as the hours ticked away. His right arm, then his left arm, began to swell from the I.V.'s. About 7:00 A.M. the next morning, a nurse rubbed his back and changed his linen. She noticed that an inflamed area had appeared on his right arm.

At 5:00 P.M., some twenty-four hours after the accident, the doctors decided to do a sternal bone marrow biopsy. Several physicians said the biopsy probably was done to determine whether Cecil was a candidate for a bone marrow transplant, which was still a new procedure in the late 1950s. But a document provided to his wife and daughter during the discovery stage of their lawsuit suggests the procedure was simply another way to collect data on the effects of radiation. Writing to a colleague a week after the accident, Los Alamos doctor Thomas Shipman observed:

> From the very beginning it was obvious that this man had received a massive dose. We are currently estimating it in excess of 12,000 rem. He died in thirty-five hours, but I am sure would have died in two or three hours had we not treated his shock. He was in a state of profound shock on admission to the hospital and this was the principal problem as far as treatment was concerned. Because of the size of the dose, it seemed obvious that he would die a central nervous system death, so we never seriously considered bone marrow transfusions.

The operating room equipment was taken to Cecil's bedside. His chest was scrubbed with soap, water, alcohol, and draped in a sterile cloth. Then an incision was made over what was thought to be his sternum. A "good deal" of material was removed, but it did not seem to include any bone marrow. The doctor suddenly realized he had made the incision in the wrong place. That wound was closed with fine silk sutures and another incision made. Cartilage, a small piece of muscle, and "a great deal of red marrow was obtained for slides," physician W. R. Oakes later wrote.

Doris's stomach churned as she witnessed the procedure: "What they pulled out was slop. They put a syringe in his chest and pulled it out. It was just mush." Cecil lived another ten hours. The nausea and cramping came and went. His arms and legs continue to swell. Six hours before his death he mumbled to a nurse his chest felt as if "it was beginning to thaw out." But then the restlessness and thrashing set in again. He complained of pains in his chest, abdomen, and arms and finally grew so agitated that he pulled the intravenous needles from his arms. He was sedated with morphine and luminal. He began having "frog type" respirations, which gradually became slower over the next fifteen minutes. "Pulse unobtainable—heart tones quite distant . . . respiration had ceased—no response—pronounced dead at 3:15 A.M.," Benson wrote in Cecil's medical chart.

It was New Year's Day of 1959, exactly thirty-four hours and forty-five minutes since the accident occurred. In the hospital room at the time of Cecil's death were physicians John Benson, Robert Grier, and Clarence Lushbaugh, a laboratory pathologist who would soon perform the autopsy. Several visitors who were en route to Los Alamos, including Louis Hempelmann, who had overseen the medical care of Harry Daghlian and Louis Slotin, were contacted and told to go back home. Hempelmann said he would be available for consultations by telephone if anyone needed him.

After his death, Cecil's corpse was dragged by sled through the snow to a steel-lined building that contained a whole-body counter. "He was so loaded with everything, the counter just went berserk," recalled Earl Kinsley, an Air Force health physicist assigned to the lab at the time of the accident. At 6:00 A.M. on New's Year Day, Clarence Lushbaugh began an autopsy.

Lushbaugh was struck by the waterlogged appearance of Cecil's tissues. (The physicians had been pumping fluids into him to keep up his blood pressure and had "nearly drowned" him in their efforts, Thomas Shipman would later write.) Lushbaugh dutifully recorded the two incisions on Cecil's chest and the "numerous needle puncture marks" on his forearms and lower legs. Not surprisingly, he found some of the same kind of hemorrhages that Stafford Warren and Shields Warren had observed years earlier on the Japanese atomic bombing victims. The abdominal cavity, the gastrointestinal tract, and the heart were covered with small hemorrhages. "Rigor mortis is exceptionally strong and the muscles more contracted than usual," Lushbaugh wrote. Cecil's heart, lungs, liver, kidneys, adrenal glands, stomach, colon, lymph nodes, gonads, and brain were removed and stored for later analysis.

Following the accident, telegrams poured into Los Alamos from all over the world. They were not sympathy messages but requests from researchers who wanted bits and pieces of Cecil's body for study. Clarence Lushbaugh shipped Cecil's brain in a wide-mouthed mayonnaise jar to the Armed Forces Institute of Pathology. When Lushbaugh was asked in a deposition who gave him authority to send the brain there, he responded, "God did."

Scientists at the Armed Forces Institute of Pathology compared Cecil's brain to the brains of monkeys that were also being blasted with huge doses of radiation. The findings were so interesting that one of the scientists, Webb Haymaker, asked Lushbaugh for permission to discuss the case at a meeting at Walter Reed Hospital.

Pieces of Cecil's frozen liver and lymph nodes were mailed to Hanford. Twenty-five ccs of his urine were sent to Oak Ridge. For many months after the accident, Los Alamos scientists churned out biomedical and dosimetry reports based on data from the deceased man's body parts and his clothing, including the brass buttons on his coveralls.

But the most important postmortem study was the one to find out if the plutonium in Kelley's body matched what scientists had predicted. Using nose counts, urinalyses, and Wright Langham's formula, the group predicted that Cecil had eighteen nanocuries, or a little less than half of the so-called maximum permissible body burden. When they reduced his organs to solution, they found his body content was nineteen nanocuries. The agreement was so close that Wright Langham considered it "undoubtedly fortuitous." But the scientists were nevertheless disturbed because the amount of plutonium in the lungs and pulmonary lymph nodes was much greater than they had predicted.

While Los Alamos scientists performed their mathematical calculations and began preparing their findings for publication, officials at AEC headquarters in Washington, D.C., were in a dither about whom to blame. Not surprisingly, Cecil Kelley became the scapegoat. It is difficult to reconstruct from documents exactly how the criticality accident occurred, but apparently three "improper transfers" of solutions were made that resulted in the excess of plutonium in the tank. It's not clear whether the transfers were made by Kelley or by workers on the preceding shift. Ironically, the lab was in the process of reviewing the safety aspects of its plutonium recovery program when the criticality occurred.

To his credit, lab director Norris Bradbury informed the Atomic Energy Commission that "no single cause" triggered the accident. "It was made possible by a complicated set of circumstances and coincidences, no one of which can be considered wholly responsible." But the AEC nevertheless went ahead and issued a press release blaming the entire incident on Cecil. "The accident was directly attributable to errors on the part of the deceased operator."

The AEC press release didn't sit well with Thomas Shipman. "I feel quite strongly that the statement as given is manifestly unfair to Kelley himself and does not give a true picture of the whole affair," he told Bradbury. Shipman also strongly protested the AEC's statement in a letter to Charles Dunham, who by then was in charge of all the AEC's biomedical programs:

> In stating that the accident was "directly" attributable to mistakes made by Kelley it was untrue. I am sure that you are sufficiently familiar with the facts to realize that Kelley could have continued to do all of the things he did had it not been for things beyond his control and beyond the knowledge of anyone concerned. . . . On the whole, the people around here know pretty well what had happened, and this new publicity has left them quite bewildered, and they feel that a man who is unable to defend himself—and who possibly could have defended himself—has been very unjustly treated.

Cecil was given a military burial and a twenty-one-gun salute. A three-cornered American flag went to Doris. His daughter, Katie, then a small girl clad in a navy-blue sailor suit and a blue hat, tossed a handful of dirt on the casket. Doris received $7,000 from Los Alamos; another $3,000 went to Kelley's first wife. Doris, who worked as a secretary at the lab for forty-seven years, said lab officials also promised to pay for her children's college education, buy her a house, and give her a salary increase. But none of those promises were kept. With two fatherless children to raise, the family gradually slipped into poverty.

The laboratory also returned to Doris her husband's gold Bulova wristwatch, and his wallet. In the wallet was Cecil's 1958 Los Alamos Golf Association membership card, his Eight Balls Bowling League card, a New Mexico hunting and fishing license, and a charge card to Pflueger's Smart Footwear in Santa Fe. Behind the bright-red Atomic Energy Commission identification card, Cecil kept a one-dollar bill, soft as tissue paper and dated May 18, 1914. The dollar bill was given to him by his father-in-law and was supposed to have been his good-luck charm.

With the death of Cecil Kelley, Los Alamos's human tissue program began in earnest. Between 1959 and 1985 the body parts of 1,712 human beings, including nearly a dozen whole cadavers, were shipped to Los Alamos and analyzed for their plutonium content. The original objective of the program was to see if the amount of plutonium in deceased nuclear workers agreed with predicted amounts derived from exposure records.

The Los Alamos investigators obtained organs and cadavers from people who died in other parts of the country for a "control group." Those analyses also helped scientists estimate how much plutonium the American people were accumulating from the bomb tests. The human organs were dried in ovens, converted into ash, then dissolved in an acid solution so they could be analyzed. For many years, anyone who died in the town of Los Alamos was autopsied, including visitors, whom pathologist Clarence Lushbaugh called "extras."

Atmospheric Test Series/Human Studies

Series/Name/Date	Maneuver Troops	Officer Volunteer Observers	Psychological Tests (HumRRO)	Flash-blindness	Decontamination	Cloud Sampling/Tracking	Body Fluids (urine & blood)
TRINITY July 16–Aug 6, 1945							
CROSSROADS Jul 1–Aug 31, 1946					X	X	X
SANDSTONE Apr 15–May 20, 1948					X	X	
RANGER Jan 27–Feb 6, 1951					X	X	
GREENHOUSE Apr 8–Jun 20, 1951					X	X	
BUSTER-JANGLE Oct 22–Dec 20, 1951	X		X	X	X	X	
TUMBLER-SNAPPER Apr 1–Jun 20, 1952	X		X	X	X	X	
IVY Nov 1–Dec 31, 1952					X	X	
UPSHOT-KNOTHOLE Mar 17–Jun 20, 1953	X	X	X	X	X	X	

Series/Name/Date	Maneuver Troops	Officer Volunteer Observers	Psychological Tests (HumRRO)	Flash-blindness	Decontamination	Cloud Sampling/Tracking	Body Fluids (urine & blood)
CASTLE Mar 1–May 31, 1954					X	X	X
TEAPOT Feb 18–Jun 10, 1955	X	X			X	X	X
WIGWAM May 14–15, 1955					X		
REDWING May 5–Aug 6, 1956					X	X	X
PLUMBBOB May 28–Oct 22, 1957	X	X	X	X	X	X	
HARDTACK I Apr 28–Oct 31, 1958					X	X	
ARGUS Aug 27–Sep 10, 1958							
HARDTACK II Sep 19–Oct 31, 1958				X	X	X	
DOMINIC I Apr 25–Dec 31, 1962				X	X	X	
DOMINIC II Jul 6–Aug 15, 1962	X				X	X	

*SOURCE: DEFENSE NUCLEAR AGENCY

PART FOUR

"The Buchenwald Touch"

33

"MICE OR MEN?"

One by one the doctors crossed the lobby of the Carlton Hotel and took a right toward the big ballroom. With its gilded ceilings and elegant furnishings, the hotel resembled an Italian Renaissance palace. Just two blocks away was the White House. The spring sun poured through the tall windows, showering light on the stragglers making their way toward the smell of coffee and the unmistakable hubbub of a meeting about to begin. When they were assembled, with steaming cups of coffee in hand, there were twenty-six of them. It was April 3, 1949, a Sunday morning in Washington, D.C.

Robert Stone, who would deliver the key presentation that day, saw many familiar faces when he looked around the room. Stafford Warren and Andrew Dowdy had flown in from Los Angeles, Hymer Friedell had come from Cleveland, Robley Evans from Boston. For Shields Warren, it was a quick cab ride from AEC headquarters to the gracious hotel at 16th and K streets. Joseph Hamilton was a member of the committee, but he was unable to attend. Wright Langham, a consultant, was absent, too.

The Manhattan Project veterans, their AEC counterparts, and other physicists and scientists present that morning were members of a medical advisory committee for the Nuclear Energy Propulsion for Aircraft, or NEPA, a project to build a long-range bomber powered by a nuclear reactor. Instinctively recognizing that such a project would not work, J. Robert Oppenheimer and Harvard president James Conant had recommended in 1947 that the aircraft proposal be "terminated promptly." But the Atomic Energy Commission and the Air Force were forging ahead, and the project would not be canceled until 1963 when President Kennedy acknowledged "the possibility of achieving a militarily useful aircraft in the foreseeable future is still very remote."

In the 1940s and early 1950s, though, many scientists and engineers still believed it was possible to construct such an aircraft. One of the key questions confronting the plane's designers was how much radiation an air crew could tolerate, which in turn would dictate the amount of shielding that was necessary to protect the crew. As one participant put it, "The weight of this shielding is large, and is the most critical item of weight in the design of the aircraft: the shield weight must therefore be known with high relative accuracy." Not surprisingly, the weight of the shielding would determine whether the bomber would fly.

The Manhattan Project veterans had been brought in to help the aircraft builders get some concrete answers about the effects of radiation on humans. A subcommittee headed by Robert Stone had concluded that the only way to get reliable answers was through radiation experiments on healthy humans. But Stone, as well as the other doctors attending the Carlton Hotel meeting, knew that those experiments would pose an ethical dilemma because the exposures could increase the risk of cancer, shorten the lives of the subjects, and produce genetic mutations. Still, Stone's subcommittee believed that the experiments were necessary and should be performed as long as they followed the three ethical guidelines embraced by the AMA in 1946 as the Nazi doctors' trial opened in Nuremberg: the voluntary consent of the individual, previous animal experimentation, and proper medical supervision.

Before the group took a vote on the issue, blue, legal-size packages were handed out to participants with security clearances. The word "restricted" was stamped across the front of the books. Inside was information culled from the Manhattan Project's TBI experiments and data from the individuals exposed to radiation during the Los Alamos criticality accidents. Andrew Dowdy, chairman of the medical advisory group, said the report was classified at the AEC's request because it contained data about some unresolved accident cases (a possible reference to the Allan Kline case) and not because there was any information that would jeopardize national security.

Sometime before lunch, Robert Stone submitted for approval a draft statement from his subcommittee endorsing the experiments. The declaration noted that such studies had been "countenanced" in the past when there was no other way to get the data. Some information on human responses to TBI had been obtained from sick patients, the statement acknowledged, but those data were limited because the patients' responses varied greatly, depending on their physical condition. Likewise, the researchers had obtained some data from accident cases, but that information was also limited because "the number of individuals so exposed has been too few to provide statistically significant results and the conditions of exposure are not sufficiently well known." In conclusion, the group submitted a resolution to go forward: "The information desired is sufficiently important to the safety of the U.S.A. that we believe the use of humans is justified. It is understood that any such experimentation would be carried out in accordance with the principles laid down by the Judicial Council of the A.M.A. in 1946."

When Andrew Dowdy, the chairman, opened the floor for comment, Shields Warren was one of the first to speak. Reflecting perhaps on the difficulties surrounding the plutonium injections, he recommended that any such experiments be unclassified. "I would say not only the information obtained, but the experiments as well," he said. "I think it very important in something of this sort that there be no suspicion that anything is being hidden or covered up, that it is all being done openly and straightforwardly." Robley Evans agreed. "We don't have to advertise it, but at the same time it doesn't want to be concealed, as Dr. Shields Warren has said."

Hymer Friedell objected to the TBI recommendation coming only from the NEPA committee: "I am just wondering whether someone else ought not to hold the bag along with us with regard to making such a recommendation. Previously in medical experiments the physicians and doctors have made such recommendations because the problem was primarily a medical one—I think this is something larger than that. It is really not a medical problem alone. It has to do with how critical this is with regard to safety of the nation."

Others objected to the wording in the resolution, "sufficiently important to the safety of the U.S.A." But Stone said conditions "have got to be pretty nearly necessary before you go giving people . . . ," his sentence trailing off.

Stafford Warren wanted to make sure the TBI studies would have a long-term component. "Those of us in the Manhattan tried to start it at the beginning of the war and couldn't because there was a shortage of men and materials. We tried to start it immediately after the war, and it has hung just because nobody would come forth and say 'This has got [to be] a must.'"

Although Robert Stone and his colleagues did not describe the kind of "volunteers" they hoped to sign up for such experiments, in a paper published ten months later Stone suggested that prisoners serving life sentences be used as subjects because they could be easily tracked for a long time. "Life prisoners are the one group of people that are likely to remain in one place where they can be observed for a great many years."

The experiment, Stone wrote, could begin by exposing volunteers to twenty-five roentgens. If no changes occurred, he said, "The next logical step would be to give fifty roentgens and repeat it in a week; if nothing happened at this level they could then proceed to expose normal people to one hundred roentgens and probably to one hundred and fifty roentgens." Stone and the other members of the medical committee felt that as long as exposures were kept below 150 roentgens, there would be only a small chance of producing delayed effects such as leukemia:

> To be able to tell a group of pilots that normal human beings had been voluntarily exposed without untoward effects to larger doses than they would receive while carrying out a particular mission would be of inestimable value. The extremely small hazard of undetectable genetic effect, undetectable effect on the life span and possibly slight effect on the blood picture are the extremely small hazards that must be weighed against the value of having actual experience with exposure of humans.

Contrary to Stone's assertion that 150 roentgens presented an extremely small risk of cancer, some doctors at the time felt such exposures would produce a "considerable chance" of cancer in the future. In 1995 President Clinton's Advisory Committee calculated that such doses would increase the risk of leukemia by a factor of seven and double the risk of many other cancers.

By 4:15 P.M. on that spring day, the NEPA medical committee unanimously endorsed Stone's proposal and was ready to adjourn. Stone, after all, had been preaching to the converted. Before the experiments could begin, however, they had to be approved by two panels in the Pentagon: the Joint Panel on the Medical Aspects of Atomic Warfare and the Committee on Medical Sciences. The Joint Panel, the civilian-military group that oversaw the biological and medical research at the proving grounds, wholeheartedly supported the experiments and formally approved them in June of 1949, two months after the Carlton Hotel meeting.

But over the next year and a half, there would be wrenching debates about the ethical implications of such studies at the next level, the Committee on Medical Sciences. In addition to those debates, even compulsive experimenters such as Joseph Hamilton began having second thoughts. After Stone had recommended using prisoners as the experimental subjects, Hamilton rethought his position and, in a letter dated November 28, 1950, advised Shields Warren that for "both politic and scientific" reasons it would be better to secure the data through animal experiments:

> If this is to be done in humans, I feel that those concerned in the Atomic Energy Commission would be subject to considerable criticism, as admittedly this would have a little of the Buchenwald touch. The volunteers should be on a freer basis than inmates of a prison. At this point, I haven't any very constructive ideas as to where one would turn for such volunteers should this plan be put into execution. There is much to recommend the use of adult males past the age of 50 in good physical status. However, one can't be certain that those people would respond in a similar manner to the 20 to 40 age group.

Long before Hamilton sent that letter, Shields Warren had already begun having qualms about irradiating healthy humans, confessing in a letter to Robert Stone that he was taking "an increasingly dim view" on human experimentation. "The more I consider this problem the more reluctant I am to go along with experiments of this type," he said in the July 11, 1949, letter. "Consequently, record me as voting against human experimentation."

The Pentagon's Committee on Medical Sciences approved the experiments on November 8, 1949. But when it learned that the AEC's Shields Warren did not favor them, it revoked its endorsement and sent the proposal back to the Joint Panel for further study. The panel merely reaffirmed its position and shuffled the proposal back to the committee.

On May 23, 1950, when the Committee on Medical Sciences met again to consider the experiments, the AMA principles were read into the transcripts. The horrifying knowledge of the atrocities committed by the Nazi doctors was still fresh in the minds of several of the military officers. Colonel Elbert "Frenchy" DeCoursey, the deputy director of the Armed Forces Institute of Pathology who went to Japan after the bombings and later coauthored a paper with Shields Warren on the casualties, said, "I must say that in my own mind I realize that all of these things are important to know and we must know them, but it is difficult for me to

come to a decision of whether or not you should go into human experimentation on this because of the world opinion on the experimentation
in Germany. That bothers me."

Admiral Frederick Greaves, a lifelong career officer who had been
awarded a Bronze Star and a Gold Star for his role in the amphibious
invasion of Sicily, Italy, and southern France, was also uncomfortable
with the idea of human experimentation. "I find it very difficult, too," he
confessed.

Wallace Fenn, a University of Rochester professor and friend of
Shields Warren, said he questioned whether the end would justify the
means. "I think the important thing is whether you take the decision to
go down this road of human experimentation and work on prisoners,
even though they are volunteers, and start the idea that as long as they
are prisoners it really doesn't matter very much what you do to them, and
it is no great loss to society, which I think it isn't, but it is a bad decision."

Although the members of the Committee on Medical Sciences had
strong reservations about the experiments, they nevertheless approved
the experiments at their May 23 meeting. The Office of the Secretary of
Defense wanted the AEC's Shields Warren on board too. But this was
one of the occasions where Warren, exquisitely aware of how human
experiments could damage the prestige and public relations of the commission, refused to abandon his principles. Thereupon General James
Cooney, the military officer who vigorously supported the atomic maneuvers and downplayed the dangers of fallout, led a last-ditch effort to get
Shields Warren to change his mind.

On November 10, 1950, eighteen months after the meeting at the Carlton Hotel, Cooney and other officers from the Army, Navy, and Air Force
sat down with Warren and his colleagues at AEC headquarters. The
bleak November light cast watery shadows over the starched uniforms
and polished shoes of the generals and admirals. The mood of the room
was undoubtedly somber. The Korean War had erupted on June 25, and
many military men believed that it would be only a matter of time before
nuclear weapons were used in battle.

In an extraordinarily candid transcript of the meeting, which was not
made public until 1995, General Cooney argued that the experiments
needed to go forward in order to give line officers more information
about what would happen to soldiers during an atomic attack. "I think

the one big problem that we have and the one becoming more acute and the one which I feel we do not have the answer for, is the reaction of a soldier to ionizing radiation. I believe it is becoming more acute because I think that the use of the weapon as a tactical weapon has now gone beyond the realm of possibility and into the realm of probability."

Beneath the courtly civility of the military, there was a growing sense of frustration over Warren's intransigence. The AEC, an exasperated Cooney said, didn't have to grapple with the tough issues facing the military. "I think it is just until the bomb goes off. When the bomb goes off, then the problem exists, and it doesn't exist now to the Commission. They are not faced with this problem."

It was not easy to be a man of conviction, or a man of science, in 1950; Joseph McCarthy was making charges in the Senate that the AEC had ignored the Communist leanings of many scientists, and earlier that spring Klaus Fuchs had been arrested. The year 1950 was a "skittish time," Warren recalled in an interview shortly before his death. "Some thought World War III was on the way."

Cooney, the veteran of two test series at the Pacific Proving Ground, pressed on with his argument, pointing out that if an A-bomb "is used tactically on a corps or on a division, and if we have, say, 5,000 troops who have received 100 R radiation, the Commander is going to want to know from me, 'Is it all right for me to reassemble these men and take them into combat?' I don't know the answer to that question."

Cooney proposed doing an experiment that was similar to the one outlined by Robert Stone—only his proposal apparently would include military volunteers also. He suggested that 200 volunteers be exposed to varying amounts of whole-body radiation, beginning with 25 roentgens and going up to 150 roentgens. "I feel that we can get volunteers both officer and enlisted to take up to as much as 100 R and 150 R, whole body radiation," he said.

Cooney compared the proposed TBI experiments to the human experiments performed by Walter Reed, the turn-of-the century researcher who discovered that mosquitoes carried yellow fever. There were significant differences, though, between Reed's human experiments and the one Cooney was proposing; for one, soldiers were dying from yellow fever when Reed did his experiments, but no soldier had yet died from an overexposure to radiation. "Personally I see no difference in subjecting men to this than I do to any other type of experimentation that has ever been carried on," Cooney argued. "Walter Reed killed some people. It was certainly the end result that was very wonderful."

None of the arguments raised by Cooney, not even the possibility that the United States was on the brink of a nuclear war, could persuade Warren that the TBI experiments were necessary. Warren re-emphasized that the medical establishment had already gathered a large amount of animal data as well as human data from the victims of the Hiroshima and Nagasaki bombings. "Actually, we have got the results of an enormous experiment. We have the experiment involving over 200,000 people in the Nagasaki and Hiroshima areas, and I think that those results are real. I was there, and I saw the people when they got sick," he said.

Since humans varied greatly in their response to radiation, Warren continued, it would be impossible to obtain accurate results without undertaking a huge study. "I don't see how it is possible to have an answer that means anything, over and above what we already have in our animal data and our scattered human data, without going to tens of thousands of individuals," he said. "That at once puts in the question of, 'Is such a thing practicable?' If we were considering things in the Kremlin, undoubtedly it would be practicable. I doubt that it is practicable here."

Warren, who had managed to keep the plutonium injections and other controversial human studies conducted by the Manhattan Project doctors from becoming public, again stated his vigorous opposition to human experiments. "I would not be quite honest in saying what I am saying," he confessed, "if I were not to add that personally I am very much opposed to human experimentation when it isn't for the good of the individual concerned and when there is any other way of solving the problem."

Cooney conceded that a small experiment with 200 volunteers would not prove anything statistically but argued the results of such an experiment would give his military leaders a degree of comfort. "Generals are hard people to deal with, and if I tell a general that 'Your men might get sick with 50 R,' or 'They might not get sick until they get 150 R' that is a very unsatisfactory answer for him, and he will not accept it. I don't think that we are interested in pushing this thing to the point of finding lethality but I do believe if we had two hundred cases whereby we could say that these men did or did not get sick up to 150 R, it would certainly be a great help to us."

"I wonder if it would really be a help if it came to the final analysis," mused Warren. "I can think in terms of times when even if everybody on a ship was seasick, you would still have to keep that ship operating."

Warren was an intimidating opponent, eloquent and imposing, and filled with what many colleagues viewed as a maddening self-righteous-ness. Sensing a deadlock approaching, Admiral Greaves stepped in to smooth the waters and lend support to his fellow officer. "I am very glad that this question of human experimentation has come up in the open so quickly and so frankly," he said in a conciliatory tone. "I certainly agree with everything you have said, Dr. Warren, and I appreciate that the idea of human experimentation within this country is certainly repugnant." In fact, Greaves had said much the same thing himself during the Commit-tee on Medical Sciences meeting some months before.

Nevertheless, he continued, "We have a problem to answer, the same thing that General Cooney says. We are going to have it [the prob-lem of radioactive materials] if we have this type of submarine that we are talking about. The Air Force is going to have it if we get that kind of stuff in their planes. . . . I think our position in this matter of human experimentation is the same as everybody else. We don't want to do it if we can get out of doing it, but if that is the only way we can get the answer, that certainly is going to be more economical in the long run to take a few chances now and perhaps not lose a battle or even worse than that . . . lose a war."

Warren said total body irradiation shortened the lives of animals and that he expected Cooney's planned experiment would also shorten the lives of the human subjects. "We can say, I think, with a good deal of certainty that 25 R is safe. We know that an appreciable proportion of any group of individuals will be seriously ill at 200 R, and that some will die at 200 R. We can say with a fair degree of assurance that with 100 R, other casualties such as burns will be materially complicated and the lethality of minor injuries will arise, and there is a great deal of perma-nent damage that is done to the organism as well as transient damage at the 100 R level."

Warren pointed out that the fatigue and stress of battle also would radically alter how soldiers responded to radiation. But Cooney doggedly insisted that his field commanders needed to make decisions based on experimental data involving human beings.

"When I start talking about animal experimentation," Cooney said, "as one general said to me: 'What are we—mice or men?' "

"I think one of the things that is very important is that we are in part mice, and only in part men," Warren responded.

Stone had recommended that prisoners serving life sentences be used, another idea that Warren had roundly rejected. Toward the end of the meeting, Admiral Greaves brought up the use of prisoners again.

Under Stone's original proposal, the military would have been responsible for making arrangements for the experiments. Although the military was interested in obtaining the data, it would not look good if the armed forces were actually conducting the experiments on prisoners, Greaves said. "That type of experimental work is a little difficult for the armed forces to engage in."

"Is this civilian prisoners, you mean?" asked Alan Gregg, an ally of Shields Warren.

"Yes," responded the admiral.

"Doesn't that fall in the category of cruel and unusual punishment?" Gregg asked.

"It would be on an absolutely volunteer basis, and under every safety precaution that could be built up around it. I don't think so, and it didn't strike me as being cruel and unusual," Greaves responded.

"It is not very long since we got through trying Germans for doing exactly that thing," Warren warned.

"That wasn't voluntary when they did it, they made them do it," Greaves responded. "I think that there are a lot of prisoners and I am given to understand that there are plenty of people in our prisons who will volunteer for that kind of work."

"Always for a quid pro quo," Warren responded.

Shields Warren and his civilian colleagues were successful that day in blocking the military's efforts to conduct TBI experiments on prisoners. But it was a Pyrrhic victory at best. Even as they were standing up to the military, the Air Force, unbeknownst to them, was moving forward on a study to be conducted at the M.D. Anderson Cancer Center in Houston. Experiments done on sick cancer patients at Anderson were to provide the military with data on human responses to radiation.

The M.D. Anderson study was one of five postwar TBI experiments funded by the military and was the first to be set in motion. The Department of Defense stressed that the military funds paid only for data collection and not for the irradiation of the patients, but one prominent researcher admitted in 1994 that he probably would not have pursued the experiment if he had not received military funding. The five studies and their host institutions were as follows:

• The M.D. Anderson Cancer Center in Houston, Texas, from 1951 until 1956. This study involved 263 patients and was sponsored by the Air Force School of Aviation Medicine, which performed the early flashblindness studies at the Nevada Test Site.

• Baylor University College of Medicine in Houston, Texas, 1952 until 1964. This study involved 112 patients and was sponsored by the Armed Forces Special Weapons Project or its successor, the Defense Atomic Support Agency, the organization that coordinated the atomic maneuvers in Nevada.

• Sloan-Kettering Institute for Cancer Research in New York City, 1954 to 1964. Sponsored by the Armed Forces Special Weapons Project and later the Defense Atomic Support Agency, this experiment involved 34 patients. James J. Nickson, the Met Lab physician who assisted in the TBI studies and the Chicago plutonium injections, and who also served as Allan Kline's physician, conducted the experiment.

• U.S. Naval Hospital, Bethesda, Maryland. Funded by the Navy, the experiment was conducted from 1960 to 1961 and involved 17 people.

• University of Cincinnati College of Medicine in Cincinnati, Ohio. This study, sponsored by Defense Atomic Support Agency, ran from 1960 to 1972 and involved 90 patients.

(One other large TBI study was done at the small research hospital in Oak Ridge, Tennessee. There, some 194 patients were exposed to total-body irradiation in one of the hospital's two specially enclosed chambers between 1957 and 1974. Some of the money for this TBI study came from the National Aeronautics and Space Administration, or NASA.)

In the military studies alone, which spanned 1951 to 1972, approximately 500 people with cancer were exposed to radiation over their entire bodies. Some patients received large, single blasts of radiation. Others were exposed to repeated, low doses along the lines of what Robert Stone had suggested. The TBI experiments were classic examples of the dual-purpose studies pioneered by the Manhattan Project. While the patients ostensibly were irradiated for their diseases, doctors collected data for the military on the side.

The official reports on the experiments invariably claim that the exposures made the patients feel better and reduced the size of their cancers. But other records indicate that the radiation caused excruciating pain and led to the premature deaths of a number of patients.

The Army, Navy, and Air Force hoped to obtain data from the patients to predict how soldiers, sailors, and pilots would behave when they were exposed to radiation on the nuclear battlefield. Ever mindful of the devastating radiation sickness they had witnessed in Japan, the military leaders were desperate to learn more about the effects of radiation. When did nausea and vomiting set in? How long before the effects of radiation showed up on the bone marrow? Could exposure impair intellectual and decision-making capabilities? What about the ability to perform simple motor tests? Was there some kind of medicine that could be taken beforehand that would protect the troops? What happened to soldiers exposed to small, repeated doses? The questions were never-ending, and ultimately the answers proved unsatisfactory because, as Robert Stone and his colleagues had recognized at the Carlton Hotel meeting, healthy young soldiers and sick cancer patients don't necessarily respond in the same way to radiation.

In all five of the postwar TBI experiments, the researchers conducted extensive analyses on the blood and urine of the patients in an effort to find a "biological dosimeter"—that is, some kind of chemical marker that would reveal how much radiation a person had absorbed. In the early days at the Met Lab, Robert Stone had instructed his employees to look for a similar marker but none had been found. The military's search for a biological dosimeter was relentless. A simple test administered on the battlefield would help doctors know who was worth saving and who was going to die. "Ever since the damaging effects of ionizing radiation in biological systems were realized," an Air Force official wrote in 1963, "interested observers have been searching for some biochemical, histological or clinical indicator that would assess this damage in a manner closely related the magnitude of dose."

Significantly, many of the patients used in the TBI experiments suffered from "radioresistant" tumors, or solid cancers of the liver, pancreas, bladder, breast, and other parts of the body, which were usually treated with thousands of rads of local radiation. Total-body irradiation was normally not used on such cases because the doses necessary to destroy the tumors were so high that they could also kill the patients. Other types of cancers that have spread through the body, such as leukemia and lymphoma, are "radiosensitive," and TBI was considered an appropriate treatment at that time and is still used today. But scientists preferred to use patients with radioresistant tumors because often their blood counts were nearly normal and the radiation effects were not obscured by the products released by the widespread destruction of tumor cells.

Blood cells, chromosomes, amino acids, enzymes, plasma proteins, and lipids of the irradiated patients were intensively studied. But the military doctors never found a reliable marker and ultimately had to rely on the same symptoms of radiation sickness they had first chronicled in the criticality victims and the Japanese bombing victims—onset, severity, and duration of nausea, vomiting, anorexia, and hair loss. These are to this day the best indicators of the degree of radiation to which a person has been exposed.

HOUSTON'S "PAPERCLIP" DOCTOR

Air Force leaders had seen the handwriting on the wall long before Shields Warren gave the official AEC thumbs-down to total-body irradiation experiments on healthy volunteers. So they simply did an end run around him. While the TBI proposal was still winding its way through the Pentagon's chain of command and being debated at meetings like the one in which Warren took his firm stand, officials from the School of Aviation Medicine in San Antonio, Texas, began looking for a research hospital where they could piggyback simple coordination and psychological tests onto medical treatments in which patients were irradiated for their diseases. Air Force officials began discussing the studies in March 1950 with Randolph Lee Clark, the director of the M.D. Anderson Cancer Center in Houston. Clark, a handsome, athletic man who had been the National Amateur Middleweight Wrestling Champion, was no stranger to the School of Aviation Medicine, having been its director of surgical research prior to his hospital appointment.

The contractual details with M.D. Anderson were finalized in October, a month before General James Cooney and Shields Warren locked horns. Explaining the M.D. Anderson contract to his superiors at the Air Material Command, a young lieutenant said the experimental data was "urgently required" by the U.S. Air Force in connection with the NEPA Project:

> It is clear that before attempting to operate its proposed nuclear powered aircraft, the U.S. Air Force must evaluate its radiation

hazards. There are no scientific data with which to assess these dangers of the NEPA aircraft in terms of their probable effects upon crew performance and well-being. The most direct approach to this information would be by human experiments in specifically designed radiation studies; however, for several important reasons, this has been forbidden by top military authority. Since the need is pressing, it would appear mandatory to take advantage of investigation opportunities that exist in certain radiology centers by conducting special examinations and measures of patients who are undergoing radiation treatment for disease. While the flexibility of experimental design in a radiological clinic will necessarily be limited, the information that may be gained from studies of patients is considered potentially invaluable; furthermore, this is currently the sole source of human data.

(Although Shields Warren was adamantly opposed to TBI experiments on healthy volunteers, he apparently saw nothing wrong with the School of Aviation Medicine's planned research on sick cancer patients. In 1953, a year after Warren resigned his position at the AEC, he became a medical consultant to the Aircraft Nuclear Propulsion program, the successor to the nuclear-propelled aircraft project, and was present at an organizational meeting in May of 1953 when M.D. Anderson's TBI experiment was discussed. There is no record of his posing any objection to the study. Other consultants included Manhattan Project veterans Andrew Dowdy and Simeon Cantril and MIT's Robley Evans.)

The School of Aviation Medicine assigned one of its newest Paperclip arrivals, Herbert Gerstner, to the TBI project. A stocky physiologist with a saberlike scar on his left cheek, Gerstner had been smuggled out of Germany's Russian Zone in 1949 and brought to San Antonio, Texas, where a number of his German colleagues were already working. By the time he arrived, most of his countrymen had already adapted to their new homeland. The fiery food, the jalapeños, salsa, and chorizo-and-egg breakfast tacos took some getting used to, and when temperatures soared toward the 100-degree mark, many of the scientists undoubtedly yearned for the cool cities of northern Europe. But through the efforts of the school's commandant, Harry G. Armstrong, a disarming medical doctor with an infectious enthusiasm, much of the hostility and resentment aimed at the foreigners following World War II had faded away. Intelligent, circumspect, and hardworking, the Germans had quietly resumed their research in the nondescript laboratories at Randolph Air Force Base.

There were at least twenty German Paperclip specialists at the School when Gerstner and his wife, Helga, a lovely green-eyed blonde sixteen years his junior, arrived in San Antonio in January of 1950. Hubertus Strughold, the intellectual leader of the small band of German specialists and the man whose own retinal burn had inspired the early flashblindness studies at the Nevada Test Site, was probably among those who greeted the couple. Strughold had helped Armstrong select the German scientists recruited for the school and no doubt was also aware of some of the circumstances behind the couple's escape.

Gerstner's personnel records, which are on file at the National Archives, show that he was a member of the Hitler Youth from 1935 to 1938, but say nothing about whether he was a member of the Nazi Party. His wife, Helga, said in an interview in 1995 that her husband was not a party member. But *The Texas Observer* reported in 1997 that Gerstner became a party member in May 1937 and was assigned the membership number 5815500 "when the party re-opened its ranks to Nazis who had proven themselves active and devoted."

Drafted into the German Medical Corps in 1939, Gerstner was first dispatched to France as a soldier and then worked as a doctor on military hospital trains in Russia. He was assigned to the Academy for Military Medicine in Berlin in 1940, where he began investigating the effects of loud sound on guinea pigs. The research was stimulated by the constant shelling that German soldiers were receiving in their bunkers. As a result of his work, Gerstner had developed a list of sound intensities and knew how long humans could be exposed to those sounds without suffering permanent hearing damage.

Two years later, Gerstner was transferred to the University of Leipzig, where he focused on the effects of electricity on animal and human skin. At Leipzig, he studied the victims of "electrical accidents" and concluded that they died from an extraordinary increase in blood pressure when blood was squeezed out of peripheral vessels and into their hearts and abdominal cavity. In subsequent studies he noted that "electrical skin resistance" was higher in cancer patients. "It has not been investigated, however, whether a diagnostic method for cancer can be developed from this. (Resumption of work on this problem is difficult since all statistical data have been lost due to war events)," Gerstner wrote.

Gerstner had just begun working at the University of Griefswald in northern Germany's Russian Zone in 1949 when an intermediary for the Central Intelligence Agency contacted him, his wife said. The couple made inquiries about the visitor through a trusted friend. Then Gerstner camouflaged himself and went to the CIA's offices in West Berlin. "As a citizen of Russian-occupied Germany, you can't go to the CIA in West Berlin and think that you're going to be safe coming back or not disappear or whatever," Helga Gerstner said. "So they indeed camouflaged him and made him look like an American GI. They insisted he had to come there in person because none of this information would be given out other than one on one."

A CIA official explained Operation Paperclip to Gerstner, but the scientist was worried that the Americans were more interested in denying him to the Soviets and were planning to "dump" him in the United States. So he again camouflaged himself as an American GI and went to Heidelberg where he was able to confirm that there was, in fact, a job waiting for him in the United States.

The Gerstners were flown from Berlin to Frankfurt by a military aircraft in a snowstorm around Christmas of 1949. From there they took a train to Landshut, Bavaria, the collection point for Paperclip scientists. A telegram dated December 27 stated that Gerstner was "available for shipment to U.S. in Jan. 50."

Gerstner was one of thirty-four Paperclip specialists employed by the School of Aviation Medicine. The Army and the Navy, even some private companies, also recruited the scientists. At least 1,600 German specialists and their dependents were imported to the United States by Paperclip and its successor projects through the early 1970s.

Many of the nation's most brilliant scientists, among them Albert Einstein and Hans Bethe, opposed the importation of German researchers. The Manhattan Project's Leslie Groves also had warned against letting Germans worm their way into America's atomic energy programs. But the American military could not be dissuaded. Not only did the Army, Navy, and Air Force crave the Germans' ingenious inventions and scientific data, but, just as Gerstner suspected, they also wanted to keep the information and the scientists from falling into Soviet hands. By 1950, less than a year after the Soviets had detonated their first atomic bomb, security concerns about Nazis had been subsumed by massive preparations for nuclear war. Communism, not Nazism, had become the greatest threat to the free world. "To continue to treat Nazi affiliations as significant considerations has been aptly phrased as 'beating a dead Nazi horse,'" Bosquet Wev, a Navy captain who directed Project Paperclip, wrote in a 1948 letter to the State Department.

Ostensibly Gerstner was recruited for the School of Aviation Medicine because of his expertise in acoustics. Instead he was assigned to the new radiation project at the M.D. Anderson Cancer Center. Gerstner had no expertise to speak of when it came to ionizing radiation. "He really got into the radiation effects area once he came to the School of Aviation Medicine," Helga Gerstner said. "It was a field of interest to him but it was not his first and foremost one."

The M.D. Anderson was Houston's pride and joy. Named after a wealthy cotton broker who left his fortune to "good works" and administered by the University of Texas, by the early 1950s the hospital was rapidly becoming one of the most respected research institutions in the country. Gone were the large noisy wards and drab corridors of yesteryear. Pictures were changed often in the private and semiprivate rooms, but if a patient couldn't stand a painting any longer, he could turn it around to a "contrasting but harmonious" color. The exterior of the hospital was covered by an inch of pink Georgia marble.

Most of the patients used in the TBI study were outpatients capable of "light tasks" and many apparently were African Americans, according to the minutes of a 1954 Air Force Research Council meeting. The purpose of the TBI treatment, wrote Gerstner and two coexperimenters, was to find out whether TBI would provide some "palliative" relief from cancer symptoms.

During the first phase of the study, 233 patients were exposed to doses ranging from 15 to 200 roentgens. During the second phase, an additional 30 patients were exposed to a single dose of 200 roentgens. School of Aviation Medicine scientists had found the first part of the experiment in which the patients were given small doses "unproductive." But when cancer specialists at M.D. Anderson began increasing their doses, the military researchers felt they, too, were beginning to make headway.

The patients who were given 200 roentgens purportedly had diseases that were so far advanced that conventional treatments offered no benefit. Yet, they were still ambulatory and clear-headed enough to take the battery of pre- and postirradiation tests prepared by the school's doctors. Three psychomotor tests were administered before the patients were irradiated: The Air Force SAM Complex Coordination Test required participants to coordinate movement of a stick and rudder bar to match the position of three red lights and three green lights. The Two-Hand Coordination Test required patients to operate two crank handles to keep a cursor positioned on a moving target. And the Rotary Pursuit Test required participants to follow a rotating target with the tip of a stylus. The tests were repeated the day after the TBI treatment and again nine days later. "These tests were chosen because of their proven relationship to the skills required in basic pilotry," School of Aviation Medicine scientists stated.

Just as Shields Warren had predicted, the patients' response to the radiation varied greatly. A thirty-three-year-old minister who was irradiated with 200 roentgens went home and had a meal and his customary one-hour nap. Then he worked at his ministerial duties till 9:00 P.M. and ten hours a day on the succeeding days. At the other end of the spectrum was a young man suffering from testicular cancer. After he was irradiated with 200 roentgens, he developed such severe nausea and vomiting that he had to be transported by stretcher and required a liter of intravenous saline solution.

Thirteen of the thirty patients who received 200 roentgens of TBI died within sixty days of the treatment, the time frame in which the effects of radiation damage to the bone marrow generally will appear. The average survival time was 4.4 months. All thirty patients died within twenty months. Because of the variability in subjects and the lack of a control group, the experimenters said it was "difficult to assess the extent to which radiation had affected the life expectancy of the patients." But for a small group of lung cancer patients, the researchers concluded that the radiation may have actually extended their lives by a few days.

As for the cancer itself, the scientists admitted that the TBI treatment did not really significantly alter the course of the disease, but it did seem to produce a transitory and clinically unsupported sense of well-being in three subjects. "Close similarity seems to prevail," they added, "between systemic effects produced in cancer patients by whole body X-irradiation and those caused in healthy human beings by nuclear explosions."

When the M.D. Anderson experiment was over, Gerstner turned his attention to the civil defense aspects of acute radiation sickness. Like General James Cooney, Gerstner believed the public was overly frightened of atomic energy and argued that human beings could recover physically from a wide range of radiation exposures and resume "useful" lives. In a 1960 paper he wrote:

Obviously, nuclear disasters can assume such dimensions that exposed persons, in order to reach medical facilities, may have to endure several hours of driving or walking through streets congested by vehicles and panic-stricken people. Thus, while on their way, they become affected by the disturbance and, thereby, suffer reduction of fitness at a time when ultimate physical and mental efforts are necessary for survival. In a small group of hypersensitive persons, reactions probably will attain such severity as to imperil escape from the disaster area without aid. Therefore, the disturbance must be taken into account by authorities designing evacuation plans and other emergency measures which require active participation of exposed populations.

Gerstner, who had witnessed the unpredictability of war in France and on the Russian Front, did not particularly enjoy the civil defense work. "He was not very happy with that aspect," his widow said, "but he was often called on as an expert." Gerstner left the School of Aviation Medicine in 1960 and went to the Oak Ridge Institute for Nuclear Studies. There he obtained his medical license and worked for a short while in the hospital. Occasionally he went to Cincinnati to see radiologist Eugene Saenger, the lead investigator for the TBI experiment at the University of Cincinnati. Sometimes Saenger visited Gerstner in Oak Ridge. "There was a connection," Helga Gerstner said. "They had some joint project. What he did and what they cooperated on, I don't know. I just know they worked together on something."

Herbert Gerstner was involved in the first military-sponsored TBI experiment of the Cold War, and Eugene Saenger oversaw the final one. While no documents have surfaced to indicate that Gerstner had any hands-on involvement whatsoever in Saenger's TBI project, the two scientists, both closely allied with the U.S. military and civil defense planners, had much in common.

35

CINCINNATI'S BATTLEFIELD

Around the time that Eugene Saenger, a young radiologist at the University of Cincinnati, went to listen to a talk given by General James Cooney, he was beginning to wonder if his medical career was ever going to amount to anything more than doing barium enemas and diagnostic X rays. Thanks to the Atomic Energy Commission's aggressive radioisotope distribution program and its concomitant public relations program, nuclear medicine was becoming a hot field, and Saenger was eager to get in on the action. He had taken a training course on radionuclides at the Oak Ridge Institute for Nuclear Studies, where he had learned "how to pipette, how to dilute, how to count," but he felt sure there was more to nuclear medicine than that. Then he heard the presentation by General Cooney, one of the nation's foremost experts on atomic energy. Perhaps Cooney talked that day about how the power unleashed by the atom could be harnessed to cure the ills of mankind—one of his standard themes as he barnstormed the country in his role as cheerleader for the atom. Whatever he said, Saenger was impressed. He was soon to do his two years of military service and wondered if Cooney might be able to help him find a placement that would take advantage of his training. Afterward he went up and introduced himself.

"Listen, I'd like to [get] into some of this nuclear energy stuff when I get into the Army," he told the general.

"Saenger," the general snapped, "you come and see me."

When Saenger joined the Army Medical Corps in 1953, he took Cooney up on his word and visited him. "I was treated as if I was king of the mountain," Saenger remembered. "His secretary knew I was coming and they made a big fuss, and we became very good friends, the Cooneys and my wife and I."

Saenger was first dispatched to Sandia Air Base in Albuquerque, New Mexico, the field command for the Armed Forces Special Weapons Project. Although Saenger had no interest in attending a weapons test ("you get all this crud coming down your neck, to me it was useless"), he did get a good introduction to "bombology." Six months later he was transferred to Brooke Army Hospital in San Antonio, where he was made chief of the Radioisotope Laboratory. Saenger remained at Brooke, the Army's leading burn research center, until he was discharged in 1955. While Saenger spent only two years in the Army, he maintained his military connections for the rest of his life.

After his tour of duty was over, he returned to Cincinnati, a sprawling city on the banks of the Ohio River that has the feel of a sleepy southern town but resembles Detroit. Located across the river from Kentucky, Cincinnati historically has been a major connecting point between the North and South. With some 2,000 industrial plants, the city has long been a destination for poor whites and African Americans from southern states. Racial tensions have occasionally run high, and in 1968 the city exploded in riots following the assassination of Dr. Martin Luther King Jr.

Handsome and confident, Saenger had strong ties to the medical school and the city itself. Except for his two-year military stint and four years as an undergraduate at Harvard, Saenger has lived his entire life in Cincinnati. His uncle was the medical school's first professor of radiology, and Saenger worked in his lab when he was young. After receiving his medical degree in 1942 from the University of Cincinnati College of Medicine, he went on to do his internship and his residency at Cincinnati General Hospital, becoming a board-certified radiologist in 1946. Saenger later directed three or four campaigns that raised millions of tax dollars for the hospital. His "small expertise," he once confessed in a letter to Los Alamos's Wright Langham, was "political rather than scientific."

In 1955, the year Saenger was mustered out of the Army, he began preparing a research proposal to study the effects of total-body irradiation on cancer patients. Saenger probably learned of the military's interest in TBI when he was in the Army. But his proposal was also fueled in part by the chairman of the pediatrics department, who made the offhand comment one day that no radiologist had ever done any decent scientific research. "That really upset me. That really annoyed me. I have never forgotten that," Saenger told staffers from the Advisory Committee on Human Radiation Experiments. "I sort of thought, dammit, I'm going to show people I know how to do something, not that it's been very momentous but it's kept me interested."

Saenger had also learned from one of his close friends, John Lawrence, the brother of Ernest Lawrence, that it was better to get contracts than grants. "We were on a boat one time in Florida and we were talking about grants and contracts and I said to him, 'These grants are really sort of a pain.' He said, 'You mean to tell me you're still going after grants?' I said, 'John, what should I be doing?' He said, 'Contracts, my boy, contracts.' And it was very interesting because a contract would run forever."

In 1958, Saenger submitted his application to the Research and Development Division of the Army Surgeon General's Office. The Army seemed like a "logical source of funds," Saenger told interviewers, because of its interest in the effects of radiation on humans. General Cooney also happened to be the deputy surgeon general at that time.

The year that Saenger submitted his application, the United States and the Soviet Union had just agreed to temporarily halt atmospheric testing of atomic weapons largely because of strong opposition to fallout. Within eighteen months, though, the troops and the cloud samplers would be back in Nevada and the Pacific Proving Ground for another season before the aboveground tests were finally halted for good.

According to Saenger's original application, entitled "Metabolic Changes in Humans Following Total Body Radiation," one of the chief goals of his proposed study was to find a biological dosimeter—the goal that for all practical purposes would elude most of the researchers who ever pursued it, to the great frustration of their military sponsors. Saenger stated that he intended to use well-nourished adult males with widespread cancer and exclude women of child-bearing age because their amino acids fluctuated too much during the menstrual cycle.

Defense Department officials who reviewed Saenger's application had mixed feelings about his proposal. James Hartgering, a former Armed Forces Special Weapons Project official who was privy to many of the high-level discussions on troop maneuvers at the Nevada Test Site, said he did not believe Saenger's research would yield anything useful but felt the experiment should be supported anyway. Hartgering wrote, "There are so few radiologists in the country willing to do total body radiation that those that are should be encouraged more. His past research experience has been good and I feel that he is a very reliable investigator. If he is supported I am sure he will soon decide that some other phase of the radiation program should be investigated and switch to this." Arthur Sullivan, another scientist, believed Saenger's experiment would "augment" the TBI studies under way at Baylor and Sloan-Kettering and might lead to a "possible biological dosimeter."

Only one Army official, Colonel John Isherwood, chief of radiological services, suggested Saenger's work might have a potential benefit to the patient. "Any correlation of tumor response to total dose of irradiation by such means as prepared by this project would be of great value in the field of cancer. In addition if by means such as those proposed accurate knowledge of the total dose of radiation received could be determined it would be of inestimable value in case of atomic disaster or nuclear warfare."

The first of several contracts between the University of Cincinnati and the Defense Atomic Support Agency, AFSWP's successor, was signed in early 1960. Saenger headed the TBI project, but he scrupulously avoided choosing the patients who were to be irradiated, leaving that task to others. The first patient who received total body irradiation was a sixty-seven-year-old African American with cancer of the left tonsil. The disease had spread to his palate and throat. He received 66 rads and died seventy-three days later. Over the next eleven years, some eighty-nine additional patients were administered TBI.

In the ten reports that Saenger submitted to the Defense Atomic Support Agency or its successor, he says almost nothing about the therapeutic effects of TBI on the cancer patients. "These studies," he wrote in his first report, "are designed to obtain new information about the metabolic effects of total body and partial body irradiation so as to have a better understanding of the acute and sub-acute effects of irradiation in the human." In his second progress report, he added, "This information is necessary to provide knowledge of combat effectiveness of troops and to develop additional methods of diagnosis, prognosis, prophylaxis and treatment of these injuries."

Saenger has said he did not include information in his progress reports on the positive medical effects of the TBI because the military was not interested in that portion of the study. The total-body irradiation was administered to the patients for "palliative purposes," he said. In other words, the treatment would not cure the patients but it might shrink their tumors, reduce pain, and possibly extend their lives. However, no written protocol has been found showing that palliation was the primary purpose of the study. Furthermore, Saenger and his colleagues did not publish a scientific report comparing the benefits of TBI to other cancer treatments until 1973, a year after the study had ended and the experiment had received widespread negative publicity. In Saenger's 1973 paper, he states that whole-body radiation and partial-body radiation had some "beneficial effects" in controlling certain advanced cancers and that its palliative effects compared favorably with those induced by other drugs.

Saenger initially planned to start with doses of 100 rads, gradually increasing exposures to 150, 200, 250, 300, and finally 600 rads. Like Shields Warren, Saenger was aware that individuals varied greatly in their response to radiation exposure and that some people might die at the higher doses without therapeutic intervention. In a handbook on radiation accidents published three years after the study began, Saenger wrote:

Fatalities may begin to occur at 200 rad and possibly approach 50 percent at 450–500 rad. Statements such as these involving percentages serve to emphasize the factor of individual sensitivity which may be of the greatest importance. One man, for instance, may show prostration resulting from a dose of total body irradiation of, say 100 rad, whereas another man may show no appreciable disability.

Saenger never exposed any patient in the Cincinnati study to the higher doses he had proposed in his initial report to the Pentagon. According to Defense Department records, the largest dose of total-body irradiation administered to any one subject appears to have been 200 rads, with a few patients receiving 300 rads of partial-body irradiation.

In a 1962 memo entitled "An Appraisal of Human Studies in Radiobiological Aspects of Weapons Effects," Saenger brought up the possibility of using "healthy volunteers" in his experiment. "Once patients from the therapy group are being managed so that their hematologic consequences of radiation have been controlled then it will be advisable to utilize a less ill, more normal group of individuals for study." However, there is no evidence that he went ahead with any plan to irradiate healthy people.

Ultimately, the Defense Atomic Support Agency contributed a total of $671,000 toward the Cincinnati study. Saenger has emphasized repeatedly that the funds were used to pay only for the observational data and extensive laboratory tests. The military was not involved in the choice of patients, doses, treatment, or care. Cincinnati General Hospital spent some $483,000 of its own funds on patient care.

As in other TBI studies, researchers specifically sought patients with radioresistant tumors who had a stable blood picture and normal kidney function. That profile, of course, closely resembles that of a healthy soldier or nuclear worker and would enable scientists to hunt more easily for a biological dosimeter and conduct their psychological tests. But TBI is generally not used for such tumors. Indeed, a year before the study began no less an authority on the subject than Shields Warren himself had written in *Scientific American:* "Radioresistant tumors are generally not treated with radiation because the damage to surrounding tissue is too great."

Efforts were made to exclude patients who had already received local radiation or chemotherapy in order not to confound the results. Like the School of Aviation Medicine's Herbert Gerstner, the Cincinnati group early on recognized that patients already exposed to radiation suffered more deleterious effects the second time around.

All the patients enrolled in the TBI experiment had widespread cancer, but many were still leading relatively normal lives. In their report for the first year of the experiment, Saenger and his colleagues wrote, "Our patients of course all have incurable and/or metastatic cancer, and although in reasonably good clinical condition, cannot be considered as normal." Later progress reports stated that the subjects were "in relatively good health," "clinically stable, many of them working daily," and able to "perform activities of daily living."

Following a long tunnel with overhead, exposed pipes that wound its way through the basement of Cincinnati General Hospital, the patients arrived at the irradiation chamber. Inside was a Cobalt 60 Teletherapy Unit, surrounded by several feet of lead. The experimental subjects were homemakers, seamstresses, maids, salesmen, carpenters, and clerks. Sixty-two percent were African American. Most were poor or had such low-paying jobs they could not afford private physicians. Many had very little formal education.

The patients were led into the room where they were placed in a sitting position 282 centimeters, or about nine feet, from the source.

Their legs were raised and their head tilted slightly forward. Half the exposure was delivered laterally through one side of the body. Then the patient was turned and the remaining radiation delivered. The treatment usually took one-half to one hour.

Toward the end of the eleven-year study, Saenger informed the Defense Department that he hoped to expose some patients with a blast of radiation from one direction. "Whenever possible unidirectional radiation will be attempted since this type of exposure is of military interest." David Egilman, a physician and professor at Brown University and long-time critic of the experiment, maintained the crouched position and "unidirectional" radiation closely resembled how soldiers would be exposed on the nuclear battlefield. There is no evidence, however, that the unidirectional radiation was given, pointed out R. Joseph Parker, Saenger's attorney.

The subjects, of course, did not feel anything while the radiation was being delivered. But Saenger acknowledged in his 1973 paper that the exposures could have initiated the hematologic form of the acute radiation syndrome in some patients. Bone marrow failure is the cause of death in this syndrome, but many other organs of the body are also damaged. In his handbook on radiation accidents, Saenger compared the acute radiation syndrome to a viral infection or an illness caused by chemical poisoning.

In the "prodromal phase" of the acute radiation syndrome, nausea, vomiting, weakness, and fatigue usually begin several hours after exposure. These symptoms subside two or three days later and then the patients enter a latent period in which they generally feel no symptoms. The latent period lasts about twenty days. Then acute illness sets in. Many symptoms occur during this period—vomiting, diarrhea, abdominal pain, fever, disorientation, shock, hemorrhage—but one of the most dangerous symptoms is infection. This danger period lasts about thirty to forty days, and then recovery usually begins. If exposures are high enough, the various stages of the acute radiation syndrome can be compressed, with the latent period disappearing altogether.

Saenger said in his 1973 paper that the TBI could have contributed to the death of eight patients if the disease and effects from previous therapy were excluded. A University of Cincinnati faculty committee that reviewed the experiment later found nineteen patients died between twenty and sixty days after the TBI treatment and "could have died from radiation alone."

One of the first patients to receive 200 roentgens—a dose that both Shields Warren and Eugene Saenger said could produce fatalities—was John Edgar Webster, Patient No. 021, a country musician and custodian at an elementary school. He was examined by doctors at Cincinnati General Hospital in April 1962 and diagnosed with bowel cancer that had spread to his left lung. Several weeks later he returned to the hospital to receive the "miracle" treatment that family members thought would cure his cancer. After the so-called cure, Webster planned to take a trip to California to see his eldest son. "My mother was extremely excited after hearing the news of this newly discovered treatment," Webster's granddaughter, Peggy Carboina, said in written testimony to a congressional subcommittee. On April 28, 1962, Webster became the third patient bombarded with 200 rads of total-body irradiation.

Webster had a severe reaction to the TBI. He could not get out of bed following the treatment. Nor could he keep down food or water. He began to lose weight rapidly. "He would cry due to such pain. We heard him pray that God would take him so the pain would stop," his granddaughter remembered. Chest X rays showed an invasive substance in the lung that appeared to be either tumor or pneumonia. "His course was progressively downhill, and he expired June 3, 1962 (36 days post TBR)," a Defense Department report states. Webster's relatives told medical officials they did not want an autopsy performed, but years later they discovered that an autopsy was done anyway.

Another patient who had a severe reaction was Patient No. 045, Maude Jacobs. She was a beautiful blond woman who radiated happiness despite a life of severe hardship and continual poverty. Born in Hazard, Kentucky, she was orphaned at ten, married at the age of twelve, and had her first child at thirteen. She washed windows, cleaned houses, and did other people's laundry. Her formal education ended after third grade, but she struggled to teach herself how to read and write.

In the summer of 1964, the doctors at Cincinnati General Hospital diagnosed Jacobs as having breast cancer that had spread to the bone. She was forty-nine years old and had seven children, six girls and one boy. Chemotherapy helped the primary tumor, but the bone cancer continued to spread. "I don't think the doctors noes [sic] what is wrong with me," she said in a letter to her sister, Arlie, two months before her death.

One day Jacobs forced her swollen feet into a pair of dress shoes and took a taxi to the hospital. There she was irradiated with 150 rads. She began vomiting immediately and continued to vomit for the next twenty-four hours despite a dose of antinausea medication. "She went out of her mind," said daughter Lillian Pagano. Jacobs regained her sanity briefly when the priest came to administer last rites. They prayed together and then he asked her, "Are you ready to meet the Lord?" She responded, "Yes, I am, Father."

According to a Defense Department report, Jacobs had a normal blood count prior to the treatment. Seven days after she was irradiated, her white blood cell count began falling. The platelet count began to fall fourteen days later. She grew short of breath, her heart started to gallop, and chest films showed a diffuse infiltrate in the left lower lung and collapse of the right lower lung. She was started on antibiotics and other medications but nothing helped. She died December 2, 1964, twenty-five days after the total body irradiation had been administered.

Jacobs's death came so suddenly that she was unable to make arrangements for her children. Three of her youngest were sent to an orphanage. Family members said they were never informed of the TBI treatment. "My version of this is they burned her alive," Lillian Pagano said. "They killed her. They actually took part of her life away."

For Grey Spanagel, Patient No. 077, death also came soon after irradiation. Spanagel had throat cancer and had already undergone two surgical procedures and two localized radiation treatments. Nevertheless, he was still working and walking every day when Cincinnati doctors recommended that he be given total-body irradiation. Spanagel drove himself to the hospital for the treatment.

He was irradiated with 200 rads on November 9, 1967. Prior to the procedure, some of his bone marrow was removed and stored. Two days after irradiation, the bone marrow was infused back into his body. Spanagel tolerated both the TBI and bone marrow procedure well and was sent home the following day. Twenty days later his blood counts began to fall. "His condition continued a downhill course," the doctors wrote, "and on Dec. 9, 1967, he expired, thirty-one days post TBR."

Spanagel's wife, Madge, told *The Cincinnati Enquirer* that she and her husband were informed by doctors in separate interview sessions that the treatment was for the throat cancer. The doctors never told them the results might be used to help soldiers on the nuclear battlefield, she recalled.

In quiet laboratories far from the day-to-day horrors of the cancer wards, Saenger's team of researchers painstakingly studied urine and blood samples from the patients. Some of the serum was shipped to an Army researcher in Fort Knox, Kentucky. The samples were scrutinized for biochemical changes caused by the radiation. When the researchers could not find a reliable radiation marker in the urinary amino acids, they began studying antibody responses, chromosome abnormalities, and other biochemical and cellular changes. Saenger said many years later that he might have moved on to something else if he had found a clear biological dosimeter in the first ten to twelve patients. "We kept being on the edge of finding what we were looking for so we kept on treating the patients. . . ."

The patients' nausea and vomiting were carefully observed. Saenger said the military wanted the information not because "you fall down and vomit and have a fit and become confused and all that, but that your judgment would be impaired, that you couldn't fly the plane through the cloud or you couldn't make it all the way through the cloud and back and so on." The patients were not given antinausea medications for up to three days following the total-body irradiation, a procedure that critics said was consistent with a military experiment but not appropriate for patients undergoing therapy for a disease.

In order to avoid tainting the data, hospital staffers were instructed not to discuss any possible side effects with the patients. "The patient is told that he is to receive treatment to help his sickness. There is no discussion of subjective reactions resulting from the treatment." Certainly withholding information is not consistent with the principle of informing patients of the possible consequences of their treatment.

Saenger told a congressional subcommittee that he didn't tell the patients of the possible side effects to avoid provoking the symptoms through the power of suggestion. "We found, as I think many of us observe in raising children and so on, if you ask leading questions, you very often elicit responses, particularly for things which are somewhat suggestive such as nausea and vomiting." The patients were given antinausea medication if they "complained," he added.

Often the patients were moved to a private room after irradiation so that their mental state could be better evaluated. What's more, the doctors told their military funders, "there are no other patients receiving radiation therapy with whom the patient can exchange experiences." These psychological studies were another important component of the experiment and became more elaborate as the years went on. Tests were administered to measure the patients' depression, hope, denial, and pessimism. Brief interviews were conducted before and after irradiation and then "scored" for cognitive dysfunction. Many of the patients were so sick after they were irradiated that they could not complete all the testing. Herb Varin remembers his mother, Nina Cline, complaining about the constant barrage of questioning. "I tell them I'm feeling terrible but they just want to talk to me," Varin recalled his mother saying. The psychological research was pertinent to the military, the Cincinnati doctors wrote, because of the way TBI affected thought processes:

> Following exposure to acute whole or partial body radiation it is possible that there will be significant impairment of the decision making capability of key personnel who have major command responsibilities. This concern has become more important in recent years since the findings that complex electronic systems can be rendered inoperative by very high doses of radiation. Thus it is necessary to maintain dependence on the human being. It is quite possible that even moderately high doses or dose rates could produce impairment of cognitive processes either of an obvious or of a subtle nature which in moments of stress would impair or defeat a military operation. In order to gain understanding of such possible changes it is necessary to seek changes in cognitive processes and decrease in the capability to perform highly technical processes.

The Cincinnati doctors were aware of the life-threatening dangers of TBI, the military reports reveal. Only one year into the study, Saenger and colleague Benjamin Friedman hypothesized that sick patients may be "unusually susceptible" to radiation. "We have had two cases, one at 150 and one at 200 rad, expire while manifesting the hematologic abnormalities of group III of the acute radiation syndrome," they remarked in their 1962 paper to the Defense Atomic Support Agency. A progress report summarizing the first five years of the experiment noted that "severe hematologic depression was found in most patients who expired." In the same report, the doctors observed, "Several of the patients have had the manifest illness stage of the acute radiation syndrome. . . . Ten of the patients died within thirty-seven days following treatment." For the report period ending April 30, 1967, the doctors wrote that "marked hematological depression occurred in all eighteen patients who received more than 125 rad total body radiation." And finally, in 1969 the Cincinnati group remarked that under one classification system used to describe radiation injury, four of eleven patients who received 200 rads of TBI "would have been classified as having sustained 'very severe' injury; three 'severely' injured and five only 'moderately' injured."

Saenger and his colleagues in the early to mid-1960s began to prepare facilities that would allow them to do autologous bone marrow transplants, a procedure in which some of the patient's bone marrow is withdrawn before the irradiation and returned to the body after the treatment is done. The Cincinnati doctors hoped the procedure would prolong the lives of patients whose bone marrow was severely damaged by the radiation exposures they were administering.

Five years were to pass before the doctors succeeded in performing their first successful bone marrow transplant. In the meantime, they continued to administer high doses of total-body irradiation and partial-body irradiation to numerous patients without the supporting bone marrow transplants. In 1969, just two years before the program was terminated, the physicians admitted, "In view of the life threatening hematologic abnormalities we have encountered in patients receiving 150–200 rad (226 to 336R) total body radiation, marrow storage is felt to be mandatory."

At the time, the process of withdrawing the marrow and reinfusing it back into the patients was itself extremely risky. The subjects were placed under general anesthesia for one and a half to two hours while about a pint of marrow was aspirated from sites in the hips and sternum. The marrow was put into storage and then infused back into the patients' veins after the TBI treatment. From there the marrow traveled through the bloodstream to the red bone marrow cavities, where it produced new cells.

According to Defense Department or university records, thirteen patients received bone marrow transplants. Margaret Bacon, an eighty-year-old woman who had been diagnosed with bladder cancer and did not want radical intervention, suffered a stroke when she was anesthetized for the bone marrow removal procedure on June 4, 1969. The doctors, apparently unaware of the stroke, proceeded to give her 150 rads total-body irradiation the same day and she died six days later.

The informed consent procedures went through a series of changes over the eleven years of the project. Between 1960 and 1964, the hospital's general consent form for all medical and surgical procedures was used. Members of Saenger's team said the patients were verbally informed of the nature of the experiment and asked for their agreement to participate in the project.

The first written consent form for the TBI treatment came into use in 1965. The document contains no specifics on what exactly the patients were told: "The nature and purpose of this therapy, possible alternative methods of treatment, the risks involved, the possibility of complications and prognosis have been fully explained to me. The special study and research nature of this treatment has been discussed with me and understood by me."

The doctors submitted the bone marrow portion of the project in 1966 to the Faculty Committee on Research, which had been created the previous year to oversee human experimentation at the medical center. "This work," physician-investigator Benjamin Friedman explained to the Faculty Committee, "is considered to be of vital importance not only for improving the survival of patients with far advanced cancer but for the survival of the citizens of this nation in the event of nuclear warfare or a major peacetime radiation accident."

Its "vital importance" notwithstanding, the project's protocol drew harsh criticism from several university reviewers. One doctor, George Shields, withdrew from the subcommittee studying the proposal because of close professional and personal ties with the investigators. In his withdrawal notice, Shields recommended the study be disapproved because of the high risks. "The radiation proposed has been documented in the author's own series to cause a 25 percent mortality," he said. The consent forms, he advised, should also contain a statement that "a 1 in 4 chance of death within a few weeks due to treatment, exists, etc." He added:

> The third purpose, "to determine whether autologous bone marrow therapy may play a role in treatment of bone marrow depression following acute radiation exposure in warfare or occupationally induced accidents" is not the subject of this experiment because normal individuals are not being tested. It is problematic whether the information gained in this study will apply to normal individuals following acute radiation exposure. Therefore it is my definite opinion that the third purpose of this experiment would not justify the risk entailed.

Another member of the review committee, Thomas Gaffney, also questioned the wisdom of expanding the TBI study given its "considerable morbidity." Gaffney was also highly critical of the study design and predicted that the experiment would not yield meaningful data:

> When this deficiency in experimental method is placed next to their previously observed poor result and high morbidity with this type of treatment in a "variety of neoplasms" I think it is clear that the study as proposed should not be done. I have the uneasy suspicion, shored up by the revised statement of objectives, that this revised protocol is a subterfuge to allow the investigators to achieve the purpose described in their original application; namely to test the ability of autologous marrow to "take" in patients who have received high doses of total body radiation. This latter question may be an important one to answer but I can't justify 200 rad total body radiation simply for this purpose, "even in terminal case material."

Despite the reviewers' reservations, the experiment was allowed to proceed. Another thirty to thirty-five patients were irradiated before the experiment became public and was terminated four years later. Edward Radford, one of the faculty members who sat on the review committee, recalled that the panel was a little intimidated by Saenger. "We hadn't thought through the whole moral morass quite as thoroughly as people have now," he told a reporter. "And Dr. Saenger was irate. He said, 'Who are these guys telling me how to do my research?' He was still living in the period when the doctor was God."

The consent forms underwent two more revisions. In a 1967 form, the patients were informed that the experiment might not benefit them but could advance medical knowledge "which may result for the benefit of mankind." They also were informed that the risks of TBI included the "chance of infection or mild bleeding to be treated with marrow transplant, drugs, or transfusion as needed."

The third and final consent form, which came into use in 1971, went into greater detail but still did not disclose that the patient might die from the procedure: ". . . if you receive a dose of 200 rads or more, which your doctor will tell you, your blood counts will fall to levels where infection or bleeding could be a problem. The bleeding can be treated by transfusion of red cells and platelets and the infection by antibiotics. In addition, we prevent such low blood counts with the use of a bone marrow transplant which will be discussed with you in a separate voluntary consent statement. . . ." In the later years Saenger and his coresearchers said they began a two-day consent process. The TBI treatment was explained to the patient during the first day. The consent form was signed on the following day after the patient talked the matter over with his or her family.

The military's oversight of the experiment was virtually nil. Occasionally military representatives would visit Cincinnati and Saenger would show them around, but no specific suggestions regarding the research were offered. During the last six years of the experiment, Saenger was a consultant to a medical advisory committee established by the Defense Atomic Support Agency, the very organization that was funding his project.

In 1969 the National Institutes of Health declined to fund the experiment on "ethical grounds." The NIH again declined to fund the experiment in 1973. Despite the rejections, Donald Chalkley, described in press reports as the NIH's "ethics watchdog," later praised the Cincinnati experiment, noting that it had promised to be "a significant addition to our armamentarium against metastatic cancer."

36

THE CHAMBERS OF OAK RIDGE

Woodrow Wilson Litton felt perfectly healthy when he was admitted for the first time to the small research hospital in Oak Ridge, Tennessee. His dark eyes and black hair gleamed with vitality and he had the loose, graceful frame of an athlete. He was forty-one years old, a materials dispatcher at one of the uranium production plants, and had missed only three days of work over the past ten years. During a routine physical in the spring of 1961, a plant doctor had discovered that Litton had several swollen lymph nodes in his neck and groin area. The nodes were about the size of peas and not at all painful. Litton had noticed them, too, but wrote them off as harmless. The doctor was concerned, though, and referred him to an Oak Ridge physician, who removed one of the nodes. The physician's findings came as a shock: Litton, he concluded, had lymphoma, or cancer of the lymph system.

Litton was then referred to the Medical Division Hospital run by the Oak Ridge Institute of Nuclear Studies, frequently referred to as ORINS. The hospital was one of the three cancer research facilities established by Shields Warren in the late 1940s and was originally assigned space in a wing of the former Manhattan Engineer District hospital where Ebb Cade had been injected with plutonium. Eventually the ORINS hospital, related laboratories, and treatment rooms occupied the entire building. The patients were required to sign various papers prior to admittance. The forms disclosed that the treatments were experimental and held no definite promise of benefit or cure, but they did not reveal the possibility that procedures might increase the patients' pain or hasten their deaths.

One of the first doctors to examine Woodrow Wilson Litton was Herbert Gerstner, the Paperclip specialist from the School of Aviation Medicine, who had gone to ORINS to get his medical license and worked briefly at the Oak Ridge hospital. Gerstner listened to the slow thump of Litton's heart, the clear, unobstructed breathing, and then questioned him about his family's medical history. Litton was the nineteenth child in a family of twenty-one children. There was no history of cancer or unusual childhood diseases. "Physical examination reveals a well-developed white male who is very alert and cooperative," Gerstner remarked. Thinking perhaps of his research in Germany, he added that Litton "hears perfectly well."

Litton underwent a series of diagnostic tests over the next two days. "The findings," Gerstner wrote, "were not sufficient to establish the diagnosis of malignant lymphoma with absolute certainty." Litton was discharged, but was to return to the hospital many times over the next four years. Gerstner's name does not show up again in his medical records.

Litton's diagnosis was difficult to verify. ORINS pathologists disagreed among themselves about whether his lymph cells were truly cancerous and decided to do another node biopsy. Some of the biopsy material was forwarded to consultants at the University of Cincinnati and the University of Chicago. Two consultants said it was lymphoma; two said it wasn't. One of the Chicago physicians said that she had seen nodes such as Litton's stabilize or regress and that active treatment wasn't necessarily required.

Litton, meanwhile, was seen regularly at the research hospital by a doctor named D. A. White. He had no complaints. He was eating, sleeping, and working hard. On one occasion, he said he had an odd sensation "like water slipping through a vessel" on his left lower leg. Almost a year to the day after the discovery of the cancer, lab reports showed an increase in his white blood cells. Although Litton felt fine, ORINS doctors decided to give him fifty roentgens of total-body irradiation in a state-of-the-art chamber called the Medium Exposure Rate Total Body Irradiator, or METBI, which had been in operation since 1960. His physician, D. A. White, wrote on May 1, 1962, "Mr. Litton seemed quite pleased when I suggested that I thought it would be well to arrange for him to have total-body irradiation in the near future."

Litton was readmitted to the hospital a few days before the TBI procedure was scheduled. At 6:30 A.M. on May 22, the date of his irradiation, he was given a radioactive concoction containing lanthanum-140 and iron-59. Then he was given 90 ccs of water and breakfast. The medical records say nothing about the function of the radioisotopes, but they apparently were administered as part of another, separate experiment.

An hour and a half after Litton had ingested the radioactive isotopes, he was escorted down a twisting corridor to METBI. The chamber was a concrete-shielded room eight feet wide, eight feet high, and eight feet long. Litton climbed into an aluminum bed suspended in the middle of the room. When everyone had left, the protective shields covering eight radioactive sources located in the floor and ceiling slid back and he was bombarded from all sides with radiation. Using a series of mirrors, the operator could watch Litton from a control panel as the radiation was administered. The procedure began at 9:31 A.M. and was completed at 10:43. Litton suffered no ill effects from the fifty roentgens or the radionuclides. When he was discharged several days later, he was given ice cream containers for his stool samples and told to return them to the hospital. A page in his medical records clearly refers to the TBI treatment as an "experiment."

Litton continued to lead an active and normal life for more than two years after the first TBI treatment. He worked long hours, painted his house, and even dabbled in politics. But the ORINS doctors were uneasy about taking such a wait-and-see approach to his disease. On November 17, 1964, Dr. White wrote, "I told him that the time would be coming when we would undoubtedly wish to give him some additional treatment, probably 100 r total-body irradiation . . . but felt it would be reasonable to defer this for the present."

A month later ORINS doctors decided to administer 2,400 rads of local radiation to Litton's groin and iliac area after they noticed that nodes in those areas had become swollen. Litton tolerated the local radiation well, but six months later he was back in the hospital with a mass the size of a large orange in his upper abdomen. The doctors decided the time had come to give Litton a second round of total-body irradiation in METBI even though they knew from experience that localized radiation would work better.

On June 29, 1965, Litton climbed back into the aluminum bed. This time he was irradiated with 100 roentgens. He tolerated the treatment well, suffering only a transient nausea. A "TBI Work Sheet" described the biochemical changes in his body. A few days before his discharge, some of his bone marrow was removed and carefully examined.

A profound change came over Litton when he returned home. Overnight, it seemed, he developed the look of someone who was chronically ill. His dark complexion turned ashen, his muscular frame withered. For the first time in his life he began to suffer from insomnia and nervousness. He was home for less than a week following the TBI treatment when he developed severe abdominal pain. He returned to the hospital on July 9 and more or less remained there until he died five months later. During the ensuing months, Litton was administered a dizzying assortment of drugs and treatments. He was given another 2,225 rads to his abdomen to relieve his "discomfort and constipation." He also was given two more radionuclides—400 microcuries of iodine-123 and 97 microcuries of iodine-131. Family members now believe the radioactive iodine was administered to help calibrate ORINS' new counting chamber.

"I think he knew he was dying," his son, Gary Litton, recalled. "I helped him take a shower one day. He held on to the towel rail and told me, 'I just wish they would let me alone.'" A handwritten note dated October 28, 1965, stated Litton had shown a "poor response" to the total body irradiation and the localized radiation. Despite this observation, the very next day Litton was given 220 rads of another planned round of 2,200 rads of local radiation. His condition grew worse, and a day later he died. "His last 25 days in the hospital," a physician remarked on his chart, "were pitiable."

Five years after Woodrow Wilson Litton died, ORINS scientists published an in-house report describing the results of a ten-year experiment in which patients suffering from lymphoma, leukemia, and polycythemia vera, a blood disorder, were given single doses of 50 roentgens or 100 roentgens of total-body irradiation. Litton was one of those patients. The report disclosed that the primary purpose of the experiment was to gain "information that might lead to improved radiation therapy" and to "acquire radiobiologic information"—with nothing said about helping the patient. In fact, the doctors admitted that even before they began the experiment they knew that the TBI would not give "better clinical results" than local applications or fractionated doses of radiation. "At present we feel that some pattern of fractionated exposure . . . probably offers a preferable approach for total-body radiotherapy." The physicians also revealed that the information from the irradiated patients was being utilized by NASA.

The medium-exposure facility, or METBI, was constructed in 1959, a year after eight workers were injured in a criticality accident at one of

Oak Ridge's uranium production plants. ORINS researchers had already begun investigating the effects of total-body irradiation on patients suffering from blood-related diseases, but the accident whetted their desire to learn more. Among other things, accident investigators had learned that film badges worn by workers were "unreliable indicators" of actual exposures. Oak Ridge scientists, like the Defense Department, became intensely interested in finding a biological dosimeter that would more accurately reveal the amount of radiation absorbed by employees in the weapons plants.

At about the time that METBI began operating, NASA was also becoming interested in the effects of radiation on humans. Scientific investigations spread out in quirky new directions as the space agency raced to put a man on the moon. How much radiation would the astronauts be exposed to when their space craft hurtled through the Van Allen belts, regions of high-energy charged particles located thousands of miles from Earth's surface? What would happen to astronauts lumbering over the surface of the moon if a solar flare suddenly erupted from the sun? Would the steady stream of background radiation dull the senses of the highly trained astronauts and prevent them from completing a mission? How would the weightlessness of space combined with low, steady doses of radiation affect the space travelers? The questions were endless, and in the unforgiving environment of space, the answers had to be right.

NASA turned to the Atomic Energy Commission for help. The AEC, which had been groping with related questions for decades, was only too happy to oblige. NASA was everything the embattled commission had once been and was no more: admired by the public and awash in taxpayers' money. In 1964 an interagency agreement was drawn up between NASA and the AEC to explore a dozen tasks related to the health impacts of space radiation. One of those tasks was a two-part study designed to refine the scientific understanding of man's sensitivity to radiation. The first part was a massive "retrospective" study that involved collection and analysis of data on some 3,000 people from over forty institutions who had received total-body irradiation accidentally or for therapeutic purposes. The second and much more controversial part was a "prospective" study that involved the collection of data for NASA from cancer patients undergoing total-body irradiation for their diseases.

ORINS was assigned the two-part study. The principal investigator was Clarence Lushbaugh, a high school classmate of Eugene Saenger's and the pathologist at Los Alamos National Laboratory who had autop-

Shields Warren (no relationship to Stafford Warren) oversaw the vast expansion of the Atomic Energy Commission's biological programs in the late 1940s and early 1950s. (FROM THE SHIELDS WARREN COLLECTION, DEPARTMENT OF SPECIAL COLLECTIONS, BOSTON UNIVERSITY)

The one thousandth shipment of radioisotopes produced in a nuclear reactor in Oak Ridge, Tennessee, is delivered by airplane to the U.S. Public Health Service in Washington, D.C. (NATIONAL ARCHIVES)

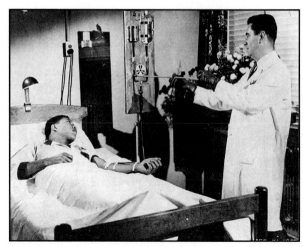

Using a long instrument, an Oak Ridge doctor demonstrates how to adjust the clamp that regulates the drip speed of radioactive gallium. (NATIONAL ARCHIVES)

Helen Hutchison, who received one of the radioactive Vanderbilt "cocktails" when she was six months pregnant, out on the town with her husband and daughter. Bizarre health problems plagued both Helen and the child she was carrying for many years after an apparently uneventful birth. (COURTESY OF HELEN HUTCHISON)

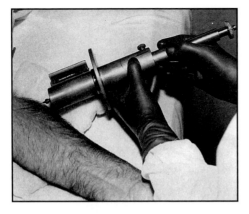

Physicians in Oak Ridge used lead-covered syringes and lead-lined gloves to protect themselves from radiation when they injected radioisotopes into humans. (OAK RIDGE ASSOCIATED UNIVERSITIES)

Lead capes, such as the one being draped around this test pilot who participated in Operation Ivy during the fall of 1952, could weigh as much as fifty-five pounds. (NATIONAL ARCHIVES)

VIPs don protective goggles during Operation Greenhouse, a 1951 test series at the Pacific Proving Ground. (NATIONAL ARCHIVES)

Brig. Gen. James Cooney (fifth from left), a tireless proselytizer of the atomic age, believed Americans needed to acquire a "practical attitude" toward the bomb. (COURTESY OF JAMES COONEY, JR.)

Thousands of soldiers watch the developing mushroom cloud produced by Shot Dog, an atomic bomb detonated on November 1, 1951, at the Nevada Test Site. (NATIONAL ATOMIC MUSEUM, ALBUQUERQUE, NEW MEXICO)

Nuclear scientist Willard Libby, standing behind President Dwight Eisenhower, once remarked that "if anybody knows how to do a good job of body snatching, they will really be serving their country." To the right of Eisenhower is AEC Commissioner Lewis Strauss, an ardent believer in the curative power of radioisotopes. (NATIONAL ARCHIVES)

Cecil Kelley's wallet, containing his bright red Atomic
Energy Commission identification badge and his supposedly lucky dollar bill, were
returned to his wife, Doris,
after his terrible death. (EILEEN
WELSOME)

Herbert Gerstner was one of the
German scientists brought to the
School of Aviation Medicine in San
Antonio, Texas, after World War II.
(NATIONAL ARCHIVES)

Eugene Saenger led a Pentagon-funded study at Cincinnati
General Hospital in which some ninety patients received whole
body radiation. (REPRINTED WITH PERMISSION OF *THE CINCINNATI ENQUIRER*)

Maude Jacobs, mother of seven who was diagnosed with breast cancer when she was forty-nine, died a painful death twenty-five days after her irradiation at Cincinnati General Hospital. Her deterioration was so rapid that she never had a chance to make arrangements for her children. (COURTESY OF LILLIAN PAGANO)

Clarence Lushbaugh, a Los Alamos pathologist, moved to Oak Ridge, Tennessee, because he wanted to work on living patients. (EILEEN WELSOME)

Woodrow Wilson Litton, a dispatcher at an Oak Ridge uranium plant, underwent numerous experimental procedures at the Oak Ridge hospital and suffered an excruciating death. (COURTESY OF GARY LITTON)

The low exposure total body irradiator, or LETBI, was designed to look like a room at the Holiday Inn. (OAK RIDGE ASSOCIATED UNIVERSITIES)

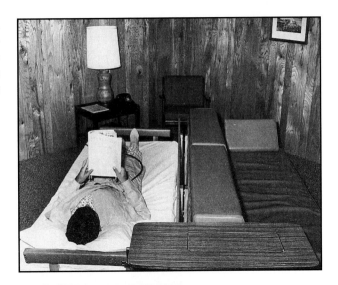

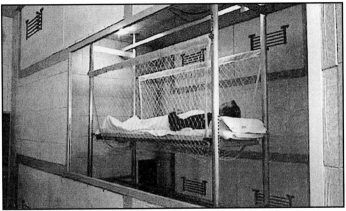

The medium exposure total body irradiator, called METBI, exposed patients to a sea of radiation. (NATIONAL ARCHIVES)

Carl Heller considered the maximum-security prison in Salem, Oregon, his most "prized facility." (COURTESY OF META HELLER)

Paul "Connie" Tyrrell, a convict "volunteer" who participated in Carl Heller's hormone and radiation experiments, had tumors removed from both breasts and died of heart failure in 1995. (EILEEN WELSOME)

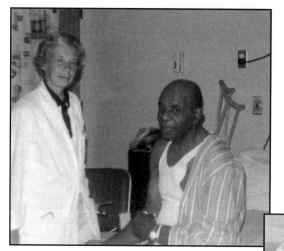

Elmer Allen has his temperature taken by physician Christine Waterhouse during a follow-up study at Strong Memorial Hospital in Rochester, New York, in June 1973. (COURTESY OF ELMERINE ALLEN WHITFIELD BELL)

Department of Energy Secretary Hazel O'Leary attacked the decades-old culture of secrecy that kept the American people in the dark about the plutonium injections and thousands of other government-sponsored nuclear experiments. (COURTESY OF HAZEL O'LEARY) sied Cecil Kelley. Lushbaugh was born in 1916 in Covington, Kentucky, across the river from Cincinnati. Saenger was the rich boy. "Lush" was the poor boy, the son of a deceased railroad freight handler and a working mother. Lushbaugh and Saenger both attended Cincinnati's Walnut Hills High School and competed against each other for class president during their senior year. Lushbaugh, who describes himself as a "cantankerous bastard," won.

After three years of study at the University of Cincinnati, Lushbaugh transferred to the University of Chicago, where he eventually received a bachelor's degree in anatomy, a Ph.D. in pathology, and a medical degree. He moved to Los Alamos in March of 1949. "I wanted to go where the action was, so to speak," he recalled.

Lushbaugh held three positions in Los Alamos: lab scientist, pathologist at the local AEC-owned hospital, and the assistant district health officer for Los Alamos County, a job akin to county coroner. Between 1949 and 1963 he autopsied nearly everyone who died in Los Alamos. Many of the deaths were suicides, he recalled. "People don't like being walled in," he said. "They want to escape and the best way to escape a walled-in situation is to commit suicide."

From the Los Alamos hospital, Lushbaugh obtained tissue and fluids from patients for laboratory experiments. He also participated in the numerous tracer studies. "I liked working in Los Alamos. We used to have high-explosive accidents there, in which trucks carrying various Spanish-Americans from down the hill would get blown up," the seventy-eight-year-old scientist recalled in an oral history. "We used to find that the best ways to find missing parts in an explosives accident was to go out with a pair of binoculars and watch the birds around radioactive dumps. You'd see the crows come in and take parts of persons that had been blown up into the trees."

Lushbaugh said he left Los Alamos to go to Oak Ridge because he had recently gotten a divorce and wanted to get away from his ex-wife. At Oak Ridge, he said, he also had the opportunity to do research on living subjects. "In Los Alamos, I only had dead patients."

Lushbaugh joined ORINS in 1963. The following year Oak Ridge researchers began the arduous task of collecting raw data for NASA from patients irradiated in hospitals and in nuclear accidents. The information was fed into a computer so analyses could be made to determine precisely the relationship between radiation dose and nausea, vomiting, diarrhea, fatigue, weight loss, fever, hair loss, anemia, cellular damage, resistance to infection, decreased antibody synthesis, accelerated aging, and carcinogenesis. Into the data bank went information from the criticality accident victims and from patients irradiated at M.D. Anderson, Baylor, and the University of Cincinnati. Saenger's patients, said Lushbaugh, came from the "slums" of Cincinnati:

> In such typical slums, these persons don't have any money and they're black and they're poorly washed. These persons were available in the University of Cincinnati Center to Dr. Saenger as persons who needed to be total body irradiated, and they were given total body irradiation by Dr. Saenger. I was on his committee, by the way, and I did review what he was doing, and I thought it was actually well done.

In 1965 ORINS proposed to the AEC that a new irradiation chamber be constructed that would deliver a uniform dose of radiation to patients at 1.5 roentgens per hour, or one-sixtieth the dose rate of METBI. Doctors theorized the low doses would kill leukemia and lymphoma cells but would not produce the side effects such as nausea and vomiting. At the same time, ORINS also suggested that NASA could use the information from the new irradiation chamber for its space research. The low-dose chamber, Lushbaugh later told a congressional committee, enabled NASA to observe in "real time" the signs and symptoms of radiation exposure that had been collected from the 3,000 patients during the retrospective study.

The second irradiation chamber came on-line in 1967. It was called LETBI, or the Low Exposure Rate Total Body Irradiator. LETBI was a room within a room. The inner shell, covered with dark paneling, was furnished to look like a Holiday Inn. There was a television, chairs, bed, and an adjoining bathroom. Patients could live for days, or even weeks, in the chamber.

The radiation sources were located in a larger, outer, heavily shielded room. The patients were able to move about freely while they were continuously exposed to a low-level sea of radiation. Attached to the patient's body were electrodes and an umbilical cord that measured cardiac and respiratory signals. The data were fed into a computer and stored for later analysis by NASA. Occasionally rats were hung in cages between the walls of the two rooms and irradiated simultaneously with the human patients.

LETBI cost $26 million. The AEC picked up the tab for the design and construction of the chamber and NASA contributed $2.2 million, which was used mostly to pay the salaries of Lushbaugh and a technician, and to buy some monitoring equipment.

A third high-dose irradiation facility was constructed at the animal research laboratory run by the University of Tennessee's School of Agriculture. Referred to in some documents as HETBI, an acronym which apparently stood for the High Exposure Rate Total Body Irradiator, the chamber delivered massive doses of radiation within minutes to plants, seeds, and large animals such as cows and horses. It became operational in 1970 and was used by ORINS researchers to irradiate four patients undergoing bone marrow transplants. One worker who was irradiating seeds accidentally received a large dose of radiation in the high-exposure facility and developed acute leukemia ten years later.

The exposures in LETBI mimicked the low, chronic radiation doses that astronauts were likely to encounter when they traveled through space. The information, wrote the Oak Ridge scientists, was "increasingly more relevant to the occupational medical needs of deep space exploration where exposures are expected to be small, multiple and randomly timed." The HETBI data would be useful in the event of a serious accident "like that which could occur during extra-vehicular activities in space from the unexpected occurrence of a large solar flare or in an accident resulting from the use of nuclear energy propulsion systems."

Records also reveal that the Army was funding a study on the irradiated patients to find out how single, repeated, or protracted doses affected the intestinal bacteria of exposed patients. NASA was also provided this data "without additional costs." Thus the data from patients irradiated in METBI and LETBI were used in multiple investigations: Oak Ridge scientists used the information in their search for a biological dosimeter and to better learn how to treat accident victims; NASA used the data in its space missions; and the Army used the findings to better predict soldiers' reactions on the nuclear battlefield.

There were many similarities between Oak Ridge's TBI experiment and the TBI experiment in Cincinnati. NASA, like the Defense Nuclear Agency, said it was merely interested in the data and did not attempt to influence the selection of patients, treatment, or doses administered to the subjects. Although nearly 200 patients were irradiated in the two chambers over almost fifteen years, no scientific report comparing total-body irradiation to other cancer treatments was ever published in any recognized journal. "We never considered them to be of enough scientific quality," Lushbaugh is quoted as saying in an article published in 1981 in *Mother Jones.*

Similarities aside, there was one critical difference between the Cincinnati and Oak Ridge experiments: The Oak Ridge patients had *radiosensitive* cancers such as leukemia or lymphoma and other blood diseases. TBI was considered an experimental but medically plausible way to treat such patients at that time. In fact, ORINS doctors said in 1966 that it would be "unethical" to treat patients with radioresistant tumors with TBI:

> The suggestion is made that we should treat carcinoma of the breast, gastroenteric tract, and urogenital tract by total body irradiation. These groups of patients have been carefully considered for such therapy, and we are very hesitant to treat them because we believe there is so little chance of benefit to make it questionable ethically to treat them. Lesions that require moderate or high doses of local therapy for benefit, or that are actually resistant (gastroenteric tract), are not helped enough by total body irradiation to justify the bone marrow depression that is induced. Of course, in one way these patients would make good subjects for research because their hematologic responses are more nearly like those of normals than are the responses of patients with hematologic disorders.

After Saenger's experiment became public in the early 1970s, the Atomic Energy Commission sent a group of six outside consultants, including Shields Warren, to Oak Ridge to review its TBI program. The committee members found no ethical problems with the Oak Ridge experiments:

> In the Cincinnati program, one of the major issues raised was the Department of Defense support of the studies. Again, we think the situation at Oak Ridge is quite different. While NASA funds are involved for evaluation of effects of total body radiation, the selection of patients for the program and their continuance in the program is clearly in the hands of a clinical group who is responsive to patient care needs and to the need of optimal therapy as opposed to the needs of the investigative protocol of NASA.

Lushbaugh said the patients exposed in the low-dose chamber actually felt better afterward. "The person who was going to be irradiated would usually have arthritis or difficulty untying his shoes, or taking off his pants or getting out of bed," he said. "After he had been irradiated for a couple of weeks, and I do mean a couple of weeks, he would now be able to walk."

The AEC in 1974 decided to close the Oak Ridge hospital after a highly critical report of the research program was completed. Government reviewers found the clinical facilities "substandard," the animal facilities "strikingly inadequate," and the staffers intellectually isolated. "The METBI and LETBI programs were viewed as evolving without adequate planning, criticism, or objectives, and have achieved less in substantial productivity than merits continued support." Lushbaugh and other scientists maintain the real reason the AEC shut down the hospital was because of budget problems. The AEC's cancer research hospitals at Chicago and Brookhaven were also closed about the same time.

37

CAPTIVE VOLUNTEERS: PRISONERS IN
OREGON AND WASHINGTON

The convicts always knew when Carl Heller, the doctor in charge of the
medical experiments, was inside the Salem penitentiary. They could tell
by the footsteps, the brisk tap-tap of his wingtips as he came and went
from the prison hospital at all hours of the day and night. Decades later a
few still remembered his rich-man look; the expensive suits, the silk
shirts and cuff links, the pipe clenched between his teeth. He had thinning brown hair, soft pale cheeks, and lived in a beautiful home, all glass
and steel, on a rainy spit of land in northwestern Washington. From his
living room, he could watch the clouds sweep across the Olympic Mountains. Surrounding him were abstract paintings, sculpture, and artifacts
from Indians who once lived on the fog-shrouded coast. Not far from the
house was an aviary flooded with the milky light of the Pacific Northwest
and filled with the flashing wings of exotic birds—Venezuelan screamers,
Peking robins, spoonbills, blue-cheeked borbets. At symposiums in Mexico City, London, Berlin, and São Paulo, Heller shared the breakthroughs he was making in unraveling the secrets of male fertility and
the complex process of spermatogenesis, the origin and development of
sperm cells in the human male. The raw material for his studies was
provided by convicts at the maximum security facility in Salem, Oregon.
Carl Heller had discovered that Robert Stone was right about prisoners:
They did make ideal test subjects. The penitentiary, Heller once wrote,
was "our most unique and prized facility."

Every few weeks Heller made the 422-mile round trip to the penitentiary where he conducted his hormone experiments. Built in 1886,

the prison was surrounded by high walls topped with dense coils of concertina wire. Armed guards prowled the towers overlooking the yard. Visitors, including Heller, had to pass through as many as seven gates to reach the area where the male prisoners lived. Some of the convicts liked Heller; others said he gave them the creeps.

In exchange for participating in his experiments, the inmates got cash payments that were equal to hundreds of times what they would have earned in daily prison wages. With the money, they bought cigarettes, coffee, toothpaste, shampoo, tools for the hobby shop. When they underwent a vasectomy or a testicular biopsy, they sometimes got high on Nembutal and Demerol. Many viewed Heller as a ticket to heaven, a fleeting ride that lasted a month or a day. But over the following years, the following decades, there was hell to pay. And pay. And pay.

Educated at the University of Wisconsin, where he obtained a medical degree and two Ph.D.'s, Carl Heller was one of the world's leading endocrinologists when he began his hormone experiments at the Salem prison in the late 1950s. (His brother was Walter Heller, President John F. Kennedy's economic advisor.) Married four times and the father of three children, Heller was in search of a male birth control pill because he thought "the woman's involvement was emotional, whereas the man's was rational." His research agenda broadened in September of 1962 when he attended a three-day conference in Fort Collins, Colorado, on the effects of radiation on the reproductive system. Sponsored by the Atomic Energy Commission, the conference occurred about a year after the AEC and NASA had begun developing a cooperative research program to study the biological impact of space radiation on astronauts. C. Alvin Paulsen, one of Heller's former protégés, was also at the conference. Paulsen had helped Heller with some of the hormone experiments at the Salem penitentiary, but after completing his residency, Paulsen had struck out on his own and had already begun to develop a reputation as a talented endocrinologist in his own right.

Heller and Paulsen were experts on the human reproductive system but had only recently become acquainted with radiation. Heller got his introduction when he began injecting radioactive thymidine, also called tritiated thymidine, into the testicles of prisoners in an effort to better understand the complex process by which male sperm developed. A newsletter published by the Pacific Northwest Research Foundation, the

Seattle research laboratory where Heller worked (today known as the Fred Hutchinson Cancer Research Center), described the radioactive material as "highly dangerous." Paulsen had received his introduction to radiation when he was called in as a consultant after three men were accidentally irradiated in an accident in April of 1962 at the Hanford Reservation.

Scientists from all over the world who were investigating the effects of radiation on the reproductive systems of animals attended the Fort Collins symposium. "The whole conference," Heller recalled in a deposition taken in 1976:

> finally focused on man. A given group at Fort Collins was working on mice and another group was working on bulls, and then they concluded what would happen to man. They extrapolated the data from bulls or mice to man. I commented one day to Dr. Henshaw, who was then the medical graduate with the AEC, that if they were so interested in whether it was happening to man, why were they fussing around with mice and beagle dogs, and canaries and so on? If they wanted to know about man, why not work on man? That interested enough people from the Atomic Energy Commission present that they got together a formal meeting to see what we might do, what questions we might answer with our setup in Salem.

Paul Henshaw was not a "medical graduate" but an old hand at the AEC who ended up serving as the liaison between Carl Heller and C. Alvin Paulsen and the commission during the early years of the prisoner experiments. Henshaw was also director of research from 1952 to 1954 for the Planned Parenthood Federation of America, the organization that donated some of the seed money to the research effort to find a birth control pill. Meta Heller, who worked closely with her husband, described Henshaw as a distinguished-looking man in his fifties: tall, well proportioned, with dark graying hair.

Henshaw had worked as a biologist at the Met Lab during the Manhattan Project. A year and a half after the Nagasaki and Hiroshima bombings, he and another Met Lab colleague, Austin Brues, were sent to Japan in order to advise the Secretary of War and the National Academy of Sciences about the feasibility of setting up a long-term study of the survivors. In a breezily cheerful account of their mission before the Chicago Literary Club, Brues later recalled: "Happily enough, nobody higher up had got interested enough in our business to dignify it with some title such as 'Operation Meathead.' Somewhere along the line, while standing on a windy corner waiting for transportation, Paul got the idea that we should have a name and suggested the 'Atomic Bomb Casualty Commission' because it would be called ABCC. We put that in a couple of reports and ever since then that has been the designation of the entire project whose feasibility we were to consider." (The project is still ongoing and is today called the Radiation Effects Research Foundation.)

One of the long-term effects the ABCC would attempt to track was the impact of the bombings on the reproductive system. Stafford Warren and Joseph Howland had detected severe testicular atrophy and sterility in men exposed to radiation from the two bombs immediately after they arrived in Japan with the Manhattan Project survey team. "As early as the fourth day definite changes were noted in the testes," they wrote. Even more disturbing, the two doctors also discovered changes among Japanese men who were not in the immediate vicinity of the blast area. "A definite decrease in the sperm count of patients in areas adjacent to the bomb explosion was found to be apparently a result of exposure to low dosages." Most worrisome to the A-bomb doctors were the mutations that Nobel laureate Herman Muller had warned might take 1,000 years to become manifest. Such concerns had not diminished with time. In his closing address to the Fort Collins participants, Henshaw himself noted that 50 to 100 rads doubled the number of mutations in some species.

Inspired by what he had heard at the Fort Collins conference, Heller returned to his laboratory and began drafting a proposal. By February 1963, less than six months later, the AEC had a neatly typed package from him describing a new series of experiments he hoped to perform at the Oregon State Prison: "We propose to apply known amounts of ionizing radiation directly to the testes of normal men," the first page began. Among other things, Heller's team planned to determine the minimum amount of radiation that would cause "permanent damage" of sperm cells and how testicular changes caused by radiation affected the secretion of various hormones. "Dr. Heller," the proposal continued, "has spent enough time behind bars to complete a one-year sentence (with time off for good behavior!). Considered neither a 'cop' nor a 'con,' he has the kind of rapport so necessary for investigations with a convict population."

At about the same time that Heller sent his proposal to the AEC, Paulsen, who was on friendly but competitive terms with Heller, submitted his own plan for a prison study to be performed at the Washington State Prison in Walla Walla. Paulsen had begun developing his proposal several months *before* the Fort Collins conference. "And how shall I put it? He (Heller) became aware of what I was doing and he initiated his study of effects of radiation," a still-competitive Paulsen told advisory committee staffers in 1994.

In his research proposal Paulsen explained that he had discovered the paucity of data on the effects of radiation on the human testes when he was called to evaluate the "gonadal consequences" for the three men injured in the Hanford accident. With space travel and the construction of nuclear power plants under way, Paulsen said he felt it was essential to acquire more information. "In our atomic age society, there is always present the possibility of radiation accidents resulting in significant radiation dose to one or more people," he wrote. "The ultimate accident would be a nuclear war involving multitudes of people."

The procedures and goals of the two experiments were very similar, but the type of radiation that the doctors planned to administer to the prisoners' testicles was different. Heller proposed to bombard testicles with X rays. Paulsen intended eventually to irradiate the testicles of the Washington prisoners with neutrons from a generator developed by scientists from Hanford. But until the generator was ready, his plan was to use a radium source. Paulsen also hoped to explore various substances that could protect against radiation damage, noting that Berkeley scientists had achieved promising results by injecting olive oil in the testes of rats.

Scientists at AEC headquarters and their consultants were simultaneously excited and a little squeamish at the prospect of these experiments. "Because of the uniqueness of this experiment, including the experimental material available, I feel that no opportunity should be overlooked for getting the maximum possible amount of information out of it," wrote Lauriston Taylor, one of the scientists who helped Robley Evans set the first radiation standards. "I think one should also bear in mind the possibility that at some time some 'do-gooder' organization may suddenly realize that we are doing radiation experiments on prisoners and cause such a furor as to bring about a political decision to stop the work. This, incidentally, makes it highly important in reporting the work, to pay a good deal of attention to the public relations aspects."

The long-term consequences of radiation for the human reproductive system had been on the minds of the Manhattan Project/AEC doctors for at least two decades. Hundreds of animal experiments with mice, rats, sheep, dogs, and donkeys had been performed. But no scientist from within the weapons establishment had ever dared to do the experiments Heller and Paulsen were about to begin. "This proposal is a direct attack on our problem," wrote Charles Edington, an AEC official from headquarters. "I'm for support at the requested level as long as we are not liable." Then, almost as an afterthought, he mused, "I wonder about possible carcinogenic effects of such treatments."

In July of 1963 the AEC approved both contracts. The commission apparently saw the two studies as a once-in-a-lifetime opportunity to get the data it needed and to relate and compare the results. Both Heller and Paulsen were asked to proceed cautiously and to "minimize publicity" associated with the program.

Human experimentation, particularly with unproven drugs, was widespread in prisons throughout the United States at the time the testicular radiation experiments began. But some scientists were already growing uneasy with medical research on captive populations. An official at the National Institutes of Health in 1964 wrote that convicts could not be volunteers in the same sense as free men and women. Prisoners were subject to tacit forms of coercion and more prone to being exposed to risky experiments. "For these reasons it is especially important to discourage prisoners from volunteering for medical projects; and when they are used at all, to utilize projects of truly minimal risk, if any." Meta Heller said scientists and corrections officials felt that it was only a matter of time before such studies would be banned. "They knew the clock was ticking, you bet." Before the clock stopped, Heller and Paulsen in separate experiments irradiated the reproductive organs of 131 men.

Sixty-seven convicts at the Oregon State Prison had their testicles bombarded with anywhere from 8 to 600 rads of radiation between 1963 and 1971. The subjects also underwent numerous testicular biopsies and were vasectomized when their participation was concluded. In addition to the tritiated thymidine, some of the inmates may have been injected with carbon-14, a radioactive tracer. The prisoners generally received $5 per month while they were in the program, $10 for each biopsy and $100 for the vasectomy at the conclusion of the program. Heller received a total of $1.12 million in grant money from the AEC.

At the Washington State Penitentiary in Walla Walla, sixty-four men were irradiated between 1963 and 1969 with anywhere from 7.5 to 400 rads. The prisoners in Paulsen's study were paid approximately $5 a month during the observation period, $25 in the month the testicular biopsies were performed, and $100 when they underwent a vasectomy. Paulsen received $505,000 from the AEC.

Heller and an assistant initially made the round-trip from Seattle to Salem every other week, working two full days and two full evenings in the penitentiary. Warden C. T. Gladden, in a 1963 letter to Oregon Attorney General Robert Thornton, complained that Heller had "taken advantage of our good will by violating many of our custodial regulations such as having close custody inmates out of their cells for participation in the program during late evening hours."

The warden also confessed in his letter that he had grave misgivings about the Heller program. "I cannot help but believe that the program is potentially dangerous or at least embarrassing to this institution and the state of Oregon." The penitentiary's Catholic chaplain, he continued, "raised strenuous objections" to the program and forbade any registered Catholic from participating. "As a matter of fact, the Catholic chaplain has been successful in establishing an agreement with Dr. Heller that he will not accept registered Catholics as patients in his programs."

Heller had the use of a completely equipped operating room, scrub room, and hospital beds. The convicts themselves served as nurses, orderlies, and lab technicians. Heller developed a close relationship with some of the inmates and tried to help them when they were paroled from prison. He wrote letters of recommendation for the inmate technicians and even loaned money to a few of the men when they were released from the penitentiary. One of the convicts, Baxter Max Hignite, worked for several months at Heller's Seattle laboratory when he was paroled from prison and even lived in Heller's house for a short time. In the 1970s, he was one of several inmates who sued Heller.

Hignite served as Heller's right arm in the penitentiary. An intelligent, muscular man with thick brown hair, Hignite recruited many of the convicts for the radiation experiment and assisted in the medical procedures. Harold Bibeau, who was then twenty-two years old and serving a twelve-year sentence for manslaughter, was one of the inmates recruited by Hignite. The older man warned Bibeau to stay away from the hormone program because of the "weird medical effects" but assured him the radiation program was perfectly safe. Initially Bibeau was rejected for the program because prison records listed him as Catholic, but Heller eventually accepted Bibeau after he assured the doctor he wasn't "really

Catholic." Bibeau said Heller often talked to him about the Nuremberg Code and medical ethics. Heller also told Bibeau the data from the experiment would be used to help NASA and the space program.

Heller interviewed the prospective candidates to make sure they were healthy and that they would be cooperative subjects—that is, show up for irradiation and biopsy appointments; provide urine, blood, and semen samples; and undergo a vasectomy at the conclusion of the experiment. (The vasectomy was administered in order to prevent genetic mutations from being passed down.) A prison psychologist interviewed the candidates to make sure they understood the consequences of the experiment. The psychologist wrote of Bibeau: "Never married, quite vague about future. Feels he doesn't want children—shouldn't have any. I agree. No contraindication to sterilization."

The prison psychologist was also supposed to evaluate and screen out candidates who had severe emotional problems. But a convict named Canyon Easton, who had been sent to prison on a rape charge and on several occasions had attempted to castrate himself, actually was *recommended* for the program. A psychologist wrote on September 3, 1964, "I feel this man is a likely candidate for benefit from Dr. Heller's program. I'll recommend him for inclusion if he qualifies otherwise. . . ." Easton participated in Heller's hormone and radiation experiments and underwent fourteen testicular biopsies. When he enrolled in the Heller program, Easton said he was filled with shame. "I felt I was beyond the pale."

Once he was paroled from prison, Easton went through several stormy relationships. One woman whom he was dating actually became frightened that she could contract cancer after she learned of his involvement in the radiation experiment. "On Dec. 22, 1975," he told an Oregon legislative committee, "I castrated myself so I would not have to deal with sexual problems again." Easton was reincarcerated in 1986 for castrating another man who attempted to rape his nieces. When asked about the incident, he explained: "I did castrate the man who told me 'Get one of the twins!' I asked, 'Which one?' He said, 'It doesn't make any difference!' I asked, 'Why do you want her?' He said, 'I'm going to fuck her!' I told him, 'I'm going to cut your nuts off!' He whined a bit but no more than my twelve-year-old nieces would have if he would have raped them."

On August 17, 1963, the testicles of the first Oregon inmate were bombarded with 200 rads of radiation by a crude-looking apparatus that had been designed by Heller and his colleagues. The machine looked like two orange crates stuck together and mounted on wheels for easy movement. Each of the "crates" consisted of an X-ray unit in a lead-lined box. Between the two boxes was a small Plexiglas cup filled with water.

The penises of the test subjects were taped to their bellies and a torn bed sheet about one-half-inch wide and a few inches long was tied above the testicles to keep them extended away from the body. Then the men lay facedown over the machine and lowered their organs into the cup. The water was maintained at 93 to 94 degrees to encourage the testicles to drop and to ensure the radiation was evenly distributed. A series of peepholes and mirrors enabled the technician to see that the testicles were properly positioned in the cup. A control panel was located in an outer room.

The AEC asked Heller to start with 600 rads. Although he did eventually irradiate fifteen men with 600 rads (one actually received a total of 708 rads in three separate doses), initially Heller was hesitant to administer such large amounts. Mavis Rowley, Heller's longtime assistant, recalled:

> I mean he felt a little uncomfortable about doing 600, but at that time, they had said that 600 rads was probably around the LD-50 dose for humans [the dose that produces sterility in 50 percent of those exposed], and so they wanted to start in there and see, okay, where are you going with your population survival. Are they going to be able to have children? And what are their children going to be like, and so forth. So we were having those kind of what, I thought, were odd conversations.

The convicts said they felt nothing, except perhaps a slight tingling or warmth, as the radiation was delivered. Afterward they said they developed rashes, peeling, and blisters on their scrotums. In the months and years following the exposure, many also said that they experienced pain during sexual intercourse, had difficulty maintaining erections, and their testicles shrank in size.

The biopsies were done anywhere from minutes, to days, weeks, even months after the exposure. The men usually were taken from their cells to the prison hospital the night before the biopsy. The next morning they received a powerful mixture of painkillers and were wheeled into surgery. Baxter Hignite said in one of the depositions that were part of the inmates' lawsuit against Heller that several prisoners usually assisted in the surgery. One convict held the testicles of the patient for the doctor and several others stood by to hold down the arms or legs of the subject in the event he began flailing.

The testicles were bathed in Novocain and the anesthetic was also injected into the skin. Then the doctor made an incision in the scrotal sac and removed a small sliver of flesh. No matter how deadened the flesh or how powerful the medication, many of the convicts said they invariably experienced excruciating pain. "Most of the times it felt like he took a pair of pliers and pulled a chunk of meat off my testicles. That's the kind of pain I would feel," Baxter Hignite said in his deposition. Donald Mathena, who was serving a sentence for armed robbery and underwent sixteen or seventeen biopsies, said he almost vomited the first time. "Right in the middle of your stomach, you can feel them. It don't feel like they're cutting. Even though they are, it feels like they're just tearing it." Ivan Dale Hetland, who was doing time for manslaughter, also said he could feel the surgery "way up" inside his stomach. "Made me want to draw my legs up. And it made me grunt." Heller boasted in a 1965–1966 progress report to the AEC that he had access to a "virtually 'inexhaustible' supply of fresh testicular biopsy material from physically normal men." One AEC official, in an apparent attempt at humor, referred to the testicular samples as "pounds of flesh" then crossed off pounds and wrote "grams of flesh."

Some of the men who participated in the experiments and were still in the Salem penitentiary said in 1994 interviews that drug abuse and homosexual behavior often occurred during the experiment. Remembered inmate Paul "Connie" Tyrrell, "They had a homosexual up there. I won't give you his name. I don't need to. He would orally get these guys off, spit it in a jar for them." Some of the inmates assisting in the experiment ingested the drugs that were supposed to be given to the biopsy patients. "Used to be inmates would pass out from the medication," recalled Tyrrell. "If they liked you, you got a little extra. If they didn't like you, you were SOL (shit out of luck)." Tyrrell participated in both the hormone and the radiation experiments. He had tumors removed from both breasts and died of heart failure in 1995 at the age of fifty-four. He was serving a life sentence for robbery and assault.

Dale Hetland said in a deposition that he underwent a vasectomy without any local anesthetic because an inmate with whom he had had a fist fight filled a syringe with sterile water instead of Novocain. "It hurt bad and I complained to the doctor at the time that it hurt, and he said it shouldn't hurt, and I said it did hurt." Hetland was irradiated twice, underwent twenty-four biopsies, and was injected twice in the testicles with tritiated thymidine. "They brought a little box in, a little tin box or a lead box with a handle on it. And when I asked what that was, they said it had a syringe with some radiation in it. And he explained to me that he was going to inject it into me. And he said it wouldn't hurt me or nothing, it would just sting a little bit. Which wasn't the truth. It stung a whole lot and hurt a whole lot." Hetland said he developed degenerative bone disease of the spine and lost part of his stomach as a result of the radiation. He wrote in 1985: "It was no better than the experiments conducted by the Germans on prisoners in concentration camps in my opinion—this experiment on me with live radiation has caused me over twenty years of pain and it has nearly destroyed my body." Another inmate, Art Clawson, told a reporter for the *Oregon Times Magazine*, "I spent years in jail, and I've never done a crime like these experiments. The only word I can think of is crime. When you start playing with people's physical well-being, their body and emotions, that's got to be one of the worst laws you can break."

Many of the convicts also said that the inmates operated the X-ray machine. "I operated the control panel myself," Baxter Hignite said when questioned under oath about the experiment.

"Did you set the dial for the amount of radiation that was to be administered?" an attorney asked.

"No. Usually there would be another inmate do that."

"Who was that?"

"Well, there's been several of them over the years. . . ."

"You say that these men set the amount of radiation?"

"Yes. And they assisted in the same ways that I have too."

"Were there occasions when only inmate technicians were in the control room?"

"Yes."

"Was that the normal procedure?"

"No. Usually there was a doctor in the hospital. Dr. Heller or one of his designates. Dr. Warner, Dr. Howieson."

"Were there ever occasions when there were no doctors in the immediate area where this was taking place?"

"Yes."

"While someone was being radiated?"

"Yes."

The men who participated in the Heller program said they did it for the money, pure and simple. The payments seemed like a pittance to outsiders. But to convicts with no money, friends, or family, the Heller program was a gold mine and the payments undoubtedly constituted a coercive factor in the informed consent process. Prisoners at that time received twenty-five cents a day in wages. Just for being on the Heller program, they got five dollars a month, which was the equivalent of twenty days of work. A biopsy on one testicle brought in ten dollars, equal to forty days' pay. And the hundred-dollar payment for the vasectomy was the equivalent of 400 days of work.

"So whenever you needed some money you would ask for a biopsy?" an attorney asked Dale Hetland.

"Yeah, I would like to have had one every month if I could have had one, for the money. I didn't like them. I liked the money."

The AEC established an advisory committee composed of radiation consultants to oversee both the Heller and Paulsen programs. The committee met in Seattle in 1963, 1965, and 1967. The AEC commissioners themselves were briefed on the experiments in 1968 when Glenn Seaborg was chairman. The function of the Seattle meetings, according to one AEC document, was to conduct a "penetrating" review of the two experiments with "the view being the opportunity to repeat or extend this type of work probably will not occur again soon, and that every effort should be made to assure project objectives." Walter Snyder, an Oak Ridge scientist who attended the first meeting, likened the risks from the experiment to "perhaps smoking, being overweight, etc."

Following the first meeting, Heller was encouraged to study the effects of radiation on the male chromosomes, a complex and difficult endeavor in which he had little experience. The AEC also was interested in the effects of low chronic doses of radiation on the testes. Heller subsequently irradiated the testicles of one convict over an eleven-week period with five rads of radiation per week. He remarked in his progress report for 1965–1966 that small chronic doses delivered over a long period of time caused more damage than the same amount of radiation delivered at once. By 1968 the AEC knew that as little as eight rads produced a detectable decrease in sperm counts.

The AEC's Paul Henshaw visited the Oregon State Prison on July 21, 1964. On the day of his visit, Heller zapped his first subject with 600 rads: a forty-nine-year-old convict and the oldest man in the program. In a memo to his files, Henshaw said nothing about that procedure but described in glowing terms the cooperative attitude of the inmates and prison officials:

It was apparent at once that there was indeed an attitude of eagerness about the work—a feeling of pride about being able to participate in the investigative program. Participants were seen to assist in record keeping, management of program schedules and equipment, and even in doing some of the technical work (e.g. sperm counts). It was obvious, also, that whatever elements of derision associated with the necessary sexual aspects, which can so easily become a feature, were either nonexistent, essentially, or had been overcome. The men seemed to be proud of their part in a scientific program and pleased with the prospect of vasectomy as a final result. Actually, as Dr. Heller manages the selection of subjects for participation, they must express a desire and actually ask for a vasectomy. Of interest is the fact that some of the participants have willingly agreed to accept dosages that will produce some degree of scrotal skin burn. This seems clearly understood and anticipated as a matter of routine. After seeing the participants, the writer was taken to meet Warden Clarence T. Gladden. He was matter-of-fact in his manner and his reference to the study being promoted. He gave no indication of dissatisfaction concerning it. Although matter-of-fact in manner, he expressed a feeling that scientific studies, such as the one being performed by Dr. Heller, actually exerts a favorable influence on prison life. While he did not say as much directly, he made the writer feel that he was—the Warden— pleased that the Atomic Energy Commission is maintaining direct contact with the work he is promoting in his institution.

Around Christmas of 1964, Heller got a letter from Douglas Grahn, a scientist at Argonne National Laboratory who cochaired a panel formed in 1961 to evaluate radiation exposure during manned space flights. The panel was reconstituted in 1964 to reevaluate the biological problems of space radiation when NASA began considering flights lasting from two weeks to a year or more.

In his letter, Grahn said the space panel (which included a number of old hands, among them Shields Warren, Wright Langham, James Nickson, and Clarence Lushbaugh) was concerned about radiation damage to the testicles of astronauts. He asked Heller if he would be interested in sharing his information as a consultant to the panel. An Oak Ridge doctor, Grahn confided, "indicated you do have some very critical information for our consideration, and we certainly hope that you will be able to help us one way or another."

Eleven days later Heller sent Grahn a three-page letter outlining how various radiation doses affected the male testes and sperm development. "Have you or your panel any suggestions regarding other information you should like to have, or other parameters that might be worth studying?" Heller queried. "This opportunity afforded to us, which may or may not be repeated or continued, should be made to yield the greatest possible pertinent information."

The following year Heller attended two meetings of the Space Radiation Study Panel at the National Academy of Sciences headquarters in Washington, D.C. Ironically, after military and civilian experts had spent many years and hundreds of thousands of dollars, Heller believed he had found the ideal dosimeter: human testicles. Heller told NASA officials that he could estimate precisely the radiation doses received by astronauts if he was allowed to do testicular biopsies before and after the space missions. But the astronauts had no desire to submit to such a procedure. Said Meta Heller, "They only cared about the adventure. They just weren't scientifically oriented."

One of Heller's ideas, she said, was to have testicular biopsies done on all men working in the weapons plants. Then if a worker was involved in an accident, the doctors could take a second testicular biopsy, compare it with the sample on file, and accurately assess the radiation dose. "It would have been good industrial medicine, you know, because everybody knew the goddamn dosimeters weren't all that accurate," Meta Heller said.

Grahn said he was somewhat uncomfortable around Heller. There was a "certain collegiality" among the members of the space panel that went back decades. But Heller was "too pushy," he said. "At the same time, there was a little sense of insecurity."

C. Alvin Paulsen did not have much contact with Heller while the two radiation experiments were under way. Paulsen said he was intent upon establishing his own identity in the scientific world and had face-to-face meetings with Heller only when they were cohosting one of the marathon "show-and-tell" meetings of the AEC's outside advisory committee. Paulsen, who was sued in the mid-1990s by several men after the case received widespread publicity, said in a deposition, "The Atomic Energy

Commission, when they came here for reviews, based on efficiency in economics, required us to be in the same room, both teams reporting the data. There was no collaboration of a scientific nature."

Paulsen had worked for Heller when he was a medical student at the University of Oregon Medical School from 1947 to 1952. Then he moved east to Detroit, where he did his internship and residency at the Detroit Receiving Hospital, the same hospital where Heller had done his training. When Paulsen returned to the West Coast, he joined the Pacific Northwest Research Foundation and resumed his research with Heller. At that time, Heller was conducting the hormone experiments at the Oregon State Penitentiary. Although Paulsen has played down his involvement in the hormone experiments, he is listed as a coauthor on several scientific papers written about those studies.

Paulsen worked at the Pacific Northwest Research Foundation from June of 1958 until 1961 and then became a full-time faculty member at the University of Washington and chief of endocrinology at the U.S. Public Health Service Hospital. Heller was disappointed about losing Paulsen but recognized that he "was gaining a certain amount of stature on his own," Meta Heller recalled.

Paulsen said he was apparently chosen by Hanford officials to examine the three men injured in the April 1962 accident because of a textbook article he had written on the testes. Two months later, he was talking with AEC officials in Washington, D.C., about a possible research proposal. Dave Bruner, the AEC's assistant director for medical and health research, wrote in a letter to Paulsen, "I personally do not see why people are nervous about such research, but it is somewhat unconventional and it does deal with a peculiarly sensitive area of human individual rights."

Paulsen said in his deposition that he consulted with numerous corrections and medical officials about the experiment, including Lauren Donaldson, an old buddy of Stafford Warren's who had established an elaborate program to study how the radioactive waste discharged into the Columbia River might affect the salmon population. Then Paulsen came up with his proposal to irradiate prisoners' testicles.

Paulsen said he secured the approval to proceed with the experiment from the superintendent of the state penitentiary, the director of state institutions, the assistant dean at the University of Washington's medical school, and the chairman of the medical school's Clinical Research Committee. Initially Paulsen planned to use a radium source on the prisoners' testicles, but he switched to X rays after he was told the dose would be too uncertain.

An energetic scientist with dark hair and bushy eyebrows, Paulsen was usually surrounded by a group of uncommunicative assistants when he visited the prison. Although he was amiable enough, he always seemed to be in a rush. "Now he looks old. But back then, he was on fire," Don Byers, an inmate who was serving time for armed robbery at the Airway Heights Correctional Center in Washington state, said in an interview in 1995. Rob White, another former prisoner, said Paulsen "had a magnetic personality. He didn't talk down to us. He seemed to accord us some dignity as human beings."

White, now a retail clerk at a garden center in Seattle, was a radiation volunteer, or RV No. 14. White said he joined the program because of the money and the fact that the experimenters promised to write the parole board. While the experimenters did not reveal what they intended to say to the board, the convicts nevertheless viewed it as a strong incentive. "That was rather important to most of us," White recalled. "The money was also important, of course, because we were making fourteen cents an hour making license plates."

White said Paulsen made the experiment sound like "glorified chest X-rays," telling the men they might experience a "sunburn type of reaction." White and other former test subjects said Paulsen never warned them of the possibility that they might contract cancer, but Paulsen said in his deposition the prisoners were orally informed of that risk.

The convicts were irradiated in a specially designed room in the basement of the Washington State Penitentiary, the maximum-security facility in the eastern part of the state. White said the room looked like any ordinary X-ray facility. There was a long flat table, an overhead machine, and a lead-lined wall behind which the technician operated the equipment. Once the men were lying on their backs, their penises were taped to their bellies. Then a bag of sugar, four to five inches wide and about a foot long, was placed over the penis and the lower abdomen area. A "bolus" of sugar in a plastic container also was placed beneath their testicles. (The sugar apparently was used because it scattered the X rays back into the exposed tissue.) The technician lowered the cone-shaped apparatus to within a few inches of the testicles, then stepped behind the wall and turned on the switch.

White, who was twenty-two years old and serving a sentence for assault, was irradiated with 400 rads to the testicles, the highest dose administered to any of the Washington prisoners. It took twenty minutes and six seconds. Several hours later, he said, he became nauseous and the skin in his groin area turned red. His thighs, abdomen, and buttocks began peeling a few days later.

While Paulsen was irradiating prisoners with X rays, scientists at what was then called the Battelle Pacific Northwest Laboratory in Hanford were doing dosimetry studies with a neutron generator that was to be used on the convicts during the final phase of the experiment. Preliminary studies with mannequins had revealed that the eye, base of the sternum, urethra, bladder, anus, and rectum also would get some radiation.

No documents have surfaced indicating that the neutron generator was actually used on the prisoners. But Don Byers, known as RV No. 71, is certain that he was irradiated with neutrons. In a telephone interview from the Airway Heights Correctional Center, he said, "I was told at the time I was getting 300 or 400 rads of neutrons." However, Byers's medical records state only that he received 100 rads of X-ray radiation.

Byers's recollection of the irradiation procedure also differed from White's. Byers said he was taken to a room in the basement of the hospital building and placed on a tilted table. His legs were spread, his knees were drawn up, and sandbags were stacked against him to hold him in place. "My first impression of the room was the *extreme* thickness of the walls—probably a foot thick at least; and an extremely heavy door," he wrote. "When the door was closed, it was exactly like a tomb—and the room was the most absolutely *SILENT* place I have ever been. There was an aperture in the wall across from me that looked like an arrow slit in the wall of a medieval castle. I had been cautioned to remain perfectly still until the door was opened—and that it would be approximately 30 minutes for the procedure to be run."

Documents released in 1994 show that scientists working at Pacific Northwest Laboratory, a research lab at the Hanford site where the dosimetry studies with the neutron generator were performed, sought to insulate themselves from any direct involvement with the medical aspects of the experiment. The reason for their action is unclear, but records suggest they were concerned about the possible legal liability. In 1967 a group of officials from the lab, including a scientist named Carlos Newton, attended the AEC's review of the Heller-Paulsen experiments in Seattle. In a trip report, Newton stressed that the scientists deliberately attempted to avoid any discussion of the medical effects of the experiments. "Our position of furnishing technical information in the physical sciences seemed to be well established. No medical information was either asked of or volunteered by us." Newton concluded his trip report with a "strictly private item" to his supervisor: "In private discussions it appears that the personnel from the AEC were interested in completing the project as it now stands, but dead set against any expansion of the program. A fair statement would be that they feel 'let's finish this up and get out.' A good BNW [Battelle Northwest] position also!"

Paulsen had hoped to begin bombarding the testicles of the Washington prisoners with neutrons by mid-1964, but it was not until 1968 that he sought approval from several University of Washington review committees to actually begin the procedure. Neutrons, which have no electric charge, deposit much larger amounts of radiation in living tissue and are on average ten times more damaging than X rays.

In October 1968 the University of Washington's Radiation Safety Committee approved the study provided the following conditions were observed: The maximum neutron dose be limited to fifteen rads; no more than twenty subjects be irradiated; and Paulsen's consent forms be modified to include the possibility that the procedure carried a very small risk of testicular cancer. The proposal was then forwarded to the University Hospital Clinical Investigation Committee, which had approved Paulsen's X-ray studies in 1963 and 1966. The committee chose to reject the neutron experiment in 1969 on the grounds that the subject selection was inappropriate and that the potential hazards to the subjects exceeded the potential benefits to society. The chairman of the committee noted that Paulsen's experiment had begun before federal regulations governing human experiments were issued and questioned whether the study had ever been thoroughly reviewed by an institutional review board.

Paulsen then appealed the decision to two additional committees, both of which also rejected the neutron study on the same grounds. Discouraged but not yet defeated, Paulsen then abandoned the neutron study and substituted a new proposal to irradiate another twenty-four prisoners with thirty rads of X rays. Twelve of those men were to be given testosterone prior to radiation in order to determine whether the male hormone was effective in reducing radiation injury.

The revised plan was approved. But from within the prison system came a new opponent: Audrey Holliday, a blunt-speaking administrator and the first woman to head the research division of the Department of Institutions. At a great personal price, Holliday was ultimately successful in halting an experiment that numerous academic committees couldn't, or wouldn't, bring to an end. Leonard Schroeter, a Seattle lawyer, remembered Holliday as a fearless woman who hated injustice. "I just loved her. She was a small, slim, Jean Arthur-ish person with a husky voice and a burning intensity."

Holliday learned of the experiment around July of 1969 from a doctor who had sat on one of the University of Washington review committees. She immediately wrote to Paulsen and demanded that all work stop until the Department of Institutions' Research Review Committee had a chance to analyze the study. Holliday was appalled by several "rather disturbing elements" of the Paulsen experiment, including the fact that many of the men who were irradiated and given vasectomies were relatively young. "To be utterly frank with you," she told George Farwell, the University of Washington's vice president for research, "we never would have approved this research, regardless of the action of the university committees, if it had come to the attention of the Department of Institutions Research Review Committee, which was, of course, not in existence at the time Dr. Paulsen accomplished the major portion of his work." In a letter to her boss, William Conte, who was in favor of letting Paulsen complete his studies, Holliday wrote:

> I do not think we have a single leg to stand on if we allow this study to continue. . . . If, as the University Committee suggests, the research is of an essential nature, if there is no danger from the X-ray procedure itself, and if the research is ethically sound, then Dr. Paulsen should have no difficulty getting graduate students, medical students, his own patients, persons who want a vasectomy, other physicians, etc. to volunteer. If he does have difficulty getting them to volunteer, then I think that simply proves the point I'm trying to make, namely, that we have to consider there is high risk, that there is special psychologic and financial etc. inducement for this particular captive audience to volunteer for this type of study. We need, I think, to stand in a special relationship to captive populations and make certain that they are not operating on the assumption that they are already destroyed as human beings, that they do not see $100 for a vasectomy as being inducement enough to volunteer away their human rights, etc.

Several months later the department's Research Review Committee unanimously rejected Paulsen's proposal. "The Committee felt strongly that the Paulsen project is inconsistent with general professional standards obtaining for the protection of the individual as research subject. For example, it seems clearly inconsistent with the standards laid down by the Nuremberg Code."

The committee's findings finally persuaded Holliday's boss, William Conte, to halt the experiment permanently. Paulsen said that he quarreled with Conte when he was told to end the experiment. "Needless to say I was distressed because I wanted to follow some of them longer," he recalled in 1994. Paulsen also got a call from Shields Warren while he was attending a meeting in New York. "Look," Paulsen remembered Warren saying, "your questions have been answered." Warren informed Paulsen that he would be receiving official notice shortly from the AEC that the program was canceled. Although Warren had nothing to do with the experiment, he probably had gotten involved in the controversy because he was still a consultant to the commission and was considered one of the world's leading experts in radiation effects.

Despite the cease-and-desist orders, Paulsen apparently was still doing "some kind of unauthorized research" at the penitentiary a year later, according to a confidential memo from Robert Sharpley, an official with the state of Washington's Department of Social and Health Services. Sharpley then met with George Farwell, the University of Washington's vice president for research. The two agreed that further research by Paulsen would have to be cleared through Farwell's office and that no experiments could be undertaken without review and approval by both the university and the Department of Social and Health Services.

Sharpley then met with Paulsen for two hours. According to Sharpley's memo, he "left no doubt" that neither the university or the Department of Social and Health Services would tolerate further "unauthorized research or any attempts to bypass" the review requirements of the two institutions. "It is probably true," Sharpley wrote, "to say that the Paulsen Case more than any other single research undertaking in the former Department of Institutions had a pronounced effect on general departmental research policy, research rules and regulations, and on formal review procedures." As for Holliday, her efforts had provoked so much hostility from her boss that she began looking for another job. "I decided what the hell and left as soon as I could find a suitable position," she is quoted as saying in a 1976 letter to Dan Evans, then the governor of Washington.

———

While Paulsen slugged it out with various committees, Carl Heller's testicular irradiation study in Salem, Oregon, was also drawing to a close. The last inmate in Oregon had been irradiated on May 6, 1971, and Heller and his assistants had been analyzing samples and performing testicular biopsies since that time. Heller suffered a debilitating stroke in December 1972 that paralyzed the left side of his body. Soon afterward Amos Reed, the administrator for Oregon's Corrections Division, ordered the shutdown of all medical experiments at the penitentiary. The announcement took Heller's research team by surprise, and several weeks later Mavis Rowley, C. Alvin Paulsen, and Daniel DiIaconi, the physician who performed the testicular biopsies, met with the administrator. Rowley hoped that Oregon prison officials would allow Paulsen to supervise the medical follow-up of Heller's test subjects.

On top of Reed's desk was a copy of an *Atlantic Monthly* article by investigative journalist Jessica Mitford describing several experiments that were going on in the nation's prisons at the time. "He pulled that article out and said that he wanted nothing like that to happen in terms of publicity nor in terms of future legal hassles, and therefore, that was it," Rowley recalled. In a memo summarizing the meeting, Reed later wrote that the "experimenters" were very concerned about the termination of the project and strongly urged him to reconsider his decision. "I asked if Dr. Paulsen, his family or his professional associates were undergoing radiation experimentation and was told 'no.' I opined that if the project was so worthwhile and so safe it would be encouraging to others if they became personally involved." Reed also said he believed the inmates could not really give informed consent. "I saw these projects as exploitation of disadvantaged people."

Heller's stroke had occurred while he was trying to work out the details of a long-term medical monitoring program for the former subjects with the Atomic Energy Commission. Locating convicts who had been released from prison posed some difficult issues, particularly regarding privacy rights, but both Heller and the AEC agreed the prisoners should be followed for at least twenty to twenty-five years. In one letter Heller noted that the men should be given routine chest X rays because any tumor found in the testis was most likely to metastasize to, and often was revealed first, in lung tissue. Heller's stroke, combined with Reed's decision to halt the experiments, put an end to any medical follow-up efforts. It was the first of many failed attempts to come to terms with the experiment and provide proper care for former subjects.

38

The Plutonium Experiment: Phase Two

By the late 1960s, nearly all of the major human radiation experiments of the Cold War were under way. Scientists at Vanderbilt University in Nashville, Tennessee, had just completed collecting the data for a follow-up study of the pregnant women who drank the radioactive iron cocktails; Eugene Saenger and his team in Cincinnati were struggling to work out the kinks in their bone marrow transplant program; the Holiday Inn–styled chamber in Oak Ridge that subjected patients to the low, chronic doses of radiation similar to what astronauts would experience in space had just begun operating; Carl Heller was discovering the incredible sensitivity of human testes to radiation; and C. Alvin Paulsen was about to submit to reviewers his proposal to irradiate prisoners' testicles with neutrons.

Countless radioactive tracer experiments also were ongoing at civilian and military hospitals and research institutions throughout the country. Many of these experiments were aimed at better understanding how fallout moved through the food chain. At the National Reactor Testing Station in Idaho, for example, radioactive iodine was intentionally released into pastures. Cows were led onto the contaminated pastures, where they grazed for several days, then they were milked, and humans drank the milk. The University of Chicago and Argonne National Laboratory conducted an experiment between 1961 and 1963 in which real and simulated fallout and solutions of strontium and cesium were fed to 102 subjects. At Hanford, humans were fed radioactive fish. Fifty-seven workers at Los Alamos ingested small spheres containing radioactive uranium-235 and manganese-54 so scientists could assess the potential hazards from the atmospheric reentry and burnup of rockets propelled by nuclear reactors or radioactive power supplies.

The studies weren't limited to humans; insects, birds, honeybees, wild animals, even forests and grasslands were subjected to experimentation. Many of the most bizarre of these experiments were carried out at the Savannah River Site's Ecology Laboratory. Located near Augusta, Georgia, Savannah River is a 300-acre site established in 1950 to produce plutonium and tritium, which is used in thermonuclear bombs. Five production reactors and two chemical separation plants are located there.

In one experiment, two persimmon trees were injected early in the growing season with calcium-45. Web worms were placed on the trees to feed, then their larvae were transferred to uncontaminated leaves in a laboratory to establish calcium-45's half-life. Sixteen loblolly pines were "inoculated" with strontium-89. Field mice were fed peanut butter laced with iron-59, zinc-65, and iodine-131. Red-winged blackbirds and sagebrush lizards were injected with tritium. Yellow-bellied slider turtles were fed calcium-47. Tantalum wires were inserted in the tails of salamanders. The larvae of houseflies contaminated with radioactive zinc were fed to spiders. An "old field" was subjected to short-term gamma radiation and a stand of hardwood trees was irradiated.

In the frenzy of ongoing experimentation aimed at better understanding atmospheric fallout, criticality injuries, nuclear battlefield casualties, and space radiation, the plutonium injections had been more or less forgotten. But in 1967 the old experiment was revived when an AEC official from headquarters placed a call to Berkeley's Patricia Durbin, the student who had once washed beakers in Joseph Hamilton's laboratory. The AEC official wanted to know more about the comparative toxicity of plutonium and americium following an accident at Rocky Flats, a plant outside Denver, Colorado, which made triggers for thermonuclear bombs. Durbin, by then a respected biophysicist, began looking up scientific reports and eventually found herself reviewing her mentor's old work. Exactly two decades had elapsed since Elmer Allen, the last of the eighteen patients, had been injected.

Durbin was astounded to discover that Allen, code-named CAL-3, was still alive. Then she drove up to Santa Rosa, California and poured through death certificates at the county courthouse. To her amazement she discovered that Albert Stevens, CAL-1, the housepainter from Healdsburg, California, had died in 1966, only one year before her search began. He had lived for more than two decades after being given a so-called lethal dose of plutonium. Durbin wondered what had become of the other patients. "Like a drunk or a gambler, a little bit whets your appetite," she recalled in an oral history interview.

Slowly she began pulling the data together. She persuaded officials at the Atomic Energy Commission headquarters to declassify the 1950 Los Alamos report written by Wright Langham and Samuel Bassett and retrieved the records of Joseph Hamilton from storage. (Durbin ruefully acknowledged in 1994, after the injections had become the subject of intense publicity and legal action had been taken against the scientists and institutions who were responsible, that it might have been better if the Berkeley lab had thrown away Hamilton's data. "It was stupid. It was like Richard Nixon taping in the White House.") In a letter to a hospital administrator dated April 23, 1969, she explained that there had been a furor within the newly formed Atomic Energy Commission when offi-cials learned that some of the plutonium patients had been misdiag-nosed:

> Most of the patients injected with Pu were studied at other hospitals around the country, and although most were elderly and expected to have short life expectancies at the time of injec-tion, some were misdiagnosed. Because of this, there was an understandably great uproar when the civilian A.E.C. took over from the Manhattan Engineer District. As a result, the human data thus obtained was classified "Secret," and so it remained for some years. All efforts to follow up on those persons who had been injected ceased abruptly, and no other human being has been deliberately injected with Pu since. . . . Unfortunately, the material from three of the four patients injected by Dr. Ham-ilton has never been made available to anyone. . . .

As she went about her data gathering. Durbin also contacted Wright Langham, who was still working at Los Alamos. Langham was pleased to learn that Durbin was interested in the fate of the plutonium injectees but did not want any active role in a follow-up study. Durbin confided in a letter to her supervisor that Langham was tired of being identified with the experiment and had grown weary of discussing the project at meet-ings and conferences. "He is, I believe, distressed by this and other aspects of the study itself—particularly the fact the injected people in the HP series [the Rochester patients] were unaware that they were the subjects of an experiment," she wrote. "I believe that in retrospect he wishes there had been some other way to obtain the needed relationships between Pu excretion and body burden." Despite his regrets, Langham couldn't pass up the opportunity to obtain some fraction of the excretion samples from the test subjects. "He said that if such material were available, the Los Alamos group would be interested in participating, but that they did not want to be directly responsible nor in direct contact with whomever was actually obtaining samples," Durbin wrote. "He summed up his feelings as follows: 'I'll be delighted to hold your coats while you other fellows fight.' " (Langham did not live long enough to see the results of the study: He died in 1972 in a plane crash in Albuquerque, New Mexico.)

Durbin soon learned that besides Elmer Allen, three patients injected with plutonium at the University of Rochester's Strong Memorial Hospital were also still living—homemaker Eda Schultz Charlton, handyman John Mousso, and Janet Stadt, the pain-wracked scleroderma patient. Durbin proposed that a complete follow-up study be undertaken. This meant obtaining additional urine and stool samples from the four survivors and exhuming the bodies of the deceased subjects. In a letter to an official at AEC headquarters, she acknowledged the proposed study was "messy," but suggested that perhaps the families of the deceased could be offered "something" in order to get them to cooperate. Durbin wanted to headquarter the project at Lawrence Berkeley Laboratory, but her boss quickly rejected the idea, fearing "the introduction of exhumed bodies into the politically charged Berkeley atmosphere might even result in picketing of the laboratory by students."

Without laboratory support, Durbin could proceed no further, and in December of 1972, she reluctantly turned over copies of the data she had so painstakingly collected to Robert Rowland, the first director of the Center for Human Radiobiology at Argonne National Laboratory, a sprawling complex that had evolved out of the Met Lab and was located some twenty-seven miles southwest of downtown Chicago. The center, which is now defunct, had been set up to do just the type of follow-up studies that Durbin envisioned for the plutonium patients. Formally established by the AEC in 1969, largely through the urging of Robley Evans, the center was devoted to studying individuals who had ingested or been injected with large amounts of radium. Deep within the bowels of the building was a whole-body counter that measured the radium content of both the living and the dead. "We had cadavers laid out and being deskeletonized one door away from the waiting room to the whole-body counter," Rowland recalled in a 1995 oral history interview. "If somebody [opened] that door by mistake, we [would be] in deep trouble."

When Robley Evans retired from MIT and moved to Scottsdale, Arizona, he and his assistant, Mary Margaret Shanahan, were put on the payroll of the Center for Human Radiobiology. Evans and Shanahan then operated a "CHR satellite" from Shanahan's home in Phoenix called the Southwest Field Station of the Massachusetts Institute of Technology Radioactivity Center. The purpose of the CHR satellite was to track down radium patients and get permission from relatives for exhumations. Evans was very powerful, Rowland recalled, and "very, very intimately involved in ways I don't understand with the Atomic Energy Commission and the Atomic Energy commissioners and the headquarters people at Germantown."

Durbin had identified most of the plutonium patients by name when she gave her information to Rowland's group. She also had secured the cooperation of Christine Waterhouse, the Rochester doctor who had taken care of Eda Schultz Charlton and John Mousso for many years. With Waterhouse's help, Rowland and his staff began making arrangements for follow-up studies of the surviving plutonium patients, to be conducted the following spring at Strong Memorial Hospital, the very hospital where eleven of the eighteen patients had been injected nearly 30 years earlier. Waterhouse later told investigators that she didn't want to tell Charlton and Mousso, both in their seventies by then, of the injections because she thought disclosure might be harmful in terms of their "advanced age and ill health."

The Chicago scientists wanted a complete collection of the patients' urine and stool samples; vials of blood for clinical analysis and chromosome research; and complete or partial X rays. Soon after receiving Durbin's files, Rowland dashed off a memo to his staff that included the following instructions: "Please note that outside of CHR we will never use the word plutonium in regard to these cases. 'These individuals are of interest to us because they may have received a radioactive material at some time' is the kind of statement to be made, if we need to say anything at all."

Rowland told Department of Energy interviewers in 1995 that he issued those instructions at the behest of James Liverman, who held essentially the same job Shields Warren had once held in what had been renamed the Division of Biomedical and Environmental Research of the AEC. Rowland said he was able to get AEC approval for the follow-up studies only on the conditions that he took the funding from his own budget and that he not tell the patients they had plutonium in their bodies. "That was Jim Liverman (who) requested that in no uncertain terms," Rowland told DOE interviewers. "So I agreed. I mean, he's the boss; he funds us, you know. You do what he tells you. And he said, 'Do it, but don't tell them they have plutonium in them.' " (Liverman did not respond to inquiries about the matter. His wife said he had been instructed by his attorneys not to speak to the media.)

Andrew Stehney, who worked closely with Robert Rowland, said scientists at the Center for Human Radiobiology didn't tell the patients the truth because everybody was "leery of getting these people all excited." He added, "We were told these people were pretty elderly and might get very upset if we started talking about radioactivity in their bodies."

Robley Evans and Mary Margaret Shanahan were given the job of locating the relatives of the ten deceased plutonium patients and obtaining permissions to exhume the bodies. They worked with a scientist in Philadelphia named Jan Lieben. "I was what you'd call a 'procurer.' I would get the names of these people, and if they were dead, we wanted to see where the plutonium was and what the excretion pattern was," Lieben said. "We were trying to establish if the bomb were dropped and people were exposed to radioactive material such as plutonium and other products, what their prognosis would be."

Officials at the Center for Human Radiobiology instructed Lieben not to tell the families that their loved ones had been injected with plutonium. "An appropriate approach would be to say that the Center was investigating the composition of radioactive materials that had been injected at an earlier date in an experimental type of treatment; and that since the composition of the mixture was not well known, there would be considerable scientific interest in investigating the nature of the isotope and the effects that it might have had." With the decision not to disclose the nature of the long-ago injections to either the living patients or the families of those who had died, the stage was set for the second phase of the experiment and the second phase of the cover-up.

Eda Schultz Charlton was the first of the plutonium survivors brought into the University of Rochester's Strong Memorial Hospital. Elmer Allen was second and John Mousso was third. Janet Stadt, the fourth patient, refused to participate.

Eda was hospitalized on the metabolic ward from January 28 to February 28, 1973. According to an admission note written by Christine Waterhouse, the hospitalization was prompted by a four-day bout of abdominal pain. During Eda's stay, doctors removed two lesions from her abdomen and biopsied them. They took X rays of her abdomen, pelvis, and spine and conducted a complete blood test. Waterhouse instructed staffers to begin collecting Eda's urine and stool samples, but she mentioned nothing in Eda's medical records about the long-ago plutonium injection or that the samples were to be sent to Chicago's Center for Human Radiobiology. John Rundo, the scientist who oversaw the chemical analyses, said the plutonium was "easily" measurable in Eda. "I was surprised at how much plutonium was in the feces, how much in the blood," he recalled.

Elmer Allen was 2,000 miles from Rochester and didn't like to fly, so getting him into Strong Medical Hospital required more planning. The first official contact with Elmer's doctor was made by Austin Brues, who at the time was serving as the medical director of Argonne's Center for Human Radiobiology. Brues, then in his mid-sixties, was another veteran of the bomb program. He had worked under Robert Stone at the Met Lab and accompanied Paul Henshaw to Japan in 1946. He also stumped the country with James Cooney, trying to defuse the public's fear of atomic weapons, and served as a consultant on panels that dealt with rad warfare and the nuclear-propelled aircraft. He was bright, articulate— and deceitful.

Brues wrote a letter to Elmer's doctor in Italy, Texas, in March of 1973 stating the Center for Human Radiobiology was interested in doing a follow-up study of his patient. Brues did not disclose the fact that Elmer had been injected with plutonium in 1947, and he lied about the purpose of the follow-up study:

> We are trying to locate a patient of yours by the name of Elmer Allen in order to do a follow-up study on treatment he received for a sarcoma in July, 1947. We are especially interested in cases of this sort, and his is of particular interest since he has this unusual malignant tumor and has shown such a long survival time. If he is able and willing we would like him to participate in a metabolism study at Strong Memorial Hospital in Rochester, New York, for about ten days. Please assure him it would only be for observation and collection of excreta.

Brues also told Elmer's doctor that the center would pick up the tab for hospital and transportation costs and pay Elmer for participating in the study.

Brues was part of the clique of Met Lab doctors who had been doing the quick and dirty animal experiments during the war. In a formerly secret report written in 1945, he described an experiment in which dogs were injected with varying amounts of plutonium. "From what we know at the present time," he wrote, "it seems reasonable to expect malignancy to occur following the administration of plutonium, as is seen after prolonged radiation in general, and to expect that bone may be a favorable site for plutonium carcinogenesis." Brues also contributed some of the information used in the definitive 1950 Los Alamos report and reviewed the manuscript. Despite the evidence, Brues told AEC investigators in 1974 he was not familiar with the injections.

Elmer agreed to participate in the follow-up study, and on a muggy evening in early June of 1973, he and Fredna took their seats in Car 1635, Drawing Room D, of the *Texas Chief,* an overnight train bound for Chicago. The Allens were on the trip of their life, a nineteen-day whirlwind that would take them to Chicago and then hundreds of miles northeast to Rochester. Limousines, fresh flowers, private train compartments, and immaculate hotel rooms awaited them. The government underwrote the trip and also paid Elmer $140 for participating in the study and $13 a day in expenses. "My mother thought this was big stuff coming from Italy, Texas," recalled Elmer's daughter, Elmerine. "She thought she was the queen of England. It wasn't like they said, 'We're testing you guys because we injected you with plutonium.'"

At Union Station in Chicago, a driver from Travelers Limousine Service picked up the Allens and whisked them off to the Hinsdale Ramada Inn, where a bouquet of flowers awaited them. The next day Fredna went sightseeing and Elmer was taken to Argonne National Laboratory. There he was placed in a whole-body counter and samples of his urine collected and studied for traces of plutonium from the long-ago injection. Scientists at the lab took numerous X rays of his entire body and detected changes in the bones of his shoulders that were "consistent [with] early radium deposition." His jawbone also showed abnormal changes "suggestive of damage due to radiation."

The limo driver picked the couple up the following evening and drove them to the Greyhound Station in Chicago, where they boarded a bus bound for Rochester. When the Allens arrived in Rochester, they took a cab to Strong Memorial Hospital. Elmer was checked into the metabolic ward, where he was scheduled to stay from June 13 to June 25.

In a detailed hospital admission note recounting Allen's medical history, Waterhouse wrote that his left leg had been amputated after he was told he had a tumor in the knee. The admission note disclosed nothing about the plutonium injection. Fredna said she had no idea what the doctors were doing. "Every time I went to see him, he was in bed. They would study the food he would eat," she said. For two weeks, Elmer's urine and stool samples were collected. John Rundo, the scientist overseeing the analyses, said the plutonium in Elmer was barely detectable. "His excretion rate was very low." On the day Elmer was to be discharged, he had a seizure and the couple stayed an extra day.

John Mousso, the man from East Rochester, was the third patient hospitalized for the follow-up studies. He was at Strong Memorial Hospital from June 21 to July 1, 1973. As with Eda, the plutonium injected into Mousso twenty-seven years earlier was easily detectable in his urine, stools, and blood.

Robert Rowland and Patricia Durbin, in a scientific paper published in 1976, said John was one of the six plutonium patients who received radiation doses to the bone "high enough to be considered carcinogenic." The others were Albert Stevens, Eda Schultz Charlton, Janet Stadt, Amedio Lovecchio, and Daniel Nelson. The two scientists estimated that John's endosteal membranes, the sensitive tissue lining the bone cavities and surfaces, had by 1975 received 973 rads of radiation—far more than the 600 rads that Durbin thought might produce bone tumors.

Three months after the last living patient was hospitalized, the exhumations began. On September 24, 1973, scientists exhumed the body of Jean Daigneault, HP-4, the young Rochester patient who suffered from Cushing's syndrome. Several months earlier Robley Evans and Mary Margaret Shanahan had driven from Phoenix to Tucson, where Jean's older sister, Ruth Brown, lived, in order to get permission to exhume the body.

Brown said that she was under the impression that Evans wanted to exhume her sister because he was doing research on pituitary disorders. She said Evans did not disclose that her sister had been injected with plutonium. Once the exhumation papers were signed, Brown said she never heard from him again. Evans and Shanahan later told AEC investigators there was "no need to introduce the reasons for the injection of the isotopes since no questions by the persons contacted were raised with respect to that point."

Jean's organs and brain had been removed during an autopsy at the time of her death. When scientists opened the casket, they saw that the body was still well preserved. The diaphragm, thigh muscle, several nerves, both eyes, the trachea with larynx, and skin from the thigh were removed. "The subject's hair was removed from the remains with the scalp intact." The hair was dried at 100 degrees Centigrade for forty-eight hours, then cut away from the scalp as closely as possible. Then it was washed, rinsed with water and "air-dried." Scientists found traces of plutonium in Jean's hair, leading them to theorize that hair possibly could be used to determine how much plutonium the body had absorbed.

The follow-up studies were rolling along nicely when serious questions about the ethics of the project were raised within the AEC. It's not clear who, or what, triggered the concern, but the studies were not brought to the attention of the Argonne human use committee until November of 1973—after the three hospitalizations and one exhumation had already occurred. This committee, which was supposed to review all human research projects, had been formed in 1970, after the AEC had adopted the revised guidelines issued by the National Institutes of Health governing research with human subjects. The NIH guidelines required the establishment of committees to oversee human research and laid out the basic elements of informed consent. Those elements included:

1. A fair explanation to the patient of the procedure to be followed, including an identification of those procedures which are experimental.

2. A description of the attendant discomforts and risks.

3. A description of the benefits to be expected.

4. A disclosure of appropriate alternative procedures that would be advantageous for the subject.

5. An offer to answer any inquiries concerning the procedures.

6. An instruction that the subject is free to withdraw his or her consent and discontinue participation in the project or activity at any time.

All of the national laboratories, such as Argonne, agreed to abide by those guidelines and each year were required in budget documents to state their intent to uphold the rules. In an agreement dated June 19, 1970, the Argonne laboratory duly noted:

The Argonne National Laboratory has formally adopted the principles expressed in the Nuremberg Code as its guide in research
which makes use of human subjects. To implement these principles, and to verify that all such research is in compliance with
the Nuremberg Code, a Review Committee for Research Projects Involving Human Subjects will be established at the Argonne National Laboratory. This committee will receive all
proposals involving research on human subjects. No research
will be undertaken without the prior approval of the Review
Committee.

Despite the lab's promises, there was a delay of nearly a year before
the Argonne human use committee found out about the follow-up studies of the plutonium patients. The committee met on March 14, 1974, to
discuss the study and several weeks later issued a report urging the
involved scientists to inform the patients of the true purpose of the
examination: "It is our opinion that the CHR should not be involved in
examination of patients believed to have a body burden of plutonium, or
excreta from such subjects, unless the patients have been informed that
the examination is to establish the presence or absence of residual radioactivity stemming from the plutonium they received many years ago."
Lab officials later said that one reason they didn't submit the follow-up
studies to the committee was because "the nature of the studies was to
be suppressed to avoid embarrassing publicity for the AEC."

John Erlewine, general manager of the AEC, officially ordered an
internal probe into the experiment on April 17, 1974. But James
Liverman and an associate, Sidney Marks, had already begun an investigation and had met with National Institutes of Health officials to discuss
the problem a month earlier. One of the NIH representatives present at
the meeting was Donald Chalkley, the same official who had praised
Eugene Saenger's total-body irradiation project. Not surprisingly, the
AEC was concerned about minimizing any adverse publicity and considered having the National Academy of Sciences issue a committee report.
"A NAS committee report, which could be appropriately published,
would be likely to have wide acceptance, and the existence of the report
might limit the duration of any controversy that may arise," an AEC
official speculated.

The official inquiry essentially had three parts: Investigators wanted
to find out, first, if the patients injected with plutonium gave their informed consent at the time the injections were administered; second,

whether the plutonium survivors studied in 1973 gave their informed consent for the follow-ups; and third, whether the relatives of deceased patients were informed about the true purpose of the exhumations. Two divisions of the AEC, the Division of Biomedical and Environmental Research and the Division of Inspection, jointly conducted the inquiry. Liverman, who headed the biomedical division, had asked the Division of Inspection to examine the contemporary period because of "conflict of interest considerations." The two principal investigators were Sidney Marks, from the AEC's biomedical division, and Leo Miazga, from the inspection division. Liverman told Marks that the inquiry had top priority and all of his other duties should be set aside.

As the "official" investigation was getting under way, Dixy Lee Ray, chairman of the AEC, ordered one of her top aides, Dave Bruner, to quietly snoop into the issue. As one of the scientists who had encouraged C. Alvin Paulsen to pursue the testicular irradiation experiment, Bruner may not have been the most objective person Ray could have asked. He then contacted Hymer Friedell and several other scientists. "If Bruner is making phone calls, he should be called off! It will only 'muddy' the water," a scientist warned Liverman.

AEC investigators fanned out across fourteen cities, examining records and talking to researchers involved in both phases of the experiment. More than 250 documents were copied and brought back to AEC headquarters. Many of those documents were declassified and publicly released in 1994 and 1995. They were the same ones that DOE officials had said on numerous occasions didn't exist.

The investigators were instructed to handle the Manhattan Project doctors, by then venerable, white-haired authorities in their field, with kid gloves. "During interviews, every effort will be made to avoid causing distress to the persons interviewed although it is recognized that some distress may inevitably result from discussions centering around the issue of informed consent." The AEC investigators prepared detailed memos of their discussions with the bomb doctors. The memos reveal how uneasy the original participants felt about the experiment twenty years later. Several denied any involvement whatsoever in the project; others claimed their memories were hazy; a few even pointed the finger at other scientists. The following are excerpts from some of the interviews, which were all conducted in the spring of 1974:

• Stafford Warren was interviewed on April 22 at his office in the UCLA Laboratory of Nuclear Medicine and Radiation Biology. Warren, the medical director of the Manhattan Project who reported directly to General Leslie Groves and supervised the overall injection program, left the investigators confused about his role in the experiment. "He did not indicate that he himself was opposed to such a program; however, he also did not indicate that he had specifically authorized one," Sidney Marks later wrote. But coinvestigator Leo Miazga had a different interpretation of Warren's remarks. "Leo felt that Dr. Warren had indicated tacit consent to the program being carried out whereas I had the impression that Dr. Warren had not participated in the meetings where final decisions were reached to go forward with the program," Marks wrote.

• Andrew Dowdy was contacted by telephone by the two AEC investigators while they were still in Stafford Warren's office. Dowdy, the supervisor of the University of Rochester's Manhattan Annex, had attended the September 5, 1945, planning meeting for the Los Alamos–Rochester portion of the experiment and later had advised against the distribution of the Wright Langham–Samuel Bassett report because of possible "unfavorable public relations" and "legal entanglements." Wrote Marks: "During the conversation, Dr. Dowdy said that he knew something of what went on but very little about the details. I asked whether Sam Bassett had reported to him and he said that Sam Bassett had, but this would be at intervals like every 6 months or so, but that he did not have intimate knowledge of the goings-on in connection with this study." Marks wanted to visit Dowdy, who was in retirement at Laguna Hills near Los Angeles, but Dowdy told him that he felt that visit would not be "sufficiently rewarding" to justify the trip.

• Robert Fink was also contacted by telephone by the two investigators while they were in Stafford Warren's office. Fink, according to documents, was designated to calibrate the plutonium solutions for injection at Rochester and also attended the September 5, 1945, planning meeting. Fink was reluctant to discuss the matter, Marks wrote, questioning "whether our credentials were proper and whether we might not be reporters rather than official personnel. I told him that we would be glad to present our credentials to him when we would visit with him and that we were very interested in finding out what he might know since Dr. Warren felt that he would have known something about the situation." Fink agreed to meet with the two AEC investigators, but before they had left Stafford Warren's office, he called back and canceled. "He said that he had confused the issue of polonium with plutonium and that it was only the polonium patients that he had worked on at all. In other words, that he would have had no knowledge of the plutonium cases."

• Hymer Friedell, Stafford Warren's second-in-command, was interviewed on April 25 at his office at Case Western Reserve University. Friedell, who had attended the Los Alamos meeting at which it was agreed that a human being would be injected with plutonium, told the two investigators he was "not present at any meeting when the decision to proceed with the program was actually taken." Wrote Marks: "Dr. Friedell virtually denied any direct involvement in the injection at Oak Ridge and also in any of the programs conducted at the other three sites."

• Louis Hempelmann, the young, panicky doctor who had pumped out Don Mastick's stomach some thirty years earlier, was questioned on April 17 and again on May 1. Hempelmann told AEC investigators he had little knowledge of the plutonium injections carried out in Rochester, Chicago, and Berkeley. The AEC investigators then showed Hempelmann the memo he had written to J. Robert Oppenheimer urging that a patient in Rochester or Chicago be injected with plutonium. "When we showed that memo to Dr. Hempelmann, he could not recall the meeting clearly nor that particular discussion." Hempelmann continued to maintain his ignorance of the experiment, and in an interview in 1992, a year before his death, he said, "I don't know what was done at the time or what was found."

• Joseph Howland, described by some of his colleagues as a "manic depressive," met with an AEC investigator on April 24 at the Holiday Inn in Chapel Hill, North Carolina. Howland never wavered in the version of the story he had been telling since 1948. He said he injected Ebb Cade with plutonium, but only after he had been ordered to do so by Hymer Friedell. "Dr. Howland emphatically stated that no consent was obtained from the patient at any time."

• Kenneth Scott was interviewed on April 18 at his home in California. Scott, who assisted in the California plutonium injections, was as plainspoken as Joseph Howland. Scott said he prepared the solution to be injected into Albert Stevens and took it to Earl Miller in San Francisco. He said he was not present when the actual injection was made and couldn't comment on who made the actual injection or whether the patient was properly informed.

• Earl Miller was contacted on the afternoon of April 17. Miller was the radiologist at the University of California Hospital in San Francisco who, according to medical records, received the plutonium-laced body parts from Albert Stevens and Simeon Shaw. He told AEC officials that he had no knowledge whatsoever of any plutonium injections. Oddly enough, "he also volunteered the opinion that the matter were best allowed to languish and not be disclosed publicly until all individuals had died."

• Leon Jacobson was interviewed on April 16 in his office. Jacobson was a hematologist who had worked as Robert Stone's deputy at the Met Lab and went on to become chairman of the department of medicine at the University of Chicago and director of the Argonne Cancer Research Hospital. At Jacobson's request, three other gentlemen were present in the room for the interview: Jacobson's administrative assistant and two professors from the medical school. Jacobson was alleged by scientist Edwin Russell to have performed the actual injections of the Chicago patients, but when questioned "stated repeatedly that he knew very little about it, next to nothing." He did suggest, however, that investigators talk to a Stanford University professor named J. Garrot Allen, who also had a security clearance and would have been "more likely to have known something about those patients than Dr. Jacobson himself." The investigators subsequently interviewed Allen, who knew nothing about the project and whose name does not appear in any documents or scientific reports related to the injections.

• J. J. Nickson, coauthor of the scientific paper describing the injections of Chicago patients Arthur Hubbard and Una Macke, was questioned on April 23 in Memphis, Tennessee. Nickson had seemed "perfectly willing" to discuss the experiment when the AEC investigators contacted him by phone. "When we arrived at Dr. Nickson's office," Marks wrote, "his attitude seemed to have changed in that the frankness that seemed to prevail during our telephone conversation was replaced by a considerable reticence to enter into any substantive discussions. During the interview he claimed that he did not have any detailed knowledge of the matter and had handled only the isotope end of it but that he had not had contact with the patients. We showed him documents including a paper that he had co-authored with Ed Russell that went into considerable detail about the clinical summaries and the analyses on the two Chicago patients. He went through the document but indicated that that did not improve his memory of the situation. We also showed him a number of monthly reports that he had written to either Dr. Stone or Dr. Jacobson that dealt with the follow-up of analyses on these patients but he again refused to elaborate on the contents of those reports or to indicate that they had jogged his memory."

• Shields Warren was interviewed at his laboratory in Boston on April 9. Warren already knew that four of the injectees were still alive because both Patricia Durbin and Robert Rowland had contacted him. Warren told AEC investigators about his long-ago conversation with Joseph Hamilton and the steps he took to make sure no such injections ever happened again.

Despite the stonewalling by the original experimenters, AEC officials had a fairly accurate picture of what had occurred during both phases of the experiment. In a report stamped "official use only," they concluded that "certain violations of ethical standards" had taken place. Specifically, they found:

• Written evidence that disclosure had been made to only one patient. (That patient was Elmer Allen, but the consent form in his medical records does not describe what Allen was told or that he was injected with plutonium.)

• Informed consent was not obtained from the surviving patients involved in the 1973 follow-up studies. However, the AEC officials added there was no reason to believe the patients "suffered harm or discomfort" as a result of the studies.

• Disclosure to all but one of the next of kin of the deceased plutonium patients "could be judged misleading" because the radioisotopes were represented as having been injected as an experimental treatment for the patients' diseases.

Officials at AEC headquarters ordered scientists from the Center for Human Radiobiology to inform the family doctors of the surviving patients of the injections. Those physicians then were asked to break the news to the patients. Scientists were also to recontact the family members of deceased patients and inform them of the real reason why the AEC wanted to exhume the bodies of their relatives.

James Liverman, in a memo to his files, noted that the planned disclosures alarmed several high-ranking military officials. U.S. Army Brigadier General R. W. Green, deputy surgeon general of the Army, was particularly worried. "General Green was considerably concerned that no good was to be achieved in his view by surfacing a whole series of issues when nothing could in fact be done at this point in time with regard to changing those issues and that the patients or their relatives might in fact be worse off because of the public, social or psychological trauma."

Robert Sproull, then the president of the University of Rochester, was also disturbed. "His response was immediate and unrestrained in his view that 'no useful purpose could be served to the patients, the University, or the Commission by informing these patients at this point in time of an event now thirty years past,'" Liverman wrote. "He felt that the value to be gained was so far offset by the possible hazards that we should face the need for a response in the event of public disclosure rather than inform the people of long past events."

Sproull said in an interview in 1992 that he couldn't recall whether the memo accurately reflected his sentiments at the time. "Things were done then during the war that would not be done at all now. You don't use the word 'nigger' now at all. But if you uncovered something fifty years old and somebody used the word 'nigger,' it would sound as if he was a terrible person. So it was done in a different society, a different world, really. . . . In the spirit of the time, the people treating them thought they were actually doing a favor to the patients because the patients were about to die and there was some possibility that this foreign stuff, this unknown stuff, might in fact help them, and without that help, they were guaranteed to die. The curious thing was that they didn't."

Christine Waterhouse agreed to tell Eda Schultz Charlton and John Mousso. But Waterhouse said in an interview many years later that she couldn't remember whether she told them or not. "The telling of the patients, or the telling of the relatives, was not a significant enough factor for me so that I can remember distinctly telling them or not telling." Janet Stadt was never informed of the injection because her doctor "concluded that the mental status of the patient precludes proper disclosure."

Austin Brues was instructed by the AEC to make a personal visit to Elmer Allen's physician in Texas and inform him of the long-ago plutonium injection. Brues agreed to make the disclosure, but he also took the opportunity to persuade Elmer's doctor to help the AEC with future follow-up work. He took a night flight to Dallas on May 21, 1974. He met Walter Weyzen, an AEC official from headquarters, near the Dallas–Fort Worth airport and the two drove to Milford, Texas, to meet with Dewey Roberts, who was then Elmer's physician. Brues summarized the discussion in a trip report:

I told him we found that the patient had received plutonium into the muscle of the sarcomatous leg three days before it was amputated, not enough in our belief to cause any trouble or to have any effect on the tumor, but that he should be carefully followed in any case because of the very small number of such cases that are living. I pointed out why we are extremely anxious to have an autopsy in the event of his death, also that we would like to be able to check him again at intervals. He will cooperate and wants advice as to whom to call in the event of serious illness or death. He said these old fellows with hypertension, in his experience, are likely to go to sleep some night and not wake up.

Elmer's physician "was quick to form the belief" the plutonium injection may have cured the tumor, Brues wrote. "We tried to cool this but with questionable success. (I had given warning of this possibility before accepting the assignment.)" Brues asked the physician to inform Elmer about the nature of the injection, adding that "the record seems to indicate only that he gave voluntary consent to an injection of radioactive material."

On his way out of town, Brues decided to pay a "social visit" to Elmer. He got directions to Elmer's house from the post office. Fredna was at the zoo in Dallas with her grade-school class, but Elmer was home and pleased to see Brues. Elmer said he would be willing to return to Chicago for another examination as long as he didn't have to fly. Several weeks later Brues contacted Elmer's physician to find out if he had informed Elmer of the injection. The doctor told him, "The patient was aware of the injection, and wasn't much concerned, although he did not know what it was that had been injected."

Despite the ethical abuses and the potential negative publicity, the AEC decided to continue with the exhumation program after a committee of outside consultants agreed the scientific results were worth the risk—provided enough bodies could be exhumed. Eugene Cronkite, a Brookhaven National Laboratory scientist who had studied the Marshall Island residents exposed to fallout following the 1954 Bravo shot, wrote: "If all were exhumed and total body plutonium determined along with tissue distribution it would be of great importance to do so even over the refusal of the next of kin. However, if only one or two are feasible, the interest is proportionately less and would not justify the adverse publicity of resorting to court action to reverse exhumation refusals of next of kin."

Most of the families did refuse to grant permission for the exhumations, but the Center for Human Radiobiology eventually succeeded in exhuming the bodies of Arthur Hubbard, the first Chicago patient injected with plutonium, and Fred Sours, one of the Rochester patients.

On a rainy morning in June of 1975, Hubbard's body was exhumed from his grave at the Mount Calvary Cemetery in Austin, Texas, by "two Mexican laborers" and J. E. Farnham, an Argonne employee. "As I sifted through each shovel-full I began to find pieces of glass and metal," wrote Farnham. "This appeared to be the remains of a metal casket which had a glass viewing window. Eventually I began to locate pieces of very eroded bone." Farnham packed the skeletal remains in plastic bags. He then asked one of the cemetery officials to go buy a "cheap suitcase" so Farnham could take Hubbard's remains back to Chicago with him. "He came back unsuccessful. As it was late and I had only thirty minutes left to catch my flight, I changed clothes in the car, washed at the garden hose faucet, and requested Mr. Lozano to ship the remains as biological specimens via Air Express, and then quickly left for the airport." Hubbard's remains were shipped to Chicago on Braniff Air Lines Flight No. 126 on June 12, 1975.

The Center for Human Radiobiology had obtained permission for the exhumation from Hubbard's children. The consent forms state the purpose of the exhumation was to advance "medical and scientific research and education" but disclose nothing about the plutonium injection. Three years after the exhumation, one of Hubbard's daughters wrote Jan Lieben, inquiring why her father's remains had not been reinterred in the promised one-year time period. Andrew Stehney telephoned her and said that Hubbard's remains were being shipped back to the cemetery. "I said that we had obtained new information about plutonium that we could not have otherwise obtained, and I thanked her for her cooperation," Stehney wrote in a April 7, 1978, memo to the files.

Several weeks later, when the snow and ice that had lain over Rochester's Holy Sepulchre Cemetery all winter had finally retreated, a group of scientists gathered at the grave of Fred Sours, HP-9, the politician from Gates, New York. He had been buried in a metal vault and his skeleton was almost intact. "The skeleton and casket were in excellent shape considering a 31-year interment," a report notes. "The skeleton was relatively free of soft tissue and, at most, only clothing material had to be scraped from it." Sours's remains were slipped into a body bag and shipped to Chicago. His body was reinterred in 1981 after remaining at the Center for Human Radiobiology for three years.

Albert Stevens's cremated remains, which had been sitting in the bronze urn at the Chapel of the Chimes in Santa Rose, California, since 1966, were also shipped to the Center for Human Radiobiology on October 16, 1975. The consent form states only that the ashes were to be used "for the purposes of advancing medical and scientific research and education." Again, there was no mention of plutonium.

When Albert's ashes arrived, Robert Schlenker examined them. "Those remains, as I recall, were a pulverized mass. It was impossible to identify what portion of the skeleton a particular piece of ash came from." Much of the plutonium, he said, had "translocated" to points in the skeleton that were distant from cells sensitive to radiation. "I was at least able to tell that much, and that much, I think, was significant."

What happened to the ashes after Schlenker finished his studies is not clear. A memo in Albert's medical files indicates the remains were shipped back to the Chapel of the Chimes in August 1978. But the chapel manager said Albert's ashes weren't returned. "They left here in October 1975, and nothing's ever come back. I've gone to the location and looked. It's empty."

Some of Albert's ashes were transferred to a repository in Spokane, Washington, called the National Human Radiobiology Tissue Repository. The repository has tissue samples from about 500 people exposed to plutonium and other similar radioactive elements. Albert's daughter, Evelyn, said, "It makes me sick to think of it. To use a person's body while they're still alive and then to continue. It's so ghoulish."

Fighting his real and imaginary ghosts, Elmer Allen continued to live out his days in Italy, Texas. About four years after he and Fredna had taken their whirlwind trip, he was admitted to the hospital after a bad drinking bout. Fredna had found him on the floor with a belt around his neck. Elmer denied having any suicidal tendencies but was taken to the hospital anyway. He had been in a fight over the weekend and had to have his left ear stitched.

Somehow Austin Brues, the scientist at the Center for Human Radiobiology, learned that Elmer was in the hospital and sent a memo to David Williams, the physician who had diagnosed Elmer as a paranoid schizophrenic. In a December 12, 1977, memo, he wrote, "In the event he should show terminal signs at any time, we would appreciate a collect call to us at Argonne."

39

"Tragic Deaths Full of Pity and Sorrow"

Although information on the human radiation experiments occasionally made its way into obscure journals, the scientists managed to pursue their studies without drawing much public attention to their projects. This was due in large part, of course, to the deliberate efforts on the part of the researchers and their government funders to keep the experiments quiet. But the silence was also the result of the media's complacency and lack of sophistication. Activities related to nuclear weapons involved a labyrinthine bureaucracy and complicated scientific and technical issues, and spokesmen for the nuclear weapons industry were adept at manipulating the press. Controversial information was difficult to obtain, and oftentimes documents were deliberately classified to keep them away from reporters. With tight deadlines and long obstacles, many journalists wound up reporting what they were told. Slowly, though, the wall of silence began to crack.

In the fall of 1971, Stuart Auerbach, a reporter for the *Washington Post,* began looking into Eugene Saenger's experiment in Cincinnati. At the time, the total-body irradiation study was in its eleventh year and Saenger had become as optimistic as his old mentor, General James Cooney, about nuclear energy. In a statement to the Joint Committee on Atomic Energy the previous year, he had declared that "any part of the field of nuclear medicine should be as good or better an investment than IBM or Coca-Cola."

Auerbach contacted the Defense Nuclear Agency, which was the third incarnation of the Armed Forces Special Weapons Project, and requested a copy of the contract for Saenger's study. John Watson, a contracting officer, suggested the reporter drop by the following morning, read the contracts, then select the pages he wanted copied. The conversation was amiable, but documents show Watson was worried.

Upon hanging up with Auerbach, Watson contacted Lieutenant Colonel John W. Cable, a veterinarian who was the DNA's medical officer for the Saenger project. Together they put in a joint phone call to Saenger. Saenger informed the DNA officials that two television producers, a trade paper, and author Roger Rapoport recently had contacted him. "Dr. Saenger suggested that Auerback [sic] be referred to him as he could explain clearly the method of approach for the persons selected for the treatments under the research being conducted, as well as other matters concerned."

Watson then informed several other people of the newspaper's inquiry—the DNA's public information officer, the agency's chief of staff, and its deputy director for science and technology. Later that afternoon he also placed a call to the Department of Defense's Office of General Counsel. "It was agreed that the request should be handled in routine manner; that is, without delay and with low emphasis," Watson later wrote in an October 6, 1971, memo to his files.

Three days later the story appeared on the front page of the *Washington Post*. Eugene Saenger was quoted as saying the total-body irradiation was a "helpful" way to treat patients, but a radiologist at Memorial Sloan-Kettering Cancer Research Institute in New York City said the treatment "approaches what happens in an atomic accident."

The story drew worldwide attention. The *Times* (London) published an editorial entitled "Hospital Wards Are Not Battlefields." *L'Exprès* of Paris ran a story headlined *"Les Cobayes* [guinea pigs] *de Cincinnati."*

"The whole question this morning," asked a reporter at a press conference three days after the story broke, "is whether we have guinea pigs in Cincinnati or not."

"No, I do not believe we had guinea pigs in Cincinnati. Absolutely not," Saenger responded.

"Did any of the patients die as a result of negative reaction to the radiation?" another journalist asked.

"Not insofar as we could tell. Some of these patients were quite ill and died, but not as far as we could see from the treatment," Saenger responded.

Events moved quickly after the story broke. Three reviews of the experiment began almost simultaneously: Senator Mike Gravel, a Democrat from Alaska, asked the American College of Radiology to evaluate the experiment; the dean of the University of Cincinnati medical school appointed an eleven-member committee to review the project; and a group of junior faculty members at the university prepared their own independent findings. The experiment also drew the interest of Senator Edward Kennedy, a Massachusetts Democrat who chaired a Senate sub-committee on health issues.

Saenger played an important role behind the scenes, according to documents released by the university in 1994. He helped shore up the University of Cincinnati's defense of the experiment; he arranged the appointments for reviewers from the American College of Radiology; and he even helped the Defense Nuclear Agency polish a draft paper on the experiment (". . . would avoid the word *experiment* in this circum-stance. Suggest *study, investigation, research* instead," he advised.)

The first panel to weigh in was the American College of Radiology. Saenger sat on four of the ACR's subcommittees or commissions. The group's president, Robert W. McConnell, was a personal friend of Saenger's and was clearly annoyed by Gravel's and Kennedy's involve-ment: "I have a certain feeling about the involved congressmen, but am trying to cut down on the use of copulative verbs," he stated in an undated memo.

Not surprisingly, the ACR report was highly supportive of the experi-ment. Saenger's study conformed with good medical practice, the proce-dure for obtaining patient counsel was valid and consistent with the practices of the day, and the program deserved further support. "The project is validly conceived, stated, executed, controlled and followed up," the ACR panel concluded.

The group of junior faculty members, next to present their judg-ments, was as critical as the ACR was supportive. Martha Stephens, who went on to become a fiction writer and a tenured English professor at the University of Cincinnati, hounded Edward Gall, then director of the medical center, for copies of the Defense Department reports after read-ing about the study in the *Village Voice*. When Gall finally gave Stephens the reports, she drove back to the English Department, pulled the papers into her lap, and began to read. "I read for about an hour, and afterward, it was as if I could hardly recognize what was around me. Everything I saw looked different to me," she later wrote. "I was used to reading in plays and novels about tragic deaths full of pity and sorrow. But I was not used to *this* pity, *this* sorrow of powerless and sick people asking for help and then being brutally abused. Many of these deaths seemed to me executions. And they still do today."

Over the Christmas holidays of 1971, Stephens and several of her colleagues analyzed the material, interviewed doctors, and wrote a summary of how the patients had died. The report, which has become known as the JFA Report, pointed out that twenty-one patients, or 24 percent, died within thirty-eight days of treatment. The group also observed that the TBI experiment began only after Department of Defense funding was in place and that the Saenger team had not published one paper in the general scientific literature on the efficacy of total- or partial-body radiation for cancer treatment. "Is it conceivable that in an authentic cancer research study, no results would be reported after eleven years and the radiation of 87 patients? If no pattern had emerged after the irradiation of 87 patients—indeed after 10 or 20—would this in itself not have been worth communicating to other cancer specialists?" the group asked.

The third group to weigh in with its analysis of the experiment was the blue-ribbon committee appointed by the dean of the medical school and chaired by Raymond Suskind, director of the university's environmental health center. The "Suskind Report" was generally supportive of the TBI studies but contained some pointed criticisms as well. Among the most stunning was the finding that nineteen of the patients could have died from the radiation alone. The committee also found that the University of Cincinnati appeared to be the only institution in the country that was using TBI to treat radioresistant tumors. The panel pointed out that Saenger and his colleagues had not incorporated into the experiment appropriate measures to evaluate palliation—the very thing that Saenger said he was studying. Despite the findings, the committee urged that the study be continued provided certain changes were made in the design and a new funding source found.

The Suskind committee was fraught with conflicts of interest, a campus newspaper later revealed. One committee member was part of Saenger's research team, and four others were members of or advisors to the faculty panel that had just reviewed—and approved—the experiment. "Could one be led to believe," an editorial asked, "they would have voted, say, to discontinue a project they just recently approved of this past summer as faculty research committee members?"

Kennedy sent staffers to Cincinnati in early December 1971 to learn more about the experiment and to interview patients. But the university fought hard to keep the investigators away from the patients. The medical school argued that the interviews would be harmful to the patients' well-being and got two outside doctors to support its position. But an attorney identified as "Roscoe," who was representing the university, questioned whether the strategy would work: "Can this (psychological harm) be said of all the patients? Query whether patients who can stand total body radiation would be harmed by 'talking about their operation.' "

Saenger was worried the congressional investigators would take the patients' comments out of context. "This is a personal impression of mine," he wrote, "but there is no question in my mind that these men would dearly love to get directly at the patients and exploit them in any way possible to make a public issue out of the fact that one or more of these sick and infirm and poorly educated people could be maneuvered into a statement that they did not really remember as to just why they were being treated and that they might be experimented on without their knowledge."

A member of Saenger's team, Edward B. Silberstein, contacted the surviving patients and the parents of several children who underwent the TBI treatment. Transcripts of these interviews show Silberstein took the opportunity to prep the patients (described in one Pentagon document as "humble, mild and conforming") about a possible interview with Kennedy's investigators. In an interview with a patient identified as J.D., Silberstein pointed out:

"I might remind you about the way that the Defense Department, which did pay for the research, never paid for any of your treatment or made us make any decisions about how to do our tests or how to treat you in any way. Do you understand that?"

"Yes sir," J.D. responded.

Kennedy's inquiry into the experiment also drew the ire of Ohio's powerful senator, Robert Taft. "Senator Taft just went bonkers on the thing," Ellis Mottur, one of the Kennedy aides who had gone to Cincinnati, told reporters many years later. "It was clear he [Taft] was going to cause us a lot of trouble if we went any further with this Cincinnati thing." Kennedy eventually backed off the Cincinnati experiment and went on to hold the sensational hearings in 1973 on the infamous Tuskegee study, in which 400 impoverished African Americans who had syphilis were tracked for forty years but not given any treatment.

Martha Stephens tried to interest several legal groups in filing a lawsuit against the university after she learned Kennedy wasn't going to hold a hearing. But none of the patients had come forward or been identified, and Stephens couldn't find any attorney interested in pursuing the case. She bundled up the reports and carted them down to her basement. There they would sit for another twenty-two years.

Saenger's career, meanwhile, flourished. He went on to write more than 100 scientific articles and serve on numerous committees, many of which were involved in setting radiation standards for workers and the general public. He testified on behalf of the government in radiation injury cases and served as a consultant to the Justice Department, the Energy Department, the Food and Drug Administration, Brooke Army Hospital, Lackland Air Force Base, Wright-Patterson Air Force Base, and the Air Force Surgeon General. He was also among the international experts called in to evaluate the effects of the Chernobyl disaster. "There are two possible attitudes toward the holocaust which can be produced by nuclear warfare," he once wrote. "One is total despair and confusion. The alternative is the adoption of an attitude of making the best of an admittedly bad situation. . . ."

The Atomic Energy Commission's worst nightmare came true in October 1975 when *The National Enquirer* broke a story on the testicular irradiation experiment at the Oregon penitentiary. The tabloid reported that the sixty-seven men who participated in Carl Heller's experiment "could be walking around with cancer" but couldn't be notified because nobody knew where they were. In fact, many of the test subjects were still locked up in the penitentiary, and they were frightened and angered by the story.

A month later Heller's top assistant, Mavis Rowley, and Glenn Warner, another scientist, went to the prison to answer their questions. When the inmates asked Rowley what the purpose of Heller's program was, she is quoted as saying "It helped in genetic counseling."

The meeting only "heightened the emotionalism and confusion of mind," one convict later wrote. Eventually a dozen subjects who participated in the Heller experiment filed a lawsuit against the AEC, prison and state officials, and the doctors. It was during the depositions taken from prisoners that some of the brutal details of the experiment were revealed.

Carl Heller, still suffering the effects of the debilitating stroke that had occurred four years earlier, had his deposition taken in 1976 at his home on the Olympic Peninsula. The morning of the deposition, a friend helped Meta Heller move her husband into the living room where he was placed on a plastic mattress. Heller's long-term memory was still excellent, but he had a hard time with short-term recall. His assistant, Mavis Rowley, was questioned under oath simultaneously in an apparent effort to conserve Heller's strength. Rowley answered most of the attorneys' queries. Only the most critical questions were directed at Heller.

"What was the primary purpose of the radiation program?" asked David Hilgemann, an attorney representing the prisoners.

"The primary purpose was to discover the effects of radiation on the human body, objectively," Heller responded.

Later in the deposition Hilgemann asked, "What were the potential dangers, as you saw them, of the radiation aspect of the program?"

"The possibility of tumors of the testes," responded Heller.

"Are you talking about cancer?"

"I didn't want to frighten them so I said tumor; I may on occasion have said cancer."

Finally Hilgemann asked Heller whether he thought the convicts could honestly be considered volunteers: "Considering the inmates' attitude toward the money, do you really think that they voluntarily entered into this program and continued on with it?"

Heller responded, "Well, that's a very difficult question to answer. I could answer it in two ways: One, the inmates would tell me that they had been bad guys all their lives. Now they were going to do something good for humanity. Then perhaps weeks or months later they would say, 'You know, Dr. Heller, that was a lot of bull that I told you. I really joined the program only for the money.' This reminds me of a discussion with some of the NIH people who brought up the same question. One of the NIH people who were interested in our program and had been following it indicated the following answer: He said, 'Well, isn't money the reason that most people do things in our society?' "

Heller then looked up from his sickbed at the prisoners' attorney and asked, "Isn't that why you are here?"

Although Dr. Heller was a very sick man, the comment showed that he had lost none of his shrewdness—or combativeness. After the disposition was completed and the court reporter and the lawyers had packed up and left, Heller swallowed a Benadryl tablet, drank a glass of orange juice, and ate two egg sandwiches. Then he asked to be propped up in bed so he could enjoy the view.

Heller's health continued to decline, and he died in 1982. The small group of prisoners who filed the lawsuit eventually settled out of court for payments totaling about $9,000. But the settlement didn't resolve the issue of medical follow-ups, a question that officials for the state of Oregon and the penitentiary continued to grapple with for the next decade or so.

Officials at the Center for Human Radiobiology were analyzing the remains of plutonium injectees Arthur Hubbard, Fred Sours, and Albert Stevens in the spring of 1976 when Arthur Kranish, the editor and publisher of *Science Trends,* a Washington, D.C., newsletter covering technology and federal agencies, spotted something about the experiment in an official report. Kranish was astonished by the information and published a lengthy article about the experiment in February 1976. Officials of the Energy Research and Development Administration, the AEC's successor, refused to divulge the names of the patients or the experimenters, telling Kranish it wasn't even clear who ordered the experiment. Always eager to put the best spin on an admittedly bad situation, they also declared that the experiment suggested that plutonium might actually be "less carcinogenic" than expected.

Kranish's story was immediately picked up by the *Washington Post* and other newspapers. In the *Post* story, an unnamed official said the commission "has no plans to launch an investigation to try to learn more about the injection program." The official neglected to mention the extensive inquiry that had just been concluded or the exhumation program that was still ongoing. In a somewhat more frank interview with a Rochester *Democrat and Chronicle* reporter, William Bale, the scientist who "activated" the metabolic unit at the University of Rochester's Strong Memorial Hospital where the injections were carried out, said the test subjects "did not come voluntarily to the project." He added, "It is my impression they did not know they were being treated with plutonium."

As he lay dying of leukemia in a Veterans Administration hospital in Salt Lake City, Paul Cooper, a highly decorated Army officer, decided in the spring of 1977 to go public with his story about the atomic tests he participated in two decades earlier. In numerous interviews with print and broadcast reporters, Cooper said he was certain his disease was caused by radiation he received during Shot Smoky, the fifth of twenty-four nuclear detonations and six safety experiments conducted during the 1957 Operation Plumbbob series. "It was like getting too close to a campfire with tight Levis on," he said of the heat released by the bomb. Although he was lying flat on his back, Cooper still looked like a sandy-haired soldier who was merely resting. But soon after the wave of publicity the disease worsened and he banished his wife and children from the hospital because he didn't want them to see his wasted body.

Several soldiers who had also participated in Operation Plumbbob happened to see Cooper's interview on television. One was Charles Broudy, a retired Marine Corps major from California who was dying of lymphoma. Broudy was a highly decorated pilot with a deep loyalty to the Marine Corps. Nevertheless, he recognized immediately that Cooper was on to something. That evening he called Cooper in Salt Lake City. Cooper advised him to file a claim as soon as possible with the Veterans Administration.

Broudy followed Paul Cooper's advice, but his claim was denied by the VA. He appealed the denial, but before a decision was rendered, he died. "He was a very loyal Marine but I was not a happy Marine's wife," said his widow, Pat Broudy. The dying Marine had urged his wife to file a wrongful death lawsuit against the federal government. Eventually she filed two lawsuits. Both were dismissed, but her legal effort attracted the attention of thousands of veterans who had participated in the atomic maneuvers.

Broudy began making numerous television appearances with Orville Kelly, an Army sergeant who had witnessed some two dozen detonations and was suffering from lymphoma. When he was too weak to make any more television appearances, he returned home and formed the National Association of Atomic Veterans. Pat Broudy became a member of that group and also helped form the National Association of Radiation Survivors. For two decades she has been lobbying Congress for compensation for the atomic veterans and has helped many individual veterans with their claims.

Paul Cooper's story caught the attention of the Centers for Disease Control in Atlanta. Investigators there did an epidemiological study and discovered there was indeed an excess of leukemias among the participants of Operation Plumbbob. Cooper's story also prompted a remarkable hearing on Capitol Hill in 1978. For perhaps the first time in history, the civilian and military officials responsible for the nuclear weapons program were put on the defensive as congressmen Paul Rogers, a Democrat from Florida, and Tim Lee Carter, a Democrat from Kentucky and medical doctor whose son had died of leukemia, peppered them with questions about the atomic maneuvers. The congressmen also delved into the efforts by the weaponmakers to quash reports on excess cancer rates among nuclear workers and the dangerous effects of low-level radiation. The testimony from representatives of the Defense Nuclear Agency and its related organizations revealed how reckless and haphazard the testing program was. The officers didn't know what groups participated in the tests or where records were stored. After the committee had heard hours of testimony, U.S. Representative Henry Waxman, a Democrat from California, observed, "It seems the Army sent men out to be exposed to radiation dangers and did not advise them—if that was the case—that they were subjecting themselves to possible health hazards. Then afterward the Army denied any liability for it because it did not seem to fit into their plans."

A strong grassroots movement was triggered by the 1978 congressional hearing. Thousands of atomic veterans, or their widows and children, began demanding more information on the testing program. Nuclear workers and people who lived near weapons sites also became concerned about radioactive contaminants. The following year an accident occurred that dealt a severe blow to the civilian nuclear power industry and further encouraged antinuclear activists.

On March 28, 1979, the cooling system of one of the reactors at the Three Mile Island nuclear power plant in Harrisburg, Pennsylvania, malfunctioned. As radioactive gases spewed into the atmosphere, the governor ordered pregnant women and children living near the plant to leave. Utility officials worked frantically to dissipate a huge hydrogen bubble which had formed inside the reactor and threatened to explode. Although utility officials managed to bring the situation under control, the Three Mile Island incident provoked worldwide demonstrations against nuclear power. Coincidentally, just two weeks before the crisis developed, the movie *China Syndrome* had been released. The film, which starred Jane Fonda, Jack Lemmon, and Michael Douglas, revolved around efforts by utility executives to suppress news of an accident that almost resulted in a core meltdown at a fictional nuclear power plant near Los Angeles.

Not long after the Three Mile Island accident, Howard Rosenberg, a reporter working for muckraking columnist Jack Anderson, began digging into the total body irradiation studies at Oak Ridge. Using the Freedom of Information Act, he gathered hundreds of documents and wrote an investigative article about the experiment that was published in 1981 in *Mother Jones* magazine. "It took eighteen months before I wrote a word," he told a journalist.

Rosenberg's piece centered around a little boy named Dwayne Sexton who had leukemia and died in 1968. The child actually underwent two experimental treatments. The first was an unproven therapy in which bone marrow from the child was removed, irradiated to kill leukemia cells, and then reinjected in the mother. Two weeks later, serum from the mother was reinjected back into the child with the hope that antibodies built up in the mother's blood might kill the child's leukemia cells. The experiment failed and the child was soon given traditional chemotherapy drugs. He lived for another three years before he had a severe relapse. At a loss over what to do, Oak Ridge doctors irradiated him in METBI, the Medium Exposure Total Body Irradiator. He died less than a month later.

The *Mother Jones* article triggered a hearing before the House Subcommittee on Investigations and Oversight. Vice President Al Gore, then a young congressman from Tennessee, chaired the hearing and soon zeroed in on the key issue: "Now the critical question, again, around which this entire investigation revolves is were the treatments for the patients altered in order to satisfy or facilitate the acquisition of the data?"

Gore had pinpointed the conflict inherent in all the dual-purpose radiation experiments carried out during the Cold War. In other words, did the experiment benefit the patient or the agency that funded it? The ACE's Carroll Wilson had tried to address the conflict in 1947 when he instructed scientists that no radiation experiment should be carried out unless it held therapeutic promise for the patient. But Wilson's directive, as well as other established rules and ethical guidelines, had taken a backseat during the Cold War.

Gore questioned Clarence Lushbaugh about a statement in which he disclosed that the doses being given to cancer patients in the low-exposure chamber had no therapeutic value but were "radiobiologically of great interest." "It is a provocative quotation," Gore continued, "because at a time when NASA was becoming more interested in the smaller and smaller doses, a couple of patients were given smaller and smaller doses." Lushbaugh could not explain his remarks, but in a follow-up letter, he said the low doses were given to two patients to accommodate their schedules.

Although Gore's committee eventually issued an equivocal statement noting that the experiments were "satisfactory, but not perfect," the information that came out during the hearing was extremely damaging. The highly embarrassing internal reviews about the Oak Ridge hospital were put into the record, and NASA's involvement was fully documented.

In subsequent years various people around the country began delving into the human radiation experiments. In Cincinnati David Egilman, a medical doctor, and Geoffrey Sea, an activist, started looking into Saenger's project and other experiments on employees at a uranium production facility near Fernald, Ohio, that was given the misleading name of the Feed Materials Production Center during the Cold War. In Tennessee, Cliff Honicker, a young student working on his master's thesis, discovered a cache of extraordinary documents written by Stafford Warren. The file contained records on more than two dozen people, including Allan Kline, one of the victims of the 1946 Los Alamos criticality accident. The Atomic Energy Commission apparently had asked Warren, whose fear of lawsuits bordered on an obsession, how to proceed with the claims.

Honicker, Sea, and several other activists and union representatives then met with staff members of Richard Ottinger, a New York Democrat who in the spring of 1984 chaired the House Subcommittee on Energy Conservation and Power. Ottinger, a member of the subcommittee that had grilled the military representatives on the atomic maneuvers six years earlier, initiated an investigation into the human radiation experiments.

More than two years passed while subcommittee staffers collected information. Edward Markey, a Democrat from Massachusetts, became chairman of the subcommittee in January of 1985 and continued to press the DOE for documents. Finally, in November of 1986, the subcommittee released a report on thirty-one human radiation experiments involving nearly 700 people.

The plutonium injections were the first experiment described in the report. Also included was a brief description of the testicular irradiation studies, the cloud fly-through experiments, and numerous fallout studies. Although the experiments described in the Markey report represented only the tip of the iceberg, the report nevertheless represented the first time any comprehensive effort was made to examine the experiments. The study correctly noted that the government covered up the evidence of many of the studies from the victims or surviving kin and that informed consent often was not obtained. "Although these experiments did provide information on the retention and absorption of radioactive material by the human body, the experiments are nonetheless repugnant because human subjects were essentially used as guinea pigs and calibration devices."

Although Markey's report was explosive, it received only cursory media coverage. The wire services reduced it to a several-hundred-word report. Many of the major papers ran the story on their inside pages or not at all. The report had not identified any of the subjects, and without the ability to convert statistics into names and faces, the story seemed little more than a bizarre collection of events that had occurred in the distant past.

Markey urged the DOE to make every effort to find the experimental subjects and compensate them for damages. But his instructions were blatantly ignored by DOE officials who were confident that if they stonewalled long enough the controversy would blow over. Department of Energy officials not only knew who had conducted the experiments, but the names of some of the subjects. As of November 1986, they knew, for example, that Elmer Allen was still alive in Italy, Texas.

The other three long-term survivors had passed away the previous decade. Janet Stadt, who had not participated in the follow-up studies, died in a nursing home on November 22, 1975. She had metastatic cancer of the larynx as well as far-advanced scleroderma and had lived for nearly thirty years after she had been injected with plutonium.

Eda Schultz Charlton, the lonely housewife who had been misdiagnosed and injected with plutonium on a wintry day in 1945, lived for thirty-seven years with the radioactive material circulating in her body. She died on January 24, 1983, but the government's interest in her case continued. Two years after her death, Argonne officials were still trying to obtain X rays from her physician. "I explained how important these X-rays are to the study and he promised to see if he could have them sent to us on loan," wrote an Argonne official in an April 18, 1985 memo.

John Mousso died at home on April 6, 1984. Given a "terminal" prognosis by the Manhattan Project doctors, Mousso carried plutonium in his body for thirty-eight years and outlived his beloved wife, Rose. According to his death certificate, he died after suffering from a massive cerebral hemorrhage.

As for Elmer Allen, there was no pot of gold waiting for him, no government men who came to Italy in his waning years to try to make good. He lived almost another five years after the Markey committee published its findings. He spent some of his last days at Italy's nursing home, a quiet place shaded by a large cottonwood tree. There among the other aged residents, the cheerful nature of the amputee described by surgeons so many years earlier was still evident. "I knew he didn't want to be here, but he wasn't mean to us because he didn't want to be here. He tried to do quite a bit of stuff for himself," said Alithea Brown, a licensed vocational nurse at Italy's Convalescent Center. She added, "He wasn't a conversation starter. He would talk to you if you talked to him. I just never asked him how he lost his leg."

Elmer died on June 30, 1991, of respiratory failure caused by pneumonia. He was eighty years old. On his death certificate, his occupation was listed as Pullman porter.

Elmer Allen, John Mousso, and Eda Schultz Charlton had managed to outlive many of the experimenters. Stafford Warren, the architect of the injection study, was quieter than usual when a small group of friends gathered in his southern California home in the summer of 1981 to help him celebrate his eighty-fifth birthday. Five weeks later, after spending a few relaxing days at his mountain retreat, he told his second wife that he felt a little weary and wanted to take a nap instead of eating lunch. On the afternoon of July 26, he died in his sleep.

Shields Warren, who had replaced him when the AEC came into being, tended an oyster farm on his beloved Cape Cod after he retired. He, too, had died in his sleep, one year earlier, on July 1, 1980.

The

Reckoning

40

"WE'RE COMING CLEAN"

Hazel O'Leary looked every inch the establishment lawyer when she appeared for her confirmation hearing before a Senate committee in January of 1993. President Clinton had nominated her as his new energy secretary, but no one knew much about her except that she had been a utility executive at Northern States Power Company in Minneapolis, Minnesota, and had worked decades ago in the administrations of Presidents Ford and Carter. She was an African American, fifty-six years old, married three times, with a bachelor's degree from Fisk University and a law degree from Rutgers.

Sounding like a Republican, O'Leary emphasized her experience in both the private and public sector, pointing out how poorly crafted regulations could negatively impact jobs and the economy. In soothing corporate tones, she told the senators of her plans to integrate and balance the "Three Es"—energy, the environment, and the economy. "We've got to do it all," she said.

"Female and black, she was a walking advertisement for diversity, which Clinton made a very public priority," *Rolling Stone* magazine later wrote. "That, combined with the apparently last-minute, second-string quality of her selection, all but howled of tokenism."

As O'Leary spoke to the committee members, her long hands moved in graceful circles. She had light skin, and her face and neck were smooth and nearly free of wrinkles. Her language often slipped into corporatese but that habit was barely noticeable because of her ability to connect with audiences. Although she had no experience in the nuclear weapons field, which gobbled up 70 percent of the Department of Energy's budget, the committee was impressed by her presentation, and two days later she was confirmed by the full Senate. With her silvery wedge cut and silky designer suits, O'Leary didn't look like a revolutionary who would send shock waves through the Department of Energy's fossilized nuclear weapons establishment. But that's exactly what she did.

Born in 1937, a year when many of the great physicist-refugees from Europe were already at work in the American laboratories that would become part of the Manhattan Project, O'Leary was a member of the first generation of Americans who grew up with the knowledge that annihilation of the human race was possible. She was a child when two atomic bombs were dropped on Japan, a teenager when the first atmospheric detonation took place in Nevada, a young housewife entering Rutgers when atmospheric testing finally stopped.

But it wasn't the Cold War that shaped her political views. She was a black child raised in the South, and the most powerful influences on her life were segregation and the civil rights movement. Newport News, Virginia, the mosquito-infested city where she grew up, was a "thoroughly and severely segregated society" until the 1960s, novelist William Styron once said. "It was a world apart." There were separate birth announcements for whites and "Negroes" in the local newspapers, separate schools, churches, restaurants, and shops.

O'Leary was buffered from the harsh realities of segregation by her family's affluence and the vigilance of both her parents. Her father, a surgeon, chauffeured her and her sister to their after-school activities. Her stepmother, a schoolteacher, carefully planned shopping trips for them to "Overtown," the white business center in Newport News early in the day. "It was because in those days black women couldn't try clothes on. But we had this privilege as doctors' daughters. We could try them on during off hours—if nobody saw us," she told a journalist.

But with the special status came the burden of expectations. O'Leary would have to be a shining example of her race. "My parents taught me that if you were reverent, honorable, clean, well-educated and smelled good—for some reason smelling good has always been important to my [stepmother]—you could transcend any obstacle," she said in another interview.

With her appointment to President Clinton's cabinet, O'Leary had fulfilled everything anyone could have expected of her. But her work as energy secretary was just beginning. She soon learned that the agency she was charged with overseeing, the Department of Energy, was one of the most wasteful and distrusted bureaucracies in the federal govern-

ment. During its fifty years of operation, the weapons complex had manufactured tens of thousands of warheads and detonated more than one
thousand bombs. The U.S. Nuclear Weapons Cost Study Project, a four-
year research project directed by Stephen Schwartz, a guest scholar at
the Brookings Institution, estimated that the U.S. nuclear weapons program cost taxpayers some $5.5 trillion in 1996 dollars.

Although bomb makers recognized as far back as 1948 that disposal
of radioactive wastes presented the "gravest of problems," they focused
only on the arms race against the Soviet Union and passed the daunting
and unglamorous task of cleanup to future generations. By the mid-
1990s, many facilities in the weapons complex had been shut down
because of health and safety dangers. Plutonium, uranium, and other
fission products had leaked into the groundwater and soil surrounding
the plants and laboratories. A paper prepared by the DOE summarized
the problems that existed at the beginning of O'Leary's tenure:

> . . . the inheritance of 1993 was a work force committed to
> maintaining a nuclear deterrent capability that did not take into
> account the Cold War had ended; programs devoid of focus on
> the challenges and opportunities presented by the global market-
> place; years of a command and control management style; a
> monumental Cold War legacy of nuclear waste and environmen-
> tal degradation at the former weapons sites; secrecy that acted as
> a cloak to evade accountability to the American public; and a
> deteriorating environment reflected in part by a global warming
> that threatened the nation's health, its environment and its econ-
> omy.

The elaborate efforts by the DOE's predecessors to protect the
agency's prestige and avoid public relations debacles had backfired with a
vengeance. The credibility gap opened in the mid-1950s when serious
concerns were first raised about the effects of fallout from atmospheric
testing. Scandal after scandal ripped through the nuclear weapons complex. The defensive strategy was almost always the same: Deny the
charges, classify the data, and destroy the reputation of the accuser. The
modus operandus was developed by the veterans of the Manhattan Project and handed down from bureaucrat to bureaucrat in each of its successor agencies: the Atomic Energy Commission, the Energy Research
and Development Administration, and, finally, the Department of
Energy.

O'Leary, the first woman and the first African American to serve as energy secretary, waded fearlessly into the department's macho world of nuclear weapons, a rarefied domain in which only a handful of women had succeeded in penetrating the uppermost ranks in fifty years. She was a striking contrast to her predecessor, Admiral James B. Watkins. She swore prodigiously, sweated in a noontime aerobics class, and was seen around headquarters from time to time in pink Lycra pants. A quick study, O'Leary had the ability to zero in on key issues during staff meetings. She was also imperious, egotistical, and sometimes difficult to get along with. "She could cut your legs off and you wouldn't even know it until you walked out of the room," said one staffer.

Just a few months after her swearing-in, O'Leary was asked to sign off on a document that would have given the green light for an additional fifteen underground detonations at the Nevada Test Site. Even though atmospheric testing had stopped in the 1960s, underground explosions had continued for the next three decades. In all, some 1,030 nuclear weapons had been exploded either above or below the ground. The last underground bomb, Divider, was detonated on September 23, 1992, just four months before O'Leary arrived.

O'Leary was hesitant to approve the tests and went to the Joint Chiefs of Staff to find out if they were necessary. "She had the courage, as I understand it, to go down to the Pentagon, to essentially go to the Joint Chiefs and say, 'Hey, why should we do this?'" Ray Kidder, a retired nuclear weapons designer from Lawrence Livermore National Laboratory, recalled. O'Leary then summoned the directors of the nation's weapons labs and several outside arms control experts to Washington for a top-secret meeting on May 18 and May 19, 1993. The meeting was held in a tomblike room known as a SCIF, or Sensitive Compartmented Information Facility, located in the basement of the DOE headquarters. There, in the windowless, carpeted room that radio transmissions could not penetrate or escape, the weapons experts gave their opinions. "I'd characterize it as a Quaker meeting in the sense there was lots of time," said Frank von Hippel, a respected physicist from Princeton University who attended.

Following the meeting, O'Leary and her staff concluded the tests weren't needed. When she recommended they be canceled, President Clinton agreed with her and announced the indefinite extension of the testing moratorium on July 4, 1993. Although the bomb builders now knew that this energy secretary was different from any who had ever occupied the seventh-floor suite of DOE's headquarters in downtown

Washington, the public would not have occasion to find out for another few months.

The test ban victory notwithstanding, O'Leary recognized that if she was going to succeed in making any permanent, long-term reforms, she would have to begin by reversing the "culture of secrecy" that had been created by the Manhattan Project. That meant, among other things, declassifying documents and revising the long-standing practice of compartmentalization—the old idea promulgated by General Leslie Groves that workers should know only what they need to know to do their jobs and nothing more. Groves's policy was beginning to backfire. As Jim Werner, director of strategic planning and analysis in DOE's Environmental Management Office, put it, "The way secrecy works is you have to compartmentalize so that people know what they need to know and nothing more. When trying to clean up a nuclear weapons site, that's just not very helpful."

After five decades of indoctrination, though, the culture of secrecy was an integral part of the department, like the recycled air that streamed through vents at its headquarters in downtown Washington or its ancillary headquarters in Germantown, Maryland, which was built in the mid-1950s to ensure that the important functions of the AEC would continue even if the Capitol was flattened by an atomic attack.

Wanting to let some fresh air in, O'Leary made both sites more accessible to the public. She disarmed the security guards who stood at the entrance to the buildings, giving them billy clubs instead of guns. She also eliminated the requirement that they escort visitors to their destinations and to the bathroom (a policy that is still in place at other DOE facilities and at the nation's weapons labs). The glass doors in the hallway leading to her suite were thrown open, the security officer who guarded the corridor was clothed in a dark business suit instead of a uniform, and benign images of windmills and other renewable energy sources replaced the doomsday photos that once lined the walls leading to the inner sanctum. As a sign of her intentions, O'Leary also changed the name of the Office of Classification to the Office of Declassification and instructed A. Bryan Siebert, the director, to develop a plan for making more documents available to the public. Siebert readily embraced O'Leary's orders: "I have been in the program for twenty to thirty years and it has been clear to me that classification has been used against the public time and again. I thought it was wrong," he said.

Siebert spearheaded the effort to declassify and review some 3 million documents. The declassification effort was greeted with resistance, even outright hostility, by some of DOE's entrenched bureaucrats. Some viewed it as a threat to national security; others as a threat to themselves. "They acted as if something personally were being taken away from them," Siebert recalled. When Siebert and his team of reviewers began examining the files, they discovered a vast amount of information that could be released to the public without threatening national security or divulging important nuclear data. Page by page, DOE's declassification experts began poring over the documents, making sure the records earmarked for release contained no information that could help anyone build a bomb. As the months passed, the pile grew.

On December 7, 1993, almost a year after she had been named energy secretary, O'Leary invited reporters to a press conference in the auditorium of the DOE headquarters. On the podium behind her was the first stack of newly declassified documents. It was the first of several "Openness Initiative" press conferences held by O'Leary, and it catapulted her from a relatively obscure member of President Clinton's cabinet into one of the highest-profile figures of his first administration.

With a bank of cameras pointing at her on that cold December morning, O'Leary made a conscious effort to break with her predecessors, a line of steely-eyed patriots that stretched back to Leslie Groves. "We were shrouded and clouded in an atmosphere of secrecy. I would even take it a step further and call it repression," she began.

Trim and confident looking, O'Leary paced back and forth across the stage, pausing occasionally to put up a transparency on an overhead projector to emphasize a point she was making. "The Cold War is over . . . we're coming clean," the first transparency announced. In the space of an hour or so, O'Leary disclosed many of the secrets that the DOE's predecessors had struggled to keep under wraps for decades. Among them were the following: Weapons scientists had exploded 204 more nuclear bombs, or 20 percent more weapons, than the figure previously made public; nearly three-quarters of a million pounds of mercury—the equivalent of some 11 billion thermometers—had been dumped into a creek in Oak Ridge; the United States had manufactured eighty-nine tons of plutonium during the Cold War. Many tons of the highly radioactive material were stored at various research sites across the country, including Hanford, Los Alamos, and Argonne—just thirty miles from downtown Chicago.

Toward the end of the press conference, O'Leary paused and then put one of her last remaining transparencies on the overhead screen. In bold letters, it read, "The Human Radiation Experiments." The department, she admitted, had conducted several hundred radiation experiments on American citizens, including one in which eighteen people were injected with plutonium. O'Leary said she was shocked and appalled by the experiments and had hired an ethicist to look into them. "What I've read," she said of the plutonium injections, "leads me to believe that by the standards of today informed consent could not have taken place." O'Leary said she had hoped to release the names of the plutonium patients but had been advised against it by the department's attorneys. "I'm attempting not to be sensational, but to balance the needs of the families with the public's desire to know more."

The acknowledgment of the radiation experiments was an astounding mea culpa for a high government official and certainly underscored the department's new commitment to openness. The only hitch was that O'Leary's admission wasn't entirely voluntary. Her comments were prompted by the forty-five-page series the *Albuquerque Tribune* had published on the plutonium injections three weeks earlier. Nevertheless, her acknowledgment was a historic break with her predecessors. She was the leader of the department that in earlier incarnations had carried out the injections and had covered them up. O'Leary had not only confirmed that the federal government had sponsored these experiments, she had gone a step further and admitted that she found them appalling. Her reaction was exactly the same as my own, six years earlier, when I first stumbled across the footnote describing the injections.

From a darkened room at DOE's regional office in Albuquerque, I watched O'Leary's press conference by satellite. I had driven over to their office to see the briefing after hearing rumors that she might discuss the experiments. Sitting at the long table with me were a handful of DOE employees and a reporter for the competing newspaper. With each new graphic O'Leary put up on the overhead screen, the bureaucrats' scowls seemed to deepen.

Although O'Leary portrayed the DOE as a revitalized department committed to openness and trust, the government employees I was dealing with still seemed to be part of the same old Cold War machine. My work on the plutonium experiment had begun long before O'Leary arrived, but the newspaper's intense legal battle to obtain records occurred during her first ten months on the job. The DOE had steadfastly refused to provide the names of the patients, even though they were all dead and had no privacy rights.

While the legal skirmishes were going on, I followed the paper trail, hoping to uncover the identities of the patients on my own. After finding the footnote in 1987, it had taken me five years to uncover the identity of Elmer Allen. But when I returned to the story full-time in the spring and summer of 1993, I was able to find four other patients in quick succession by using the same kinds of clues that had helped me find Elmer.

The second patient I found was Albert Stevens, CAL-1, the California housepainter injected in California. The document that helped me unravel his identity came from history professor Barton Bernstein, whom I had met during my 1991–92 journalism fellowship at Stanford University. Bernstein just happened to be one of the few historians in the country who knew something about Joseph Hamilton and Robert Stone and their human experiments at Berkeley. I called him one afternoon and we talked at length about the two scientists. A couple of weeks later I received an unsolicited document in the mail from him. It was a copy of the July 7, 1945, letter that Hamilton wrote to Stone asking him whether he could pay CAL-1 fifty dollars a month to keep him in the Berkeley area.

The letter contained three clues: It identified the subject as a "Mr. Stephens," disclosed that he was a housepainter, and that he owned property in 1945 in Healdsburg, California. But how was I to find a man with such a common last name who had owned property in a small town fifty years ago? On a whim, I contacted a local museum in Healdsburg to find out what historical records were available. An official there suggested that I call a genealogist named Lorlei Metke. I left a message on Metke's answering machine, doubting that she would call me back or even be able to help me.

Late one Friday evening, as I was locking the door to the press room, the phone rang. It was Lorlei Metke. When I explained what I was looking for, she responded crisply, "I'll see what I can do." Metke proved to be an indefatigable and resourceful researcher. She plowed through city directories, phone books, marriage records, death records, voting records, and finally consulted some of her old friends.

She discovered there was indeed a housepainter who lived in Healdsburg in 1945. But his name was Albert *Stevens*, not *Stephens*. She also tracked down the whereabouts of Albert's two children. His son, Thomas, was retired and living in Michigan, and his daughter, Evelyn, was still living in California. Metke was convinced Joseph Hamilton had misspelled the name of the man he had injected with plutonium. I hoped she was right but needed further corroboration.

One of my first calls was to Albert's son, Thomas, who is now deceased. Briefly I described the plutonium experiment and explained why I thought his father might have been one of the subjects. Thomas was startled by the news, but offered to help me in any way he could. He confirmed that his father did undergo a serious stomach operation in San Francisco in 1945. He also remembered that following the procedure, his father kept urine and stool samples in the shed behind his house for some people who came up from Berkeley. And Thomas recalled one more strange thing. In the early 1970s, he said, he had received a phone call from someone inquiring about Albert's cremated remains. He couldn't remember much more about the inquiry or what happened after that.

Thomas's recollections dovetailed closely with what I knew about CAL-1. But I still needed further proof that Albert Stevens and "Mr. Stephens" were one and the same person. I ordered a copy of Albert Stevens's death certificate by mail from the state of California. When it arrived, the certificate indicated that Albert had been cremated by the Chapel of the Chimes in Santa Rosa, California. Thinking back to the mysterious phone call Thomas had received, I called the funeral home one afternoon and asked the woman who answered the telephone if Mr. Stevens's cremated remains were still there. She put me on hold while she looked up the records. When she returned to the telephone, she said, They're gone. Where? I asked her. They were shipped to Argonne National Laboratory in 1975, she responded.

I thanked her and slowly put down the receiver. Then I got up and walked around the newsroom several times to give myself a few moments to absorb what I had heard. Why would a national laboratory want the ashes of a California housepainter? It could only be because the plutonium they wanted to measure was still in those ashes. The pieces had fallen into place. Eventually I received a copy of the official permit releasing Albert's remains to Argonne. At last I had incontrovertible, written proof that "Mr. Stephens" and Albert Stevens were indeed the same person.

As the story progressed, I kept in touch with Thomas Stevens. The surprise that he initially felt upon hearing that his father had been injected with plutonium had begun to turn into indignation—a reaction experienced by many relatives of the plutonium patients. "It's inconceivable that anything like this could have occurred. You think of something like this happening in other countries," he said during one interview.

Gradually our conversation turned to Albert himself. One of

Thomas's most vivid memories was the intoxicating year the family made their way from Ohio to California in the cramped Model-T. They had pitched their nine-by-twelve-foot tent in the snows of Colorado and under the shade of New Mexico's cottonwood trees. Thomas sent me a photograph of his father that had been taken on the road. He is standing in the middle of the desert with his hands on his hips and smiling as if he owns the mountain behind him. Although he is miles from civilization, he is dressed like a gentleman, wearing a white shirt and tie beneath his old-fashioned driving suit.

While I was trying to obtain more information on Elmer Allen and Albert Stevens, documents began trickling in from the DOE in response to the newspaper's Freedom of Information Act request. Clues in those documents helped me uncover the identity of several more patients. One was Eda Schultz Charlton, HP-3, the misdiagnosed housewife.

One afternoon I received a thick manila envelope of documents from the Energy Department. My response to these packages was nearly always the same: a sense of anticipation followed by sharp disappointment as I skimmed the contents and realized the envelope contained mostly duplicate and triplicate copies of scientific reports and press releases that I already had. This thick package promised to be no different. Nevertheless, I took it home that night and dumped the contents onto the floor of my living room. Carefully I sorted through the papers. Mixed in with the official reports were a few records I hadn't seen before. Perhaps something on one of those papers—a word or a phrase—might yield information that would lead to more names. I examined each page carefully, looking at the dates, signatures, even the declassification stamps. From the stack, I pulled out one document. It was an unsigned and undated note on which the following words were scrawled: "Charlton—died 198?"

My mind immediately leapt to the two unidentified Rochester patients, a man and a woman, who had participated in the follow-up studies and died in the 1980s. Could "Charlton" be the last name of one of those patients? From my reporting, I knew that Christine Waterhouse had cared for those two patients. She was retired and living in Maine and I had spoken to her on the phone several times. Although she was pleasant enough, she couldn't remember much about the study. "This was war," she said during one of our first interviews. "There were a lot of things condoned for the good of the many."

I put the scrap of paper in my notepad and went to bed. When I arrived in the newsroom the following morning, I dialed Christine Water-house's number again. Was "Charlton" the name of one of your patients, I asked her, slowing spelling out the last name.

"Edith Charlton. That's the first time I remembered it. Edith Charl-ton. Now that you bring that up, I do remember her better. I did take care of her for a long time, too." Of course, her first name was Eda, not Edith. Although Waterhouse said she didn't think Eda had any close relatives, I began calling funeral homes in Canandaigua, New York, where Eda had died. If she did have any relatives, the funeral home that handled her burial arrangements would have their names. From one of those funeral homes, I eventually discovered that she indeed had a son, Luther Fred Schultz, and that he was living in Geneva, New York.

Soon I was talking on the telephone with Fred and his wife, Helen. In a matter-of-fact voice, Helen volunteered in the first few minutes of our conversation that her mother-in-law had once told her that she had been injected with plutonium. "We didn't know what to think about that," Helen said. Although the comment clearly indicated that Eda had been informed of the plutonium injection at some point in her life, Helen said that her mother-in-law really didn't understand what pluto-nium was or what it meant to her health. "She couldn't understand why they were always checking her for radiation and why she was having to go in and stay in the hospital and be on a special diet and have her speci-mens collected and all that."

Eventually I met Fred and Helen during one of two research trips to upstate New York. They were a lovely, trusting couple who welcomed me into their home. Both are now dead. As Eda grew older, Helen often prepared soups and stews for her mother-in-law and drove her to her doctor's appointments at Christine Waterhouse's office.

During Eda's final days in the nursing home, when senility was mov-ing across her mind like an eraser and bananas had become her chief delight, Helen put together a photograph album of Eda's life, hoping the images would lessen her mental confusion. As I sat on their couch, Helen pulled the thick photo album down from a shelf and placed it in my lap. Suddenly the life story of Eda, HP-3 as she was referred to in all the study documents, opened before me—the shy, pensive daughter, the young wife, the mother, and finally the grandmother, an old woman struggling to corral the fleeing memories.

Dr. Waterhouse herself volunteered the identity of the other Roches-ter patient during one of our conversations. His name was John Mousso.

"I took care of him for a long time. I can even visualize him," she said. Waterhouse said she had no idea where Mousso lived or if he had any children.

I enlisted the aid of a second genealogist, named Richard Halsey, to help me in that search. He was an easygoing man of forty-three who worked on the shipping docks at Kodak and had been doing genealogy research as a hobby for nearly twenty years. Halsey sent me a list of all the Moussos in the Rochester telephone book. Slowly, I began working my way down the list.

Late one evening I reached Jerry Mousso, a retired school administrator in Rochester. When I explained who I was looking for, he said, "You know, that sounds a lot like my uncle."

Jerry gave me the name and telephone number of his uncle's son, Robert Mousso, who lives in a small town outside Rochester (and wasn't on my list). When I contacted Robert, he confirmed that Waterhouse was indeed his father's physician and that his father suffered from Addison's disease. The fact that he had the same doctor and suffered from the same disease as HP-6 convinced me I'd found the right John Mousso.

Robert talked at length about his father and about the severe hardship the family had endured as a result of his long illness. "Before he was sick, he was always working. When he was sick, he was always in hospitals." After his mother died, Robert drew closer to his father. One summer he put in a garden for him. On warm summer nights, with the water running on the vegetable plants, they would sit on apple crates and talk. The elder Mousso often reminisced about his youth, the time before the sickness set in. He came from a tribe of French Canadians who had worked in the Adirondacks as miners and lumberjacks and then moved to East Rochester in the early 1920s to work in the "carshops," the railroad yards where refrigerator cars were built.

I sent Robert some documents about the experiment. A few days later I called him again and asked him what he thought of it. "It's unbelievable. It's unbelievable. It's here in black and white, but I say to myself, my God, where is the humanity to do something like that?" Robert was disturbed by the information but subsequently decided that he didn't want to cooperate further in the story. "He's gone. It happened years ago. I want my father to have his privacy."

But John Mousso's nephew, Jerry Mousso, disagreed. "I just have a gut feeling my uncle would want to fight this. This guy was a fighter. He had a lot of self-respect and I think he would be indignant, just like I'm indignant." Jerry Mousso subsequently became deeply involved in the controversy, testifying before Congress and acting as a spokesman for the Rochester families.

I uncovered the identity of a fifth patient, Fred Sours, HP-9, the politician from Gates, New York, with another document that we had received under the Freedom of Information Act. That document was a summary memo containing statistical data on the eighteen patients. Included were the exhumation dates of three of the patients. Although the document did not disclose where the exhumations had taken place, I figured at least one may have occurred in Rochester, since that's where most of the injectees lived.

I got a list of the largest cemeteries in Rochester from genealogist Richard Halsey and began another round of phone calls. Using the exhumation dates together with the birth and death dates, I thought I might be able to work backward and find the names of the patients. Exhumations, after all, aren't everyday affairs. But most of the cemetery officials I contacted said they couldn't help me without a name. Rochester's Holy Sepulchre Cemetery was the last number on my list. I dialed the cemetery halfheartedly and for the umpteenth time explained to the employee who answered the phone, John Moore, what I was looking for. Instead of giving me the usual negative response, Moore sounded interested. He put me on hold while he looked up some records. Then he came back on the line and said, "Yup, we got one."

Moore had found a person buried in Holy Sepulchre Cemetery who had the same birth date, death date, and exhumation date as one of the plutonium patients I was looking for. But the clincher came when he told me the remains of the man had been shipped to Argonne National Laboratory.

What's his name? I asked, trying to tamp down the excitement in my voice.

Fred C. Sours, he responded.

Richard Halsey retrieved an obituary of Sours from the microfilm archives of a Rochester newspaper. Sours had no children, and I was unable to locate any living relatives. His life would have to be reconstructed from official records only. (Some relatives eventually were found after my series was published.)

Halsey also went through reel after reel of microfilmed newspaper obituaries at the Rochester public library, hoping to find some of the unidentified plutonium patients by matching their birth and death dates with the published notices. I soon learned that obituaries are often inaccurate and that not everybody who dies has one. Halsey came up with some promising names, but none of them panned out. We had reached a dead end as far as obits went.

In the meantime, several of the families gave me permission to obtain the medical records of their relatives. From the San Francisco hospital, I received copies of Albert Stevens's records and Elmer Allen's records. Albert's records did not say anything about the plutonium injection, but Elmer's contained the so-called consent form written so many years earlier by Bertram V. A. Low-Beer. From Strong Memorial Hospital in Rochester I obtained more than 300 pages of records describing Eda's medical history dating back to 1945. The word "plutonium" was not mentioned anywhere.

Following other leads, I tracked down John Abbotts, a former staffer for congressman Edward Markey, who located a copy of the 1974 AEC report describing the internal investigation into the plutonium experiment and sent it to me. The report, which was stamped "Official Use Only," was difficult to follow because the DOE had deleted the names of the scientists and the names of the patients. Nevertheless, it provided many important details about both the original injections and the follow-up study. I also interviewed Christine Waterhouse, Patricia Durbin, and Hymer Friedell on numerous occasions and talked with Argonne scientist Robert Rowland and others involved in the follow-up study. Although the DOE refused to confirm the names of any of the patients or even that the experiment had taken place, the documentation was solid, and we decided to publish what we had.

As the series was being edited, I went over again and again in my mind the documentary evidence proving that CAL-1 was Albert Stevens; CAL-3, Elmer Allen; HP-3, Eda Schultz Charlton; HP-6, John Mousso; and HP-9, Fred Sours. I was sure these people were five of the plutonium patients, but without official DOE confirmation, it was impossible to be 100 percent certain.

So it was with considerable apprehension that I watched that morning as Hazel O'Leary placed one transparency after another on the overhead screen. When she mentioned the plutonium experiment at the end of the press conference, my pen stopped moving. For one brief moment, I thought she was going to deny what the newspaper had printed and was grateful for the darkened room. Instead she said she was disturbed by the experiments and that the department was looking into them. Numb with relief, I resumed my note taking. With the help of Karen MacPherson, the newspaper's Washington correspondent who had attended the press conference, we got a story on the front page two hours later.

O'Leary told me in an interview in 1997 just days before she stepped down as energy secretary that the question of whether the radiation experiments should be discussed at the press conference was a matter of "hot debate" within the department for a brief period. "I came pretty quickly to the decision that we had to go with it and it was just good common sense."

Although O'Leary had touched on many issues at the press conference, the national media focused on disclosures about the human radiation experiments. It was the first time any sustained attention had been given to the experiments. Within days of her admission, the Department of Energy was deluged with inquiries. A hot line was established as thousands of calls poured in. A staff of three telephone operators mushroomed to a staff of thirty-six. The hot line "overloaded" by 10,000 attempted calls in one day, according to one press release. Through January 4 of 1994, it was receiving 6,000 to 10,000 calls a day. Many callers never got past the busy signal.

O'Leary conceded on a CNN program that individuals who had been harmed by the radiation experiments might be entitled to compensation, an admission that led to even more frenzied news coverage and worried some officials at the White House. "There was this four-day period where the middle-level minions in the White House were tearing me apart because they weren't sure whether the news would turn out to be positive or negative," O'Leary remembered. "In the midst of all that, I got a call from the president of the United States saying, 'I think you're doing just the right thing. Keep on doing it.'"

41

REVELATIONS AND TRIBULATIONS

On November 30, 1993, Eugene Saenger was awarded the Gold Medal, the highest honor given out by the Radiological Society of North America. He thought the TBI controversy, a musty scandal more than two decades old, had finally been put to rest. "It was the trial of my life," he would later tell the *Cincinnati Enquirer*.

Just a week after he received the award, when Energy Secretary Hazel O'Leary confirmed that Cold War scientists had used American citizens as guinea pigs, Saenger found himself back on trial. Martha Stephens, the young faculty member who nearly twenty-five years earlier had helped write the scathing indictment of Saenger's experiment, was determined not to let the story fade away this time. She went down to her basement, retrieved the old reports, and gave them to reporters. In early 1994, the *Cincinnati Post* published a lengthy article about the experiment. More comprehensive than anything written in the 1970s, the story stirred up a frenzied wave of publicity.

Stephens and a graduate student identified nearly twenty patients by cross-referencing statistics in the Department of Defense documents with other publicly available records. The city's two newspapers unraveled the identities of other test subjects, while still other relatives of deceased patients came forward on their own after reading or listening to news reports.

With names, the faceless, hopelessly ill cancer patients suddenly became flesh and blood: They were mothers, fathers, grandparents, aunts, and uncles. Day after day the sorrowing relatives appeared on television or in the newspaper recalling their loved ones' last miserable weeks. Family members alleged the doctors killed their relatives or, at the very least, shortened their lives and increased their suffering.

It was a public relations nightmare for the University of Cincinnati. A hot line set up by the medical center initially logged some 500 callers. There were rumblings of a criminal probe. The university's Board of Trustees held a special meeting to address the issue in early 1994, and two weeks later, 5,000 pages of documents, some quite damaging, were released by UC president Joseph Steger.

With publicity at a fever pitch, a congressional field hearing was held in Cincinnati on April 11, 1994. The federal courtroom was packed with community leaders and public officials. Many of the relatives of the cancer patients couldn't get in and were forced to listen to the testimony on a speaker that had been hurriedly placed in a hallway. After the Department of Defense, the doctors, and the families had testified, Eugene Saenger rose from the audience and took a seat alone at the witness table. He was then seventy-seven years old, erect and confident, and recovering from bladder cancer. A murmur went up from the crowd.

If the relatives had come to hear a plea for forgiveness, a few words of regret, they were to be sorely disappointed. Saenger stuck to the same remarks he had made more than twenty years earlier; he said the patients were gravely ill and the purpose of the TBI treatment was to relieve pain, shrink the tumors, and improve their well-being. He also retracted his statement made in the 1973 paper that eight of the patients may have died from radiation. "We have looked at these charts recently and find the course of these patients—the downhill course of these patients to have been due to cancer."

Sitting at the witness table, a manila folder opened in front of him, Saenger was still the military consultant who believed the world was on the brink of nuclear war. "Our work," he told the congressmen, "has contributed significantly to the better treatment of patients with far advanced cancer and to our better understanding of the effect of radiation on humans in a time when nuclear warfare once again seems possible." But one of his most inadvertently revealing comments came later, in an interview with staffers from President Clinton's Advisory Committee, when Saenger admitted he didn't know whether he would have proceeded with the experiment if he had not secured the DOD funding.

"Would you have done it [the total body irradiation experiment] if you hadn't gotten the DOD funding, or could you have?" asked staffer Gary Stern.

"I think we certainly could have. What we would have done, I don't know," Saenger responded.

The families eventually filed a class-action lawsuit in federal court. Although the obstacles were daunting, U.S. District Judge Sandra Beckwith, a Republican appointed to the federal bench in 1992 by President George Bush, issued an early ruling favorable to the plaintiffs. Beckwith said she found it "inconceivable" that the doctors "when allegedly planning to perform radiation experiments on unwitting subjects, were not moved to pause or rethink their procedures in light of the forceful dictates of the Nuremberg Tribunal." She added, "The Nuremberg Code is part of the law of humanity. It may be applied in both civil and criminal cases by the federal courts in the United States."

In Massachusetts, Sandra Marlow's ears perked up when she heard the Department of Energy was going to come clean on the human radiation experiments. After her father died in 1977 of a rare form of leukemia, she had begun delving into the atmospheric testing program in her spare time. Her father had been an Air Force colonel and had been exposed to radiation during a training course on one of the contaminated Operation Crossroads ships towed back to California and as a participant in the 1955 Operation Teapot.

When Secretary O'Leary made her announcement, Marlow just happened to be working as a librarian at the Walter E. Fernald State School in Waltham, Massachusetts—the institution where the boys had eaten the radioactive oatmeal decades' earlier. While organizing the library's historical collection, she had come across numerous yellowing reprints describing the radioactive iron and calcium experiments. Some of the studies, she noticed, were funded by the Atomic Energy Commission. Why was the AEC, she wondered, sponsoring radiation research at a state institution for the mentally retarded? A few days after O'Leary's announcement, Marlow and one of her friends, Dan Bernstein, a lawyer for the Center for Atomic Radiation Studies in Brookline, Massachusetts, tipped off the *Boston Globe* to the studies.

When the newspaper published an account of the experiment on December 26, 1993, the article touched off a furor. Some of the Science Club members, such as Gordon Shattuck, learned about the experiment when they were contacted by reporters. Others "self-identified" themselves after reading or listening to news reports about the experiments. The memories of the long-forgotten injustices—the mattress springs, the rope rubbing, the back-breaking farm labor—came flooding back, along with the stinging knowledge that the state officials charged to protect them had used them as test subjects. The institution, Shattuck said bitterly, used the boys as "guinea pigs and farm rats."

Less than three weeks after the article appeared, Senator Edward Kennedy and Representative Edward Markey were conducting a field hearing at Fernald. Markey was outraged that the experiment had not been disclosed when he was conducting his investigation. "I fear that past human radiation experimentation may prove much wider than we found in 1986," he said.

Austin LaRocque and Charles Dyer, two of the men who had been subjected to the experiments during their boyhood days at Fernald, testified at the hearing. A. Bertrand Brill, the scientist who had helped analyze the doses that the Vanderbilt children had received in the womb, represented the scientific point of view. As Markey tried to pin down Brill, Austin LaRocque turned to Senator Kennedy and said, "Can I ask one question please?"

"Sure," responded Kennedy.

"To this gentlemen here," LaRocque said, nodding at Brill. "If you had your son here, would you have allowed this to happen, knowing what you know about radiation?"

"Well, I have, you know, many of us in medicine, when we are investigating new phenomena will take radioactive tracers and study ourselves. I've done it so many times," Brill responded.

LaRocque pressed on, going straight to the heart of the matter. "But you didn't answer my question directly. I want to know, if it was your son, would you have accepted it?"

The audience suddenly erupted in applause, nearly drowning out Brill's response. "Knowing what I know now, I would," he said. "But at that time, I don't know . . ."

The Massachusetts Department of Mental Retardation assembled the Task Force on Human Subject Research to investigate the experiments. Following a four-month inquiry, the task force found the studies violated the "fundamental human rights" of the patients. The parents were not adequately informed, and the Science Club constituted a "potentially coercive factor" in getting the children to cooperate.

The task force also concluded that the doses were too small to produce "significant health effects." But many of the former Fernald residents don't believe the experiments were harmless. They have lost their teeth. They have lumps, cysts, deteriorating disks, and prostate problems, and they don't know if the ailments are related to aging, radiation, or both.

"They bribed us by offering us special privileges, knowing that we had so little that we would do practically anything for attention," Fred Boyce, one of Fernald's former residents, said at a hearing in Washington, D.C. "It was cruel and unusual punishment in the name of science. Keep in mind, we didn't commit any crimes. We were just seven-year-old orphans."

While they were making dinner, driving their cars, or watching TV during the Christmas season of 1993, the women who attended Vanderbilt University's prenatal clinic listened in astonishment to news reports about an experiment that had been conducted there after the war. As in Cincinnati, a media frenzy had erupted in Nashville when a reporter for the *Nashville Tennessean* wrote a story about the Vanderbilt study. So much time had elapsed. The mothers had lived through births, deaths, divorces. They were grandmothers with gray hair and long lives etched into their faces and bore little resemblance to the young women who obligingly drank the cocktails the doctors handed them.

They sifted through their memories. The dates fit. But the thought that Vanderbilt would do something like that didn't. The idea challenged their sense of orderliness, the way the world had operated for fifty years. When Helen Hutchison heard the news, she told her daughter, "Vanderbilt couldn't do anything like that. I just don't believe anything like that happened. They wouldn't do that to us."

Vanderbilt found several boxes of records on the experiment in a remote warehouse. With those records, the university was able to identify approximately 240 of the 829 women given radioactive iron.

Helen Hutchison was one of them. In March of 1994, she received records confirming that she had been given 4.16 milligrams of radioactive iron on July 25, 1946. "It's unthinkable," she said. "To take something that powerful and that unknown and test it on women, it's beyond comprehension."

Vanderbilt began aggressively defending itself against charges that the experiment was unethical and unsafe. "While it would not be acceptable today to give radioactive isotopes to pregnant women, it is also clear that this was carefully evaluated at the time, and there was a feeling then it was safe," Joseph C. Ross, Vanderbilt's associate vice chancellor for health affairs, told the *New York Times*. "We want to be as helpful as we can, but to create the feeling that we've done something wrong, we don't want to do that."

Vanderbilt University officials enlisted the aid of scientists and statisticians to refute its own report, which found cancers in the children exposed in utero to the radioactive iron. Henry N. Wagner, a professor of medicine and radiology at Johns Hopkins University School of Medicine, said Ruth Hagstrom's study was riddled with errors. Her conclusion that three of the malignancies constituted a statistically significant increase was "totally unwarranted by the data," he claimed in a court affidavit.

Hagstrom agreed with her critics and downplayed the cancer deaths. But when the publicity had subsided and I asked her in a telephone interview two years later whether she personally believed the radioactive iron caused the malignancies, she responded, "I don't know. We don't know any better now than we knew then. I mean, the data's just not there. All we can say is what's in the paper."

Scientists in Oak Ridge reanalyzed the Vanderbilt data and came up with "a few tens of millirads" for the total fetal doses. These were the lowest exposures ever assigned to the unborn infants and many times lower than what the original experimenter Paul Hahn had estimated. The Oak Ridge scientists conceded that it would "never be absolutely determined" whether the malignancies in the Vanderbilt infants were caused by radiation exposure, but they added that most experts believed that fetal abnormalities occur when the doses are much higher.

The Oak Ridge analysis drew strong criticism from Roland Finston, a retired Stanford University health physicist and an expert witness hired by attorneys representing the mothers. Finston, who had helped me calculate the radiation doses to the plutonium patients, contended the malignancies found among the children present a "convincing profile" of cancers that might be expected from in-utero exposure to radioactive iron. "All of these cancers are either known to be radiogenic, or are closely associated with the hematopoetic and lymphatic systems where radioiron would be expected to have its effects. We can also be sure that the Vanderbilt experiment has already resulted, or will inevitably result in the future, in several 'genetic deaths' in the descendants of the exposed women and children, as well as genetic diseases of varying severity."

Emma Craft called the hot line set up by the Department of Energy. When she got a busy signal, she sat down and wrote a letter to U.S. Senator Jim Sasser, a Democrat from Tennessee. Apparently tipped off by Sasser, reporters began knocking at her door. One of them showed her the Ruth Hagstrom report, which described the eleven-year-old girl who died from the synovial sarcoma.

The description of the unnamed child fit her daughter, Carolyn Bucy. They were the same age, the same gender, and the cancer started in the same place in the same leg. Emma said she knew immediately that it was her daughter. "I knew it explained my baby. And I knew that was her. And I can't tell you how mad I got. I was hurt, mad and upset all at the same time because I knew it was her when I read the report."

Emma did not receive documents from Vanderbilt confirming that she had received the radioactive iron. But the similarities between Carolyn and the unnamed eleven-year-old cancer victim described in Ruth Hagstrom's report were too numerous to be coincidental. Emma said that the Vanderbilt doctors closely monitored her daughter's illness and later tried to obtain her body for an autopsy. All the grief she suffered when her daughter died came surging back. At first she sought only an apology from Vanderbilt and an acknowledgment of what they had done. When the apology failed to materialize, she joined the class-action lawsuit. "What I went through was for no reason at all," she said in her deposition. "I could accept God taking her but not man."

U.S. District Judge John T. Nixon refused to dismiss the class action lawsuit against Vanderbilt University and the other parties. A jury, he said, could "reasonably find" that the university and its doctors fraudulently concealed the nature of the experiment from the women. The judge pointed to the fact that Darby told the women the radioactive drink was a "cocktail" and that the letters sent to the women in the follow-up study did not disclose that they had been given radioactive iron. Furthermore, he said, there is a suggestion that the university may "have lost or destroyed records while on notice of liability."

Emma was not in the best of health and worried about whether she would live long enough to see the case through to a conclusion. An apology from Vanderbilt, she said, would no longer do.

Harold Bibeau, who had been irradiated in Oregon, read about Hazel O'Leary's press conference in a Portland newspaper one morning. He decided to go public with his story on *Northwest Reports,* an investigative television news program in Portland. For Bibeau, who had managed to rebuild his life when he was released from prison, the decision did not come easily. He was married and had a nine-year-old son. Except for his wife and a few close friends, nobody, not even his son, knew about his past, and going public carried a large personal risk. "Something had to be done. And as far as I knew, nobody else was willing to do it."

Although it was the first time many Oregonians had ever heard of the experiments, corrections officials had been trying to find a way to provide follow-up care to Carl Heller's subjects for years.

The Oregon legislature had passed a law in 1987 requiring that the Department of Corrections provide a free annual examination to individuals who had taken part in the Heller program. Oregon prison officials asked James Ruttenber, then with the Centers for Disease Control, to develop a protocol for medical follow-up. Ruttenber recommended that all of Heller's subjects, including those who were in the hormone experiments, undergo annual exams.

Ruttenber also contacted C. Alvin Paulsen, Heller's protégé, to see if a similar program could be set up for the Washington prisoners. Paulsen was "noticeably defensive" and unwilling to provide any information, Ruttenber said. "I think he even implied at one point in the discussion that providing information would be potentially incriminating. I don't think he meant that in the sense that he had done anything criminally wrong but that he would be providing information that would be against his interest."

By the time Hazel O'Leary held her press conference, corrections officials had begun providing physical exams for a handful of subjects irradiated by Carl Heller who were still in prison and a few living in the community. But Oregon authorities felt that since the federal government funded the program, it should also pick up some of the tab. "I hope that you will consider making available some kind of medical surveillance for these people through the federal government that does not require that they first identify themselves as a prisoner," Frank Hall, director of Oregon's Department of Corrections, said in a letter to O'Leary.

The atomic veterans, who had been battling to get adequate compensation since the 1978 congressional hearings prompted by Paul Cooper's story, felt they had something in common with the other experimental subjects. As the *Atomic Veteran's Newsletter* put it:

> We were the victims of radiation experiments too. They exposed
> over 200,000 of us in over 200 atmospheric atomic and hydrogen
> bomb tests between 1945–1962. They deliberately bombed us

with nuclear weapons and exposed us to deadly radioactivity to see how it would affect us and our equipment in nuclear warfare on land, on sea and in the air. They didn't need our informed consent because we were under military discipline. They devalued our lives too! They made us sterile! They crippled and killed our children! They made widows of our wives! Then denied repeatedly and publicly that there was ever any danger! "Say the same lie often enough, the people will believe it."

In countless newspaper articles published throughout the United States, aging vets described the glowing fireballs that came up over the Pacific Ocean, the choking dust they breathed in at the Nevada Test Site.

Some veterans and civilians began talking about the bizarre medical treatments in which rods tipped with radium were placed in their nostrils for disorders ranging from earaches to infected tonsils. Wilhelm Hueper, the scientist who had once provoked the wrath of Shields Warren when he wrote about the dangers in the uranium mines, had warned of the unforeseen risks of nasopharyngeal treatment in 1954. But Hueper's warning went largely unnoticed and the treatment was widely used. The Centers for Disease Control has estimated that between 8,000 and 20,000 servicemen were treated with nasopharyngeal irradiation and that a total of 500,000 to 2 million Americans may have received the treatment.

That number is huge, but what makes it even more worrisome is the fact that several contemporary researchers have warned that patients who received the nasopharyngeal irradiation run a greater risk of contracting head and neck cancers. A Dutch researcher calculated that individuals exposed to radium rods in the Netherlands appear to have twice as many verified cancers as a nonexposed control group. And American patients typically received doses that were nearly four times larger than the Dutch patients received.

Cherie Anderson, a California woman now in her fifties, received the nasal radium treatments for sinus problems when she was about six years old. Her mother told her the rods looked like Fourth of July sparklers. She developed polio when she was eight; had two benign breast tumors removed at age twenty-two; developed strange red blood cells at thirty and nodules on the thyroid at thirty-five; and by forty-one, had lost almost all of her teeth. Anderson believes the radiation damaged her immune system and upset her hormonal balance. "The dentists said a woman my age should have all her own teeth," she told a reporter. "They were baffled. But when I mentioned the radiation treatments, they said, 'Ah, ha, that's it.' "

In a house trailer in Edgewood, New Mexico, a three-hour drive from Los Alamos National Laboratory, Katie Kelley pored over documents she had received from the lab about her father, Cecil, the plutonium worker who received the massive dose of radiation in the 1958 criticality accident. "A wide-mouthed mayonnaise jar. They packed my father's brain in a wide-mouthed mayonnaise jar," she said, her voice filled with disbelief. Katie had been trying since 1974 to obtain information from Los Alamos National Laboratory about her father's death. But she said lab officials had repeatedly rebuffed her efforts, claiming the data on her father was classified.

But times had changed. In early 1994, the lab had sent her a stack of records on her father's accident. Only when she read those records did Katie realize for the first time that her father's organs had been shipped to researchers throughout the country. "The cutting him up makes me nuts. I don't think they have a right, government or not, to chop up my father's parts without his family's knowledge," she said.

The Cecil Kelley story was only one of the articles that surfaced in early 1994 about the laboratory's ghoulish "human tissue analysis project," the decades-long program in which organs, tissues, or even whole cadavers were sent to Los Alamos and analyzed for plutonium content. In a 1994 press release, lab officials said they had obtained consent for the tissue samples, but Jim McInroy, the lead scientist in the study, admitted in a private meeting a few months later that "people did not know they were sent to Los Alamos."

The organs from Michael Brousseau, a fifteen-year-old boy who died in Los Alamos in 1968 from complications caused by a birth defect, were among the body parts analyzed. His father, Armand Brousseau, a retired engineer, told reporters he never gave permission for the analysis. "This place," he said of Los Alamos, "is full of gods."

In one of its most embarrassing disclosures, the lab admitted that it still had seven small unanalyzed bone samples from Karen Silkwood, an employee at the Kerr-McGee Nuclear Corporation in Crescent, Oklahoma. Silkwood, a union worker, was killed in a car crash on November 13, 1974, when she was on her way to meet with *New York Times* reporter David Burnham about safety violations at the plant. The accident became the subject of a highly successful movie starring Cher and Meryl Streep.

The day before the accident, she had flown to Los Alamos, where she had undergone tests aimed at measuring the plutonium in her body. She had been placed in the lab's whole-body counter, and she provided scientists with urine and stools samples, which were then analyzed with an improved version of the chemical process worked out by Wright Langham decades earlier. George Voelz, a close friend of Louis Hempelmann's, and Don Petersen, Wright Langham's old friend, helped decipher the data.

Following the car crash, George Voelz flew to Oklahoma for the autopsy and took back to Los Alamos some of Silkwood's organs, including her brain. The organs were reduced to 113 small flasks containing solvent and a small amount of dissolved tissue. The flasks remained at Los Alamos until 1992 and were then shipped to the DOE's National Human Radiobiology Tissue Repository in Spokane, Washington (the same place where some of Albert Stevens's ashes wound up).

Bill Silkwood, Karen's father, was shocked when he learned that Los Alamos had kept his daughter's body parts. He said the lab did not have the family's permission to take the organs in the first place. "They stole those organs. How else can you put it?" But the lab said its authority to take the organs came from the Oklahoma medical examiner.

Alan McMillan, head of the lab's Human Studies Project Team, offered in 1994 to return the bone chips to Karen's father. "Since the amount of plutonium present is so small and would present no hazard, the lab could send them to you in their current state. Or they could be cremated and sent to you in a proper container. Please let me know what you would like us to do with regards to these remains," he wrote.

Silkwood wanted the bone chips back so that he could bury them in Texas. But in an interview two years later, he said he never heard another word from Los Alamos. "They were supposed to apologize and everything but I never heard nothing. You know how the government is. They tell you one thing and do another."

As the public pressure mounted, the Department of Energy finally released the medical records on all eighteen plutonium patients. Although their names and other identifying factors were deleted, or "redacted," the files nevertheless provided enough information for me and several other reporters to unravel the identities of all the remaining patients except for

CHI-3, the young man from Chicago who was injected with a massive amount of plutonium.

When stories about the patients began appearing in the Rochester newspapers, Mary Jeanne Connell, an elderly woman living in the Rochester area, read them closely. There were so many aspects of the experiment that seemed familiar to her. She, too, had been hospitalized on Samuel Bassett's metabolic ward at Strong Memorial Hospital in the mid-1940s. Her urine and stool specimens had been collected in special containers. And, like Eda Schultz Charlton, she also had been sent on shopping trips where she was accompanied by hospital personnel.

With a sickening feeling in the pit of her stomach, Connell realized that she must have been used in a similar experiment. But as it turns out, she had been injected with uranium—not plutonium. She was the youngest of the six patients injected with uranium and is the only known living survivor from that experiment. "All these things have been in my mind all these years," she said a year or so after her participation had been confirmed.

A shy young woman raised on a sheep farm in upstate New York, Connell was twenty-four years old when her doctor referred her to the metabolic ward in September 1946. She was five feet two inches tall and weighed eighty-four pounds. Although she was perfectly healthy, the physician wanted to find out why she couldn't gain weight. (Slenderness, she said, runs in the family.)

Soon after she was admitted to the ward, she was taken to an animal laboratory on two occasions. The experience, she said, upset her "something terrible." During one of the visits, her white-coated chaperon made several oblique remarks about how slowly their animal experiments were going, how they needed human subjects to continue their work. "I think that's when they decided they were going to have me," she said.

Connell found herself lying on a gurney with straps across her chest and ankles when she woke up one morning. A large group of doctors had gathered at her bedside and one of them was trying to open a small vial of orange-colored liquid. Everyone in the room appeared to be afraid of the mixture. There was no cork, no cap, no way to open the sealed bottle. Finally someone smashed the vial against of the edge of a table and a small amount of the orangey stuff trickled onto the floor. Connell looked over the edge of the table and couldn't believe her eyes: The material had burned a hole in the floor. "I never forgot that," she said.

One of the doctors then injected the mixture into her veins. As the radioactive material flooded through her body, she said, "I felt like I was laying on hot coals. I almost passed out." Later she was woozy and sick to her stomach. Numerous doctors came in and looked at her. "They didn't say anything. They just stood around looking at me."

The date was October 1, 1946. Connell had just been injected with 584 micrograms of enriched uranium, twice the amount researchers at the time believed would cause kidney damage. Her urine and stool samples were collected and a woman stood guard over her day and night. Occasionally two or three attendants took her out for a shopping spree. One of the nurses joked that she was the most famous person in the hospital, but five decades would elapse before Connell finally understood what she meant.

Connell was discharged about three weeks later. The injection forced her to urinate frequently. Over the years, she has suffered from persistent urinary tract infections, kidney pain, and high blood pressure. She doesn't know if she is still excreting uranium but said she often caused electronic equipment at her job to malfunction.

Bassett and his colleagues did not inform Connell of what was in the vial nor did she give consent for the uranium injection. "I feel hurt and humiliated, everything all at once," she said. "The doctors were probably saying to themselves, 'Well, she isn't much good for anything. If she dies, so what?'"

42

January 1994: The Advisory Committee on Human Radiation Experiments

Less than a month after Hazel O'Leary's disclosures, President Clinton ordered all federal agencies to comb their records for any documents related to human radiation experiments and make them public. He also established the Advisory Committee on Human Radiation Experiments to investigate the studies. With that action, the attention shifted from the Department of Energy and Hazel O'Leary to Ruth Faden and the Advisory Committee.

Faden chaired the committee. She was a bioethicist at the Johns Hopkins School of Hygiene and Public Health and a scholar at Georgetown University's Kennedy Institute of Ethics. Forty-four years old and coauthor of an authoritative book on informed consent, Faden told a reporter she viewed the appointment as a chance to "rewrite the history of ethics and research on human subjects in this country."

Both of Faden's parents were survivors of the Holocaust. Her father spent two years in Auschwitz, and her mother was in Birkenau for two years. But Faden said she had a "deep aversion" to drawing any analogies to the Holocaust or trading in any way on that experience. "I don't think I have any special claim to anything because of who I am, or more importantly, who my parents are and what they experienced. Nor do I want to draw any straight line analogies between what we're studying and the Nazi experience. At the same time, obviously I am the product of that horrible event."

Because of what her own family had gone through, Faden said she recognized how important it was for the committee to leave behind an accurate historical record of the radiation experiments. "There's nothing more terrifying for survivors of a horrible event than to hear other people trivialize it, or even worse, raise skepticism about whether the event ever occurred. Maybe my sensitivity to the importance of leaving the historical record irrefutably straight comes out of that experience."

The White House appointed thirteen other people to the panel. They included two more ethicists, five medical doctors, two lawyers, two scientists, a historian, and a bank vice president. The group met roughly once a month in Washington, D.C., for two to three days from April of 1994 to October of 1995. In general, the first hour or two was set aside for witness testimony; the remaining time was reserved for debate and discussion among the committee members themselves.

The committee's headquarters, located at 1726 M Street in downtown Washington, had the chaotic feel of a law firm on the eve of a big trial. The hallways were stacked with boxes of documents from various federal agencies. Desks and floors were piled high with records and paper coffee cups. In one room, two industrial-size copying machines ran twelve to fifteen hours a day, spitting out thousands of pages.

The creation of the committee changed the way the media covered the controversy. Instead of digging up their own stories, reporters began relying on what the panel had found. The committee had two press spokesmen, and its executive director, Dan Guttman, was an affable Washington lawyer who enjoyed schmoozing with the media. Before each monthly meeting, the panel would gather up a package of the most sensational documents and release them to the press. This process guaranteed that at least once a month the group would be portrayed in countless news reports as "uncovering," "revealing," or "disclosing" some new Cold War horror. Although staffers did find many important documents, much of the work was done by the legions of anonymous Energy and Defense Department employees working in the bowels of various federal archives. The monthly releases also enabled the Clinton administration, whether intended or not, to regain control of the controversy and, as one of O'Leary's aides explained, "slow things down."

None of this was apparent at first. The committee's formation was viewed with great optimism by activists and the experimental subjects. Finally, they thought, here was an independent panel of experts not connected to the nuclear weapons establishment who would conduct a complete and unbiased investigation of this chapter in Cold War history.

A staff of about seventy people was hired to review documents, provide historical context, and help organize the monthly meetings. The staffers for the most part were young and liberal, but the fourteen people the White House appointed to the commission itself were members of the nation's scientific and academic elite. In fact, they bore a remarkable resemblance to the experimenters they were investigating: They came from the same socioeconomic class, attended the same colleges, and worked at the same universities that sponsored the experiments. Ruth Faden's employer, for example, Johns Hopkins University, developed and refined the radium nasal treatments, which were administered by doctors throughout the country and significantly increased the subjects' risks of cancer and other diseases. None of the victims of the experiments or their relatives were appointed to the panel, even though many presidential committees are required to include a representative from the affected community.

Counting the staffers and the appointed members, the committee had about eighty-five people working on the radiation experiments, but it quickly became apparent that not even that large a group would be able to keep up with the tidal wave of documents. Almost immediately, the panel was deluged with tens of thousands of records that the federal agencies had uncovered in response to Clinton's search directive.

In all, an estimated 6 million pages related to the government's little-known radiation studies were gathered up by the federal agencies and the military branches between late 1993 and 1997 and made available. A small percentage of the documents had been declassified, but the majority were records technically open to the public but not readily accessible. They came from federal repositories, university archives, storage rooms, filing cabinets, personal files, and even family garages.

Faden acknowledged in December of 1994 that the committee was overwhelmed by the documents. Despite this admission, she actually broadened the scope of the panel's work to look at how well the rights of patients in *contemporary* experiments were being protected. At her direction, two large projects examining contemporary experiments were undertaken by outside contractors at a cost to taxpayers of several hundred thousand dollars. One involved interviewing 1,900 patients in waiting rooms throughout the country; the other was a detailed analysis of 125 contemporary research projects.

The General Accounting Office in December of 1994 noted that the committee "had done little of the ethical and scientific analysis called for in its charter." Yet, the GAO added, "Despite these difficulties, the Committee has chosen to expand the overall scope of its work." Faden staunchly defended the expansion, saying the panel couldn't make any meaningful statements about the past without investigating whether similar problems were occurring in contemporary experiments. "We have to look at the contemporary situation and say, 'OK, what is the likelihood that this could happen now?' And if there's any plausibility to the view it could happen today, what do we need to do to change it?"

The committee attacked its assignment on several fronts simultaneously. Some staff members reviewed, analyzed, and searched for documents while others crisscrossed the country interviewing the scientists who had conducted the experiments. At the monthly meetings, the appointed members listened to personal testimony from witnesses who had firsthand experience with the horrors being investigated or whose family members had been victimized. They then tried to develop an ethical framework that they could use to judge the experiments and make recommendations for medical monitoring or financial compensation.

Between meetings, the members exchanged copious e-mail messages. For Faden, a handsome woman with curly, dark hair, chairing the meetings was exhausting work: ten minute breaks, hour lunches, then back to the table for more debate. "Totally draining," she said after one of the marathon sessions. "You have to be vigilant every single minute. This must be what it feels like if you're a good judge or a good trial attorney."

Faden almost always lived up to her Solomon-like duties. She was courteous to the witnesses and solicitous of her colleagues. But there was an edgy quality to her and she could be extremely abrupt. One of her most important tasks was to keep the committee—a group of congenial, high-powered professionals such as herself—from becoming splintered as it worked in a fishbowl of public scrutiny for eighteen months. The committee's recommendations would carry more weight if a unanimous report was delivered to President Clinton. Dissenting opinions, which were not infrequent on ethics panels, would weaken the report's impact.

Although the committee's job was to analyze the unethical radiation experiments that had taken place during the Cold War, some of the members seemed uncomfortable when the victims actually appeared before them. The committee members had little knowledge of the nuclear weapons complex or its history, and they were understandably confused when the speakers began talking about atmospheric test series with names like Buster-Jangle, Tumbler-Snapper, and Upshot-Knothole. Oftentimes an embarrassing silence followed the testimony. Faden usually instructed the speakers to leave their records with the staff. Implicit in the instructions was the promise that the cases would be investigated. But hundreds of thousands of records were already flowing in, and some of the documents, which often had taken the witnesses years to collect, were forwarded without much scrutiny to the National Archives when the committee was disbanded eighteen months later.

43

HARVEST OF SORROW

By train, plane, and automobile, in buses and carpools, the witnesses traveled what were often thousands of miles to speak at hearings in Washington, D.C., or at outreach meetings in San Francisco, Cincinnati, Spokane, Sante Fe, and Knoxville. Eager to maintain its neutrality, the Advisory Committee gave the speakers no funds for travel expenses, no money for hotels, no petty cash for copying fees. But that policy did not deter these people. Many had been waiting years to tell their stories of deception and betrayal. Their testimony demonstrated in a dramatic way the breadth of the experimentation program and the deep distrust many Americans felt toward the nuclear weapons complex.

Some witnesses broke down in tears as they paced the hallway before the meetings. Others cried as they unwrapped family photographs and propped them up at witness tables so the world could see that the mother, father, grandparent who was irradiated was a human being and not a laboratory animal. In halting and unpolished voices, they gave witness to outlandish and bizarre Cold War events that one committee member later described as "surrealistic."

The meetings drew dozens of residents who lived downwind of Hanford, Los Alamos, and Oak Ridge, who testified that they, too, had been exposed to dangerous amounts of radiation and were unwitting guinea pigs in America's Cold War. Uranium miners recounted the extraordinary lung cancer epidemic that struck their villages after they began digging the ore from mines on the Colorado Plateau. Representatives from Inupiat villages of the North Slope of Alaska told of an experiment in which eighty-four Eskimos, seventeen Indians, and nineteen whites were given iodine-131. Marshall Islands residents, often accompanied by interpreters, noted the vast increase in illness and disease following years of atmospheric testing on their tropical atolls. "The only thing we knew is what we were observing and that the children that were born were like animals and they weren't children at all," said a Ms. Matayoshi through an interpreter.

The first "outreach" meeting was held from October 11 to 13, 1994, in San Francisco, a block or so from Union Square. In a booming voice, atomic veteran Israel Torres described the July morning in 1957 when Shot Hood rocked his trench. Hood was a seventy-four-kiloton bomb, more than three times the size of the weapon dropped on Nagasaki and the largest ever detonated at the Nevada Test Site. "I was thrown from wall to wall in the trench. It felt like a giant vacuum was trying to suck me out, but I fought the suction," he remembered.

As she waited to speak at the San Francisco meeting, Darcy Thrall, born and raised five miles from the Hanford plutonium complex in Washington state, fingered a mysterious dog tag that she had been given by scientists when she was in the second grade. One day, she told the panel, a man came into her classroom in Richland, Washington, and escorted her to a room where some bottles and cups were sitting on a table. She was given a white substance to drink and then taken outside to a waiting van. Inside the van were men and women in white uniforms. She was instructed to lie on her back and was sent through a noisy, tube-shaped machine. Afterward, she was given a log book in which her parents were to write down everything she ate and drank. Her family grew their own vegetables, raised their own cattle, and ate fish from the Columbia River. Several weeks later the scientists returned to her second-grade classroom and sent her through the machine again. She was given the dog tag and instructed to wear it at all times. The tag is engraved with her name and address and has the initials "R-P" in the left-hand corner and "S" in the right corner.

Although the significance of the dog tag is unknown and it is unclear what Thrall drank, documents show that scientists working at Hanford regularly monitored school children to determine what kind of radionuclides were in their bodies. Researchers were particularly interested in families such as Thrall's because they would have absorbed larger amounts of radionuclides than someone who purchased "store-bought" food. The van that Thrall was taken to was undoubtedly one of the two mobile whole-body counters operated by Batelle Pacific Northwest Laboratory. The children were often given comic books to read while they waited to be measured. "None of the more than 3,000 children measured in the mobile whole-body counter to date," wrote a scientist sometime after 1967, "have had body burdens of radionuclides outside the range anticipated on the basis of our known environmental conditions."

When Darcy Thrall went public with her story in 1994, she received many threats, and one of her pets was killed at her home in Washington state. "I had a great, huge, old, old turkey. And one morning I woke up and when the sun came up I could see steam rising in the pasture. And I went out there and found my turkey, and he had been stabbed over and over again so far I could put my hand this deep in his chest. He was still alive." Thrall was afraid for her daughter and her other animals and asked the committee to help her. "It's something that happened. I don't know any, any big secrets, or anything."

At the Cincinnati meeting held October 21, family members remembered the tears and vomit of loved ones who underwent total-body irradiation. "I believe my father was in the wrong place at the right time," Katherine Hagar observed. Hagar's father, Joseph Mitchell, Patient No. 51, was scheduled for surgery for lung cancer. Instead he was given 150 rads of total-body radiation and died seventy-four days later. Doris Baker spoke lovingly of her great-grandmother, Gertrude Newell, Patient No. 20, who was exposed to 200 rads of total body radiation. "Will someone please tell me why our government let this happen?" she pleaded.

Other witnesses who worked at nearby weapons plants also spoke at the Cincinnati meeting. Owen Thompson, who said he was "just a dumb hillbilly, big and strong," was assigned to a special team that buried radioactive wastes at night while guards with machine guns stood by. The waste was brought by hay wagons to the dump site, and giant bulldozers used in strip mining plowed the material into the ground. "I did my country wrong," Thompson confessed.

Gene Branham, a union representative and longtime worker at a uranium production facility outside Cincinnati, talked about the network set up by the government to snatch the body parts of deceased workers before they were embalmed. The body snatching got so bad, he said, union members often set up vigils to make sure that the DOE didn't grab the corpse before it was buried.

A frigid wind blew through downtown Spokane on November 21 as dozens of residents who once lived on or near Hanford piled into a chilly meeting room. Nodding in the direction of the highly contaminated complex 130 miles away, they described immune system diseases, thyroid disorders, cancer, allergies, and reproductive problems that they believed were caused by radioactive emissions. Gertie Hanson, who grew up in northern Idaho about 140 miles from Hanford, did an informal survey of young girls who graduated from high school in the early 1950s. Twenty-nine percent of the forty-nine women who responded to her survey had suffered miscarriages in their early childbearing years, she said.

Pat Hoover, in a written statement, recalled that when she was about thirteen or fourteen men clad in white coats would visit her physical education class or her health class. "We assumed that these were doctors. Now looking back, I have no idea if they were doctors, chemists or workers from the Hanford plant with no medical background; but they came in looking like doctors, stood behind us and felt our throats with their hands." Many teenage girls had odd fingernails with horizontal ridges, she said, and were given a chemical supplied by Pacific Northwest Laboratory that would "fix" the problem. (The "doctors" were probably palpating the girls' necks for thyroid nodules; the ridged fingernails could be a sign of hypothyroidism, or underactive thyroid, which can be caused by radiation exposure.)

Brenda Weaver lived for most of her life seven miles from Hanford in an area known as Death Mile. Her family, she said, always seemed sick with "something weird." Weaver was put on thyroid medication at the age of twelve and had an ovary removed at age fourteen. Her brother was taken to the hospital when his eyes began bleeding. In the early 1960s, the sheep on her father's farm were born with missing legs, missing body parts, and missing eyes. Her daughter, Jamie, was born in 1965 without eyes. "She has eyelashes and eyelids and tear ducts, but no eyes. It makes life difficult, it's hard to be blind."

Weaver said she believes wholeheartedly her daughter's birth defect and those in the sheep were caused by the radioactive emissions from Hanford. "We were irradiated, used as guinea pigs by our government. I could hardly believe it, but I do remember, as a kid, men in white coats with Geiger counters coming to the farm. They were out in the fields taking parts of dead animals, food. The weather balloons would come over onto our property," she said. "We thought that this meant that our government was taking care of us, and if there was anything going on at Hanford, surely they would tell us, right?"

In Hanford's early years, scientists intensively studied the animal and plant life surrounding the nuclear complex, often posing as cowboys or ropers or agricultural agents. Accompanied by two Manhattan Project security officers, a scientist named Karl Herde pretended he was an animal husbandry specialist in 1946 when he measured radioactive iodine in the thyroids of farm animals. "I was successful in placing the probe of the instrument directly over the thyroid at times when the owner's attention was focused on the next animal or some concocted distraction," he later wrote. "At that time the revelation of a regional iodine-131 problem would have had a tremendous public relations impact and furthermore the presence of other nuclides (some known but some not recognized or identified) was of possible National Defense significance."

The Spokane meeting drew speakers with other kinds of stories to tell. Kathy Jacobovitch said her father worked on the three "hot" Navy ships hauled back from the Pacific Proving Ground and died of advanced lung cancer. Jacobovitch, who was asked by her mother to look into her father's radiation exposure after his death, learned from military records that her father was exposed to 135 hours of radiation. "I noticed that while my dad was coming home 'hot,' mom was pregnant with me." Jacobovitch has been diagnosed with lupus disease, an autoimmune disorder she believes is related to the exposure she received in the womb.

Harold Bibeau, who participated in the testicular irradiation experiments at the Oregon State Penitentiary, read an excerpt from Carl Heller's deposition in which the doctor admitted under oath he didn't fully disclose the cancer risk to the convicts because he didn't want to frighten them. Dr. Heller "must have taken Personal Ethics 101 at the University of Buchenwald," Bibeau said, referring to the infamous Nazi death camp.

In Sante Fe, New Mexico, several inches of powdery snow covered the roof of the brown adobe building where one of the Advisory Committee's last outreach meetings was held on January 30, 1995. Scattered through the audience were atomic veterans, uranium miners, Native Alaskans, the son and grandson of two of the plutonium patients, the wives of several former Utah convicts, and scientists who worked down the road at Los Alamos National Laboratory.

Bill Holmes, the grandson of Albert Stevens, the first California patient injected with plutonium, strongly condemned the scientists who performed the experiment: "The people who did this to my grandfather had only to ask themselves how they would feel if they were in his place. Any code of ethics or scientific experiment involving humans must, it seems to me, begin and end with that very simple question."

Rosalie Jones and Bernice Brogan traveled down from Utah to tell the panel how their husbands, former convicts at Utah State Prison, received multiple injections of radioactive materials. Four of the babies fathered by ten of the men in the experiment subsequently died of birth defects. "The path to hell is paved with good intentions," said Brogan, one of the women whose infants died. "Us mothers, we were given the path to hell."

William Tsosie worked at a uranium mine near Shiprock, New Mexico, for seven and a half years. His clothes covered with uranium dust, he went home to his wife and children at the end of each shift. He often ate supper or played with the children without changing clothes or bathing. Tsosie once took back to his trailer a chunk of high-grade uranium ore and placed the rock on the window above his bed. "We never been told what it is until later on, and it's too late. We're already contaminated. We're already exposed," he said.

Barney Bailey was ordered onto the battleship *New York* two hours after the underwater bomb, Shot Baker, was detonated during Operation Crossroads. Located near the center of the bull's-eye, the battleship was listing badly when the young man boarded. "We were there three days, three days and three nights on that ship. No warning, no protective clothing. We never heard of radiation. We were seventeen-year-old kids, most of us. We had no idea."

The Santa Fe audience stirred angrily as three retired Los Alamos scientists walked to the witness table. Among them where George Voelz, who had examined Karen Silkwood, and Don Petersen, who had scraped Cecil Kelley's diarrhea and vomit from the walls and floor of the emergency room. Petersen vividly described the scientific "stampede" to get radioisotopes after the war. "Now all of a sudden there was this bonanza. You could ask Oak Ridge, and Oak Ridge would provide you with information and with a tracer, a radiotracer, and you could approach your experiment in a way that had never been possible before. Now that enthusiasm overshadowed any soul searching about ethical considerations."

Petersen was so excited about the possibilities of radioisotopes and so confident that small amounts posed little risk that he used two of his own children in radioactive iodine tracer studies. "My five-year-old took one look at this, and she said she didn't want anything to do with it, so she got to stay home. The six-year-old and the eight-year-old were very interested in this, and they participated." Each of the children received about fifteen millirem of radiation, the equivalent of what a tourist in Sante Fe gets in thirteen days, he recalled. (Sante Feans are exposed to more radiation because the city is more than a mile above sea level.)

"I guess it's a fine line," remarked committee member Duncan

Thomas, "between a child consenting in full knowledge of all the facts, and being consented by their parents who are talking them into it." Petersen responded, "There is no question but what their daddy talked them into it but he was only two-thirds successful."

The final outreach meeting was held March 2 in the grand ballroom of Knoxville's Radisson Summit Hill Hotel. In their neatly coiffed hairdos and carefully pressed dresses, the women who once attended Vanderbilt University's prenatal clinic ticked off the strange illnesses that had befallen them or their children after they drank the radioactive iron cocktails. Emma Craft said, "I want you to tell President Clinton that I want an apology from somebody and I want some answers." Ron Hamm, whose mother was pregnant with him when she drank the cocktail, said, "We were violated in the worst possible way. I was a fetus, I had no choice. My mother was an unsuspecting young lady and she had no choice. But what did happen to her in that room, in my estimation, was tantamount to rape."

Frank Comas, a physician, appeared before the president's Advisory Committee to defend the work done by the Oak Ridge doctors. "It is with some sadness and also some annoyance, I must confess, that I am obliged to try to exonerate ourselves for something perceived by some as devilish acts where science was God and damn all other considerations."

44

CLOSING THE BOOK

As the hearings progressed, the committee tried to figure out a way to judge the experiments. A subtle rift soon appeared in the companionable facade the group presented to the public. According to an executive order from President Clinton, the committee's task was to find out whether there was a clear medical or scientific purpose for the experiments; whether appropriate medical follow-up was conducted; and whether the experiments met the ethical and scientific standards, including the standards of informed consent, that prevailed at the time and that exist today. Once that evaluation had been completed, the group could then make recommendations about the need for notification and medical follow-up for the experimental subjects or their descendants.

The instructions from the president clearly indicated that the committee would have to make judgments. But most of the members were hesitant to do so. Instead they wanted to write a descriptive account of the experiments and focus their energy on trying to make recommendations that would ensure that unethical experiments would not occur in the future. "We don't want to pass severe moral judgments, particularly because it's much more important to really look at the present," said Jay Katz, a venerable ethicist from Yale University who had escaped Nazi Germany with his family when he was a child. Although Katz was a gentle and empathetic man, he, like other committee members, seemed to treat the radiation experiments as if they were an abstract, historical event. He frequently argued that the 1940s, 1950s, and 1960s were a period of "ethical chaos" in medicine and that the radiation experimenters shouldn't be singled out. Paternalism governed the relationship between doctor and patient during that period, he asserted, and patients were rarely informed of anything.

The other panelists shared Katz's reluctance to make judgments about the individual experimenters. But their hesitation was based more on the sketchy nature of the documents and the fact that the experimenters weren't alive or available to defend their actions. Patricia King, one of the two attorneys, said, "I felt then and I feel now that we were not structured to make judgments in individual cases absent some pretty clear evidence." The idea of judging also didn't sit well with Henry Royal, a radiologist at Washington University who perhaps more than anyone else represented the experimenters' viewpoint. The doctors, he argued, may have gotten oral consent from the patients. "What I would like to know," he said in an interview, "is what did the investigator say to the patient?"

Ruth Macklin, a professor at Albert Einstein College in the Bronx and perhaps the most eloquent of the three ethicists, refused to let her colleagues off the hook so easily. If the panel did not want to make judgments, she said, "then we can't talk about anyone having been wronged by the conduct and we can't begin to talk about remedies." Macklin argued that the committee needed to hold individuals accountable in order to deter future researchers from performing unethical experiments and to provide justice to the victims.

Eventually the group came up with an ingenious compromise that sidestepped the issue of whether individuals should be held culpable and ensured that a unanimous report would be delivered to the president. The committee declared that separate judgments could be made about the *wrongness* of an action and the *blameworthiness* of the person who committed the act. Simply put, it separated the experiments from the experimenters. "If experiments violated basic ethical principles, institutional or organizational policies or rules of professional ethics," the panel wrote, "then they were and will always be wrong. Whether and how much anyone should be blamed for these wrongs are separate questions."

While the committee was trying to develop its ethical framework, the political atmosphere in Washington shifted dramatically. For the first time in forty years, Republicans captured a majority in both houses of Congress during the November 1994 elections. Social programs were out; fiscal austerity was in. Some panelists said the changed atmosphere didn't color their work at all. But others confessed it had a profound effect on their deliberations and the recommendations they eventually sent to President Clinton. Remembered panelist Eli Glatstein, a radiation oncologist: "The mind-set of the Republicans, particularly the young House members, was so extreme and so partisan that it toned down virtually every decision that the committee could reach. It was very clear that we wanted to have recommendations that Congress would take up. It was clear that our scope had to be toned down after that election. The last thing the committee wanted was to make recommendations that would be refused."

One immediate response to the changed political climate was the committee's reluctance to ask the White House for an extension to complete its work. By December of 1994, a month after the elections, it was clear the group was not going to finish its assignment in its one-year time frame. Eventually the panel did get a six-month extension and a pared-down staff to help draft its final report, but it was not nearly enough time to adequately analyze and synthesize the voluminous documentary record.

Many contemporary scientists defended the Cold War experiments when the controversy first erupted, claiming that ethical standards were different in the past from what they are today. But the documents clearly showed that government officials recognized decades ago that the voluntary and understanding consent of the human subject was essential for an experiment to be ethical. The Atomic Energy Commission had rules by 1947 and the Defense Department by 1953 requiring researchers to obtain the consent of sick patients for therapeutic and nontherapeutic experiments.

Furthermore, the documents show that the experimenters understood the rules. Thomas Shipman, the physician who supervised Los Alamos's health division through much of the Cold War, advised the Los Alamos Medical Center in 1951 that patients should not be given nontherapeutic irradiation unless the procedures were explained and consent obtained. "In other words, we should not carry out on a patient a procedure even mildly experimental while intimating to the patient that this is part of his regular treatment. The situation, it seems to me, is quite comparable to the use of a relatively new drug."

The writings of Robert Stone, an inveterate experimenter, also show that physicians, even during World War II, recognized that they needed the consent from sick patients for experiments. Of the patients exposed to total body irradiation during the Manhattan Project, Stone wrote, "No signed consent was received from the patient, but the treatment was explained to them by the physicians and they, in full knowledge and facts, accepted the treatments."

While Stone may not have always followed the rules, records show that he was also extremely familiar with the AMA's code of ethics and the Nuremberg Code. During a meeting at UCSF's Cancer Board in 1952, he argued against an experiment in which an investigator proposed transferring malignant melanoma cells to terminally ill patients. "Dr. Stone stated that he felt such a procedure was not in line with the basic principles governing human experimentation outlined at the War Crimes Tribunal at Nuremberg or the code of ethics regarding human experimentation adopted by the American Medical Association. In particular, the investigator could not terminate the experiment and it would not seem to serve any purpose to benefit humanity." The Cancer Board subsequently refused to allow the experiment to proceed.

The formerly classified transcripts of the TBI debates held at the Pentagon demonstrate clearly that both military and civilian scientists were familiar with the Nuremberg Code. The code was even read aloud at the Pentagon during a November 10, 1952 meeting of the Committee on Chemical Warfare.

Despite the new evidence, Jay Katz continued to assert his long-held belief that the researchers did not think the Nuremberg Code had practical bearing on their work. "The Nuremberg Code is an aspirational code and, as I've observed, it speaks to the stars," he declared at one meeting. "It is a document not for earthlings, but for the heavens." Although many new declassified documents showed unequivocally that there were rules and ethical guidelines governing the radiation experiments, Katz dismissed them as bureaucratic "lip service." In a separate statement appended to the committee's final report, he wrote: "Most references to consent (with rare exceptions) that we uncovered in governmental documents or in exchanges between officials and their medical consultants were meaningless words, which conveyed no appreciation of the nature and quality of disclosure that must be provided if patient-subjects were truly to be given a choice to accept or decline participation in research. Form, not substance, punctuated most of the policies on consent during the Cold War period." (Katz makes the same argument about the consent process in many contemporary experiments.)

The Advisory Committee also asserted that experimenters had a tradition of obtaining consent from "healthy subjects" but not from "patient-subjects." For some reason, the committee expended considerable intellectual effort trying to prove there were different practices for these two groups, but the theory is not substantiated by the written evidence.

Although hopes were high for the committee, it became apparent over a matter of months that the group didn't have the political will or the desire to thoroughly probe the Cold War experiments. Both Ruth Faden and Jay Katz appeared to be more interested in finding out whether informed consent rules were being followed by contemporary experimenters—certainly a worthwhile endeavor but not the one for which they had been hired. Other members, such as Henry Royal, were determined to see that the reputation of the radiation research community was not unduly smeared. And Kenneth Feinberg, the other lawyer on the committee, was alleged by critics to have been placed on the panel to ensure that compensation to subjects would be kept low. Feinberg denied the allegations, but he did argue at one meeting that the evidence was too "marginal" for the committee to use as a basis for remedies. "It's interesting. It tells a story. But it's hardly the stuff for recommending to the Congress that somebody get $50,000 or medical monitoring or a life insurance policy or health insurance or even a letter of apology."

With the conservative political atmosphere, the group also was not about to recommend remedies or medical monitoring that would have cost millions of dollars and have required congressional approval. Oncologist Eli Glatstein said any effort to recommend compensation for the veterans, for example, "went out the window" when the Republicans took over Congress. "There was no sympathy for that." Still, there was a voluminous record that unequivocally showed that thousands of unethical experiments had occurred during the Cold War. How was the panel to deal with that?

Again they invoked the difference between actor and act, condemning the experiment but not the experimenter. In their final report, which numbers 925 pages, the group did find that many of the studies were unethical, that doctors routinely violated their patients' trust, and that subjects were not fully informed. With few exceptions, though, the panel declared no one was harmed, no one was to blame, and no one needed medical monitoring. "This report is the worst thing to happen to medical ethics since the Bible," said David Egilman, a physician and professor at Brown University, and one of the people who helped spur the congressional investigation into the human experiments in the mid-1980s. "It's constructed so that you can knowingly do something wrong to someone and not be punished; not only not punished but not even found responsible. Think about applying that to anything else in life!"

In brief, the committee managed to come up with only one very small group that was eligible for monetary compensation. In a tortuously worded statement, the panel declared that anyone who had been used in an experiment in which the government tried to keep information secret out of fear of embarrassment or potential liability should be compensated. Although deception was rife in all the experiments, and in many of them for precisely those reasons, the only experimental subjects the panel specified as fitting into this category were the relatives of the plutonium injectees, a woman known as CAL-Z, who was injected with zirconium in 1948 by Berkeley scientists, and the fourteen people used in the Met Lab's total-body irradiation experiment at the Chicago Tumor Clinic. Practically speaking, the only people who would actually receive any money were the families of the plutonium injectees because the identities of the zirconium patient and the fourteen TBI subjects have never been revealed.

The committee also made a general recommendation that subjects who were harmed in experiments that were not intended to have any therapeutic benefit be compensated. Many of the controversial projects, such as the testicular irradiation experiments, fell into this category. But the panel said it could not make specific recommendations about those experiments because it didn't have time to undertake the individualized fact-finding.

Finally, the committee recommended that people who were used in radiation experiments in which they were not harmed but did not give their informed consent should be given a personalized apology. This recommendation was directed at the "tracer" studies, which comprised the majority of experiments done during the Cold War. With scant scientific data on which to base their conclusion and no information whatsoever about the identities of people used in the experiments, the Advisory Committee asserted repeatedly that most of the "tracer" studies caused no physical harm. But some of the tracer studies did, in fact, deliver large doses, and it's impossible to say with certainty that no harm occurred without going to individual cases.

The Advisory Committee also constructed a peculiar ethical argument that linked the wrongness of an experiment to physical harm. "It should be emphasized," the final report observed, "that often these non-therapeutic experiments on unconsenting patients constituted only minor wrongs. Often there was little or no risk to patient-subjects and no inconvenience. Although it is always morally offensive to use a person as a means only, as the burden on the patient-subject decreased, so did the seriousness of the wrong."

Many critics took aim at this position, including editorial writers at the *Boston Globe,* the newspaper that broke the first stories on the radioactive breakfast cereal experiments done at the Fernald school. The *Globe* editorial said:

> Beyond the question of harm, beyond the evil of duplicity, the most unfortunate casualty of the Cold War radiation agenda was the simple capacity of individuals to make informed decisions about their own bodies. Unfortunately, the committee does not seem to lend the principle of self-determination the same value it accords some of the others in its list of moral precepts. Rather, it seems to focus on risks to patients. The panel admits that the nonconsensual use of humans in nontherapeutic experiments is always an affront, but it says, "As the burden on the patient-subject decreased, so too did the seriousness of the wrong." That construction lets the government off too easily, for it does not assign blame based upon the essential nature of the action it-self—the use of an innocent person as a test animal—but rather, fosters a retrospective opinion that allows less-bad outcomes to ameliorate the action's inherent wrong. The committee's recommendation that some of those experimented upon without consent deserve only apologies is informed by this belief.

Once the panel had determined that most of the experiments were harmless, troublesome questions about whether the thousands of Americans who had been used in the studies should be notified and offered medical monitoring went away. If no one was harmed, then there was no need for notification and medical monitoring. In an early draft of its final report, the group did recommend medical monitoring for prisoners who had their testicles irradiated, but the panel changed its mind after it concluded that the cancer risk to the subjects was even smaller than what the original experimenters had calculated. Even Carl Heller, disabled by a stroke and lying on a plastic mattress, told attorneys in 1976 that the prisoners should be monitored for the rest of their lives. If the committee had recommended medical monitoring for one group of test subjects, it would have been hard-pressed not to recommend the same follow-up for people used in other experiments.

The panel based its recommendation against notification and medical monitoring on an unusual set of guidelines that were much more restrictive than what other public health agencies use. The criteria were (1) whether the person would have a greater than a 1 in 1,000 chances of dying from a *fatal* cancer as a result of the radiation exposure and (2) whether early detection and treatment would medically benefit the test subject.

In a paper sharply critical of the committee's work, Brown University's David Egilman points out that other federal agencies, such as the National Institute of Occupational Safety and Health, have determined that all participants in any research study must be notified of the results, even if they show no health risk. Furthermore, he added that most agencies use a threshold of 1 in 1 million when evaluating health risks. By limiting the analysis to cancer mortality only, Egilman said the panel also avoided the sticky issue of other radiation-induced diseases and nonfatal malignancies, such as thyroid tumors, which are extremely painful and dependent on early intervention and medical monitoring for cure.

Even using its own highly restrictive guidelines, the committee found several groups of experimental subjects who were at risk of contracting a fatal malignancy as a result of their radiation exposure, including those who had undergone nasopharyngeal radium treatments and children who were the subjects of radioactive iodine studies. But the panel concluded notification and follow-up was still not warranted because screening methods were not very good and there was no evidence that the subjects would receive any medical benefit from early detection and treatment.

Ironically, the National Institutes of Health had recommended in 1977 that children who received the nasal radium treatments be examined every one to two years, Egilman points out. And early detection and treatment did benefit some experimental victims. John McCarthy, a political science professor in California subjected to the radium nasal treatments as a child, decided to get a check up after reading a 1994 newspaper article about the procedure. During the exam, his doctor found two small tumors on his thyroid. "I've got pretty good odds," he told a reporter. "Had I not known about the risk of these treatments and begun to do some routine monitoring, I probably would not have addressed it for another five to eight years and the prognosis would have gone down sharply."

Radiation oncologist Eli Glatstein believed patients given the radium nasal treatments should be medically monitored but was outvoted thirteen to one. Glatstein later told Stewart Farber, a Rhode Island health physicist who first brought the experiments to the public's attention, that it was "not salable in today's political environment" to recommend screening for so many victims.

The committee did not hold one scientist accountable nor did it single out any institution for blame. Instead, it chose to condemn the entire federal government and the medical profession, a condemnation so broad that it was the equivalent of blaming no one. Even the generic condemnation of physicians was written in a timid, tentative voice:

> To characterize a great profession as having engaged over many years in unethical conduct—years in which massive progress was being made in curbing mankind's greatest ills—may strike some as arrogant and unreasonable. However, fair assessment indicates that the circumstance was one of those times in history in which wrongs were committed by very decent people who were in a position to know that a specific aspect of their interactions with others should be improved.

Despite the hundreds of intentional releases of radioactive material that took place over population centers without the public's knowledge, the Advisory Committee did not recommend that such releases be banned. Instead the group advised that an independent panel review any proposed releases in the future to make sure the secrecy was being maintained for bona fide national security reasons and that measures were taken to reduce risk. Along similar lines, the committee also did not advocate that classified research with human subjects be outlawed. "Important national security goals," the group wrote, "may suffer if human subjects research projects making unique and irreplaceable contributions were foreclosed." Instead the panel urged the Clinton administration to develop regulations so that subjects of future classified research would be protected, adequately informed, and the documents declassified as soon as possible. (The federal government did subsequently develop new rules for classified research.)

The panel also failed to lay to rest the long-standing and bitter controversy involving the atomic veterans; it simply chastised the military for not keeping accurate records and urged that epidemiological tables used in compensating veterans be updated. The Advisory Committee was well aware that the federal government has spent millions on questionable dose reconstructions and, by comparison, pennies on veterans. But instead of issuing a strong statement that would help correct this grave injustice, the panel merely urged the government to determine whether existing laws were being administered in ways that "best balance allocation of resources between financial compensation to eligible atomic vet-

erans and administrative costs, including the costs and scientific credibility of dose reconstruction."

Although Ruth Faden had pledged to leave the record "irrefutably
straight," the panel left the historical record in some ways, murkier than
ever. Not surprisingly, its findings were a great disappointment to the
experimental subjects and their families. Jerry Mousso, the nephew of
one of the Rochester plutonium patients, said, "I guess the government
really won. All the culprits that planned and executed this thing got away
with it." Brenda Weaver, the Hanford woman whose daughter was born
without eyes, observed, "A book has been opened, a page read, and then
it's been closed." Fred Boyce, one of the Fernald boys who participated
in the Science Club, said, "For them to turn around and say that a little
apology is enough . . . is just beyond belief." And finally, Ron Hamm,
who was exposed as a fetus to radiation when his mother was given the
radioactive iron cocktail at Vanderbilt University, spoke for many when
he said, "I do feel betrayed and I feel abused by this committee's report."

45

A PRESIDENTIAL APOLOGY

President Clinton formally accepted the Advisory Committee's final report in a quiet ceremony at the White House on the morning of October 3, 1995. Hoisting the heavy blue volume into the air, he said, "This report I received today is a monumental document in more ways than one. It is a very, very important piece of America's history."

The president then condemned the experiments in straightforward language, leaving out all the caveats that muddied the committee's report. He admitted that thousands of government-sponsored radiation experiments took place at hospitals, universities, and military bases throughout the United States during the Cold War. "While most of the tests were ethical by any standards, some were unethical, not only by today's standards, but by the standards of the time in which they were conducted. They failed both the test of our national values and the test of humanity."

Many of the experiments were performed on the atomic veterans and on the sick and the poor, he admitted, without their having any idea of what was being done to them. "Informed consent means your doctor tells you the risk of the treatment you are about to undergo. In too many cases, informed consent was withheld. Americans were kept in the dark about the effects of what was being done to them. The deception extended beyond the test subjects themselves to encompass their families and the American people as a whole, for these experiments were kept secret. And they were shrouded not for a compelling reason of national security, but for the simple fear of embarrassment, and that was wrong."

The president acknowledged that the subterfuge used during the

Cold War had added to the mistrust many Americans feel toward their government. "Because of stonewalling and evasions in the past, times when a family member or a neighbor suffered an injustice and had nowhere to turn and couldn't even get the facts, some Americans lost faith in the promise of our democracy. Government was very powerful, but very far away and not trusted to be ethical."

Although the committee had labored over the question of whether the radiation victims should receive an apology, Clinton swept away all the conditions and spontaneously offered an apology to all of the people who had been used in the radiation experiments. The government leaders responsible for the experiments were no longer alive to apologize to the people and communities whose lives were "darkened by the shadow of the atom," he began. "So today, on behalf of another generation of American leaders and another generation of American citizens, the United States of America offers a sincere apology to those of our citizens who were subjected to these experiments, to their families and to their communities."

Clinton was such a polished speaker, his words came so effortlessly, that the historic significance of what he was saying almost slipped by the audience. He was the first president born after the bombings of Hiroshima and Nagasaki, and he had just broken with the official pattern of denial, cover-up, and secrecy that had characterized nearly every controversial issue surrounding the atomic bomb, including the building and dropping of the bomb itself. His speech took sixteen minutes.

With the president's apology, the day of reckoning had finally come for the scientists, doctors, and bureaucrats who schemed for decades to keep knowledge of the plutonium injections and other radiation experiments from becoming public. Lawsuits were being brought, public denunciations made, but most of the experimenters were dead and spared the consequences they had feared so long.

Most Americans, in fact, paid little attention whatsoever to Clinton's speech. Two hours later a jury in Los Angeles returned to the courtroom with its verdict in the sensational murder trial of football legend O. J. Simpson. In the frenzied media coverage that followed the innocent verdict, Clinton's remarks on a much vaster question of guilt were reduced to sound bites on the evening news and stories on the inside pages of the nation's newspapers. Not even the clever doctors of the Manhattan Project could have dreamed up such a diversion.

46

"NEVER AGAIN"

With the pronouncements by the Advisory Committee and President Clinton's apology, the controversy over the human radiation experiments began to slip from public view. Although her stint as energy secretary was nearly over, Hazel O'Leary was not yet through with her involvement in the horrific scandal she had helped bring to light.

O'Leary's public image had changed dramatically in the three years since her December 7, 1993 press conference. She also had made many formidable enemies as she went about trying to reform the DOE's anachronistic bureaucracy and to dismantle its creaky cold war machinery. When she recommended in the spring of 1993 that the fifteen underground tests planned at the Nevada Test Site be canceled, powerful officials in the Pentagon began viewing her with suspicion. Was the elegant corporate lawyer in the bright tropical suits an antinuclear activist? Many thought so.

"She was not seen by the Defense Department, at least initially, as especially supportive of the weapons program," said Al Narath, the former director of Sandia National Laboratories and one of the three weapons lab directors who was summoned to Washington for the debate in the tomblike room in the basement of DOE headquarters. "She and I never talked about this, but my guess is she came into the job with sort of a natural, anti-nuclear weapon inclination."

John Nuckolls, the former director of Lawrence Livermore National Laboratory who was also summoned to Washington, said he was taken aback by the way O'Leary had conducted the meeting. "And I was most startled when she invoked her grandmother in response to some of the arguments for why the tests needed to be done, saying she couldn't convince her grandmother of that. That's THE memorable remark of the meeting. I think I would have felt more comfortable if the issue had been addressed on its merits for the national security of the United States and not for what she, with her lack of understanding and appreciation, could explain to her grandmother. So she suddenly introduced this way of thinking about the problem—can we convince the non-technically trained and oriented person of the validity of these requirements. And I would say I was astonished when she did that."

Frank Gaffney, a former assistant secretary in the Defense Department during the Reagan administration, compared her 1993 press conference to the Japanese attack at Pearl Harbor: "It is somehow fitting that the Secretary of Energy, Hazel O'Leary, chose Pearl Harbor Day 1993 to launch what was, arguably, the most devastating single attack on the underpinnings of the U.S. national security structure since Japan's lightning strike on the 7th Fleet fifty-two years ago."

Many active and retired scientists viewed her remarks about the radiation experiments as a slap in the face. In the weapons labs, the dislike for O'Leary was almost palpable. Some officials openly ridiculed her, calling her "Witch Hazel."

But O'Leary airily dismissed the criticisms in the waning weeks of her four-year tenure. She told *Inside Energy*, a trade newspaper that covers her department, that she credited her achievements to the "audacity of this sort of aging, old broad, who doesn't sit at the table and never sat at the table before, to walk in and say, 'Uh-uh, I'm not certifying [fifteen nuclear] tests. I don't think so.' I'm proud of having the guts to say, 'Why are we doing this? Would you tell me again why we're doing this?'"

By the time she made those remarks, she was practically out the door. Partly due to her own mismanagement, in the latter part of her tenure O'Leary had found herself facing hostile questions from Republicans regarding expenditures on trade missions to India, Pakistan, China, and South Africa. Although O'Leary, unlike other members of President Clinton's cabinet, was not accused of self-enrichment, she found her folk-hero status evaporating as she was portrayed in hearing after hearing as a high-flying Evita Perón intent on seeing the world at taxpayers' expense. Her trade missions may have been overstaffed, but none of the documents and testimony submitted in the course of numerous congressional hearings revealed any criminal or ethical wrongdoing.

In an interview just two weeks before leaving the office, O'Leary said that she viewed the congressional inquires as a personal attack by Republicans bent on destroying her. She said that she believed her "tear-down" was also related to the fact that she refused to seek help from Washington's power brokers. One congressman believed she had been "too uppity," she confided. "Do you know that word? It's a very Southern word. And by that he meant—and this is a congress person—that I was self-assured, extremely direct and never needy. And there was something about that in a woman which was unseemly; to be so self-assured, to be so large and never to be asking for help. And that my sin was not that I had been extraordinary to the positive but that I had been too large and too uppity; that I should have been quieter, softer and needy of the supportive protection of others. And the way I translate that is, I rarely asked for permission."

O'Leary pointed out that while congressional investigators had found no evidence of either criminal or unethical behavior on her part, several of her fellow cabinet officers, by contrast, were mired in serious criminal probes. "What I've learned is that I'm a lot tougher than anyone ever thought. And that we have managed to get our work done and I'm still standing. If I had done something terribly wrong, I wouldn't be the longest serving secretary of energy in the history of the United States of America—and I am." A few minutes later, she added, "I feel like a tough old chick who's been through an extraordinary four years and I'm extremely proud of every outcome."

O'Leary held one more "Openness" press conference just five days before she left her job. Among the items she released was an extraordinary report on weapons tests and peaceful nuclear explosions conducted in the former Soviet Union between 1949 and 1990. The report, received from the Russian Federation for Atomic Energy, was a mirror image of the study O'Leary made public in 1993 on U.S. tests. She also released the first batch of some 6,500 government films chronicling the troop maneuvers in Nevada and other spectacles of the atomic age. Perhaps more than anything else, the films capture the arrogance and ignorance of the nuclear weapons program.

On an overcast, cold day in mid-December of 1996, O'Leary flew to Rochester, New York. When she had discussed the experiments at her first press conference three years earlier, she had vowed to meet personally with the families of the plutonium patients. Now she was fulfilling that pledge in a private meeting room at the Radisson Hotel. The lawyers were asked to leave the room. For forty-five minutes, O'Leary talked with the families of several of the patients.

Present were the relatives of Amedio Lovecchio, HP-1, the maintenance man who each fall buried his fig trees in the ground to protect
them from the harsh winter; Jean Daigneault, HP-4, the young woman
who craved hot dogs when she went on a rice-and-raisin diet; and Paul
Galinger, HP-5, the tall man with trembling hands. Also in attendance
were family members of John Mousso, HP-6, the gentle man from East
Rochester; Janet Stadt, HP-8, the woman who suffered from scleroderma; and Fred Sours, HP-9, the politician with the red, swollen face
whose body was analyzed for plutonium even as his constituents
mourned his death.

After the meeting, O'Leary vowed, "My commitment is: Never
Again. This should never happen again in government." Standing among
the family members was Mary Jeanne Connell, the only known survivor
of the injection experiments at Rochester's Strong Memorial Hospital.
The sting of the humiliation that Connell felt when she learned she had
been used as a laboratory animal was still with her. O'Leary's "never
again" promise was reassuring, but for Connell the world had become a
less trustworthy place. She told a Rochester reporter, "I'm afraid it's
going to happen again, you know."

47

WHITEWASHES, RED HERRINGS, AND COLD CASH

Ultimately, the subjects used in the Cold War radiation experiments went to court to seek justice. The legal hurdles were immense and the lawsuits extremely difficult to pursue. Decades had passed since the experiments had taken place. Many of the subjects and scientists were dead. Key documents had been lost or destroyed. Then there was the question of harm, the nearly impossible task of linking a long-ago radiation exposure to health problems, some of which hadn't shown up for decades, or might be dormant even now—still waiting for the right trigger.

Relatives of the plutonium patients were among the first to file lawsuits in federal court. Some families banded together and filed joint lawsuits, others filed individually. Eventually the federal government settled out of court with sixteen of the eighteen plutonium families. The relatives of thirteen patients received approximately $400,000 each. The surviving kin of Una Macke's family received $300,000; Simeon Shaw's family, $262,500; and Edna Bartholf's relatives, $160,000. Mary Jeanne Connell, who was injected with uranium, also received $400,000.

As for the remaining two patients, CHI-3, the young Chicago patient, was never identified, and the family of William Purcell, one of the Rochester injectees, chose not to participate in the lawsuit.

In Massachusetts, a lawsuit was filed on behalf of the boys who were enticed into eating radioactive oatmeal at the Walter E. Fernald State School. The petition claimed that the state owed the children "the highest duty of care, including the duty not to use them as human guinea pigs." In April 1998 Quaker Oats and MIT agreed to pay $1.85 million to settle the claims against them. The money will be split among forty-five of the former test subjects. The commonwealth of Massachusetts has also agreed to pay another $676,000 to twenty-seven participants. Other state claims, as well as federal claims, are still pending.

In Cincinnati, five years of rancorous legal proceedings came to an end on May 4, 1999, when a federal judge approved a $5.4 million settlement. Eugene Saenger, wearing a gray suit and red bow tie, was present in the courtroom for the judge's ruling but declined to talk with reporters afterward. Under the terms of the settlement, most of the families will receive about $50,000 each. In addition, a large plaque commemorating the victims of the Pentagon-funded study will be placed in a courtyard at the University of Cincinnati hospital. Many families also wanted a personal apology from physician Eugene Saenger, but Saenger's attorney, R. Joseph Parker, said Saenger felt he had done nothing wrong and that an apology was "non-negotiable."

In Oak Ridge, relatives of Woodrow Wilson Litton retained flamboyant San Francisco lawyer Melvin Belli, the "king of torts," to represent them in a lawsuit against the government. But the case fell into limbo when Belli filed for bankruptcy protection and later died. The lawsuit was dismissed in 1996 by a federal judge.

Attorneys for Vanderbilt University fought hard to get the class-action lawsuit brought by the women who unknowingly drank the radioactive iron cocktails thrown out of court. But a federal judge kept rejecting their arguments. Kenneth Feinberg, one of the two attorneys who served on the Advisory Committee, eventually was appointed to serve as a mediator in the case. The lawsuit was settled in the spring of 1998 for approximately $10.3 million with $3 million earmarked for attorneys' fees.

The class-action lawsuit initiated by Harold Bibeau, a former convict who had his testicles irradiated in Oregon, was dismissed by a federal judge because of statute-of-limitations considerations. Attorneys representing Bibeau have appealed the ruling and also have filed a lawsuit in state court to compel authorities to establish a fund for the medical monitoring of the prisoners. About half of the men who participated in Heller's experiment are dead.

In Washington State, a lawsuit filed by prisoners irradiated by C. Alvin Paulsen was faring better. A federal judge ruled in early 1999 that the case could go forward, but dismissed two contractors and the federal government from the lawsuit. In a sworn deposition taken in September of 1998, Hazel O'Leary said that Paulsen's subjects could not have obtained information from the Department of Energy about the experiment before December 1993, when she held her press conference. She continued, "If information was deemed to be embarrassing, it was simply not made available. I might add that the department had a culture of punishing people . . . when they delivered bad information."

In comparison to the mild criticism levied by the Advisory Committee, several federal judges presiding over the cases had harsh words for the experimenters. "This was an atrocity," snapped U.S. District Judge Michael A. Telesca of Rochester during a preliminary proceeding in one of the plutonium cases. In Cincinnati, U.S. District Judge Sandra Beckwith wrote, "The allegations in this case indicate that the government of the United States, aided by the officials of the City of Cincinnati, treated at least eighty-seven of its citizens as though they were laboratory animals. If the Constitution has not clearly established a right under which these plaintiffs may attempt to prove their case, then a gaping hole in that document has been exposed. The subject of experimentation who has not volunteered is merely an object."

Almost without exception, the universities and hospitals named in the lawsuits were bellicose and defensive about their role in the experiments, downplaying their involvement and the harm to the patients, or even going so far as to rewrite history. The institutions hired top-flight lawyers to represent them. There is nothing wrong with that, but it's worth noting that the American taxpayers wound up picking up the tab because of policies dating back to the Manhattan Project, which indemnify contractors if they are sued in the course of carrying out their duties.

The University of California at San Francisco assembled a "fact-finding" committee in early 1994 to probe the three plutonium injections performed at the University of California Hospital. In its final report, the committee occasionally referred to the experiment as an "intervention" and to the subjects as "plutonium recipients." With no direct evidence to support the claim, the panel put forth the speculative hypothesis that Simeon Shaw, CAL-2, and Elmer Allen, CAL-3, were not part of the Manhattan Project's plutonium experiment but participants in a legitimate university research effort to discover a treatment for bone cancer. Similarly, the panel hypothesized that the injection of americium into Hanford Jang, the sixteen-year-old from China, was also part of the researchers' efforts to find a cure for bone cancer. The panel reluctantly conceded that Albert Stevens and Simeon Shaw's guardian didn't give their informed consent for the injections, but it noted, "The committee found no evidence that the experiment was designed with malevolent intentions."

The report revealed more about the bunker mentality of UCSF in the 1990s than the plutonium experiment in the 1940s. All but one of the committee members were employed by UCSF, which in essence meant the university was investigating itself. In addition, several multi-million-dollar lawsuits were filed against the university by relatives of the plutonium patients while the group was meeting, making it even more doubtful that an unbiased report would emerge. Ruth Macklin, a member of the president's Advisory Committee, dismissed the UCSF findings at a public meeting as a "whitewash."

The report may have been a whitewash and its contents a classic case of counterspin, but the findings actually were used by lawyers representing UCSF to pressure the family of Simeon Shaw into settling for $262,500. Simmy was an Australian citizen and the youngest patient used in the plutonium experiment. Yet his family received one of the smallest awards.

Joshua Shaw, Simmy's brother, said that with the public attention waning, attorneys representing UCSF felt free to play hardball. The immorality of the experiment meant nothing to them, he said. "Morality has to be accounted for. The Nazis tattooed numbers on their victims' arms. The American government gave Simeon Shaw the number 'CAL-2.'"

In face-to-face negotiations with Joshua Shaw in the spring of 1997, attorneys for UCSF argued that the injections didn't kill Simmy, that the child was going to die anyway, and that physicians at the University of California Hospital were trying to find a cure for one of mankind's most dreaded diseases. "They said UCSF doctors were looking for a cancer cure and that's why he was given the extra injections," Joshua said. "But there is nothing in the documents that indicate they were looking for a cure for cancer. It was just another red herring."

In Rochester, Strong Memorial Hospital officials initially expressed regret about the experiment. But the repentant attitude hardened into a defensive posture as debate over the experiment raged. Hospital spokesman Robert Loeb described the plutonium injections as a "covert extracurricular activity" of which the university was not aware and did not approve. When advocates for the experimental subjects called for a criminal investigation, Loeb labeled it "a suggestion full of sound and fury, signifying nothing." He added, "As far as they concern UR Medical Center, these cries for a criminal investigation are utterly ridiculous. There is no basis for criminal charges whatsoever."

With scores of foreign journalists knocking at their doors and helicopter-borne camera crews buzzing the air space above them, officials at

Los Alamos National Laboratory decided to take a proactive stance toward the radiation experiments. A task force called the Human Studies Project Team was assembled, and beginning in January of 1994, the group released documents on a regular basis to public reading rooms. The weekly disclosures contained a few juicy items, but many of the documents consisted of previously published reports or memos already in the public domain. Los Alamos also sought to put a favorable spin on the documents in press statements accompanying the releases. The manipulation notwithstanding, the fact that the lab was making public anything at all was a historic event. Los Alamos was the heart and soul of the weapons complex. From the remote mesa in northern New Mexico, it had operated in virtual secrecy for fifty years. But the lab could not escape the public scrutiny of the radiation experiments and was under intense pressure from the Department of Energy to cooperate with the national search effort ordered by President Clinton.

During a "close-out" news conference, lab officials concluded no Los Alamos scientist had acted improperly. But Joan McIver Gibson, a medical ethicist from the University of New Mexico and a paid consultant on the document-release project, afterward told a reporter that she didn't know if the public should believe the lab had told all it knew. "There is an insularity at the lab, a lack of practice and experience in talking to the community," she said. "We don't have a clue to a lot of things that have gone on here."

Even though President Clinton, Energy Secretary Hazel O'Leary, and the Advisory Committee had publicly acknowledged that many of the experiments were unethical, many scientists couldn't accept the idea that they or their peers had committed any wrongs. They maintained their belief that the ends they had pursued justified the means they used, expressed little or no remorse for the experimental subjects, and continued to bash O'Leary and the media for blowing the controversy out of proportion.

Don Petersen, one of the old hands who was brought back to the lab to help with the search effort and who had testified at one of the outreach meetings about giving his own children trace amounts of radioiodine, told a reporter he would be willing to drink a solution of radioactive plutonium if it would help researchers. "The abject terror of plutonium is unfounded," he said.

Patricia Durbin, the Berkeley scientist who worked for Joseph Hamilton and initiated the follow-up study of the plutonium patients, was still irritated when I contacted her by telephone at her home in Berkeley three years after the story broke. The controversy over the plutonium injections, she said, took a year out of her life. "When you're approaching seventy, you can't afford years out of your life. I spent the better part of a year in interviews, hearings, depositions, consultations with lawyers, writing reports and so on. I got tired of it."

Durbin said she and her colleagues hoped to publish a comprehensive scientific report on the plutonium experiment "when the dust settled." She said she would also like to see the rest of the plutonium patients exhumed. The data are so important, Durbin continued, that she and several colleagues considered having themselves injected with plutonium before their deaths and then donating their bodies to science.

Officials in the Department of Energy were quick to reject the offer. Lori Azim, an aide to Tara O'Toole, the DOE's assistant secretary for environment, safety, and health, told a Rochester newspaper she couldn't imagine anyone endorsing that idea. "Frankly, we're not interested in that anymore."

EPILOGUE

When Energy Secretary Hazel O'Leary acknowledged that the federal government had conducted radiation experiments on its own people, thousands of callers flooded a hot line set up by the DOE: What was going on? Had we become a nation of paranoiacs? A country of guinea pigs? Or had O'Leary touched on something that resonated deeply with the American public?

Certainly the radiation experiments raised complex questions that go to the core of our society: the trust between a government and its people, the subjugation of individuals to the interest of the state, and the ethical dilemma associated with the development of weapons of mass destruction.

But what O'Leary did in a dramatic and unexpected way was confirm the hunch that all was not well beneath the soothing no-harm, no-danger statements that accompanied the reports of nuclear blasts, spills, and accidents of the Cold War. Her admission produced an electrifying response, something akin to the emotions a person might feel after being subjected to a lifetime of vague allusions and abrupt silences and suddenly learning a dark family secret he or she had always suspected.

When the Nevada Test Site opened in 1951, the Atomic Energy Commission warned its public relations men to approach the tests "matter-of-factly" and not go overboard in emphasizing how safe the explosions were going to be. Such a campaign might be interpreted as one of the "lady doth protest too much," an AEC official cautioned.

The bomb project's public relations machine succeeded in keeping a lid on the experiments for fifty years. Its spokesmen were able to blame the fallout controversy, the illnesses of the atomic veterans, and the diseases of the downwinders on sudden wind shifts, misinformed scientists, the overactive imaginations of aging soldiers, and even Communist propagandists. But the radiation experiments revealed a deliberate intent, a willingness to inflict harm or the risk of harm, which could not be explained away so easily. Somebody inserted the needle into the human vein, mixed the radioisotopes in the paper cup, or flipped the switch that delivered a potentially lethal dose of whole-body radiation. There is no denying that:

• Thousands of Americans were used as laboratory animals in radiation experiments funded by the federal government. Many of the subjects were not asked for their consent or given accurate information about the nature of these experiments. Some didn't learn they or their loved ones had been used as guinea pigs until 1994 or 1995. Some still don't know, and never will.

• Many of the doctors and scientists who performed these experiments routinely violated their patients' trust and engaged in deception. They ignored the Hippocratic Oath, the 1946 American Medical Association guidelines, the Nuremberg Code, as well as policies adopted by the Atomic Energy Commission in 1947 and by the Defense Department in 1953. Civil and criminal laws also may have been broken. Beyond everything else, the experimenters violated a fundamental right that belongs to all competent adults: the right to control one's own body.

• Although the majority of the experiments were the so-called tracer studies, which involved administering radioactive materials in quantities so small that they probably caused no harm, most scientists agree that no dose can absolutely be called safe.

• Some studies are known to have had very serious consequences. The total-body irradiation experiments caused intense suffering and premature death in some patients. The radium rod treatments and some of the radioactive iodine experiments increased the risk of head, neck, and thyroid cancers and other secondary disorders.

What can be said about the scientists and doctors involved in these experiments? Like professionals in every field, some were extremely accomplished and others were hacks. A few of the experiments increased scientific understanding and led to new diagnostic tools, while others were of questionable scientific value. The plutonium experiment is a prime example of bad science. It was a poorly designed experiment for several reasons, including the fact that the sample size was too small and the patients varied greatly in age and type of disease. Beyond those obvious flaws, the experimental results led the Manhattan Project doctors to erroneous assumptions. From the excretion data, they concluded that urine could be used to determine the body burden of any compound of plutonium that is inhaled or ingested. But William Jay Brady, the scientist who spent four decades at the Nevada Test Site and is now helping the atomic vets, said that just isn't true.

The eighteen patients were injected with plutonium citrate or plutonium nitrate, both soluble forms of plutonium that are excreted in the urine. But only a few thousand people, at most, who worked in the weapons complex over the last fifty years have been exposed to those particular plutonium compounds. As Brady explains it, the majority of the world's population, including test-site participants, have been exposed to plutonium *oxide,* a compound that is created during a nuclear detonation. And plutonium oxide, for the most part, stays in the lungs and lymph nodes and cannot be detected in the urine. Thus the data from the injectees are applicable to perhaps a few thousand workers in the nuclear weapons complex and not to the many hundreds of thousands of people exposed to global fallout.

During the heyday of the atmospheric testing program, thousands of urine samples were taken regularly from test-site workers and, to a lesser extent, military troops and examined for plutonium. Those test results invariably produced false negatives—that is, no evidence of contamination that could be confirmed. In fact, Brady said, many of the soldiers and test-site workers could have had a significant amount of plutonium in the lungs, but it would not have been detectable in the urine. "How ironic," he added. "The federal government has spent millions of dollars analyzing urine samples for something we now know doesn't even show up in urine!"

One of the most disturbing revelations was the pervasive deception that the doctors, scientists, and military officials routinely engaged in even before the first bomb had been detonated. And General Leslie Groves lied egregiously when he testified to Congress in 1945 about the radiation effects of the bomb. "A pleasant way to die," he said—fully aware of how dreadful such deaths really are. Groves knew what happened to the Japanese victims, and he knew what had happened a great deal closer to home, when one of the scientists in the Los Alamos lab was fatally injured. His sidekick, Stafford Warren, downplayed the fatalities and lingering deaths in Japan. By not fully disclosing the human suffering caused by those bombings, they did a grave disservice. Furthermore, General Groves got it exactly backward when he told congressmen, "In the end, I think that the atomic bomb will be considered as a byproduct of the atomic age."

The culture bred by the Manhattan Project caused a blanket of secrecy to be thrown over everything related to atomic weapons. The secrecy was essential during the Manhattan Project, but it hardened into a protective and impenetrable shell after the war. The secrecy cut researchers off from the healthy sunlight of inquiry that would surely have put a stop to some of the experiments and perhaps reduced the number of atmospheric tests. Many of the scientists, such as Carl Heller and C. Alvin Paulsen, were instructed to avoid publicity, and several studies, such as Eugene Saenger's, were halted only after they received public attention.

Working behind their security fences, the scientists developed a them-against-us mentality. This attitude was often manifested in a distrust of the public and disdain for scientific opponents. The "cleared" researchers even began to think alike, which accounts in part for the remarkably similar statements issued whenever a controversy erupted. The web of deception and denial looks in retrospect like a vast conspiracy, but in actuality it was simply a reflection of the shared attitudes and beliefs of the scientists and bureaucrats who were inducted into the weapons program at a time of national urgency and never abandoned their belief that nuclear war was imminent. This collective body of ideas was passed down through the generations and is only now beginning to be dislodged. But the intensity of the attacks upon Hazel O'Leary, who played an active role in trying to dismantle this culture of secrecy, shows what a hold it has on us still. In fact, the pendulum began swinging back toward secrecy in the spring of 1999 when allegations emerged that China may have stolen some of our nuclear secrets. Numerous steps were undertaken to bolster security in the nation's weapons labs, and the Office of Declassification was renamed the Office of Nuclear and National Security to reflect the changed priorities.

As far back as 1947 much of the secrecy was prompted by fear of lawsuits and adverse public relations. But where did this worry over lawsuits, the fretting about public relations, come from? After all, this was a patriotic era when most Americans trusted their government, when conspiracy theories did not abound, and when lawsuits were not filed over a spilled cup of coffee.

The fear of lawsuits dates back to the 1920s and 1930s, when the young women who painted the watch dials inadvertently ingested radium and later developed cancer. Their deaths triggered numerous lawsuits and an outpouring of sympathy throughout the world. Many of the Manhattan Project doctors, such as Stafford Warren, Louis Hempelmann, Robert Stone, and Joseph Hamilton, were acutely aware of the tragedy and sought to avoid similar lawsuits from being filed by workers in the nation's nuclear weapons complex.

During the war, the bomb makers believed that lawsuits would jeopardize the secrecy of the project. After the war, they worried that lawsuits would jeopardize the continued development of nuclear weapons.

The Veterans Administration in 1947 considered establishing a "confidential" Atomic Medicine Division to deal with potential disability claims from soldiers and sailors involved in the weapons tests. Wrote one physician, "It was felt unwise to publicize unduly the probable adverse effects of exposure to radioactive materials. The use of nuclear energy at this time was so sensitive that unfavorable reaction might have jeopardized future developments in the field."

As a public information officer for the AEC explained after the first series of bombs were detonated in Nevada: "During the period from August 1945 until early 1951, the public had been subjected to a diet of Sunday-magazine sensationalized reports of atomic weapons. There had been created a mass fear of radioactive effects and perhaps a feeling that if one atomic bomb were exploded many cities in areas distant from the site would be disintegrated."

Thus the weaponeers recognized that they would have to allay the public's fear of atomic weapons in order to keep the production plants operating and nurture the budding fields of nuclear medicine and nuclear power. This meant an aggressive propaganda campaign about the "friendly atom" and the suppression of all potentially negative stories about health hazards related to atomic energy.

It's difficult to describe how pervasive, how all-encompassing this propaganda campaign was. In the films of the atmospheric testing program now being declassified by the Department of Energy, military officials continually emphasize how safe the bomb tests are, how vital they are to the security of the free world, how glorious the future of mankind will be when the full potential of the atom has been realized. "It's a huge fraternity, this order of the mushroom, and it's growing all the time," one narrator crowed.

AEC officials routinely suppressed information about environmental contamination caused by the weapons plants and the health risks posed by fallout from the atmospheric testing program. In the case of the people who lived downwind of the Nevada site or the atomic plants, the suppression continued even when scientists knew the public should be warned of dangerous levels of radioactivity in order to protect themselves. "The functionaries who executed this policy were not evil men, but rather loyal men who wore blinders and fulfilled their missions with such dedication and zeal that these virtues, in excess, resulted in dishonorable deeds," wrote Stewart Udall, a former secretary of the interior as well as an attorney who has represented Nevada's downwinders and the uranium miners.

For five decades the public remained largely ignorant of the systematic nature of human radiation experiments. Secrecy, compounded by the insular, inbred nature of the atomic establishment, helped keep the experiments from becoming known. But the fact is, the Manhattan Project veterans and their protégés controlled virtually all the information. They sat on the boards that set radiation standards, consulted at meetings where further human experimentation was discussed, investigated nuclear accidents, and served as expert witnesses in radiation injury cases. The Manhattan Project researchers also worked in a professional world that remained remarkably stable. Once the project itself had been disbanded, the scientists got jobs in the weapons laboratories and at universities, many of which had contracts with the Atomic Energy Commission, and they remained in these jobs for the rest of their lives.

The experiments conducted after the war generally were not secret. But the results were published in obscure journals or laboratory health reports that were inaccessible to the public. Furthermore, many of the policy discussions surrounding the purpose of the experiments were kept secret.

As the oral histories conducted by the Advisory Committee show, the radiation experiments were not an anomaly. Unethical human experimentation occurred in many medical fields in the decades following World War II. Money was plentiful and scientists were eager to conduct research, publish scientific papers, and climb the academic ladder. It was a time when certain medical doctors acted like predators and viewed their patients as little more than white mice. Although human experimentation is necessary to eradicate disease, there is nevertheless something unsettling about the powerful deciding that the powerless should sacrifice themselves to science.

Another of the ethical horrors was the melding of military and medical agendas. The large total-body irradiation experiments conducted after the war probably would not have been done without funding by the armed forces. Eugene Saenger said he didn't know if he would have conducted the TBI experiment had he not gotten money from the military. Saenger also said that he might have halted the experiment had investigators found a biological marker, or "dosimeter," which could have been used to accurately measure radiation exposure.

The low-dose irradiation chamber in Oak Ridge was built at a time when NASA was exploring the effects of low-level radiation on astronauts. Those experiments, too, probably would never have gone forward without the space agency's interest. Carl Heller and C. Alvin Paulsen had no experience using radiation and most likely would never have proceeded with their testicular irradiation experiments without encouragement and funding from the AEC.

It was not until 1993, with the admission by Energy Secretary Hazel O'Leary, that the size of the experimentation program began to be revealed. O'Leary's acknowledgment was a radical departure for a bureaucracy steeped in secrecy and arrogance. President Clinton supported O'Leary's efforts to make all documents public, and even notoriously closed agencies like the Central Intelligence Agency were dragged into the search effort. But Hazel O'Leary was the public official who took the greatest risk and paid the greatest price for making public such a controversial chapter in Cold War history. Through her efforts, a massive and secretive bureaucracy was nudged farther into the bright light of truth.

By contrast, the findings of the Advisory Committee on Human Radiation Experiments were disappointing and timid. Even committee member Jay Katz admitted in an interview after the panel had been disbanded that the members did not "sufficiently condemn" many of the experiments. Although the group's final report is factual and contains much new information, its conclusions are weak and fail to come to terms with many of the controversial studies.

Collectively, the documents show that the atomic veterans were put at risk without their knowledge. The extent of the risk will probably never be known with certainty because the passage of time has obliterated information trails and record keeping was shoddy and incomplete. Many veterans were put in harm's way for a frivolous and unconscionable purpose: public relations. Military leaders, such as General James Cooney, wanted to prove to the troops and the American public that the scorched earth left by an atomic detonation was perfectly inhabitable soon after the blast. The federal government, as California Senator Alan Cranston observed in 1984, has a moral obligation to the atomic veterans that has not been fulfilled.

Residents who lived downwind of Hanford and other weapons sites arguably could also be considered subjects of what the Advisory Committee termed "experiments of opportunity." Certainly the residents were not told of the dangers from the plant emissions and many were the subsequent objects of scientific study, which was not identified as such.

Although many of the experimental subjects and their relatives were disappointed by the government's response, the American people nevertheless gained a vast amount of knowledge from the documents about the Cold War. It's as if a submerged continent has risen to the surface. There are peaks and valleys and still lots of shadows, but the contours are better understood.

Much of the information is disturbing, shocking, and will serve as a cautionary tale about the corrupting power of secrecy, the danger of special interest groups, the excesses of science and medicine, and the need to monitor closely the activities of civilian and military weapons makers. "The breathtaking advances in science and technology demand we always keep our ethical watch light burning. No matter how rapid the pace of change, it can never outrun our core convictions that have stood us so well as a nation for more than two hundred years now, through many different scientific revolutions," President Clinton observed when he accepted the Advisory Committee's report.

In the records are the voices of the little-known men who walked the corridors of power during the Cold War. In his humorless reports to the Manhattan Engineer District, a careful reader can ferret out the callous recklessness that drove Joseph Hamilton to take such risks with his life and the lives of others. The fear and frustration that scientists at Los Alamos felt as the kilogram amounts of plutonium began arriving is almost palpable in the exchange of memos between Louis Hempelmann and J. Robert Oppenheimer. Los Alamos chemist Wright Langham and physician Samuel Bassett reveal their capacity for self-deception as they struggle to maintain a gentlemanly decorum in the midst of discussions about blood, urine, and feces. Nobel laureate Willard Libby strikes one of the most lunatic notes of the Cold War when he turns to his peers and wistfully remarks, "If anybody knows how to do a good job of body snatching, they will really be serving their country."

Most of the men who wrote the memos and reports, delivered their opinions behind closed doors, are dead. The committees and boards they once served on are defunct and forgotten. Even the buildings where they once met have been razed. Still, there is an invisible but nonetheless real thread connecting that past to our present and even our future. These scientists helped to shape the policies that have affected the health of thousands of Americans. Indeed, we are still reaping the consequences.

Scientists at the National Cancer Institute in late 1997 estimated that bomb tests conducted in Nevada during the 1950s may cause 10,000 to 75,000 extra thyroid cancers. Seventy percent of the cancers, or as many as 52,500 malignancies, have yet to be diagnosed. Three-fourths of the cancers are expected to develop in people who were younger than five at the time of the exposure. These current and future cancer patients are the baby boomers who guzzled milk from the cows that grazed on the contaminated fields that Stafford Warren warned about in his 1947 speech at Yale University. "There were few, if any, Americans in the contiguous forty-eight states at the time that were not exposed to some level of fallout," Dr. Richard D. Klausner, director of the National Cancer Institute, said in 1997.

The NCI's fallout study, which took fourteen years to complete, does not take into account the vast amounts of radioiodine released from tests at the Pacific Proving Ground or the radioiodine released into the atmosphere by nuclear tests conducted by other countries. Nor do the results address the health effects caused by long-lived isotopes of cesium, strontium, plutonium, and carbon, which were released during the blasts and found their way into the bodies of the people living on the planet. All of the baby boomers, a few retired weapons scientists said with an almost macabre cheeriness, have a few atoms of plutonium in their bones.

The documents go far in demystifying some of the most secretive aspects of the weapons program. With the unveiling comes understanding and perhaps a basis for communication. President Clinton said he hoped the massive release of records would help rebuild the public's trust in the government. But trust occurs when behavior is consistent and honest over a long period of time. The track record of openness is short. The pitfalls ahead are many. Unnecessary secrets and vast distances still exist between the people inside and outside the fences.

ACKNOWLEDGMENTS

I am indebted to the many people who enabled me to write this book. It seemed that whenever I hit a rough spot—whether it was in the research, the writing, or the editing phase—someone appeared and extended a helping hand. In particular, I want to thank the relatives of the deceased people who were unwittingly used in these experiments, as well as those subjects who are still living, who so generously gave of their time, recounting painful moments in their lives and providing me with invaluable documents and photographs.

One of the people whom I will never be able to repay is William Jay Brady, who became my unofficial scientific advisor for the project. Having worked at the Nevada Test Site since 1952, Jay not only possesses a firsthand knowledge of many of the events and scientists described in this book but also has a brilliant scientific mind and an almost photographic memory. He read the manuscript twice and spent many hours tutoring me in physics, mathematics, and radiation biology. Other scientists who helped were Bill Bartlett, John Gofman, Darrell Fisher, George Voelz, William Moss, Roland Finston, John Cobb, and Arthur Upton.

My heartfelt thanks also go to Mary Diecker, an indefatigable researcher who appeared at my house week after week with her arms laden with books and scientific reports. Many of the extraordinary details described in this book were uncovered by Mary during her many trips to the library. I also received research assistance from Albert Lukban, Lily Wound, Lorlei Metke, and Richard Halsey.

Countless government officials went out of their way to help me. Among the most helpful were employees in the Department of Energy, the very agency that had been so uncooperative when I began this project twelve years ago. I owe a very large thank-you to the DOE's Lori Azim, a lovely and efficient young woman who sent me dozens of documents. I also am grateful to Martha DeMarre, Jeff Gordon, and former staffer Cynthia Ashley at the DOE's Coordination and Information Center in Las Vegas, Nevada, for the rapidity with which they responded to my requests for documents. Evie Self, a declassification official at DOE headquarters in Washington, D.C., worked a minor miracle when she managed to get the accident report of Jimmy Robinson declassified by both the Department of Energy and the Department of Defense. The report had languished in Washington for more than two years and was in danger of being lost until she stepped in. Other government employees who helped were Diana Joy Leute, Ellyn Weiss, Bob Alvarez, Jim Solit, Rick Ray, Pam Bonee, Cheri Abselnour, and Col. Claud Bailey.

Staffers from President Clinton's Advisory Committee on Human Radiation Experiments were of tremendous assistance. In particular, I want to thank Dan Guttman, the committee's executive director, with whom I had many lively discussions. Dan literally opened the committee's doors to me, allowing me to copy hundreds of documents before they were boxed up and shipped to the National Archives. Lanny Keller, Trad Hughes, Gil Whittemore, Patrick Fitzgerald, Gregg Herken, James David, Patricia Perentesis, Jon Harkness, Kristin Crotty, Stephen Klaidman, Gary Stern, Gail Javitt, and Ronald Neuman were also helpful.

Loretta Garrison, formerly an attorney with the Baker & Hostetler law firm, was instrumental in getting many important documents on the plutonium experiment released under the Freedom of Information Act. Loretta and her husband, David, also opened their home to me on my many research trips to Washington, putting me up in their spare bedroom and supplying me with maps, subway passes, and umbrellas as I negotiated my way through Washington's archives and reading rooms. James Houpt, another attorney with the Baker & Hostetler firm, helped keep my original notes and documents on the Cecil Kelley case from being subpoenaed by Los Alamos.

Many records used in this book came from the private collections of individuals. One of the most generous was Harold Bibeau, a subject in Carl Heller's testicular irradiation experiment, who sent me the bulk of the documents used in the chapter on the prisoner experiments. Other people who opened their personal files included Pat Broudy, Stewart

Udall, Katie Kelley, Jackie Kittrell, Doris Baker, Martha Stephens, Sandra Marlow, Peter J. Thompson, Venlo Wolfsohn, Langdon Harrison, and Ubaldo Arizmendi.

Doe West, who chaired the Massachusetts task force that investigated the radiation experiments at the Fernald state school, spent hours tracking down photographs for me. I also received help from numerous professional archivists and librarians, including Margaret Moseley, a librarian in Newport News; Loretta Hefner, formerly with Lawrence Berkeley Laboratory; Roger Mead, the archivist at Los Alamos; Terry Fehner, a historian at DOE headquarters in Germantown, Maryland; Sandy Smith, at the National Archives; and Valerie Komor, at the Rockefeller Archive Center.

Scott Ware, the editor of the *Albuquerque Tribune,* gave me permission to use many of the documents and photographs from the original series. Colleagues Dennis Domrzalski, Ed Asher, Dan Vukelich, and Bob Benz were a great help, as were reporters in other cities, including Corydon Ireland, Tim Bonfield, Karen Dorn Steele, Mary Manning, and Keith Rogers. Countless other individuals provided assistance, including Oscar Rosen, Robert Campbell, Don Arbitblit, William Burleson, R. Joseph Parker, E. Cooper Brown, Thomas Fisher, David Egilman, Cliff Honicker, Kitty Alvarez, John Abbotts, James P. Cooney Jr., Meta Heller, John Daniel, Madonna Daniel, Don Byers, James Brascoe, Jeff Petroculley, Ray Heslin, and David Hilgemann.

I am also indebted also to Jim Bettinger, the deputy director of the John S. Knight Fellowship Program at Stanford University, who took time out of his busy schedule to plow throught the first draft of my manuscript, offering many intelligent suggestions for the revisions and much-needed encouragement. Luis Tovar and Diane Edwards also read the first draft, gently pointing out the rough spots that needed to be smoothed.

I cannot begin to express my thanks to my dear friend, Loydean Thomas, who listened patiently to my ordeals over the years. I also owe a special thanks to my next-door neighbor, Dena Daniel, now eighty-four, who cruised the airwaves, capturing on tape anything that might be related to the project and leaving it on my doorstep each evening.

I am also indebted to my literary agent, Lisa Bankoff, for her unwavering support, as well as to the people at The Dial Press who saw this book through to publication. I have an abiding gratitude to my two wonderful editors, Beth Rashbaum and Susan Kamil. With a ruthless pen and gentle heart, Beth took a grocery bag's worth of manuscript pages and turned them into this book. Susan guided the project through all its twists and turns. Her commitment was constant, her enthusiasm unflagging, her advice inspiring. I also want to thank Zoë Rice, for her incalculable assistance and unfailing courtesy; Random House's Bill Adams, for his superb legal review; Virginia Norey, Brian Mulligan, and Roberto de Vicq de Cumptich, who worked on everything from the jacket to the interior design of the book; Susan Schwartz, publishing manager, and Johanna Tani, chief copy editor, who shepherded the book through the production process; and copy editor Debra Manette, who culled out more errors than I believed were possible. Those that remain are my own.

And finally to my husband, Jim, I owe my deepest gratitude. He has always believed in this book. More than anything else, it was his love and confidence that carried me through the years. He read the manuscript at least four times, offered many invaluable suggestions, and endured years of endless discussion about the people and events described here. It is not an exaggeration to say that without Jim, I might not have completed the journey.

NOTES

A Note on Sources

Two of the major sources used in this book consist of government documents and oral histories. Many of these documents can be obtained from the National Archives, the Department of Energy's reading rooms, or at the DOE's Coordination and Information Center in Las Vegas, Nevada, a repository that contains a vast amount of material related to the nuclear weapons testing program and the human radiation experiments. But the simplest way to retrieve these records is through the Internet. Complete and fully searchable texts of more than 250,000 documents from the Department of Energy, Department of Defense, and other federal agencies can be found at http://hrex.dis.anl.gov. Other bibliographic information can be found by going to www.doe.gov. and clicking on OpenNet.

In addition to being interviewed by me, a number of the scientists mentioned in this book were also interviewed by historians and/or government officials. For simplicity's sake, I have grouped all of those interviews as oral histories. They can be divided into three groups: those done by academic historians in the 1960s, 1970s, and 1980s; oral histories conducted between 1978 and 1982 by J. Newell Stannard, a scientist who wrote a monumental, three-volume work for the DOE entitled *Radioactivity and Health*; and oral histories taken in 1994 and 1995 by staffers from the Department of Energy or the Advisory Committee on Human Radiation Experiments. Complete transcripts of many of these interviews are also available on the Internet.

ACRONYMS AND ABBREVIATIONS

ABCC	Atomic Bomb Casualty Commission
ACBM	Advisory Committee for Biology and Medicine
ACHRE	Advisory Committee on Human Radiation Experiments
AEC	Atomic Energy Commission
AFSC	Air Force Systems Command
AFSWP	Armed Forces Special Weapons Project*
AJ	*Albuquerque Journal*
AJR	*American Journalism Review*
AT	*Albuquerque Tribune*
AIP	American Institute of Physics
ANL	Argonne National Laboratory
AFSWL	Air Force Special Weapons Laboratory
AO	*Archives of Ophthalmology*
AP	Associated Press
CDC	Centers for Disease Control
CE	*Cincinnati Enquirer*
CHR	Center for Human Radiobiology
CIC	Coordination and Information Center, Las Vegas, Nevada
Cong.	Congressional
DASA	Defense Atomic Support Agency
DBM	Division of Biology and Medicine
DNA	Defense Nuclear Agency
dep.	deposition
DOD	Department of Defense
DOE	Department of Energy
DOE/OHRE	Department of Energy, Office of Human Radiation Experiments
DOE-OR	Department of Energy, Oak Ridge Reading Room
ERDA	Energy Research and Development Administration
ES	Eugene Saenger
FOIA	Freedom of Information Act
GAO	General Accounting Office
HB	Harold Bibeau personal papers
HSPT	Human Studies Project Team
int.	interview
JAMA	*Journal of the American Medical Association*
JGH	Joseph Gilbert Hamilton

JNS	Jay Newell Stannard
JWH	Joseph Wiseman Howland
LANL	Los Alamos National Laboratory
LASL	Los Alamos Scientific Laboratory
LAT	*Los Angeles Times*
LBL	Lawrence Berkeley Laboratory
MED	Manhattan Engineer District
MP	Manhattan Project
m.r.	medical records
NCI	National Cancer Institute
NA	National Archives
NEPA	Nuclear Energy for the Propulsion of Airplanes
NIH	National Institutes of Health
NTPR	Nuclear Test Personnel Review
NYT	*New York Times*
NIH	National Institutes of Health
OH	oral history
ORINS	Oak Ridge Institute for Nuclear Studies
ORISE	Oak Ridge Institute for Science and Education
OSP	Oregon State Prison
PNL	Pacific Northwest Laboratory
PNRF	Pacific Northwest Research Foundation
RDC	*Rochester Democrat & Chronicle*
RW	radiological warfare
SAM	School of Aviation Medicine
TBI	total body irradiation
UC	University of Cincinnati
UCLA	University of California, Los Angeles
UCSF	University of California, San Francisco
USAF	United States Air Force
UW	University of Washington
WP	*Washington Post*

*The Armed Forces Special Weapons Project, created from remnants of the Manhattan Project, has undergone numerous name changes since it was founded in 1947. Its successor agencies include the Defense Atomic Support Agency (1959–1971), the Defense Nuclear Agency (1971–1996), and the Defense Special Weapons Agency (1996–1998). It was folded into a new DOD agency called the Defense Threat Reduction Agency on October 1, 1998.

PROLOGUE

1: someone from the post office: Historical committee, "Italy, Texas, 1879–1979," n.d.

4: "to a physician": Robert G. Sachs to James Liverman, "Plutonium Studies at the Center for Human Radiobiology," enclosure, Nov. 13, 1973. This is one of the hundreds of documents that the DOE eventually provided to the *Albuquerque Tribune* in response to an August 28, 1992, FOIA request. Unless otherwise specified, all documents described as "FOIA" are a result of the 1992 request. Many of these documents can be found on the Internet or at the CIC.

4: plunged a hypodermic needle: AEC, "Report of Investigation," Aug. 16, 1974 (File No. 44-2-326), FOIA, pp. 7–8.

5: "He told me they": Welcome, "Plutonium Experiment," *AT*, series reprint, Nov. 15–17, 1993, p. 7.

6: "I'm not angry": Ibid., p. 6.

6: "I'm very upset": Ibid.

7: "I was appalled and shocked": DOE, *Openness Initiative*, Videocassette, Dec. 7, 1993.

9: "We're trying every angle": DOE, *Operation Tumbler Snapper,* Videocassette, 1952 (CIC 0800011).

9: "same old chestnuts": Thomas Shipman to Shields Warren, Jan. [date illegible], 1952, ACHRE, p. 1.

9: "From past experience we know": Shipman to Charles Dunham, Oct. 7, 1957, ACHRE, p. 2.

10: "People have got to learn": AEC Meeting No. 1062, Feb. 23, 1955 (CIC 14021), p. 121.

CHAPTER 1

16: crew developed a flow chart: LANL, *Radiation Protection,* p. 187.

16: "They were prepared to tear": Louis Hempelmann dep., p. 31.

16: "not pleasant": LANL, *Radiation Protection,* p. 186.

17: "I could taste the acid": Description of accident and quotes in this chapter come from documents and author interviews with Don Mastick conducted on Oct. 26, 1993, May 16, 1995, Nov. 27, 1995, and Aug. 6, 1998.

17: "deluge shower baths": LANL, *Radiation Protection,* p. 130.

17: "unusual hazards": Hempelmann, "History of the Health Group (A-6), March 1943–November 1945" (LANL-HSPT-94-105), p. 1.

17: "Louie did his first sternal puncture": Agnew OH, JNS, pp. 11–12.

18: he prepared two mixtures: Hempelmann to Stafford Warren, Aug. 2, 1944, ACHRE.

18: one-half microgram of plutonium: Ibid.

18: Sippy alkaline powders: Hempelmann, "Health Report for Month Ending Sept. 30, 1944" (LANL-HSPT 94-250), p. 4.

19: "I was sorry to bother": Hempelmann to Stafford Warren, Aug. 2, 1944.

19: "There were all sorts of problems": Hempelmann dep., p. 10.

CHAPTER 2

21: selling kitchenware from farm to farm: Rhodes, *Making of the Atomic Bomb*, pp. 143–144.

21: bright red coupe: Davis, *Lawrence and Oppenheimer*, p. 11.

22: "fly inside a cathedral": Ibid., p. 17.

22: gray suit and round-toed black shoes: Chevalier, *Oppenheimer: The Story of a Friendship*, p. 20.

23: In 1935 John Lawrence: Davis, *Lawrence and Oppenheimer*, p. 67.

24: "Lawrence, with his cyclotron": Waldo Cohn OH, p. 10.

24: "He got me on the platform": Davis, *Lawrence and Oppenheimer*, pp. 67–68.

25: "We thought or hoped": Ibid., p. 72.

25: "big grandstand act": Scott OH, p. 26.

25: "She was the very first": Davis, *Lawrence and Oppenheimer*, p. 77.

26: injected two leukemia: Hamilton and Stone, "Administration of Radio-Sodium," *Radiology*, pp. 178–188.

26: "stimulated me": Stone, Transcript of tape-recorded memoir, 1964, p. 5.

26: Born in Canada: Brown, "Obituary—Robert Stone," *Radiology*, pp. 807–808.

26: "Ernest Lawrence was a great stimulus": Stone memoir, p. 2.

26: bombarded some 128 patients: Stone and Larkin, "Treatment of Cancer with Fast Neutrons," *Radiology*, pp. 608–620.

27: "Dr. Stone's wealthy patients": Scott OH, p. 29.

27: likened to armor plates: Int. Robert Kallman, Jan. 11, 1997.

27: "He was just a young resident": Scott OH, p. 35.

27: "He was the kind of guy": Ibid., p. 55.

28: "He didn't have any warm": Int. Anne De Gruchy Low-Beer, May 29, 1995.

28: "would have been very much at home": Durbin OH, ACHRE, p. 170.

28: treating many well-known personalities: Int. Christine Alan, April 17, 1995.

28: son had sucked: Hamilton, *Introduction to Objective Psychopathology*, pp. 302–303.

28: Hamilton attended schools: Lawrence and Garrison, "J.G. Hamilton," *Science*, p. 294.

28: owned a log cabin: Int. Christine Alan.

29: "We considered him": Stafford Warren OH, p. 580.

29: "what he liked to do" Durbin OH, DOE/OHRE, p. 30.

29: "Then he would walk across the room": Welsome, "Plutonium Experiment," p. 27.

29: flying through radioactive clouds: Hamilton to [name deleted], March 27, 1951, Call No. 72/117C, Box 32, Folder 21, p. 1. (Hamilton's papers can be found in the Ernest O. Lawrence papers, Joseph Hamilton correspondence, Call No. 72/117c, Bancroft Library, Berkeley, CA. Hereafter those papers will be noted as "JGH.")

29: "I tried to talk to him": Miller OH, DOE/OHRE, p. 5.

29: "had already had it": Scott OH, p. 46.

30: "looked like a ghost": Int. John Gofman, Jan. 24, 1996.

30: "I would be willing": Int. Patricia Durbin, Sept. 3, 1992.

30: "I wrote to Dr. Stone": Friedell OH, DOE/OHRE, p. 9.

30: treated a few of his patients: Ibid., p. 10.

30: The radiophosphorous seemed especially: Ibid., p. 13.

30: patients had almost died: Joseph Hamilton to Shields Warren, Nov. 28, 1950, Box 32, Folder 21, JGH, p. 2.

30: Hamilton was confused: Int. Hymer Friedell, Sept. 23, 1992.

30: "I was assigned a project": Friedell OH, JNS, p. 27.

31: Washington University was his alma mater: Miller and Koszalka, "Obituary—Louis Hempelmann," *Radiation Research*, pp. 435–438; Hempelmann dep., pp. 4–5.

31: After four months in Berkeley: Hempelmann dep., p. 5.

31: Nearly twenty ships and 292 aircraft: Rhodes, *Making of the Atomic Bomb*, p. 392.

CHAPTER 3

32: scientists climbed the stairs: Compton, *Atomic Quest*, pp. 80–81.

33: she calculated the energy: Ibid., p. 18.

34: "extremely powerful bombs": Libby, *Uranium People*, inside cover.

34: After McMillan moved east: Seaborg, *Plutonium Story*, p. 14.

35: "The new land": Seaborg, "Plutonium Revisited," *Radiobiology of Plutonium*, p. 6.

35: By Tuesday, February 25, 1941: Seaborg, *Plutonium Story*, p. 29.

35: the men donned goggles: Ibid., pp. 30–34.

35: "It really should have been called": Welsome, "Plutonium Experiment," p. 6.

35: "super bomb": Smyth, *Atomic Energy for Military Purposes*, p. 65.

37: "You'll never get the chain reaction": Compton, *Atomic Quest*, pp. 80–81.

37: "The project for producing plutonium": Ibid., p. 82.

37: arrived in Chicago: Seaborg, *Plutonium Story*, pp. 109–110.

38: "He could give us enough ideas": Groueff, *Manhattan Project*, p. 25.

38: "I'm cutting off": Compton, *Atomic Quest*, p. 126.

38: "special category of secrecy": Seaborg, *Plutonium Story*, p. 117.

38: "At Berkeley, we have": Ibid., p. 119.

39: The Chicago chemists: Cunningham, "The First Isolation of Plutonium," in Coffinberry and Miner, eds., *The Metal Plutonium*, p. 15.

39: From those eleven pounds: Ibid., pp. 16–17.

39: 50 micrograms of plutonium: Ibid.

39: helping out on the cyclotron: Hempelmann dep., p. 5.

39: "irreversible toxic effects": Hemplemann et al., "Hematologic Complications," *Journal of Laboratory and Clinical Medicine*, 1944, p. 1041.

39: "It is the first time that element 94": Seaborg, *Plutonium Story*, p. 177.

40: contents spilled on a Sunday edition: Ibid., p. 178.

40: "absolutely crazy": Int. Ed Hammel, Aug. 5, 1998.

40: "Plutonium is so unusual": Groueff, *Manhattan Project*, pp. 151–152.

40: "live rabbit": Libby, *Uranium People*, p. 171.

40: "I held in my hand": Compton, *Atomic Quest,* p. 213.

41: easy as driving a car: Libby, *Uranium People,* p. 123.

CHAPTER 4

42: "knew what had happened": Compton, *Atomic Quest,* p. 177.

43: "Stone's exceptional qualification": Ibid.

43: "offer the possibility of infecting": Hamilton to Robert Stone, "A Brief Review of the Possible Applications of Fission Products in Offensive Warfare," May 26, 1943, Carton 8, Folder 25, JGH, p. 3.

43: "I think that we should not attempt": J. Robert Oppenheimer to Enrico Fermi, May 25, 1943, Elmerine Allen Whitfield personal papers.

44: There were three major sections: Smyth, *Atomic Energy,* p. 150.

44: he directed his staff: Stone, "Health Protection Activities of the Plutonium Project," *Proceedings of the American Philosophical Society,* p. 12.

45: "rem," a term: Hacker, *Dragon's Tail,* p. 42.

45: "It must be remembered": Metallurgical Project, "Health Division Program," May 10, 1943 (CIC 717325), p. 1.

46: "The hair at the temples": No author, "Deleterious Effects of X Rays on the Human Body," *Electrical Review,* Aug. 12, 1896 (CIC 702392).

46: Within a year: Hacker, *Dragon's Tail,* p. 10.

46: hundred radiation pioneers: Stone, "Concept of a Maximum Permissible Exposure," *Radiology,* May 1952, p. 641.

46: limited to 0.1 roentgen: Hacker, *Dragon's Tail,* p. 18.

46–47: "that dose of radiation": Stone, "Maximum Permissible Exposure," p. 642.

47: "very sketchy": Stone, "The Plutonium Project," *Radiology,* p. 364.

47: "It is our hope": Metallurgical Project, "Health Division Program," pp. 1–2.

47: "Clinically, I couldn't diagnose": Lang, *From Hiroshima to the Moon,* p. 390.

47: "radium jaw": Ibid.

48: some 4,000: Denise Grady, "A Glow in the Dark, and a Lesson in Scientific Peril," *NYT,* Oct. 6, 1998, p. F-4.

48: 800 of whom: Lang, *Hiroshima to the Moon,* p. 389.

48: caused tiny scintillations: Martland, "Occupational Poisoning," *JAMA,* p. 466.

48: 250 to 300 watch dials: Evans, "Radium Poisoning," *American Journal of Public Health,* p. 1019.

48: "Depending on their skill": Ibid.

48: One of the first dial painters: Martland et al., "Some Unrecognized Dangers," *JAMA,* pp. 1769–1776.

49: "I would be only too happy": Lang, *Hiroshima to the Moon,* p. 393.

49: settled out of court: Martland, "Occupational Poisoning," p. 472.

50: "debutante fatigue": Evans OH, AIP, p. 51.

50: 1,000 to 1,500 bottles: Macklis, "The Great Radium Scandal," *Scientific American,* p. 95.

51: proved "fatal": Evans, "Radium Poisoning," p. 1019.

51: threatened to draft: Evans OH, AIP, p. 83.

51: "Well, my feeling": Evans OH, JNS, p. 7.

51: examined some 2,000 people: LANL, *Radiation Protection*, p. 232.

52: "The Health Division": Low-Beer and Stone, "Hematological Studies on Patients," *Industrial Medicine on the Plutonium Project*, p. 338.

53: "extremely worked up": Stone, "Obituary—Bertram V. A. Low-Beer," *Radiology*, pp. 284–285.

53: exposure did reduce: Low-Beer and Stone, "Hematological Studies," p. 417.

53: "most difficult part of the project": Craver, "Tolerance to Whole-Body Irradiation," *Industrial Medicine*, p. 486.

53: "such doses of radiation": Ibid., p. 498.

54: A third TBI experiment: Nickson, "Blood Changes in Human Beings," *Industrial Medicine*, pp. 308–337.

54: "particular interest": Ibid., p. 336.

54: "What are the first changes": Stone, "The Plutonium Project," *Radiology*, p. 364.

CHAPTER 5

56: To Groves, Leo Szilard: Ermenc, *Atomic Bomb Scientists*, p. 248.

56: "I suspected that Compton": Ibid., p. 247.

56: "It must have been": Libby, *Uranium People*, p. 96.

56: "depressing effect": Groves, *Now It Can Be Told*, pp. 65–66.

57: "The geographically enforced isolation": Ibid., p. 67.

57: "My two great loves": Rhodes, *Making of the Atomic Bomb*, p. 451.

57: Oppenheimer wanted John Lawrence: Hacker, *Dragon's Tail*, p. 59.

57: his duties would be: Ibid.

57: Until enough housing: Hawkins, *Project Y*, p. 9.

58: packed up his belongings: Hempelmann dep., p. 5.

58: "He was my first paying boss": Fermi, *Atoms in the Family*, p. 228.

59: "Nobody could think straight": Wyden, *Day One*, p. 95.

59: "rather odd orders": Friedell OH, DOE/OHRE, pp. 20–22.

60: "He thinks I'm the world's": Friedell OH, JNS, p. 31.

60: the executive officer: Nichols, *Road to Trinity*, p. 122.

60: "You're too young": Friedell OH, JNS, p. 5.

60: "General Groves was": Stone to Compton, Feb. 15, 1943, University of Washington Manuscripts and University Archives Division, Herbert M. Parker papers, Accession No. 3616, Box 5, Robert Stone folder.

61: wearing combat boots: Weisgall, *Operation Crossroads*, p. 208.

61: "She was very anemic": Stafford Warren OH, p. 358.

61: In a 1937 paper: Stafford Warren et al., "Artificially Induced Fever," *JAMA*, pp. 1430–1435.

62: twenty-two year-old boxer: Ibid., p. 1433.

62: "Why do you want": Nichols, *Road to Trinity*, p. 123.

62: "Of course, the colored people": Stafford Warren OH, pp. 679–680.

62: "My rule was simple": Groves, *Now It Can Be Told*, p. 140.

63: "When the general decided": Friedell OH, JNS, p. 1.

63: "He thought we had some special": Ibid., p. 5.

63: "We wouldn't go and say": Ibid., pp. 1–2.

63: "The rest of the places": Friedell OH, ACHRE, pp. 30–31.

63: "We didn't know what to do": Stafford Warren OH, p. 965–966.

CHAPTER 6

65: "stand-in" isotopes: Hawkins, *Project Y*, p. 72.

65: "You're going to have grams": Gofman OH, p. 12.

65: "After about three weeks": Ibid., pp. 12–13.

65: published a follow-up study: Evans, "Protection of Radium Dial Workers," *Journal of Industrial Hygiene and Toxicology,* pp. 253–269.

66: "first bullet of a repeating gun": Ibid., p. 254.

66: With proper precautions: Ibid., p. 257.

66: "quite likely": Int. Glenn Seaborg, Aug. 10, 1998.

66: two milligrams of plutonium: LANL, *Radiation Protection,* p. 182.

66: "It was only when the plutonium appeared": Seaborg OH, p. 3.

66: "It has occurred to me": Glenn Seaborg to Stone, "Physiological Hazards of Working with Plutonium," Jan. 5, 1944 (CIC 708058).

67: "Oh, God, no": Welsome, "Plutonium Experiment," p. 17.

67: "We were working" Int. Seaborg, Aug. 10, 1998.

67: "The question of tracer studies": Stone to Seaborg, "Health Hazards of Working with Plutonium," Jan. 8, 1944 (CIC 708278).

67: first milligram amounts: A. V. Peterson to Compton, "X-49 Deliveries," Jan. 29, 1944, Bill Moss personal papers.

67: "poisonous nature of product": "Project Council—Policy Meeting," Jan. 19, 1944 (CS-1262), p. 4.

68: "potentially extremely poisonous": Ibid.

68: Hamilton received eleven milligrams: Hamilton, "Metabolism of Product," Report for Period Ending Oct. 15, 1944 (CIC 180070), p. 3.

68: approved by J. Robert Oppenheimer: "X-49 Deliveries."

68: Luminous Paint Company: Hempelmann, "History of the Health Group (A-6), March 1943–November 1945," p. 5.

68: "We were always very careful": Evans OH, AIP, p. 99.

68: floors and walls: Evans, "Protection of Radium Dial Workers."

69: "conscientious objectors": Evans to Joseph Howland, Oct. 28, 1944, DOE-OR (1017).

69: Before the vial: Nichols, *Road to Trinity,* pp. 133–134.

69: scientists were "individualists": Hempelmann dep., p. 46.

69–70: "Unfortunately, the more scholarly": Ibid., p. 61.

70: "very high counts": Chemistry and Metallurgical Division, "Health and Safety Report," July 1944 (LAMS-119), p. 4.

70: "She was well endowed": Shipman, "H Division Activities," May 6, 1969 (LANL-HSPT-94-108), p. 6.

70: 1,578 . . . 40,000: "Health and Safety Report," pp. 2–3.

70: "infinite": Hempelmann dep., p. 62.

70: workers' respirators: "Health and Safety Report," p. 2.

70: fifty counts per minute: Hempelmann dep., p. 37.

70: "The lack of records": Hempelmann, "History of the Health Group (A-6), March 1943–November 1945," p. 15.

71: "Mr. Oppenheimer, I believe": J. F. Mullaney to Norris Bradbury, "Report by J. G. Hoffman on Biological Effects of July 16th Explosion," Jan. 3, 1946, LANL.

71: "I realize that analogies": Hamilton to Stone, "[More?]Concerning Accidental Introduction of Product into the Body by Way of Penetrating [illegible]," May 5, 1944, LANL.

71: received fifty-one grams: Oppenheimer to Groves, Aug. 31, 1944, Moss personal papers.

71: metallurgist was exposed: Moss OH, pp. 7–8.

71: plutonium in powder form: R. A. Popham to Hempelmann, "Accident in Room D-101," Aug. 22, 1944 (CIC 90514).

71: An open beaker: Popham to Hempelmann, "Accident in Room D-117," Aug. 30, 1944 (CIC 90515).

71: D Building was: LANL, *Radiation Protection,* p. 130.

71–72: "As has been anticipated": Hempelmann, "Health Report," Aug. 30, 1944 (LANL-HSPT-94-237), p. 2.

72: "A great deal of concern": Hempelmann to Oppenheimer, "Health Hazards Related to Plutonium," Aug. 16, 1944, LANL.

72: "It would not seem out of place": Ibid.

72: "As for the biological sides": Oppenheimer to Hempelmann, "Your memorandum of Aug. 16, 1944," Aug. 16, 1944, LANL, p. 1.

72: "not equipped for biological experiments": Oppenheimer to Compton, Feb. 11, 1944, telegram, ACHRE.

73: 1,500 . . . 8,200: Truslow, *Manhattan District History,* p. 101.

73: The project was to have: Hempelmann to Oppenheimer, "Medical Research Program," Aug. 29, 1944, LANL, p. 1.

73: contamination-free laboratory: Hempelmann, "History of the Health Group," p. 8.

73: "They were just frightfully high": Hempelmann dep., p. 34.

74: "It was not until the first human tracer": Hempelmann, "History of the Health Group," p. 8.

CHAPTER 7

75: "I used him for my 'crying wall' ": Stafford Warren OH, p. 793.

75: fix a flat tire: Friedell OH, DOE/OHRE, p. 34.

76: the first kilogram amounts: Nichols, *Road to Trinity,* p. 141.

76: transported by Army ambulances: Groueff, *Manhattan Project,* p. 311.

76: "if it had not been": Hempelmann dep., p. 39.

77: Los Alamos and Pueblo creeks: W. H. Hinch to Hempelmann, "Report on the Contamination of Creek Water," Oct. 15, 1945 (LANL HSPT-94-201), p. 4.

77: 144,000 disintegrations per minute: Ibid.

77: "It's quite possible": Hempelmann to R. C. Hill, July 1, 1947 (LANL-HSPT-94-205), p. 2.

77: "Everybody had his own": Shipman, "H Division Activities," May 6, 1969, p. 12.

77: Scientists detected plutonium: Hinch, "Report on the Contamination of Creek Water," p. 4.

77–78: "In conjunction with": Hymer Friedell, "Program for Product Research 5 December 1944," Jan. 19, 1945, DOE-OR (1006).

78: On Friday, March 23: Hempelmann to Oppenheimer, "Meeting of Chemistry Division and Medical Group," March 26, 1945, LANL, p. 1.

78: "occasionally" dropped in: Friedell OH, DOE/OHRE, p. 34.

78: lab was not getting: Hempelmann, "History of the Health Group (A-6), March 1943–November 1945," p. 2.

78: wasn't "terribly enthusiastic": Friedell OH, DOE/OHRE, p. 35.

78: "Now my own recollection": Ibid., p. 34.

78: Born in Winsburro: Wright Haskell Langham, "Biographical Data," LANL.

78: "ingenious studies": Hempelmann, "Obituary—Wright Langham," *Radiation Research,* pp. 419–421.

79: "He came over": Hempelmann dep., p. 54.

79: "underlying gentleness": Hempelmann, "Obituary—Wright Langham," p. 420.

79: thirty times *more* hazardous: Nickson, ed., "Report of Conference on Plutonium," p. 47.

79: "radio-sensitive bone marrow": Hamilton, "A Report of the Past, Present, and Future Research Activities for Project 48-A-1," n.d., ACHRE.

79: "It is suggested": Hempelmann to Oppenheimer, "Meeting of Chemistry Division and Medical Group," March 26, 1945, LANL, p. 1.

80: "I should like to add": Oppenheimer to Stafford Warren, March 29, 1945, LANL.

80: having prostate surgery: Friedell OH, ACHRE, p. 39.

80: "primarily responsible": Langham et al., *Distribution and Excretion of Plutonium,* p. 2.

80: "Tracer experiments on humans": Stafford Warren, Memorandum for the Files, "Medical Experimental Program on Radium and Product," Dec. 2, 1944, Carton 5, Folder 9, JHG.

81: "not the kind of thing": John Lansdale, letter to author, June 24, 1995.

81: "I think he was": Friedell OH, DOE/OHRE, p. 37. During his oral history interview, Friedell seemed unsure about Groves's involvement, but at a meeting in San Francisco several months earlier, he told that same interviewer that he was fairly certain that Groves was aware of the plan to test plutonium in humans.

Chapter 8

82: soft-spoken man: Int. Pauline Jones, March 10, 1996; int. Mary Frances Cade Derr, May 21, 1996.

82: left eye was completely blind: "Experiment 1 on p. 49 + 4," DOE-OR (1003).

82: About 6:30: Wilson O. Edmonds to Jon Anderson, "Memorandum Report," July 15, 1974 (CIC 701184), p. 2.

83: bustling facility: Stafford Warren, "The Role of Radiology in the Development of the Atomic Bomb," p. 874.

83: Ebb's nose and lip: "Experiment 1."

83: Smith, was hospitalized: "Memorandum Report," p. 2.

83: "completely obliterated": "Experiment 1."

83: "He was a well developed": Ibid.

83: second set of instructions: Wright Langham to Friedell, April 6, 1945 (ACHRE No. DOE-120894-E1).

83: "My experience has been": Ibid., p. 1.

83: "you may have a better idea": Ibid., p. 2.

83: "care was taken to avoid leakage": "Experiment 1."

84: five times the amount: Langham to Friedell, May 21, 1945, ACHRE, p. 1.

84: dose equal to eighty: LANL, *Radiation Protection,* p. 209.

84: "Everything went smoothly": Friedell to Hempelmann, April 11, 1945 (ACHRE No. DOE-121294-D-1), p. 1.

84: he did it under protest: Walter Weyzen, "Visit with Dr. Joe Howland, Chapel Hill Holiday Inn," April 24, 1974, FOIA.

84: "Interviewer: Were you there": Friedell OH, ACHRE, pp. 49–50.

85: suffered a nervous breakdown: Howland, "Experience in Nuclear Medicine," n.d., p. 3.

85: "a command performance": Ibid., p. 2.

85: "Holland: One other thing": Transcript of telephone conversation, Jan. 9, 1948 (ACHRE No. DOE-120894-E-63). Another document that supports Howland's version of the story is a Feb. 18, 1947, letter from Andrew Dowdy, the director of Rochester's Manhattan Annex, to Friedell. In that letter Dowdy states: "It is my understanding that it was your idea [the Oak Ridge injection] and that Major Howland and Captain Goldring were the two who actually carried out the administration."

86: "The subject was": Langham, "Report of Talk Given at the Chicago Meeting," July 30, 1947, p. 7.

86: "This presumably would produce": Ibid.

86: 332 counts per minute: Ibid., p. 12.

86: 2.2 counts: Ibid., p. 11.

86: "than with rats": Ibid., p. 7.

86: experiment was flawed: "Experiment 1," p. 3.

87: Fifteen of Ebb's teeth: David Goldring to Langham, Sept. 19, 1945, FOIA.

87: "He was just moaning": Int. Lawrence Suchow, March 30, 1994.

87: "is at a loss": Bill Clarkson to Friedell, "Request for Possible Information on Case of Jesse Smith," April 25, 1947, ACHRE.

87: "Joe Howland actually": Friedell to Clarkson, April 28, 1947, Elmerine Allen Whitfield personal papers.

CHAPTER 9

88: As a young man: Int. Velin Hubbard Hughes, Jan. 5, 1998; int. B. L. Guess, Jan. 6, 1998; Rita Delmar correspondence to author.

88: "hen's egg": R. C. Weber, "Autopsy Report," Oct. 3, 1945, Hubbard m.r., p. 5.

89: "We knew they": Int. B. L. Guess.

89: "seven different plastic": Weber, "Autopsy Report," p. 5.

89: dose equal to 120 times: LANL, *Radiation Protection*, p. 209.

89: "seal-fast" cardboard: Russell and Nickson, *Distribution and Excretion of Plutonium*, p. 2.

89: "Since people were of necessity": Ibid., p. 1.

90: "to undertake, on a limited scale": Hamilton to Compton, Jan. 11, 1945 (LANL-HSPT-94-375), p. 2.

90: "clinical material": Hamilton to Col. E. B. Kelly, "Summary of Research Program for Contract #W-7405-eng-48-A," Aug. 28, 1946, DOE-OR (1008), p. 2.

90: extremely sharp pains: G. S. Feher, "X-ray Consultation Request," May 6, 1945, Stevens m.r.

90: another put it at forty: "Abstract of Hospital Record," n.d., FOIA.

90: local physician suspected: UCSF Ad Hoc Fact Finding Committee, *World War II Human Radiation Experiments*, Appendix 18, p. 2.

91: $5.25 a day: Ibid.

91: suggested a gastroscopy: Ibid.

91: Kenneth Scott, the chubby: Scott OH, p. 49.

92: animal tumors with LSD: Ibid., p. 64.

92: "beer party": Scott OH, p. 13.

92: "carcinogenic dose": Int. Patricia Durbin, July 6, 1992.

92: five rats were injected: Crowley et al., *Metabolism of Plutonium in Man and the Rat*, p. 2.

92: Earl Miller injected: Scott OH, p. 49.

92: acting chief of the radiology: Miller OH, DOE/OHRE, pp. 66, 83.

92: "I never, never, never": Int. Earl Miller, May 3, 1995.

92: "These people": Miller OH, ACHRE, p. 240.

92: "huge, ulcerating, carcinomatous mass": "Description of Operation," June 6, 1945, Stevens m.r.

92: specimens were handed: UCSF, *World War II Human Radiation Experiments*, Appendix 18, p. 8.

93: "special studies": Ibid.

93: "The patient withstood": S. Johnson, "Description of Operation," May 31, 1945, Stevens m.r.

93: "saved for Mr. Scott": UCSF, *World War II Human Radiation Experiments*, Appendix 18, p. 8.

93: "All specimens going": Ibid., p. 9.

93: "benign gastric ulcer": James F. Rinehart, "Pathological Report," May 18, 1945, Stevens m.r.

93: "radical procedure": UCSF, *World War II Human Radiation Experiments*, Appendix 18, p. 8.

93: "he just didn't have it": Scott OH, p. 48.

93: "I thought they were morally": Scott OH, pp. 47–49.

94: document declassified in 1994: T. S. Chapman to Area Engineer, "Human Experiments," Dec. 30, 1946, ACHRE.

95: "Kenneth [Scott] and I": Hamilton to Stone, July 7, 1945, Barton Bernstein personal papers, p. 1.

95: "financial embarrassment": Joseph Howland to Area Engineer, "Status of Experimental Subject," July 12, 1945, Carton 28, Folder 41, JGH.

95: "They sent an intern": Welsome, "Plutonium Experiment," p. 23.

95: "My mother and I": Ibid.

96: "The fate of plutonium": Crowley et al., *Metabolism of Plutonium in Man and the Rat,* p. 1.

96: "Four days after": Ibid., p. 2.

96: "the problem of chronic plutonium": Ibid., p. 7.

96: "It contains material": C. L. Marshall to W. H. Zinn, "Document Refused Declassification," May 23, 1947, Carton 5, Folder 12, JGH.

CHAPTER 10

97: Nobel laureate James Franck: Compton, *Atomic Quest,* p. 235.

98: "There were few who sensed": Ibid., p. 241.

99: "Now before the war": Stafford Warren OH, p. 784.

99: called Project TR: Hawkins, *Project Y,* p. 234.

99: "Everybody was too busy": Stafford Warren OH, p. 783.

99: "hangers on": Friedell OH, JNS, p. 3.

99: "In spite of all this": Joseph O. Hirschfelder, "Scientific-Technological Miracle at Los Alamos," in Badash et al., eds., *Reminiscences of Los Alamos,* p. 75.

99: Warren's "chief helpers": Ibid., p. 75.

100: "We suddenly discovered": Stafford Warren OH, p. 792.

100: "I asked for a couple of hundred": Ibid., p. 797.

100: ferry four psychiatrists: Ibid., p. 804.

100: "One of the big problems": Ibid., p. 780.

101: "or I will hang you": Szasz, *Day the Sun Rose Twice,* p. 77.

101: "Let's synchronize watches": Lamont, *Day of Trinity,* p. 222.

101: "Keep this line open": Ibid.

101: "They were embarrassed": Stafford Warren OH, pp. 805–806.

102: "Now I am become Death": Kunetka, *City of Fire,* p. 170.

102: "When I went to Warren's": Groves, *Now It Can Be Told,* p. 299.

102: "You boys must have been": Hirschfelder, "Scientific-Technological Miracle," p. 77.

102: "They told me": Int. William Wrye, June 29, 1998.

102–103: sedan with a flat tire: Grilly OH, p. 21.

103: four roentgens per hour: Hirschfelder, "Scientific-Technological Miracle," p. 78.

103: "By being at Bingham": Hemplemann, "Itinerary of Trip Made by Colonel Warren, Captain Whipple and L. H. Hempelmann on 12 August 1945" (CIC 90351), p. 3.

103: "being covered with light snow": Hempelmann, Memo to Files, "Trip to ranches of [deleted] and Mr. [deleted] on Sunday, 11th, November 1945" (CIC 90368), p. 2.

103: "nervousness, tightness in the chest": Hempelmann, "Itinerary of Trip," p. 3.

103: "slightly anemic": Hempelmann, "Trip to ranches," p. 1.

103–104: "One of the dogs": Ibid., p. 2.

104: forty-seven roentgens: Hacker, *Dragon's Tail,* p. 104.

104: "I was slick-faced": Int. William Wrye, June 29, 1998.

104: "According to neighbors": Hempelmann to files, "Follow-up of Outlying Area Contaminated by Trinity Cloud," Dec. 1, 1945 (CIC 90369), pp. 2–3.

104: discovered 1,100 miles away: Szasz, *Day the Sun Rose Twice,* p. 135.

CHAPTER 11

105: "I can't stand": Int. Don Mastick, Aug. 6, 1998.

105: Morrison would sit: Cong. hearing, *Atomic Energy,* 1945, pp. 234–235.

106: "prompt and utter destruction": Rhodes, *Making of the Atomic Bomb,* p. 692.

106: "The mushroom itself": Ibid., p. 711.

106: "The banks of the river": P. Siemes, "Eyewitness Account," Vol. 1, Physical Damage, Hiroshima, Japan. Prepared by Major Noland Varley, 77-VH, Records of Office of Chief of Engineer, Box 1, NA, p. 13.

106: "small piece of the sun": Cong. hearing, *Atomic Energy,* 1945, pp. 236–237.

107: "A human dam!": Chie Setoguchi, "The Human Dam," in *Testimonies of the Atomic Bomb Survivors,* p. 13.

108: "like a tattered old rag": Sumiteru Taniguchi, "Eternal Scars," in ibid., p. 46.

108: As she felt the heat: Hisae Aoki, "Back from Death's Doorstep," in ibid., pp. 82–93.

108: most anguishing experience: "Translator's Note," ibid., pp. iv–v.

108: "employ a new and most cruel bomb": Rhodes, *Making of the Atomic Bomb,* p. 745.

108: another round of interviews: Stafford Warren OH, p. 615; Hempelmann, "Itinerary of Trip," p. 1.

109: Daghlian left the regular: Paul Aebersold et al., "Report on Accident of Aug. 21, 1945, at Omega Site," Aug. [day illegible], 1945, LANL, p. 2.

109: Suddenly the brick: Ibid., p. 3.

109: eight people were exposed: Hempelmann to Files, "Accident Report at Omega," July 6, 1945, LANL.

109: "tingling sensation": Aebersold et al., "Report on Accident," p. 3.

110: "grease gauze dressings": "Attending Physician's Report," Labor and Industrial Commission of New Mexico, Department of Claims, Sept. 1, 1945, LANL.

110: "The death toll at Hiroshima": Stoff, Fanton, and Williams, eds., *The Manhattan Project,* pp. 258–262.

111: "Number dead or injured": Wyden, *Day One,* p. 325.

112: "like kittens with paper shoes": G. Millard Hunsley, "Big Saucer-Like Crater Marks Site of Bomb Test," *AJ,* Sept. 12, 1945, p. 1.

112: "The tour's purpose": Howard M. Blakeslee, "Party of Newsmen Inspects Scene Near Alamogordo," *AJ,* Sept. 12, 1945, p. 1.

112: "There were evidences": Ibid., p. 2.

112: "there would be no indirect": Ibid., p. 2.

112: "It seemed certain": "New Mexico's Atomic Bomb Crater," *Life,* Sept. 24, 1945, pp. 27–31.

113: "give us the maximum": Cong. hearing, *Atomic Energy,* 1945, p. 42.

113: on September 19, General MacArthur: Wyden, *Day One,* p. 326.

113: "When we got there": Stafford Warren OH, p. 647.

115: "oozing that continued to death": Stafford Warren, "The Role of Radiology," p. 901.

115: "prove there was no radioactivity": Donald Collins, "Pictures from the Past," in Kathren and Ziemer, eds., *Health Physics: A Backward Glance,* p. 41.

115: "It often took an hour": Cong. hearing, *Atomic Energy,* 1945, pp. 511–512.

115: "I think the radiation": Ibid., p. 513.

115: number of people killed: Hacker, *Dragon's Tail,* p. 113.

116: "When we came out the other side": Shields Warren OH, p. 70.

116: *ketsueki . . . ikutsu:* Shields Warren diary, Boston University, Mugar Memorial Library, Special Collections, Box 3, Sept. 25, 1945.

116: "Rats, flies, mosquitoes": Ibid.

116: "Few transfusions given": Ibid.

117: "A greater number of injuries": Shields Warren, "Pattern of Injuries Produced by the Atomic Bombs," *Naval Medical Bulletin,* p. 1350.

117: The first troops: DNA fact sheet, "Hiroshima and Nagasaki Occupation Forces," pp. 10, 12.

117: "I don't know what the purpose": Int. Bill Griffin, May 1, 1996.

118: "The radioactive casualty": Cong. hearing, *Atomic Energy,* 1945, p. 37.

118: "We had no operating accidents": Ibid., p. 56.

118: "There is none": Ibid., p. 33.

119: "There was no radioactivity damage": Ibid., p. 36.

119: "If the bomb had exploded": Ibid., p. 37.

119: "few tens of millirem": Int. D. Michael Schaeffer, May 2, 1996.

CHAPTER 12

120: "Everybody had parties": Feynman, "Los Alamos from Below," in Badash et al., eds., *Reminiscences of Los Alamos,* p. 132.

120: "If atomic bombs": Hawkins, *Project Y,* pp. 260–261.

120: Bradbury agreed: Bradbury, "Los Alamos—The First 25 Years," in Badash et al., *Reminiscences of Los Alamos,* p. 161.

121: "that the situation seems": LANL, *Radiation Protection,* p. 201.

121: "the patient was ambulatory": Goldring to Langham, Sept. 19, 1945, FOIA.

121: "We just loved to talk": Int. Mary Frances Cade Derr, May 21, 1996.

121: "I believe the old days": Chris Gachet, "Her 107th Birthday Like Any Other Day," *Hickory (NC) Daily Record,* July 8, 1981, p. B-1.

122: plutonium did not seem to concentrate: Russell and Nickson, *Distribution and Excretion of Plutonium,* p. 27.

122: "It got to the point": Welsome, "Plutonium Experiment," p. 26.

122: 6,400 rem: LANL, *Radiation Protection,* pp. 198–199.

122: developed a list: Nickson, *Report of Conference on Plutonium,* pp. 1–4.

123: "the medico-legal aspect": Langham to Friedell, May 21, 1945, ACHRE.

123: lowered the tolerance: Langham et al., "The Los Alamos Scientific Laboratory's Experience with Plutonium," *Health Physics,* pp. 753–754.

123: "It has been indicated": Stafford Warren to Kenneth Nichols, "Purpose and Limitations of the Biological and Health Physics Research Program," April 17, 1945 (CIC 719448).

C H A P T E R   1 3

124: larger, planned study: Andrew Dowdy to William Bale, "Metabolism Studies," June 5, 1945, FOIA.

124: "they were loyal American": No author, "The Rochester Story," n.d., DOE-OR (296).

125: "He, of course, was": Stafford Warren OH, p. 410.

125: "activated" the ward: Samuel Bassett to Bale, "Proposal of Work for Metabolism Section," Dec. 2, 1947, ACHRE, p. 1.

125–126: "numerous conversations": Langham, "Revised Plan of 'Product' Part of Rochester Experiment" (ACHRE No. DOE-121294-D), p. i.

126: only two subjects: Ibid., p. 1.

126: "human product": Hannah E. Silberstein to Langham, Oct. 25, 1945 (ACHRE No. DOE-121294-D-19), p. 1.

126: "At the meeting it seemed": Langham, "Revised Plan," p. 2.

126: "We considered doing": Rex Graham, "Scientists Shunned N-Tests on Employees," *AJ* (north edition), April 5, 1994, p. 1.

127: "The period of indoctrination": Bassett, "Excretion of Plutonium Administered Intravenously to Man," n.d. (ACHRE No. DOE-121294-D-10), p. 2.

127: "any leakage which might": Ibid., p. 3.

127: Lieutenant Valentine perform: Langham, "Revised Plan," p. 7.

127: Bassett made the first: Silberstein to Langham, Oct. 23, 1945 (ACHRE No. DOE-121294-D-19), p. 1.

127: "quite positive": "Comments on meeting with Dr. Hempelmann on April 17, 1974," FOIA, p. 1.

127: "deliberate decision" was made: Ibid.

127: "well preserved for his years": Bassett, "Excretion of Plutonium," p. 14.

127: two fig trees: Welsome, "Six More Test Victims Revealed," *AT,* March 5, 1994, p. 6.

127: "with no ill effects": Silberstein to Langham, Oct. 23, 1945, ACHRE, p. 1.

128: red-haired Irishman: Welsome, "Six More Test Victims."

128: "The reason being": Bassett to Langham, Oct. 24, 1945, FOIA.

128: craved a hot dog: Int. Ruth Brown, May 7, 1996.

128: "So far he has cooperated": Bassett to Langham, n.d., FOIA.

128: "This may be counting": Bassett to Langham, Jan. 14, 1946, FOIA.

129: "We arrived after": Bassett to Langham, May 21, 1946, FOIA.

129: "The specimens from both": Bassett to Langham, May 7, 1946, FOIA.

129: "It begins to look now": Bassett to Langham, date unknown, FOIA.

129: "well developed, but thin male": Bassett, "Excretion of Plutonium," p. 22.

130: "Her church was the thing": Welcome, "Six More Test Victims," p. 7.

130: "poorly nourished, weak, thin male": Bassett, "Excretion of Plutonium," p. 28.

130: "I hope this next part": Bassett to Langham, Feb. 27, 1946, FOIA.

130: "We were somewhat pressed": Bassett to Langham, Feb. 27, 1946, FOIA.

130: "This would permit": Langham to Bassett, March 13, 1946 (ACHRE No. DOE-121294-D-4).

131: "This case did turn out": Bassett to Langham, March 27, 1946, FOIA.

131: "thin and pale female": Bassett, "Excretion of Plutonium," p. 24.

131: "I had to get up": Transcript, ACHRE meeting, Jan. 30, 1995, p. 108.

131: received 1,000 rem: LANL, *Radiation Protection*, p. 209.

131: "My mother": Transcript, ACHRE meeting, p. 111.

132: "Man appears chronically ill": Bassett, "Excretion of Plutonium," p. 26.

132: "His honesty was known": Welcome, "Plutonium Experiment," p. 44.

132: "I would like to suggest": Langham to Bassett, Nov. 12, 1945, ACHRE.

132: "very peculiar" diet: Bassett to Langham, Nov. 19, 1945, ACHRE.

133: "would not be taken up": Bassett, "Excretion of Plutonium," p. 5.

133: "The amazing feature": Langham to Bassett, May 28, 1946 (CIC 719236).

133: "With regard to ultimate": Bassett, "Excretion of Plutonium," p. 29.

133: "a miscellaneous group": Ibid., p. 1.

134: "suffering from chronic disorders": Langham et al., *Distribution and Excretion of Plutonium*, p. 10.

134: "hopelessly sick": ACHRE staff, "Additional Documentation on the Plutonium Injection Experiments," Jan. 10, 1995, p. 1.

134: "terminal": Langham et al., "The Los Alamos Experience with Plutonium," *Health Physics*, p. 755.

134: "We were finally successful": Helen Van Alstine to Langham, July 10, 1946, ACHRE.

134: string of misfortunes: Welcome, "2 More Victims Discovered," *AT,* March 8, 1994, p. 1.

135: "The second test at Bikini": Langham to Bassett, Aug. 29, 1946 (CIC 719252).

135: "Shall we try": Bassett to Langham, Aug. 20, 1946 (CIC 719229).

135: "I think we should": Langham to Bassett, Aug. 29, 1946 (CIC 719252).

CHAPTER 14

136: sat on a high stool: Admission notes, Nov. 2, 1945, Charlton m.r.

137: "Her nutrition has been poor": Ibid.

137: "We have also taken": Bassett to Langham, Nov. 14, 1945, ACHRE.

137: "I think she had": Welcome, "Plutonium Experiment," p. 34.

138: "Cover with acid": Doctor's orders, Charlton m.r.

138: "She feels that her ankles": Physician notes, Ibid.

138: "The plutonium solution was injected": Langham et al., *Distribution and Excretion of Plutonium*, p. 15.

138: "For obvious reasons": Langham, "Revised Plan," p. 7.

138: dose of 880 rem: LANL, *Radiation Protection*, p. 209.

138: "Collect urine Spec.": Doctor's orders, Charlton m.r.

139: "I talked to Colonel Warren": Langham to Bassett, Oct. 25, 1946 (CIC 719260).

139: "A woman aged 49": Bassett, "Excretion of Plutonium," p. 2.

139: "I don't remember": Welsome, "Plutonium Experiment," p. 34.

140: "I am still hammering": Bassett to Langham, Oct. 17, 1946, ACHRE.

140: "very rare": Laboratory report, Dec. 12, 1962, Charlton m.r.

140: "Even one sample": Langham to Howland, April 15, 1950 (CIC 709723).

141: "I never knew": Welsome, "Plutonium Experiment," p. 35.

141: "classified information" until 1972: Ibid., p. 33.

141: "My feeling was": Ibid., p. 35.

142: "The X-rays seem": Langham to Howland, Oct. 2, 1950 (ACHRE No. DOE-121294-D-11).

142: "There are some interesting": Radiology report, April 11, 1953, Charlton m.r.

142: "The patient in question": ACHRE, *Final Report,* p. 258.

142: "soft, rubbery mass": Pathology report, June 6, 1953, Charlton m.r.

142: "Patient is a thin": Admission note, Dec. 12, 1962, Charlton m.r.

143: "Because Mrs. Charlton": Int. Joseph Guattery, July 8, 1993.

143: "She said to me one day": Welsome, "Plutonium Experiment," p. 36.

143: "Dr. Waterhouse gave me": Ibid., p. 36.

143: ". . . she feels that this weight increase": Ibid., p. 38.

143–144: "The doctor was being very careful": Ibid., p. 36.

144: "Patients of this character": Ibid.

144: "Mrs. Charlton says": Ibid., p. 38.

144: 1976 [Day illegible]: Ibid., pp. 38–39.

145: "At no time": Joseph Guattery to Gail Knasko, Dec. 6, 1984, FOIA.

145: "Do you suppose that stuff": Welsome, "Plutonium Experiment," p. 39.

CHAPTER 15

146: lookout for "moribund": JWH, "Santa Fe Conversations," n.d., DOE-OR (1020), p. 1.

146: faint bluish tint: Pathology report, Jan. 13, 1946, Macke m.r., p. 1.

146: John Shillito Company: Ed Asher and Dennis Domrzalski, "17th Victim Died 17 Days After Injection," *AT,* Aug. 17, 1994, p. 1.

147: "U" medication was started: Pathology report, p. 5.

147: "On the head": Ibid., p. 1.

147: "The muscles are thin": Ibid., p. 4.

147: "was induced by the medication": Ibid., p. 6.

147: emitting 1,399 counts: Russell and Nickson, *Distribution and Excretion of Plutonium,* p. 32.

148: 94.91 micrograms: Nickson to Stone, "Monthly Summary for Section H-III," Jan. 19, 1946, FOIA.

148: 1,700 times the radiation: LANL, *Radiation Protection,* p. 209.

148: Russell told AEC investigators: Draft memo, "Visit with Edwin Russell, Savannah River Plant, April 23, 1974," FOIA.

148: "knew very little": Draft memo, "Interview with Dr. Leon Jacobson, Mr. Kupferberg, his administrative assistant, Dr. John Rust, and Dr. George V. LeRoy in Dr. Jacobsen's office at the University of Chicago medical school by Marks at Miazga at about 1:30 P.M. on 4/16/74," FOIA.

148: drank a plutonium solution: "Studies Conducted Without ANL Involvement But for Which ANL Has Records," DOE search records, n.d.

148: tasted like "lemonade": Int. Robert Carr Milham, May 2, 1995.

CHAPTER 16

149: "That's been my work": Int. Christine Alan, April 17, 1995.

149: "The next human subject": Hamilton, "Technical Progress Report on the Metabolic Properties of Plutonium and Allied Materials," September 1945, UCSF, *World War II Human Radiation Experiments,* Appendix 27.

150: Around January 6: Admittance note, n.d., Shaw m.r.

150: "There is a whole blank": Int. Joshua Shaw, March 17, 1994.

150: An Australian doctor: British Medical Association House to Dr. J. Hoets, April 1, 1946, FOIA.

151: "Major Davis through the Red Cross": Admission note, Shaw m.r.

151: American troops headed home: "Plane Flies Sick Boy to U.S.A.," undated newspaper clipping (ca. April 16, 1946), Shaw family records.

151: prepared a fresh bed: Harry J. White to Samuel Shaw, April 16, 1946, Shaw family records.

152: "Inside of one hour": "Australian Boy Is Flown Here for Treatment at U.C.," undated newspaper clipping (ca. April 16, 1946), Shaw family records.

152: "They say if I go": Telephone transcript, April 26, 1946, Shaw family records.

152–153: injected with three radioisotopes: "Report on [name deleted], n.d., FOIA.

153: "oblong section": Operation Note, May 3, 1946, Shaw m.r.

153: "responsible individuals": LeRoy C. Abbott to Whom It May Concern, "Re Simeon Shaw U 127513," June 11, 1946, Shaw family records.

153: "If I had any contact": Int. Earl Miller, May 3, 1995.

153: Russian-born father: Int. Joshua Shaw.

153: "They have given him": Telephone transcript, April 26, 1946, Shaw family records.

154: "This afternoon they said": Telephone transcript, May 9, 1946, Shaw family records.

154: tumor actually was increasing: "X-Ray Consultation Request," June 5, 1946, Shaw m.r.

155: "At last I have": Mrs. O. S. Adams to Mrs. Sam Shaw, n.d., Shaw family records.

155: "The last time I went": Int. Joshua Shaw, March 17, 1994.

155: "From Simeon's death onward": The Nine Network of Australia, *60 Minutes,* "Betrayal of Simeon," March 20, 1994.

155: "We realize you may have": A. Jorgenson to Mrs. [name deleted], Feb. 11, 1949, FOIA.

155: pleading with the Manhattan: Hamilton to Area Engineer, "Request for Radioactive Isotopes," Nov. 15, 1946, Carton 5, Folder 11, JGH.

156: "An injection has been given": Sidney Marks, "Summary description of medical records of Albert Stevens and Hanford Jang," April 29, 1974, FOIA.

156: "make arrangements": K. S. S. to Joe, n.d., in UCSF, *World War II Human Radiation Experiments,* Appendix 25.

156: the americium measured: DOE, *Human Radiation Experiments Associated with the U.S. Department of Energy,* p. 53.

156: "no evidence of disclosure": Welsome, "Plutonium Experiment," p. 9.

156: "I don't think Dr. Hamilton": Durbin OH, DOE/OHRE, p. 49.

157: "We were optimistic": Int. Fredna Allen, July 1992.

157: "The principal picture": Lloyd Fisher to Dr. Cappellar, June 13, 1947, Allen m.r.

158: Rent was $35: Application Record, June 20, 1947, Allen m.r.

158: "but the probability": R. S. Sherman, Jr., "X-ray consultation request," June 25, 1947, Allen m.r.

158: "This is probably": Ibid., July 3, 1947, Allen m.r.

158: microscopic examination: James Rinehart, "Pathological Report," July 14, 1947, Allen m.r.

158: "postponed until Monday": Doctor's orders, Allen m.r.

158: "The experimental nature": Ibid.

159: "If they told my father": Int. Elmerine Allen Whitfield, July 8, 1992.

159: "No blood appeared": Doctor's orders, July 18, 1947, Allen m.r.

159: "no pain or discomfort": Ibid.

159: "to pathology and radiological study": Ibid.

159: "Feeling much better": Ibid.

159: "It just takes big beakers": Int. Patricia Durbin, Sept. 3, 1992.

160: "For large, grossly contaminated": Nickson, *Report of Conference on Plutonium,* p. 57.

160: Hempelmann had begun excising: Langham et al., "Los Alamos Scientific Laboratory's Experience with Plutonium," *Health Physics,* p. 758.

160: "He wanted to make": Int. Fredna Allen, July 1992.

160: "He was disgusted": Int. Fredna Allen, Jan. 26, 1993.

160: "He could do anything": Welsome, "Plutonium Experiment," p. 12.

160: "He would chew the spoon": Int. Elmerine Allen Whitfield, July 8, 1992.

161: David Williams, a doctor: Welsome, "Plutonium Experiment," p. 12.

161: "I wondered": Ibid.

161: "passionately dedicated": Int. Anne De Gruchy Low-Beer, May 29, 1995.

162: "He became sad": Earl Miller OH, DOE/OHRE, p. 37.

162: "He was very sad": Int. Grace Walpole, June 1, 1995.

162: "You know": Durbin OH, DOE/OHRE, p. 31.

CHAPTER 17

165: "the most important federal bureau": Lang, *Hiroshima to the Moon,* p. 82.

165: "God Almighty": Cong. Record, U. S. Senate, 79th Cong., 1st sess., Nov. 28, 1945, pp. 11085–11087.

165: Should the bomb: Weisgall, *Operation Crossroads*, p. 12.

166: The Navy was the first: Ibid., pp. 13–14.

166: "If such a test": Ibid.

166: The May-Johnson bill: Hewlett and Anderson, *New World*, pp. 428–445.

167: "reluctant lobby": Ibid., p. 445.

167: "The question is": Lang, *Hiroshima to the Moon*, p. 56.

167: "The scientists quickly discovered": Ibid., p. 58.

167: "His nibs (G.G.)": Hewlett and Anderson, *New World*, p. 487.

167: birth of Jesus Christ: Ibid., p. 436.

168: "They felt that an army": Lang, *Hiroshima to the Moon*, p. 61.

168: "The study was a peculiar one": Ibid., p. 67.

169: Under the terms: Glenn Seaborg, foreward to Weisgall, *Operation Crossroads*, pp. ix–xii.

170: "special attributes of the atom bomb": Stafford Warren OH, p. 861.

170: "Mark III" lead jockstrap: Ibid., p. 878.

170: "I had to practically browbeat": Ibid., p. 890.

170: "I felt they might be": Ibid., p. 886.

170: threw their scientific notebooks: Bradley, *No Place to Hide*, pp. 5–6.

170: "A little eggshell of coral": Ibid., p. 11.

171: 42,000 men . . . 242 ships: Dennis Domrzalski, "Deadly Cleanup" *AT*, April 26, 1994, p. C-1.

172: "Through the glasses": Stafford Warren OH, p. 904.

172: boats were recovering: Weisgall, *Operation Crossroads*, p. 228.

173: "They might have passed": Stafford Warren OH, p. 909.

173: "Our cook had never been": Ibid., p. 934.

173: "Since they couldn't taste": Stafford Warren to Viola Warren, Aug. 11, 1946 (CIC 140498).

173: "You could just feel": Stafford Warren OH, pp. 909–910.

174: "reassure Col. Warren": R. R. Newell, "Report of the Medico-Legal Board," June 8, 1946, Pat Broudy personal papers.

174: 0.1 roentgen per day: Stafford Warren to Commander, Joint Task Force One, "Review of Radiological Safety Situation," Aug. 3, 1946, Broudy papers, p. 2.

174: "insidiously toxic": Stafford Warren to Commander, Joint Task Force One, "Occupancy of Target Vessels as Influenced by Intensity of Radiation of Various Types on Target Vessels," Aug. 7, 1946, Broudy papers, p. 2.

174: "The majority of personnel": Stafford Warren, "Radiological Safety Situation," p. 3.

174: "We worked there": Dennis Domrzalski, "One Family's Agony," *AT*, April 28, 1994, p. C-2.

174: "Mac, that's hot": Domrzalski, "Diver Probed Depths of Radioactive Cesspool," *AT*, April 27, 1994, p. C-1.

175: "It was often a matter": Domrzalski, "In Harm's Way," ibid.

175: "They checked our clothing": Domrzalski, "Sailor Spent Two Weeks on Contaminated Ship," ibid.

175: a decade later: Stafford Warren to Ralph B. Snavely, Aug. 2, 1957, Stewart Udall personal papers.

175: "Boxes, mattresses, life belts": Bradley, *No Place to Hide,* p. 74.

177: "That is part": Cong. hearing, *Atomic Energy,* 1945, p. 46.

177: "national suicide": Ibid., p. 49.

177: "We cannot shut down": Ibid., p. 47.

177: "For I was no longer": Groves, *Now It Can Be Told,* p. 391.

177: "The whole purpose": Ibid., p. 400.

CHAPTER 18

178: other talks were: Stafford Warren to Groves, "Clearance of 'Discussion on product contamination after underwater bomb detonation,' during part of informal talks on safety at Bikini," Oct. 9, 1946, Broudy personal papers, p. 1.

178: "is probably the most toxic": Ibid., p. 2.

179: "Soon the number of bombs": Stafford Warren, Transcript of Lecture, Oct. 7, 1946, Broudy papers, p. 27.

179: "You need only": Ibid., pp. 21–22.

179: "It has recently come to my attention:" Don Mastick to Hempelmann, June 6, 1947, ACHRE.

179: "You know Staff": Hempelmann to Mastick, July 23, 1947, ACHRE.

180: three years and two days: Stafford Warren OH, p. 999.

180: start-up medical school faculty: Ibid., p. 1085.

180: "They were afraid": Ibid., p. 1089.

180: *extremely* low morale": LeRoy G. Augenstine, "Report of Visit to UCLA," Trip Report, March 19, 1959, ACHRE, p. 1.

180: Under an AEC contract: Paul Lavik to Norma Shinn, "Summary of Research Activities Under USAEC Contract No. W31-109-eng-78," Oct. 30, 1961, Case Western Reserve University, University Archives.

181: "He wasn't about": Stafford Warren OH, pp. 928–929.

181: He believed Warren: Udall, "Memorandum of telephone conversation with Pete Scoville," Feb. 21, 1979, Udall papers.

181: "He was tremendously": Int. James P. Cooney Jr., April 27, 1995.

182: "walker in the corridors": Int. Patricia Durbin, Sept. 3, 1992.

182: "One of the principal strategic uses": Hamilton to Nichols, "Radioactive Warfare," Dec. 31, 1946, ACHRE, p. 6.

182: plane tracking the radioactive: Hamilton to [address deleted], March 27, 1951, Box 32, Folder 21, JGH.

182: According to the Clinton: ACHRE, *Final Report,* pp. 518–524.

183: "The technical developments": Cong. hearing, *Investigation into the Atomic Energy Project,* July 6, 1949, p. 774.

183: "With the lifting of security": James Nolan, "History of Health Group During Interim Period (November 1945–May 1946)" (LANL HSPT-94-104), p. 2.

183: "milk route": Ibid., p. 3.

184: Slotin was an intense-looking: Jungk, *Brighter Than a Thousand Suns,* p. 194.

184: "Keep doing that": Weisgall, *Operation Crossroads,* p. 138.

184: some forty times before: Stewart Alsop and Ralph E. Lapp, "The Strange Death of Louis Slotin," *Saturday Evening Post,* March 6, 1954, p. 90.

184: hollow beryllium hemisphere: Roy Reider to D. F. Hayes, Nov. 16, 1955, enclosure (LAMD-1387).

184: "You can guess the rest": Norris Bradbury to Marshall and Roger, May 23, 1946, LANL, p. 1.

185: 800 roentgens: "Part I, Estimate of Radiation Dosage in Nuclear Accident, May 21, 1946," LANL.

185: "This is not because": Alvin Graves to Stewart Alsop, Dec. 3, 1953, Rick Ray personal papers, p. 2.

185: "When we were alone together": Ibid., p. 3.

186: "Nothing could be done": J. Garrot Allen, "Death Will Be Slow Agony for Victims," *LAT,* n.d., Ray personal papers.

186: pair of opera glasses: Major Sidney Newburger Jr., "Possessions of Louis Slotin," June 5, 1946, LANL.

186: Alvin Graves suffered from nausea: "Clinical Histories of Alvin Graves, Allan Kline and Theodore Perlman," LANL, pp. 2–3.

186: "concocted in the minds": Udall, *Myths of August,* p. 243.

186: "cut finger not requiring": Graves, "Radiation Exposures," n.d., Udall papers, p. 2.

186: Allan Kline, who was standing: "Clinical Histories."

187: took a radically different: Clifford T. Honicker, "The Hidden Files," *New York Times Magazine,* Nov. 19, 1989, p. 98.

187: physician was J. J. Nickson: "Abstract of History of Allan Kline taken from records of Argonne National Laboratory," n.d., LANL.

187: "unusually shabby treatment": Paul Stickler to Brien McMahon, Aug. 15, 1949, ACHRE, p. 2.

187: "I was actually used": Allan Kline, "Estimated Damages to S. Allan Kline Resulting from Radiation Accident at Los Alamos, New Mexico in 1946," enclosure to Stickler letter, ACHRE.

188: Hempelmann carefully collected: "Meeting of the Biological and Medical Committee," Dec. 8, 1950, ACHRE, pp. 9–15.

CHAPTER 19

189: stroke of midnight: Hewlett and Duncan, *Atomic Shield,* p. 18.

189: "The first paragraph": Nichols to the Area Engineer, "Administration of Radioactive Substances to Human Subjects," Dec. 24, 1946, DOE-OR (No. 1009).

190: "suitable solutions": Hamilton, "Progress Report for the Month of November 1946," UCSF, *Addendum to the February 1995 Report,* Appendix 4.

190: "Until the Atomic Energy Commission": E. E. Kirkpatrick to Area Engineer, "Administration of Radioactive Substances to Human Subjects," Jan. 8, 1947 (CIC No. 707075).

190: "In the American army": "The Brutalities of Nazi Physicians," *JAMA,* pp. 714–715.

191: "doubts were expressed": Sidney Marks, "Patients Injected with Plutonium (Chronology)," n.d., FOIA.

191: "It is the opinion": Stafford Warren to Carroll Wilson, Jan. 30, 1947, DOE-OR.

191: Al Capone: AEC press release, "Former Secret Service Chief Names Security Consultant to U.S. Atomic Energy Commission," Jan. 25, 1947.

192: "should be susceptible": Wilson to Stafford Warren, April 30, 1947, DOE-OR, p. 2.

192: guidelines to be circulated: Robert J. Buettner to B. M. Brundage, May 12, 1947, DOE-OR.

193: "The atmosphere of secrecy": Wilson to Stone, Nov. 5, 1947 (ACHRE No. DOE-052295-A-1).

193: earliest known use: ACHRE, *Final Report,* p. 90.

193: "Maybe it means": Int. Ruth Faden, April 11, 1997.

194: "inconceivable that [Wilson]": Int. Joseph Volpe, May 21, 1997.

194: "There are a large number": "Medical Policy," Oct. 8, 1947 (CIC 707132), p. 8.

195: "This document appears": "Excerpts from statements of reviewers," n.d. (ACHRE No. 113094-B-9).

195: "It would be unwise": Brundage to Declassification Section, "Clearance of Technical Documents," March 19, 1947 (CIC 712320).

196: "attitude taken by the AEC": Bassett to Stafford Warren, Sept. 12, 1947 (CIC 724059).

196: "I make this suggestion": Andrew Dowdy to Bradbarry [sic], Feb. 18, 1947 (ACHRE No. DOE-121294-D-6).

196: "It is desired": O. G. Haywood Jr. to Dr. Fidler, "Medical Experiments on Humans," April 17, 1947 (CIC 703001).

CHAPTER 20

197: "People more alert": quoted in John Z. Bowers, "The ABCC: Its Creation and First Years (1946–1952)," unpublished manuscript, p. 19. The diary that Bowers is quoting from is apparently Shield Warren's red diary dated April 21, 1947, to June 8, 1947. Warren's diaries and papers are in the Special Collections section of the Mugar Memorial Library at Boston University. That diary is listed in a logbook but not among the diaries in Box 3 of the collection. Also missing is a gray book, dated September 16, 1945, to December 29, 1945, the period covering Warren's first Japan trip, and a gray Crossroads book dated May 19, 1946, to August 17, 1946. BU archivists said the collection represents what was donated to the library by Warren's family. They have no explanation for the absent diaries.

197: "compulsive zeal": Ibid., p. 60.

197: "Stoicism of Japanese": Ibid., p. 33.

198: "told me that I had": Shields Warren OH, p. 59.

198: "There were so many opportunities": National Library of Medicine, *Shields Warren,* Videotape, 1974.

198: "gentle stammer": Int. William McDermott, May 18, 1995.

198: lymphatic system: Shields Warren obituary, *The Annual Obituary,* 1980, p. 395.

199: "ominous" implications: Wendell Latimer and Hamilton to Shields Warren, "Review of the Gabriel Project Report," Oct. 4, 1949 (CIC 26588).

199: no-danger chorus: Divine, *Blowing on the Wind,* p. 134.

200: "He was a god": Int. Clarence Lushbaugh, March 3, 1995.

200: "I considered him": Int. John Pickering, Sept. 28, 1995.

200: "I was never quite sure": Andrews OH, Dec. 3, 1994, p. 36.

200: "was too swift": Int. Herman Wigodsky, June 2, 1995.

200: "kind of a turkey": Pace OH, p. 9.

200: "You must realize": Udall, "Memorandum of Conversation with Dr. Shields Warren," July 11, 1979, Udall papers.

200: One of his grandfathers: Shields Warren OH, pp. 2, 4.

200: philosophy professor: Ibid., p. 11.

201: "The mortality was terribly": Ibid.

201: "I decided the best": Ibid., pp. 12–26.

201: "Apparently nobody knew": Ibid., p. 51.

201: "The Effects of Radiation on Normal Tissue": AEC press release, "Dr. Shields Warren Appointed Interim Director of Biology and Medicine," Oct. 24, 1947.

202: no "epidemics" brewing: L. A. Miazga, Sidney Marks, and Walter Weyzen, "Interview with Shields Warren," April 9, 1974 (CIC 719365), p. 8.

202: "interplanetary rockets": "Medical Policy," Oct. 8, 1947 (ACHRE DOE-051094-A-502), p. 7. The memo does not include author's name, but other AEC records suggest it was written by Albert Holland.

202: radioactivity levels in fish: Gerber, *On the Home Front,* pp. 118–119.

202: "It is recommended that all river": Wendell Crane to Milton Cydell, "Meeting of the Committee of Senior Responsible Reviewers—Statement of Hanford Operations Office Problems," Dec. 17, 1948 (CIC 006217).

202: "When I took over": Miazga et al., "Interview with Shields Warren," pp. 3–4.

202: "isotopic injection": Ibid. All of Shields Warren's statements about the meeting with Joseph Hamilton taken from this document.

203: ". . . feels fine": Orthopedic clinic, Dec. 3, 1947, Allen m.r.

204: refused to declassify: Shields Warren to Albert Holland, "Declassification of Documents," March 2, 1948 (CIC 707058).

204: given a "confidential" classification: Walter Claus to Langham, Aug. 30, 1950 (CIC 709725).

205: "With regard to the first statement": Stone to Shields Warren, Oct. 6, 1948 (CIC 714416).

205: "highly significant decreases": Norman C. Knowlton, "Changes in the Blood of Humans Chronically Exposed to Low Level Gamma Radiation" (LADC 587), 1948.

205: "The results of the studies": Anthony Vallado to Clyde Wilson, "Review of Document by Knowlton," Dec. 8, 1948 (ACHRE No. DOE-120894-E-32).

205: has "no idea": Int. Norman Knowlton, April 24, 1996.

206: "to be made into a scientific liar": Wilhelm Hueper, "Adventures of a Physician," unpublished manuscript, p. 178.

206: nasopharyngeal irradiation: Hueper, "Recent Developments in Environmental Cancer," Vol. 6, Hueper papers, p. 55.

206: Warren did not dispute: Udall, *Myths of August,* p. 192.

CHAPTER 21

207: "our very survival": Cong. hearing, *Investigation into the United States Atomic Energy Project,* July 11, 1949, p. 881.

208: "The radioactive isotopes": Evans, "The Medical Uses of Atomic Energy," *Atlantic Monthly,* January 1946, p. 71.

208: 1,092 shipments: AEC press release, "Background Material on Activity in First Year of Distribution of Pile-Produced Radioisotopes," Aug. 3, 1947.

208: "The liberal establishment": ACHRE, *Final Report,* p. 72.

208: "would aid in showing": AEC, "Report of the Medical Board of Review," June 20, 1947, p. 5.

208: $5 million: Shields Warren to M. W. Boyer, "Biology and Medicine Cancer Program," Oct. 3, 1951, Udall papers.

209: Armed with $1.1 million: Gil Whittemore, "Shields Warren Papers," Oct. 6, 1994, ACHRE, p. 4.

209: "The emphasis on": AEC, "Medical Board of Review," p. 8.

209: "no romance": AEC, "Meeting of the Biological and Medical Committee," Dec. 8, 1950 (ACHRE No. DOE-012795-C-1), p. 145.

209: "time consuming and rather unspectacular": Stafford Warren, "Radioactivity, Health and Safety," April 1, 1947, p. 29, in George Darling, MSS 770, "Radioactive Materials Research" Folder, Yale University Library.

209: "Several members [of the Advisory]": Bob Tumbleson to Morse Salisbury, "Visit to Los Alamos with Medical Advisory Board," Jan. 13, 1948, DOE archives.

210: "One had the feeling": Bale OH, JNS, p. 40.

210: "It was fantastic": Stanton Cohn OH, JNS, p. 29.

210: "I am black and blue": Shipman, "H Division Activities," May 6, 1969 (LANL-HSPT-94-108) p. 34.

210: By the 1950s: Hewlett and Holl, *Atoms for Peace and War,* p. 264.

210: "Never before in history": Behrens, *Atomic Medicine,* p. 3.

211: "Pretty soon it makes": Morgan OH, JNS, p. 9.

211: "The backers": Jungk, *Brighter Than a Thousand Suns,* p. 254.

211: "This was, to borrow": Rothman, *Strangers at the Bedside,* p. 51.

211: "In some cases, basic": GAO, *Human Experimentation,* p. 1.

212: "Some of my peers": Silverman OH, p. 75.

212: "Doctors who were doing": Leonard Sagan OH. Excerpt courtesy of Jon Harkness.

213: pertained only to patients: Grodin, "Historical Origins of the Nuremberg Code," in *Nazi Doctors and the Nuremberg Code,* p. 124.

213: William Beaumont: Ibid., p. 125.

213: "will not protect": "Element of Consent in Surgical Operations," *JAMA,* p. 402.

213: "In the case at hand": *Schloendorff v. Society of New York Hospital,* 105 NE 92 (1914).

213: by the 1920s the Army: ACHRE, *Final Report,* p. 780.

213: "It is the most fundamental": Cong. hearing, *Radiation Testing on Humans,* 1994, p. 74.

214: "The connection between": Silverman OH, pp. 87–88.

214: "The model was in religion": Ibid., p. 7.

214: "It's very easy": Finch OH, p. 52.

215: "I must also tell you": Silverman OH, pp. 113–114.

215: "We were taking care of them": Beeson OH, p. 39.

215: "One of the fellows in the cardiac": Ibid., p. 27.

215: "I may be phrasing this crudely": Ibid., p. 28.

215: "It brings up the sociological": Ibid.

216: African American mothers: DOE, *Experiments Associated with the U.S. Department of Energy,* p. 186.

216: tens of thousands of hours: Int. Gary B. Ellis, July 23, 1997.

217: "some of which": "Medical Policy," Oct. 8, 1947 (ACHRE DOE-051094-A-502), pp. 3–4.

217: AEC researchers didn't really: Shields Warren to Albert Holland, "Basic Policy Concerning Human Administration of Isotopes," Dec. 7, 1948, Jacqueline Kittrell personal papers.

218: Aebersold as a "nut": Eisenbud OH, p. 19.

CHAPTER 22

219: The waiting room: Description of clinic and experiment performed on Helen Hutchison taken from Hutchison's medical records and numerous author interviews conducted with Hutchison between 1994 and 1998.

221: "an energetic and competent": C. S. Robinson to E. W. Goodpasture, May 9, 1946, Kittrell personal papers.

221: protégé of Stafford Warren's: Hahn application, Tennessee State Department of Public Health, Dec. 1, 1943, Kittrell personal papers.

221: largest number of radioisotope: AEC press release, "Background Material on Activity in First Year of Distribution of Pile-Produced Radioisotopes," Aug. 3, 1947, p. 8.

221: "There were signs": Nancy Humphrey, "Darby Recalls His Life's Work Improving Human Nutrition," *VUMC Reporter,* Jan. 14, 1994.

221: simple and straightforward: Hahn et al., "Iron Metabolism in Human Pregnancy," *Journal of Obstetrics and Gynecology,* pp. 478–486; "Flow Sheet for Nutrition Study of New White Patients," Sept. 4, 1945, Kittrell papers.

222: drinks as "cocktails": Darby dep., May 20, 1994, Kittrell papers, p. 244.

222: he was "certain": Keith Schneider, "Scientists Are Sharing the Anguish Over Nuclear Experiments," *NYT,* March 2, 1994, p. A-9.

222: "We did not decide": Darby dep., p. 235.

222: no therapeutic purpose: Ibid., p. 283.

222: "In fact, it": Ibid., p. 427.

222: discussed "isotopes": Excerpt, Stafford Warren diary, Oct. 28, 1945, Kittrell personal papers.

222: "while a recent supply": Press release, Vanderbilt University News Office, Dec. 13, 1946.

223: "considerable radiation": Edgar J. Murphy to J. C. Stewart, Nov. 18, 1947, Kittrell personal papers.

223: "Radioactive iron regardless": Hahn to Zaven M. Seron, Feb. 17, 1947, in Donald C. Arbitblit statement to ACHRE, Oct. 12, 1994.

223: "must not be too long": Hahn and C. W. Sheppard, "Therapeutic Use of Radioactive Elements," *Annals of Internal Medicine,* pp. 598–606.

224: "What is it that you": Emma Craft videotaped deposition, Sept. 13, 1994. Unless otherwise specified, details and quotes involving Craft's case taken from videotaped deposition.

224: "They had to carry me": Int. Emma Craft, July 10, 1996.

226: The research community: Stewart, Webb, and Hewett, "Survey of Child-hood Malignancies," *British Medical Journal,* pp. 1495–1508.

226: An independent study: MacMahon, "Prenatal X-Ray Exposure," *Journal of the National Cancer Institute,* pp. 1173–1191.

226: "Ruth Hagstrom did": Int. A. Bertrand Brill, July 14, 1996.

227: "He helped to find": Ibid.

227: mothers were informed: Schneider, "Scientists Are Sharing."

227: "This lady called": Int. Helen Hutchison, Sept. 17, 1994.

227: "I filled it out": Craft dep.

227: "You may remember": Ruth Hagstrom to [name deleted], Jan. 29, 1965, Arbitblit statement, Oct. 12, 1994.

228: "suggests a cause": Hagstrom et al., "Long Term Effects of Radioactive Iron," *Journal of Epidemiology,* pp. 1–10.

CHAPTER 23

230: "He molested me": Int. Gordon Shattuck, May 29, 1996. Description of daily life at Fernald also have been compiled from interviews with Austin La-Rocque, May 24, 1996; Charles Dyer, May 29, 1996; Albert Gagne, May 29, 1996.

230: divided into "idiots": Wallace, *History of the Walter E. Fernald,* p. 108.

231: seventy-four Fernald boys: Int. Doe West, May 27, 1996.

231: first permanent school: Wallace, *History of the Walter E. Fernald,* p. 27.

231: Florence Nightingale: Ibid., p. 4.

232: His wife was Julia: Chip Brown, "The Science Club Serves Its Country," *Esquire,* December 1994, p. 124.

232: Edward W. Emerson: Wallace, *History of the Walter E. Fernald,* p. 97.

232: "The social and economic": Clarke and Clarke, *Mental Deficiency,* p. 16.

232: "deviants and defects": Int. Doe West.

233: "zoo": Ibid.

233: air-conditioning repairmen: Account taken from letters and undated newspaper clippings received from James Brasco, of the Brasco & Sons Memorial Chapel in Waltham, which buried the heads; undated document entitled "Fernald School Specimens," received from Sandra Marlow.

233: Many human experiments: "A Listing of Some of The 'Non-Radioactive' Studies Found," n.d., Marlow personal papers.

234: "moribund gargoyle patient": Bronner et al., "Calcium Metabolism in a Case of Gargoylism," *Journal of Clinical Investigation,* pp. 139–147.

234: "hot spots": Evans to Aebersold, March 1949, in Task Force on Human Subject Research, *Research that Involved Residents of State-Operated Facilities within the Commonwealth of Massachusetts,* p. B-2/A.

234: "additional studies": Rand Sunshine Project, Dec. 16–18, 1953, DOE archives, p. 35.

235: "potentially coercive factor": Task Force, *Research that Involved Residents of State-Operated Facilities*, p. 28.

235: "In previous years": Clemens Benda to [parent's name deleted], May 28, 1953, Ibid., p. B-23.

C H A P T E R   2 4

239: afternoon of September 3: Hewlett and Duncan, *Atomic Shield,* p. 363.

239: One filter paper: Halberstam, *The Fifties,* p. 25.

239: "Keep your shirt on": Hewlett and Duncan, *Atomic Shield,* p. 369.

239: including Leslie Groves: Nichols, *Road to Trinity,* p. 272.

240: "weapon of genocide": Hewlett and Duncan, *Atomic Shield,* p. 384.

240: "necessarily an evil thing": Ibid.

240: "hydrogen bombs by the thousands": Shelton, *Reflections of a Nuclear Weaponeer,* p. 6–2.

240: President Truman reluctantly: Hewlett and Duncan, *Atomic Shield,* p. 408.

240: three men had helped: Halberstam, *The Fifties,* p. 46.

241: "Will that include": Hewlett and Duncan, *Atomic Shield,* p. 532.

241: on St. Patrick's Day: Biographical sketch, James P. Cooney, Department of the Army, Center of Military History, Washington, D.C.

242: Japanese were not prepared: "General Minimizes Fear of Atom Bomb Effects," undated newspaper clipping, James Cooney Jr. personal papers.

242: Hoover dropped him: J. Edgar Hoover to James P. Cooney, May 4, 1949, Cooney Jr. personal papers.

242: "He was a wonderful": Int. Charles Gingles, May 2, 1995.

242: Huge blisters appeared: Hacker, *Elements of Controversy,* p. 34.

242: psychological training: Cooney, "Psychological Factors in Atomic Warfare," Speech before the American Public Health Association, Boston, MA, Nov. 12, 1948, DOE archives.

242–243: "An Irishman is no good": NEPA Medical Advisory Panel Subcommittee No. II, "An Evaluation of the Psychological Problem of Crew Selection Relative to the Special Hazards of Irradiation Exposure," July 22, 1949, ACHRE, p. 11.

243: "I have observed": Cooney, "Psychological Factors."

243: Soviets might try: AP, "U.S. Planned for Soviet Siege of Nuclear Test Site," *AT,* Aug. 23, 1995, p. A-7.

243: study called "Nutmeg": Director of Military Application, "Selection of a Continental Atomic Test Site," Dec. 13, 1950, DOE archives.

243: "A good place to throw": Rosenberg, *Atomic Soldiers,* p. 17.

244: thriving ecosystem: Goin, *Nuclear Landscapes,* pp. 17–18.

244: atomic tests could be justified: Hewlett and Duncan, *Atomic Shield,* p. 535.

244: statesmen of the Manhattan: Frederick Reines, "Discussion of Radiological Hazards Associated with a Continental Test Site for Atomic Bombs," Sept. 1, 1950 (LAMS-1173), DOE archives.

244: "serious oversight": Udall, "Memorandum of Conversation with Shields Warren," July 5, 1979, Udall papers.

244: "omitting insofar as possible": Reines report, p. 5.

245: "generally accepted": Ibid., p. 6.

245: "quite wrong": Udall, "Memorandum of Conversation."

245: "one would have to ingest": Reines report, p. 7.

245: "unduly alarming miners": Bale to Files, "Measurements of Air-borne Radioactivity in a Colorado Plateau Uranium Mine," July 17, 1951, Udall papers.

246: "It should be emphasized": S. T. Cantril, "Biological Bases for Maximum Permissible Exposures," *Industrial Medicine,* p. 54.

246: "Even the lightest type": Bale to James Cooney, "Relative Dosage from Beta and Gamma Radiation to Individuals Exposed to Fission Product Fall-Out Following A-Bomb Detonation," Aug. 22, 1950, Appendix II, Reines report, p. 4.

246: "people will receive": Reines report, p. 23.

246: Enrico Fermi wanted: Ibid., p. 21.

246: "make the atom routine": Hacker, *Elements of Controversy,* p. 43.

247: Two series of atmospheric tests: Dates compiled from DNA reports and numerous interviews with scientist William Jay Brady.

247: "sunburns": Udall, *Myths of August,* p. 227.

CHAPTER 25

249: Huddled in the cold: Description of Shot Fox comes from April 2, 1996, interview with Jerry Schultz and his Oct. 25, 1995, recollection entitled "Remembrance of Operation Ranger."

250: lasted just thirteen days: DNA fact sheet, "Operation Ranger."

251: Because the exercises: William Jay Brady, "Problems with Radiation Dose Reconstructions and Unassigned Doses for Atomic Veterans," Paper presented at University of Lethbridge, Lethbridge, Canada, June 25–30, 1995.

251: "Doom Town": Mary Manning, " 'Doom Town' Builder's Demise," *Las Vegas Review Journal/Sun,* July 3, 1994, p. 6-D.

251: 2,000 to 3,000: ACHRE, *Final Report,* p. 455.

252: "Fear of radiation": Richard L. Meiling, "Military Medical Problems Associated with Military Participation in Atomic Energy Commission Tests," June 27, 1951 (ACHRE No. DOD-122794-B).

252: "A tactical exercise": Ibid.

252: "negative, defensive attitude": Sven A. Bach, "Conference at OCAFF, Fort Monroe, Virginia, re Past and Future Atomic Weapons Tests," July 12, 1951 (ACHRE No. NARA-042295-C).

253: "more realistic tolerance levels": Ibid.

253: "It was generally agreed": Ibid.

253–254: "It is, of course, obvious": "Biomedical Participation in Future Atomic Weapons Tests," Joint Panel on the Medical Aspects of Atomic Warfare, Sept. 20, 1951 (ACHRE No. DOE-072294-B).

CHAPTER 26

255: "A person in the vicinity": "Public Health Convention Will End Here Today," *AT,* May 23, 1951, p. 10.

256: "In Los Alamos": Lyon and Evans, eds., *Los Alamos: The First Forty Years,* p. 57.

256: "meddlers, peddlers": Ibid., p. 117.

256: One bomb would: Hacker, *Elements of Controversy,* pp. 60–61.

256: "It is not possible": Shields Warren to James McCormack, "Health Hazards Associated with Underground Burst in Nevada," Feb. 21, 1951 (CIC 103851).

257: Fifty-five pages: "Notes on the Meeting of a Committee to Consider the Feasibility and Conditions for a Preliminary Radiologic Safety Shot for Jangle," May 21–22, 1951, ACHRE.

258: one to two microns: Glasstone, *Effects of Nuclear Weapons,* pp. 597–600.

258: "would appear most ominous": Latimer and Hamilton to Shields Warren, "Review of the Gabriel Project Report," Oct. 4, 1949 (CIC 26588).

258: "The particle size problem": "Notes," p. 6.

259: "One point makes me": Ibid., p. 26.

259: "Our safe region": Ibid., p. 29.

259: "From our experience": Ibid., p. 26.

259: "We are faced": Ibid., p. 40.

260: "One thing I'm afraid": Ibid., p. 52.

260: "The hazard in the lung": "Summary of Jangle Meeting," attachment to "Notes."

260: "Distant or worldwide": "Dr. Warren: Stevenson Statement Should be Corrected," *U.S. News & World Report,* Oct. 26, 1956, p. 127.

CHAPTER 27

261: The GIs lived: In addition to individuals cited below, description of Desert Rock compiled from interviews conducted between March and May of 1996 with Robert Hall, John Dishong, Billy Sykes, Wordell Woolridge, Glenn Stuckey, Louis Silva, Albert Remavich, Dan Pfahl, and Filiberto Uriegas.

262: no free betting: Venlo Wolfsohn, "Recollection of Operation Buster-Jangle's Shot Dog," n.d.

262: "The ground was running": Int. William Brecount, March 20, 1996.

262: an oven door: Int. Robert Saunders, May 1, 1996.

262: rocks falling: Int. Ubaldo Arizmendi, March 20, 1996.

262: "Though they drove": "New Weapon for the GIs," *Life,* Nov. 12, 1951, pp. 37–39.

263: "If the radiation intensity": "History of the Battalion Combat Team (BCT) During Shot Dog Operation Buster-Jangle (1951)," Venlo Wolfsohn personal papers.

263: found the troops' confidence: Rosenberg, *Atomic Soldiers,* pp. 46–47.

263: 7,500 roentgens: Hacker, *Elements of Controversy,* p. 70.

263: "The absence of film badges": Ibid., p. 71.

264: "So strong is the feeling": Director of Military Application, "Troop Participation in Operation Tumbler-Snapper," n.d., ACHRE, p. 3.

264: "Accidents occurring": Shields Warren to K. E. Fields, "Draft Staff Paper on Troop Participation in Operation Tumbler-Snapper," March 25, 1952 (CIC 18863).

264: "from two and one half": Gordon Dean to H. B. Loper, April 2, 1952 (ACHRE No. DOD-100694-A).

264: "Here again": L. L. Lemnitzer to U. S. Rep Carl T. Durham, Feb. 11, 1953, ACHRE.

265: launched a campaign: John T. Hayward to John C. Bugher, "Exposure Standards for Personnel at AEC Weapons Tests," Sept. 19, 1952 (CIC No. 72699).

265: "Our position": George Kraker to Fields, "Troop Participation in Upshot-Knothole," Oct. 7, 1952, enclosure (CIC 72699), p. 28.

265: "*close* atomic support": John C. Oakes to Assistant Chief of Staff, "Indoctrination of Personnel in Atomic Warfare Operations," June 3, 1952 (ACHRE No. NARA-112594-A).

265: selected soldiers: K. D. Nichols to Chief of Staff, U.S. Army, "Positioning Troops at Atomic Explosions," Feb. 3, 1953, ACHRE.

265: "must have sufficient": Carl Jark, "Instructions for Positioning DA [Department of Army] Personnel at Continental Atomic Tests," Feb. 20, 1953, ACHRE.

265–266: "Volunteers in foxholes": R. C. Morris to Army Chief of Research and Development, "Proposed Project Regarding Blast Injury Evaluation," Nov. 15, 1955 (ACHRE No. DOD-030895-F).

266: "It is evident": "Detailed Explanation of AFSWP Comments on Feasibility of Human Volunteer Program," n.d. (ACHRE No. DOD-030895-F).

266: no more "useful": Ibid.

267: handful of excess cancer deaths: ACHRE, *Final Report,* p. 482.

267: "There were also": Jordan OH, JNS, p. 14.

268: "I thought it was": Int. William Jay Brady, May 12, 1999.

268: erroneously included 4,500: ACHRE, *Final Report,* p. 480.

268: study of Crossroads: Institute of Medicine, *Mortality of Veteran Participants in the Crossroads Nuclear Test.*

268: 500 of the 450,000: Int. Pat Broudy, May 12, 1997.

269: "creates the unmistakable": William Taft IV to G. V. (Sonny) Montgomery, Sept. 4, 1981, Broudy personal papers.

269: fewer than fifty: Int. Patricia Broudy, July 7, 1997.

269: "were in the hundreds": Cong. hearing, *Effects to Veterans of Exposure to Ionizing Radiation,* p. 72.

CHAPTER 28

270: "The Atomic Energy Commission does not": John Bugher to Walter Aleen, April 14, 1953, ACHRE. Letters from volunteers also obtained from ACHRE.

CHAPTER 29

272: four fighter pilots cruised: Details of this flight taken from April 12, 1952, accident report entitled "Major Aircraft Accident, F-84G, Eniwetok" (Doc. No. TR-9141, E8, 56B), which was jointly declassified in 1998 by DOE and

DOD. Also Leland Taylor, *History of Air Force Atomic Cloud Sampling,* published in January 1963 by Air Force Systems Command. Some specific references cited below.

272: column was twenty miles: Shelton, *Reflections of a Nuclear Weaponeer,* pp. 5–38.

272: diaphanous cloud: Taylor, *History of Air Force Atomic Cloud Sampling,* p. 105.

273: "A dingaling": Int. William Wright, Oct. 20, 1995.

273: the stem was highly radioactive: Taylor, *Atomic Cloud Sampling,* p. 105.

273: When the head: Ibid.

273–274: "When he reached the cloud": Ibid., p. 71.

274: "Inside the cloud Colonel Meroney": Ibid.

275: electromagnetic interference: The declassified accident report on Jimmy Robinson discloses that a major factor leading to the fatality was the electromagnetic interference from Shot Mike, which caused the "breakdown of communications and electronic equipment during and after shot time in the area." Interestingly enough, the Air Force history, which was originally classified as "Secret," makes no mention of the electromagnetic interference, an omission which demonstrates that sensitive information occasionally was withheld even from classified documents.

276: seven-member crew received: DNA, *Operation Ivy,* p. 255.

276: They found an oil slick: Taylor, *Atomic Cloud Sampling,* p. 74.

276: "a miserable thing": Halberstam, *The Fifties,* p. 42.

276: "gently and irregularly moving": Edward Teller, "The Work of Many People," *Science,* p. 274.

276: "was the motion": Ibid., p. 275.

277: "how to take psychological": Nichols, *Road to Trinity,* p. 291.

277: "It was an awesome": Truman, *Years of Trial and Hope,* Vol. 2, p. 314.

277: 4,000 people: GAO, *Radiation Exposures for Some Cloud-Sampling Personnel Need to Be Reexamined,* p. 8.

278: "simply overwhelmed": Taylor, *Atomic Cloud Sampling,* p. 213.

278: "volunteered to get": Ibid.

278: "must maintain a minimum": Randall Beck, "Hazardous Duty," *Knoxville Journal,* Nov. 14, 1985, p. A-17.

278: Fermi rumbled to Ground Zero: Taylor, *Atomic Cloud Sampling,* p. 2.

278: "As I recall, he would not": Stafford Warren OH, p. 808.

278: developed stomach cancer: Gottfried, *Enrico Fermi,* p. 123.

278: no "ill effects": Taylor, *Atomic Cloud Sampling,* p. 21.

279: a lead-glass vest: GAO, *Radiation Exposures,* p. 12; Taylor, *Atomic Cloud Sampling,* p. 87.

279: rose-colored glasses: "The Target of the 4926th Is the Bomb Cloud," *ARDC Newsmagazine,* March 1957, p. 15, Langdon Harrison personal papers.

279: gold face shields: Int. Langdon Harrison, Oct. 19, 1995.

279: "Its members during test operations": "The Target of the 4926th," p. 14.

280: "Needed for planning purposes": Taylor, *Atomic Cloud Sampling,* p. 209.

280: "The same for ground personnel": Ibid., p. 193.

280: "A scarcity of information": Ibid., p. 230.

280: 3.9 roentgens: Shields Warren to Carroll Tyler, "Permissible Levels of Radiation Exposure for Test Personnel," Oct. 11, 1951 (CIC 39084).

280: permitted up to 50 roentgens: W. M. Canterbury to Chief of Staff, USAF, "Radiation Dosage Required for Project 2.66, Operation Redwing," Oct. 4, 1955 (CIC 76977).

280: 42.5 roentgens: Int. Cheri Abdelnour, April 19, 1996.

280: exposures were underestimated: GAO, *Radiation Exposures,* p. 2.

280: "As a result a radiation flux": Taylor, *Atomic Cloud Sampling,* p. 211.

281: special forklifts were rolled: Int. William Wright, Oct. 20, 1995.

281: "Those aircraft never": Ibid.

281: Duz, a common laundry: Int. Jim Braddock, March 6, 1996.

281: compound called "Gunk": Taylor, *Atomic Cloud Sampling,* p. 85.

281: "grease spots collected": Ibid., p. 230.

281: "Our experience in nuclear tests": Ibid., p. 236.

281: "We have always gone": Shipman to Alvin Graves, "Decontamination of Aircraft at Tests," March 29, 1957, ACHRE.

282: 100 roentgens per hour: Taylor, *Atomic Cloud Sampling,* p. 225.

282: "neither crew or passengers": Ibid., p. 193.

282: "After we went": Langdon Harrison, Transcript of Personal Hearing before Veterans Administration Regional Office Rating Board, Albuquerque, NM, Aug. 8, 1985.

282: 0.2 to 0.3 roentgens: DNA, *Operation Ranger,* p. 95.

282: "Since there is a lack": Canterbury to Chief of Staff, "Operation Redwing," p. 1.

283: swallowed a film packet: DNA, *Operation Teapot, 1955,* pp. 96–98.

283: seventeen to forty-one minutes: DNA, *Operation Teapot: Manned Penetrations of Atomic Clouds,* April 30, 1958.

283: Langham was brought: Pinson et al., *Operation Redwing—Project 2.66A, Early Cloud Penetrations,* Feb. 24, 1960.

284: "wholly insignificant": Ibid., p. 42.

284: "no action": Ibid., p. 51.

284: "The whole thing was fraught": Gallagher, *American Ground Zero,* p. 97.

CHAPTER 30

285: 100 people: ACHRE, *Final Report,* p. 465.

285: "24 rem initial gamma": Irving Branch, "Detailed Explanation of AFSWP Comments on Feasibility of Human Volunteer Program," Jan. 20, 1956 (ACHRE No. DOD-030895-F), p. 2.

286: *"Prior to final acceptance":* Robert A. Hinners, "Report of Participation in Selected Volunteer Program of Desert Rock V-7," April 25, 1953. It is not known whether Hinners suffered any ill effects from the blast. A FOIA request filed with DOD's Radiation Experiments Command Center yielded little additional information on him.

CHAPTER 31

290: Normally the weapons: Int. William Jay Brady, April 9, 1996.

290: S.H., was the last: Landesberg, "Chorioretinitis Produced by Atomic Bomb Explosion," *AO,* pp. 539–540. The DOD's Radiation Experiments Command Center had no information on S.H.

291: Everyone heeded: Szasz, *The Day the Sun Rose Twice,* pp. 82–83.

291: "I'm probably the only guy": Feynman, *Surely You're Joking, Mr. Feynman,* p. 134.

291: "Calls about cyclotron eyes": Whittemore, "Shields Warren Papers," Oct. 6, 1994, ACHRE, p. 12.

291: eyes of eleven scientists: L. W. Tuttle to Warren and Bowers, "Report on Oak Ridge Activities, Feb. 10 and 11, 1949," Feb. 15, 1949, DOE archives.

291: Forty "certain" cases: AEC press release, "Atomic Bomb Casualty Commission to Continue Studies of Japanese Atomic Bomb Survivors," June 18, 1950, p. 2.

291: "Should the central vision": J. C. Clark to Kenner Hertford, March 5, 1952, attachment (ACHRE No. DOE-020795-C).

292: permanent eye damage: Byrnes et al., "Chorioretinal Burns Produced by Atomic Flash," *AO,* pp. 351–364.

292: "That's the thing": Int. John Pickering, June 5, 1995.

292: "His successful career": ACHRE staff, "Post-World War II Recruitment of German Scientists—Project Paperclip," April 6, 1995, Attachment 7.

293: Heinrich Rose, a diminutive scientist: "Chronological Record of Full Time Employment and Military Service," RG330, Records of the Office of the Secretary of Defense, Foreign Scientist Case Files, Heinrich W. Rose file, NA.

293: member of the Nazi Storm Troopers: Verdict, Denazification Court, Heidelberg, ibid.

293: "While a member of the SA": Rose affidavit, Aug. 8, 1947, ibid.

293: According to a security report: Office of the Military Government, Security Report, Feb. 8, 1947, ibid.

293: not a party member: Rose affidavit, Aug. 8, 1947, ibid.

293: highest civilian honor: "Air Force Award Goes to Ex-German Surgeon," *NYT,* Oct. 9, 1956, ibid.

293: "especially qualified in the field": Walter R. Agee to Director, Joint Intelligence Objectives Agency, "Procurement of Paperclip Specialists," Feb. 25, 1949, ACHRE, pp. 1–2.

293: Konrad Buettner, a slender: RG 330, Records of the Office of the Secretary of Defense, Foreign Scientist Case Files, Konrad Buettner file, NA.

294: "under pressure" from party: Affidavit, Jan. 12, 1948, ibid.

294: cared little for "material advantages": Sworn statement, Wilhelm Hornberger, Nov. 24, 1947, ibid.

294: "very elegant dwelling": Sworn statement, Hans Olaf Hudemann, ibid.

294: not in "sympathy": Office of the Military Government, Revised Security Report, ibid.

294: "Experiments with human beings": Biographical and Professional Data," n.d., ibid.

294: "correlation of skin": Buettner, "Effects of Extreme Heat and Cold," *Journal of Applied Physiology,* pp. 207–220.

294: "Its significance in civil defense: Ibid., p. 218.

294: twenty-five volunteers: AEC press release, Test Information Office, April 14, 1952 (CIC 33279), p. 2.

295: "serious visual handicap": Byrnes, *Operation Buster,* p. 2.

295: "determine accurately what": Carroll Tyler to Kenneth Fields, "Responsibility for Injury to Human Subjects in Test Operations at Nevada Proving Grounds," March 19, 1952 (CIC 18862).

295: The AEC, which had demanded: Ibid.

295: A light-tight trailer: Byrnes, *Operation Snapper.*

295: "The shutters remained open": Ibid., p. 4.

295: two men developed retinal burns: Ibid., p. 15.

295: "completely recovered": Ibid.

295: "Consequently we assume": Rose et al., "Human Chorioretinal Burns from Atomic Fireballs," *AO,* p. 210.

295: "Due to the concentration": Byrnes et al., *Operation Upshot-Knothole,* March–June 1953 (CIC No. 34219), p. 4.

296: the initials C.B.: Ibid., p. 24.

296: "When the time came" Pickering OH, pp. 54–55.

296: About 700 rabbits: Byrnes et al., "Chorioretinal Lesions Due to Thermal Radiation," *AO,* pp. 909–914.

296: tiny explosions occurred: Byrnes et al., "Retinal Burns—New Hazard of the Atomic Bomb," *JAMA,* pp. 21–22.

296: began boiling: Byrnes et al., "Chorioretinal Lesions Due to Thermal Radiation."

296: "yellowish white plaque": Byrnes et al., "Chorioretinal Burns Produced by Atomic Flash," *AO,* p. 356.

296: "One must consider": Ibid., p. 359.

297: "It can be assumed": John McGraw to Director, Atomic Energy Commission, "Examination of the Retina of Individuals Exposed to Recent Atomic Detonation," March 20, 1954 (ACHRE No. DOE-090994-C).

297: "Because of the implications": Branch to Assistant Secretary of Defense, "Status of Human Volunteers in Bio-medical Experimentation," March 5, 1954 (ACHRE No. DOD-042595-A).

297: "In Nov. 53": Ibid., attachment.

298: Wilson had signed: Secretary of Defense to the Secretary of the Army, Secretary of the Navy, Secretary of the Air Force, "Use of Human Volunteers in Experimental Research," Feb. 26, 1953 (ACHRE No. DOD-082394-A).

298: Operation Plumbbob: Gully et al., *Operation Plumbbob.*

298: Dominic I: Hill, Chisum, and Richardson, *Operation Dominic.*

298: rabbits on barges: Int. John Pickering, Jan. 24, 1995.

CHAPTER 32

299: fallout, like sunshine: Hewlett and Holl, *Atoms for Peace and War,* p. 266.

299: largest of fifty-nine: GAO, *DOE's Human Tissue Analysis Work,* pp. 2–3.

300: "nutritional" study: A. R. Luedecke to Surgeon General, USAF, "Fall-Out Studies," Dec. 16, 1954 (ACHRE No. DOD-090994-C), p. 2.

300: "next to weapons": Willard Libby to Sunshine group, draft remarks, Feb. 4, 1957, DOE archives, p. 1.

300: "active Communist": Libby OH, UCLA, p. 18.

300: "For some reason, Oppenheimer": Ibid., p. 35.

300: Bravo was the largest: Hacker, *Elements of Controversy,* pp. 136–152.

301: men left footprints: Lang, *Hiroshima to the Moon,* p. 372.

301: Libby and his fellow scientists: AEC transcript, "Biophysics Conference," Jan. 18, 1955 (ACHRE No. DOE-040395-A).

301: "shows no signs": Ibid., p. 7.

301: "If anybody knows how": Ibid., p. 8.

302: "I don't know how: Ibid., p. 12.

302: "Down in Houston": Ibid., p. 81.

302: Kulp told a reporter: Shankar Vedantam, "N-Scientists Discount Harm of Radiation Experiments," *AT,* July 15, 1995, p. A-5.

302: "I think you will find": AEC transcript, "Biophysics Conference," p. 65.

303: "bad actor": J. Newell Stannard, letter to author, Jan. 30, 1995.

303: children on average had: GAO, *DOE's Human Tissue Analysis Work,* May 1995, p. 9.

303: "We knew in one week": Welsome, "Thyroid Was Clue to Global Contamination," *AT,* Dec. 21, 1993, p. A-6.

303: "Dr. Van Middlesworth is": Hamilton to Walter Claus, June 18, 1954, Carton 5, Folder 23, JGH, p. 2.

304: "playing down": Claus to Hamilton, June 30, 1954, ibid.

304: "It was not as helpful": Welsome, "Thyroid Was Clue."

304: thirty cases of leukemia: Wright Langham, "The Problem of World-Wide Radioactive Fallout from Nuclear Weapons Testing" (LANL-HSPT-94-438), p. 22.

304: "There is no doubt": Ibid., pp. 1–2.

304: 1,165 human thyroid: GAO, *DOE's Human Tissue Analysis Work,* p. 10.

305: plutonium processing operator: LANL, *Radiation Protection,* pp. 250–251.

305: seven and one-half pounds: Norris Bradbury to AEC, Feb. 4, 1959 (LANL-HSPT-94-148), p. 7.

305: seventy-five times before: Ibid., p. 4.

306: "I'm burning up": Shipman, "Description of Accident and Subsequent Events," *Journal of Occupational Medicine,* pp. 147–149.

306: 10,000 and 12,000: Shipman, "A Case of Radiation Fatality," p. 23, Katie Kelley personal papers.

306: "nice pink skin": Shipman, "Description of Accident," p. 149.

306: "The skin of the chest": Admission note, Kelley m.r.

306: "I was on call": Welsome, "Family Decries Treatment of Accident Victim," *AT,* Feb. 23, 1994, p. 6.

306: "When seen in the ER": Admission note, Kelley m.r.

306: Using a tongue depressor: Petersen dep., pp. 72–76.

306: "We weren't going to lose": Ibid., p. 69.

307: 15 millirad per hour: Shipman, "A Case of Radiation Fatality," p. 10.

307: Langham met her: Welsome, "Missing Parts," *AT*, Feb. 12, 1994, p. 5.

307: "severe chills": Doctor's notes, Kelley m.r.

308: "From the very beginning": Shipman to [name illegible], Jan. 6, 1959, Kelley personal papers.

309: A "good deal" of material: W. R. Oakes, "Sternal Biopsy," Kelley m.r.

309: "What they pulled out": "Missing Parts," p. 5.

309: "Pulse unobtainable": Doctor's notes, Kelley m.r.

309: Several visitors who were: D. M. Stearns, Memo to File, "Cecil Kelley Accident," Jan. 7, 1959 (LANL-HSPT-94-196).

309: "He was so loaded": Welsome, "Family Decries Treatment," p. 6.

309: Clarence Lushbaugh began: Autopsy report, Kelley m.r.

309: "nearly drowned": Shipman, "A Case of Radiation Fatality," p. 37.

310: wide-mouthed mayonnaise jar: Webb Haymaker to Langham, Jan 5, 1959, LANL.

310: "God did": Clarence Lushbaugh dep., p. 41.

310: The findings were so interesting: Clarence Lushbaugh, "Transcript of Telephone Conversation with Webb Haymaker on Jan. 13, 1959," LANL.

310: Cecil had eighteen nanocuries: LANL, *Radiation Protection*, p. 236.

311: "improper transfers": Marvin M. Mann and Peter A. Morris, AEC Division of Inspection (Report CF-94), n.d., Kelley personal papers, p. 3.

311: "no single cause": Bradbury to AEC, telegram, pp. 8–9.

311: "The accident was directly": AEC press release, March 2, 1959 (LANL-HSPT-94-155), p. 2.

311: "I feel quite strongly": Shipman to Bradbury, "AEC Release of Kelley Incident," Feb. 24, 1959 (LANL-HSPT-94-152).

311: "In stating that the accident": Shipman to Charles Dunham, March 3, 1959, Kelley personal papers.

311: lab officials also promised: Plaintiff Doris E. Kelley's Answers to Defendant Regents of the University of California's First Set of Interrogatories, Santa Fe District Court (CV No. SF-96-2430), p. 4.

312: 1,712 human beings: GAO, *DOE's Human Tissue Analysis Work*, p. 10.

312: called "extras": Ed Asher and Dennis Domrzalski, "Body-Parts Testing Done Without Knowledge, Consent of Kin," *AT*, June 10, 1995, p. 11.

CHAPTER 33

317: doctors crossed the lobby: Transcript, "NEPA Advisory Committee on Radiation Tolerance of Military Personnel," April 3, 1949 (ACHRE No. DOE-120994-B-1).

317: "terminated promptly": Udall, *Myths of August*, p. 137.

318: "the possibility of achieving": Hogerton, *Atomic Energy Deskbook*, pp. 15–20.

318: "The weight of this shielding": NEPA Medical Advisory Committee, "Recommendations to NEPA," Jan. 5, 1950 (ACHRE No. DOE-060295-C-1), p. vii.

318: blue, legal-size packages: Transcript, "Radiation Tolerance," p. 10.

319: "The information desired": Ibid., pp. 38–39.

319: "I would say not only": Ibid., p. 40.

319: "We don't have to": Ibid., p. 42.

319: "I am just wondering": Ibid., p. 41.

320: "Life prisoners are": Stone, "Irradiation of Human Subjects as a Medical Experiment," Jan. 31, 1950 (ACHRE No. NARA-070794-A), p. 7.

320: "To be able to tell": Ibid., p. 4.

320: "considerable chance": Transcript, Committee on Medical Sciences, May 23, 1950 (ACHRE No. DOD-042994-A-15), p. 6.

320: risk of leukemia: ACHRE, *Final Report,* pp. 375–376.

321: "both politic and scientific": Hamilton to Shields Warren, letter, Nov. 28, 1950, Box 32, Folder 21, JGH, p. 3.

321: "an increasingly dim view": Shields Warren to Stone, July 11, 1949, ACHRE.

321: "I must say": Transcript, Committee on Medical Sciences, p. 14.

322: "I find it very difficult, too": Ibid., p. 15.

322: "I think the important thing": Ibid., p. 18.

322–323: "I think the one big problem": Partial transcript, ACBM, Nov. 10, 1950 (ACHRE No. DOE-012795-C-1), pp. 5–6. All subsequent meeting quotes taken from this transcript.

323: "skittish time": Udall, "Interview with Shields Warren," July 5, 1979.

326: The M.D. Anderson Cancer Center: Miller, Fletcher, and Gerstner, "Radiobiologic Observations on Cancer Patients Treated with Whole-Body Radiation," *Radiation Research,* pp. 150–165.

327: Baylor . . . U.S. Naval Hospital: DOD, *Search for Human Radiation Experiment Records,* pp. 23–36.

327: University of Cincinnati: There have been conflicting reports about the number of people irradiated in Cincinnati, with the figures ranging from eighty-two to eighty-eight. Martha Stephens, who has followed the case for many years, said in January 1998 that documents submitted in federal court now indicate that ninety people were exposed to TBI.

327: small research hospital: ACHRE, *Final Report,* p. 397.

328: "Ever since the damaging": Lawrence T. Odland, "Biological Dosimetry of Ionizing Radiation as Applied to Triage Casualties Following a Thermonuclear Detonation," AFWL (No. RTD TDR-63-3049), October 1963, p. 2.

CHAPTER 34

330: "It is clear that": Lando Haddock to Commanding General, Air Material Command, "Negotiation of Cost Reimbursement Contract," Oct. 19, 1950 (ACHRE No. DOD-062194-B-3), p. 3.

331: In 1953, a year after: Minutes, "The Organizational Meeting of the ANP Medical Advisory Group," Aero Medical Laboratory, Wright-Patterson AFB, Ohio, May 25–26, 1953 (CIC 727115).

331: A stocky physiologist: RG 319, Records of the U.S. Army Staff, G-2 "Paperclip" personnel files, Box 100, Herbert Gerstner file, NA.

332: not a party member: Int. Helga Gerstner, March 4, 1995.

332: became a party member: Linda Hunt, "Nazi Braceros: Hitler's Doctors in Texas Hospitals," *Texas Observer,* Feb. 28, 1997, p. 14.

332: Drafted into the German: "Basic Personnel Record for Paperclip Specialist," Gerstner file.

333: Central Intelligence Agency: Int. Helga Gerstner.

333: thirty-four Paperclip: Armstrong OH, p. 69.

333: 1,600 German specialists: ACHRE staff, "Post–World War II Recruitment of German Scientists," April 6, 1995.

333: opposed the importation: Groves to Major General S. J. Chamberlin, "Exploitation of Foreign Scientists," Nov. 27, 1946, ACHRE.

333: "To continue to treat": Bosquet Wev to Hamilton Robinson, March 17, 1948, ACHRE.

334: "contrasting but harmonious": "Pink Palace of Healing," *Time,* Dec. 13, 1954, pp. 44–47.

334: small doses "unproductive": Minutes, SAM Research Council Meeting, Jan. 14, 1954 (ACHRE No. DOD-092894-A-1).

334: Three psychomotor tests: DOD, *Search for Human Radiation Experiment Records,* p. 27.

335: Thirteen of the thirty: Miller et al., "Systemic and Clinical Effects Induced in 263 Cancer Patients," pp. 15–16.

335: "Close similarity seems": Ibid., p. 19.

335: public was overly frightened: Gerstner, "Acute Radiation Syndrome in Man," *Armed Forces Medical Journal,* pp. 313–354.

336: "Obviously, nuclear disasters": Levin et al., "Initial Clinical Reaction to Therapeutic Whole-Body X-Radiation," pp. 14–15.

CHAPTER 35

337: barium enemas: Saenger OH, Sept. 15, 1994, pp. 3–4.

337: "how to pipette": Ibid., p. 9.

337: "Listen, I'd like to": Ibid., p. 5.

337: "I was treated": Ibid.

338: "you get all this crud": Ibid., p. 15.

338: His "small expertise": Saenger to Langham, Sept. 8, 1969, LANL.

338: "That really upset": Saenger OH, p. 31.

339: "We were on a boat": Ibid., pp. 11–12.

339: In 1958, Saenger: Cong. hearing, *Experiments Conducted by the University of Cincinnati,* 1994, p. 36.

339: well-nourished adult: Ibid., p. 333.

339: "There are so few": James Hartgering to A. D. Sullivan, Nov. 7, 1958, ACHRE.

340: "augment" the TBI: Sullivan to Colonel Hullinghorst, Nov. 12, 1958, ACHRE.

340: "Any correlation": Cong. hearing, *Experiments Conducted by University of Cincinnati,* p. 222.

340: The first patient: UC College of Medicine, "Metabolic Changes in Humans Following Total Body Irradiation," Report for Feb. 1960–Oct. 1961 (DASA 1422 Supplement), p. 27. DOD reports and other documents related to Saenger's study can be found at UC under the following citation: *Unpublished work. Eugene*

Saenger et al., Whole Body Radiation Study, Cincinnati Medical Heritage Center, University of Cincinnati. Documents from this collection hereafter noted as "ES."

340: "These studies": Ibid., p. 1.

340: "This information is necessary": Report for Nov. 1, 1961–April 30, 1963 (DASA 1422), ES, p. 1.

340: Saenger has said: Cong. hearing, *Experiments Conducted by University of Cincinnati,* p. 278.

341: "beneficial effects": Saenger et al., "Whole Body and Partial Body Radio therapy of Advanced Cancer," *American Journal of Roentgenology,* p. 683.

341: "Fatalities may begin": Saenger, *Medical Aspects of Radiation Accidents,* p. 66.

341: "Once patients": Cong. hearing, *Experiments Conducted by University of Cincinnati,* p. 361.

341–342: $671,000 . . . $483,000: Ibid., p. 174.

342: "Radioresistant tumors": Shields Warren, "Ionizing Radiation and Medicine," *Scientific American,* p. 170.

342: "Our patients of course": Report for Feb. 1960–Oct. 1961 (DASA 1422 supplement), ES, p. 20.

342: "relatively good health": Report for May 1, 1968–April 30, 1969 (DASA 2428), ES, p. i.

342: "clinically stable": Report for May 1, 1969–April 30, 1970 (DASA 2599), ES, p. 1.

342: and able to "perform": Report for May 1, 1970–April 30, 1971 (DNA 2751T), ES, p. 4.

342: placed in a sitting: Report for Nov. 1, 1961–April 30, 1963 (DASA 1422) ES, pp. 4–6.

343: "Whenever possible unidirectional": Saenger to Ralph E. Ballinger, July 29, 1969, attachment, ES, p. 6.

343: acute radiation syndrome: Saenger et al., "Whole Body and Partial Body Radiotherapy," p. 676.

343: viral infection: Saenger, *Medical Aspects of Radiation Accidents,* p. 63.

343: death of eight patients: Saenger et al., "Whole Body and Partial Body Radiotherapy," p. 677.

343: nineteen patients died: The Ad Hoc Review Committee of the University of Cincinnati ("Suskind Report"), Jan. 1972, ES, p. 65.

344: One of the first patients: Report for Feb. 1960–April 30, 1966 (DASA 1844), ES, p. 105.

344: "My mother was extremely": Cong. hearing, *Experiments Conducted by University of Cincinnati,* p. 389.

344: "His course was progressively": Report for Feb. 1960–April 30, 1966 (DASA 1844), ES, p. 105.

345: "She went out": Int. Lillian Pagano, June 16, 1994.

345: Jacobs had a normal: Report for Feb. 1960–April 30, 1966 (DASA 1844), ES, pp. 133–134.

345: working and walking: Martha Stephens, "An Annotated Record of Certain Short Survivors," Sept. 7, 1994, p. 2.

345: "His condition continued:" Report for May 1, 1967–April 30, 1968 (DASA 2168), ES, pp. 45–46.

345: doctors never told: Tim Bonfield, "Widow: Man Believed Radiation Would Help," *CE*, Feb. 5, 1994, p. 1.

346: "We kept being": Saenger OH, p. 94.

346: "you fall down": Ibid., p. 66.

346: "The patient is told": Report for Feb. 1960–Oct. 1961 (DASA 1422 Supplement), ES, p. 3.

346: Saenger told a congressional: Cong. hearing, *Experiments Conducted by University of Cincinnati*, pp. 284–285.

346: "there are no other patients": Report for Feb. 1960–Oct. 1961 (DASA 1422 Supplement) ES, p. 4.

347: "I tell them": Int. Herb Varin, June 16, 1994.

347: "Following exposure": Saenger to Ballinger, attachment, July 29, 1969, ES, p. 12.

347: "We have had": Saenger and Ben I. Friedman, "An Appraisal of Human Studies in Radiobiological Aspects of Weapons Effects," Nov. 14, 1962, ES, pp. 2–3.

347: "severe hematologic depression": Report for Feb. 1960–April 30, 1966 (DASA 1844), ES, p. 17.

347: "Several of the patients": Ibid., p. 9.

347: "marked hematological depression": Friedman and Susan J. Toler, "The Effects of Filtration on Stored Human Bone Marrow," attachment to Report for May 1, 1966–April 30, 1967 (DASA 2179), ES.

348: "would have been classified": Report for May 1, 1968–April 30, 1969 (DASA 2428), ES, p. 6.

348: "In view of the life threatening": Saenger to Ballinger, attachment, July 29, 1969, p. 10.

348: suffered a stroke: Stephens, "Annotated Record," pp. 2–3.

348: Members of Saenger's team: Cong. hearing, *Experiments Conducted by University of Cincinnati*, pp. 223–228.

349: "The nature and purpose": Ibid., p. 223.

349: "This work": Friedman and Saenger, "The Therapeutic Effect of Total Body Irradiation Followed by Infusion of Stored Autologous Marrow in Humans," 1967, ES, p. 13.

349: "The radiation proposed": George Shields to Edward Gall, "Protection of Humans with Stored Autologous Marrow," March 13, 1967, ES.

349–350: "considerable morbidity": Thomas Gaffney to Gall, April 17, 1967, ES.

350: "We hadn't thought": Keith Schneider, "Cold War Radiation Test on Humans to Undergo a Congressional Review," *NYT*, April 11, 1994, p. 12.

350: "which may result": Cong. hearing, *Experiments Conducted by University of Cincinnati*, p. 225.

350: ". . . if you receive": Ibid., p. 227.

351: Saenger was a consultant: Ibid., p. 188.

351: "ethical grounds": Chairman, Faculty Committee on Research, to Members of Faculty Committee on Research, April 18, 1969, ES.

351: "a significant addition": Cong. hearing, *Experiments Conducted by University of Cincinnati*, p. 266.

CHAPTER 36

352: Litton felt perfectly healthy: All details and quotes on Litton case taken from medical records. Some specific sources listed below.

353: "Physical examination reveals": Gerstner, "History and Physical," May 10, 1961, Litton m.r.

353: "Mr. Litton seemed": D. A. White, "Outpatient Note," May 1, 1962, Litton m.r.

354: "experiment": "Low Dose Total Body Irradiation," Litton m.r.

354: "I told him": D. A. White, "Outpatient Note," Nov. 17, 1964, Litton m.r.

355: "I think he knew": Int. Gary Litton, Sept. 18, 1995.

355: "His last 25": "Final Summary," Litton m.r.

355: ORINS scientists published: Andrews et al., "Hematologic and Therapeutic Effects of Total-Body Irradiation," pp. 1–2.

356: "unreliable indicators": Cong. hearing, *Total Body Irradiation at Oak Ridge*, p. 132.

356: two-part study: Ibid., pp. 159–163.

357: "cantankerous bastard": Int. Clarence Lushbaugh, March 3, 1995.

357: "I wanted to go": Ibid.

357: "People don't like": Ibid.

357: "I liked working": Lushbaugh OH, pp. 25–26.

357: "In Los Alamos, I only had": Int. Clarence Lushbaugh.

358: "In such typical slums": Lushbaugh OH, p. 19.

358: ORINS proposed: Cong. hearing, *Total Body Irradiation at Oak Ridge*, p. 134.

358: "real time": Ibid., p. 198.

359: LETBI cost $26 million: Ibid., p. 157.

359: irradiate four patients: Hubner OH, pp. 12–13.

359: developed acute leukemia: Vodopick OH, pp. 18–19.

359: "increasingly more relevant": Cong. hearing, *Total Body Irradiation at Oak Ridge*, p. 390.

359: "like that which could occur:" Ibid., p. 379.

359: "without additional costs": Ibid., p. 366.

359: merely interested in the data: Ibid., p. 158.

360: "We never considered them": Howard Rosenberg, "Informed Consent: How Much Radiation Can an Astronaut Withstand? NASA Used Dwayne Sexton to Find Out," *Mother Jones*, Sept./Oct. 1981, p. 37.

360: "The suggestion is": Cong. hearing, *Human Total Body Irradiation at Oak Ridge*, p. 252.

360: "In the Cincinnati program": Ibid., p. 115.

361: "The person who was going": Lushbaugh OH, p. 28.

361: "substandard": Charles E. Carter to James Liverman, "Program Review of the Medical Division of Oak Ridge Associated Universities," attachment, April 16, 1974.

CHAPTER 37

362: The convicts always knew: Description compiled from interviews with the following prisoners who were still incarcerated in 1994 in the Oregon State Penitentiary: Paul Tyrrell, Canyon Easton, Russell Obremski, Dwain Little, John Atkinson, and Charles Evans.

362: ideal test subjects: Heller et al., "Effects of Progesterone," *Federation Proceedings,* p. 1057.

362: "our most unique": PNRF, "Effects of Ionizing Radiation on the Testicular Function of Man," renewal proposal, Aug. 1, 1970, Harold Bibeau personal papers, p. 41.

363: "the woman's involvement": William Boly, "The Heller Experiments," *Oregon Times Magazine,* November 1977, p. 45.

364: "highly dangerous": William Hutchinson, "Your Tomorrow," May 1961, Harold Bibeau personal papers. (Hereafter records obtained from Bibeau will be identified as "HB.")

364: "finally focused": Rowley and Heller joint dep., July 19, 1976, p. 18.

364: distinguished-looking man: Int. Meta Heller, Sept. 30, 1996.

364: "Happily enough, nobody": Austin Moore Brues, "The Chrysanthemum and the Feather Merchant," Speech to Chicago Literary Club, Feb. 13, 1961, John Z. Bowers Papers, p. 3.

365: "As early as the fourth": Howland and Stafford Warren, "Effects of the Atomic Bomb Irradiation on the Japanese," Jan. 13, 1948, Department of Special Collections, UCLA Research Library, Stafford Warren Papers, MED Papers, Box 68, Folder 8, Item 13, p. 23.

365: "We propose to apply": PNRF, "Effects of Ionizing Radiation on the Testicular Function of Man," Proposal for U.S. AEC, February 1963, HB, p. 1.

366: "And how shall I": Paulsen OH, p. 8.

366: "In our atomic age": Paulsen, "Preliminary Research Proposal for the Study of Irradiation Effects on the Human Testis," April 21, 1963, UW, p. 1.

366: "Because of the uniqueness": Lauriston S. Taylor to Paul Henshaw, Dec. 9, 1965, HB.

367: "This proposal is a direct": Charles Edington, "Summary of Review of Research Proposal," April 14, 1963, HB.

367: "minimize publicity": "Assistance to Dr. Paulsen—University of Washington Medical School," July 2, 1963 (PNL 9076).

367: "For these reasons": NCI, "Clinical Research and the Medical Treatment of Patient-Volunteers," Dec. 2, 1964, HB, p. 4.

367: "They knew the clock": Int. Meta Heller, Sept. 30, 1996.

367: injected with carbon-14: PNRF to USAEC, "Effects of Ionizing Radiation on the Testicular Function of Man," Renewal Proposal, February 1964, HB, pp. 6–7.

367: Total of $1.12 million: Phil Garon, "AEC Human Testicular Irradiation Project," Feb. 23, 1976 (CIC 703558).

367–368: $5 a month: Paulsen, "The Study of Radiation Effects on the Human Testis," renewal request, n.d. (circa 1965–1966), UW.

368: "taken advantage of our": C. T. Gladden to Robert Y. Thornton, "Carl G. Heller, M.D. Medical Research Programs," Sept. 9, 1963, HB.

368: lived in Heller's house: Hignite dep., p. 59.

368: "weird medical effects": Bibeau dep., p. 44.

368–369: wasn't "really Catholic": Ibid., p. 47.

369: "Never married": "Psychiatric examination," Nov. 4, 1964, HB.

369: "I feel this man": "Psychiatric examination," Sept. 3, 1964, Canyon Easton m.r.

369: "I felt I was": Int. Canyon Easton, Nov. 28, 1994.

369: "I castrated myself": Easton, "Testimony before Senate Human Resources Committee," 1987, HB.

369: "I did castrate": Easton, letter to author, Dec. 31, 1996.

370: "I mean he felt": Rowley OH, p. 37.

371: "Most of the times": Hignite dep., p. 67.

371: "Right in the middle": Mathena dep., p. 24.

371: "Made me want": Hetland dep., p. 19.

371: "virtually 'inexhaustible' supply": PNRF to USAEC, "Effects of Ionizing Radiation," Renewal Proposal, February 1965, HB, p. 10.

371: "grams of flesh": Jared J. Davis, "Comments on Carl Heller request for additional funds," Sept. 2, 1964, HB.

371: "They had a homosexual": Int. Paul "Connie" Tyrrell, November 1994.

371: "It hurt bad": Hetland dep., p. 30.

372: "They brought a little box": Ibid., pp. 41–42.

372: "It was no better": Hetland, Survey response, June 7, 1985, HB.

372: "I spent years": Boly, "Heller Experiments," p. 48.

372: "I operated the control": Hignite dep., pp. 104–105.

373: "So whenever you": Hetland dep., p. 48.

373: AEC commissioners themselves: AEC Meeting 2348, Oct. 4, 1968 (CIC 107664).

373: conduct a "penetrating": AEC Headquarters, "Radiation and Human Spermatogenesis, an In-Progress Program Review," August 26–27, 1965, UW.

373: "perhaps smoking": Walter S. Snyder to Paul Henshaw, Nov. 26, 1963, HB.

373: small chronic doses: Heller, "Third Yearly Progress Report," February 1966, HB, pp. 12–13.

374: "It was apparent": Henshaw to Files, "Visit to the Laboratories of Dr. Carl Heller," Aug. 20, 1964, HB.

374: "indicated you do have": Douglas Grahn to Heller, Dec. 23, 1964, HB.

375: "Have you or your panel": Heller to Grahn, Jan. 4, 1965, HB.

375: Heller attended two meetings: PNRF, "Effects of Ionizing Radiation on the Testicular Function of Man," Third Yearly Progress Report, February 1966, HB, p. 68.

375: "They only cared": Int. Meta Heller, Nov. 14, 1994.

375: "It would have been good": Ibid., Nov. 25, 1994.

375: "certain collegiality": Int. Douglas Grahn, May 1, 1995.

375–376: "The Atomic Energy Commission": Paulsen dep., p. 65.

376: "I personally do not see": H. D. Bruner to Paulsen, June 19, 1962, UW.

376: secured the approval: Paulsen, "Preliminary Research Proposal for the Study of Irradiation Effects on the Human Testis," April 21, 1963, UW, p. 2.

377: "Now he looks old": Int. Don Byers, Oct. 26, 1996.

377: "That was rather important": Int. Rob White, Oct. 10, 1996.

377: prisoners were orally: Paulsen dep., p. 21.

378: studies with mannequins: K. L. Swint to W. E. Wilson, "Fast Neutron Medical Research Facility Dosimetry for 2.5 MeV Neutrons," April 11, 1967 (PNL-9669), p. 3.

378: "I was told": Int. Don Byers.

378: "My first impression": Byers to Nancy Oreskovich, "Radiation Program Recollections," Nov. 12, 1995.

378: "Our position of furnishing": C. E. Newton to P. A. Fuqua, "Trip Report—Review of Dr. Paulsen's Project," Dec. 18, 1967 (PNL 9316).

379: Radiation Safety Committee: Peter Wootton to Paulsen, "Use of Tritiated Targets for Neutron Production in the Study of Neutron Radiation Effects in Human Testicles," Oct. 22, 1968, UW.

379: The committee chose: Robert Bruce to Paulsen, April 4, 1969, UW.

379: questioned whether the study: Bruce to Wil B. Nelp, May 20, 1969, UW.

379: Twelve of those men: "Minutes—Research and Clinical Investigations Committee," Dec. 10, 1969, UW.

380: "I just loved": Int. Leonard Schroeter, Nov. 26, 1996.

380: "rather disturbing elements": Holliday to George W. Farwell, "Dr. Alvin Paulsen—Research," July 25, 1969, HB, p. 4.

380: "I do not think": Holliday to William Conte, "Dr. Paulsen: X-ray Study, Atomic Energy Commission," Jan. 29, 1970, HB, p. 2.

380: "The Committee felt": Research Review Committee to Holliday, "Disposition of Division Review Committee in Regard to Irradiation Project of Dr. C. Alvin Paulsen at the State Penitentiary," March 13, 1970, HB, p. 2.

381: "Needless to say": Paulsen OH, p. 60.

381: "Look," Paulsen remembered: Ibid.

381: "some kind of unauthorized": Robert Sharpley, "Summary of Review File on the X-Irradiation Studies by Dr. C. Alvin Paulsen at the Washington State Penitentiary," n.d., HB.

381: "I decided what the hell": Karen Dorn Steele, "Psychologist Pays Price to Stop Experiments," *Spokesman-Review,* June 19, 1994, p. A-8.

382: Rowley hoped: Rowley dep., Oct. 10, 1996, p. 136.

382: "He pulled that article": Rowley and Heller joint dep., p. 55.

382: "I asked if Dr. Paulsen": Amos Reed, "OSP Radiation Experiment (Heller Project)," 1973, HB, p. 2.

382: tumor found in the testis: Heller to Frank Brooks, Feb. 25, 1971, p. 1.

CHAPTER 38

383: Cows were led: Cong. report, *American Nuclear Guinea Pigs,* pp. 22–23.

383: real and simulated fallout: Ibid., p. 31.

383: radioactive fish: Ibid., p. 35.

383: Fifty-seven workers: Ibid., p. 13.

384: persimmon trees . . . stand of hardwood: Savannah River Ecology Laboratory, Annotated Bibliography, DOE Search Records.

384: old experiment was revived: AEC, Office of Investigations, "Report of Investigation" (File No. 44-2-326) Aug. 16, 1974, pp. 7–8.

385: "Like a drunk": Durbin OH, DOE/OHRE, p. 41.

385: "It was stupid": Durbin OH, ACHRE, p. 94.

385: "Most of the patients": LANL, *Radiation Protection,* p. 217.

385: "He is, I believe": Durbin to James L. Born, Dec. 10, 1971, FOIA, p. 2.

386: study was "messy": AEC, "Report of Investigation," p. 8.

386: "introduction of exhumed bodies": Ibid., p. 9.

386: "We had cadavers": Rowland OH, p. 23.

387: "very, very intimately involved": Ibid., p. 22.

387: Chicago scientists wanted: Robert Rowland to Christine Waterhouse, Jan. 4, 1973, FOIA, p. 1.

387: "Please note": AEC, "Report of Investigation," p. 19.

388: "That was Jim Liverman": Rowland OH, p. 53.

388: "leery of getting these people": Welsome, "Plutonium Experiment," p. 14.

388: "I was what you'd call": Ibid., p. 45.

388: "An appropriate approach": AEC, "Report of Investigation," pp. 20–21.

389: "I was surprised": Welsome, "Plutonium Experiment," p. 36.

389: "We are trying to locate": Austin Brues to Dr. A. O. Dykes, March 7, 1973, FOIA.

390: "From what we know": Brues, "Clinical Picture Following Plutonium Administration," in Nickson, ed., *Report of Conference on Plutonium,* p. 21.

390: Brues also contributed: Langham et al., *Distribution and Excretion of Plutonium,* p. 3.

390: Brues told AEC: Sidney Marks, "Interview with Dr. Austin Brues," April 15, 1974, FOIA, p. 2.

390: "My mother thought": Welsome, "Plutonium Experiment," p. 12.

390: "consistent [with] early radium": I. E. Kirsh, "Radiologist's Report," June 13, 1973, Allen m.r.

390: The limo driver: Trip itinerary, Allen family records.

391: "Every time I went": Welsome, "Plutonium Experiment," p. 13.

391: "His excretion rate": Ibid.

391: As with Eda, the plutonium: Ibid., p. 36.

391: John was one of the six: Rowland and Durbin, "Survival, Causes of Death, and Estimated Tissue Doses in a Group of Human Beings Injected with Plutonium," in Jee, ed., *Symposium on Health Effects of Plutonium and Radium,* pp. 329–341.

391: John's endosteal membranes: Ibid., p. 334.

391: pituitary disorders: Int. Ruth Brown, May 7, 1996.

391: "no need to introduce": Marks, "Summary of interview with Robley Evans and Mary Margaret Shanahan," April 22, 1974, FOIA.

392: diaphragm, thigh muscle: Joe Farnham, "Pathology Report," June 1974, Daigneault m.r., p. 2.

392: "The subject's hair": Toohey et al., "Concentration of Plutonium in Hair," *Health Physics,* p. 882.

392: Those elements included: AEC, "Report of Investigation," p. 16.

393: "The Argonne National Laboratory": Ibid., p. 15.

393: "It is our opinion": Ibid., p. 17.

393: "the nature of the studies": "Briefing on Plutonium Project by Dr. James Liverman on April 29, 1974," p. 8.

393: "A NAS committee report": "Meeting at NIH Regarding Patients Injected with Plutonium," n.d., FOIA, p. 2.

394: "conflict of interest": AEC, "Report of Investigation," p. 1.

394: "If Bruner is making": Handwritten note from unidentified scientist that appears at bottom of memo written by Sidney Marks to James Liverman, March 26, 1994, FOIA.

394: "During interviews": "Memo to DBER and Division of Inspection from GM," April 12, 1974, FOIA, p. 2.

394: Stafford Warren was interviewed: Quotes from MP doctors taken from a compilation of rough draft memos written by AEC investigators and obtained by the *Tribune* in its 1992 FOIA request.

398: "certain violations of ethical standards": James Liverman to John Erlewine, "Remedial Actions Based Upon a Report of Disclosure to Patients Injected with Plutonium," n.d., FOIA, p. 1.

398: "General Green was": Liverman to Files, "Meeting with the Army general counsel and deputy surgeon general with regard to plutonium in people," April 10, 1974, FOIA.

398: "His response was immediate": Liverman to Files, "Proposed program regarding persons injected with plutonium 1945–47," April 9, 1974, FOIA.

399: "Things were done": Welsome, "Plutonium Experiment," p. 38.

399: "The telling of the patients": Ibid., p. 36.

399: "concluded that the mental": Liverman to Erlewine, "Remedial Actions," p. 1.

399: "I told him we found": Brues to Rowland, "Trip Report—Visit to Milford and Italy, Texas," May 31, 1974, FOIA.

400: "The patient was aware": AEC, "Report of Investigation," p. 19.

400: "If all were exhumed": E. P. Cronkite to Liverman, May 29, 1974, FOIA, p. 2.

401: "As I sifted": Farnham to CHR-RR, "Disinterment of Mr. [name deleted], June 13, 1975, Hubbard m.r.

401: "I said that we": Andrew Stehney to CHR Records File, "Return of remains of Case No. 40–004," April 7, 1978, Hubbard m.r.

401: "The skeleton and casket": J. W. Forkal, "Report of Skeletal Inspection," May 26, 1978, Sours m.r.

402: "for the purposes": Stevens m.r.

402: "Those remains": Welsome, "Plutonium Experiment," p. 26.

402: "They left here in October": Ibid., p. 26.

402: "It makes me sick": Ibid.

402: bad drinking bout: Hospital note, Dec. 7, 1977, Allen m.r.

402: "In the event he": Brues to David W. Williams, Dec. 12, 1977, Allen m.r.

CHAPTER 39

403: "any part of the field": Rapoport, *Great American Bomb Machine,* p. 90.

403: Auerbach contacted: John Watson, memo for record, "Washington Post Request for Copy of Contract DASA 01-69-C-0131 University of Cincinnati," October 6, 1971, ES.

404: "Dr. Saenger suggested": Ibid.

404: "It was agreed": Ibid.

404: "approaches what happens": Stuart Auerbach and Thomas O'Toole, "Pentagon has Contract to Test Radiation Effect on Humans," *WP,* Oct. 8, 1971, p. 1.

404: "The whole question": Transcript, "Press Conference Held at Cincinnati General Hospital," Oct. 11, 1971, ES.

404: Events moved quickly: Cong. hearing, *Experiments Conducted by the University of Cincinnati,* pp. 50–55.

405: ". . . would avoid": Saenger to John A. Northrop, Nov. 26, 1971, ES, p. 1.

405: Saenger sat on four: Cong. hearing, *Experiments Conducted by the University of Cincinnati,* p. 191.

405: "I have a certain feeling": Robert McConnell, n.d., ES.

405: "The project is validly": Cong. hearing, *Experiments Conducted by the University of Cincinnati,* p. 247.

405: "I read for about an hour": Stephens, "A Tragic and Terrible Tale," *CE,* Feb. 16, 1994.

406: "Is it conceivable": Junior Faculty Association, "A Report to the Campus Community," Jan. 25, 1972, p. 3.

406: nineteen of the patients: "Suskind Report," Jan. 1972, ES, p. 65.

406: fraught with conflicts: Lew Moores, "Suskind Comm.—Conflict of Interest?" *University of Cincinnati News Record,* Feb. 11, 1972, n.p., ES.

406: "Could one be led": Editorial, "The Suskind Committee," *News Record,* n.d., ES.

407: "Can this (psychological harm)": Tim Bonfield, "Radiation: Legal Strategy Revealed," *CE,* May 21, 1994, p. B-1.

407: "This is a personal impression": Saenger, "An interview with Dr. Silberstein and Mr. Motter [sic] and Dr. Caper representing Senator Kennedy," ES, p. 7.

407: "I might remind you": Transcript of interview with "J.D," Jan. 3, 1971, ES.

407: "Senator Taft just went": Paul Barton and Howard Wilkinson, "Ex-aide: Taft Blocked UC Probe," *CE,* Feb. 9, 1994, p. B-1.

407: She bundled up: Int. Martha Stephens, June 15, 1994.

408: "There are two": Saenger, "Radiation Casualities," *New York State Journal of Medicine,* pp. 309–314.

408: "could be walking around": Jan Goodwin, "67 Ex-convicts, Who Volunteered for Useless Radiation Experiments, Could Now Be Unknowing Victims of Cancer," *National Enquirer,* Oct. 21, 1975, n.p.

408: "It helped in genetic": Hal Waltz, "Radiation Meeting," Nov. 21, 1975, HB.

408: "heightened the emotionalism": Ibid.

409: "What was the primary": Rowley-Heller joint dep., p. 17.

409: Later in the deposition: Ibid., p. 32.

409: Finally Hilgemann asked: Ibid., p. 53.

409: Heller swallowed a Benadryl: Excerpt from nursing log, July 19, 1976, Meta Heller personal papers.

410: Arthur Kranish, the editor: Debra D. Durocher, "Radiation Redux," *AJR,* March 1994, pp. 34–37.

410: "less carcinogenic": Arthur Kranish, "Plutonium Experiment," *Science Trends,* Feb. 23, 1976, p. 128.

410: "has no plans": George C. Wilson, "18 Injected in 1945 Plutonium Testing," *WP,* Feb. 22, 1976, p. 1.

410: "did not come voluntarily": Maurice H. Thompson, "Humans Injected with Plutonium at Strong," *RDC,* Feb. 22, 1976, p. 1.

410: "It was like getting": Todd Ensign and Michael Uhl, "A Victim of the Tests," *The Progressive,* March 1978, p. 8.

411: "He was a very loyal Marine": Int. Pat Broudy, May 11, 1998.

411: remarkable hearing on Capitol Hill: Cong. hearing, *Effects of Radiation on Human Health,* 1978.

412: "It seems the Army": Ibid., p. 168.

412: he gathered hundreds: Howard L. Rosenberg, "Informed Consent," *Mother Jones,* Sept.–Oct. 1981, pp. 31–44.

412: "It took eighteen months": Durocher, "Radiation Redux."

413: "Now the critical question," Cong. hearing, *Human Total Body Irradiation Program at Oak Ridge,* p. 177.

413: "radiobiologically of great interest": Ibid., p. 269.

413: "It is a provocative": Ibid., p. 271.

413: "satisfactory, but not perfect": ACHRE, *Final Report,* p. 400.

414: The file contained: Clifford Honicker, "The Hidden Files," *New York Times Magazine,* Nov. 19, 1989, p. 99.

414: Honicker, Sea, and several other: Int. Clifford Honicker, March 25, 1998.

414: "Although these experiments": Cong. report, *American Nuclear Guinea Pigs,* p. 7.

414: The wire services reduced: Durocher, "Radiation Redux," p. 35.

415: they knew, for example: John Herrington to Edward Markey, Addendum to letter, Feb. 10, 1987, p. 2.

415: cancer of the larynx: Christine Waterhouse to John Rundo, Dec. 26, 1975, Stadt m.r.

415: "I explained how important": Gail Knasko to File, "X-ray film for [name deleted], April 18, 1985, Charlton m.r.

415: "I knew he didn't want": Welsome, "Plutonium Experiment," p. 15.

416: Stafford Warren, the architect: Paul Dodd, Introduction to Stafford Warren OH, p. xii.

416: tended an oyster farm: "Obituary—Shields Warren," *Radiation Research,* 1981, p. 434.

CHAPTER 40

419: "We've got to do it all": Hazel R. O'Leary, *Current Biography Yearbook,* 1994, pp. 410–414.

419: "Female and black": Francis Wilkinson, "Power to the People," *Rolling Stone,* March 24, 1994, p. 33.

420: powerful influences in her life: Int. Hazel O'Leary, Jan. 9, 1997.

420: "thoroughly and severely": John V. Quarstein and Parke S. Rouse Jr., "Newport News: A Centennial History," *City of Newport News,* 1996, pp. 179–180.

420: "It was because in those days": Linda Witt, "Balance of Powers," *San Jose Mercury News, West Magazine,* May 8, 1994, p. 8 ff.

420: "My parents taught": David Grogan, Linda Witt, and Sarah Skolnik, "Spilling Secrets," *People,* Jan. 31, 1994, p. 77–78.

421: Stephen Schwartz, a guest: Brookings Institution press release, "Atomic Audit," June 30, 1998, p. 1.

421: "gravest of problems": DOE, *Closing the Circle,* p. 8.

421: ". . . the inheritance" DOE, "Four Years of Changes and Advances," draft paper, Jan. 7, 1997, p. 3.

422: The last underground bomb, Divider: Int. Jonathan Ventura, March 12, 1997.

422: "She had the courage": Int. Ray Kidder, Feb. 11, 1997.

422: "I'd characterize it": Int. Frank von Hippel, Jan. 30, 1997.

423: "The way secrecy": Int. Jim Werner, Jan. 31, 1997.

423: "I have been": Int. A. Bryan Siebert, Feb. 3, 1997.

424: "They acted as if": Ibid.

424: "We were shrouded and clouded": DOE, *Openness Initiative,* Videotape, Dec. 7, 1993.

424: 204 more nuclear bombs: Department of Energy fact sheets, Dec. 7, 1993.

425: "What I've read": DOE, *Openness Initiative.*

427: "It's inconceivable": Welsome, "Plutonium Experiment," p. 22.

428: "This was war": Int. Christine Waterhouse, Feb. 26, 1993.

429: "Edith Charlton. That's": Welsome, "Plutonium Experiment," p. 35.

429: "We didn't know": Int. Helen Schultz, June 18, 1993.

429: "She couldn't understand": Welsome, "Plutonium Experiment," p. 35.

430: "I took care of him": Ibid., p. 41.

430: "You know, that sounds": Ibid.

430: "Before he was sick": Ibid., pp. 40–41.

430: "It's unbelievable": Ibid., p. 41.

430: "I just have a gut feeling": Ibid.

433: "I came pretty quickly": Int. Hazel O'Leary, Jan. 9, 1997.

433: 6,000 to 10,000 calls: DOE press release, "Human Radiation Experiments: Chronology of Recent Events," Jan. 3, 1994.

433: "There was this": Int. Hazel O'Leary.

C H A P T E R   4 1

434: "It was the trial": Tim Bonfield, "Life of Achievements, Accusations," *CE*, March 13, 1994, p. 1.

435: If the relatives had come: Cong. hearing, *Experiments Conducted by the University of Cincinnati*, p. 177.

435: "We have looked": Ibid., p. 277.

435: "Our work": Ibid., p. 176.

435: "Would you have done": Saenger OH, ACHRE, Sept. 15, 1994, p. 52.

436: found it "inconceivable": Judge Sandra S. Beckwith, Opinion and Order, U.S. District Court for the Southern District of Ohio Western Division (Case No. C-1-94-126), Jan. 11, 1995, pp. 57–58.

436: Marlow just happened: Int. Sandra Marlow, June 18, 1996.

436: tipped off the *Boston Globe:* Int. Sandra Marlow, May 21, 1998; Int. Dan Bernstein, June 10, 1998.

437: "I fear that past": Cong. hearing, *Human Subjects Research*, Jan. 13, 1994, p. 5.

437: "Can I ask": Ibid., p. 22.

437: "fundamental human rights": Task Force, *Research that Involved Residents of State-Operated Facilities within the Commonwealth of Massachusetts*, p. 43.

437: "potentially coercive factor": Ibid., p. 28.

437: "significant health effects": Ibid., p. 44.

438: "They bribed us": Transcript, ACHRE hearing, Dec. 16, 1994, p. 87.

438: "It's unthinkable": Int. Helen Hutchison, Sept. 17, 1994.

438: "While it would not be": Keith Schneider, "Scientists Are Sharing the Anguish Over Nuclear Experiments on People," *NYT*, March 2, 1994, p. 9.

439: "totally unwarranted": Henry N. Wagner, affidavit, July 11, 1994.

439: "I don't know": Int. Ruth Hagstrom, July 14, 1996.

439: "a few tens of millirads": M.G. Stabin et al., "Review of the Radiation Doses Received by Infants Irradiated in Utero," draft paper, ORISE, March 2, 1995, p. 10.

439: "All of these cancers": Roland Finston, "Doses Received by Mothers and Fetuses in the Vanderbilt Radioiron Experiment," n.d., p. 7.

440: "I knew it explained": Int. Emma Craft, July 18, 1996.

440: doctors closely monitored: Int. Emma Craft, July 10, 1996.

440: "What I went through": Craft dep., Sept. 13, 1994.

440: "reasonably find": John T. Nixon, Memorandum and Order, Aug. 26, 1996, U.S. District Court, Middle District of Tennessee at Nashville (CV No. 3: 94–0090).

441: "Something had to be": Int. Harold Bibeau, May 27, 1998.

441: "I think he even implied": Int. James Ruttenber, Oct. 25, 1996.

441: "I hope that you will": Frank Hall to Hazel O'Leary, Jan. 21, 1994, HB.

441: "We were the victims": *Atomic Veteran's Newsletter,* Winter 1993, p. 1.

442: 8,000 . . . 2 million: DOD, *Search for Human Radiation Experiment Records,* p. 40.

442: A Dutch researcher: Lawrence Spohn, "Nasal Rods Doubled Risk of Cancer, Study Says," *AT,* Dec. 16, 1996, p. 1.

442: Cherie Anderson, a California: Ed Asher, "A Lifetime of Hurt," *AT*, Feb. 7, 1994, p. 1.

443: "A wide-mouthed mayonnaise jar": Welcome, "Missing Parts," *AT*, Feb. 12, 1994, p. 5.

443: "The cutting him up": Ibid.

443: 1994 press release: LANL fact sheet, "The Los Alamos Human Tissue Analysis Project," Feb. 7, 1994.

443: "people did not know": "Tissue Study Close-Out Meeting," Aug. 24, 1994, LANL.

443: "This place": Ed Asher and Dennis Domrzalski, "Body-parts Testing Done Without Knowledge, Consent of Kin," *AT*, June 10, 1995, p. 11.

443: samples from Karen: Alan C. McMillan to Billie Silkwood, Feb. 18, 1994 (LANL-HSPT-94-107).

444: 113 small flasks: McMillan to Silkwood, attachment to letter.

444: "They stole those organs": Domrzalski and Asher, "Silkwood Dad Still Angry with Lab," *AT*, Feb. 22, 1994, p. 1.

444: "Since the amount of plutonium present": McMillan to Silkwood.

444: "They were supposed to": Int. Bill Silkwood, Oct. 8, 1997.

445: so many aspects: Int. Mary Jeanne Connell, Oct. 24, 1996.

CHAPTER 42

447: "rewrite the history": Philip J. Hilts, "Study on Tests: Dream Job for Ethicist," *NYT*, Jan. 30, 1994, p. 15.

447: Both of Faden's parents: Int. Ruth Faden, Jan. 26, 1995.

447–448: "There's nothing more terrifying": Ibid.

449: estimated 6 million pages: Human Radiation Interagency Working Group, *Building Public Trust,* 1997, p. 3.

449: "had done little": Karen MacPherson, "GAO: Not All Radiation Victims Will Be ID'd," *AT*, Dec. 1, 1994, p. 1.

450: "We have to look": Int. Ruth Faden.

450: "Totally draining": Ibid.

CHAPTER 43

452: described as "surrealistic": Transcript, ACHRE meeting, Nov. 14, 1994, p. 163.

452: eighty-four Eskimos: ACHRE, *Final Report,* p. 598.

453: "The only thing we knew": Transcript, ACHRE meeting, April 10–12, 1995, p. 96.

453: "I was thrown": Transcript, ACHRE meeting, Oct. 11–13, 1994, p. 215.

453: Darcy Thrall, born and raised: Ibid., pp. 331–349.

454: "None of the more": J. F. Honstead, "A Program for Evaluating Environmental Radiation Dose to Children" (BNWL-SA 1288), n.d., p. 7.

454: "I had a great": Transcript, ACHRE meeting, Oct. 11–13, 1994, p. 336.

454: "I believe my father": Transcript, ACHRE meeting, Oct. 21, 1994, p. 201.

454: "Will someone please": Ibid., pp. 25–26.

454: "just a dumb hillbilly": Ibid., p. 107.

454: "I did my country wrong": Ibid., p. 104.

454: Gene Branham, a union: Ibid., pp. 176–184.

455: Gertie Hanson, who grew: Transcript, ACHRE meeting, Nov. 21, 1994, p. 35.

455: "We assumed that these": Ibid., p. 286.

455: "She has eyelashes": Ibid., pp. 109–111.

456: "I was successful": Stannard, *Radioactivity and Health,* pp. 761–762.

456: "I noticed that while my dad": Transcript, ACHRE meeting, Nov. 21, 1994, p. 191.

456: "must have taken Personal Ethics 101": Ibid., p. 52.

456: "The people who did this": Transcript, ACHRE meeting, Jan. 30, 1995, p. 56.

457: "The path to hell": Ibid., p. 72.

457: "We never been told": Ibid., pp. 181–183.

457: "We were there three days": Ibid., p. 75.

457: "Now all of a sudden": Ibid., p. 19.

457: "My five-year-old": Ibid., p. 27.

457: "I guess it's a fine line": Ibid.

458: "I want you to tell": Transcript, ACHRE meeting, March 2, 1995, pp. 136–138.

458: "We were violated": Ibid., pp. 138–146.

458: "It is with some sadness": Ibid., pp. 162–170.

CHAPTER 44

459: order from President Clinton: White House, "Advisory Committee on Human Radiation Experiments," Executive Order, Jan. 18, 1994.

459: "We don't want to pass": Transcript, ACHRE meeting, Nov. 14, 1994, p. 42.

460: "I felt then": Int. Patricia King, April 4, 1997.

460: "What I would like": Int. Henry Royal, April 7, 1997.

460: "then we can't talk": Transcript, ACHRE meeting, Nov. 14, 1994, meeting, pp. 43–44.

460: "If experiments violated": ACHRE, *Final Report,* p. 211.

461: "The mind-set of the Republicans": Int. Eli Glatstein, April 1, 1997.

461: "In other words, we": Shipman to Executive Committee, Dec. 19, 1951, LANL.

461: "No signed consent": Stone to Alan Gregg, letter, Nov. 4, 1948, Call No. 80/80c, Robert Stone Carton, Letters I–Z Folder, Bancroft Library, Berkeley, CA, p. 3.

462: "Dr. Stone stated": Transcript, Cancer Board Meeting, April 23, 1952, received from UCSF Public Information Office.

462: code was even read: Transcript, Committee on Chemical Warfare, Nov. 10, 1952, pp. 121–124, ACHRE.

462: "The Nuremberg Code": Transcript, ACHRE meeting, April 10–12, 1995, Vol. 2, p. 312.

462: "Most references to consent": ACHRE, *Final Report,* p. 850.

463: too "marginal": Transcript, ACHRE meeting, Dec. 15, 1994, p. 77.

463: "went out the window": Int. Eli Glatstein, April 1, 1997.

463: "This report is the worst thing": Int. David Egilman, March 26, 1997.

464: "It should be emphasized": ACHRE, *Final Report,* p. 220.

465: "Beyond the question": Editorial, "Ethical Trimming on Radiation," *Boston Globe,* Oct. 4, 1995, p. 18.

466: all participants in any research: Egilman et al., "Ethical Aerobics," p. 40.

466: National Institutes of Health: Ibid., p. 48.

466: "I've got pretty good": Dennis Domrzalski, "Man Reads About Woman's Nasal Radium Treatments, Finds He Has Tumors," *AT,* July 30, 1994, p. 1.

466: "not salable in today's": Egilman et al., "Ethical Aerobics," p. 35.

467: "To characterize a great profession": ACHRE, *Final Report,* p. 220.

467: "Important national security goals": Ibid., p. 829.

467: "best balance allocation": Ibid., p. 812.

468: "I guess the government": A. S. Zaidi, "Rochester, Radiation, and Repression," Z *Magazine,* April 1997, p. 11.

468: "A book has been opened": AP, "Downwinders Criticize Radiation Tests Report," *Oregonian,* Oct. 9, 1995, p. B-4.

468: "For them to turn": *Boston Globe,* Sept. 29, 1995, p. 33.

468: "I do feel betrayed": Transcript, Stakeholder Workshop, Feb. 26–27, 1996, pp. 217–218.

CHAPTER 45

469: "This report I received": Interagency Working Group, *Building Public Trust,* Appendix A.

CHAPTER 46

471: "She was not seen": Int. Al Narath, March 5, 1997.

471: "And I was most startled": Int. John Nuckolls, Feb. 24, 1997.

472: "It is somehow fitting": Center for Security Policy, "U.S. 'De-Nuclearization': Who Is Minding the Store?" Decision Brief (No. 93-D 103), Dec. 9, 1993.

472: "audacity of this sort": David Kramer, "O'Leary Faults Lab Board Report; Asks, 'What's Wrong with Them?' " *Inside Energy,* Jan. 27, 1997, p. 3.

473: personal attack by Republicans: Int. Hazel O'Leary, Jan. 9, 1997.

473: "too uppity": Ibid.

473: "What I've learned": Ibid.

473: Among the items: DOE fact sheets, "Openness: The Way to Do Business," Jan. 15, 1997, p. 45.

474: "My commitment is": Corydon Ireland, "U.S. Apology Hits Home," *RDC,* Dec. 17, 1996, p. 1.

474: "I'm afraid it's": Ireland, "Survivor Afraid It Will Happen Again," *RDC,* Dec. 17, 1996, p. 11.

CHAPTER 47

475: $400,000 each: J. Patrick Glynn to Eva Plaza, "Response to Questions Posed by Eileen Welsome," memorandum, U.S. Dept. of Justice, Civil Division, July 2, 1997.

475: "the highest duty of care": Plaintiff's Complaint and Demand for a Jury

Trial, *Gordon Shattuck et al. v. Massachusetts Institute of Technology et al.,* U.S. District Court, District of Massachusetts (95-12605GAO), Dec. 1995, p. 2.

475: $1.85 million: Int. Jeff Petrucelly, March 6, 1999.

476: $5.4 million: AP, "Settlement Ok'd in Radiation Case," *AJ,* May 5, 1999, p. 12.

476: "non-negotiable": Int. R. Joseph Parker, July 10, 1997.

476: lawyer Melvin Belli: James H. Jarvis, Order, *Dorothy McWright et al. v. Oak Ridge Institute of Nuclear Studies et al.,*U.S. District Court, Eastern District of Tennessee at Knoxville (No. 3:95-cv-14), May 31, 1996.

476: $10.3 million: Int. Don Arbitblit, May 28, 1998.

476: lawsuit initiated by Harold Bibeau: Michael Hogan, Order, *Harold Bibeau et al. v. Pacific Northwest Research Foundation et al.,* United States District Court, District of Oregon (CV No. 95-06410-HO), July 28, 1997, p. 24.

477: "If information was": O'Leary dep., p. 42.

477: "This was an atrocity": Ireland, "Bid to Cut Names from Suit Denied," *RDC,* April 4, 1996, p. B-1.

477: "The allegations in this case": Sandra S. Beckwith, Opinion and Order, U.S. District Court for the Southern District of Ohio, Western Division (Case No. C-1-94-126), Jan. 11, 1995, p. 58.

477: experiment as an "intervention": UCSF, *World War II Radiation Experiments,* pp. 28, 17.

477: "The committee found": Ibid., p. 33.

478: "whitewash": Author notes, ACHRE meeting, May 8–10, 1995.

478: "Morality has to be": Int. Joshua Shaw, March 26, 1997.

478: "They said UCSF doctors": Ibid.

478: "covert extracurricular activity": Zaidi, "Rochester, Radiation, and Repression," pp. 11–12.

478: "a suggestion full of sound": Ireland, "Further Radiation Inquiry Sought," *RDC,* Dec. 22, 1996, p. 1.

479: "There is an insularity": Rex Graham, "LANL Fails to Find N-Test Wrongdoing," *AJ,* Oct. 7, 1994, p. 1.

479: "The abject terror": Ibid.

480: "When you're approaching": Int. Patricia Durbin, Jan. 5, 1997.

480: "Frankly, we're not": Ireland, "Scientist: Exhume Radiation Subjects," *RDC,* April 5, 1994, p. 1.

EPILOGUE

481: "lady doth protest": Tyler, "Operation Ranger: Administrative Summary Report," July 1952, ACHRE, p. 43.

483: "How ironic": Int. William Jay Brady, May 28, 1998.

484: "In the end, I think": Cong. hearing, *Atomic Energy,* 1945, p. 60.

485: "It was felt unwise": William S. Middleton, "Recommendation for Administrator's Exceptional Service Award," May 13, 1959, ACHRE.

485: "During the period": Tyler, "Operation Ranger: Administrative Summary Report," p. 41.

485: "It's a huge fraternity": DOE, *Operation Tumbler-Snapper,* videotape.

486: "The functionaries who": Udall, *Myths of August,* p. 179.

487: "sufficiently condemn": Int. Jay Katz, March 24, 1997.

488: "The breathtaking advances": Interagency Working Group, *Building Public Trust,* p. A-5.

489: 10,000 to 75,000: NCI press release, "Questions and Answers on the NCI Fallout Report," Aug. 1, 1997.

489: "There were few": Matthew L. Wald, "Thousands Have Thyroid Cancer from Atomic Tests," *NYT,* Aug. 2, 1997, p. 6.

MAJOR SOURCES USED IN NOTES

BOOKS

Annas, George, and Michael Grodin, eds. *The Nazi Doctors and the Nuremberg Code*. New York: Oxford University Press, 1992.

Badash, Lawrence, Joseph O. Hirschfelder, and Herbert P. Broida, eds. *Reminiscences of Los Alamos, 1943–1945*. Dordrecht, Holland: D. Reidel Publishing Company, 1980.

Behrens, Charles Frederick, ed. *Atomic Medicine*. New York: Thomas Nelson & Sons, 1949.

Blumberg, Stanley A., and Louis G. Panos. *Edward Teller: Giant of the Golden Age of Physics*. New York: Charles Scribner's Sons, 1990.

Bower, Tom. *The Paperclip Conspiracy: The Hunt for the Nazi Scientists*. Boston: Little, Brown and Company, 1987.

Boyer, Paul. *By the Bomb's Early Light*. New York: Pantheon Books, 1985.

Bradley, David. *No Place to Hide*. Boston: Little, Brown and Company, 1948.

Chevalier, Haakon. *Oppenheimer: The Story of a Friendship*. New York: George Braziller, 1965.

City of Nagasaki. *Testimonies of the Atomic Bomb Survivors*. Nagasaki: City of Nagasaki, 1985.

Clarke, Ann M., and A.D.B. Clarke, eds. *Mental Deficiency: The Changing Outlook*. New York: Free Press, 1966.

Coffinberry, A. S., and W. N. Miner, eds. *The Metal Plutonium*. Chicago: University of Chicago Press, 1961.

Committee for the Compilation of Materials on Damage Caused by the Atomic Bombs in Hiroshima and Nagasaki. *Hiroshima and Nagasaki*. New York: Basic Books, 1981.

Compton, Arthur. *Atomic Quest*. New York: Oxford University Press, 1956.

D'Antonio, Michael. *Atomic Harvest: Hanford and the Lethal Toll of America's Nuclear Arsenal*. New York: Crown Publishers, 1993.

Davis, Nuel Pharr. *Lawrence and Oppenheimer*. New York: Simon and Schuster, 1968.

Divine, Robert A. *Blowing on the Wind: The Nuclear Test Ban Debate 1954–1960.* New York: Oxford University Press, 1978.

Ermenc, Joseph J., ed. *Atomic Bomb Scientists: Memoirs, 1939–1945.* Westport, CT: Meckler Corporation, 1989.

Fermi, Laura. *Atoms in the Family: My Life with Enrico Fermi.* Chicago: University of Chicago Press, 1954.

Feynman, Richard P. *Surely You're Joking, Mr. Feynman: Adventures of a Curious Character.* New York: W. W. Norton, 1985.

Fradkin, Philip L. *Fallout: An American Nuclear Tragedy.* Tucson: University of Arizona Press, 1989.

Gallagher, Carole. *American Ground Zero: The Secret Nuclear War.* Cambridge, MA: MIT Press, 1993.

Gerber, Michele Stenehjam. *On the Home Front: The Cold War Legacy of the Hanford Nuclear Site.* Lincoln: University of Nebraska Press, 1992.

Gerstner, Herbert B. *Mankind's Quest for Identity.* Park Forest South, IL: Pathotox Publishers, 1981.

Glasstone, Samuel. *Sourcebook on Atomic Energy.* New York: D. Van Nostrand, 1950.

Gleick, James. *Genius: The Life and Science of Richard Feynman.* New York: Pantheon Books, 1992.

Gofman, John W. *Radiation and Human Health.* San Francisco: Sierra Club Books, 1981.

Goin, Peter. *Nuclear Landscapes.* Baltimore: John Hopkins University Press, 1991.

Gottfried, Ted. *Enrico Fermi: Pioneer of the Atomic Age.* Makers of Modern Science. New York: Facts On File, 1992.

Griffiths, Joel, and Richard Ballantine. *Silent Slaughter.* Chicago: Regnery, 1972.

Groueff, Stephane. *Manhattan Project: The Untold Story of the Making of the Atomic Bomb.* Boston: Little, Brown and Company, 1967.

Groves, Leslie R. *Now It Can Be Told: The Story of the Manhattan Project.* London: Andre Deutsch Publishers, 1963.

Hacker, Barton C. *The Dragon's Tail: Radiation Safety in the Manhattan Project, 1942–1946.* Berkeley: University of California Press, 1987.

———. *Elements of Controversy: The Atomic Energy Commission and Radiation Safety in Nuclear Weapons Testing 1947–1974.* Berkeley: University of California Press, 1994.

Halberstam, David. *The Fifties.* New York: Villard Books, 1993.

Hamilton, G. V. *An Introduction to Objective Psychopathology.* St. Louis: C. V. Mosby, 1925.

Hawkins, David, Edith C. Truslow, and Ralph Carlisle Smith. *Project Y: The Los Alamos Story.* Los Angeles: Tomash Publishers, 1983.

Hershey, John. *Hiroshima.* New York: Modern Library, 1946.

Hewlett, Richard, and Oscar E. Anderson Jr. *The New World: A History of the United States Atomic Energy Commission, 1939–1946.* Vol. 1. University Park: Pennsylvania State University Press, 1962.

Hewlett, Richard, and Francis Duncan. *Atomic Shield: A History of the United States Atomic Energy Commission, 1947–52.* Vol. 2. University Park: Pennsylvania State University Press, 1969.

Hewlett, Richard, and Jack Moll. *Atoms for Peace and War: Eisenhower and the Atomic Energy Commission: 1953–1961.* Vol. 3. Berkeley: University of California Press, 1989.

Hogerton, John F. *The Atomic Energy Deskbook.* New York: Reinhold Pub. Corp., 1963.

Hunt, Linda. *Secret Agenda.* New York: St. Martin's Press, 1991.

International Physicians for the Prevention of Nuclear War and the Institute for Energy and Environmental Research. *Plutonium: Deadly Gold of the Nuclear Age.* Cambridge, MA: International Physicians Press, 1992.

Jee, Webster S. S., ed. *Symposium on Health Effects of Plutonium and Radium, Sun Valley, Idaho, 1975.* Salt Lake City: JW Press, 1976.

Jette, Eleanor. *Inside Box 1663.* Los Alamos: Los Alamos Historical Society, 1977.

Jungk, Robert. *Brighter Than a Thousand Suns: A Personal History of the Atomic Scientists.* Translated by James Cleugh. New York: Harcourt Brace, 1958.

Kathren, Ronald L., and Paul L. Ziemer, eds. *Health Physics: A Backward Glance: Thirteen Original Papers on the History of Radiation Protection.* New York: Pergamon Press, 1980.

Katz, Jay. *The Silent World of Doctor and Patient.* New York: Free Press, 1984.

Kunetka, James W. *City of Fire: Los Alamos and the Birth of the Atomic Age 1943–1945.* Englewood Cliffs, NJ: Prentice-Hall, 1978.

Lamont, Lansing. *Day of Trinity.* New York: Atheneum, 1965.

Lang, Daniel. *From Hiroshima to the Moon.* New York: Simon and Schuster, 1959.

Lasby, Clarence G. *Project Paperclip: German Scientists and the Cold War.* New York: Atheneum, 1971.

Lawren, William. *The General and the Bomb: A Biography of Leslie R. Groves, Director of the Manhattan Project.* New York: Dodd, Mead, 1988.

Libby, Leona Marshall. *The Uranium People.* New York: Crane. Russak, 1979.

Lilienthal, David. *The Journals of David E. Lilienthal.* Vol. 2. *The Atomic Energy Years 1945–1950.* New York: Harper & Row, 1964.

Low-Beer, Bertram V. A. *The Clinical Use of Radioactive Isotopes.* Springfield, IL: Charles C Thomas Publisher, 1950.

Lyon, Fern, and Jacob Evans, eds. *Los Alamos: The First Forty Years.* Los Alamos: Los Alamos Historical Society, 1984.

Nichols, K. D. *The Road to Trinity: A Personal Account of How America's Nuclear Policies Were Made.* New York: William Morrow, 1987.

O'Neill, Dan. *The Firecracker Boys.* New York: St. Martin's Press, 1994.

Pizzarello, Donald J., and Richard L. Witcofski. *Basic Radiation Biology.* Philadelphia: Lea & Febiger, 1975.

Rapoport, Roger. *The Great American Bomb Machine.* New York: E. P. Dutton, 1971.

Rhodes, Richard. *The Making of the Atomic Bomb.* New York: Simon and Schuster, 1986.

Roff, Sue Rabbit. *Hotspots: The Legacy of Hiroshima and Nagasaki.* London: Cassell, 1995.

Rosenberg, Howard L. *Atomic Soldiers: American Victims of Nuclear Experiments.* Boston: Beacon Press, 1980.

Rothman, David. *Strangers at the Bedside: A History of How Law and Bioethics Transformed Medical Decision Making.* New York: Basic Books, 1991.

Shelton, Frank H. *Reflections of a Nuclear Weaponeer.* Colorado Springs, CO: Shelton Enterprises, 1988.

Shirabe, Raisuke. *My Experience of the Nagasaki Atomic Bombing and an Outline of the Damages Caused by the Explosion.* n.c.: n.p., n.d.

Smyth, Henry DeWolf. *Atomic Energy for Military Purposes.* Princeton, NJ: Princeton University Press, 1945.

Stoff, Michael B., Jonathan F. Fanton, and R. Hal Williams, eds. *The Manhattan Project: A Documentary Introduction to the Atomic Age.* Philadelphia: Temple University Press, 1991.

Stone, Robert, ed. *Industrial Medicine on the Plutonium Project: Survey and Collected Papers.* New York: McGraw-Hill, 1951.

Stover, Betsy, and Webster Jee, eds. *Radiobiology of Plutonium.* Salt Lake City: J. W. Press, 1972.

Sylves, Richard T. *The Nuclear Oracles: A Political History of the General Advisory Committee of the Atomic Energy Commission 1947–1977.* Ames: Iowa State University Press, 1987.

Szasz, Ferenc Morton. *The Day the Sun Rose Twice: The Story of the Trinity Site Nuclear Explosion, July 16, 1945.* Albuquerque: University of New Mexico Press, 1984.

Truman, Harry S. *Years of Trial and Hope.* Memoirs. Vol. 2. New York: Doubleday, 1956.

Uhl, Michael, and Tod Ensign. *GI Guinea Pigs: How the Pentagon Exposed Our Troops to Dangers More Deadly than War: Agent Orange and Atomic Radiation.* Chicago: Playboy Press, 1980.

Udall, Stewart. *The Myths of August: A Personal Exploration of Our Tragic Cold War Affair with the Atom.* New York: Pantheon Books, 1994.

Wasserman, Harvey, and Norman Solomon, with Robert Alvarez and Eleanor Walters. *Killing Our Own: The Disaster of America's Experience with Atomic Radiation.* New York: Delacorte, 1982.

Weisgall, Jonathan. *Operation Crossroads: The Atomic Tests at Bikini Atoll.* Annapolis: Naval Institute Press, 1994.

Wyden, Peter. *Day One: Before Hiroshima and After.* New York: Simon and Schuster, 1984.

GOVERNMENT PUBLICATIONS AND REPORTS

Advisory Committee on Human Radiation Experiments. *Final Report.* Washington, D.C.: Government Printing Office, 1995.

Andrews, G. A., F. V. Comas, C. L. Edwards, R. M. Kniseley, C. C. Lushbaugh, and Helen Vodopick. "Hematologic and Therapeutic Effects of Total-Body Irradiation (50r–100r) in Patients with Malignant Lymphoma, Chronic Lymphocitic and Granulocytic Leukemias, and Polycythemia Vera." Oak Ridge: U.S. AEC Division of Technical Information, December 1970 (ORAU-112).

Armed Forces Special Weapons Project. *Radiological Defense: The Principles of*

Military Defense Against Atomic Weapons. Vol. 2. Washington, D.C.: Armed Forces Special Weapons Project, 1951.

Byrnes, Victor A. *Operation Buster, Project 4.3, Flash Blindness.* Oak Ridge: AEC Technical Information Service, March 1952 (CIC 64562).

———. *Operation Snapper, Project 4.5, Flash Blindness.* Oak Ridge: AEC Technical Information Service, March 1953 (CIC 49283).

Byrnes, Victor A., D. V. L. Brown, H. W. Rose, and Paul Cibis. *Operation Upshot-Knothole, Project 4.5, Ocular Effects of Thermal Radiation From Atomic Detonation—Flashblindness and Chorioretinal Burns.* March–June 1953 (CIC 34219).

Clinton Laboratories. *Minutes of Project Council Policy Meeting.* Oak Ridge, TN: DOE Office of Scientific and Technical Information, Jan. 19, 1944 (CS-1262).

Crowley, J., H. Lanz, K. Scott, and J. G. Hamilton. *A Comparison of the Metabolism of Plutonium (Pu 238) in Man and the Rat.* Oak Ridge, TN: DOE Office of Scientific and Technical Information, May 31, 1946 (CH-3589).

Defense Nuclear Agency. *Nuclear Test Personnel Review.* Public Affairs Office Fact Sheet, Jan. 14, 1994.

———. *Hiroshima and Nagasaki Occupation Forces.* Public Affairs Office Fact Sheet, Aug. 6, 1980.

———. *Sandstone.* Public Affairs Office Fact Sheet, n.d.

———. *Operation Ranger.* Public Affairs Office Fact Sheet, Feb. 26, 1982.

———. *Greenhouse.* Public Affairs Office Fact Sheet, n.d.

———. *Operation Buster-Jangle.* Public Affairs Office Fact Sheet, June 21, 1982.

———. *Operation Tumbler-Snapper.* Public Affairs Office Fact Sheet, June 14, 1982.

———. *Operation Upshot-Knothole.* Public Affairs Office Fact Sheet, Jan. 11, 1982.

———. *Operation Castle.* Public Affairs Office Fact Sheet, Dec. 1, 1982.

———. *Teapot Series.* Public Affairs Office Fact Sheet, Nov. 23, 1981.

———. *Operation Redwing.* Public Affairs Office Fact Sheet, Jan. 20, 1983.

———. *Plumbbob Series.* Public Affairs Office Fact Sheet, Sept. 15, 1981.

———. *Hardtack.* Public Affairs Office Fact Sheet, n.d.

———. *Operation Hardtack II.* Public Affairs Office Fact Sheet, Dec. 3, 1982.

———. *Dominic I.* Public Affairs Office Fact Sheet, n.d.

———. *Operation Dominic II.* Public Affairs Office Fact Sheet, Jan. 31, 1983.

Defense Nuclear Agency. *Operation Crossroads: 1946.* U.S. Atmospheric Nuclear Weapons Tests. Nuclear Test Personnel Review. Report DNA 6032F, May 1, 1984.

———. *Operation Ranger: Shots Able, Baker, Easy, Baker-2, Fox, 25 January–6 February 1951.* U.S. Atmospheric Nuclear Weapons Tests. NTPR. Report DNA 6022F, Feb. 26, 1982.

———. *Shots Able to Easy: The First Five Tests of the Buster-Jangle Series, 22 October–5 November 1951.* U.S. Atmospheric Nuclear Weapons Tests. NTPR. Report DNA 6024F, June 22, 1982.

———. *Shots Sugar and Uncle: The Final Tests of the Buster-Jangle Series, 19*

November–29 November 1951. U.S. Atmospheric Nuclear Weapons Tests. NTPR. Report DNA 6025F, June 23, 1982.

———. *Operation Greenhouse, 1951.* U.S. Atmospheric Nuclear Weapons Tests. NTPR. Report DNA 6034F, June 15, 1983.

———. *Operation Ivy, 1952.* U.S. Atmospheric Nuclear Weapons Tests. NTPR. Report DNA 6036F, Dec. 1, 1982.

———. *Operation Teapot, 1955.* U.S. Atmospheric Nuclear Weapons Tests. NTPR. Report DNA 6009F, Nov. 23, 1981.

———. *Operation Redwing, 1956.* U.S. Atmospheric Nuclear Weapons Tests. NTPR. Report DNA 6037F, Aug. 1, 1982.

———. *Plumbbob Series, 1957.* U.S. Atmospheric Nuclear Weapons Tests. NTPR. Report DNA 6005F, Sept. 15, 1981.

———. *Operation Hardtack I, 1958.* U.S. Atmospheric Nuclear Weapons Tests. NTPR. Report DNA 6038F, Dec. 1, 1982.

———. *Operation Dominic I, 1962.* U.S. Atmospheric Nuclear Weapons Tests. NTPR. Report DNA 6040F, Feb. 1, 1983.

———. *Operation Teapot: Manned Penetrations of Atomic Clouds, Project 2.8b.* Washington, D.C.: Defense Nuclear Agency, Sept. 1, 1980 (CIC 12800).

Department of Defense. *Report on Search for Human Radiation Experiment Records 1944–1994.* Vol. 1. Springfield VA: Department of Commerce, Technology Administration, National Technical Information Service, 1997.

Department of Energy. *Human Radiation Experiments: The Department of Energy Roadmap to the Story and the Records.* Springfield, VA: Department of Commerce, Technology Administration, National Technical Information Service, 1995 (DOE/EH-0445).

———. *Human Radiation Experiments Associated with the U.S. Department of Energy and Its Predecessors.* Springfield, VA: Department of Commerce, Technology Administration, National Technical Information Service, 1995 (DOE/EH-0491).

———. Office of Environmental Management. *Closing the Circle on the Splitting of the Atom.* Washington, D.C.: Department of Energy, 1995.

———. Office of Inspector General. *Inspection of the Secretary of Energy's Foreign Travel.* Oak Ridge, TN: Office of Scientific and Technical Information, 1996 (DOE/IG-0397).

Glasstone, Samuel, and Philip J. Dolan, eds. *The Effects of Nuclear Weapons.* Washington, D.C.: Government Printing Office, 1977.

Government Accounting Office. *Radiation Exposures for Some Cloud Sampling Personnel Need to Be Reexamined.* Washington, D.C: U.S. Government Accounting Office, 1987 (GAO/RCED-87-134).

———. *Examples of Post World War II Radiation Releases at U.S. Nuclear Sites.* Washington, D.C.: U.S. Government Accounting Office, 1993 (GAO/RCED-94-51FS).

———. *Human Experimentation: An Overview on Cold War Era Programs.* Washington, D.C.: U.S. Government Accounting Office, 1994. (GAO/T-NSIAD-94-266).

———. *Information on DOE's Human Tissue Analysis Work.* Washington, D.C.: U.S. Government Accounting Office, 1995 (GAO/RCED-95-109FS).

————. *Unsubstantiated DOE Travel Payments*. Washington, D.C.: U.S. General Accounting Office, 1995 (GAO/RCED-96-58R).

————. *Some Unsubstantiated Payments for the Secretary's Foreign Travel*. Washington, D.C.: U.S. General Accounting Office, 1996 (GAO/T-RCED-96-59).

————. *Energy Department Trade Missions: Authority, Results, and Management Issues*, Washington, D.C.: U.S. General Accounting Office, 1996 (GAO/T-NSIAD-96-151).

Gulley, Wayne T., Robert D. Metcalf, Mathew R. Wilson, and Jerome A. Hirsch. *Operation Plumbbob, Project 4.2, Evaluation of Eye Protection Afforded by an Electromechanical Shutter*. Headquarters, Field Command, Defense Atomic Support Agency, Sandia Base, Albuquerque, NM, April 29, 1960 (CIC 6308).

Hill, J. H., Gloria Chisum, R. A. Richardson. *Operation Dominic, Christmas Series, Project 4.2, Photoelectric and Psychophysical Measures of Weapons Flashes*. Washington, D.C.: Defense Nuclear Agency, Sept. 1, 1985 (CIC 51093).

Human Radiation Interagency Working Group. *Building Public Trust: Actions to Respond to the Report of the Advisory Committee on Human Radiation Experiments*. Washington, D.C.: Government Printing Office, 1997 (DOE/EH-04542).

Lalos, George, ed. *Film Badge Dosimetry in Atmospheric Tests*. Washington, D.C.: National Academy Press, 1989.

Langham, Wright, ed. *Radiobiological Factors in Manned Space Flight*. Washington, D.C.: National Academy of Sciences, National Research Council, 1967.

Langham, Wright, Samuel H. Bassett, Payne S. Harris, and Robert E. Carter. *Distribution and Excretion of Plutonium Administered Intravenously to Man*. Los Alamos: Los Alamos Scientific Laboratory, Sept. 20, 1950 (LA-1151).

Levin, William C., Martin Schneider, and Herbert Gerstner. "Initial Clinical Reaction to Therapeutic Whole-Body X-Radiation." School of Aviation Medicine, Randolph AFB, TX, 1960.

Los Alamos National Laboratory. *Radiation Protection and the Human Radiation Experiments. Los Alamos Science*, no. 23, 1995.

Medical Follow-up Agency, Institute of Medicine. *Mortality of Veteran Participants in the Crossroads Nuclear Test*. Washington, D.C.: National Academy Press, 1996.

Metallurgical Project, Health Division. *Report for Month Ending Feb. 29, 1944*. Oak Ridge, TN: DOE Office of Scientific and Technical Information, March 1944 (CH-1459).

Miller, Lowell S., Gilbert H. Fletcher, and Herbert Gerstner. "Systematic and Clinical Effects Induced in 263 Cancer Patients by Whole-Body X-Irradiation." School of Aviation Medicine, Randolph AFB, TX, 1957.

Nickson, J. J., ed. *Report of Conference on Plutonium—May 14th and 15th*. Oak Ridge, TN: DOE Office of Scientific and Technical Information, July 23, 1945 (CN-3167).

Parker, Herbert. *Status of Product Monitoring by Health-Physics Section*. Oak Ridge, TN: DOE Office of Scientific and Technical Information, Jan. 2, 1945 (CN-1892).

Pinson, Ernest A., Kermit C. Kaericher, James E. Banks, and John d'Hord. *Opera-

tion Redwing—Project 2.66A, Early Cloud Penetrations. Washington, D.C.: Defense Nuclear Agency, March 20, 1987 (CIC No. 0051870).

Russell, E. R., and J. J. Nickson. *The Distribution and Excretion of Plutonium in Two Human Subjects.* Argonne, IL: Argonne National Laboratory, Oct. 2, 1946 (CH-3607).

Saenger, Eugene L. *Medical Aspects of Radiation Accidents: A Handbook for Physicians, Health Physicists and Industrial Hygienists.* Washington, D.C.: Government Printing Office, 1963.

Stannard, J. Newell. *Radioactivity and Health: A History.* 3 vols. Oak Ridge, TN: Office of Science and Technical Information, 1988. (Available from Batelle Press, Columbus, OH.)

Task Force on Human Subject Research. *A Report on the Use of Radioactive Materials in Human Subject Research that Involved Residents of State-Operated Facilities within the Commonwealth of Massachusetts from 1943 through 1973.* Commonwealth of Massachusetts, Office of Health & Human Services, Department of Mental Retardation, 1994.

Taylor, Leland. *History of Air Force Atomic Cloud Sampling.* Air Force Systems Command, Historical Publications Series 61-142-1. Kirtland Air Force Base, NM: Air Force Special Weapons Center, January 1963.

Truslow, Edith. *Manhattan District History: Nonscientific Aspects of Los Alamos Project Y, 1942 through 1946.* Los Alamos Scientific Laboratory (LA-5200) 1973.

UCSF Ad Hoc Fact Finding Committee. *Report of the UCSF Ad Hoc Fact Finding Committee on World War II Human Radiation Experiments.* San Francisco: UCSF, February 1995.

———. *Addendum to the February 1995 Report of the UCSF Ad Hoc Fact Finding Committee on World War II Human Radiation Experiments.* San Francisco: UCSF, September 1995.

University of Texas. *The First Twenty Years of the M. D. Anderson Hospital and Tumor Institute.* Houston: The University of Texas M. D. Anderson Hospital and Tumor Institute, 1964.

U.S. Congress. Senate. Special Committee on Atomic Energy. *Atomic Energy.* Hearings. 79th Cong., 2nd sess., Nov. 27–30, Dec. 3, 1945.

U.S. Congress. Joint Committee on Atomic Energy. *Investigation into the Atomic Energy Project.* Hearings. 81st Cong., 1st sess., 1949.

U.S. Congress. Joint Committee on Atomic Energy, Special Subcommittee on Radiation. *The Nature of Radioactive Fallout and Its Effects on Man.* Hearings. 85th Cong., 1st Sess., May 27–June 7, 1957.

U.S. Congress. House. Committee on Interstate and Foreign Commerce, Subcommittee on Health and the Environment. *Effect of Radiation on Human Health: Health Effects of Ionizing Radiation.* Hearings. 95th Cong., 2nd sess., Jan. 24–26, Feb. 8, 9, 14, 28, 1978.

U.S. Congress. House. Committee on Science and Technology, Subcommittee on Investigations and Oversight. *Human Total Body Irradiation (TBI) Program at Oak Ridge.* Hearings. 97th Cong., 1st sess., Sept. 23, 1981.

U.S. Congress. House. Committee on Energy and Commerce, Subcommittee on Energy Conservation and Power. *American Nuclear Guinea Pigs: Three De-*

cades of Radiation Experiments on U.S. Citizens. Report. 99th Cong., 2nd sess., November 1986.

U.S. Congress. Senate. Committee on Labor and Human Resources. *Human Subjects Research: Radiation Experimentation.* Hearings, 103rd Cong., 1st sess., Jan. 13, 1994.

U.S. Congress. House. Committee on Energy and Commerce, Subcommittee on Energy and Power. *Radiation Testing on Humans.* Hearings. 103rd Cong., 2nd sess., Jan. 18, 1994.

U.S. Congress. House. Committee on the Judiciary, Subcommittee on Administrative Law and Governmental Relations. *Government-Sponsored Testing on Humans.* Hearings. 103rd Cong., 2nd sess., Feb. 3, 1994.

U.S. Congress. House. Committee on the Judiciary, Subcommittee on Administrative Law and Governmental Relations. *Radiation Experiments Conducted by the University of Cincinnati Medical School with Department of Defense Funding.* Hearings. 103rd Cong., 2nd sess., April 11, 1994.

U.S. Congress. Joint Hearing before the Subcommittee on Oversight and Investigations and the Subcommittee on Energy and Power of the Committee on Commerce. *Department of Energy: Misuse of Federal Funds.* Hearings. 104th Cong., 1st sess., Nov. 17, 1995.

U.S. Congress. House. Committee on Commerce, Subcommittee on Oversight and Investigations. *Department of Energy: Travel Expenditures and Related Issues.* Hearings. 104th Cong., 2nd sess., Jan. 4, March 8, 1996.

U.S. Congress. House. Committee on Commerce, Subcommittee on Oversight and Investigations. *Department of Energy: Travel Expenditures and Related Issues (Part 2).* Hearings. 104th Cong., 2nd sess., April 24, 1996.

U.S. Congress. House. Committee on Commerce, Subcommittee on Oversight and Investigations. *Department of Energy: Travel Expenditures and Related Issues (Part 3).* Hearings. 104th Cong., 2nd sess., June 12–13, 1996.

U.S. Congress. House. Committee on Veteran's Affairs, Subcommittee on Compensation, Pension, Insurance, and Memorial Affairs, *Effects to Veterans of Exposure to Ionizing Radiation, Subsequent Treatment and Compensation,* Hearings. 104th Cong., 2nd sess., April 30, 1996.

Wallace, Anna M. *History of the Walter E. Fernald State School,* Waltham, MA: Fernald Corp., 1948.

Warren, Stafford. "The Role of Radiology in the Development of the Atomic Bomb." *Radiology in World War II.* Washington, D.C.: Office of the Surgeon General, Department of the Army, 1966, pp. 831–921.

SCIENTIFIC ARTICLES

"Acute Radiation Death Resulting from an Accidental Nuclear Critical Excursion." *Journal of Occupational Medicine,* Special Supplement (March 1961).

"Address on the Present Status and Future Tendencies of the Medical Profession in the United States." *Journal of the American Medical Association,* 1, no. 2 (July 21, 1883), 33–42.

Aub, Joseph, Robley Evans, Louis Hempelmann, and Harrison Martland. "The

Late Effects of Internally Deposited Radioactive Materials in Man." *Medicine*, 31 (1952), 221–329.

Balfour, W. M., P. F. Hahn, W. F. Bale, W. T. Pommerenke, and G. H. Whipple. "Radioactive Iron Absorption in Clinical Conditions: Normal, Pregnancy, Anemia, and Hemochromatosis." *Journal of Experimental Medicine*, 76 (1942), 15–30.

Brill, A. Bertrand, Masanobu Tomonaga, and Robert M. Heyssel. "Leukemia in Man Following Exposure to Ionizing Radiation." *Annals of Internal Medicine*, 56, no. 4 (1962), pp. 590–609.

Bronner, Felix, Clemens Benda, Robert Harris, and Joseph Kreplick. "Calcium Metabolism in a Case of Gargoylism, Studied with the Aid of Radiocalcium." *Journal of Clinical Investigation*, 37, part 2 (February 1958), 139–147.

Bronner, Felix, Robert S. Harris, Constantine Maletskos, and Clemens E. Benda. "Studies in Calcium Metabolism. Effect of Food Phytates on Calcium 45 Uptake in Children on Low-Calcium Breakfasts." *Journal of Nutrition*, 54, no. 4 (December 1954), 523–542.

———. "Studies in Calcium Metabolism. The Fate of Intravenously Injected Radiocalcium in Human Beings." *Journal of Clinical Investigation*, 35 (January 1956), 78–88.

———. "Studies in Calcium Metabolism. Effect of Food Phytates on Calcium 45 Uptake in Boys on a Moderate Calcium Breakfast." *Journal of Nutrition*, 59, no. 3 (July 1956), 393–406.

Brown, Reynold. "Obituary—Robert Stone." *Radiology*, 88 (April 1967), 807–808.

Brues, Austin. "Obituary—Shields Warren." *Radiation Research*, 88 (1981), 430–435.

"Brutalities of Nazi Physicians." *JAMA*, 132, no. 12 (Nov. 23, 1946), 714–715.

Buettner, Konrad. "Effects of Extreme Heat and Cold on Human Skin III. Numerical Analysis and Pilot Experiments on Penetrating Flash Radiation Effects." *Journal of Applied Physiology*, 5 (November 1952), 207–220.

Byrnes, Victor A. "Eye Injuries in Nuclear Warfare." *Military Medicine*, 118 (April 1956), 286–292.

———. "Flash Blindness and Chorioretinal Burns Produced by Atomic Flash." *JAMA*, 168 (October 1958), 178–179.

Byrnes, Victor A., David V. L. Brown, H. W. Rose, and Paul A. Cibis. "Chorioretinal Burns Produced by Atomic Flash." *Archives of Ophthalmology*, 53 (March 1955), 351–364.

———. "Retinal Burns—New Hazard of the Atomic Bomb." *JAMA*, 157, no. 1 (June 1955), 21–22.

———. "Chorioretinal Lesions Due to Thermal Radiation From the Atomic Bomb." *Archives of Ophthalmology*, No. 55 (June 1956), 909–914.

"Castration Recommended as a Substitute for Capital Punishment." *JAMA*, 18 (April 1892), 499–500.

Cibis, Paul A. "Retinal Adaptation in Night Flying." *Journal of Aviation Medicine*, 23 (April 1952), 168–176.

Cibis, Paul A., Werner K. Noell, and Bertram Eichel. "Ocular Effects Produced by High Intensity X-Radiation." *Archives of Ophthalmology*, 53, no. 5 (May 1955), 651–663.

Egilman, David, Wes Wallace, Cassandra Stubbs, and Fernando Mora-Corrasco. "Ethical Aerobics: ACHRE's Flight from Responsibility." *Accountability in Research,* 6, nos. 1, 2 (January 1998), 15–61.

"Element of Consent in Surgical Operations." *JAMA,* 15 (Sept. 13, 1890), 401–402.

Evans, Robley. "Radium Poisoning: A Review of Present Knowledge." *American Journal of Public Health,* 23, no. 10 (October 1933), 1017–1023.

———. "Protection of Radium Dial Workers and Radiologists from Injury by Radium." *Industrial Hygiene and Toxicology,* 25, no. 7 (September 1943), 253–269.

———. "The Medical Uses of Atomic Energy." *Atlantic Monthly* (January–June 1946), 68–73.

"Experiments on Prisoners." *Science News Letter,* 53 (February 1948), 117.

Gerathewhohl, S. J., and H. Strughold. "Motoric Responses of the Eyes When Exposed to Light Flashes of High Intensities and Short Duration." *Journal of Aviation Medicine,* 24 (June 1953), 200–207.

Gerstner, Herbert B. "Acute Radiation Syndrome in Man: Military and Civil Defense Aspects." *United States Armed Forces Medical Journal,* 9, no. 3 (March 1958), 313–354.

———. "Acute Clinical Effects of Penetrating Nuclear Radiation," *JAMA* (Sept. 27, 1958), 381–388.

Hagstrom, Ruth M., S. R. Glasser, A. B. Brill, and R. M. Heyssel. "Long Term Effects of Radioactive Iron Administered During Human Pregnancy." *American Journal of Epidemiology,* 90, no. 1 (1969), 1–10.

Hahn, P. F., and C. W. Sheppard. "The Therapeutic Use of Radioactive Elements in Malignancy." *Annals of Internal Medicine,* 28 (Jan.–June 1948), 598–606.

Hahn, P. F., E. L. Carothers, W. J. Darby, et al. "Iron Metabolism in Human Pregnancy as Studied with the Radioactive Isotope, Fe 59." *American Journal of Obstetrics and Gynecology,* 61, no. 3 (March 1951), 477–498.

Hamilton, G. V. "A Study of Sexual Tendencies in Monkeys and Baboons." *Journal of Animal Behavior,* 4, no. 5 (September–October 1914), 295–318.

Hamilton, Joseph, and Robert Stone. "The Intravenous and Intraduodenal Administration of Radio-Sodium." *Radiology,* 28, no. 2 (1937), 178–188.

Harkness, Jon. "Nuremberg and the Issue of Wartime Experiments on US Prisoners." *JAMA,* 276, no. 20 (Nov. 27, 1996), 1672–1675.

Heilbron, J. L., Robert W. Seidel, and Bruce R. Wheaton. "Lawrence and His Laboratory: Nuclear Science at Berkeley." *LBL News Magazine* 6, no. 3 (Fall 1981).

Heller, Carl, Donald J. Moore, C. Alvin Paulsen, Warren O. Nelson, and William Laidlaw. "Effects of Progesterone and Synthetic Progestins on the Reproductive Physiology of Normal Men." *Federation Proceedings,* 18, part 2 (1959), 1057–1065.

Heller, Carl, Warren O. Nelson, Irvin B. Hill, Edward Henderson, William O. Maddock, Edwin Jungck, C. Alvin Paulsen, and Glenn E. Mortimore. "Improvement in Spermatogenesis Following Depression of the Human Testis with Testosterone." *Fertility and Sterility,* 1, no. 5 (1950), 415–422.

Hempelmann, Louis. "Obituary—Wright Langham." *Radiation Research,* 52, no. 2 (November 1972), 419–421.

Hempelmann, Louis, Edward H. Reinhard, Carl V. Moore, Olga S. Bierbaum, and Sherwood Moore. "Hematologic Complications of Therapy with Radioactive Phosphorous." *Journal of Laboratory and Clinical Medicine* (October 1944), 1021–1041.

Heublein, Arthur C. "A Preliminary Report on Continuous Radiation of the Entire Body." *Radiology,* 18, no. 6 (June 1932), 1051–1062.

Ivy, A. C. "Nazi War Crimes of a Medical Nature." *JAMA,*139, no. 3 (January 1949), 131–134.

———. "The History and Ethics of the Use of Humans in Medical Experiments." *Science,* 108 (July 1948), no. 1–5.

Jacobs, Melville L., and Fred J. Marasso. "A Four-Year Experience with Total-Body Irradiation." *Radiology,* 84 (March 1965), 452–456.

Landesberg, Jacques. "Chorioretinitis Produced by Atomic Bomb Explosion." *Archives of Ophthalmology,* 54 (October 1955), 539–540.

Langham, W. H., J.N.P. Lawrence, Jean McClelland, and Louis Hempelmann. "The Los Alamos Scientific Laboratory's Experience with Plutonium in Man." *Health Physics,* 8 (1962), 753–760.

Lawrence, Ernest, and Warren M. Garrison. "J. G. Hamilton, Medical Physicist and Physician." *Science,* 126 (Aug. 16, 1957), 294.

Liebow, Averill, Shields Warren, and Elbert DeCoursey. "Pathology of Atomic Bomb Casualties." *American Journal of Pathology,* 25, part 2 (1949), 853–945.

Macklis, Roger. "The Great Radium Scandal." *Scientific American,* 269 (1993), 94–99.

MacMahon, Brian. "Prenatal X-Ray Exposure and Childhood Cancer." *Journal of the National Cancer Institute,* 28, no. 5 (1962), 1173–1191.

Martland, Harrison, Philip Conlon, and Joseph P. Knef. "Some Unrecognized Dangers in the Use and Handling of Radioactive Substances." *JAMA,* 85 (Dec. 5, 1925), 1769–1776.

———. "Occupational Poisoning in Manufacture of Luminous Watch Dials." *JAMA,* 92 (Feb. 9, 1929), 466–473.

Medinger, Fred G., and Lloyd Craver. "Total Body Irradiation." *American Journal of Roentgenology,* 48, no. 5 (1942), 651–671.

Miller, Lowell S., Gilbert H. Fletcher, and Herbert B. Gerstner. "Radiobiologic Observations on Cancer Patients Treated with Whole-Body X-Irradiation." *Radiation Research,* 4 (1958), 150–165.

Miller, Robert W., and Thomas Koszalka. "Obituary—Louis H. Hempelmann." *Radiation Research,* 136 (1993), 435–438.

Pommerenke, W. T., P. F. Hahn, W. F. Bale, and W. M. Balfour. "Transmission of Radioactive Iron to the Human Fetus." *American Journal of Physiology,* 137 (1942), 164–170.

Report of a Committee Appointed by Gov. Dwight H. Green. "Ethics Governing the Service of Prisoners as Subjects in Medical Experiments." *JAMA,* 136, no. 7 (February 1948), 457–458.

Rose, H. W., David L. Brown, Victor A. Byrnes, and Paul A. Cibis. "Human

Chorioretinal Burns from Atomic Fireballs." *Archives of Ophthalmology,* 55 (February 1956), 205–210.

Saenger, Eugene. "Radiation Casualties: Newer Aspects of Mass Casualty Care." *New York State Journal of Medicine,* 64, part 1 (January 1965), 309–314.

Saenger, Eugene, Edward Silberstein, Bernard Aron, Harry Horwitz, James Kereiakes, Gustave Bahr, Harold Perry, and Ben Friedman. "Whole Body and Partial Body Radiotherapy of Advanced Cancer." *American Journal of Roentgenology,* 117, no. 3 (March 1973), 670–685.

Shipman, Thomas. "A Case of Radiation Fatality Resulting from a Massive Over-Exposure to Neutrons and Gamma Rays." Paper, Joint meeting of International Atomic Energy Agency and the World Health Organization, Geneva, Switzerland, October 1960.

Stewart, Alice, Josefine Webb, and David Hewitt. "A Survey of Childhood Malignancies." *British Medical Journal,* 1 (June 28, 1958), 1495–1508.

Stone, Robert. "Health Protection Activities of the Plutonium Project." *Proceedings of American Philosophical Society,* 90 (January 1946), 11–19.

————. "The Plutonium Project." *Radiology,* 49 (September 1947), 364–365.

————. "The Concept of a Maximum Permissible Exposure." *Radiology,* 58, no. 5 (May 1952), 639–660.

————. "Obituary—Bertram V. A. Low-Beer." *Radiology,* 66 (1956), 284–285.

Stone, Robert S., and John C. Larkin. "The Treatment of Cancer with Fast Neutrons." *Radiology,* 39 (1942), 608–620.

Stone, Robert S., John Lawrence, and Paul Aebersold. "A Preliminary Report on the Use of Fast Neutrons in the Treatment of Malignant Disease." *Radiology,* 35 (1940), 322–327.

Teller, Edward. "The Work of Many People." *Science,* 121 (February 1955), 267–275.

Toohey, R. E., C. G. Cacic, R. D. Oldham, and R. P. Larsen. "The Concentration of Plutonium in Hair Following Intravenous Injection." *Health Physics,* 40 (June 1981), 881–886.

Warren, Shields. "The Treatment of Leukemia by Radioactive Phosphorous." *New England Journal of Medicine,* 223, no. 19 (November 1940), 751–754.

————. "The Retention of Radioactive Phosphorous in Leukemic Patients." *Cancer Research,* 3 (1943), 872–876.

————. "The Pattern of Injuries Produced by the Atomic Bombs at Hiroshima and Nagasaki." *U.S. Naval Medical Bulletin,* 46, no. 9 (September 1946), 1349–1353.

————. "The Nagasaki Survivors as Seen in 1947." *Military Surgeon,* 102 (1948), 98–100.

————. "Radiation Cataracts." *JAMA,* 141 (1949), 407.

————. "Ionizing Radiation and Medicine." *Scientific American,* (September 1959), 165–176.

Warren, Stafford. "Differential Diagnosis of Gonococcal Arthritis." *Journal of Laboratory and Clinical Medicine,* 22 (1936), 44–47.

Warren, Stafford, Winfred Scott, and Charles M. Carpenter. "Artificially Induced Fever for the Treatment of Gonococcic Infections in the Male." *JAMA,* 109, no. 18 (1937), 1430–1435.

DEPOSITIONS

Atkinson, John. Conducted Oct. 14, 1976. *Donald Mathena et al. v. Amos Reed et al.* U.S. District Court, District of Oregon, CV Nos. 76–326, 76–327, 76–328, 76–329, 76–330.

Bibeau, Harold. Conducted Sept. 17, 1996. *Harold Bibeau et al. v. Pacific Northwest Research Foundation et al.* U.S. District Court, District of Oregon, CV No. 95-06410-HO.

Craft, Emma. Conducted Sept. 13, 1994. *Emma Craft et al. v. Vanderbilt University et al.* U.S. District Court, Middle District of Tennessee at Nashville, CV No. 3: 94–0090.

Hempelmann, Louis. Conducted Dec. 20, 1979. *Bernice Lasovick v. United States of America.* U.S. District Court, District of New Mexico, CV No. 77-323-M.

Hetland, Ivan Dale. Conducted Oct. 14, 1976. *Donald Mathena et al. v. Amos Reed et al.* U.S. District Court, District of Oregon, CV Nos. 76–326, 76–327, 76–328, 76–329, 76–330.

Hignite, Baxter. Conducted Oct. 13, 1976. *Donald Mathena et al. v. Amos Reed et al.* U.S. District Court, District of Oregon, CV Nos. 76–326, 76–327, 76–328, 76–329, 76–330.

Liverman, James. Conducted Oct. 30, 1996. *Harold Bibeau et al. v. Pacific Northwest Research Foundation et al.* United States District Court, District of Oregon, CV No. 95-06410-HO.

Lushbaugh, Clarence. Conducted Dec. 3, 1997. *Doris E. Kelley et al. v. Regents of the University of California et al.* First Judicial District Court, Santa Fe, New Mexico, CV No. SF-96-2430.

Marks, Sidney. Conducted Jan. 13, 1997. *Harold Bibeau et al. v. Pacific Northwest Research Foundation et al.* United States District Court, District of Oregon, CV No. 95-0641-HO.

Mathena, Donald Eugene. Conducted Oct. 14, 1976. *Donald Mathena et al. v. Amos Reed et al.* U.S. District Court, District of Oregon, CV Nos. 76–326, 76–327, 76–328, 76–329, 76–330.

O'Leary, Hazel. Conducted Sept. 1, 1998. *Robert White et al. v. Dr. C. Alvin Paulsen et al.* United States District Court, Eastern District of Washington, CV No. CS-97-0239-RHW.

Paulsen, C. Alvin. Conducted Aug. 12, 1996. *Melvin Briggs v. C. Alvin Paulsen et al.* United States District Court, Eastern District of Washington, CV No. CS-96-0005-WFN; *Don Byers et al. v. C. Alvin Paulsen et al.*, CV No. CS-95-00573-WFN.

Petersen, Don. Conducted Oct. 28, 1997. *Doris E. Kelley et al. v. Regents of the University of California et al.* First Judicial District Court, Santa Fe, New Mexico, CV No. SF-96-2430.

Rowley, Mavis. Conducted Oct. 10, 1996. *Harold Bibeau et al. v. Pacific Northwest Research Foundation et al.* United States District Court, District of Oregon, CV No. 95-0641-HO.

Rowley, Mavis, and Carl Heller. Joint deposition conducted July 19, 1976. *Donald Mathena et al. v. State of Oregon et al.* U.S. District Court, District of Oregon, CV Nos. 76–326; 76–327, 76–328, 76–329, 76–330.

Sexton, Mary Sue. Conducted April 11, 1983. *Mary Sue Sexton et al. v. Oak Ridge*

Associated Universities. Circuit Court for Anderson County, Tennessee, CV No. L-2728.

Totter, John R. Conducted Jan. 9, 1997. *Harold Bibeau et al. v. Pacific Northwest Research Foundation et al*. United States District Court for the District of Oregon, CV No. 95-0641-HO.

UNPUBLISHED MANUSCRIPTS AND MEMOIRS

Bowers, John Z. "The ABCC: Its Creation and First Years (1946–1952)." in the John Z. Bowers Papers (unprocessed), Rockefeller Archive Center, Tarrytown, NY.

Howland, Joseph. "Experience in Nuclear Medicine." n.d. University of Rochester, Edward C. Miner Library, Papers of Joe W. Howland, Box 11, Folder 4.

Hueper, Wilhelm. "Adventures of a Physician in Occupational Cancer: A Medical Cassandra's Tale." Bethesda, MD: National Institutes of Health, National Library of Medicine, History of Medicine Division.

Stone, Robert. Transcript of recording. UCSF Library, Special Collections, July 1964 (OH-23).

ORAL HISTORY TRANSCRIPTS

Agnew Harold. Interviewed by J. Newell Stannard, La Jolla, CA, May 2, 1980 (PNL-9575).

Andrews, Howard. Interviewed by ACHRE staff, Middletown, RI, Dec. 3, 1994.

Armstrong, Maj. Gen. Harry (ret.). Interviewed by John W. Bullard and T. A. Glasgow. Brooks Air Force Base, TX, April 6, 8, 13, 20, 1976.

Bagshaw, Malcolm. Interviewed by ACHRE staff, Palo Alto, CA, Feb. 13, 1995.

Bair, William. Interviewed by DOE/OHRE staff, Richland, WA, Oct. 14, 1994 (DOE/EH-0463).

Bale, William. Interviewed by J. Newell Stannard, Atlanta, GA, Nov. 5–6, 1979 (PNL-9594).

Beeson, Paul. Interviewed by Susan Lederer, Seattle, WA, Nov. 20, 1994.

Cohn, Stanton. Interviewed by J. Newell Stannard, Brookhaven National Laboratory, Sept. 16, 1982 (PNL-9611).

Cohn, Waldo. Interviewed by DOE/OHRE staff, Oak Ridge, TN, Jan. 18, 1995 (DOE/EH-0464).

Durbin, Patricia. Interviewed by DOE/OHRE staff, Berkeley, CA, Nov. 11, 1994 (DOE/EH-0458).

Durbin, Patricia. Interviewed by ACHRE staff, Berkeley, CA, n.d.

Eisenbud, Merril. Interviewed by DOE/OHRE staff, Chapel Hill, NC, Jan. 26, 1995 (DOE/EH-0456).

Evans, Robley. Interviewed by Charles Weiner, Cambridge, MA, American Institute of Physics, Neils Bohr Library, 1972, 1974, 1978.

Evans, Robley. Interviewed by J. Newell Stannard, Scottsdale, AZ, April 26, 1978 (PNL-9622).

Finch, Stuart. Interviewed by ACHRE staff, Washington, D.C., Dec. 6, 1994.

Foreman, Nadine. Interviewed by DOE/OHRE staff, Sebastopol, CA, Aug. 19, 1994 (DOE/EH-0465).

Friedell, Hymer. Interviewed by J. Newell Stannard, Cleveland, OH, May 27, 1981 (PNL-9884).

Friedell, Hymer. Interviewed by ACHRE staff, Aug. 23, 1994.

Friedell, Hymer. Interviewed by DOE/OHRE staff, Cleveland, OH, Jan. 28, 1995 (DOE/EH-0466).

Grilly, Julie Langham. Interviewed by DOE/OHRE staff, Los Alamos, NM, Feb. 3, 1995 (DOE/EH-0469).

Gofman, John. Interviewed by DOE/OHRE staff, San Francisco, CA, Dec. 20, 1994 (DOE/EH-0457).

Healy, John. Interviewed by DOE/OHRE staff, Los Alamos, NM, Nov. 28, 1994 (DOE/EH-0455).

Himmelsbach, Clifton. Interviewed by ACHRE staff, Washington, D.C., Nov. 2, 1994.

Hubner, Karl. Interviewed by DOE/OHRE staff, Knoxville, TN, Dec. 30, 1994 (DOE/EH-0470).

Jordan, Harry. Interviewed by J. Newell Stannard, Los Alamos, NM, Sept. 22, 1981 (PNL-9893).

Kohn, Henry I. Interviewed by DOE/OHRE staff, Berkeley, CA, Sept. 13, 1994 (DOE/EH-0471).

Lasagna, Louis. Interviewed by ACHRE staff, Washington, D.C., Dec. 13, 1994.

Libby, Willard. Interviewed by Mary Terrall, Santa Monica, CA, UCLA Oral History Program, 1978.

Libby, Willard. Interviewed by Greg Marlowe, Santa Monica, CA, American Institute of Physics, Niels Bohr Library, April 12, 1979.

Lushbaugh, Clarence. Interviewed by DOE/OHRE staff, Oak Ridge, TN, Oct. 5, 1994 (DOE/EH-0453).

Maletskos, Constantine. Interviewed by DOE/OHRE staff, Gloucester, MA, Jan. 20, 1995 (DOE/EH-0473).

Miller, Earl. Interviewed by DOE/OHRE staff, San Rafael, CA, Aug. 9, Aug. 17, 1994 (DOE/EH-0474).

Morgan, Karl Z. Interviewed by J. Newell Stannard, Atlanta, GA, April 20, April 22, 1979 (PNL-9905).

Morgan, Karl Z. Interviewed by DOE/OHRE staff, Indian Springs, FL, Jan. 7, 1995 (DOE/EH-0475).

Moss, William. Interviewed by DOE/OHRE staff, Los Alamos, NM, Nov. 30, 1994 (DOE/EH-0459).

Pace, Nello. Interviewed by DOE/OHRE staff, Berkeley, CA, Aug. 16, 1994 (DOE/EH-00476).

Paulsen, C. Alvin. Interviewed by ACHRE staff, Seattle, WA, Sept. 8, 1994.

Perry, Seymour. Interviewed by ACHRE staff, Washington, D.C., Jan. 4, 1995.

Petersen, Don. Interviewed by DOE/OHRE staff, Los Alamos, NM, Nov. 29, 1994 (DOE/EH-0460).

Pickering, John. Interviewed by ACHRE staff, Albuquerque, NM, Nov. 2, 1994.

Richmond, Chet. Interviewed by DOE/OHRE staff, Oak Ridge, TN, Jan. 24, 1995 (DOE/EH-0477).

Rowland, Robert E. Interviewed by DOE/OHRE staff, Batavia, IL, Jan. 27, 1995 (DOE/EH-0461).

Rowley, Mavis. Interviewed by ACHRE staff, Seattle, WA, Sept. 8, 1994.

Saenger, Eugene. Interviewed by ACHRE staff, Cincinnati, OH, Sept. 15, Oct. 20, 1994.

Sagan, Leonard. Interviewed by ACHRE staff, Washington, D.C., Nov. 17, 1994.

Scott, Kenneth. Interviewed by Sally Smith Hughes, History of Science and Technology Program, University of California, Berkeley, Dec. 17, 1979.

Seaborg, Glenn. Interviewed by ACHRE, n.d.

Silverman, William. Interviewed by ACHRE staff, Greenbrae, CA, Feb. 14, 1995.

Stephens, Martha. Interviewed by ACHRE staff, Cincinnati, OH, Oct. 20, 1994.

Tobias, Cornelius A. Interviewed by DOE/OHRE staff, Eugene, OR, Jan. 16, 1995 (DOE/EH-0480).

Totter, John. Interviewed by DOE/OHRE staff, Oak Ridge, TN, Jan. 23, 1995 (DOE/EH-0481).

Vodopick, Helen. Interviewed by DOE/OHRE staff, Oak Ridge, TN, Dec. 28, 1994 (DOE/EH-0482).

Voelz, George. Interviewed by DOE/OHRE staff, Los Alamos, NM, Nov. 29, 1994 (DOE/EH-0454).

Warren, Shields. Interviewed by Peter D. Olch, Bethesda, MD, National Institutes of Health, History of Medicine Division, National Library of Medicine, Oct. 10–11, 1972.

Warren, Stafford. "Stafford Warren: An Exceptional Man for Exceptional Challenges." 3 vols. Interviewed by Adelaide Tusler, Los Angeles, CA, UCLA Oral History Program, 1966–1967.

Wigodsky, Herman. Interviewed by ACHRE staff, Washington, D.C., Jan. 17, 1995.

Woodward, Theodore. Interviewed by ACHRE staff, Walter Reed Army Institute of Research, Dec. 14, 1994.

Volpe, Joseph. Interviewed by ACHRE staff, Washington, D.C., Oct. 6, 1994, May 18, 1995.

VIDEOTAPES

Betrayal of Simeon. Length 26 min. Sydney, Australia: The Nine Network of Australia. *60 Minutes.* March 20, 1994.

Dwayne Sexton. Length 12 min. New York: CBS *60 Minutes.* March 13, 1994.

Openness Initiative. Length 55 min. Washington, DC: Department of Energy, Dec. 7, 1993.

Operation Tumbler-Snapper. Length 47 min. Coordination and Information Center, Las Vegas, NV: (CIC No. 0800011) 1952.

Shields Warren. Leaders in American Medicine. Length 90 min. Alpha Omega Alpha. Bethesda, MD: National Institutes of Health, National Library of Medicine, History of Medicine Division, 1974.

Techniques of Nuclear Cloud Sampling. Length: 38 min. Los Alamos, NM: Los Alamos National Laboratory, 1966.

INDEX